The Right to Development in Africa

Studies in Critical Social Sciences

Series Editor
David Fasenfest
(*Wayne State University*)

VOLUME 201

New Scholarship in Political Economy

Series Editors
David Fasenfest
(*Wayne State University*)
Alfredo Saad-Filho
(*King's College London*)

Editorial Board
Kevin B. Anderson (*University of California, Santa Barbara*)
Tom Brass (*formerly of SPS, University of Cambridge*)
Raju Das (*York University*)
Ben Fine ((*emeritus*) SOAS *University of London*)
Jayati Ghosh (*Jawaharlal Nehru University*)
Elizabeth Hill (*University of Sydney*)
Dan Krier (*Iowa State University*)
Lauren Langman (*Loyola University Chicago*)
Valentine Moghadam (*Northeastern University*)
David N. Smith (*University of Kansas*)
Susanne Soederberg (*Queen's University*)
Aylin Topal (*Middle East Technical University*)
Fiona Tregenna (*University of Johannesburg*)
Matt Vidal (*Loughborough University London*)
Michelle Williams (*University of the Witwatersrand*)

VOLUME 11

The titles published in this series are listed at *brill.com/nspe*

The Right to Development in Africa

By

Carol Chi Ngang

BRILL

LEIDEN | BOSTON

Cover illustration: Courtesy of David Fasenfest, 2021.

Library of Congress Cataloging-in-Publication Data

Names: Ngang, Carol Chi, author.
Title: The right to development in Africa / by Carol Chi Ngang.
Description: Leiden ; Boston : Brill, [2022] | Series: Studies in critical
    social sciences, 2666-2205 ; volume 201 | Includes bibliographical
    references and index.
Identifiers: LCCN 2021041853 (print) | LCCN 2021041854 (ebook) |
    ISBN 9789004467811 (hardback) | ISBN 9789004467903 (ebook)
Subjects: LCSH: Right to development–Africa. | Law and economic
    development–Africa. | Sustainable development–Africa. | Natural
    resources–Africa–Management.
Classification: LCC HC800.Z9 E4464 2022 (print) | LCC HC800.Z9 (ebook) |
    DDC 338.96–dc23
LC record available at https://lccn.loc.gov/2021041853
LC ebook record available at https://lccn.loc.gov/2021041854

Typeface for the Latin, Greek, and Cyrillic scripts: "Brill". See and download: brill.com/brill-typeface.

ISSN 2666-2205
ISBN 978-90-04-46781-1 (hardback)
ISBN 978-90-04-46790-3 (e-book)

Copyright 2022 by Carol Chi Ngang. Published by Koninklijke Brill NV, Leiden, The Netherlands.
Koninklijke Brill NV incorporates the imprints Brill, Brill Nijhoff, Brill Hotei, Brill Schöningh, Brill Fink,
Brill mentis, Vandenhoeck & Ruprecht, Böhlau Verlag and V&R Unipress.
All rights reserved. No part of this publication may be reproduced, translated, stored in a retrieval system,
or transmitted in any form or by any means, electronic, mechanical, photocopying, recording or otherwise,
without prior written permission from the publisher.
Authorization to photocopy items for internal or personal use is granted by Koninklijke Brill NV provided
that the appropriate fees are paid directly to The Copyright Clearance Center, 222 Rosewood Drive, Suite
910, Danvers, MA 01923, USA. Fees are subject to change.

This book is printed on acid-free paper and produced in a sustainable manner.

*To my father, Bernard Ngang Amungwa (of blessed memory)
and mother, Grace Alieh Ngang for the encouragement they instilled in
me to strive for the utmost in life in spite of a difficult background*

∵

Contents

Preface XI
Acknowledgements XIV
Acronyms and Abbreviations XV

1 Introduction – Africa's Development Setbacks in Context 1
1   Overview 1
2   Background 6
   2.1   *A Wrongly Conceived Development Trajectory* 6
   2.2   *Starting Point* 9
3   Approach and Structure 10
   3.1   *Theory Base* 10
   3.2   *Scope and Delineation* 14
   3.3   *Significance of the Book* 15
   3.4   *Outline of Chapters* 16

2 Historical Account on the Right to Development 18
1   Introduction 18
2   Origins of the Right to Development 20
   2.1   *Africa's History of Development Injustices* 22
      2.1.1   Slavery and the Impact on Development in Africa 23
      2.1.2   Iniquities of Colonialism 25
   2.2   *Decolonial Revolution* 29
      2.2.1   The Quest for Independence 30
      2.2.2   Post-independence Difficulties 36
3   Evolution of the Right to Development 38
   3.1   *Latent Manifestations* 38
      3.1.1   Self-Determination 39
      3.1.2   Third World Aspirations for Global Balance 41
   3.2   *Formal Recognition* 43
      3.2.1   Proclamations on the Right to Development 44
      3.2.2   Legal Recognition and Protection 47
4   Conceptual Clarity 53
   4.1   *Nature of the Right to Development as a Human Rights Concept* 53
      4.1.1   Defining Characteristics 54
      4.1.2   Substantive Entitlements 56
      4.1.3   Legal Entitlements 59
      4.1.4   Normative Standards 61

	4.2	*Nature of the Right to Development as a Development Paradigm* 68		
		4.2.1	Specific Components for Realisation	69
		4.2.2	Right to Development Goals	75
5	Concluding Remarks	81		

3 Global Dynamics and the Geopolitics of Development Cooperation 83

1	Introduction	83		
2	Cooperation Framework for Development	87		
	2.1	*Origins of Development Cooperation*	87	
		2.1.1	Brief Historical Account	87
		2.1.2	Definitional Problem	89
	2.2	*Basic Features of Development Cooperation*	91	
		2.2.1	Motives behind Development Cooperation	91
		2.2.2	Operational Modalities	93
		2.2.3	Patronage and Paternalism	100
	2.3	*Cooperation Patterns*	102	
		2.3.1	North-South Cooperation	102
		2.3.2	South-South Cooperation	104
		2.3.3	Multilateralism and Global Partnership	107
3	Development Cooperation and the Right to Development	111		
	3.1	*Determining the Connection*	111	
	3.2	*Political Nature and the Indeterminate Motives of Cooperation*	114	
		3.2.1	Self-Interest	115
		3.2.2	Desire to Dominate	117
	3.3	*Hurdles to Africa's Development Prospects*	119	
		3.3.1	Economic Sabotage	119
		3.3.2	Military Disruptions	122
4	Asserting the Right to Development in Africa	125		
	4.1	*Modalities for Realisation*	125	
		4.1.1	Individual State Responsibility	125
		4.1.2	Shared Responsibility for Concerted Action	128
	4.2	*Human Rights and Development Practice*	131	
		4.2.1	The Law on Human Rights and Development in Africa	131
		4.2.2	Normative Requirements for Cooperation	133
		4.2.3	Continental Framework Mechanisms for implementation	141
5	Concluding Remarks	150		

CONTENTS   IX

4 A Dispensation for Socio-economic and Cultural Self-Determination 153

1   Introduction   153
2   Framework for Implementation   155
   2.1 *Right to Development Dispensation*   155
      2.1.1 Soft Law Provisions on the Right to Development   156
      2.1.2 African Treaty Provisions on the Right to Development   159
      2.1.3 Constitutional Guarantees   167
   2.2 *Entitlement to Self-Determination*   173
      2.2.1 The Rule of Law   174
      2.2.2 Associated Legal Responsibilities   176
3   Safeguard Measures   181
   3.1 *The Duty to Protect*   182
   3.2 *Enforcement Mechanisms*   184
      3.2.1 African Commission on Human and Peoples' Rights   184
      3.2.2 African Court on Human and Peoples' Rights   185
      3.2.3 Domestic Courts of First Instance   187
      3.2.4 National Human Rights Institutions   190
   3.3 *Access to Justice and Means of Redress*   192
      3.3.1 Procedural Considerations   192
      3.3.2 Litigation   194
      3.3.3 Nature of Remedies   205
   3.4 *Critique of the Regime of Protection*   208
      3.4.1 Extraterritoriality and the Constraints of International Law   208
      3.4.2 Inadequacies within the African Human Rights System   211
4   Concluding Remarks   215

5 Right to Development Governance for Africa 218

1   Introduction   218
2   Incongruities and the Complex Dynamics in Africa   221
3   Right to Development Regulatory Mechanisms   225
   3.1. *Mandated Entities for Development Policy Making*   226
      3.1.1 African Union (AU)   226
      3.1.2 States Governments – Selected Country Analysis   227
   3.2 *Implication for Ineffective Implementation*   248

X — CONTENTS

    3.3 *On the Decoloniality of Thought in Development Programming* 251

        3.3.1 Insufficiency in Development Cooperation Approaches 251

        3.3.2 Some Major Impediments 256

        3.3.3 The Obligation to Fulfil 263

        3.3.4 The Right to Development as a Tool for Policy Making 264

4   Right to Development Governance 266

    4.1 *Conceptual Formulation* 266

        4.1.1 Definition and Justification for the Model 266

        4.1.2 Functional Requirements 271

        4.1.3 Capacity to Fulfil 274

    4.2 *Operational Considerations* 279

        4.2.1 Collective Socio-economic and Cultural Freedoms 279

        4.2.2 Non-regression in the Enjoyment of Existing Rights 283

    4.3 *Relevance of the Right to Development Governance to Africa* 287

5   Concluding Remarks 290

6 Conclusion – Right to Development Imperatives for Africa 293

1   Concluding Highlights 293

    1.1 *Summary Observations* 294

    1.2 *Alternative Perspective to Development Thinking* 296

2   Imperative for Political Action 299

    2.1 *African Union (AU)* 299

        2.1.1 Africa's Common Policy Principle 299

        2.1.2 Financing for Development 300

        2.1.3 On Skills and Technology Transfer 302

        2.1.4 On Attaining the Superior Purpose for Development 303

    2.2 *States Governments* 305

        2.2.1 Socio-economic and Cultural Transformation 305

        2.2.2 Transformative Leadership 307

        2.2.3 Basis for Making Political Choices 308

3   Final Remarks 309

Bibliography 313

Index 369

Preface

This book provides a conceptual analysis of the right to development in Africa with a decolonial critique of the requirement to have recourse to development cooperation as a mechanism for its realisation. The analysis is intended to account for the fact that the setbacks to development in Africa are not necessarily caused by the absence of development assistance but principally as a result of the lack of an operational model to steer the processes for development towards the highest attainable standard of living for the African Peoples. The arguments are situated within the framing of the decolonial and capability theories to justify the need for Africa to dissociate from paternalistic colonial models and the rationale for a shift in development thinking towards an alternative model embodied in the right to development.

As a point of departure, the claim is stated that the mechanism of development cooperation is conceptually opposed to the African conception of the right to development, which guarantees an entitlement to socio-economic and cultural self-determination in the making of development choices and policy alternatives. To justify this claim, a historical account on the origins of the right to development is detailed out. In tracing its origins in this way, further illustration is provided on how the right to development has evolved in Africa not as a solicitation for foreign aid but essentially as an assertion of self-determination against the development injustices that deprive the peoples of Africa of their inherent entitlement to socio-economic and cultural development.

The right to development in Africa is, accordingly, portrayed as having a dual nature; on the one hand, as a human rights concept intended to ensure that development processes are informed and regulated by the principles of justice and equity and on the other hand, as a development paradigm that envisages improved well-being and better living standards for the peoples of Africa. Pertaining to the central enquiry whether the right to development in Africa is achievable through development cooperation, it is argued that the probability is minimal, owing to the geopolitical motives behind prevailing patterns of development cooperation, which are innately lopsided and intended primarily to safeguard the interests of foreign stakeholders. In disagreement with arguments in favour of development cooperation as a means to achieve the right to development, it is argued that the right to development in Africa was originally conceived as a remedy mechanism to redress endemic development injustices on the continent.

In effect, the right to development entails the fulfilment of three normative requirements: sovereignty in domestic development policy making; the obligation to eliminate obstacles to development; and the need for an enabling environment for the actualisation of socio-economic and cultural development. However, in spite of the range of instruments, which African states have committed to in ensuring that the right to development becomes reality, effective implementation remains problematic due to a combination of factors including the dominant influence of foreign stakeholders, which despite evidence of violations of the right to development resulting from their actions and operations, remain insulated from legal accountability. On this note, the dimension of the right to development as a paradigm for development is examined with clarification that its transformative potential is yet to be explored to the benefit of the peoples of Africa.

The argument is then further advanced for a shift in development thinking from dependence on development assistance to a reading of the right to development as an alternative functional model for development suited to Africa. This model is defined as *the right to development governance* and demonstrated to have the potential to accelerate the processes for transformation and sustainable development within the context of Agenda 2063 among other development initiatives. A number of policy recommendations are outlined on priority measures and actions that need to be taken both at the continental level by the African Union and at national levels by African states governments as a guarantee that envisaged economic, social and cultural development is achieved in Africa.

While the book broadly focuses on Africa, specific illustrations are drawn from a few countries including Cameroon, Libya, South Africa, Ethiopia and Nigeria, selected randomly from the five principal geopolitical regions that make up the economic building blocs of the continent. A cursory reference is also made to a few other countries in the course of the discussions to illustrate a point. While the analysis on these five countries may not present an accurate picture of the 55 sovereign states in Africa with disparate dynamisms and diversities in the development challenges they experience, the argument is sustained that the idea of a human right to development is much more profound and suited to redressing the setbacks to development on the continent as a whole and thus, cuts across the borderlines of state sovereign.

It is hoped that this book will make a noteworthy contribution to the evolving discourse on the right to development in Africa and globally, and possibly also broaden the debate on human rights and development and rights-based approaches to development more generally. The motivation to write the book draws from the deep-seated socio-economic and cultural challenges and the global contradictions that subject the impoverished peoples of Africa to a seemingly endless struggle against domination. It contains exciting insights and novel perspectives, which with anticipation, will open up avenues for further research and robust academic engagements. It would be of great satisfaction therefore, if the book achieves the intended purpose of motivating other African scholars in taking the interest to drive the discourse on the right to development in Africa much further.

Acknowledgements

I acknowledge with gratitude the guidance of Prof Danie Brand, Prof Serges Djoyou Kamga, Prof Frans Viljoen, Dr Donald Rukare and Prof Babatunde Fagbayibo whose critique and comments on earlier drafts contributed to ensuring that this book is of the finest quality. I am thankful to Prof Michelo Hansungule who significantly shaped my views on the right to development. The material and moral support of Dr Justin Wanki, Dr Fred Sekindi, Dr Solomon Abegaz, Mr James Nyondo (of blessed memory), Ms Bih Fomukong and other esteemed friends were a sustainable source of strength.

I am indebted to my treasured wife, Mrs Mercy Ngang and kids; Joey Maformbah, Ngang Thercy Fusi and Ngang Myra Wuffi-Manyonga for their undiluted love, support and encouragement while I burnt the mid-night oil and deprived them of precious family time. All other well-wishers whose assistance contributed in one way or the other, great or small also merit my appreciation. I exalt the heavenly Father for illuminating my path.

I grateful to the Department of Public Law and Centre for Human Rights, University of Pretoria; Cegla Centre for Interdisciplinary Research in Law, Tel Aviv University; Law and Development Research Group, University of Antwerp and Free State Centre for Human Rights, University of the Free State for utilising their academic space in conducting the research that resulted in the publication of this book. I am thankful to the anonymous peer reviewers and the Brill editorial and production teams. Any errors, omissions or inaccuracies contained herein are the unintentional result of my shortcomings and I take full responsibility for them.

Acronyms and Abbreviations

ACB	African Central Bank
ACHPR	African Commission on Human and Peoples' Rights
ACIL	Amsterdam Centre for International Law
ACP	African, Caribbean and Pacific countries
AEC	African Economic Community
AfCFTA	African Continental Free Trade Agreement
AHRLJ	African Human Rights Law Journal
AHRLR	African Human Rights Law Report
AIB	African Investment Bank
AMF	African Monetary Fund
APRM	African Peer Review Mechanism
ASEAN	Association of South East Asian Nations
ATPC	African Trade Policy Centre
AU	African Union
AUDA	African Union Development Agency
BBC	British Broadcasting Corporation
BRICS	Brazil, Russia, India, China and South Africa (economic bloc)
BSAC	British South Africa Company
CAPPE	Centre for Applied Philosophy and Public Ethics
CDDRL	Centre on Democracy, Development and the Rule of Law
CEMIRIDE	Centre for Minority Rights Development
CEPR	Centre for Economic Policy Research
CFA	Communauté Financier Africaine
CIA	Central Intelligence Agency
COMESA	Common Market for Eastern and Southern Africa
CSO	Civil Society Organisation
DANIDA	Danish International Development Agency
DRC	Democratic Republic of Congo
DRtD	Declaration on the Right to Development
EAU	East African Union
ECCAS	Economic Community of Central African States
ECOSOC	Economic and Social Council
ECOWAS	Economic Community of West African States
ESCR	Economic, social and cultural rights
FES	Friedrich-Ebert-Stiftung
FOCAC	Forum for China-Africa Cooperation
GDP	Gross Domestic Product

HRW	Human Rights Watch
ICCPR	International Covenant on Civil and Political Rights
ICESCR	International Covenant on Economic, Social and Cultural Rights
IDS	Institute of Development Studies
IMF	International Monetary Fund
IOM	International Organisation for Migration
MDGS	Millennium Development Goals
MINEPAT	Ministry of the Economy, Planning and Regional Development
MPRA	Munich Personal RePEc Archive
NANHRI	Network of African National Human Rights Institutions
NATO	North Atlantic Treaty Organisation
NGO	Non-governmental organisation
NHRI	National Human Rights Institutions
NIEO	New International Economic Order
NORAD	Norway Agency for Development Cooperation
ODA	Official Development Assistance
ODI	Overseas Development Institute
OECD	Organisation for Economic Cooperation and Development
OIC	Organisation of Islamic Cooperation
SADC	Southern African Development Community
SADPA	South African Development Partnership Agency
SAHRC	South African Human Rights Commission
SAIFAC	South African Institute for Advanced Constitutional, Public, Human Rights and International Law
SAIIA	South African Institute of International Affairs
SAP	Structural Adjustment Programme
SDGS	Sustainable Development Goals
SERAC	Social and Economic Rights Action Centre
SESRTCIC	Statistical, Economic and Social Research Training Centre for Islamic Countries
SIDA	Swedish International Development Agency
SRSG	Special Representative of the United Nations Secretary General
TST	Technical Support Team
UN	United Nations
UNCTAD	United Nations Conference on Trade and Development
UNDP	United Nations Development Programme
UNECA	United Nations Economic Commission for Africa
UNEP	United Nations Environment Programme
UNESCO	United Nations Education, Scientific and Cultural Organisation
UNICEF	United Nations International Children's Fund

ACRONYMS AND ABBREVIATIONS

UNOHCHR	United Nations Office of the High Commissioner for Human Rights
UNU	United Nations University
US	United States
USAID	United States Agency for International Development
USD	United States Dollar
WEO	World Economic Outlook
WIDER	World Institute for Development Economics Research
ZANU-PF	Zimbabwe African National Union Patriotic Front

CHAPTER 1

Introduction – Africa's Development Setbacks in Context

1   Overview

Africa has, in spite of its extensive natural resources as well as socio-economic and cultural potential, often been presented in very negative light as the least developed region in the world: a birthplace of conflicts and instability, disease, extreme levels of poverty, endemic corruption and insensible leadership, democratic insufficiencies, governance malpractices and general decline. These downbeat characteristics combine in a cyclical manner to sustain the unacceptably low standards of living on the continent. While interventions have multiplied over the years and Africa is reported to have experienced unprecedented economic growth, living standards have not improved for a large proportion of the populations across the continent. In the face of these challenges, the law provides that all the peoples of Africa are entitled to the right to socio-economic and cultural development, which is granted to be claimed and enjoyed in all freedom.[1]

However, regardless of the African origins of the right to development, which was conceived at inception as a remedy to the development injustices that the peoples of Africa have had to endure for centuries, attention has rather increasingly been directed towards the paternalistic model of development cooperation. As it is argued in this book, the requirement to have recourse to the mechanism of development cooperation as a means for the realisation of the right to development does not come short of a deliberate attempt to narrow into insignificance and consequently, subsume the claim to a human right to development into the framework of global coloniality that accentuates the ascendancy of donor developed countries over the recipient claimants of the right to development.

This book provides a conceptual analysis of the right to development in Africa, with a decolonial critique of the requirement of development cooperation for its realisation as envisaged in the Declaration on the Right to

---

1   African Charter on Human and Peoples' Rights adopted by the Organisation of African Unity in Nairobi Kenya on 27 June 1981, OAU Doc CAB/LEG/67/3 rev. 5; 1520 UNTS 217 preamble & art 22(2).

© CAROL CHI NGANG, 2022 | DOI:10.1163/9789004467903_002

Development among other international instruments and mechanisms for global development. The purpose is to advance the argument that Africa has remained underdeveloped not necessarily because of the absence of material help in the form of development assistance to accelerate development on the continent but essentially, as a result of the lack of an operational model to steer the processes for development towards the highest attainable standard of living for the African Peoples. The term "underdeveloped" is used not necessarily in the manner in which global narratives categorise Africa in relation to other regions of the world but in essence, with the purpose to inspire critical consciousness of the reality that existing systems and the applicable models and approaches to development on the continent do not demonstrate sufficient capacity for socio-economic and cultural self-determination.

Development as a concept is noted to be quite complex and not subject to any exclusive uniform applicable definition. This claim is anchored on the understanding that development and human rights cannot be divorced from each other. This tends to fuel misunderstanding about the claim to development as a human right, which despite universal acceptance, still raises practical and conceptual questions with regard to its realisation. The complexity relating to the concept of human rights and of development notwithstanding, for the purpose of the argumentation in this book, it is important to clarify that no matter how human rights or development are conceived or whatever form they take, both concepts aim ultimately at securing better living standards and the attainment of improved well-being for the human person.

While some scholars argue that well-being is a complex concept, multifaceted, intangible and difficult to define and even harder to measure,[2] Geir Asheim provides a simple definition of well-being as an "indicator of the situation under which the people within a generation live".[3] Asheim's definition fits appropriately with the notion of development that is articulated in this book as aiming to improve the situation under which the peoples of Africa live. The right to development in Africa is conceived from this viewpoint to mean entitlement to the highest attainable standard of living, which in accordance with article 22 of the African Charter, is guaranteed to be achieved through asserting socio-economic and cultural self-determination. Although the African Charter explicitly obligates state parties to create the conditions for the peoples of

---

2   Thomas, J. Corbett "Current measures and the challenges of measuring children's well-being" (2009) Office for National Statistics – Working Paper 11; Pollard, Elizabeth & Lee, Patrice "Child well-being: A systematic review of the literature" (2003) 61:1 *Social Indicators Research* 60.

3   Asheim, Geir B. "Intergenerational equity" (2010) 2 *Annual Review of Economics* 198.

INTRODUCTION – AFRICA'S DEVELOPMENT SETBACKS IN CONTEXT

Africa to exercise that right, development assistance has instead largely been propagated as the mechanism through which the right to development is guaranteed to all peoples is envisaged to be achieved.[4]

Even as Africa is pulled into expectation and probably convinced to believe in the promise of foreign assistance as a supplementary source of financing to its onerous efforts to achieve comprehensive development, the same donor developed countries from which such assistance is expected refuse to acknowledge that they owe any legal obligation to fulfil the right to development in developing countries.[5] Despite affirmation in the Vienna Declaration that the right to development forms an integral part of fundamental human rights – meaning they are accorded the same status in law[6] – unlike other human rights that are protected by legally binding instruments, the Declaration on the Right to Development has since its adoption in 1986, retained the status of soft law without any universally binding effect. This lapse in the recognition of human rights under international law is innately detrimental and has meant that the right to development can primarily only be achieved through the conditionality of having to depend on the benevolence of developed country to provide needed assistance for development.

Philipp Dann notes that while conditionality requirements compel recipient developing countries to be accountable and show evidence of good governance in the administration of development assistance, donor countries

---

4 Declaration on the Right to Development Resolution A/RES/41/128 adopted by the UN General Assembly on 4 December 1986 art 3(3) & 4(2); Charter of the United Nations adopted in San Francisco on 26 June 1945 arts 1(3), 55 & 56; Arts, Karin & Tamo, Atabongawung "The right to development in international law: New momentum thirty years down the line?" (2016) 63:3 Neth Int'l Law Rev 239–242; De Feyter, Koen "Towards a framework convention on the right to development" (2013) Friedrich Ebert Stiftung 17; Mahalu, Costa R. "Human rights and development: An African perspective" (2009) 1:1 Leiden J Int'l L 16; Felice, William F. "Right to development" in Forsythe, David P. (ed) Encyclopaedia of Human Rights (2009) 21; Salomon, Margot E. "Legal cosmopolitanism and the normative contribution of the right to development" in Marks, Stephen P. (ed) Implementing the Right to Development: The Role of International Law (2008) 17; Sengupta, Arjun "Development cooperation and the right to development" (2003) Copyright©2003 Arjun Sengupta 20; Sengupta, Arjun "On the theory and practice of the right to development" (2002) 24:4 Hum Rts Qtly 880; Haüsermann, Julia "A human rights approach to development: Some practical implications for WaterAid's work" (1999) Rights & Humanity 5; Siitonen, Lauri "Political theories of development cooperation: A study of theories of international cooperation" (1990) UNU – WIDER 15–16.
5 Tadeg, Mesenbet A. "Reflections on the right to development: Challenges and prospects" (2010) 10:2 AHRLJ 339.
6 Vienna Declaration and Programme of Action adopted by the UN Conference on Human Rights UN Doc A/CONF.157/24 25 June 1993 paras I(5) & (10).

are under no obligation to demonstrate reciprocal accountability.[7] This divergence in perception and approach, characterised by the display of structural imbalance in the power matrix of global governance is reflective of a functional disconnect within the international cooperation framework, which affects the realisation of the right to development in Africa.[8] For this reason, the requirement of development cooperation for the realisation of the right to development is subjected to critical analysis. The grounds on which the arguments are framed are twofold: First, that the right to development in Africa is conceptualised as an expression of self-determination rather than a solicitation for foreign assistance. Second, that development cooperation is primarily intended to promote the geopolitical interests of donor countries and not necessarily to advance the right to development, particularly for Africa. Central to this enquiry is the question why Africa is expected to have recourse to development cooperation for the realisation of the right to development?

Complex as it may be in providing an accurate response to the above question, the context, particularly relating to the contention in acknowledging that development constitutes a human right and also with regard to divergent perspectives on the subject of development cooperation, raises other important questions that need to be explored: Whether there is a right to development in Africa? Whether that right can be achieved through development cooperation? To what extent is the right to development guaranteed as a legal entitlement to the peoples of Africa? Can the right to development be conceived to apply as an alternative model to development in Africa? What concrete measures are required to make the right to development a reality to the peoples of Africa?

In responding to these questions, the book seeks to provide clarity on the nature of the right to development in Africa and by so doing, propose a shift in the discourse from development cooperation to a decolonial thinking of the right to development as a home-grown model entailing greater collective action among African countries. This is anchored in the central argument that the essentially paternalistic nature of development cooperation runs counter to the concept of the right to development in Africa, which presupposes a claim "to be allowed the freedom and the opportunity" to make the development policy choices to enable Africa to "advance beyond prevailing circumstances".[9]

---

7 Dann, Philipp *The Law of Development Cooperation: A Comparative Analysis of the World Bank, the EU and Germany* (Cambridge: Cambridge University Press, 2013) 1.

8 Nagan, Winston P. "The right to development: Importance of human and social capital as human rights issues" (2013) 1:6 *Cadmus Journal* 30.

9 Ngang, Carol C. "Towards a right-to-development governance in Africa" (2018) 17:1 *Journal of Human Rights* 113.

Considered severally, the response drawing from the first question provides justification to the argument that in spite of opinions to the contrary, the right to development is established to have originated from Africa as an affirmation of emancipation from colonial rule and a legitimate claim to be liberated from foreign domination and external influences. Thus, the right to development is presented as aiming to accomplish two main purposes; on the one hand, to ensure that development is achieved with justice and equity and on the other hand that the well-being and the betterment of living standards for the peoples of Africa is guaranteed.

With this conception of the right to development, it is argued with regard to the second question that prevailing patterns of development cooperation neither provide assurance for development to be achieved with justice and equity nor guarantee well-being for the peoples of Africa. This is explained by the fact that development cooperation is designed to promote the interest of donor countries, which is underlined by the desire to dominate global politics through the mechanism of aid dependency. The correlation is difficult to establish, and it is hard to locate how the right to development could realistically be achieved through development cooperation.

In response to the third and fourth questions relating to the actual dimensions of the right to development, a description of the context within which the right to development is established by law to apply as a human rights concept and as a development paradigm is provided. This context is designated as the right to development dispensation on the basis of the range of legal instruments that guarantee self-determination in formulating domestic policies and in setting development priorities that are relevant to Africa. Attention is further drawn to the fact that because of the dominant influence of foreign stakeholders within the framework of development cooperation, which in itself lacks the potential to drive development in Africa, the context necessitates a radical shift from prevailing patterns of development cooperation that primarily only create dependency on foreign stakeholders to fostering collective action among African countries. From this perspective and drawing from propositions to move away from economic growth models to rights-based approaches to development, the argument is made in favour of exploring the right to development not only as a claimable entitlement but essentially as a development model for Africa, which is proposed to be conceptualised as *right to development governance*.

The analyses and the accompanying arguments ultimately draw to the conclusion that the right to development in Africa is not an objective required to be achieved through development cooperation but rather the means by which Africa's development aspirations could be realised and consequently

6 CHAPTER 1

also suggests how Africa ought to be governed. As a justification for this claim, explanation is provided why it is relevant to prioritise the right to development governance as a home-grown model for development in Africa. The policy recommendations outlined in the concluding chapter are intended to ensure practical application of the right to development governance model in driving the agenda for development in Africa.

2 Background

2.1 A Wrongly Conceived Development Trajectory

With this background overview, a brief explanation is provided on how Africa came to be where it is today and how the right to development has evolved in that process as a potential remedy to the problem of underdevelopment, which supposedly is envisaged to be redressed through development cooperation. Way back in 1949, United States (US) President, Harry Truman, in his inaugural speech drew world attention to the fact that certain parts of the world were "underdeveloped" and needed some form of "civilisation", which according to him was only possible through the charitable assistance of the industrialised world.[10] Truman's statement established the biased barometer by which the world has largely been gauged either as "developed" in terms of industrial advancement or "underdeveloped"/"backward" in terms of the lack thereof. By this estimation, underdevelopment can only be redressed through the benevolence of developed countries, the basis on which development cooperation has eventually been structured as illustrated in chapter three.

The parts of the world, which Truman referred to as underdeveloped of course, did not choose to be so; they were rendered underdeveloped by the industrialised countries.[11] Campaigns for decolonisation and subsequent demands for a more equitable global system challenged Truman's preconceptions that the peoples in underdeveloped countries only needed to be rescued from misery and sufferings. The decolonisation campaign demonstrated the capabilities of the "underdeveloped" peoples to seek justice and freedom from domination rather than charitable assistance.[12] The idea of wanting to

---

10   Truman, Harry S. "Inaugural address" (1949) available at: www.bartleby.com/124/pres53.html (accessed: 14 October 2016) paras 44-45.

11   See generally Rodney, Walter *How Europe Underdeveloped Africa* (Dar-Es-Salaam: Tanzanian Publishing House, 1973).

12   Ouguergouz, Fatsah *The African Charter on Human and Peoples' Rights: A Comprehensive Agenda for Human Dignity and Sustainable Democracy in Africa* (Dordrecht: Martinus Nijhoff Publishers, 2003) 298; Felice, *supra* note 4, 21.

INTRODUCTION – AFRICA'S DEVELOPMENT SETBACKS IN CONTEXT

be free to develop began to materialise following the massive acquisition of independence in the 1960s.[13] The right to development evolved from this background, marked by a number of initial public proclamations in the late 60s and early 70s.[14]

However, a protracted debate ensued, characterised by contestation as to the existence of such a right and a misconception as to what it actually embodies or what its realisation entails.[15] The primary focus of this book does not necessitate reigniting the debate, which in essence, has remained a major distraction to genuine effort in making the right to development become reality. Despite the arguments of proponent scholars in favour of the right to development as an instrumental human right[16] and a host of opponents who deny its legal foundation,[17] the right to development eventually gained universal

---

13 Kirchmeier, Felix "The right to development – where do we stand?: State of the debate on the right to development" (2006) *Friedrich Ebert Stiftung – Occasional Paper No 23* 8.

14 Ware, Athony "Human rights and the right to development: Insights into the Myanmar government's response to rights allegations" (2010) *Conference Paper* 3; Meilan, Laurent "Le droit au développement et les Nations Unies: Quelques réflexions" (2003) 34 *Droit en Quart Monde* 14; Rich, Roland Y. "The right to development as an emerging human right" (1983) 23 *Virg J Int'l L* 290, see footnote 10; M'baye, Kéba "Le droit au développement comme un droit de l'homme: Leçon inaugural de la troisième session d'enseignement de l'Institut International des Droits de l'Homme" (1972) 5 *Revue des Droits de l'Homme* 503.

15 Marks, Stephen P. "The politics of the possible: The way ahead for the right to development" (2011) *Friedrich Ebert Stiftung* 3; Felice, *supra* note 4, 21.

16 Chowdhury, Roy & De Waart, Paul "Significance of the right to development in international law: An introductory view" in Chowdbury, Roy; Denters, Erik M.G. & De Waart, Paul (eds) *The Right to Development in International Law* (Dordrecht: Brill/Nijhoff, 1992) 10; Bedjaoui, Mohammed "The right to development" in Bedjaoui, Mohammed (ed) *International Law: Achievements and Prospects* (Dordrecht: Martinus Nijhoff & UNESCO, 1991) 1177 & 1182; Salomon, *supra* note 4, 17; Sengupta 2002, *supra* note 4,857–867.

17 Whyte, Jamie (2007) "Book review: Development as a human right edited by Bård A Andreassen and Stephen P Marks Harvard University Press, London, England, 2006" 1:1 *Elect J Sust Dev't* 1–3; Rosas, Allan "The right to development" in Eide, Asbjørn; Krausus, Catarina & Rosas, Allan (eds) *Economic social and cultural rights* (Dordrecht: Nijhoff Publishers, 2001) 251; Bello, Emmanuel "Article 22 of the African Charter on Human and Peoples' Rights" in Bello, Emmanuel & Ajibola, Bola (eds) *Essays in Honour of Judge Taslim Olawale Elias* (Dordrecht: Nijhoff Publishers, 1992) 462; Shivji, Issa G. *The Concept of Human Rights in Africa* (London: African Books Collective, 1989) 82; Ghai, Yash "Whose human right to development?" (1989) *Commonwealth Secretariat Occasional Papers*; Rich, Roland "The right to development: A right of peoples?" in Crawford, James (ed) *The Rights of Peoples* (Oxford: Oxford University Press, 1988) 17–38; Donnelly, Jack "The right to development: How not to link human rights and development" in Welch, Claude E. & Meltzer, Roland I. (eds) *Human rights and development in Africa* (New York: SUNY Press, 1984) 261.

recognition as an inalienable human right.[18] Its realisation however, remains constrained by the absence of an acceptable modality for implementation.[19] Although recognised as an inalienable right, which means it ought to respond to universal human rights standards, defined by the duties to respect, to protect and to fulfil, a rather less compelling standard is envisaged for its achievement through the mechanism of development cooperation.

A concrete meaning of development cooperation might be necessary to be able to determine to what extent it could be relied on for the realisation of the right to development. The difficulty in constructing such a definition is that development cooperation is driven by a variety of reasons relating to issues of an economic, technical, security and environmental nature among others, and achievable through various strategies ranging from the provision of development assistance to foreign direct investment (external capital inflows) as well as more specialised technical assistance.[20] For the purpose of this book, even though reference is made to the provision of development assistance; development cooperation is used in its broadest sense, involving a range of external state and non-state actors referred to here as "foreign stakeholders" because of their vested interests in Africa.

The generality draws from the bottom-line, as it is argued in the subsequent chapters that development cooperation is generally not favourable and more so, not desirable as a model for development in Africa. Despite being one of the most favoured destinations for development assistance, the global narrative on aid ineffectiveness illustrates that there is little evidence of the

---

18   UN Human Rights (ed) *Realizing the Right to Development: Essays in Commemoration of 25 Years of the United Nations Declaration on the Right to Development* (Geneva: United Nations Publication, 2013) iii; Baxi, Upendra "The new international economic order, basic needs and rights: Note towards development of the right to development" (1983) 23 *Indian J Int'l L* 227; Alston, Philip "Development and the rule of law: Prevention versus cure as a human rights strategy" in International Commission of Jurists (eds) *Development, Human Rights and the Rule of Law* (Oxford: Pergamon, 1981) 106; United Nations General Assembly Resolution A/RES/34/46 of 23 November 1979 para 8.

19   De Feyter, Koen "The right to development in Africa" (2013) *Law & Development University of Antwerp* 7; Sengupta, Arjun *et al.* "The right to development and human rights in development: A background paper" (2004) *The Norwegian Centre for Human Rights – Research Notes 07/2004* 2.

20   Esteves, Paulo & Assunção, Manaíra "South-South cooperation and the international development battlefield: Between the OECD and the UN" (2014) 35:10 *Third World Quarterly* 1776; Killick, Tony "The developmental effectiveness of aid to Africa" (1991) *International Economics Department of World Bank – Working Paper Series 646* 10–17; IOM "International cooperation" available at: http://www.rcmvs.org/documentos/IOM_EMM/vi/ViSo7_CM.pdf (accessed: 26 May 2016) 9–17.

development gains resulting from such assistance to Africa.[21] This is so largely because of the dominant self-seeking interests of foreign stakeholders within the framework of development cooperation, which in reality is not designed to achieve the right to development. A discussion on the actual dimensions of development cooperation is given more precision in chapter three.

2.2 *Starting Point*

The nature of the right to development raises crucial questions, some of which have been explored extensively as is evident from the wide repertoire of literature on the subject. However, a scrutiny of the available literature shows a dearth of knowledge relating to why implementation of the right to development remains problematic. This book provides clarity in this regard and is intended to fill the existing gap in the discourse relating to modalities for the realisation of the right to development in Africa. A range of authors hold the conviction that the right to development is achievable through development cooperation and therefore, advocate for its recognition as a mechanism for implementation.

Margot Salomon for example, believes that the right to development demands international cooperation as a means of creating an enabling environment for the achievement of human well-being through the realisation of basic human rights and freedoms for everyone.[22] Lauri Siitonen sees development cooperation as a means to curb global inequalities through which developing countries are strengthened in their endeavour to achieve self-determination, universal human rights and poverty eradication.[23] According to Julia Haüsermann, a normative framework for cooperation combining domestic laws and international development policies is imperative as a measure of accountability for the realisation of the right to development.[24] In a related approach, Koen de Feyter proposes a framework convention as a binding legal regime to regulate the interaction between cooperating parties on the right to development.[25]

Interestingly, these affirmative views are expressed only to the extent that the right to development is seen as a problem requiring a solution. To the extent that it does not represent a problem as such, this book takes a contrary

---

21   See Ake, Claude *Democracy and Development in Africa* (Washington DC: The Brookings Institute, 1996) 103.

22   Salomon, *supra* note 4, 17.

23   Siitonen, *supra* note 4, 15–16.

24   Hausermann, *supra* note 4, 5 & 8.

25   De Feyter 2013(a), *supra* note 4, 17.

10   CHAPTER 1

and a rather more critical stance with regard to development cooperation as a means to achieve the right to development in Africa. If the right to development is to be attained, there is need to examine the concept from a pragmatic point of view. This resonates with Oduwole's perception that the right to development must be seen as imposing more of a negative obligation, requiring restraint from actions that may jeopardise the enjoyment of that right.[26] Šlaus and Jacobs share the conviction that practical solutions to the range of challenges confronting humanity can be found by exploring alternative paradigms.[27] Accordingly, Nagan argues that the right to development meets the criteria to be considered as such a paradigm.[28]

These positions suggest looking at the right to development in Africa more concretely as a mechanism for dealing with the range of development challenges that the continent is confronted with,[29] which provides the point of departure for this book. It builds into the argument that the framework for development in Africa is in need of proper conceptualisation, direction and transformative leadership, necessitating on the most part a revolutionary shift from the mindset that remedies to Africa's development setbacks can only be initiated by foreign stakeholders.

3   Approach and Structure

3.1   *Theory Base*

The analysis and the arguments advanced in this book are situated within the framing of two mutually reinforcing theories – the decolonial theory and the theory of capabilities – to justify the need for Africa to dissociate from paternalistic colonial models and the rationale for a shift in development thinking towards an alternative model embodied in the right to development. The theory base provides the framework of understanding why the level of development in Africa is as it is, and more so, how the situation could be ameliorated. Owing to the perpetuation of abuse and exploitation; buttressing my argument as highlighted above that Africa's development trajectory is from inception wrongly conceived, if the continent is to advance beyond prevailing

---

26   Oduwole, Olajumoke "International law and the right to development: A pragmatic approach for Africa" (2014) *International Institute of Social Studies* 3.

27   Šlaus, Ivo & Jacobs, Garry "In search of a new paradigm for global development" (2013) 1:6 *Cadmus Journal* 1–3.

28   Nagan, *supra* note 8, 24–27.

29   Oduwole, *supra* note 26, 3.

INTRODUCTION – AFRICA'S DEVELOPMENT SETBACKS IN CONTEXT

development injustices and challenges, it is of essence to see how the decolonial theory and the theory of capabilities could provide a framework of reasoning in this regard.

The decolonial theory otherwise referred to as decoloniality is a revolutionary form of critical reasoning and manner of doing that suggests opposition, resistance, disruption or deviation from standard theoretical narratives, derivative norms, practices and thought patterns that originate from histories of European colonial influence and distorted Western notions of civilisation and universality.[30] It is a theory that has evolved from the imagination of the oppressed to create and define the alternatives on which the future and survival of their species rest.[31] It creates an exigency for "epistemic disobedience" that compels the subjugated to dissociate from the colonial matrix of power that persistently creates an illusion of hope for in frequently reinvented universal narratives[32] that only replicate what Wanki and Ngang describe as "colonial absolutism".[33]

---

30 For a general understanding of decoloniality, see Mignolo, Walter "Epistemic disobedience and the decolonial option: A manifesto" (2011) *Transmodernity* 44–66; Ndlovu, Morgan "Coloniality of knowledge and the challenge of creating African Futures" (2018) 40:2 *Ufahamu: A Journal of African Studies* 95–112; Adams, Glen & Estrada-Villalta, Sara "Theory from the South: A decolonial approach to the psychology of global inequality" (2017) 18 *Current Opinions in Psychology* 37–42; Ndlovu-Gatsheni, Sabelo J. "Global coloniality and the challenges of creating African futures" (2014) 36:2 *Strategic Review for Southern Africa* 181–202; Bhambra, Gurminder K. "Postcolonial and decolonial dialogues" (London: Bloomsbury Academic, 2014) 17:2 *Postcolonial Studies* 115–121; Bhambra, Gurminder K. "Postcolonial and decolonial reconstructions" in Bloomsbury Collections *Connected Sociologies* (London: Bloomsbury Academic, 2014) 117–140; Ndlovu-Gatsheni, Sabelo J. "Coloniality of power in development studies and the impact of global imperial designs on Africa" (2012) *Inaugural Lecture delivered at the University of South Africa* 1–24; Grosfoguel, Ramón "Decolonizing post-colonial studies and paradigms of political-economy: Transmodernity, decolonial thinking, and global coloniality" (2011) 1:1 *Transmodernity* 1–38; Maldonado-Torres, Nelson "Thinking through the decolonial turn: Post-continental interventions in theory, philosophy, and critique – an introduction" (2011) *Transmodernity* 1–15; Mignolo, Walter D. "Delinking: The rhetoric of modernity, the logic of coloniality and the grammar of decoloniality" (2007) 21:2/3 *Cultural Studies* 449–514. Other famous African decolonial theorists include, Cheikh Anta Diop, Frantz Fanon, Ngugi wa Thiong'o, Samir Amin, Kwame Nkrumah, Steve Bantu Biko.

31 Gordon, Lewis R. "Fanon and development: A philosophical look" (2004) 29:1 *Africa Development/Afrique Development* 94.

32 Mignolo, Walter *The Darker Side of Western Modernity: Global Futures, Decolonial Options* (2011) 122–123; Mignolo 2007, *supra* note 30, 450; Mignolo 2011, *supra* note 30, 45.

33 Wanki, Justin N. & Ngang, Carol C. "Unsettling colonial paradigms: The right to development governance as framework model for African constitutionalism" (2019) 18:2 *African Studies Quarterly* 69–70.

Walter Mignolo portrays decoloniality not just as an abstract theory but indeed also as an a pragmatic project[34] that creates possibilities for radical transformation, necessitating according to Isaac Shai, a radical disruption of parochial Eurocentric narratives[35] that have become a perennial problem; challenging efforts aimed at creating sustainable futures for the peoples of Africa.[36] Ndlovu-Gatsheni situates this challenge within the understanding of decoloniality as one of asymmetrical power relations between Africa and the rest of the world. He explains that in spite of the potential to shape global politics, Africa has rather increasingly been handicapped by the degree to which dominant global forces have penetrated the continent and continue to influence the thought and doing processes.[37] Decoloniality in this context as Maldonado-Torres explains should be understood as "the unfinished project of decolonisation".[38]

In Ramón Grosfoguel's reasoning, Africa is still very much engulfed in a colonial world and needs to break from the narrow ways of thinking about colonial relations, in order to accomplish the unfinished and incomplete dream of decolonisation.[39] Driven by such thinking, the decolonial revolution of the mid 20th century birthed the African conception of the right to development, which pragmatically emboldens the peoples of Africa to define and shape its own development future based on the capability to think and to act differently. Radin's conception of pragmatism describes a results-oriented approach that evaluates theories or beliefs in terms of the success of their application in particular circumstances.[40] According to Singer, pragmatism requires focusing on the actual workings of the law within a specific context, which is ideally more important than pursuing the conceptual correctness[41] of global norms such as development cooperation, which pragmatically is not very relevant as a model for development in Africa.

---

34 Mignolo 2011, *supra* note 32, xxiv.

35 Shai, Isaac "The right to development, transformative constitutionalism and radical transformation in South Africa: Postcolonial and decolonial reflections" (2019) 19:1 *African Human Rights Law Journal* 509.

36 Ndlovu-Gatsheni 2014, *supra* note 30,181–202.

37 As above, 191.

38 Maldonado-Torres, Nelson "On the coloniality of being: Contributions to the development of a concept" (2007) 21:2/3 *Cultural Studies* 263.

39 Grosfoguel, Ramón "The epistemic decolonial turn: Beyond political-economy paradigms" (2007) 21:2/3 *Cultural Studies* 221.

40 Radin, Margaret J. "The pragmatist and the feminist" (1990) 63:2 *South Calif L Rev* 1700; Singer, *infra* note 41, 1822.

41 Singer, Joseph W. "Property and coercion in federal Indian law: The conflict between critical and complacent pragmatism" (1990) 63:6 *South Calif L Rev* 1821.

INTRODUCTION – AFRICA'S DEVELOPMENT SETBACKS IN CONTEXT 13

Inspiration is drawn from the theoretical understanding of the capabilities approach to development propounded by Amartya Sen and Martha Nussbaum as a theory base for dealing with issues relating to human rights and development.[42] Capability, according to Nussbaum, is "pragmatic", "result-oriented" and "provides a fine basis for a theory of justice and entitlement".[43] The idea of capabilities is explained to mean "the opportunity to achieve valuable combinations of human functioning".[44] It focuses on the recognition of the human potential, emphasised by the need to expand opportunities and choices and to develop productive capabilities. The theoretical underpinnings of the capabilities model provide the basis for my analysis of the right to development in Africa as a means to advance the capacity of the African peoples to freely set their own development priorities.

The analysis and argumentation in this book are anchored on the combined theories of decoloniality and capabilities to dissipate established misconceptions with regard to the realisation of the right to development through development cooperation, which as the argument is advanced in this book, is not practically possible. The theories of decoloniality and of capabilities are employed in this instance to illustrate that development cooperation is a subtle replication of colonial absolutism that perpetuates development injustices through continuous external domination in Africa.[45] It builds into the frame of decolonial thinking, necessitating the collective acceptance that the context for development in Africa does not necessitate recourse to development cooperation, which although envisaged by international law as shown in chapter three, remains fluid in its application and is unrealistic as a means to practically change the socio-economic and cultural circumstances in Africa.

Basing on the decoloniality and capabilities theories, the concept of the right to development is examined in terms of the functional dimensions of its application as an alternative model suited to drive development processes in Africa. The points advanced in this regard are anchored on the fact that Africa has both the resource potential for implementation and also the legal capacity to ensure judicial enforcement as illustrated in chapter four. As an alternative to development cooperation, chapter five described the actual functioning of

---

42   Sen, Amartya *Development as Freedom* (Oxford: Oxford University Press, 1999) 87–95; Nussbaum, *infra* note 43, 33–34.

43   Nussbaum, Martha *Creating Capabilities: The Human Development Approach* (Cambridge/ Massachusetts/London: Harvard University Press, 2011) 17–18.

44   Sen, Amartya "Elements of a theory of human rights" (2004) 34:4 *Philosophy & Public Affairs* 320.

45   AU Commission "Agenda 2063: The Africa we want" (2015) *African Union* para 59.

14   CHAPTER 1

the right to development as a development paradigm capable of redressing the prevailing development injustices, contradictions and inconsistencies in Africa. While this goal is still very much visionary as reflected in the 2063 African agenda for development, it is indeed the attainment with a proper conceptualisation of the right to development.

3.2   *Scope and Delineation*

It might seem risky to generalise about the continent of Africa as a homogenous entity. It is worth acknowledging that Africa is made up of 55 autonomous states whose sovereignty has however, increasingly dissipated, giving way to a more integrated continent, politically, socio-economically and culturally.[46] The broad focus of this book on Africa is informed by the progressive shift in the African narrative towards greater integration with emphasis on human rights protection and sustainable development as envisaged by the Constitutive Act of the African Union (AU), the 2063 agenda for development[47] and the African Charter that makes provision for the right to development.[48] It is important to also highlight the African origins of the right to development, which, as illustrated in chapter two was conceptualised to address issues pertaining to the entire continent and not to specific African countries.

A country-by-country analysis for all the 55 states of Africa would have been appropriate to determine the extent of implementation of the right to development at the domestic levels. Unfortunately, such an extensive analysis cannot realistically be achieved within the structural limitations of this book. Reference is made to a few countries not with the aim to narrow down understanding of the right to development to those particular countries; the specific examples are intended to explore the challenges with individual state efforts at implementing the right to development. The facts and lessons drawn from these examples are made understandable within the framework of the African Charter that obligates state parties to collectively ensure the realisation of the right to development guaranteed to all the peoples across the continent.[49]

Given the context, and because the book involves more of a conceptual analysis, it is expedient to explore the subject from a continental scope to determine how in conjunction with Africa's 2063 agenda for development, the right to development could be achieved. Agenda 2063 adopted by the AU

---

46   Ngang, *supra* note 9, 107.
47   Constitutive Act of the African Union adopted in Lomé on 11 July 2000 art 3(a), (h)&(j); AU Commission "Agenda 2063", *supra* note 45, para 20.
48   African Charter, *supra* note 1, art 22.
49   As above, art 22(2).

Commission in 2015 is a consolidated roadmap that aims at harmonising efforts towards sustainable development in Africa.[50] As promising as it appears, the agenda leaves unanswered questions relating to how the collective entitlement to development enshrined in the Charter could be used to achieve the outlined development aspirations, which this book endeavours to explore. By so doing, justification is provided for looking at the right to development as a context-specific model for development relevant to Africa.

3.3   *Significance of the Book*

Questions relating to human rights and development, including in particular the right to development, have formed the basis of controversial contemporary debates globally. One of the controversies emanate from the fact that in spite of its conceptual nature as an assertion of self-determination against development injustices, the right to development is often narrowly perceived as subject to development cooperation for its realisation. This book provides new insights and a broader perspective on the right to development in Africa, which is identified to be formulated not only as a claimable entitlement but also as a paradigm for development that has not sufficiently been explored. The arguments are intended to move the discourse on the right to development in Africa beyond the realm of the controversial debates towards practical modalities for its implementation.

This purpose is achieved by demonstrating how the right to development could be conceptualised to fill up the gap created by the lack of an operational model, which is argued to constitute the reason for retarded progress and development setbacks on the African continent. The concluding recommendations are framed to shift development thinking from dependency-based development cooperation,[51] towards greater focus on the right to development as a home-grown alternative model for development in Africa. Readers, particularly academics and researchers will find the book instructive as an invaluable reference material on the right to development in Africa, especially because it

---

50   AU Commission "Agenda 2063", *supra* note n 45, paras 5-8.

51   When the OAU was founded, African leaders mistakenly believed that development was achievable through international cooperation, and so article 2 of the OAU Charter which states the purpose of the organisation emphasised the need for cooperation in every aspect of African society. Fifty years after, African leaders come to the realisation that reliance on international cooperation has rather hindered than advance development on the continent. The African agenda for development named, Agenda 2063 adopted at the instance of the 50th anniversary of Africa's independence highlights the need to move away from aid dependency (para 72(o)) and to focus on self-reliant efforts to create development on the continent (para 19).

explores the concept of the right to development in Africa in greater depth and addresses in a profound manner, topical issues relating to human rights and development in Africa, which readers will find engaging.

3.4 *Outline of Chapters*

The book is structured in six chapters; including this introductory chapter, four substantive chapters and the concluding chapter. Chapter one provides the context for understanding Africa's development setbacks and the theoretical underpinnings relating to a purposive reading of the right to development as it is perceived within that context. Being the introductory chapter, it lays the groundwork on which the rest of the analysis and the arguments are put together.

A historical account is presented in chapter two to illustrate that there is indeed a human right to development, which from its deep African roots is shown to have evolved conceptually as an entitlement guaranteed to all the peoples of Africa to assert socio-economic and cultural self-determination against endemic development injustices. Contrary to the traditional understanding of human rights as fundamentally individualistic in nature, the right to development in Africa is delineated as essentially a collective right that has evolved in its dual dimension as a human rights concept and as a development paradigm.

Chapter three responds to the question with regard to whether development cooperation has the potential to facilitate the realisation of the right to development. It is explained that the mechanism of development cooperation holds the promise to assist developing countries, particularly those in Africa in their efforts to achieve development in a comprehensive manner. However, an examination of its characteristic features indicates that development cooperation is primarily paternalistic in nature and designed to promote the geopolitical interests of donor countries and not necessarily to advance the right to development in Africa.

Based on the understanding of the right to development as a human rights concept; the discussion proceeds in chapter four with a closer examination of the right to development dispensation in Africa and the entitlement to self-determination that it engenders for the formulation of development priorities that are relevant for redressing the socio-economic and cultural contradictions on the continent. Safeguard measures for consolidating the right to development are discussed with reference to case law, which as it is argued does not currently guarantee sufficient protection to the impoverished and virtually "unfree" peoples of Africa.

The enquiry in chapter five is situated within the understanding that Africa is constrained to embrace development cooperation, which allows the opportunity for abuse and exploitation by foreign stakeholders, due to the absence of an established development model for the continent. Drawing from its dimensions as a development paradigm, a lucid illustration is provided on how the right to development could be conceptualised as an alternative to development cooperation and a home-growth model for development model suited to accelerating development in Africa.

In the sixth and concluding chapter, besides providing a summary of the main arguments, the chapter further explores the alternative perspective of the right to development governance as a transformative model with the potential to drive the project of structural transformation and sustainable development that is envisaged for Africa. In accordance, a number of policy measures are recommended to be undertaken at the continental level by the AU and at domestic levels by African states governments as an assurance of setting development priorities for the continent right, on the basis of which the peoples aspire for better living standards.

CHAPTER 2

Historical Account on the Right to Development

1   Introduction

In making the determination in this chapter as to whether there is a right to development in Africa, a historical account of its African origins is given with a detailed description of how and the purpose for which it came to be conceptualised as a claimable legal entitlement. The historical account includes an explanation on how slavery and colonialism contributed to the dispossession and impoverishment of the African peoples, which eventually inspired claims for the right to development. The extensive narrative also illustrates how the right to development has evolved not only as a human right as it is generally understood, but indeed also as a development paradigm, which unfortunately has not been explored to make a radical turnaround of the legacy of historical injustices.

Given the resource potential that the continent of Africa is endowed with and the capabilitiesinherent in its peoples,[1] it is argued that with the right to development as a model for development, Africa would be able to advance much faster than by hanging on to paternalistic models such as development cooperation. The purpose of the analysis in this chapter is first and foremost, to establish the basis for interrogating in the next chapter, the proposition to have recourse to development cooperation as a mechanism for the realisation of the right to development and secondly, to rely on this background information to justify in chapters five and six, the need for a paradigm shift in development thinking from development cooperation towards greater focus on the right to development as a model for development suited to Africa.

Human rights are inherent entitlements that people possess by virtue of their humanity. For a right to be inherent does not create any legal problem. The problem arises when entitlements that are inherent to individuals or peoples come under attack or are threatened. This often then results in demands for the recognition and protection of those rights. When human rights become recognised and protected by law, they provide right holders the legitimacy to seek justice and protection under the law. To say that there is a right to

---

1   Suhfree, Cletus S. *Africa: Where Did We Go Wrong?* (Johannesburg: Muimeledi Mutangwa Publisher, 2016) 104–108.

© CAROL CHI NGANG, 2022 | DOI:10.1163/9789004467903_003

development means that the African peoples are inherently entitled to that right, which in and of itself does not create any legal problem. The fact that the peoples of Africa began to make assertions for the recognition of their right to development is indicative that this entitlement was threatened or had been contravened. Laying claim to development as a human right thus posed a legal problem in the sense that it provoked contestation as to whether there is such thing as a right to development.[2]

Owing to the controversy, the legitimacy of the idea of development as a human right requires justification of its nature as an inherent entitlement worthy of legal recognition and protection. One way of making such a determination is by looking back into history; to explore the factors and circumstances that gave birth to claims on the right to development. Scholarship on the right to development has largely associated its origins with provisions of the international bill of human rights, which has been interpreted to imply that apart from the human rights explicitly enshrined in the various instruments, there is an additional entitlement called the right to development.[3] Assuming that the idea of development as a human right originated from Africa with its complex development history, its intricate dimensions cannot be understood simply by looking at it as deriving from international human rights law. While this interpretation may not be wrong, it is misleading in that it conceals the African origins of the right to development, distorts its conceptual clarity and thus complicates the mechanism for its realisation.

---

2   Whyte, Jamie (2007) "Book review: Development as a human right edited by Bård A Andreassen and Stephen P Marks Harvard University Press London England 2006" 1:1 *Elect J Sust Dev't* 1–3; Rosas, Allan "The right to development" in Eide, Asbjørn; Krausus, Caterina & Rosas, Allan (eds) *Economic, Social and Cultural Rights* (Dordrecht: Nijhoff Publishers, 2001) 251; Shivji, Issa G. *The Concept of Human Rights in Africa* (London: African Books Collective, 1989) 82; Bello, Emmanuel "Article 22 of the African Charter on Human and Peoples' Rights" in Bello, Emmanuel & Ajibola, Bola (eds) *Essays in Honour of Judge Taslim Olawale Elias* (Dordrecht: Nijhoff Publishers, 1992) 462.

3   See Charter of the United Nations adopted in San Francisco on 26 June1945 art 55, Universal Declaration of Human Rights adopted by General Assembly Resolution 217 A(III) of 10 December 1948 arts 22 & 25-28; International Covenant on Economic, Social and Cultural Rights (ICESCR) adopted by General Assembly Resolution 2200A (XXI) 1966 art 11(1); see also Ware, Athony "Human rights and the right to development: Insights into the Myanmar government's response to rights allegations" (2010) *18th Biennial Conference of the Asian Studies Association of Australia* 3; Johnson, Glen M. "The contributions of Eleanor and Franklin Roosevelt to the development of international protection for human rights" (1987) 9:1 *Hum Rts Qtly* 36; Alston, Philip "Making space for new human rights: The case of the right to development" (1988) 1 *Hum Rts Yearbk* 5–6; Office of the High Commissioner for Human Rights "Development: Right to development" available at: http://www.ohchr.org/EN/Issues/Development/Pages/Backgroundrtd.aspx (accessed: 30 June 2015).

Relating to the origins, the background account in this chapter is aimed at providing a comprehensive understanding of the right to development with the purpose to deflate some apparent misconceptions and, therefore, pave the way for a proper enquiry into the requirement of development cooperation for its realisation. The chapter is structured as follows: Section 2 explores the genesis of the right to development, bringing into focus Africa's history of development injustices (2.1), leading to the rejection of colonialism and imperial domination (2.2). It proceeds to investigate in section 3, how the concept of the right to development has evolved, with a retrospective view on how it manifested in latent form (3.1) and also how it eventually gained formal recognition both in Africa and internationally (3.2). Section 4 presents a conceptual clarity on the right to development in Africa by exploring its theoretical nature as a human rights concept (4.1), and its pragmatic nature as a development paradigm (4.2). The discussion wraps up in section 5 with some concluding remarks.

2 Origins of the Right to Development

The historical foundations of the right to development is examined in this section with the purpose to show that although it has been part of development and human rights scholarship for over half a century, it has not yet fully impacted positively on development practice in Africa where its origins can more accurately be traced.[4] This may be explained by the fact that in spite of its African roots, the right to development has largely been abandoned in favour of development cooperation as shown in chapter three. Without this historical account, the potential value of the right to development in redressing underdevelopment in Africa might be overlooked. Much of the literature on the right to development does not give a true narrative of its actual origins and therefore, complicates its conceptual nature and modalities for implementation. Attempts to trace the origins of the right to development have rather described stages in the evolution of the concept instead of looking at the factors that caused the emergence of such a right. It is true that Africa's underdevelopment is a product of the interplay between external forces and a host of domestic factors.[5] However, a better understanding of the right to

---

4 Dąbrowska, Anna O. "Legal status of the right to development" (2010) *Haskoli Island University* 2–3.
5 Soko, Mills & Lehmann, Jean-Pierre "The state of development in Africa: Concepts, challenges and opportunities" (2011) 14:1 *J Int'l Rel & Dev't* 97.

development necessitates knowledge of the historical events that gave birth to such a right, which has to do more with the external factors from which most of the domestic factors arose.

A starting point for this analysis is the claim that Africa's underdevelopment can be directly attributed to exploitation by industrialised countries.[6] An exploration of the historical events that motivated claims for the right to development is not only necessary for an understanding of how the right came to be. Such background knowledge is also crucial in determining what the right to development is intended to achieve and to what extent development cooperation could contribute to the realisation of that purpose. The earliest origin of the right to development has been attributed to a statement made by human rights protagonist Eleanor Roosevelt in 1947, in the run-up to the adoption of the Universal Declaration of Human Rights (UDHR). She is quoted as having said that; "we will have to bear in mind that we are writing a bill of rights for the world and one of the most important rights is the opportunity for development".[7] It might not be wrong to interpret this statement as inferring a right to development. It is, however, difficult through such an interpretation to establish a connection to the events that gave birth to such a right.

The fact that the right to development as Eleanor Roosevelt might have intended it, did not find its way into the UDHR suggests that it had other, more remote origins, which did not correlate with the immediate causes that triggered the codification of the range of human rights that got enshrined in the Declaration.[8] Cornwall and Musembi explain that many of the principles that are articulated as part of the concept of the right to development have been part of struggles for self-determination and social justice, which predate the discourse on human rights.[9] This claim motivates the reason to look back

---

6   See generally Rodney, Walter *How Europe Underdeveloped Africa* (Dar-Es-Salaam: Tanzanian Publishing House, 1973); Kirchmeier, Felix; Lüke, Monica & Kalla, Britt *Towards the Implementation of the Right to Development: Field-testing and Fine-tuning the UN Criteria on the Right to Development in the Kenyan-German Partnership* (Geneva: Friedrich-Ebert-Stiftung, 2008) 7.

7   Sengupta, Argun "Realising the right to development" (2000) 31 *Development & Change* 554–555; Johnson, *supra* note 3, 36; Alston, *supra* note 3, 5–6.

8   The atrocities of the Second World War constituted the immediate causes that motivated the codification of the UDHR, following the signing of the Atlantic Charter in 1941 by Great Britain and the United States as a blueprint for post-war peace and the basis of the mutual recognition of the rights of all nations. See Facing History "Universal Declaration of Human Rights timeline" available at: https://www.facinghistory.org/for-educators/educator-resources/universal-declaration-human-rights-timeline (accessed: 15 March 2018).

9   Cornwall, Andrea & Nyamu-Musembi, Celestine "Putting the 'rights-based approach' to development into perspective" (2004) 25:8 *Third World Quarterly* 1420.

beyond 1947; to explore why and how consciousness about historical injustices gradually built up into what eventually became known as the right to development. Empirical studies suggest that Africa's entangled history with industrialised countries explains part of its current underdevelopment[10] and by implication the origins of the right to development.

2.1   Africa's History of Development Injustices

In recounting Africa's history of development injustices in this section, the purpose is to provide justification to the argument against development cooperation as a mechanism for the realisation of the right to development, which is portrayed instead a development model that Africa needs to pursue. This narrative is not intended to showcase Africa's development gains, but to describe events whose legacy continues to impede aspirations for development on the continent. It is a narrative that is characterised by dispossession, exploitation and extraction of the continent's human and material resources, accompanied by gross violations of human rights. A study on the right to development in Africa necessitates this historical perspective for the reason that what happened in the past shapes the present and determines the future.

While unfair development practices continue to prevail in Africa, two unforgettable historical processes, namely slavery and colonialism, account for a large part of the continent's current state of underdevelopment. Prior to the invasion of the African continent, the self-governing communities are reported to have been making steady and significant progress.[11] Although it cannot be stated with exactitude which developmental direction the peoples of Africa would have taken and the level to which the continent would have advanced, it also cannot be denied that the continent would not have remained stagnant were it not for slavery and colonisation. Following Walter Rodney's argument that the "magnitude of man's achievement is best understood by reflecting on the early history of human society",[12] it cannot be denied that slavery and colonialism to a large extent stalled progress on the African continent. The discussion proceeds from this understanding of African history to illustrate how the injustices stemming from slavery and colonialism contributed to depriving the African populations of the opportunity to advance their capabilities for development and thus progressively built up into resentment and rejection.

---

10   Nunn, Nathan "The long-term effects of Africa's slave trades" (2006) *J Econ Lit* 2.

11   Settles, Dwayne J. "The impact of colonialism on African economic development" (1996) *Honours Book University of Tennessee* 1; Rodney, *supra* note 6, 3–4.

12   Rodney, *supra* note 6, 3.

2.1.1 Slavery and the Impact on Development in Africa

For a period of over five centuries between the years 1400 and 1900 the African continent was raided for slaves. This decimated the once functional polities.[13] The four slave routes that operated simultaneously during the course of this period were the trans-Saharan, Red Sea, Indian Ocean and trans-Atlantic routes.[14] Through this dehumanising practice the continent suffered the extraction of millions of its competent men and women, leading to severe deterioration in the African human potential.[15] Not counting those who died in the process, the number of African men and women who were taken as slaves to the Americas alone to supply workforce in the European-established plantations is documented at between 12 and 13 million.[16] The total number that was forcefully extracted from the continent, including those who were tortured to death, is estimated at between 20 and 50 million.[17] During this period international trade was beginning to boom, which motivated the high demand for slaves from Africa to expand the production of sugar, cocoa, cotton, tobacco and coffee to supply the international market.[18]

The boom in international trade bolstered the sale of human beings through the practice of "slave trade", which in every sense was unethical considering that value of what was taken (human beings) exceedingly surpassed what was exchanged in return. African peoples with great potentials were bought like cattle and transformed into slaves; dehumanised and deprived of the opportunity to develop their own communities, the legacy of which haunts Africa to this day. Contrary to general perception, the millions of African peoples that were bundled away against their will for a surprisingly disparate exchange of firearms, gunpowder, brandy, cloth, tobacco, glassware, and iron, among others[19] were not inherently slaves but agriculturalists, potential doctors, architects and engineers among others who, for purposes of promoting European economic interests, were transformed into slaves. While they laboured in the European plantations in the Americas to boost production for international

---

13   Nunn, Nathan "The historical origins of Africa's underdevelopment" (2007) *VOX CEPR's Policy Portal* available at: http://www.voxeu.org/article/slave-trade-and-african -underdevelopment (accessed: 13 February 2016).

14   Nunn 2006, *supra* note 10, 4.

15   As above.

16   Nunn 2006, *supra* note 10, 4; Whatley & Gillezeau, *supra* note 19 below, 2.

17   Nkrumah, Kwame *Africa Must Unite* (New York: Frederick A Praeger Publisher, 1963) 5.

18   M'bokolo, Elikia "The impact of the slave trade on Africa" *Le Monde Diplomatique* available at: http://mondediplo.com/1998/04/02africa (accessed: 12 February 2016).

19   Whatley, Warren & Gillezeau, Rob "The impact of the slave trade on African economies" (2009) *Department of Economics University of Michigan* 6; M'bokolo, *supra* note 18.

trade and consequently the development of western capitalist societies,[20] it is incomprehensible how ammunitions and consumable items which were taken in exchange could contribute to developing Africa.

Without the African workforce the plantations would not have had the requisite human input for extensive commercial production. It also means that supplies from the plantations would not have been able to meet the demands of international trade and therefore also implies that international trade would have suffered tremendously. The Europeans promoted the invasion of African communities and fuelled the raid for slaves because of the cost benefits they derived from the practice – a primary source of cheap labour.[21] Terreblanche provides an elaborate explanation of how, through extensive slave raiding, the Portuguese, the Dutch, the British and the French successively reduced the peoples of South Africa into dehumanising forms of cheap labour while systematically plundering the country's resources to build the capitalist empires of the West.[22] The African person represented to the European a factor of production or "economic property", in other words, which motivated slaveholding for purposes of economic exploitation.[23]

The success of international trade and the consequent development of the western capitalist societies of Europe and America were achieved at the expense of development that would have taken effect in Africa had the slave raid not happened. The European demand for slaves severely retarded socio-economic progress,[24] while the process by which slavery took place, through domestic warfare and kidnapping also adversely impacted on long-term development prospects in Africa.[25] To prove the impact of slavery, Nathan Nunn has established empirical evidence of a direct causal link between the raid

---

20   Mazrui, Ali A. *The Africans: A Triple Heritage* (London: BBC Publications, 1986)12.

21   Williams, Carolyn " 'Am I not a man and a brother?' 'Am I not a woman and a sister?': The trans-Atlantic crusade against the slave trade and slavery" (2010) 56:1/2 *Caribbean Quarterly* 108; Dodson, Howard "How slavery helped build a world economy" (2003) *National Geographic News* available at: http://news.nationalgeographic.com/news/2003/01/0131_030203_jubilee2.html (accessed: 16 August 2017).

22   Terreblanche, Sampie *A History of Inequality in South Africa 1652–2002* (Pietermaritzburg: University of Natal Press, 2002) 8–14 & 153; Amĭn, Samir *Imperialism and Unequal Development* (New York/London: Monthly Review Press, 1977) 49–55.

23   Eltis, David "Europeans and the rise and fall of African slavery in the Americas: An interpretation" (1993) 98:5 *The American Historical Review* 1399.

24   Nunn, Nathan "Slavery, institutional development and long-term growth in Africa 1400–2000" (2005) *J Econ Lit* 4; Inikori, Joseph E. "Africa and the trans-Atlantic slave trade" in Falola, Toyin (ed) *Africa Volume 1: African History Before 1885* (Durham: Carolina Academic Press, 2000).

25   Nunn 2006, *supra* note 10, 3.

for slaves and Africa's current development challenges; indicating that the African countries from which the largest number of slaves were extracted have remained the least developed to this day.[26] The massive extraction of the human potential seriously depopulated the African continent, leaving in its wake fragile and politically fragmented states, fractionalised communities and weak judicial institutions incapable of enforcing laws to regulate the society.[27]

The legacy of poverty and deprivation as well as structural inequalities and systemic injustices contributed to weakening the African continent economically.[28] Given that slavery was outlawed, the European imperialists forged a new narrative to justify their further encroachment into Africa by advancing the "civilisation theory", which carried the explanation that the continent was backward and they had a God-ordained evangelical mission to enable the peoples of Africa to benefit from the white man's civilisation.[29] The refusal to equate the African civilisation that existed at the time to the European perception of civilisation as Suhfree explains[30] provided an unjustified basis for the colonisation of the African continent in 1885.

2.1.2   Iniquities of Colonialism

Official (direct) colonial rule in most of Africa lasted a total of approximately seventy five years from 1884 to the 1960s when the majority of the colonised territories gained political independence.[31] Some of the colonised territories like Angola, Mozambique, Zimbabwe, Namibia and South Africa only gained independence between the 1970s and 1990s. Apart from some notable development gains recorded during the colonial period, evidence abounds that African

---

26   Nunn 2006, *supra* note 10, 2; see also Sarkin, Jeremy "The coming of age of claims for reparations for human rights abuses committed in the south" (2004) 1:1 *SUR – Int'l J Hum Rts* 67–68.

27   Nunn 2006, *supra* note 10, 2.

28   Terreblanche, *supra* note 22, 382–400.

29   Sharkey, Heather J. "African colonial states" in Parker, John & Reid, Richard (eds) *The Oxford Handbook of Modern African History* (Oxford: Oxford University Press, 2013) 151–152; Mendy, Peter K. "Portugal's civilizing mission in colonial Guinea-Bissau: Rhetoric and reality" (2003) 36:1 *The International Journal of African Historical Studies* 49–57; Truman, Harry S. "Inaugural address" (1949) available at: www.bartleby.com/124/pres53.html (accessed: 14 October 2016) paras 44-45; Nkrumah, *supra* note 17, 8; M'bokolo, *supra* note 18.

30   Suhfree, *supra* note 1, 76–78.

31   Ndlovu-Gatsheni, Sabelo J. "Decoloniality in Africa: A continuing search for a new world order" (2015) 36:2 *Australian Review of African Studies* 26; Osaghae, Eghosa E. "Colonialism and African political thought" (1991) 19:2/3 *Ufahamu: A Journal of African Studies* 24; Nunn 2006, *supra* note 10, 2.

populations experienced a severe deterioration in living standards principally through land expropriation.[32] Taking South Africa for example, Heldring and Robinson explain that not only were the majority of African populations dispossessed of about 93 per cent of agricultural lands, they were also subjected to coercive labour at exploitative wage rates, which cumulatively amounted to an estimated 59 per cent decline in living standards.[33] Before the advent of colonialism, it is reported that communities in Tanzania, Malawi, Zambia and Zimbabwe practised an organised governance system of civic participation and accountability, which, experienced remarkable deterioration during the colonial period.[34]

The colonial enterprise was not designed to create development in Africa. It thrived on a policy of sustained mass "immiserization" of the African populations through extraction, dispossession, looting of the continent's wealth and resources, and also through the massive expropriation of native lands as well as infringement of indigenous property rights.[35] Colonialism as Khanya Motshabi explains, had as its core essence to "degrade, exploit and subjugate" the African peoples.[36] In the absence of legality the application of "subjugation laws" in the governance of the colonies was not intended to promote development but rather to compel the African populations to comply with colonial rule.[37] For instance, though slavery had officially been outlawed, it persisted in the colonies in the form of forced labour – such as in King Leopold's Belgian Congo Free State (which functioned as a massive labour camp) and in the Portuguese plantations in the Cape Verde and São Tomé where the local populations

---

32   Heldring, Leander & Robinson, James A. "Colonialism and economic development in Africa" (2012) *National Bureau of Economic Research – Working Paper 18566* 10–12; Bowden, Sue & Mosley, Paul "Politics, public expenditure and the evolution of poverty in Africa 1920–2009" (2010) available at: http://www.bwpi.manchester.ac.uk/resources/Working -Papers/bwpi-wp-12510.pdf (accessed: 10 February 2016); De Zwart, Pim "South African living standards in global perspective 1835–1910" (2011) 26:1 *Economic History of Developing Regions* 26.

33   Heldring & Robinson, *supra* note 32, 12.

34   As above, 14–15.

35   Robinson, James A. "Why is Africa poor" Maddison Lecture – University of Groningen 8 April 2013 19; Heldring & Robinson, *supra* note 32, 10–17.

36   Motshabi, B. Khanya "Decolonising the university: A law perspective" (2018) 40:1 *Strategic Review for Southern Africa* 109.

37   A good example is the apartheid laws that were made official from 1948 and for a period of almost 50 years used to govern most of Southern Africa; according to which the white and the black races were forced to live separately and use separate public facilities. Contact between the races was limited and only permissible under conditions of exploitation where those of the black race were required to carry "passbooks" to be able to access white areas menial job opportunities.

were constrained to work for starvation wages in order to pay arbitrary taxes imposed by the colonial administration.[38] The imperial machinery employed the strategy of "divide and rule" in many polities to create ethnic cleavages that have ended up in entrenched inequalities, political instability, conflicts and animosity among African peoples which did not exist prior to colonisation.[39] Colonialism did not only fail in advancing Africa, it also flouted the process through which development could have been achieved.

It might be true that to a certain extent colonialism brought some benefits to Africa in terms of increased income per capita, school enrolment, adult literacy, human capital and life expectancy among others.[40] However, it is difficult to be convinced that these benefits measured up as development; otherwise the peoples of Africa would not have found reason to orchestrate the collapse of the colonial system. On the contrary, colonialism rendered the African situation worse than it was before the continent was partitioned in 1885 and exploited for over 75 years. This negates any "optimistic interpretation of the impact of colonialism on development in Africa".[41] The European colonisers "set goals for the continent based on foreign interests" to the extent that Africans had no control over their own affairs and the fate of the continent.[42] Even "under the relatively less virulent forms of colonial control, such as that of the British", the proportion of resources spent on "law and order" to subjugate the African peoples, "far exceeded that spent on education, health, and social welfare combined".[43] Socio-economic and cultural rights remained a privilege within the discretion of the colonial authorities to grant to the African peoples and to withdraw at will.[44] Undeniably, the colonial administration did invest in some infrastructural projects such as railroads, forts, export systems and

---

38   M'bokolo, *supra* note 18; Boddy-Evans, Alistair "A short history of the African slave trade" *ThoughCo*, 28 December 2018 available at: http://www.thoughtco.com (accessed: 20 June 2019).

39   Heldring & Robinson, *supra* note 32, 20–21. They cite the examples of Rwanda, Ghana, Uganda and Burkina Faso where cleavages created during colonial rule have deteriorated in later years into animosity and murderous conflicts.

40   Prados de la Escosura, Leandro "Human development in Africa: A long-run perspective" (2011) *University Carlos III – Working Papers in Economic History WP 11-09*; Kenndy, Paul "The costs and benefits of British imperialism 1846–1914" (1989) 125 *Past & Present* 186; Robinson, *supra* note 35, 9–11.

41   Heldring & Robinson, *supra* note 32, 23.

42   Oloka-Onyango, Joe "Heretical reflections on the right to self-determination: Prospects and problems for a democratic global future in the new millennium" (1999) 15:1 *Am U Int'l L Rev* 171.

43   Oloka-Onyango, *supra* note 42, 172.

44   As above.

a money economy, but these were used principally to promote the colonial interest of extraction, looting, plundering and profit making rather than to empower the local populations.[45]

The levels of colonial injustices thus ignited resentment that triggered the formation of resistance movements in different parts of Africa.[46] The wave of liberation struggles swept across the continent from the late 1950s up to 1990 when apartheid – the last bastion of colonial rule – collapsed, without much to show, especially in terms of human development. It might be relevant to ask why the colonisers failed to invest in development on the colonies when the primary motivation for colonisation was supposedly to "civilise" the African peoples. It is noted for instance that over four decades of British colonial rule in Tanzania left no record of any remarkable development gains but the country is reported to have instead experienced serious deterioration when the British took over from the Germans after the First World War.[47] When Julius Nyerere took over administration of the country from the British after 43 years of colonial rule, he remarked that 85 per cent of the adult population was illiterate while the British had trained only two engineers and twelve doctors.[48] By the time he resigned in 1985, Nyerere noted that 91 per cent of the population had become literate and practically all children attended school, while thousands of engineers, doctors and teachers had been trained.[49]

In Ghana, Kwame Nkrumah lamented that all the British left was "much ignorance and few skills" and that over 80 per cent of the local population remained illiterate on account of the fact that the existing schools were

---

45   Akyeampong, Emmanuel "African socialism; or the search for an indigenous model of economic development?" (2018) 33:1 *Economic History of Developing Regions* 71; Hrituleac, Alexandra "The effects of colonialism on African economic development: A comparative analysis between Ethiopia, Senegal and Uganda" (Masters Dissertation, Aarhus University, 2011) 14–15.

46   Msellemu, Sengulo A. "Common motives of Africa's anti-colonial resistance in 1890–1960" (2013) *Social Evolution & History* 143–152; Kastfelt, Niels "African Resistance to Colonialism in Adamawa" (1976) 8:1 *Journal of Religion in Africa* 1–12; Ranger, Terence "The people in African resistance: A review" (1977) 4:1 *Journal of Southern African Studies* 125–146; Smith, Ken "Nationalism and anti-colonialism in the inter-war years" (d.n.a) 343–362; South African History Online "The fight against colonialism and imperialism in Africa" available at: http://www.sahistory.org.za/article/fight-against-colonialism-and-imperialism-africa-grade-11 (accessed: 3 March 2016).

47   Heldring & Robinson, *supra* note 32, 15.

48   Tornielli, Andrea "Former Tanzanian politician Julius Nyerere could be made a saint" *Vatican Insider* available at: http://vaticaninsider.lastampa.it/en/inquiries-and-interviews/detail/articolo/tanzania-santo-saint-santos-20322/ (accessed: 11 February 2016).

49   As above.

HISTORICAL ACCOUNT ON THE RIGHT TO DEVELOPMENT

designed to promote imperial ideologies which did not respond to local realities.[50] According to Heldring and Robinson, the British colonial expedition accomplished virtually nothing in terms of education and human development.[51] Despite the priority accorded to education as a fundamental human right, and by implication the responsibility of the European nations that assumed administration of the colonies,[52] education for the colonised peoples was barefacedly neglected.[53] French colonial policies in Morocco for instance, was designed in such a manner that "[i]t was practically impossible for a Moroccan child to get a decent education".[54]

With these clearly noticeable injustices and the increasing awareness among the peoples of Africa of the sub-standards systems to which they were confined, it is not unusual that the consciousness soon metamorphosed into a concrete determination to chase the colonisers out of Africa and collapse the colonial machinery of patrimonialism.

2.2   *Decolonial Revolution*

After over half a century of colonial engineering – a systemic attack on African cultural patterns and virtual purging of the minds and memories, self-identity and knowledge systems of the African peoples and implanting very shallow perceptions that negate African forms of reasoning and doing – it became apparent that without breaking the bonds of colonialism and imperial domination, a better future for Africa could not possibly be imagined.[55] The decolonial revolution obligated the colonised peoples of Africa to begin to imagine new horizons from a radically opposed perception to the civilising mission

---

50   Nkrumah, *supra* note 17, xiii.

51   Heldring & Robinson, *supra* note 32, 15; Nkrumah, *supra* note 17, xv.

52   France for example, practiced a colonial policy of assimilation aimed at creating a favoured class of African elites by introducing them to French culture and civilisation and raising them to the status of Frenchmen with the aim to avoid the rise of African nationalism and by so doing, guarantee hegemony over the French colonies. Like France, Portugal also pursued a colonial policy of assimilation by which its African colonies of Mozambique and Angola were regarded as integral parts of Portugal, administered by the *Ministerio do Ultramar* in Lisbon. Accordingly, Portugal granted its colonised peoples the right to become "white" by a process of law if they met with European standards; see Nkrumah, *supra* note 17, 10–12.

53   Nkrumah, *supra* note 17, 11.

54   As above 10.

55   Ndlovu, Morgan "Coloniality of knowledge and the challenge of creating African futures" (2018) 40:2 *Ufahamu: A Journal of African Studies* 95; Maldonado-Torres, Nelson "On the coloniality of being: Contributions to the development of a concept" (2007) 21:2/3 *Cultural Studies* 243.

(mission civilatrice) ideology that the peoples of Africa were indoctrinated to believe in. However, the awakening of the African peoples from the slumber of the futile promises of colonialism soon metamorphosed into widespread resistance to colonial rule and the irreversible quest for liberation from the shackles of domination and colonial governorship. The liberation struggles against colonialism were, as Jan Eckel affirms, essentially struggles for the recognition of human rights,[56] including the right to development, expressed in the quest for independence.

2.2.1 The Quest for Independence

The history of struggles for decolonisation across all of Africa points to similar fundamental causes including exploitation, dispossession, subjugation and the denial of basic rights and fundamental freedoms and the violation of inherent entitlements to well-being. The liberation struggles summed up in an overriding aspiration to achieve justice. Compared to other parts of the world, especially the countries of South-East Asia, where, after independence, colonial ties were severed, allowing the decolonised peoples to advance steadily towards accelerated development; Africa has on the contrary remained stuck to colonial systems that have caused the continent to remain wanting in many aspects of development.[57] Over half a century after independence, the story of colonial domination of parts of or the entire continent is still being told. Africa's past, present and future remains shrouded in unanswered questions, some of which are explored in this chapter. Given the reasons why European powers subjugated Africa under colonial rule (supposedly to bring civilisation to the continent), what motivated the drive for decolonisation? What did Africa envisage to achieve by seeking independent? How was independence intended to redress the wrongs of colonialism? Did the liberation struggles envisage how Africa would be governed after independence? The prevailing situation on the continent suggests that these questions might not have been

---

56 Eckel, Jan "Human rights and decolonization: New perspectives and open questions" (2010) 1:1 *International Journal of Human Rights, Humanitarianism and Development* 111–135.

57 Maathai, Wangari *The Challenge for Africa: A New Vision* (London: William Heinemann, 2002) 48–49; McAuslan, Patrick "Good governance and aid in Africa" (1996) 40:2 *Journal of African Law* 169; Vickers, B. "Africa and international trade: Challenges and opportunities" (d.n.a) *Thabo Mbeki African Leadership Institute – International Trade and Economic Development Division* 9. Vickers illustrates that: "The share of Africa's total trade in the world since 1980s has remained largely stagnant at around 2–3 percent. This compares poorly with the performance of the Asian region, where the shares of world trade have doubled over the same period, reaching 27.8% in 2006".

HISTORICAL ACCOUNT ON THE RIGHT TO DEVELOPMENT

taken into account; or maybe not seriously when the decolonisation project was initiated.

The above questions are explored in light of capabilities theory, which explains the variations of human functioning in terms of "doings" and "beings".[58] The "doing" variant translates into the freedom to choose between alternatives, which the peoples of Africa manifested by opting for decolonisation. The "being" variant found expression in expectations for improved well-being as a legitimate aspiration of the African peoples.[59] According to Nussbaum, the focus on capabilities as a theory of justice cannot look only to collective well-being but importantly to the opportunities that become available to every single person to exercise their human functioning.[60] Such an opportunity evolved as a latent manifestation of the right to development embodied in the quest for independence. As it followed, the primary reason for seeking freedom from colonial subjugation arose from the fact that the African peoples were dispossessed of the potential to manage their own affairs.[61] In seeking independence, the peoples of Africa aimed at something close to declaring a right to development as the following statement of Nkrumah suggests:

> If the outside world refuses us its sympathy and understanding, we have at least the right to ask it to leave us alone to work out our destiny in ways that seem most apposite to our circumstances and means, human as well as material. In any event, we are determined to overcome the disruptive forces set against us and to forge in Africa [...] the African's ability to manage his own affairs.[62]

2.2.1.1 In Pursuit of a Legitimate Cause

The course of events prior to the struggle for decolonisation, characterised by gross injustices provided a legitimate moral justification to seek to become free from colonial rule. The quest for independence that subsequently engulfed the entire continent in the late 1950s originated from the consciousness that in spite of its purported civilising mission, colonialism was actually not going to bring meaningful development but increased dispossession and deprivation of

---

58   Sen, Amartya *Development as Freedom* (Oxford: Oxford University Press, 1999) 87–95.

59   See Charter of the Organisation of African Unity (OAU Charter) 1963 preamble.

60   Nussbaum, Martha *Creating Capabilities: The Human Development Approach* (Cambridge/Massachusetts/London: Harvard University Press, 2011) 18.

61   Nkrumah, *supra* note 17, 10.

62   As above, xv.

the African peoples of the opportunity to explore and utilise their potentials. The enthusiasm to reject colonial rule found legitimacy in the fact that "the colonization of Africa had come with little regard for local education, health, or infrastructure", among others.[63] Land grabbing by the large European settler populations in Kenya, Zimbabwe, South Africa and Algeria among others dispossessed the African populations and thus, limited their productive capacity as they were only looked upon to provide cheap labour under slavery-like conditions.[64]

It amounted to a moral wrong that the European powers continued to enslave the African peoples through colonialism, especially as slavery had been abolished. The codification of international law in the period after the Second World War rendered colonialism unlawful and thus gave legitimacy to the decolonisation of Africa. For instance, the United Nations (UN) Charter adopted in 1945 made provision for the principle of self-determination.[65] The subsequent codification of human rights in the Universal Declaration in 1948 also exposed the illegality of colonial practices, which contravened the human rights guarantees to which the peoples of Africa were equally entitled.[66] The principle of self-determination later gained recognition as a human right in the 1970 Declaration on Principles of International Law concerning Friendly Relations and Cooperation among States.[67]

Enthusiasm for independence mounted as many Africans, through education and exposure to Western democracies, levels of advancement and standards of living were confronted with the realities of the white man's purported civilisation mission and the detriments of colonialism to development on the African continent.[68] The international law instruments that came into force

---

63   Yergin, Daniel & Stanislaw, Joseph "Excerpt from *The Commanding Heights*" available at: http://www-tc.pbs.org/wgbh/commandingheights/shared/pdf/prof_kwamenkrumah .pdf (accessed: 14 February 2016) 2.

64   Lützelschwab, Claude "Settler colonialism in Africa" in Lloyd, Christopher; Metzer, Jacob & Sutch, Richard (eds) *Settler Economies in World History* (Leiden: Brill, 2013) 141–167.

65   UN Charter, *supra* note 3, arts 2 & 3.

66   UN Universal Declaration of Human Rights adopted by General Assembly Resolution 217 A(III) 10 December 1948 art 2.

67   Declaration on Principles of International Law concerning Friendly Relations and Co-operation among States in accordance with the Charter of the United Nations Res 2625 (XXV) adopted by the General Assembly on a Report from the Sixth Committee (A/8082) on 24 October 1970.

68   Many of the liberation leaders like Kwame Nkrumah of Ghana, Jomo Kenyatta of Kenya, Julius Nyerere of Tanzania, etc were educated in missionary schools. Nkrumah, the architect of independence in Ghana and in Africa received his early education in a Catholic missionary school and later went to study at Lincoln University in the United States where he experienced a stark difference between British colonial rule and the alternative system

HISTORICAL ACCOUNT ON THE RIGHT TO DEVELOPMENT   33

provided assurance that justice could be achieved through the assertion of rights, the basis on which the idea started to form that development for Africa could be claimed as a matter of right. Although not expressly stated, it has been argued that the idea of the right to development is embedded in the concept of self-determination which drove the quest for independence. The details on this are discussed later in this chapter. However, following the unfolding of events after independence, particularly relating to concerns about livelihood and the well-being of the African peoples,[69] the question arises as to whether the timing was right and also whether Africa was prepared to embrace independence.

2.2.1.2   Operational Model Deficit

A fundamental problem that the quest for independence suffered from inception was the complete lack of a functional development model on which the independent states would operate.[70] The rise of charismatic African liberation leaders[71] embodied the fact that the African peoples could do without colonial rule and that the timing was appropriate for decolonisation. However, leadership alone does not provide sufficient ground on which to found a state. The fragmented and destabilised situation in which the slave trade and colonialism left Africa necessitated a human rights-based development model to guide the independence project.

However, owing to the lack of such an operational model the quest for independence failed in strategy. Coming from a background characterised by illegality, development injustices and massive human rights abuses, it would have been rational at the time of seeking independence to state in concrete terms the reasoning for rejecting imperialism and domination. Such a proclamation would have laid a solid foundation for independence and probably constituted the operational model to forestall imperialistic practices and also bind the political conscience of the governments that were eventually to administer

---

of governance practiced in America. He then moved to London where he mobilised other fellow Africans into a series of pan-African Congresses for the liberation of Africa from colonial rule.

69   Gassama, Ibrahim J. "Africa and the politics of destruction: A critical re-examination of neocolonialism and its consequences" (2008) 10:2 *Oregon Rev Int'l L* 328.

70   Gonye, Jaoros & Moyo, Thamsanqa "African nationalist transformative leaders: Opportunities, possibilities and pitfalls in African fiction and politics" (2013) 5:6 *Journal of African Studies and Development* 126.

71   Gassama, *supra* note 69, 334 & 350; Famous among the liberation leaders were Kwame Nkrumah of the Gold Coast (Ghana), Patrice Lumumba of the Belgian Congo (Democratic Republic of Congo), Leopold Sedar Senghor of Senegal, Julius Nyerere of Tanganyika (Tanzania), Jomo Kenyatta of Kenya, Kenneth Kaunda of Northern Rhodesia (Zambia).

the independence states from engaging in further development injustices and governance malpractices. The right to development could have provided such a model as illustrated in this chapter and in subsequent ones.

The African liberation leaders rather believed in achieving political freedom as was echoed by Kwame Nkrumah's rallying ideology to "seek [...] first the political kingdom and every other thing shall be added [...]".[72] The liberation leaders unfortunately underestimated the extent to which slavery and colonialism had ruined African societies and so engaged in the decolonisation project quite nonchalantly.[73] Nkrumah believed, albeit wrongly that: "If we get self-government, [...] we'll transform the Gold Coast [Ghana] into a paradise in ten years".[74] He based this "belief in the capacity of ordinary people to decide their own future through politics".[75] Nkrumah like many of his contemporaries, failed to realise that many of the "ordinary people" that they counted on to determine the future of Africa, were dispossessed of the requisite capacity to engage productively in politics.[76] Africa needed a pragmatic model to drive human development, socio-cultural reconstruction and economic self-determination rather than just political liberation anchored on some civil liberties and freedoms. By this is meant that there was and still is a need for a development model to shape the dysfunctional African societies.

However, because the African leaders craved political independence much more than socio-economic and cultural emancipation, the colonial masters exploited the weaknesses and shrewdly crafted and handed over to the decolonised states succession plans in the form of independence constitutions. Those constitutions, which enshrined a handful of provisions on fundamental human rights and civil liberties, caused African leaders to imagine that the attainment of political independence was bound to bring about development.[77] Unfortunately, the independence constitutions were proficiently designed to breed chaos and instability rather than sustain independence and development on the continent. For instance, it is hard to understand the rationale behind the written constitutions that the British left in their former colonies, which, together with the home government had until then never

---

72   Yergin & Stanislaw, *supra* note 62; Gassama, *supra* note 69, 352.

73   Oloka-Onyango, *supra* note 42, 171.

74   Yergin & Stanislaw, *supra* note 62.

75   Gassama, *supra* note 69, 345.

76   Keller, Edmond J. "Decolonisation, independence and the failure of politics" in Martin, Phyllis & O'Meara, Patrick O. (eds) *Africa* (Bloomington: Indiana University Press, 1995) 156–171.

77   Aguda, T. Akinola *Human Rights and the Right to Development in Africa* (Lagos: Nigerian Institute of International Affairs, 1989) 13; Suhfree, *supra* note 1, vii.

HISTORICAL ACCOUNT ON THE RIGHT TO DEVELOPMENT

been governed through a documented constitution. The constitution they fashioned for Zambia for example, created a presidential system with the name of Kenneth Kaunda enshrined in it as President. Meanwhile, Britain is governed by a parliamentary system.[78] It is doubtful how Zambia, like other independent African states was expected to succeed with the new system of governance, which in most cases was different from the systems they had become accustomed to under colonial rule.

Such manoeuvring was intended arguably, to ensure the failure of the independence project so as to justify the fact that the African peoples are incapable of managing their own affairs. In this way the opportunity was created for the colonial machinery to continue to exercise control over the colonies long after independence through the process that became known as "neo-colonialism".[79] This is not to say that colonialism and neo-colonialism were the only factors that caused the failure of the decolonised states. The inability to govern effectively drove Africa's "irresponsible leadership", as Claude Ake describes it, into corruption, embezzlement and mismanagement of public resources, which make up the political conditions that remain the greatest impediment to development on the continent.[80] However, Ake as well as Alemazung concur to the fact that the foundation for failure was laid in Africa during colonialism and has been sustained through colonial legacies with the accomplice of African ruling elites.[81]

As the African leaders became increasingly conscious that liberation meant much more than nominal political independence, they haphazardly fumbled with a couple of conflicting and poorly conceived ideologies.[82] The likes of Jomo Kenyatta and Mobutu Sese Sekou advocated for western-style capitalism while Julius Nyerere, Sedar Senghor, Kwame Nkrumah and Sekou Touré lobbied for African socialism.[83] Unfortunately, both ideologies were neither

---

78   Go, Julian "Modelling state and sovereignty: Postcolonial constitutions in Asia and Africa" in Lee, Christopher J. (ed) *Making a World after Empire: The Bandung Movement and its Political Afterlives* (Athens: Ohio University Press, 2010) 111–112.

79   See generally Nkrumah, *supra* note 17.

80   Ake, Claude *Democracy and Development in Africa* (Washington DC: The Brookings Institute, 1996) 1; Alemazung, J. Asongazoh "Post-colonial colonialism: An analysis of international factors and actors marring African socio-economic and political development" (2010) 3:10 *The J Pan Afri Stud* 62.

81   Ake, *supra* note 80, 2–6; Alemazung, *supra* note 79, 64–70; see also Pogge, Thomas "Real world justice" (2005) 9:1/2 *The Journal of Ethics* 38; see also Fanon, Frantz (tr: Markmann C.L.) *Black Skin, White Masks* (London: Pluto Press, 1986) 98.

82   Yergin & Stanislaw, *supra* note 63.

83   Ndlovu-Gatsheni 2015, *supra* note 31, 35; Akyeampong, *supra* note 45, 2; Lützelschwab, *supra* note 64, 1–22.

sufficiently conceptualised nor their implementation accompanied by the relevant institutional mechanisms and therefore, lacked the potential to protect the fragile independent African states from neo-colonial exploitation. The granting of independence thus allocated to the African states "all the classic attributes of statehood" and "judicial sovereignty" implied by the termination of colonialism.[84] However, the emerging states virtually failed to attain nationhood because without an appropriate founding model, the independent states exercised self-government, but remained porous and incapable of the economic potential to uplift the African peoples out of poverty.[85]

The internal conflicts and political instability that ensued in almost all of the new African states in the years after independence proved that the acquisition of some civil liberties and political freedoms without an appropriate framework for socio-economic and cultural development was fatally wrong. Through increased consciousness of that fact, African states quickly resorted to the codification of laws into various treaty and statutory instruments to protect the African patrimony, a project which in my opinion should have taken place prior to independence. However, as the saying goes that it is better late than never, the codification of African law, beginning with the Charter of the Organisation of African Unity (OAU) as François Borella points out, has increasingly taken a developmental orientation.[86] Such a move represents a step in the right direction in laying down the minimum standards for the legal protection of Africa's development aspirations *vis-à-vis* the exploitative behaviour of foreign stakeholders. In this light, it is argued that if the struggle and subsequent acquisition of independence was anchored on the right to development, the probability of sustained development for Africa would have been much greater.

2.2.2 Post-independence Difficulties

From the foregoing analysis, the purpose here is to establish the fact that the difficulties that Africa encountered after independence came about largely because of the lack of an operational model to drive development on the continent. The anti-colonial struggles for liberation carried great promise that things would be different and better, politically, economically, and

---

84 Le Vine, Victor T. *The Cameroons: From Mandate to Independence* (London: University of California Press, 1964) 217.

85 Le Vine, *supra* note 84, 217; Ake, *supra* note 80, 8–14; New Partnership for Africa's Development (NEPAD) Declaration, adopted in Abuja, Nigeria October 2001 paras 18–27.

86 Borella, François "Le système juridique de l'Organisation de l'Unité Africaine" (1971) 17 *Annuaire Français de Droit International* 246.

otherwise.[87] When Sen describes development as freedom, pragmatically he is saying that by exercising the capability to perform the human functioning of doing and being, the fact of that freedom should translate into development, which requires the removal of various types of "unfreedoms" that limit peoples' choices and leave them with little prospect of taking reasoned action.[88] Accordingly, with the freedom achieved through independence, the scenario was created for the peoples of Africa to proceed to transforming the continent both in terms of material acquisition and in terms of expanding capabilities and choices. However, events took a different dimension from the aspirations of the African peoples.[89]

Instead of engaging in the advancement of the human potential as the basis for consolidating independence, the immediate post-independence challenge that Africa faced as Gassama has noted, was that of struggling to define its political future amidst the complexity of domestic challenges and encroaching globalisation.[90] Africa needed, and of course still needs a post-independence strategy beyond that offered by the "generation of woefully unprepared leaders" who, instead of positioning Africa on the path of development, resorted to futile efforts in combating neo-colonialism, which simply took advantage of their lack of foresight.[91] Thus, independence brought not the destruction of colonial practices but rather just transferred colonial administration into the hands of the political elites who, backed by the powers bestowed on them by the independence constitutions, administered the fragile states with unfettered control.[92]

The OAU was established in 1963 as a post-colonial institutional mechanism to harness the gains of independence and to ensure increased well-being for the African peoples.[93] By this time most of Africa had gained independence, which presented the opportunity to right the wrongs of the past by proclaiming the right to development as the basis for the formation of the OAU. The

---

87   Bulhan, Hussein A. "Stages of colonialism in Africa: From occupation of land to occupation of being" (2015) 3:1 *Journal of Social and Political Psychology* 240; Gassama, *supra* note 69, 351–352.

88   See generally Sen, *supra* note 58.

89   Gassama, *supra* note 69, 334; Bulhan, *supra* note 87, 240.

90   Gassama, *supra* note 69, 334.

91   As above, 353.

92   Heldring & Robinson, *supra* note 32, 19; Poku, Nana & Mdee, Anna *Politics in Africa: A New Introduction* (New York: Zed Books, 2011) 18, 22; Ndulo, Muna "The democratisation process and structural adjustment in Africa" (2003) *India J Global L Stud* 333; Ake, *supra* note 80, 4.

93   OAU Charter, *supra* note 59, art 2.

wordings of the preamble to the OAU Charter and article 2 which sets out the purpose of the organisation contain elements that could have been regrouped into a binding provision on the right to development.[94] However, the African leaders lacked the foresight to do so. Such a formulation would have established the framework to drive the continent's development agenda much more effectively than has so far been achieved. By this, the claim is stated that the right to development would have laid the foundation for post-colonial development in Africa. On the basis of this argument, the assertion that the right to development in Africa is achievable through development cooperation is disputed in chapter three. Justification to the claim is further provided in chapter five, where the case is advanced for conceptualising the right to development as a development model for Africa. In the absence of such a framework model for development, Africa has been forced to rely on imported models that bear no relevance to the socio-economic and cultural development exigencies[95] that has left the continent even more vulnerable to continuous external domination and exploitation, which is explained in the subsequent chapters. In what follows, the analysis focuses on how the right to development has evolved in Africa.

3 Evolution of the Right to Development

3.1 *Latent Manifestations*
The purpose of this section is to illustrate that the idea of a right to development lingered in the African imagination but did not quickly find articulation or become reality in an instant. The idea evolved gradually and took different expressions, implicit and explicit. It also took on an international dimension within the context of decolonisation, articulated through the right

---

94 The preamble to the OAU Charter states that: "We, the Heads of African States and Governments [...]:
Convinced that it is the inalienable right of all people to control their own destiny;
Conscious of the fact that freedom, equality, justice and dignity are essential objectives for the achievement of the legitimate aspirations of the Africa peoples;
Conscious of our responsibility to harness the natural and human resources of our continent for the total advancement of our peoples in all spheres of human endeavour [...]" Have agreed to [...]
Art 2(1)(b) – "To co-ordinate and intensify their cooperation and efforts to achieve a better life for the peoples of Africa [...]".

95 Ngang, Carol C. "Towards a right-to-development governance in Africa" (2018) 17:1 *Journal of Human Rights* 113.

to self-determination, which paved the way for independence, resulting in the recognition of former colonial territories as henceforth sovereign states and subjects of international law. Subsequently, the idea of development as a human right also gained currency during the post-independence era through the campaign for a new international economic order (NIEO) by which developing countries sought to redress the prevailing *status quo* of global imbalances.

3.1.1 Self-Determination

The right to development, as many authors have noted, is inextricably bonded to or at least implied in the right to self-determination, which guarantees the right to seek political freedom and to freely pursue economic, social and cultural development.[96] When the UN Charter was adopted in 1945, it took into consideration the plight of colonised peoples and therefore stated as one of its founding principles, to promote the ideals of sovereign equality, universal respect for human rights and the *self-determination of peoples* in view of creating "conditions of stability and well-being".[97] By acknowledging the equal right of colonised peoples to self-determination, the Charter signalled the fact that colonial practices were unacceptable under international law. The right to self-determination thus, guarantees that no people have the right to dominate or exploit another as stipulated in the Declaration on the Granting of Independence:

> The subjection of peoples to alien subjugation, domination and exploitation constitutes a denial of fundamental human rights, is contrary to the Charter of the United Nations and is an impediment to the promotion of world peace and co-operation.[98]

---

96 Anghie, Anthony "Whose utopia?: Human rights, development and the third world" (2013) 22:1 *Qui Parle: Critical Humanities and Social Sciences* 66; Udombana, Nsongurua J. "The third world and the right to development: Agenda for the next millennium" (2000) 22:3 *Hum Rts Qtly* 769–770; Kamga, Serges A.D. "Human rights in Africa: Prospects for the realisation of the right to development under the New Partnership for Africa's Development" (Doctoral Thesis University of Pretoria 2011) 131–132; Oloka-Onyango, *supra* note 41, 166; see also common art 1 of the ICESCR, *supra* note 2 and International Covenant on Civil and Political Rights (ICCPR) adopted by General Assembly Resolution 2200A (XXI) 1966; Vienna Declaration and Program of Action adopted at the World Conference on Human Rights June 1993 para 1(2); Declaration on the Right to Development Resolution A/RES/41/128 adopted by the UN General Assembly on 4 December 1986 art 1(2); Declaration on Principles of International Law Concerning Friendly Relations, *supra* note 62.

97 UN Charter, *supra* note 3, arts 1(2) & 55.

98 Declaration on the Granting of Independence to Colonial Countries and Peoples adopted by General Assembly Resolution 1514 (XV) 14 December 1960 preamble.

The right to self-determination gained currency within the context of decolonisation and thus, provided the legal and political platform on which liberation of the colonised territories of Africa was achieved.[99] Entrenched within the framework of international law, the right to self-determination did not straightforwardly translate into the right to development, but contained elements of it and thus facilitated decolonisation as many of the African colonies launched their campaign for independence on the platform of self-determination. The right to self-determination thus also provided the first steps in the articulation of the right to development with clearly similar objectives, as the UN General Assembly is reported to have qualified the right to self-determination as a "prerequisite for the full enjoyment of all fundamental human rights".[100]

Apart from the UN Charter, entrenchment of the right to self-determination in other international human rights instruments guarantees that it amounts to a human rights offence to deprive a people of the opportunity for development.[101] International law recognises as an integral part of the right to self-determination: a people's right to sovereign ownership over their natural wealth and resources as a guarantee to social progress and development.[102] The idea of a right to development that emerged after independence was in effect, as Anthony Anghie correctly observes an extension of the project of decolonisation that was achieved on the platform of self-determination.[103] The right to development was born out of the consciousness as Ndlovu-Gatsheni explains that "[d]ecolonisation only led to the incorporation of African states at the lowest echelons of the asymmetrical modern global power structure without

---

99   Özden, Melik & Golay, Christophe "The right of peoples to self-determination and to permanent sovereignty over their natural resources seen from a human rights perspective" (2010) *CETIM* 1.

100   See El-Obaid, Ahmed El-O. & Appiagyei-Atua, Kwadwo "Human rights in Africa: A new perspective on linking the past to the present" (1996) 41:4 *McGill Law Journal* 839.

101   Vienna Declaration, *supra* note 94, stipulates in para 1(2) that the "denial of the right of self-determination as a violation of human rights and underlines the importance of the effective realization of this right". The preamble to the Declaration on the Principles of International Law Concerning Friendly Relations and Cooperation conveys the idea that the subjection of peoples to alien subjugation, domination and exploitation constitutes a violation of the principle, as well as a denial of fundamental human rights, and is contrary to the UN Charter. The Declaration on the Granting of Independence to Colonial Countries Peoples also establishes in para 1 that "The subjection of peoples to alien subjugation, domination and exploitation constitutes a denial of fundamental human rights, is contrary to the Charter of the United Nations and is an impediment to the promotion of world peace and co-operation".

102   Declaration on Social Progress and Development adopted by General Assemble Resolution 2542 (XXIV) 11 December 1969; Oloka-Onyango, *supra* note 42, 173.

103   Anghie, *supra* note 96, 66.

HISTORICAL ACCOUNT ON THE RIGHT TO DEVELOPMENT

destroying global coloniality".[104] Self-determination resulted in political independence, while the right to development is envisaged to facilitate socio-economic and cultural autonomy.[105] The right to development is said to be implied in the right to self-determination in the sense that both are envisaged not as individual rights but as collective entitlements.[106] Identifying with this collective entitlement, the countries of the developing world that felt sidelined within the framing of global coloniality found reason to contest the power play with the hope to achieve some form of global balance.

3.1.2   Third World Aspirations for Global Balance
The origin of the right to development can also be traced to the NIEO campaign championed largely by African countries in the 1970s as part of the quest for a just global system that reflects the aspirations of developing countries.[107] It should be noted that in the aftermath of the Second World War, following the creation of the UN and the Breton Woods institutions, these entities proceeded to establish the systems, set the standards and in effect, defined the models by which the world would be governed. In doing so, colonial territories were unfortunately not included in the global policy and decision-making processes. When these colonial territories gained independence and became part of the global framework and thus, (alienated) subjects of international law, they were by rule of law required to comply with the established norms even though they never took part in formulating those norms. It therefore became necessary, on the basis of the international law principle of sovereign equality of states, to reconceptualise the models in force, which largely disfavoured the emerging, relatively fragile developing states. This ignited the campaign for a NIEO, intended to address questions relating to the advancement of developing countries.[108]

---

104   Ndlovu-Gatsheni, Sabelo J. "Global coloniality and the challenges of creating African futures" (2014) 36:2 *Strategic Review for Southern Africa* 189; see also Grosfoguel, Ramón "The epistemic decolonial turn: Beyond political-economy paradigms" (2007) 21:2/3 *Cultural Studies* 219.

105   ICCPR, *supra* note 96, art 1(1).

106   Oloka-Onyango, *supra* note 42, 166; African Charter on Human and Peoples' Rights adopted in Nairobi, Kenya on 27 June 1981 OAU Doc CAB/LEG/67/3 Rev.5 (1981) art 22(1); UN Human Rights (ed) *Realizing the Right to Development: Essays in Commemoration of 25 Years of the United Nations Declaration on the Right to Development* (Geneva: UN Publication, 2013) 12.

107   Kwakwa, Edward "Emerging international development law and traditional international law: Congruent or cleavage?" (1987) 17:3/2 *Georgia J Int'l & Comp L* 431.

108   Nagan, Winston P. "The right to development and the importance of human and social capital as human rights issues" (2013) 1:6 *Cadmus Journal* 29.

Beside the global imbalances generated by the combination of colonial and post-colonial forces, the NIEO campaign demonstrated that the economic growth ambitions of developed countries jeopardised prospects for advancement in developing countries.[109] The campaign highlighted concerns about unfair agricultural policies and free trade rules imposed by the World Trade Organisation (WTO), which systematically disfavour developing countries and therefore only serve as a tool through which developed countries institutionalised their economic dominance.[110] As Udombana has noted, the decolonised African states were simply dragged into and constrained to abide by the rules of free trade[111] without sufficient guarantees on how they would succeed within the free trade regime which is dominated by industrialised countries. These measures proved extremely disadvantageous to developing countries, especially those in Africa, which depend heavily on agriculture for economic growth. With these frustrations, developing countries demanded significant changes in the global arrangement.[112]

To the extent that developing countries envisage achieving structural changes within the global system and a "more just global order",[113] the NIEO agenda may rightly be said to have embodied the idea that developing countries are entitled to choose their own development path. Upendra Baxi notes that although the NIEO campaign was not anchored on the language of rights, it unavoidably emphasised the idea of entitlement to work and employment, education, meaningful participation and freedom from exploitation.[114] The right to development, which conveys the idea of equality of opportunity for development as Baxi also rightly points out, evolved in principle from the same notion of basic needs and associated notions of conversion of those needs into

---

109   See generally Ngang, Carol C. "Differentiated responsibilities under international law and the right to development paradigm for developing countries" (2017) 11:2 *HR & ILD* 265–288.

110   Birovljev, Jelena & Ćetković, Biljana "The impact of the WTO Agreement on Agriculture on food security in developing countries" (2013) 135 *EAAE Seminar – Challenges for the Global Agricultural Trade Regime after Doha* 57; Schoenstein, Anna & Alemany, Cecilia "Development cooperation beyond the aid effectiveness paradigm: A women's rights perspective" (2011) *Association for Women's Rights in Development – Discussion Paper* 1; Oxfam "Rigged rules and double standards: Trade, globalisation and the fight against poverty" (2002) 23; Cornwall & Nyamu-Musembi, *supra* note 9,1422.

111   Udombana, *supra* note 96, 760.

112   Clapp, Jennifer "Developing countries and the WTO Agriculture Negotiations" (2006) *The Centre for International Governance Innovation – Working Paper No 6* 1-2.

113   Baxi, Upendra "The new international economic order, basic needs and rights: Notes towards development of the right to development" (1983) *Indian J Int'l L* 225–227.

114   As above, 231.

rights.[115] In running the campaign for an equitable global system, developing countries hoped to achieve redistributive justice as a matter of right to that which they were deprived of as a result of the imbalances created by the global arrangement.[116]

The campaign to further the cause for global equity and justice culminated in the drafting of the Declaration for a New International Economic Order in 1974, which aimed at upholding the economic position of the new sovereign participants within the global society.[117] Although the aspirations for a new global economic order failed to materialise, it paved the way for the first public pronouncement of the right to development at a conference involving the group of developing countries that championed the cause for restructuring the global order.[118] It turned out, as Margot Salomon observes, that the Declaration on the Right to Development was adopted as a follow-up to the quest by the community of developing countries for a just global system to redress the imbalances created by the prevailing economic arrangement.[119] The Declaration on the Right to Development in effect pays tribute to the resolution on the new international economic order as an important antecedent to the concept of the right to development.[120]

3.2   *Formal Recognition*

Following the events described in the previous sections, which illustrate clear manifestations of development injustices inflicted on Africa through different forms of imperial practices including slavery, colonialism and neo-colonialism, the formal recognition of the right to development happened in two stages: First, through proclamations emanating from the African continent and subsequently through the legal recognition and protection of the right to development in official instruments both at the African and at the international levels.

---

115   As above.

116   Udombana, *supra* note 96, 763.

117   Nagan, *supra* note 108, 29.

118   Ouguergouz, Fatsah *The African Charter on Human and Peoples' Rights: A Comprehensive Agenda for Human Dignity and Sustainable Democracy in Africa* (Dordrecht: Martinus Nijhoff Publishers, 2003) 298.

119   Salomon, Margot E. *Global Responsibility for Human Rights: World Poverty and the Development of International Law* (Oxford: Oxford University Press, 2008) 50.

120   Declaration on the Right to Development, *supra* note96, art 3(3).

44   CHAPTER 2

3.2.1   Proclamations on the Right to Development
Tribute has largely been paid to Senegalese Jurist Kéba M'baye for conceptualising the idea of development as a human right. However, earlier proclamations of the right to development are recorded to have been made prior to M'baye's pronouncement. It is noted for instance that while addressing the Economic Conference of the Group of 77 (currently consisting of 134) developing countries in Algiers, Algeria in October 1967, Senegalese Minister of Foreign Affairs, Doudou Thiam categorically declared that "[t]he old colonial past, of which the present is merely an extension, should be denounced" and to "proclaim, loud and clear, *the right to development* for the nations of the Third World" (emphasis added).[121] Thiam did not only state the fact that developing countries were entitled to the right to development, but made clear that the right emanated from the development injustices that characterised the colonial past, which he advocated for countries of the third world to denounce. He was thus, stating that Africa, among other developing countries have the right to be released from the injustices of socio-economic subjugation. By emphatically stating the need to proclaim the right to development, Thiam sounded loud and clear that developing countries do not need to be plugged into the systems of the industrialised world to be able to function.

Two years later in the same city of Algiers in Algeria another early pronouncement on the right to development is recorded to have been made in 1969 by the humanitarian and anti-imperialist Archbishop Emeritus, Cardinal Léon-Étienne Duval.[122] Cardinal Duval decried the development injustices perpetuated by industialised countries and thus advocated that "the right to development should be proclaimed for the Third World".[123] Kéba M'baye is rightly credited to have brought the concept of the right to development to the limelight in academic discourse in 1972 when he stated in legal terms that the right to development is indeed a human right guaranteed to be enjoyed by everybody.[124] M'baye's argument laid the foundation for conceptualising development as an inherent legal entitlement to which all other fundamental

---

121   Ouguergouz, *supra* note 118, 298; Okafor, Obiora C. "A regional perspective: Article 22 of the African Charter on Human and Peoples' Rights" in UN Human Rights (ed) *Realizing the Right to Development: Essays in Commemoration of 25 Years of the United Nations Declaration on the Right to Development* (Geneva: UN Publication, 2013) 374.

122   Ouguergouz, *supra* note 118, 298.

123   As above.

124   M'baye, Kéba "Le droit au développement comme un droit de l'homme: Leçon inaugural de la troisième session d'enseignement de l'Institut International des Droits de l'Homme" (1972) 5 *Revue des Droits de l'Homme* 505–534; Manzo, Kate "Africa in the rise of rights-based development" (2003) 34:4 *Geoforum* 439 ; Ouguergouz, *supra* note 118, 298–299.

rights and freedoms are connected to define the existence and survival of the peoples of Africa.[125] When M'baye stated the claim for a right to development, he was concerned about the exploitation of the African peoples, which in legal terms constitutes a human rights offence necessitating redress by the law.[126] After his proclamation the right to development gained widespread attention in academia and in development politics.[127] What did Thiam, Duval, and M'baye envisage when they advocated for the right to development for Africa or more broadly for developing countries?

Quite reasonably, these early proponents could not have intended to incite the peoples of Africa to assert an entitlement to development from the new states that had just emerged from decades of colonialism. Rather, they were postulating a model or an operational paradigm with the potential to determine Africa's future and its prospects for development *vis-à-vis* the aggressive imperialistic attitude of developed countries and their instruments for domination. Emerging from the continent of Africa shortly after independence, the proclamations on the right to development did not just coincide with the happenings of the time; they were informed by the same injustices that motivated decolonisation and continues to threaten the foundations of African societies. It is apparent as articulated by Ndlovu-Gatsheni that in the absence of an alternative model, Africa would not have the resilience to combat global coloniality that continues to limit development prospects for the continent.[128] The pronouncements on the right to development echoed the decolonial frame of mind to claim as a matter of entitlement the freedom to determine a development agenda that is suited to Africa and the liberty to enjoy the benefits deriving therefrom.[129]

At the dawn of independence in Africa, the proponents of the right to development were not only preoccupied with preserving the newly gained freedom, but in essence were postulating a development paradigm to drive Africa into a new era, which unfortunately was not and until recently has not been taken seriously. It is necessary to make a comparative reference to South Africa as the last kid on the block to gain independence in 1990. South Africa probably

---

125   Bulajic, Milan "Principle of international development law: The right to development as an inalienable human right" in de Waart, Paul; Paul, Peters & Denters, Erik (eds) *International Law and Development* (Dordrecht: Martinus Nijhoff Publishers, 1988) 359.

126   Shivji, Issa G. *The Concept of Human Rights in Africa* (London: African Books Collective, 1989) 30.

127   Ouguergouz, *supra* note 118, 299.

128   Ndlovu-Gatsheni 2014, *supra* note 104, 185–186.

129   See generally Ngang 2018, *supra* note 95, 107–122; Nkrumah, *supra* note 17, xv.

learnt from the experience of other African countries and therefore structured its independence within the legal framework of transformative constitutionalism.[130] There is no denying the fact that South Africa's independence has been more sustainable than the wave of independence achieved by the majority of African countries in the late 1950s and in the 1960s, which, of course, lacked a solid operational model to stand on.[131] The acquisition of independence by the American colonies under British colonial rule provides an informative example. When the thirteen American colonies achieved independence in 1776, they stated and documented in the Declaration of Independence a list of grievances and injustices that necessitated and justified their rejection of British colonial rule, which became entrenched as part of the fundamental statute law that defines American democracy.[132]

It is assumed that the injustices that the American colonies suffered under British rule were not unlike what the African colonies endured under European imperialism,[133] with the exception that the proponents of independence in the American colonies were themselves settler colonists, who were in the process of subjugating the native American peoples. This notwithstanding, it is argued that a similar obligation necessitated the decolonised African states to have formulated their rejection of colonialism in a declaration on the right to development to pilot the course of independence. However, the independence leaders opted to seek first the "political kingdom" with the anticipation that every other thing about development would eventually be added.[134] A unified

---

130 See generally Rapatsa, Mashele "Transformative constitutionalism in South Africa: 20 years of democracy" (2014) 5:27 *Mediterranean Journal of Social Sciences* 887–895.

131 Not long after independence most of the African states plunged into instability; including economic stagnation, political strive, lethal civil and ethnic conflicts, single party dictatorship, military *coup d'états* and widespread tyranny up till the 1990s when the wind of political change began to blow across the continent. Meanwhile, South Africa, although it may not represent the best example as it has its own share of weaknesses, has been able to sustain its independence relatively steadily for over twenty five years.

132 National Centre for Constitutional Studies "The Declaration of Independence part of American law" available at: http://www.nccs.net/1998-06-the-declaration-of -independence-part-of-american-law.php (accessed: 20 February 2016); The Heritage Foundation "The Declaration of Independence July 4 1776" available at: http://www .heritage.org/initiatives/first-principles/primary-sources/the-declaration-of-independence (accessed: 14 February 2016).

133 American Government "The colonial experience" available at: http://www.ushistory.org/ gov/2a.asp (accessed: 16 August 2017). It states that "British rule suppressed political, economic, and religious freedoms", coupled with arbitrary taxation which were not unlike the conditions under which African colonies were oppressed by the European colonialists.

134 See Yergin & Stanislaw, *supra* note 63, 2: Ghana's independence leader, Kwame Nkrumah whose country became the first to gain independence in 1957 inspired his peers across

HISTORICAL ACCOUNT ON THE RIGHT TO DEVELOPMENT

proclamation on the right to development, which highlights the ideas of equity and justice would have made much more sense as a development model for Africa than the nominal political independence that each of the African states achieved in isolation. The granting of political independence deflected attention away from socio-economic and cultural concerns and in effect, concealed many of the colonial injustices for which the perpetrators ought to have been held accountable. As an analogy to this point, Mamdani shows how South Africa's transition from apartheid to constitutional democracy was marred by political compromises through which perpetrators of the ills of apartheid were shielded from legal responsibility for their actions and in particular those causing the socio-economic underdevelopment of black South Africans.[135]

A uniform declaration of independence on the basis of the right to development would in my opinion have established an indomitable force to withstand any form of imperial domination. However, the right to development – an African brainchild, born out of decolonial thinking – was hijacked by international actors, who in trying to extrapolate on its meaning have actually not accomplished much, but dragged the concept into controversy and, therefore, confused its original meaning and purpose. Although the right to development has eventually become a subject of international concern, its unique dimensions as an African concept have, to some extent, been retained.

3.2.2   Legal Recognition and Protection

Legal recognition and protection refer to official guarantees and documented evidence on the right to development both in hard law and in soft law instruments. Owing to the fact that the question of development invariably connects Africa to the rest of the world, and that most of the development injustices that Africa suffers often stem from the actions of developed countries and other international actors, it is important to look at the recognition of the right to development at the African as well as at the international levels. This is to ensure a balanced determination of the extent to which foreign stakeholders are morally or legally bound by the right to development in Africa as discussed in chapters four and five.

Contrary to the conviction that the right to development was first officially documented by the UN Commission on Human Rights in 1977,[136] the right to

---

Africa with his philosophy of self-government and autonomy as preconditions for development.

135 Mamdani, Mahmoud "Amnesty or impunity?: A preliminary critique of the Report of the Truth and Reconciliation Commission of South Africa (TRC)" (2002) 32:3/4 *Diacritics* 57.

136 UN Commission on Human Rights Res 4 (XXXIII) 21 February 1977; Mahalu, Costa R. "Human rights and development: An African perspective" (2009) 1:1 *Leiden J Int'l L* 19.

development was indeed first given official statutory recognition in the 1972 Constitution of Cameroon,[137] following the public proclamations by Doudou Thiam, Cardinal Duval and Kéba M'baye. The UN Commission on Human Rights only subsequently endorsed the right to development in 1977 and went further to commission an investigation on its international dimensions as a human right.[138] Based on the findings of this investigation, the General Assembly adopted Resolution 34/46 in 1979, recognising that the right to development is indeed a human right that guarantees equality of opportunity for development as an entitlement guaranteed to states and to individuals.[139] This marked the beginning of the shift in the original formulation of the right to development as essentially a collective entitlement.

The implication for recognising the right to development, particularly at international level was that the perpetuation of development injustices was acknowledged to be unacceptable. By this assurance African governments hoped, although erroneously that it was a ticket to access some form of remedial justice against the perpetrators of the historical injustices of slavery and colonialism.[140] The race for the recognition of the right to development gathered momentum in the 1980s. Groundwork towards its codification at the international level took off in March 1981 when the UN Commission on Human Rights assigned a Working Group of Governmental Experts to investigate and draft an international instrument on the right to development, which, however, only became available five years later in 1986.[141]

Meanwhile, in Africa, the stage was set for the writing of the Charter on Human and Peoples' Rights. While commissioning the group of legal experts for the drafting of the charter, the then Senegalese President, Sedar Senghor enjoined the Committee to draw inspiration from African value systems and traditions and also to prioritise the actual needs of Africans as well as their

---

137   Constitution of the Republic of Cameroon 1972 as amended. Article 65 guarantees that the preamble forms an integral part of the Constitution, which means, although contained in the preamble, the right to development has the nature of a legally enforceable right.

138   UN Human Rights, *supra* note 106, 3.

139   UN General Assembly Resolution A/RES/34/46 of 23 November 1979 para 8; see also Rich, Roland Y. "The right to development as an emerging human right" (1983) 23 *Virg J Int'l L* 322; Tadeg, Mesenbet A. "Reflections on the right to development: Challenges and prospects" (2010) 10:2 *AHRLJ* 329.

140   Tadeg, *supra* note 139, 340.

141   UN Human Rights, *supra* note 106, 3.

HISTORICAL ACCOUNT ON THE RIGHT TO DEVELOPMENT

right to development.[142] Senghor is quoted to have stated succinctly that "[w]e want to lay emphasis on the right to development and other rights which need the solidarity of our states to be fully met".[143] In 1981, the same year that the UN Working Group was established and getting ready to start work to produce a universal document on the right to development, Africa went ahead to adopt the African Charter on Human and Peoples' Rights in which it provided legal recognition and protection of the right to development as a justiciable entitlement to the peoples of Africa.[144] As Chinedu Okafor has observed, the African Charter became the first hard law instrument to enshrine the right to development, not only within the context of Africa's evolving human rights law but also within the context of international human rights law.[145] Africa thus, made a significant contribution not only in terms of pioneering the legal recognition of the right to development but also in integrating human rights and development within a legal framework. The Charter came into force in October 1986, two months before the UN General Assembly adopted the Declaration on the Right to Development in December 1986.

Unlike the African Charter, the UN Declaration contains noticeable differences in the formulation of the right to development.[146] One of such

---

142   Centre for Human Rights *A Guide to the African Human Rights System: Celebrating 30 Years since the Entry into Force of the African Charter on Human and Peoples' Rights 1986–2016* (Pretoria: University of Pretoria Law Press, 2016) 2.

143   See *Kevin Mgwanga Gumne & Others v Cameroon* (2009) AHRLR 9 (ACHPR 2009) para 173; see also Baricako, Germain "Introductory preface: The African Charter and African Commission on Human and Peoples' Rights" in Evans, Malcom & Murray, Rachel (eds) *The African Charter on Human and Peoples' Rights: The System in Practice 1986–2006* (Cambridge: Cambridge University Press, 2008) 6; Mahalu, *supra* note 135, 23; Ouguergouz, *supra* note 117, 41; Address delivered by Mr Leopold Sedar Senghor, President of Senegal (28 November 1979), OAU DOC CAB/LEG/67/5; (The meeting for the drafting of the African Charter held in Dakar, Senegal from 28 November to 8 December 1979).

144   The African Charter was adopted on 27 June 1981 three months after the Working Group was commissioned to start work on the right to development. The Charter entered into force on 21 October 1986, two months before the UN Declaration on the Right to Development was adopted on 4 December 1986.

145   Okafor, Obiora C. " 'Righting' the right to development: A socio-legal analysis of article 22 of the African Charter on Human and Peoples' Rights" in Marks, Stephen P. (ed) *Implementing the Right to Development: The Role of International Law* (Geneva: Friedrich-Ebert-Stiftung, 2008) 52.

146   The differences in the conceptualisation of the right to development in the African Charter and the Declaration on the Right to Development include the following: 1) The African Charter makes clear that the right to development is a collective right guaranteed only to peoples, while the Declaration on the Right to Development stipulates that it is both an individual and a collective right. 2) The African Charter envisages socio-economic and cultural development as a claimable entitlement, while the Declaration on

differences is the conflicting arrangement with regard to development cooperation as a mechanism for the realisation of the right to development. Development cooperation ought to provide the framework for redressing the structural imbalances created by international actors, which in turn impacts adversely on the aspirations of developing countries.[147] However, while the African Charter enshrines the right to development as an absolute legal entitlement, the moral character of the Declaration on the Right to Development leaves questions with regard to the need to have recourse to development cooperation as a mechanism for its realisation. This is challenging, because for developed countries, cooperation provides the opportunity to dominate weaker developing countries.[148] It explains the reluctance of developed countries to commit to a legal obligation on the right to development, preferring a non-compelling approach, for example, through global partnerships in dealing with issues of human rights and development.[149]

A compromise was thus reached when world leaders attending the Millennium Summit in 2000 "committed to making the right to development a reality for everyone".[150] This, however, remains a moral commitment without any genuine obligation to ensure its realisation. By this arrangement they consented to the setting of time-bound goals for combating development challenges through a global partnership for development.[151] Although the Millennium Declaration set out to eradicate extreme poverty and to achieve human development and the realisation of human rights, the resultant Millennium Development Goals (MDG) failed to incorporate human rights. The MDGs lacked the force of law and, therefore, imposed no legally binding obligations. Consequently, Thomas Pogge has expressed reservation with regard to the framing of such global actions to eradicate global poverty owing

---

the Right to Development sees the right to development as an inalienable human right which only allows individuals and peoples to participate in, contribute to and benefit from economic, social, cultural and political development.

147   Salomon 2008, *supra* note 119, 50.

148   See Alemazung, *supra* note 79, 70–73. Alemazung explains how after independence the colonial masters sought means of protecting their interests and retaining economic control in Africa and thus introduced the (ill-intentioned) mechanism of development aid, which she says is based on the hidden intention to secure control over the resources, the economy and politics in the ex-colonies.

149   Kirchmeier, Felix "The right to development – where do we stand?: State of the debate on the right to development" (2006) *Friedrich Ebert Stiftung – Occasional Paper No 23* 13–17.

150   UN Millennium Declaration Resolution *A/55/L.2* adopted by the General Assembly on 18 September 2000 para III(11).

151   Villaroman, Noel G. "Rescuing a troubled concept: An alternative view of the right to development" (2011) 29:1 *Neth Qtly Hum Rts* 15.

to the lack of sufficient clarity on the roles and responsibilities that states are supposed to play.[152] Following after the Millennium Summit, the Durban Declaration of 2001 reaffirmed the solemn promise by all states to promote the right to development among other human rights.[153]

While the right to development continued in its strides as soft law at international level, Africa stepped decisively ahead of the international community to further develop its normative dimensions in other treaty instruments. In 2003, the African Union adopted the Protocol on the Rights of Women in Africa, which recognises the rights of women to sustainable development.[154] This is a ground-breaking achievement for Africa where women have generally been suppressed through conservative practices. In spite of pessimism, the African Commission on Human and Peoples' Rights forged ahead to demonstrate that the right to development is indeed justiciable. In 2004 the Commission dealt with the first inter-state communication in the *Democratic Republic of Congo* (*DRC*) case in which it found the respondent states in violation of article 22 on the right to development, among other provisions of the African Charter.[155] The right to development thus gained not only legal recognition but also judicial enforcement as a justiciable entitlement.

As can be observed, the African human rights system, more than any other in the world has championed the cause on the right to development, both in terms of developing its normativity and in terms of jurisprudential advancement. Another major milestone was recorded in 2006 with the adoption of the African Youth Charter, which like the other regional treaty instruments clearly guaranteed legal protection on the right to development for the youth of Africa.[156] In 2009 the African Commission further dealt with the *Darfur* case[157] and the groundbreaking *Endorois* case.[158] The litigation remains a landmark in the African Commission's jurisprudence because of the precedent it set in

---

152 Pogge, Thomas "The Sustainable Development Goals: Brilliant propaganda? (2015) *Annals of the University of Bucharest – Political Science Series ISSN 1582-2486* 1.

153 Durban Declaration adopted at the World Conference against Racism, Racial Discrimination, Xenophobia and Related Intolerance Durban, South Africa 31 August – 8 September 2001 paras 19 & 78.

154 Protocol to the African Charter on Human and Peoples' Rights on the Rights of Women in Africa adopted in Maputo Mozambique on 11 July 2003 art 19.

155 *Democratic Republic of Congo v Burundi, Rwanda and Uganda* (2004) AHRLR 19 (ACHPR 2003) para 95.

156 African Youth Charter adopted in Banjul, The Gambia on 2 July 2006 art 10.

157 *Sudan Human Rights Organisation & Another v Sudan* (2009) AHRLR 153 (ACHPR 2009) para 224.

158 *Centre for Minority Rights Development (Kenya) & Minority Rights Group International on Behalf of Endorois Welfare Council v Kenya* (2009) AHRLR 75 (ACHPR 2009).

clarifying the intricate dimensions of the right to development as a collective entitlement.[159] Following the increasing importance attached to the right to development within the African human rights system, coupled with the legal commitments undertaken under ancillary treaties and other international instruments, a number of African countries have proceeded to domesticate the right to development as an entrenched right in their national constitutions.[160] These, together with the African treaty instruments and the cases highlighted in this section, are discussed in detail in chapter three.

The fact that the right to development is guaranteed legal protection in Africa creates expectations for justice and fairness as well as liberty of action in self-determining an African development agenda. This is unlike in the instance where the power of policy-making on issues relating to development in Africa remains in the hands of foreign stakeholders.[161] The legal guarantees on the right to development in the African treaty instruments also make a normative proposition that any threat or contravention of the right would amount to an offence against the law and therefore, susceptible to adjudication.[162] It is important to note that the right to development in Africa is formulated with the realities of the socio-economic and cultural challenges in mind and the need to address those realities. The African Charter makes clear that it is primarily the duty of state parties to do so.[163] This has largely not been achieved, owing to the absence of an enabling international environment, which constitutes a critical constraint to country efforts to ensure the enjoyment of the right to development.[164] Thus, its status in law in Africa raises concerns regarding its realisation.

Concerning the requirement to have recourse to development cooperation for the realisation of the right to development, the Charter fails to take

---

159 Kamga, *supra* note 96, 382.

160 The countries include Cameroon, Malawi, the DRC, Ethiopia as well as Benin and Nigeria, which provide explicit guarantees and also South Africa, Sao Tome and Principe and Burkina Faso, which provide implicit guarantees. More explanation on this is provided in chapter five.

161 Sengupta, Arjun "The human right to development" (2004) 32:2 *Oxf Dev't Stud* 194. Fiscal and economic policies for Africa are in most cases decided by the IMF and the World Bank, in most cases without the involvement or participation of the countries concerned where the policies are to be implemented. A typical example is the structural adjustment policies that were imposed on African countries for implementation.

162 African Charter, *supra* note 106, art 22; African Youth Charter, *supra* note 156, art 10; Protocol on the Rights of Women, *supra* note 154, art 19.

163 African Charter, *supra* note 106, art 1.

164 Marks, Stephen "The human right to development: Between rhetoric and reality" (2004) 17 *Harvard Hum Rts J* 139; Kirchmeier, *supra* note 149, 12.

cognisance of the adverse influence exerted by major development stake-holders and therefore does not make provision for holding these actors legally accountable for their sometimes questionable actions in Africa.[165] The question that may be asked is whether the legal status of the right to development in Africa imposes any binding obligation on foreign stakeholders to comply with the relevant treaties on matters relating to the right to development? It is important to point out that according to international law standards, regional treaties only impose legally binding obligations on state parties, which therefore means that foreign stakeholders are insulated from legal action when they contravene the right to development in Africa, except for the extent to which African states can act toward foreign non-state actors operating in their jurisdiction through application of the domestic law, developed in accordance with the duty to protect the right to development. However, according to Mohamed Mattar, regional human rights treaties have a unique potential to combine universal norms and principles with sensitivity and responsiveness to regional particularities.[166] Mattar is correct to the extent that, as illustrated in chapters four and five below, the right to development needs to be developed even further to be able to respond adequately to the development challenges in Africa and to ensure greater protection against abuse and exploitation by foreign stakeholders. In the meantime, the analysis proceeds in the next section to establish what the right to development in Africa represents in principle.

4   Conceptual Clarity

4.1   *Nature of the Right to Development as a Human Rights Concept*
Development has until recent times, generally been equated to economic growth.[167] Drawing from that perception in relation to the right to development, the question that arises is whether there is a human right to economic growth. Of course, there is no claimable right to economic growth but there is indeed, a human right to development, understood broadly as incorporating economic, social and cultural as well as political development, which particularly in Africa, is recognised and protected by law. This section looks at the right to development as it is formulated within the African human rights

---

165   Okafor 2008, *supra* note 145, 61–62.
166   Mattar, Mohamed "Article 43 of the Arab Charter on Human Rights: Reconciling national, regional and international Standards" (2013) 26 *Harvard Hum Rts J* 91.
167   Melo, Alberto "Is there a right to development?" (2008) 1:2 *Rizoma Freireano – Instituto Paulo Freire de España* 2; Sengupta 2004, *supra* note 161, 181.

54 CHAPTER 2

system, with the aim to dispel some misconceptions with regard to its conceptual nature.

4.1.1 Defining Characteristics

The right to development does not respond to any universally acceptable definition.[168] Its formulation in Africa as a collective right creates an even more complex definitional problem, particularly in relation to the orthodox understanding of human rights as basically individualistic in nature. To ascribe a unique definition to the right to development is theoretically not possible and pragmatically not necessary, because, as it is argued here, the realisation of the right to development is context-specific and therefore, its conceptual and practical dimensions can only be understood within particular development contexts. In this regard, it is of essence to look at the defining characteristics of the right to development rather than attribute to it a straightforward definition. Literally, the right to development represents an integrated process for equalising opportunities for the advancement of all peoples to participate in and to enjoy the benefits obtaining from socio-economic and cultural development.[169] It is a subjective concept: as much as it is recognised universally as an inalienable human right, its practical dimensions remain relative to specific circumstances.

It is not unsurprising that the formulation of the right to development in Africa differs from the way it is understood under the Declaration on the Right to Development and other global instruments and regional human rights systems. Informed by the historical account of how the idea of development evolved into an entrenched human right, a description of the right to development as it envisages responding to African realities is constructed from the African Charter provision which provides that:

1) All peoples shall have the right to their economic, social and cultural development with due regard to their freedom and identity and in the equal enjoyment of the common heritage of mankind.
2) States shall have the duty, individually or collectively, to ensure the exercise of the right to development.[170]

The interpretation of this provision on the right to development in the African Charter is as follows: Originating from the legacy of injustices bequeathed by

---

168 Dąbrowska, *supra* note 4, 6.
169 Armiwulan, Hesti "Development and human rights" (2009) *China Intercontinental Press* 32.
170 African Charter, *supra* note 106, art 22.

slavery and colonialism as illustrated earlier, the right to development should be understood to mean recognition of the collective potential of all the peoples of Africa to participate freely in the development process with due regard to the liberty to determine a policy agenda that allows for equity and justice to prevail.[171] It ascribes entitlement to *exercise* the right, which means to take concrete action to ensure equitable redistribution of the benefits of development for the purpose of sustained well-being for all the peoples of Africa. The right to development in Africa also suggests that if it is to be achieved through development cooperation, my view is that the peoples of Africa should determine the terms of cooperation and not vice versa, where development cooperation has generally been donor driven.

Taking development in the broadest context as ultimately aiming to achieve human well-being and better living standards,[172] it is important to make clear that the right to development does not mean the right to economic growth as may be conceived in neo-liberal terms.[173] The Office of the High Commissioner for Human Rights has noted that "[t]he formulation of development as a right is based on the idea that it is not merely an equivalent to economic growth".[174] While the right to development generally does not mean the right to economic growth, it also does not exclude economic growth.[175] Economic growth constitutes an important component in the holistic concept

---

171 This view is opposed to the views of other scholars such as De Feyter, Koen "Towards a framework convention on the right to development" (2013) *Friedrich Ebert Stiftung* 17; Salomon, Margot E. "Legal cosmopolitanism and the normative contribution of the right to development" in Marks, Stephen P. (ed) *Implementing the Right to Development: The Role of International Law* (2008) 17; Sengupta, Arjun "Development cooperation and the right to development" (2003) *Copyright©2003 Arjun Sengupta* 20; Sengupta, Arjun "On the theory and practice of the right to development" (2002) 24:4 *Hum Rts Qtly* 880, whose propositions is for the right to development to be achieved through development cooperation, which basically takes away the right of participation and ownership of the development process from the African peoples.

172 UN Information Service Bangkok Press Release No G/05/2000 12 February 2000; Dąbrowska, *supra* note 4, 3.

173 Sengupta 2002, *supra* note 171, 853.

174 UN Office of the High Commission for Human Rights "The right to development and least developed countries" UN Human Rights, available at: http://www.ohchr.org/EN/Issues/Development/Pages/LDCIVconferenceandRighttoDevelopment.aspx (accessed: 4 November 2017).

175 Kamga, Serges A.D. & Heleba, Siyabonga "Can economic growth translate into access to rights?: Challenges faced by institutions in South Africa in ensuring that growth leads to better living standards" (2012) 9:17 *SUR – Int'l J Hum Rts* 82–104; Sengupta 2004, *supra* note 161, 184–185.

of the right to development,[176] incorporating economic, social and cultural elements.[177] It therefore suggests that effective realisation would progressively redress the plethora of development challenges without breeding new ones.[178] Accordingly, the right to development in Africa guarantees substantive entitlements in terms of the achievement of human well-being as well as legal entitlements in the sense that it can be claimed through the courts and other legal processes.

4.1.2 Substantive Entitlements

Substantive entitlement entails the material things that peoples can anticipate to achieve as a result of asserting the right to development. These entitlements guarantee the opportunity for the advancement of human capabilities and the standards of achievement for determining human well-being and living standards.[179] Generally, the substantive entitlements that can be expected from the realisation of the right to development are embodied in socio-economic and cultural as well as in civil and political rights.[180] In setting priorities right, the preamble to the African Charter highlights the imperative to direct more attention on the realisation of socio-economic and cultural rights than civil and political rights. It is not because civil and political rights are not relevant for development but rather because, as the preamble stipulates lucidly, "the satisfaction of economic, social and cultural rights is a guarantee for the enjoyment of civil and political rights". The African treaty instruments that enshrine the right to development suggest that if all peoples are allowed to exercise the right to development freely, they would invariably be entitled to enjoy well-being at the economic, social and cultural levels.[181] These instruments do not define what would amount to economic, social and cultural development, which leaves much interpretative responsibility with the judiciary.[182] However,

---

176   Sengupta, Arjun *et al.* "The right to development and human rights in development: A background paper" (2004) *The Norwegian Centre for Human Rights – Research Notes 07/2004* 6–8.

177   See African Charter, *supra* note 106, art 22(2).

178   See Ewanfoh, Obehi P. *Underdevelopment in Africa: My Hands are Clean* (Morrisville: Lulu Press, 2014) 140.

179   Sengupta 2004, *supra* note 161, 185.

180   See African Charter, *supra* note 106, preamble & art 22; Declaration on the Right to Development, *supra* note 96, art 1(1).

181   African Charter, *supra* note 106, art 22; Protocol on the Rights of Women, *supra* note 154, art 19; African Youth Charter, *supra* note 156, art 10.

182   Much of the interpretation and clarification on the nature and content of the right to development enshrined in the African Charter has been provided by the African Commission in the following cases: *Kevin Gumne, supra* note 137, paras 172-179; *DRC case,*

a scrutiny of the provisions of the African Charter reveals that the rights to property ownership, job security and income guarantee would contribute to economic development.[183] The rights to health care and education would contribute to social development.[184] Recognition of traditional values and belief systems, customary practices and an African lifestyle would lead to cultural development.[185]

In stating that the right to development is to be achieved with due regard to the defining elements of "freedom and identity",[186] the Charter establishes that its content is subject to determination only by the peoples concerned. Only a collective of people in accordance with their communal identity can state with exactitude what would constitute socio-economic and cultural development in their particular context. For instance, indigenous peoples are identified to manifest unique cultural, spiritual and lifestyle characteristics that distinguish them from other communities.[187] Their conception of development is thus unlikely to respond to the same criteria applicable to communities that live a more urbanised and modern lifestyle. In the same manner, what constitutes development for women[188] differs from what the youths envisage as development.[189]

Contrary to the view that the right to development does not create any "substantive right",[190] the right to development in Africa does guarantee entitlement to improved human well-being and better standards of living realisable through economic, social and cultural self-determination. Former UN High Commissioner for Human Rights, Navi Pillay has reiterated that the right to development contains a specific entitlement "to participate in, contribute to, and enjoy economic, social, cultural and political development".[191] Unlike in the African Charter, where political development is deliberately omitted in the formulation of the right to development, the Declaration on the Right to

---

     supra note 155, para 95; *Endorois* case, *supra* note 158, para 269-298; *Darfur* case, *supra* note 157, para 224.

183   African Charter, *supra* note 106, arts 14 & 15.

184   As above, arts 16 & 17(1).

185   As above, arts 17(2-3) & 18; see also Charter for African Cultural Renaissance adopted in Khartoum on 24 January 2006.

186   African Charter, *supra* note 106, art 22(1).

187   ILO Convention on Indigenous and Tribal Peoples 1986 (No 196) art 1; Martínez Cobo 1987 UN Doc E/CN.4/Sub.2/1986/7.

188   See Protocol on the Rights of Women in Africa, *supra* note 154, art 19.

189   See African Youth Charter, *supra* note 156, art 10.

190   Dąbrowska, *supra* note 4, 5.

191   UN Human Rights, *supra* note 106, 4.

Development includes political development as a central component for the realisation of the right to development.[192] The omission is explained to mean that in the African context, the enjoyment of civil and political rights can only be guaranteed through the fulfilment of economic, social and cultural rights.[193] Even though the Declaration on the Right to Development defines the right to development as including political development, it outlines in article 8 that in order to ensure the realisation of the right to development at the domestic level, states should guarantee "equality of opportunity for all in their access to basic resources, education, health services, food, housing, employment and the fair distribution of income". These guarantees are predominantly socio-economic in nature, which as explained in the preamble to the African Charter guarantee that when socio-economic and cultural development is achieved, political development would follow.

To seek to achieve the right to development otherwise, by prioritising political development over economic, social and cultural development only creates the opportunity for failure as has been the situation in most of Africa. In calling on states to cooperate for development, the UN Charter points to the same fact that issues that need attention are those of an economic, social, cultural or humanitarian nature.[194] It seems obvious that political issues are not considered international problems, because they have to do with state sovereignty and are therefore complex to deal with through development cooperation.[195] While political development may be relevant for the achievement of the right to development, it is not inherent to human well-being and livelihood and thus, not particularly important to prioritise over socio-economic and cultural development. The absence of political development may not necessarily devalue the right to development the way it would do when socio-economic and cultural development fails to be achieved. The point here is simply to explain why the right to development as it is conceptualised in the African Charter only envisages socio-economic and cultural development and not political development.[196]

---

192   Declaration on the Right to Development, *supra* note 96, art 1(1).
193   African Charter, *supra* note 106, preamble.
194   UN Charter, *supra* note 3, art 1(3).
195   Based on the principle of sovereign equality of states, which allows for friendly relations among states based on respect for the principle of equal rights and the right to self-determination, the UN Charter formulates the need for international cooperation to deal purposefully with "problems of and economic, social, cultural or humanitarian character, and in promoting and encouraging respect for human rights". The Charter does not make mention of issues of a political nature.
196   See African Charter, *supra* note 106, art 22(1).

HISTORICAL ACCOUNT ON THE RIGHT TO DEVELOPMENT   59

However, the preamble to the Charter underscores the fact that civil and political rights cannot be dissociated from socio-economic and cultural rights in their conception and universality, which in accordance with universal human rights standards must aim to protect the dignity and well-being of the human person. To ensure that the substantive entitlements inherent in the right to development are adhered to and fulfilled, they have had to be recognised and protected by law so as to impose binding obligations as explained in the next sub-section.

4.1.3   Legal Entitlements

The African human rights system provides extensive recognition of the right to development[197] but there is as yet no comprehensive clarification as to its precise nature. By looking at the legal nature of the right development in Africa, the aim is to explore the core dimensions of the idea of development as an entrenched entitlement under African law, which François Borella has rightly contextualised as development law.[198] Informed by the injustices that motivated the conceptualisation of development as a human right, the African Charter forbids the further subjugation of the African peoples to enslavement or domination.[199] It also guarantees protection of the African space from inappropriate invasion that may jeopardise, cause a regression to or contravene the right to development.[200] Though controversial at the level of the international community, the right to development in Africa is worth paying close attention to because of the normative impetus that it pulls together, which guarantees that it can legitimately be invoked before a court of law in accordance with the criteria necessary for making such a claim.[201]

---

197   African Charter, *supra* note 106, art 22; Protocol on the Rights of Women, *supra* note 154, art 19; African Youth Charter, *supra* note 156, art 10; African Charter on Democracy, Elections and Governance adopted in Addis Ababa 30 January 2007 preamble; Report of the Meeting of Experts of the First Ministerial Conference on Human Rights in Africa Kigali 5–6 May 2003 EXP/CONF/HRA/RPT(II) para 42; Grand Bay Declaration and Plan of Action adopted by the First OAU Ministerial Conference on Human Rights held in Grand Bay April 1999 para 2; Kigali Declaration adopted by the AU Ministerial Conference on Human Rights in Africa held in Kigali May 2003 para 3; Solemn Declaration on Gender Equality in Africa adopted by the AU Assembly of Heads of State and Government in Addis Ababa July 2004 para 6; Pretoria Declaration on Economic, Social and Cultural Rights in Africa adopted by the African Commission at its 36th Session December 2004 preamble & para 1; New Partnership for Africa's Development, *supra* note 86, para 79. These instruments are discussed a bit more elaborately in chapter four.
198   Borella, *supra* note 86, 246.
199   See Declaration on the Right to Development, *supra* note 96, art 5.
200   African Charter, *supra* note 106, preamble para 8.
201   Sengupta 2004, *supra* note 161, 186.

Reading from article 22 of the African Charter, it can be deduced that the right to development creates the condition not just for the realisation of socio-economic and cultural development but also for the exercise of legality, legitimacy, equity and justice in the development process. It imposes the obligations to respect, to protect, to fulfil and to prevent, which by extension translates into the positive duty to ensure sustained access to the material benefits corresponding to the fulfilment of each right and the negative duty necessitating restrained action to avoid a regression in the enjoyment of existing rights.[202] Drawing from universal human rights standards, these obligations are described as follows: The obligation to respect, which entails recognition of the fact that all African peoples are entitled to the inalienable right to development. The obligation to protect entails taking action in the form legislation and enforcement measures against perceived threats. The obligation to fulfil requires making available the material things that are necessary to ensure well-being, which includes ensuring access to remedies when a violation is alleged. Lastly, the obligation to prevent necessitates the ability to pre-empt and to take appropriate measures to avert a potential violation of the right to development. These obligations can be summed up into two principal duties: On the one hand, the positive duty to fulfil requires concrete action in order to achieve the substantive entitlements relating to economic, social and cultural development, which ultimately must result in the full enjoyment of well-being and improvement of the human condition.[203] This duty imposes a direct legally binding obligation on the state parties to the instruments that enshrine the right to development. On the other hand, the right to development establishes the negative duty to respect the rights of the peoples of Africa to make their own development choices, which must not be infringed upon or contravened.[204]

When development is acknowledged to constitute an entrenched human right, it empowers right-holders with the legitimacy to demand accountability by requiring of duty-bearers to honour their treaty obligations.[205] Thus as a human right, the right to development accords to the peoples of Africa a justifiable basis for claiming that their governments have certain development obligations to fulfil.[206] These obligations include protecting the right to

---

202   As above, 184.
203   As above, 187–188.
204   Oduwole, Olajumoke "International law and the right to development: A pragmatic approach for Africa" (2014) *International Institute of Social Studies* 3.
205   Sengupta 2004, *supra* note 161, 181.
206   As above, 187.

HISTORICAL ACCOUNT ON THE RIGHT TO DEVELOPMENT

development from violation, especially by foreign stakeholders.[207] The legal nature of the right to development in Africa is not only guaranteed by its normative force. The means by which it is envisaged to be achieved – through cooperation – is also guaranteed by law.[208] However, under the development cooperation framework, it is hard to envisage a directly binding obligation requiring foreign stakeholders to fulfil the right to development in Africa despite the legally bindings obligation originating from international law necessitating cooperating partners to respect such a right.[209]

4.1.4   Normative Standards

The normative standards should be understood to mean the highest attainable benchmarks that the right to development in Africa aims to achieve. Fundamentally, the right to development was conceived to establish some form of transformative justice against the negative impact of global incompatibilities that has increasingly affected development in Africa.[210] The right to development proposes an alternative model that looks at development from a rights-based point of view with the objective to ameliorate the living standards for the human person.[211] Envisaging development in Africa from a rights-based perspective carries the promise that human well-being can be attained through the concurrent realisation of economic growth and human rights. To this end, it is important to look at and include standards for up-holding human

---

207   See generally UN Guiding Principles on Business and Human Rights: Implementing the United Nations "protect, respect and remedy" Framework adopted by the UN Human Rights Council UN Doc A/HRC/17/L17/31 (June 2011).

208   The treaty instruments that impose the duty to cooperate include, the UN Charter, *supra* note 3, arts 1(3), 55 & 56); ICESCR, *supra* note 3, art 1(2); African Charter, *supra* note 105, art 22(2); Declaration on the Right to Development, *supra* note 96, art 3(3) & 4(2); Vienna Declaration, *supra* note 96, para 1(10).

209   See UN Charter, *supra* note 3, art 1(3), 55 & 56; ICESCR, *supra* note 3, art 1(2).

210   Garavito, César R.; Kweitel, Joana & Waisbich, Laura T. "Development and human rights: Some ideas on how to restart the debate" (2012) 2:17 SUR – *Int'l J Hum Rts* 6.

211   Merh, K. Williams "Bringing human rights to bear on strategies to achieve the Millennium Development Goals (2005) *Keynote address Irish Department of Foreign Affairs 7th Annual NGO Forum on Human Rights* 2. Mehr Khan notes that: "When we use the phrase – "human rights and development" – we sometimes seem to imply that the two are quite different. Indeed in the way that human rights and development have been addressed in the past, there are differences. But fundamentally the ultimate goal is the same: to contribute to enhancing the dignity of people's lives. Development aims at improvement in the lives and the well-being of all people. It does this through the delivery of services and the expansion of government capacities. This is also the process of realizing many human rights".

62 CHAPTER 2

rights and standards for promoting development, which lay the groundwork for the right to development in Africa.

4.1.4.1 *Standards for Up-holding Human Rights*

The Vienna Declaration underscores the fact that human rights and fundamental freedoms are the birthright of all human beings.[212] Besides being a right in itself, the right to development provides the means through which other human rights may be achieved. Looking at Africa's human rights record (which remains a major concern), if progress is to be made toward the realisation of the African Union Agenda 2063 for development,[213] the following standards on human rights in Africa must be adhered to.

4.1.4.1.1 Inalienability of the Right to Development

The right to development has been recognised universally and reaffirmed in many international forums as an inalienable human right. It means that the right to development is an undeniable entitlement that cannot be taken away, cannot be bartered or bargained for less than its inherent value and more so it cannot be set aside for any reason including the lack of development.[214] Sengupta explains this to mean that the right to development is absolute and cannot be negotiated.[215] According to Luo Haocai, the right to development is of primary importance to the millions of peoples in developing countries that are yet to align with the global development process, which as he argues can only be attained through claiming that right.[216] The inalienability of the right to development in Africa justifies its recognition and protection as an entitlement to the African peoples. By virtue of this fact, a compelling obligation is imposed if not positively to ensure fulfilment, at least negatively to ensure that the right to development is not violated.[217]

---

212 Vienna Declaration, *supra* note 96, para 1(1); Sengupta 2000, *supra* note 7, 558.
213 Amnesty International "African Union: President Mugabe should urgently address human rights concerns" (2015) available at: https://www.amnesty.org/en/articles/news/2015/01/african-union-president-mugabe-should-urgently-address-human-rights-concerns/ (accessed: 17 March 2016).
214 Kamga, *supra* note 96, 121.
215 Sengupta 2000, *supra* note 7, 563.
216 Haocai, Lou "Remarks at the opening ceremony of the Beijing forum on human rights" (2008) *China Hum Rts* 1.
217 See Oduwole, *supra* note 206, 3; Sengupta 2004, *supra* note 159, 183. In making this assertion, I take cognisance of the problematic in accurately distinguishing between positive and negative duties in the realisation of socio-economic rights as highlight in Brand, Danie "Introduction to socio-economic rights in the South African Constitution" in Heyns, Christof & Brand, Danie (eds) *Socio-Economic Rights in South Africa* (Pretoria: Pretoria

4.1.4.1.2 Collectivism and People-Centeredness

Acknowledging the right to development as a human right gives the impression, according to the orthodox understanding of human rights that it is vested in the individual.[218] The Declaration on the Right to Development makes a compromise by stipulating that the right to development is both an individual and a group right.[219] Fundamental to a realistic understanding of the right to development in Africa is the fact that only a collective of peoples are recognised as the subjects and beneficiaries of the right to development.[220] The African Charter enshrines the right to development as essentially a collective right.[221] This is not only informed by the values of solidarity and community living that predominate in most African societies.[222] It obtains also from the historical problem of collective disadvantage or collective dispossession, necessitating a remedy that is of a collective nature to deal with the problem. Scholarship confirms that human rights in Africa are generally communitarian in the sense that they provide protection based on ascribed status and belonging of the individual to a particular community where collective well-being is guaranteed to be enjoyed by everyone.[223] Accordingly, the individualistic or dual nature of the right to development has been argued to be irrelevant for advancing the concept of the right to development and thus, must be rejected.[224]

University Law Press, 2005) 26–29; Skogly, Sigrun I. "Extra-national obligations towards economic and social rights" (2002) *International Council on Human Rights Policy – Background Paper* 4.

218   Sohn, Louis "The new international law: Protection of the rights of individuals rather than states" (1982) 32 *Am U L Rev* 1, 48; Kiwanuka, Richard "The meaning of 'people' in the African Charter on Human and Peoples' Rights" (1988) 82:1 *Am J Int'l L* 85; Benedek, Wolfgang *et al. The Role of Regional Human Rights Mechanisms* (Brussels: European Parliament, 2010) 4.

219   Declaration on the Right to Development, *supra* note 96, art 1(1).

220   Sengupta *et al.*, *supra* note 176, 15; Declaration on the Right to Development, *supra* note 96, art 1(1).

221   African Charter, *supra* note 106, art 22(1).

222   See the preambles to the OAU Charter, *supra* note 55 and the Constitutive Act of the African Union adopted in Lomé on 11 July 2000.

223   Chirwa, Danwood M. "In search of philosophical justifications and suitable models for the horizontal application of human rights" (2008) 8:2 *AHRLJ* 303; Cobbah, Josiah A.M. "African values and the human rights debate: An African perspective" (1987) 9 *Hum Rts Qtly* 321; Mojekwu, Chris C. "International human rights: The African perspective" in Nelson, Jack L. & Green, Vera M. (eds) *International Human Rights: Contemporary Issues* (New York: Human Rights Publishing Group, 1980) 86; El-Obaid & Appiagyei-Atua, *supra* note 100, 833–834.

224   Bedjaoui, Mohammed "The right to development" in Bedjaoui, Mohammed (ed) *International Law: Achievements and Prospects* (Dordrecht: Martinus Nijhoff & UNESCO,

The concept of the right to development in Africa places an uncompromised emphasis on the fact that people constitute the drivers of the development process. As Tamara Kunanayakam puts it, the right to development demands that peoples should be seen as subjects rather than as objects of development.[225] It establishes the legal principle that an individual cannot possibly succeed with a personal claim on the right to development, but, of course, can legitimately exercise and enjoy the right to development as part of a collective.[226] In the African context the right to development can only be claimed by peoples and not by individuals, because, as established by law – in accordance with article 22(1) of the African Charter – it is an entitlement guaranteed only to peoples. The collectivism that is ascribed to the right to development constitutes an empowering tool that provides agency to the millions of impoverished and disadvantaged peoples in Africa who otherwise would not have the capacity to advance a claim on an individual basis. In contrast to the individualistic conception of human rights, the right to development as a collective entitlement does not alienate the individual, but makes provision for supportive inclusiveness based on the recognition of the collective capability to contribute to the development process and to equitably share in the benefits deriving therefrom.[227]

As Luo Haocai argues, there are no collective human rights to speak of if individual human rights are not protected – likewise, collective human rights are the prerequisite and guarantee for the full realisation of individual human rights.[228] Development is a subjective process that cannot be imposed from outside, but must be determined and driven by popular participation in accordance with peoples' aspirations to improvement of livelihood and well-being.[229] Therefore, to put people at the centre of the development process means to invest in the advancement of their capabilities and choices for the betterment of their lives.[230] This is a lofty aspiration, which under the present

---

1991) 1180; Bunn, Isabella D. "The right to development: Implications for international economic law" (2000) 15 *Am U Int'l L Rev* 1435; Villaroman, *supra* note 151, 17.

225 Kunanayakam, Tamara "Report of the Working Group on the Right to Development on its fourteenth session" (2013) *Human Rights Council A/HRC/24/37* 4–5.

226 African Charter, *supra* note 106, art 22(1).

227 Mahalu, *supra* note 136, 16–18.

228 Haocai, *supra* note 216, 4.

229 Kunanayakam, *supra* note 225, 5.

230 Gawanas, Bience "The African Union: Concepts and implementation mechanisms relating to human rights" in Bosl, Anton & Diescho, Joseph (eds) *Human Rights in Africa: Legal Perspectives on their Protection and Promotion* (Windhoek: Macmillan Education Namibia, 2009) 145.

HISTORICAL ACCOUNT ON THE RIGHT TO DEVELOPMENT 65

circumstances remains far-fetched to the poor in Africa who continue to "struggle in grinding poverty".[231] It necessitates the right to development paradigm to prioritise not only human rights standards but also standards for promoting development.

4.1.4.2 *Standards for Promoting Development*

In spite of the role that economic growth may play in the realisation of the right to development, McKay and Vizard have pointed out that focus on economic growth alone raises concerns about the impact that accelerated growth may have on the realisation of human rights.[232] This also does not negate the extent to which respect for human rights may leverage economic growth.[233] The concept of the right to development suggests a radical shift from the economic growth dominated theory of what Serges Kamga calls, "developmentalism",[234] to conceptualising development in legal terms as a human right, which entitles the African peoples to make informed development choices.[235] The right to development thus presupposes that a rights-based approach to development is crucial for Africa.

4.1.4.2.1 Rights-Based Approach to Development

Within the debate on development and human rights, Stephen Marks identifies seven different approaches for applying human rights thinking to development practice.[236] Of the seven approaches, the right to development stands out distinctly as the process by which development can be achieved with equity and justice, ultimately for the attainment of human well-being and improved living standards.[237] As Sengupta rightly illustrates, the rights-based approach requires that every development activity must be carried out in a manner that is consistent with human rights standards.[238] Unlike with

---

231 Gaeta, Anthony & Vasilara, Marina "Development and human rights: The role of the World Bank" (1998) *The International Bank for Reconstruction and Development/The World Bank* 5.

232 McKay, Andy & Vizard, Polly "Rights and economic growth: Inevitable conflict or 'common ground'?" (2005) *Overseas Development Institute* 4.

233 As above, 2.

234 Kamga, *supra* note 96, 121.

235 Gaeta & Vasilara, *supra* note 231, vii.

236 Marks, Stephen P. "The human rights framework for development: Seven approaches" (2003) *François-Xavier Bagnoud Centre for Health and Human Rights, Harvard University – Working Paper No 18* 1–29.

237 Sengupta 2002, *supra* note 171, 846.

238 Sengupta 2004, *supra* note 161, 180.

economic growth approaches, the rights-based approach envisages an alternative development model that aims at the realisation of all human rights and fundamental freedoms.[239]

Despite the critique by some scholars on the relevance of the rights-based approaches to development,[240] Selime Jahan explains that the rights-based framework (like in Africa where the right to development is recognised as law) provides the opportunity to assert a claim when that right is violated and the duty bearers can be held to legal accountability.[241] The rights-based framework looks at human rights and development holistically in terms of the processes and the goal to be achieved, which must reinforce each other.[242] It implies that if the right to development is to be achieved through development cooperation as it is envisaged, the cooperation processes for development must prioritise human rights.[243] The rights-based approach equally guarantees fairness in ensuring that development gains are evenly redistributed to ensure collective well-being.[244]

4.1.4.2.2 Model for Poverty Eradication

To talk about poverty eradication may be considered unrealistic based on the reasoning that poverty is of such a nature that it can hardly be done away with completely. This book articulates the view that the nature of poverty that is experienced in Africa can indeed be eradicated, which entails getting rid of the systems and the mechanisms that generate and sustain it.[245] Poverty has progressively been perceived and described as a violation of human rights,

---

239 Sengupta 2002, *supra* note 171, 847.
240 See for example Renard, R. "Theories of development and the emergence of rights based approaches" (2013) *Lecture notes on the Right to Development – Centre for Human Rights University of Pretoria* 1–17; Donnelly, Jack "The right to development: How not to link human rights and development" in Welch, Claude E. & Meltzer, Ronald I. (eds) *Human Rights and Development in Africa* (New York: SUNY Press, 1984) 261; Whyte, *supra* note 2, 1–3.
241 Jahan, Selime "Human rights-based approach to poverty reduction: Analytical linkages, practical work and UNDP" (2004) *UNOHCHR High-Level Seminar on Global Partnership for Development on Right to Development*, 9–10 February 2004 2.
242 Sengupta 2002, *supra* note 171, 846.
243 UN General Assembly "Human rights-based approach: Statement of common understanding" adopted at the Inter-Agency Workshop on a human rights-based approach 3 – 5 May 2003 1–3.
244 Sengupta 2002, *supra* note 171, 846.
245 Ngang, Carol C. "Systems problem and a pragmatic insight into the right to development governance for Africa" (2019) 19:1 *AHRLJ* 365–394; Ngang, Carol C. "Poverty eradication through global partnerships and the question of the right to development under international law" (2017) 47:3 *Africa Insight* 39–58; see also Wang, Xigen "Eradicating poverty and the role of the right to development" (2017) *Human Rights Institute of Wuhan*

constituting one of the major obstacles to development in Africa.[246] The idea of poverty as a violation of human rights is explained by the fact that people are not born poor but are impoverished (rendered poor) by the man-made systems that deprive them of inherent entitlements and the basic freedoms to aspire for better standards of living. Contrary to resorting to dependence on development assistance through cooperation as a means of eradicating poverty as has become the practice within the global framework for development, the African conception of the right to development provides a model through which the challenges of poverty can most effectively be redressed. Poverty is defined as "a human condition characterised by sustained or chronic deprivation of the resources, capabilities, choices, security and power necessary for the enjoyment of an adequate standard of living".[247] In practical terms, poverty is injustice resulting from the policy choices that create and sustain inequalities and power imbalances.[248] In this instance, people are not poor because they are incapable but because they are rendered poor (impoverished) by political design. This relates to Amartya Sen's description of poverty as a deprivation of the freedoms to advance the human potential.[249] Following these definitions, poverty in Africa can rightly be said to derive from several decades of development injustices that the peoples have experienced.

In this way, it is possible to argue that the right to development as an expression of self-determination provides the framework for eradicating poverty, which entails on the most part the "the integral liberation" and empowerment of the African peoples to make their own development choices.[250] It necessitates a radical shift from cooperation frameworks that unnecessarily yoke African countries with developed countries in unsustainable relationships of dependency on development assistance. The capability to achieve this has manifested previously in the instance where the colonised peoples of Africa

---

      University, China – Recommendation for the 18th Session of UN Working Group on the Right to Development 1–4.

246   Doz Costa, Fernanda "Poverty and human rights from rhetoric to legal obligations: A critical account of conceptual frameworks" (2008) 5:9 *SUR – Int'l J Hum Rts* 86–88; see also Prada, Maritza F. *Empowering Poor through Human Rights Litigation* (Paris: UNESCO, 2011) 7; Campbell, Tom "Poverty as a violation of human rights: Inhumanity or injustice?" (2003) *CAPPE – Working Paper 2003/9* 1–19; Pogge, Thomas (ed) *Freedom from Poverty as a Human Right: Who Owes What to the Very Poor?* (Paris: UNESCO, 2008) 2–11.

247   ESCR Committee "Poverty and the International Covenant on Economic, Social and Cultural Rights" Statement adopted on 4 May 2001 para 8.

248   Brand, Danie *et al.* "Poverty as injustice" (2013) 17 *Law, Democracy & Development* 273–275.

249   Sen, *supra* note 58, 87–95.

250   Brand *et al., supra* note 248, 277.

asserted with vigour the right to self-determination, which led to decolonisation and the acquisition of independence. Udombana notes that the right to development flows from the right to self-determination and has the same nature,[251] meaning that it constitutes a tool in the hands of the peoples of Africa to change the socio-economic and cultural situation on the continent.

Gauri and Gloppen point out that in the past couple of years development has increasingly been framed in the language of human rights, thus setting apart poverty eradication not only as a moral but also as a legal imperative.[252] The human rights framework for development allows for a plurality of models for achievement but as Robin Perry rightly observes, the right to development constitutes a novelty in the sense that it combines the complex relationship between development, poverty eradication and the realisation of human rights.[253] It implies as Sengupta further argues that by asserting the right to development, substantive development can be achieved with equity and justice.[254]

4.2 *Nature of the Right to Development as a Development Paradigm*

In spite of scepticism about the relevance of the right to development as a stand-alone human right,[255] its theoretical dimensions as discussed in the previous section illustrates that it is not just a human right in the traditional sense but in effect a "new paradigm in development thinking that places human rights firmly within national and international development" frameworks.[256] The Office of the UN High Commissioner for Human Rights recognises that the right to development is "a development paradigm for our globalized future".[257] As Winston Nagan puts it, "the right to development represents a concept that with proper clarification could enhance the kind of thinking that anticipates a new global economic paradigm".[258] It is a pragmatic concept that entails

---

251 Udombana, *supra* note 96, 769–770.

252 Gauri, Varun & Gloppen, Siri "Human rights based approaches to development: Concepts, evidence and policy" (2012) *World Bank Development Research Group* 2.

253 Perry, Robin "Preserving discursive spaces to promote human rights: Poverty reduction strategy, human rights and development discourse" (2011) 7:1 *McGill Int'l J Sust Dev't L & Policy* 78.

254 Sengupta 2002, *supra* note 171, 850.

255 De Feyter, Koen "Right to development: A treaty and its discontents" (2016) ©2016 *Prof Dr K. de Feyter Law & Development Research Group, University of Antwerp* 1–27; Vandenbogaerde, Arne "The right to development in international human rights law: A call for its dissolution" (2013) 31:2 *Neth Qtly Hum Rts* 197–209.

256 Ibhawoh, Bonny "The right to development: The politics and polemics of power and resistance" (2011) 33 *Hum Rts Qtly* 103; see also Udombana, *supra* note 96, 762.

257 UN Human Rights, *supra* note 106, 495.

258 Nagan, *supra* note 108, 30.

HISTORICAL ACCOUNT ON THE RIGHT TO DEVELOPMENT

functionalism; involving the engineering of human capabilities, equitable social construction and non-doctrinaire application of the legal obligations that it imposes for its realisation.[259] Accordingly, Chinedu Okafor estimates that the right to development ought to be made " 'right', not just by strengthening its normative capacity, but also its capacity to contribute to 'good' development praxis".[260]

4.2.1 Specific Components for Realisation

4.2.1.1 *Sovereign Ownership of the African Patrimony*

It takes ownership of natural wealth and resources for socio-economic and cultural development to be achieved. The African Charter establishes the fact that the right to economic, social and cultural development can only be achieved with due regard to the "freedom and identity" of the African peoples.[261] This is a particularly unique formulation that is not common with other instruments that make provision for the right to development. The guarantee of "freedom and identity" confers recognition of human potential in the peoples of Africa to refuse to be seen as "backward savages", as they have been labelled to justify the colonisation theory.[262] Freedom represents a broad range of liberties, which include liberty of mind and thought, liberty of decision-making, liberty of action and liberty of ownership of the African patrimony. Freedom further denotes the liberty to develop human capabilities, of which the African peoples have been deprived for long. Owing to the fact that development injustices in Africa were perpetuated in the form of colonisation of the African imagination, deprivation of rights and the dispossession of wealth and resources, the right to development originating from this background guarantees the freedom to make development choices and the liberty of action to translate such choices into concrete entitlements.[263]

To acknowledge that the right to development must be achieved with due regard to the freedom and identity of the African peoples articulates the right

---

259   See Amir, Shimeon *Israel's Development Cooperation with Africa, Asia and Latin America* (New York: Praeger Publisher, 1974) 1.

260   Okafor 2013, *supra* note 121, 373.

261   African Charter, *supra* note 106, art 22(1).

262   Watson, Irene *Aboriginal Peoples, Colonialism and International Law: Raw Law* (New York: Routledge, 2015) 5.

263   Sing'Oei, Korir "Engaging the leviathan: National development, corporate globalisation and the Endorois quest to recover their herding grounds" in Henrard, Kristin (ed) *The Interrelation between the Right to Identity of Minorities and their Socio-Economic Participation* (Leiden/Boston: Martinus Nijhoff Publishers, 2013) 395; *Endorois* case, *supra* note 158, para 283.

to self-determination, which the African Charter recognises as an "unquestionable and inalienable right".[264] The capability to exercise the series of liberties as the Charter makes provision for, must be accompanied by the freedom to portray a collective identity as peoples, which forms the eligibility criterion for claiming the right to development. This is embedded in the African construction of collectivism, which situates individual functioning only within the framework of the broader community.[265] It is further emphasised by the fact that the African patrimony is conceived as a "common heritage" from which its peoples are entitled to derive benefits by exercising the right to development.[266]

Freedom and identity allow for sovereignty in decision-making with regard to economic, social and cultural development.[267] It qualifies the right to development in terms of peoples' collective entitlement to define their own development priorities without subjection to economic coercion or exploitative relationships.[268] Freedom and identity constitute an empowering component of the right to development not only because they guarantee the advancement of capabilities but also because they emphasise the collective nature of that entitlement to the peoples of Africa.[269] As Ndlovu-Gatsheni rightly points out, only a politically, socially, economically, ideologically, and epistemologically liberated peoples are capable of taking charge of their destiny and creating their own futures.[270] It requires present generations of African peoples to mobilise in confronting existing "structural and agential sources of social injustices, asymmetrical power structures, patriarchal ideologies, logics of capitalist exploitation, resilient imperial/colonial reason, and racist articulations and practices".[271]

---

264   African Charter, *supra* note 106, art 20.

265   Carson, Leslie R. " 'I am because we are': Collectivism as a foundational characteristic of African American college student identity and academic achievement" (2009) 12 *Soc Psychol Educ* 327.

266   African Charter, *supra* note 106, art 22(1) states that: "*All peoples* shall have the right to their economic, social and cultural development with due regard to their freedom and identity and in the equal enjoyment of *the common heritage of mankind*" (emphasis added).

267   Declaration on the Right to Development, *supra* note 96, art 1(2).

268   Van der Have, Nienke "The right to development and state responsibility: Towards idealism without a sense of realism?" (Masters Thesis, University of Amsterdam, 2011) 4.

269   See *Endorois* case, *supra* note 158, para 157.

270   Ndlovu-Gatsheni 2014, *supra* note 104, 184.

271   As above, 186.

4.2.1.2 *Inclusive Participation*

Unlike in neo-liberal understanding where development is characterised by individualism and the accumulation of wealth,[272] the right to development allows for the inclusive participation of all peoples in the development process.[273] Accordingly, any development initiative that is crafted and superimposed on the African peoples without their free consent and active participation violates the right to development.[274] Inclusive participation entails a deep-rooted involvement that has an important effect in advancing people's capabilities in the course of creating development.[275] This is relevant in the developmental context in Africa where, in accordance with the right to development, all peoples are assured of active participation in the development process as a matter of right and to share equitably in the benefits deriving from that process.[276]

The theoretical basis for inclusive participation is contained in the African Charter and ancillary instruments such as the Protocol on the Rights of Women in Africa, which provide that the right to development is principally a collective entitlement that allows individuals inclusive participation in exercising the right to well-being.[277] Although benefits can be enjoyed individually, the right to development makes more sense as a collective entitlement for the reason that greater social justice is attained by extending benefits to a wider number of individuals. As the pioneer instrument to give the right to development hard law status, the African Charter punctured the cliché by which human rights have been regarded solely as individualistic in nature. Following Perry's estimation that participatory processes are crucial to promoting genuinely sustainable forms of development,[278] states are required to encourage popular participation as an important factor for the realisation of the right to development.[279] As a minimum standard, peoples' prior informed consent

---

272 Ball, Richard "Individualism, collectivism and economic development" (2001) 573 *The Annals of the American Academy of Political and Social Science* 59–62; Femi, Omojarabi W. "Adam Smith's view in *wealth of nations* and how it has led to the growth and consolidation of capitalism" *Academia.edu* available at: https://www.academia.edu/4057757/adam_smith_and_capitalism (accessed: 21 March 2016) 2–3.

273 African Charter, *supra* note 106, art 22(1); Declaration on the Right to Development, *supra* note 96, art 1(2).

274 See *Endorois* case, *supra* note 158, para 291.

275 As above, para 279.

276 As above, para 291.

277 African Charter, *supra* note 106, art 22(1); Protocol on the Rights of Women, *supra* note 154, art 19(b).

278 Perry, *supra* note 252, 76.

279 Declaration on the Right to Development, *supra* note 96, art 8(2).

72   CHAPTER 2

must be obtained.[280] This is established in the *Endorois* case where the African Commission held that because participation aligns with the right to development, the process must be carried out in good faith to ensure that disadvantaged communities are actively involved.[281]

4.2.1.3   *Equality of Opportunity*

The right to development in Africa provides the opportunity for the enjoyment of well-being by all peoples, which according to Stephen Marks suggests "equality of welfare".[282] The practices of slavery and colonialism deprived the African populations of the opportunity for development. The right to development on the contrary grants rights of access to opportunities which in principle, guarantee to all the peoples of Africa entitlement to basic needs and as Baxi puts it, the associated notions of conversion of such needs into rights.[283] Equality of opportunity guarantees the right to choose between alternatives, which right embodies the freedom to determine what options to trade off and what development priorities to pursue.[284] Sengupta explains this by illustrating that the state, for instance, cannot arbitrarily decide where people must live just because it provides housing, but preferably, people must be granted the freedom to choose where to live.[285] Applied in context, Africa is not obligated to remain plugged into unproductive global systems and models for development but is entitled to create its own functional alternatives. If development is understood to mean a commitment to achieve improved human well-being and social equity, which in order words is referred to as "sustainable development", equality of opportunity for development entitles present generations to satisfy their needs without compromising the rights guaranteed to future generations to also meet their own needs.[286]

---

280   *Endorois* case, *supra* note 158, paras 290-291; Kamga, Serges A. D. "The right to development in the African human rights system: The *Endorois* case" (2011) 44:2 *De Jure* 390.

281   *Endorois* case, *supra* note 158, paras 281 & 289; *Social and Economic Rights Action Centre (SERAC) & Another v Nigeria* Comm 155/96 (2001) AHRLR 60 (ACHPR 2001) para 54.

282   Marks, Stephen P. "Obligations to implement the right to development: Political, legal and philosophical rationales" in Andreassen, Bård A. & Marks, Stephen P. (eds) *Development as a Human Right: Legal, Political and Economic Dimensions* (Cambridge: Harvard School of Public Health, 2006) 59.

283   Baxi, *supra* note 113, 231.

284   Sengupta 2000, *supra* note 7, 578.

285   As above; *Endorois* case, *supra* note 158, para 278.

286   Brundtland, Gro Harlem "Report of the World Commission on Environment and Development: Our common future" (1987) *Brundtland Commission* 27.

As part of the duty to ensure the realisation of the right to development, states are required to ensure, *inter alia,* "equality of opportunity for all in their access to basic resources, education, health care, food, housing, employment and the equitable distribution of income".[287] Equality of opportunity envisaged by the right to development also means that all peoples are guaranteed equal enjoyment of the benefits of development.[288] The assurance is also contained in the Covenant on Economic, Social and Cultural Rights, which is based on the conviction that "the ideal of free human beings enjoying freedom from fear and want can only be achieved if conditions are created whereby everyone may enjoy [their] economic, social and cultural rights".[289] For Marks, equality of opportunity requires developed countries to act in ways that increase the potential for the realisation of the right to development in developing countries.[290] While the subject position advanced in this book differs with how Marks envisages the rapport between developed and developing countries, his view provides reason to look at the role of the state with regard to the obligation that the right to development imposes for its realisation.

4.2.1.4 *The Role of the State*
From the foregoing analysis, the state is directly attributed the central role to ensure the realisation of the right to development. The Office of the UN High Commissioner for Human Rights points out that the "central responsibility for protecting human rights rests with Governments" on account of their legal commitments under human rights instruments, which impose the duties to respect, to protect and to fulfil the rights contained therein.[291] It entails a duty as stipulated in article 2(3) of the Declaration on the Right to Development to create the enabling environment through appropriate national development policies to ensure that socio-economic and cultural development translates into improved well-being and better living standards for the peoples. The African Charter imposes primary responsibility on state parties to ensure the exercise and enjoyment of the right to development either through individual or collective action.[292] It obligates state parties to create the conditions and

---

287 Declaration on the Right to Development, *supra* note 96, art 8(1).
288 Declaration on the Right to Development, *supra* note 96, arts 1(1) & 6(2); Vienna Declaration, *supra* note 96, para 1(10).
289 ICESCR, *supra* note 2, preamble.
290 Marks 2006, *supra* note 281, 60.
291 UN Human Rights *National Human Rights Institutions: History, Principles, Roles and Responsibilities* (New York/Geneva: UN Publication, 2010) 5.
292 African Charter, *supra* note 106, art 22(2).

74 CHAPTER 2

the enabling environment for the African peoples to engage in the development process and to reap the benefits of doing so.

The legal provisions that define the human rights obligations of states are meant to apply in the instance where the state enjoys sovereignty to protect its people and to ensure the respect and fulfilment of their human rights. Because the right to development was born out of socio-economic and cultural deprivation, its realisation demands of African states to assert and authoritatively exercise the sovereignty to take such actions and policy measures that may deviate from or rupture established standards of subjugation. It necessitates the state to explore alternatives as may contextually be relevant and to establish appropriate systems to ensure that the right to development translates into improved well-being for the peoples of Africa.[293] The role of the state is thus one of agency in coordinating different constituencies of peoples to make development choices from a variety of options to ensure the realisation of the right to development. It implies that the state has the duty to create a scenario in which national development policies are designed to allow equal opportunity for the range of collectives that the state is composed of, to make their own socio-economic and cultural choices.[294]

The right to development does not only involve action at national level but also at the international level through cooperation. Thus, in addition to their domestic obligations, African states are further required to cooperate in order to ensure that the right to development is achieved. However, this does not provide an escape route for African countries to relinquish their sovereign obligation on the right to development and become relegated to the subordinate position of recipients of good-will donations from developed countries. Development prospects in Africa have for long been frustrated through the imperialistic interests of industrialised countries, which continue to exert a dominant influence in shaping international development policies through the globalisation agenda. As Chinedu Okafor points, the African Charter does not make provision for how state parties may deal with the exploitative behaviour of foreign stakeholders, which poses a challenge to the possibility of holding these actors accountable.[295]

---

293 See Declaration on the Right to Development, *supra* note 96, arts 3(1) & 2(3).

294 The women of Africa are guaranteed the right to sustainable development alongside other human rights under the Protocol on the Rights of Women (art 19), while indigenous peoples are guaranteed special protection under the UN Declaration on the Rights of Indigenous Peoples, which makes provision for indigenous Peoples' right "to determine and develop priorities and strategies for exercising their right to development" (art 23).

295 Okafor 2008, *supra* note 145, 61–62.

The responsibility to create development in Africa lies first and foremost with African states.[296] Exposed to international cooperation, the extent to which African states may exercise full control over the right to development becomes questionable in the context where development cooperation allows developed countries only the moral responsibility *to assist* without necessarily any legal obligation to be accountable for wrongful action.[297] The right to development is achievable through cooperation only to the extent that partner states assume mutual obligations for accountability. As Sengupta has emphasised, state responsibility to ensure the realisation of the right to development is not diminished by the absence of international cooperation.[298] The primary role of African states within the framework of development cooperation can therefore, not be circumscribed. Without international cooperation African states retain the obligation of action, the essence of which is not to become passive recipients of foreign aid but to make conditions favourable for development.[299]

4.2.2 Right to Development Goals

The question relating to what the right to development aims to achieve is relevant not only in justifying its existence but also in shaping critical thinking around its realisation through the mechanism of development cooperation. The unique formulation of the right to development in Africa both as a human right concept and a development paradigm suggests a quest to address, in a holistic manner, issues of justice and equity within a legal framework. The legal framework discussed in chapter four is described as a "right to development dispensation" on account of the range of moral and legal commitments undertaken in this regard. This integrated process, which is required to be rights-based and people-centred, must ensure that the achievement of the full range of human rights adds up to the enjoyment of well-being and amelioration of the human condition.[300] To this end, it is argued that the right to development aims at achieving two principal goals, namely, justice in development and substantive development in the form of improved livelihood as explained below.

---

296   Dąbrowska, *supra* note 4, 9.

297   Declaration on the Right to Development, *supra* note 96, art 4(2).

298   Sengupta 2002, *supra* note 171, 877.

299   Skogly, Sigrun I. "Global responsibility for human rights" (2009) 29:4 *Oxf J Leg Stud* 838.

300   Sengupta 2002, *supra* note 171, 846.

4.2.2.1 *Equity and Justice in Development*

Under-development in Africa is portrayed by extreme levels of poverty amidst an immeasurable wealth of natural resources.[301] From a "functionalist" understanding of poverty,[302] the solution is envisaged to entail cooperation between states in order to accelerate "comprehensive development" in poor countries.[303] The functionalist perception ignores the fact that poverty, and especially in Africa originates from historical disadvantage, which from a "dialectical" point of view is perceived as injustice rather than as a developmental problem.[304] In this instance, a redress of the situation requires "not development" in the sense of modernisation, technological and infrastructural advancement "but rather liberation from the [...] structures" that subjugate the impoverished.[305] Accordingly, Brand *et al.* envisage not just an approach in dealing with poverty that focuses solely on legal strategy but importantly, an approach that takes into account a politicised account of justice.[306] The understanding of poverty in Africa as injustice demands political commitment to ensure equitable opportunities as a means to advance human capabilities for the peoples of Africa. As part of the commitment, the political leadership recognise that development on the continent is threatened by external interferences,[307] consequently, requiring a legal framework to regulate the situation.

However, the *corpus* of international law, which aims partly at the duty to cooperate for development,[308] has become the dominant paradigm that has been employed in global development frameworks such as the MDGs and the Sustainable Development Goals (SDGs) among others. The norms that form the core content of international development are identified to include the principle of cooperation for global welfare, the principle of deferential treatment for developing countries, and the principle of entitlement of developing countries to development assistance.[309] The inference is that international development law envisages only positive moral obligations, which is problematic. If international development law aims at eliminating inequalities in

---

301   Suhfree, *supra* note 1, 102–106.

302   Brand *et al., supra* note 248, 275.

303   Declaration on the Right to Development, *supra* note 96, art 4(2).

304   Brand *et al., supra* note 248, 275.

305   As above, 276.

306   As above, 277.

307   African Union Commission "Agenda 2063: The Africa we want" (2015) *African Union* para 59.

308   Kwakwa, *supra* note 107, 435.

309   As above, 436.

global economic relations to the benefit of developing countries,[310] it is argued that without emphasis on the aspect of justice, it certainly does not guarantee fairness, particularly to Africa where development injustices are perpetuated with impunity. Accordingly, Emmanuel Kwakwa rightly cautions that international law must be viewed with scepticism because its application engenders a *status quo* that does not sufficiently protect developing countries.[311]

The connection between justice and development has been made clear by the UN General Assembly when it emphasised that global development should be established "on the basis of justice, equality and mutual benefit".[312] The right to development in Africa does not only impose a positive obligation for collective action for its realisation,[313] but also imposes a negative obligation for its protection.[314] The principles of cooperation and justice must be mutually re-enforcing through appropriate legislative and other measures to ensure adequate protection of the right to development, in which case, when a violation is alleged, access to a remedy must be guaranteed. The negative obligation to respect the right to development and consequently to protect it from violation is not only a question of principle but one of legal practice as illustrated by a number of instances of right to development litigation in Africa.[315]

Ultimately, the right to development requires that development be determined by considerations for equity and justice,[316] absent which, efforts aimed at the achievement of substantive gains may remain in vain. To the extent that slavery and colonialism could be considered as crimes against humanity, the ethics of equity and justice necessitate redress of some kind.[317] To proponents

---

310 As above, 453.

311 As above.

312 Preparation for an International Development Strategy for the Third United Nations Development Decade, GA Res 33/193 UN GAOR Supp (No 45) at 121 UN Doc A/33/45 (1979); Kwakwa, *supra* note 106, 449–450.

313 African Charter, *supra* note 106, art 22(2).

314 The principle of justice in development is embedded in the formulation of the right to development within the framework of international law as a human rights concept. Article 3(2) of the Declaration on the Right to Development stipulates that the "realization of the right to development requires full respect for the principles of international law concerning friendly relations and cooperation among States in accordance with the Charter of the United Nations".

315 *Endorois* case, *supra* note 158; *Darfur* case, *supra* note 157; DRC case, *supra* note 155; SERAC case, *supra* note 281; *Kevin Gumne* case, *supra* note 143.

316 Sengupta, Arjun "Conceptualizing the right to development for the Twenty-First Century" in UN Human Rights (eds) *Realizing the Right to Development: Essays in Commemoration of 25 Years of the United Nations Declaration on the Right to Development* (Geneva: UN Publication, 2013) 69; Oduwole, *supra* note 204, 19.

317 See Mamdani, *supra* note 135, 56–57.

of development cooperation, the allocation of development assistance is envisaged to constitute some form of redistributive or restorative justice.[318] Katerina Tomasevski's view is unconvincing and as such, a contrary view is expressed in chapter four with the argument that the development context in Africa demands more of liberation and preventive justice. The substantive outcomes that the peoples of Africa could anticipate to achieve from the development process are embedded in and attainable only in function of effectively asserting the right to development.

4.2.2.2   *Anticipated Substantive Development Outcomes*

The right to development incorporates the promise that certain substantive outcomes can be expected from the multidimensional processes of creating development. Recognising the human person as the central subject and the active participant and beneficiary of the right to development suggest that development of any kind will not be meaningful if it does not result in improved human well-being and better living standards.[319] When development is carried out, it creates expectations of some benefits that should contribute to improving the well-being or to bettering the living conditions of the human person. The Declaration on the Right to Development provides that in order to enjoy the benefits that flow from the development process, every individual and all peoples are "entitled to participate in, contribute to, and enjoy economic, social, cultural and political development" by which process "all human rights and fundamental freedoms can be fully realized".[320] The African Charter also guarantees that in order to reap the benefits of development, the peoples of Africa are entitled to exercise their right to socio-economic and cultural development.[321] Unlike with the provisions of the Declaration, the preamble to the African Charter stipulates that the realisation of socio-economic and cultural development is a guarantee for the enjoyment of civil and political rights.

The Charter presents political development as one of the benefits that the peoples of Africa can anticipate to enjoy as a result of achieving socio-economic and cultural development. When socio-economic and cultural

---

318   Tomasevski, Katerina *Development Aid and Human Rights: A Study for the Danish Centre for Human Rights* (London: Pinter Publishers, 1989) 48.

319   Declaration on the Right to Development, *supra* note 96, art 2(1) & (3).

320   As above, art 1(1).

321   African Charter, *supra* note 106, art 22. The African Youth Charter however, stipulates in article 10 that besides the entitlement to socio-economic and cultural development, the youths of Africa are also entitled to the right to political development, understandably reaffirming the rights of the youths to aspire for political leadership and governance as elucidated in other provisions of the Youth Charter.

development is achieved, the resultant system (devoid of corruption, democratic deficits and governance malpractices), would create the opportunity for a decent political culture where the peoples of Africa are empowered with the capacity to engage constructively in domestic politics and governance, unlike is the case with the prevailing *status quo* across the continent. To meet the aspiration of Africa becoming an "influential global player and partners with a significant role in world affairs" as contained in the 2063 African Agenda for development,[322] socio-economic and cultural development provides the only leverage to be able to shape the direction of global politics and thus, reverse the injustices that motivated the campaign for a NIEO and subsequently the right to development discussed earlier.

Because the right to development incorporates the principle of equity and justice as highlighted in the preceding sub-section, to ensure that development gains are not unreasonably accumulated in the hands of the privileged, the Declaration on the Right to Development talks about the need for equitable distribution of the benefits resulting from the development process as a means to equalise aspirations for the highest attainable standards of living guaranteed to all peoples.[323] The right to development thus, aims at breaking down the systemic barriers of structural inequalities and alternatively to standardise the level of well-being such that some peoples do not become extremely wealthy while others remain perpetually impoverished. To reaffirm the conviction that the right to development does not imply the right to economic growth but contributes to it, as much as the peoples of Africa get to develop their productive capabilities through active participation in the development process, the more they are able to contribute gainfully in advancing the economy.

The anticipation to achieve substantive development is preconditioned on the right to sovereign ownership over natural resources (the common heritage), which constitutes an inevitable recipe for creating development in Africa.[324] By implication, as part of the gains to anticipate from the development process, the peoples of Africa ought to demonstrate effective ownership and control over their natural wealth and resources, which the state may only have the right to dispose of to their exclusive interest.[325] The substantive outcomes that can be anticipated from the disposal of the peoples' wealth and

---

322   AU Commission "Agenda 2063" *supra* note 306, paras 59-63.
323   Declaration on the Right to Development, *supra* note 96, art 2(3); see also Universal Declaration, *supra* note 66, art 25(1).
324   African Charter, *supra* note 106, art 22(1); Declaration on the Right to Development, *supra* note 96, art 1(2).
325   African Charter, *supra* note 106, art 21(1).

resources include for example, the provision of material things such as educational and healthcare facilities, roads and other public infrastructures as well as non-tangible benefits in the form of public services, which the peoples are entitled to be enjoy as a right. Material things generally may not automatically translate into improved well-being, which may be used as a means to meet aspirations of well-being, which development economists, measure in terms of income per capita while rights-based proponents mostly apply the human development index in gauging living standards and human well-being around the world.

To achieve substantive development outcomes requires positive action, usually through domestic policy measures and according to the requirement of the African Charter, through collective action including for example, through initiatives such as the recently established African Continental Free Trade Area (AfCFTA), which promises to gainfully boost economic development cooperation among African countries.[326] Comparatively, after over five decades of dependency on development assistance, the development outcomes for Africa have not only been relatively minimal, the majority of African countries remain classified as the least developed in the world.[327] Accordingly, it is accurate to argue that owing to the prevailing *status quo* of endemic global imbalances and its resultant injustices, the realisation of the right to development in Africa depends largely on the extent to which the development process is shaped and defined by the substantive outcomes that the peoples of Africa can legitimately anticipate to achieve as a result of asserting that right. On the most part, these expectations are hindered by avoidable obstacles to development resulting from a calculated denial of the right to development that the impoverished peoples of Africa are inherently entitled to.[328]

---

326   The African Continental Free Trade Agreement is a trade agreement adopted in Kigali, Rwanda on 21 March 2018 with the goal of creating a single market. It achieved record ratification within the period of one year and entered into force in June 2019.

327   Nielsen, Lynge "Classifications of countries based on their level of development: How it is done and how it could be done" (2011) *IMF Working Paper WP/11/31* 20-23.

328   Statement by UN High Commissioner for Human Rights on the occasion of the 25th Anniversary of the Declaration on the Right to Development available at: www.un.org/en/events/righttodevelopment/ (accessed: 12 April 2019).

5 Concluding Remarks

By way of conclusion, it is important to recall that Africa has not only had a complicated development history, but the development challenges that it continues to experience have for several decades elevated the continent into the spotlight of international development discourse and the politics of development assistance, which in relation to the formulation of the right to development in Africa remains questionable. Owing to the complexity with regard to an accurate reading of the right to development, clarity is provided on the subject by exploring the historical events that gave birth to such a right, which as illustrated, originated from Africa. On this basis, it is further explained what the right to development in Africa actually aims to achieve.

Importantly, it is demonstrated that, rooted in a distressful history characterised by material dispossession of natural wealth and resources, deprivation of human rights and denial of the productive capacity for development, the right to development aims to achieve two fundamental goals, namely, justice in development and substantive development. Although it cannot be stated with precision the extent to which Africa would have achieved these goals, asserting the right to development suggests that the continent would not have remained underdeveloped but for the legacy of historical development injustices created by several decades of subjugation. Because of the development injustices perpetuated through the systematic schema of global coloniality, it is noted that the aspiration for substantive development is largely contingent on a legal framework to ensure that development is achieved with justice and equity.

However, questions relating to the realisation of the right to development in Africa remain complex for a number of reasons, which directly translate into operational difficulties. Without sufficient clarity on the purpose of the right to development, it is inconceivable that modalities for its implementation would become clear and straightforward. The insufficiencies that necessitated the adoption of the African Charter in 1981 and subsequently the Constitutive Act of the African Union in 2001 to replace the OAU Charter, which largely favoured development cooperation, underscored the need for a shift from dependency-based development thinking to envisaging development more in terms of self-determination and self-sufficiency as highlighted in Agenda 2063.[329] However, despite Sengupta's designation of the right to development as a rights-based process that entails equity and justice,[330] Mekuria Fikre posits that the process

---

329   African Union Commission, *supra* note 306, para 19.
330   Sengupta 2002, *supra* note 171, 846.

will not be complete without situating the role of development cooperation.[331] In substantiation of the argument in favour of the right to development as a remedy to Africa's development challenges resulting from the absence of an established development model for the continent, the next chapter explores the mechanism of development cooperation to determine its potential to facilitate realisation of the right to development in Africa.

331 Fikre, B. Mekuria "The politics underpinning the non-realisation of the right to development" (2011) 5:2 *Mizan L Rev* 256.

CHAPTER 3

Global Dynamics and the Geopolitics of Development Cooperation

1 Introduction

One of the principal arguments advanced in this chapter is that owing to the paternalistic nature of development cooperation, which runs counter to the concept of the right to development in Africa, the discourse on human rights and development in Africa ought to focus more on advancing the right to development as an alternative to development cooperation. Development cooperation is seen in this context as an extension of the colonial design, which decolonial theorists describe as global coloniality;[1] the system of patronage that portrays developing countries as constantly in need of help, even at the expense of their entitlement to self-determination and the freedom to make self-reliant development choices. This argument builds on the analysis in the previous chapter where illustration is provided on how the right to development originated in Africa as an expression of socio-economic and cultural self-determination rather than a solicitation for development assistance. In this way, it is demonstrated that the right to development is in effect

---

1 See Mignolo, Walter "Epistemic disobedience and the decolonial option: A manifesto" (2011) *Transmodernity* 44–66; Ndlovu, Morgan "Coloniality of knowledge and the challenge of creating African futures" (2018) 40:2 *Ufahamu: A Journal of African Studies* 95–112; Adams, Glenn & Estrada-Villalta, Sara "Theory from the South: A decolonial approach to the psychology of global inequality" (2017) 18 *Current Opinions in Psychology* 37–42; Ndlovu-Gatsheni, Sabelo J."Global coloniality and the challenges of creating African futures" (2014) 36:2 *Strategic Review for Southern Africa* 181–202; Bhambra, Gurminder K. "Postcolonial and decolonial dialogues" (2014) 17:2 *Postcolonial Studies* 115–121; Bhambra, Gurminder K. "Postcolonial and decolonial reconstructions" in Bloomsbury Collections *Connected Sociologies* (London: Bloomsbury Academic, 2014) 117–140; Ndlovu-Gatsheni, Sabelo J. "Coloniality of power in development studies and the impact of global imperial designs on Africa" (2012) *Inaugural Lecture delivered at the University of South Africa* 1–24; Grosfoguel, Ramón "Decolonizing post-colonial studies and paradigms of political-economy: Transmodernity, decolonial thinking, and global coloniality" (2011) 1:1 *Transmodernity* 1–38; Maldonado-Torres, Nelson "Thinking through the decolonial turn: Post-continental interventions in theory, philosophy, and critique – an introduction" (2011) *Transmodernity* 1–15; Mignolo, Walter D. "Delinking: The rhetoric of modernity, the logic of coloniality and the grammar of decoloniality" (2007) 21:2/3 *Cultural Studies* 449–514; Mignolo, Walter *The Darker Side of Western Modernity: Global Futures, Decolonial Options* (Durham: Duke University Press, 2011) 122–123.

© CAROL CHI NGANG, 2022 | DOI:10.1163/9789004467903_004

a development paradigm and therefore, a potential remedy to Africa's development challenges. This is reflected in the two-fold purpose that the right to development in Africa sets out to achieve: First, to create the context for justice in development to prevail and secondly, to ensure that well-being and an improved standard of living for the peoples of Africa is achieved.

Building on that argument, this chapter proceeds to dispute the fact that the right to development is achievable through development cooperation as envisaged under international law and in human rights and development scholarship. On account of this argument, the proposition is reiterated that if Africa is to advance beyond prevailing development challenges, there is a need to shrewdly rupture development cooperation ties and to deviate from paradigms that promote dependency on development assistance towards greater focus on the right to development as a development model for the continent.

The enquiry draws on the fact that international law demands recourse to development cooperation as a means to resolving, among others, problems of an economic, social and cultural nature and for promoting and encouraging respect for human rights and fundamental freedoms.[2] In this regard, many scholars estimate that development cooperation provides a platform on which to negotiate how the right to development is to be achieved.[3] To determine whether the right to development is achievable through development cooperation necessitates a proper analysis of how development cooperation could as a means and as a process enable the attainment of the outcomes that the right to development anticipates. The question that might not have been considered is the adverse impact resulting from the actions of foreign stakeholders within the development cooperation framework on the realisation of the right to development in Africa. With regards to the discussion in this chapter, a range of legal instruments that define the right to development dispensation

---

2 Charter of the United Nations adopted in San Francisco on 26 June 1945 art 1(3).

3 De Feyter, Koen "Towards a framework convention on the right to development" (2013) *Friedrich Ebert Stiftung* 17; Salomon, Margot E. "Legal cosmopolitanism and the normative contribution of the right to development" in Marks, Stephen P. (ed) *Implementing the Right to Development: The Role of International Law* (Geneva: Friedrich-Ebert-Stiftung, 2008) 17; Sengupta, Arjun "Development cooperation and the right to development" (2003) *Copyright©2003 Arjun Sengupta* 20; Sengupta, Arjun "On the theory and practice of the right to development" (2002) 24:4 *Hum Rts Qtly* 880; Häusermann, Julia "A human rights approach to development: Some practical implications for WaterAid's work" (1999) *Rights & Humanity* 5; Bedjaoui, Mohammed "The right to development" in Bedjaoui, Mohammed (ed) *International Law: Achievements and Prospects* (Dordrecht: Martinus Nijhoff & UNESCO, 1991) 1178; Siitonen, Lauri "Political theories of development cooperation: A study of theories of international cooperation" (1990) *UN University WIDER –Working Paper 86* 15–16.

are outlined in chapter four, which in effect obligates state parties to individually or collectively prioritise the right to development in Africa.

Africa may and has often been blamed for its own "backwardness". However, the fact that the right to development emerged from the African continent indicates that the peoples are able to locate where the problem lies. The angle from which that problem is conceived determines the extent to which strategies may be formulated to try and fix it. According to Charles Gore, the concept of development is multidimensional, which therefore implicates the way it can be understood.[4] There are exciting commentaries that present an optimistic and sometimes romanticised account of development in Africa in terms of impressive economic growth rates, emerging economies and opportunities for investment.[5] However, the approach in this book is to problematise the notion of development in Africa with the aim to advance the argument against development cooperation as an envisaged mechanism for the realisation of the right to development. This is principally because Africa's development challenges are either generated or amplified by the lop-sided global arrangement that promotes development cooperation as a *modus operandi*.

Theoretically, it is estimated that the global imbalances that tilt unfavourably towards Africa could be redressed through advancing the right to development. The intricacy follows from the way collaboration with Africa is envisaged. For instance, whereas South-South partners such as China, India and Brazil see cooperation with Africa more in terms of mutual collaboration for collective advancement, developed countries, particularly those within the Organisation for Economic Cooperation and Development (OECD), see Africa rather as facing a problem of economic growth and thus place emphasis on the provision of development assistance as a solution to the problem.[6] In accordance with this perception, the Declaration on the Right to Development is formulated to ensure that sustained action is made available, which practically translates into the provision of development assistance to enable developing

---

4 Gore, Charles "The new development cooperation landscape: Actors, approaches, architecture" (2013) 25 *J Int'l Dev't* 772.

5 See The Economist "Development in Africa: Growth and other good things" (2013) available at: http://www.economist.com/blogs/baobab/2013/05/development-africa (accessed: 10 June 2016); UNCTAD *Economic Growth in Africa Report 2014: Catalysing Investment for Transformative Growth in Africa* (New York/Geneva: UN Publication 2014); African Development Bank *Africa Development Report 2014: Regional Integration for Inclusive Growth* (2014) African Development Bank – Development Research Department.

6 Gore, *supra* note 4, 772.

countries to advance in a comprehensive manner.[7] With the anticipation to achieve some form of redistributive justice, Felix Kirchmeier notes that the promise of development assistance has caused an aid-dependency syndrome and therefore challenges the African conception of the right to development.[8]

If development assistance, which is promised and made available through cooperation, constitutes the reason for asserting the right to development in Africa, it would have featured in the instruments that enshrine such a right. It is also assume that if development cooperation has the potential to ensure the realisation of the right to development; it would by every indication contribute to redressing development injustices and improving human well-being through, for example, the eradication of poverty and the advancement of human rights in Africa. While development cooperation as envisaged for the realisation of the right to development seems unproblematic, it is taken for granted that it may not always turn out as promising as envisaged. Many developed countries, which according to the development cooperation understanding are expected to make provision for development assistance are apprehensive of any legal obligations stemming from the right to development, which is propagated principally by developing countries.[9] In exploring these issues, the theoretical and practical dimensions of development cooperation are subjected to critical examination.

The chapter is structured as follows: Section 2 interrogates the cooperation framework for development as a mechanism for the realisation of the right to development in Africa. In this regard, the origins of development cooperation is explored in (2.1), its basic features in (2.2) and the nature of two opposing cooperation patterns in (2.3); intended to illustrate that development cooperation is design not necessarily with the aim to achieve the right to development. In section 3, development cooperation is examined in relation to the right to development by looking at any possible connection that may exist (3.1), the political nature and indeterminate motives of development cooperation (3.2) and the persistent sabotage of Africa's development prospects (3.3). Section 4 further looks at the right to development in Africa in terms of the recommended modalities for its realisation in (4.1) and the actual realities of human rights and development practice in (4.2). The chapter concludes in section 5 with a summary of the principal arguments.

---

7   Declaration on the Right to Development Resolution A/RES/41/128 adopted by the UN General Assembly on 4 December 1986 art 4(2).

8   See Kirchmeier, Felix "The right to development – where do we stand?: State of the debate on the right to development" (2006) *Friedrich Ebert Stiftung – Occasional Paper No 23* 14.

9   See for example Kirchmeier, *supra* note 8, 13–14.

THE GEOPOLITICS OF DEVELOPMENT COOPERATION

2 Cooperation Framework for Development

This section examines the mechanism of development cooperation with the purpose to determine its potential as an envisaged mechanism for the realisation of the right to development and to establish whether there is in effect a causal connection between development cooperation and the right to development. Owing to the fact that the right to development in Africa is established by law to remedy development injustices and consequently lead to improved well-being, background knowledge on development cooperation as well as its status in law might help to illustrate to what extent it could contribute to achieving the intended purpose.

2.1 *Origins of Development Cooperation*

2.1.1 Brief Historical Account

Knowledge on the background to development cooperation is intended to illustrate that the post-colonial relationship that has been forged between Africa and foreign stakeholders and in most instances former colonial masters, leaves room to question what such cooperation actually aims to achieve. Drawing from the discussion in the previous chapter on how imperialist practices helped to destabilise Africa, it is worth noting that the post-World War II global arrangement established a framework for collaboration that was primarily designed to advance the colonial agenda. The history of development cooperation dates back to around 1944 with the creation of institutional frameworks for cooperation,[10] probably in anticipation of decolonisation.[11] The United Nations (UN) Charter subsequently established the legal basis that set the development cooperation framework into motion. Development cooperation as envisaged by the UN Charter to deal with global problems might have been well intended but because of Cold War politics, the 1960s experienced a radical redesigning of the meaning of cooperation to respond to western capitalist ideologies of domination and profit maximisation.[12] As a result, the

---

10 Führer, Helmut "The story of official development assistance: A history of the Development Assistance Committee and the Development Cooperation Directorate in dates, names and figures" (1996) *OECD* 4–5.

11 Jordan, Sarah (tr) "Cooperation: New players in Africa" (2010) 1 *Int'l Dev't Pol* 95–113. By the time the institutional frameworks for cooperation were established, colonised territories had not yet gained independence and so exercised no autonomy to get involved in international development politics.

12 Dann, Philipp *The Law of Development Cooperation: A Comparative Analysis of the World Bank, the EU and Germany* (New York: Cambridge University Press, 2013) 3 5 & 35–43; see also http://www.isc.niigata-u.ac.jp/~miyatah/oda/oda_top.htm "In 1960 the OECD set up

decolonised countries of the third world that regrouped as the Non-Aligned Movement became the target for development aid from the United States (US)-led capitalist bloc.[13] As Bartenev and Glazunova rightly indicate, the intentions of the US was not based on any genuine interest for cooperation on the basis of equitable partnership but as a Cold War strategy to win more allies as a means to overpower the communist bloc led by the Soviet Union.[14] The Soviet Union equally relied on the same strategy in establishing its cooperation network.

The development aid bait used by the capitalist bloc became widespread following the establishment of aid agencies such as the US Agency for International Development (USAID), the American Peace Corps, and the Alliance for Progress, which brought US presence in almost every developing country around the world.[15] The designation of the 1960s as the UN Development Decade saw the creation of an unprecedented number of cooperation agencies, financial institutions, multinational corporations and a host of others to represent and to promote the colonial, diplomatic and economic interests of the countries that established them. Accordingly, because these foreign stakeholders are mandated or regulated by their respective states, they take on accompanying legal obligations under international law, as do the countries that they represent.[16] However, by 1969 the concept of development cooperation had undergone a corrupt modification to mean the allocation of "official development assistance" to developing countries under the auspices of the OECD, with the Development Assistance Committee (DAC) as the

---

      the Development Assistance Group (DAG) as a forum for consultations among aid donors on assistance to less-developed countries. In the following year, it was reconstituted as the Development Assistance Committee (DAC)". On the other hand, in 1961, the UN General Assembly designated the 1960s as the UN Development Decade "in which Member States and their peoples will intensify their efforts to mobilize and to sustain support for the measures, required on the part of both developed and developing countries to accelerate progress towards self-sustaining growth of the economy of the individual nations and their social advancement so as to attain in each under-developed country a substantial increase in the rate of growth".

13   Bartenev, Vladimir & Glazunova, Elena *International Development Cooperation: Set of Lectures* (Moscow: The World Bank, 2013) 22.

14   Bartenev & Glazunova, *supra* note 13, 22.

15   Berg, Robert & Gordon, David F. (eds) *Cooperation for International Development: The United States and the Third World in the 1990s* (Boulder: Lynne Rienner Publishers, 1989) 1.

16   See Augenstein, Daniel & Dziedzic, Lukasz "State responsibilities to regulate and adjudicate corporate activities under the European Convention on Human Rights" (2011) *Submission to the Special Representative of the UN Secretary General on the Issue of Human Rights and Transnational Corporations and Other Business Enterprises* 5–6.

THE GEOPOLITICS OF DEVELOPMENT COOPERATION

coordinating mechanism.[17] By so doing the OECD-DAC cooperation architects skilfully removed the legal obligations attributed by international law, leaving the cooperation framework to operate on the basis of charity. It is within this framework that the bonds between former colonial masters as donors and the former African colonies as recipients of development assistance became established.[18] Many international development agencies such as the Danish International Development Agency (DANIDA), the Swedish International Development Agency (SIDA) and the Norway Agency for Development Cooperation (NORAD) for example, provide extensive development assistance to Africa not based on any colonial ties. A lot more are actually based on colonial ties, which calls into question the proper meaning of development cooperation, especially when juxtaposed with the right to development in Africa.

2.1.2 Definitional Problem

The discussion in this section is intended to establish the fact that the concept of development cooperation poses a definitional problem, which has misleadingly been normalised as standard practice according to which the right to development is envisaged to be achieved. If the right to development is to be achieved through development cooperation, both concepts need to be seen from the same perspective. However, drawing in particular from the background discussion above, development cooperation can be said to be capitalist driven while the right to development is more socialist in orientation. Most leading international development agencies programme their cooperation arrangements in line with the OECD-DAC model, which prioritises development assistance as a modality for cooperation.[19] This is problematic in the sense that development cooperation is supposed to aim at creating a global enabling environment for balanced development to take place. However, the focus has been more on development assistance, which represents just an aspect of the broader concept of development cooperation.[20] More light

---

17 Rich, Roland "The right to development: A right of peoples?" in Crawford, James (ed) *The Rights of Peoples* (Oxford: Oxford University Press, 1988) 49–50.

18 Dann, *supra* note 12, 135.

19 See for example Rijksolvereid "Interministerial policy review: Towards a new definition of development cooperation considerations on ODA" (2013) *The Netherlands Ministry of Finance* 10. Within the context of the ODA definition, the Netherlands' development cooperation policy considers that the aim of development cooperation is to promote economic development and prosperity, focusing particularly on poverty reduction.

20 See Tinbergen, Jan "Alternative forms of international co-operation: Comparing their efficiency" (1978) 30:2 *Int'l Soc Sc J* 224–225. Tinbergen identifies aspects that make up sound international cooperation to include; participation in decision making and/or policy formulation, mutual exchange of information, review and appraisal of programmes for

is shed on this in the discussion on the operational modalities for cooperation below.

Development cooperation derives from the broad concept of international cooperation, which embodies many dimensions.[21] In the context of this book, development cooperation should be understood to refer to the specific aspects of international cooperation that deals with economic, social and cultural development.[22] It is worth highlighting that the concept of development cooperation as originally envisaged by the UN Charter, existed long before the emergence of the right to development. The reason why the two concepts have become yoked together suggests, at least in principle the common purpose to promote human rights and to deal with problems of an economic, social and cultural nature. However, this bonding has been severed as a result of the fact that development cooperation has lost its original meaning. Although development cooperation is supposed to be driven by the principle of sovereign equality of states, it has instead largely become subjected to the discretion of donor countries.[23]

Consequently, in the course of developed countries providing assistance according to the contemporary understanding of development cooperation, most African countries have been rendered dependent – in contradiction to the international law principle that recognises the sovereign equality of states;[24] in contradiction to the African Charter provision that prohibits external domination;[25] and therefore also in contradiction to the right to development. If the right to development aims at achieving justice and equity in development

---

execution, non compulsory mediation, compulsory arbitration, application of sanctions and a legal framework for cooperation that must be charter-based.

21 Esteves, Paulo & Assunção, Manaíra "South-South cooperation and the international development battlefield: Between the OECD and the UN" (2014) 35:10 *Third World Quarterly* 1776; IOM "International cooperation" available at: http://www.rcmvs.org/documentos/IOM_EMM/v1/V1S07_CM.pdf (accessed: 26 May 2016) 9–17. The areas of development cooperation include among others technical, economic, security, climate, migration and military cooperation.

22 UN Charter, *supra* note 2, art 1(3); Declaration on the Right to Development, *supra* note 7, art 2.

23 Janus, Heiner; Klingebiel, Stephan & Mahn, Timo "How to shape development cooperation?: The global partnership and the development cooperation forum" (2014) *German Development Institute – Briefing Paper 3* 1; Gore, *supra* note 4, 770.

24 UN Charter, *supra* note 2, art 2(1). States may not have the same economic power but in terms of treaty recognition every state is guaranteed the right to sovereign equality, which must be respected.

25 African Charter on Human and Peoples' Rights adopted in Nairobi, Kenya on 27 June 1981 OAU Doc CAB/LEG/67/3 Rev.5 (1981) art 19.

THE GEOPOLITICS OF DEVELOPMENT COOPERATION   91

for the ultimate realisation of human well-being and an improved standard of living,[26] as a causal principle development cooperation should invariably lead to the same outcome. Theoretically, it means that in the absence of the causal factor, the consequential factor is bound to suffer setbacks, giving the impression that development cooperation is inevitable for the realisation of the right to development. On the contrary, it may not be so, especially when the right to development and development cooperation are juxtaposed in terms of their conceptual formulation.

Literally, development cooperation could be defined as the act of states working together to achieve a common development purpose. In this context, the element of "working together" would be understood to respond to the principle of sovereign equality of states, while the component of "common development purpose" may be said to represent the range of economic, social and cultural problems that need to be addressed. This entails a scenario for collective action where cooperating partners are capable of adjusting their actions and behaviours to the actual or anticipated preferences of other states.[27] On the basis of this definition it is necessary to explore the basic features of development cooperation.

2.2   *Basic Features of Development Cooperation*
2.2.1   Motives behind Development Cooperation
In analysing the motives behind development cooperation my aim is to illustrate that development cooperation is not designed to achieve the right to development. The purpose for which countries engage in development cooperation is characterised by a diversity of interests and objectives,[28] which have constantly changed over time.[29] Degnbol-Martinussen and Engberg-Pedersen identify four primary motives for giving and receiving development assistance involving moral and humanitarian considerations, political and national security concerns, economic and trade motivations as well as environmental

---

26   UN Charter, *supra* note 2, art 55; Declaration on the Right to Development, *supra* note 7, art 2; International Covenant on Economic, Social and Cultural Rights adopted by Gen Ass Res 2200A (XXI) of 16 December 1966 art 11.

27   Paulo, Sebastian "International cooperation and development: A conceptual overview" (2014) *German Development Institute* 3; Axelrod, Robert & Keohane, Robert O. "Achieving cooperation under anarchy: Strategies and institutions" (1985) 38:1 *World Politics* 226.

28   Hynes, William & Scott, Simon "The evolution of Official Development Assistance: Achievements, criticisms and a way forward" (2013) *OECD* 2.

29   Anderssen, Maria "Motives behind the allocation of aid: A case study regarding Swedish motives for aid allocation" (Masters Essay in Political Science, Goteborg Universitet 2009) 8.

considerations.[30] Of these motives, which are categorised in accordance with the parameters established by some key development cooperation actors, the one that relates closest to the issues embodied in the right to development in Africa is cooperation that is based on moral and humanitarian considerations. However, as Maria Anderssen notes, "Western powers have always been very clear that foreign aid to former colonies is not compensation for the violations and damages that colonialism imposed".[31]

Apparently, development cooperation is portrayed as intended to support developing countries through economic, financial and technical assistance and by adapting this assistance to the requirements of recipient countries.[32] However, as will be illustrated later, purely moral and humanitarian motives are uncommon in prevailing development cooperation patterns mainly because they are often overridden by the "enlightened self-interest" of donor countries.[33] This is generally informed by the dominant priority to promote their "economic and commercial interests, including continuous access to natural resources, raw materials, and markets in the former colonies".[34] According to Jean-Claude Berthélemy, the motive for giving aid is primarily commercial, in terms of which target countries for cooperation are often selected from the perspective of the potential for trade.[35] This mercantile motive often has a short-term strategy of first identifying and seizing market opportunities in the cooperating country and in the longer term to gain and expand trade and investment opportunities.[36] Unfortunately, the underlying commercial and trade interests behind development cooperation are never actually in Africa's favour. The motives that inform states' actions in their international transactions determine the operational modalities for cooperation. Two operational modalities for cooperation are examined to determine the underlining reasons for which states engage in such a practice.

---

30   Degnbol-Martinussen, John & Engberg-Pedersen, Poul *Aid: Understanding International Development Cooperation* (London/New York: Zed Books, 2005) 7–24; Anderssen, *supra* note 29, 9.

31   Anderssen, *supra* note 29, 9.

32   Hynes & Scott, *supra* note 28, 3.

33   Degnbol-Martinussen & Engberg-Pedersen, *supra* note 30, 10.

34   As above, 9.

35   Berthélemy, Jean-Claude "Aid allocation: Comparing donors' behaviours" (2006) 13 *Swed Eco Pol Rev* 75–109.

36   Anderssen, *supra* note 29, 9.

2.2.2 Operational Modalities

The two operational modalities for development cooperation examined in this section are: development assistance and development partnership, which generally apply in the context of one pattern of development cooperation or another. There are two reasons for making this distinction. The first stems from concerns relating to the effectiveness of development assistance in dealing with the challenges that impact adversely on developing countries.[37] Although development assistance is commonly understood as intended to accelerate progress in developing countries as stated in article 4(2) of the Declaration on the right to development, the reality is that it instead creates a situation where developing countries remain dependent on those that provide the assistance. The second builds on the fact that the idea of partnership has loosely been used synonymously with the concept of development cooperation.[38] Article 55 of the UN Charter for instance, underscores the idea of partnership, which must be based on the principles of sovereign equality and self-determination of states. In contrast, development cooperation is often established on the basis of dominance of the donor state over the recipient state and therefore, cannot be said to qualify as partnership. An overview of these two modalities is presented in the sub-sections that follow with the purpose to determine to what extent they could realistically actualise the right to development in Africa.

2.2.2.1 *Partnership for Development*

Not to confuse partnership for development with other forms of partnership, the discussion in this section is specifically related to development cooperation of a genuinely mutual nature between two or more actors for the purpose of creating the opportunity for socio-economic and cultural development to take place. For the reason that the law prohibits domination by one state over another, the term partnership, because it sounds more appealing has been used quite frequently as "a subtle form of external power imposition".[39] This is illustrated in the way developed countries conceptualise partnership to entail ensuring "aid effectiveness, the reduction of corruption, and the provision of assistance rather than mutual benefits and reciprocity".[40]

---

37   Bailey, Fiona & Dolan, Anne M. "The meaning of partnership in development: Lessons for development education" (2011) 13:2 *Policy & Practice: A Development Education Review* 30–31.

38   Bailey & Golan, *supra* note 37, 30.

39   Fowler, Alan "Beyond partnership: Getting real about NGO relationships in the aid system" (2000) 31:3 *IDS Bulletin* 3; Bailey & Golan, *supra* note 37, 36.

40   Bailey & Golan, *supra* note 37, 32.

There is a fundamental legal justification why it is important to focus on development partnership as an operational modality to ensure that the right to development may be achieved in the process. When development cooperation is established on the basis of partnership, it allows legal norms to become applicable, requiring cooperating partners to honour their commitments. The rationale for engaging in development partnership from a development point of view is to leverage the achievement of substantive development and from a legal point of view, to ensure justice and equity in the development process.[41] Genuine partnership for development is thus associated with and defined by the following characteristic principles: sustainable commitment, a common goal and shared responsibilities, reciprocal obligations, equality and mutual respect, transparency and accountability, joint decision making, and most importantly symmetry in power relations.[42] In the light of these defining principles, major international development fora in the course of the past decade have consistently emphasised a need for country ownership of development programmes.[43]

However, instead, Africa's development agenda has often entirely been determined by foreign stakeholders who generally determine the terms of partnership, usually without Africa's active involvement and participation in the decision-making processes.[44] At a conceptual level, development partnership seen from the perspective of rights-based approaches to development should be understood to translate from the international law principles of sovereign equality of states, the right to self-determination and the right not to be dominated by another state. The suggestion is that the formulation of partnerships for development must be based on legality to ensure greater reasonableness, transparency and accountability, especially in respect of human rights. As it stands that the right to development in Africa is guaranteed by law, it is important also to determine what the law says with regard to development cooperation.

---

41   Sengupta, Arjun "The human right to development" (2004) 32:2 *Oxf Dev't Stud* 183–184; Sengupta 2002, *supra* note 3, 848–852.

42   Communication from the Commission to the European Parliament, the Council, the European Economic and Social Committee and the Committee of the Regions Brussels "A global partnership for poverty eradication and sustainable development after 2015" 5.2.2015 COM (2015) 3–4; Bailey & Golan, *supra* note 37, 33–34.

43   The 2002 Monterrey International Conference on Financing for Development; the 2003 Rome High Level Forum on Harmonization; the 2004 Marrakech Roundtable on Managing for Development Results; the 2005 Paris High Level Forum on Aid Effectiveness; and the 2008 Accra High Level Forum on Aid Effectiveness.

44   Bailey & Golan, *supra* note 37, 35.

THE GEOPOLITICS OF DEVELOPMENT COOPERATION

Deriving from the principle of friendly relations, the motivation to engage in global partnerships for development has largely been determined by a moral commitment as laid down in soft law instruments.[45] Although these instruments are in the strict sense not absolutely binding, they provide moral guidelines that can be "used as mechanisms for authoritative interpretation or amplification of the terms of a treaty".[46] As Serges Kamga points out, most soft law instruments have come to be accepted as constituting international customary practice, which is an acceptable source of international law.[47] Besides that, the UN Charter among other international instruments stands out as the primary instrument that provides the legal framework for development cooperation as a means of solving international problems relating to human well-being.[48] Given the magnitude of development challenges that Africa is confronted with, the legal guarantee that development cooperation conveys inspires the need for effective right to development practice.[49] However, while the legal requirement for development cooperation as it applies in principle may be considered for the realisation of the right to development, some scholars have argued that it does not impose any absolute obligation.[50] Accordingly, most developed countries deny that they owe any legal obligation to cooperate

---

45   The soft law instruments that make provision for development cooperation for the realisation of the right to development include the Declaration on the Right to Development, *supra* note 7, art 3, arts 4 & 6(1), the Vienna Declaration and Programme of Action adopted at the World Conference on Human Rights June 1993 (para I(10)); UN Millennium Declaration (para III(11)); the Millennium Development Goals (goal 8) & the Sustainable Development Goals (goal 17).

46   See Mahalu, Costa R. "Human rights and development: An African perspective" (2009) 1:1 *Leiden J Int'l L* 19; Boyle, Alan E. & Chinkin, Christine *The Making of International Law* (Oxford: Oxford University Press, 2007) 216; Salomon, Margot E. *Global Responsibility for Human Rights: World Poverty and the Development of International Law* (Oxford: Oxford University Press, 2007) 89; Kirchmeier, *supra* note 8, 11.

47   Kamga, Serges A.D. "Human rights in Africa: Prospects for the realisation of the right to development under the New Partnership for Africa's Development" (Doctoral Thesis, University of Pretoria 2011) 145.

48   Fikre, B. Mekuria "The politics underpinning the non-realisation of the right to development" (2011) 5:2 *Mizan L Rev* 260; UN Charter, *supra* note 2, arts 1(3), 55 & 56; see also ICESCR, *supra* note 26, art 2(1).

49   See Marks, Stephen P. "The human rights framework for development: Seven approaches" in Sengupta, Arjun; Negi, Archna & Basu, Moushumi (eds) *Reflections on the Right to Development* (Delhi: SAGE Publication, 2005) 23–60.

50   Salama, Ibrahim "The right to development: Towards a new approach?" (2005) 10:2 *Perceptions* 58; Donnelly, Jack "In search of the unicorn: The jurisprudence and politics on the right to development" (1985) 15:3 *Calif West Int'l L J* 509; Meir, Benjamin M. & Fox, Ashley M. "Development as health: Employing the collective right to development to achieve the goals of the individual right to health" (2008) 30 *Hum Rts Qtly* 328.

for the purpose of achieving the right to development.[51] Thus, contrary to the obligation to cooperate for the purpose of equalising opportunities for development, development cooperation has rather established a situation where donor countries take liberty to patronise recipient countries through the mechanism of development assistance.

2.2.2.2 Development Assistance

In the discourse on international development, the encompassing concept of international development cooperation has unfortunately been abridged and narrowed down to the provision of development assistance. This has come about as a result of the practice where the provision of aid by developed countries and the dependence by developing countries on such aid for developmental purposes has dissipated the original meaning of development cooperation.[52] To my mind, development assistance should be regarded as only a sub category of the broad concept of development cooperation. Development assistance, which in OECD-DAC terminology is known as Official Development Assistance (ODA) consists of concessional flows of development financing by bilateral and multilateral donors to developing countries with the aim to promote their economic development and welfare.[53] It may be assumed that the motivation to advance the right to development in Africa is underlined by the desire to achieve a particular interest. If that interest is a claim to development assistance, sound logic would support the fact that such an interest would feature in the instruments that proclaim the right to development. However, a perusal of the African treaty instruments and domestic legislation that enshrine the right to development reveals nothing about a claim to development assistance as a pre-requisite for the realisation of the right to development in Africa.[54]

---

51 Nwauche, Enyinna S. & Nwobike, Justice C. "Implementing the right to development" (2005) 2:2 SUR – Int'l J Hum Rts 4.

52 Schoenstein, Anne & Alemany, Cecilia "Development cooperation beyond the aid effectiveness paradigm: A women's rights perspective" (2011) Association for Women's Rights in Development – Discussion Paper 1–2.

53 Führer, supra note 10, 24; OECD-DAC "Is it ODA?" (2008) OECD-DAC – Factsheet November 1; Draft International Development (Official Development Assistance Target) Bill presented to Parliament by the Secretary of State for International Development by Command of Her Majesty January 2010 1.

54 See the African Charter, supra note 25, art 22; Protocol to the African Charter on Human and Peoples' Rights on the Rights of Women in Africa adopted in Maputo Mozambique on 11 July 2003 art 19; African Youth Charter adopted in Banjul The Gambia on 2 July 2006 art 10; Constitution of Malawi art 30; Constitution of the DRC art 58; Constitution of

THE GEOPOLITICS OF DEVELOPMENT COOPERATION 97

The African Charter is explicit about the fact that it is the duty of state parties to either individually or collectively ensure the realisation of the right to development.[55] It is important to note that collectivism in this instance does not carry the same connotation as development cooperation in the manner that it is conceived in this book. Accordingly, it is argued that development assistance is neither the envisaged development goal that Africa aims to achieve nor is it a strategic option for advancing the right to development in Africa. For Donald Rukare, development assistance constitutes a legally binding right established through international customary law.[56] Without disputing the existence of such a right, my basic argument is that it is unproductive to pursue development cooperation (except where it plays a complementary role) because in terms of effectiveness, development assistance generally lacks the potential to facilitate the realisation of the right to development in Africa.

Arjun Sengupta has also advanced the argument that development assistance remains the most important instrument of development cooperation and therefore advocates in favour of increasing the volume of foreign aid to developing countries.[57] A couple of other scholars advance similar arguments that the legal force of the right to development is established on the duty of states to cooperate with one another.[58] A contrary argument is presented here based on a number of reasons: First, the provision of foreign aid or development assistance is a political decision that is motivated by the discretion of the donor rather than by the obligation to fulfil development obligations in another country. The criteria by which development assistance is allocated are determined primarily and often unilaterally by donor entities rather than by the exigency of the countries that might genuinely need such assistance for development purposes. Fundamentally, donors determine the criteria for allocating development assistance and formulate the policies while recipient countries are often only expected to comply with programmes implementation.[59]

Ethiopia art 43 and Constitution of the Republic of Uganda 2006, National Objectives and Directive Principles of State Policy objective six.

55   African Charter, *supra* note 25, art 22(2).

56   Rukare, Donald "The role of development assistance in the promotion and protection of human rights in Uganda" (Doctoral Thesis, University of Pretoria, 2011) 94.

57   Sengupta 2002, *supra* note 3, 880.

58   Villaroman, Noel G. "Rescuing a troubled concept: An alternative view of the right to development" (2011) 29:1 *Neth Qtly Hum Rts* 41; Iqbal, Khushid "The declaration on the right to development and implementation" (2007) 1:10 *Political Perspectives* 4; Rich, Roland "The right to development as an emerging human right" (1983) 23 *Virg J Int'l L* 291.

59   Branzick, Amelia "Humanitarian aid and development assistance" (2004) *Beyond Intractability* available at: http://www.beyondintractability.org/essay/humanitarian-aid (accessed: 18 November 2017). One of the most common features in the development

Second, considering that development from a rights-based point of view means improvement in human well-being through the realisation of all human rights, an important question is whether the volume of foreign aid that has been channelled to Africa has achieved improvement in the well-being of the African peoples? Quite to the contrary, in spite of the phenomenal flow of development assistance to Africa over the decades, human rights violations have become endemic, exacerbated by extreme levels of poverty.[60] Third, development, which Amartya Sen describes as freedom, ought to amount to the removal of various types of "unfreedom" that limit rational action and, therefore, should be seen as a process of expanding the actual freedoms and capabilities to sustain well-being and standards of living that people have reason to value.[61] Following Sen's definition, the question to ask is whether development assistance creates the kind of freedom that amounts to development? In essence, development assistance, which is often tied to conditionalities, rather creates a relationship of dominance on the part of donor countries while recipient countries are reduced to the level of subservience and dependency.[62] In this relationship recipient countries enjoy neither the freedom to make development choices, the liberty to formulate their own development policies nor the opportunity to advance the productive capabilities of their peoples.[63] In other words, apart from its ineffectiveness as a modality for development, development assistance is in fact opposed to the concept of the right to development in Africa as it is conceived of in this book.

Lastly, contrary to Rukare's view that there is a legally binding right to development assistance under international law, which implies a duty to make such assistance available to developing countries,[64] it is argued that the right to

---

cooperation arrangement is the fixing of conditionalities by donor countries, which recipient countries are obligated to comply with.

60 Statistical, Economic and Social Research Training Centre for Islamic Countries (SESRT-CIC) "Poverty in Sub-Saharan Africa: The situation in the OIC member countries" (2007) *Preliminary Report* 1–14.

61 Sen, Amartya *Development As Freedom* (Oxford: Oxford University Press, 1999) xii, 1 & 8.

62 BBC News "Kenya's Uhuru Kenyatta urges Africa to give up aid" (12 June 2015) available at: http://www.bbc.com/news/world-africa-33108716 (accessed: 14 June 2016). Although foreign aid is said to amount for about 5 to 6 per cent of Kenya's national income, President Uhuru Kenyatta, while addressing the 25th Summit of the African Union is quoted to have stated that: "The future of our continent cannot be left to the good graces of outside interests. Dependency on giving that only seems to be charitable must end. Foreign aid, which so often carries terms and conditions that preclude progress is not an acceptable basis for prosperity and freedom. It is time to give it up".

63 See Uhuru Kenyatta's statement cited in BBC News, *supra* note 62.

64 See Rukare, *supra* note 56, 94 & 321–324.

development in Africa does not create any binding obligation for reliance on development assistance. African countries are therefore, not bound to remain subject to the patronage of developed countries with the hope to develop. This argument is based on the logic that if development assistance is accepted as an operational modality for development, when such assistance becomes unavailable, development will consequently not be achieved and, therefore, the right to development would have been compromised. Relating this analysis to Radin and Singer's conception of pragmatism as a legal theory that envisages practical outcomes through the actual workings of the law,[65] it is further argued that if the right to development is to be achieved through development cooperation, cooperation arrangements must comply with the law that protects the right to development. Accordingly, the commitment undertaken by industrialised countries to provide 0.7 per cent of their national gross domestic product (GDP) as assistance to developing countries,[66] for example, ought to become a legal obligation that must be fulfilled to produce expected outcomes of well-being and better living standards. Unfortunately, that commitment has never fully been met. The 0.7 per cent GDP quota is discussed more elaborately in chapter five.

The realisation of the right to development cannot reasonably be based on the charitable provision of development assistance, which Richard Dowden observes, does not have the potential to rescue Africa from its development challenges.[67] It requires equitable balance in the global system, which entails that development cooperation must be designed to comply with the obligations imposed by the right to development enshrined in the African Charter and ancillary instruments. Even where it is established that development assistance is of relevance in order to accelerate development in Africa,[68] the contention is advanced that because of the patronising nature of development cooperation through which assistance is provided as explained below,

---

65   Radin, Margaret J. "The pragmatist and the feminist" (1990) 63:2 *South Calif L Rev* 1700; Singer, Joseph W. "Property and coercion in federal Indian law: The conflict between critical and complacent pragmatism" (1990) 63:6 *South Calif L Rev* 1821–1822.

66   Monterrey Consensus on Financing for Development adopted at the International Conference on Financing for Development, Monterrey Mexico *United Nations* 2002 para 42; UN Resolution 2626 (1970) *The International Development Strategy for the Second United Nations Development Decade*.

67   Dowden, Richard *Africa: Altered States, Ordinary Miracles* (London: Portobello Books Ltd, 2009) 508.

68   See UN Charter, *supra* note 2, art 55 & 56; Declaration on the Right to Development, *supra* note 7, art 4(2); ICESCR, *supra* note 26, art 1(2); Rukare, *supra* note 56, 94.

100   CHAPTER 3

it can ultimately only result in dependency rather than guarantee the right to
development.

2.2.3   Patronage and Paternalism

The donor-driven forms of cooperation are consistently referred to in this book
as fundamentally patronising and paternalistic in nature. Although provided
for and regulated by international law requiring states to undertake concerted
action in dealing with development challenges;[69] the development cooperation mechanism often does not espouse the principle of sovereign equality
of the states involved, especially because of the competition for hegemony
among cooperation partners and also within rival cooperation patterns.[70] The
Office of the High Commissioner for Human Rights describes development
cooperation as the space regulated by law within which the right to development can fully be realised.[71] Contrary to the general perception that development cooperation is intended to improve living conditions in poorer countries,
Janus *et al.* portray the cooperation mechanism as "part of an international
system characterised by fragmentation and limitations in global problem
solving".[72] If international law were to apply in actual terms in guaranteeing
genuine equality between developed and developing countries, development
cooperation could be counted as a means to achieve the right to development.
However, because of established global inequalities, development cooperation has rather become a mechanism through which developing countries are

---

69   See for example UN Charter, *supra* note 2, art 1(3), 55 & 56; Declaration on the Right
      to Development, *supra* note 7, art 3(3) & 4(2); ICESCR, *supra* note 26, art 1(2); Vienna
      Declaration, *supra* note 45, para 1(10); Fikre, *supra* note 48,256–257.

70   For a general discourse on development cooperation see Esteves & Assunção, *supra* note
      21, 1775–1790; Mawdsley, Emma "Human rights and south-south development coopera-
      tion: Reflections on the 'rising powers' as international development actors" (2014) 36:3
      Hum Rts Qtly 630–652; De Renzio, Paulo & Seifert, Jurek "South–south cooperation and the
      future of development assistance: Mapping actors and options" (2014) 35:10 *Third World
      Quarterly*1860–1875; Milani, Carlos R.S. & Muñoz, Echart E. "Does the South challenge the
      geopolitics of international development cooperation?" (2013) 4:1 *Geopolítica(s)* 35–41;
      Quadir, Fahimul "Rising donors and the new narrative of 'south-south' cooperation: What
      prospects for changing the landscape of development assistance programmes?" (2013)
      34:2 *Third World Quarterly* 321–338; Gore, *supra* note 4, 769–786.

71   UN Human Rights "Development is a human right for all" available at: http://www.ohchr.org/
      EN/Issues/Development/Pages/Backgroundrtd.aspx (accessed: 8 April 2016).

72   Janus, Heiner; Klingebiel, Stephan & Paulo, Sebastian "Beyond aid: A conceptual per-
      spective on the transformation of development cooperation" (2015) 27:2 *Journal of
      International Development* 155–156.

constrained to remain perpetual subordinates to donor developed countries for subsistence.[73]

San Bilal describes the approach to development cooperation of actors from the industrialised countries of the North, as framed in the ideology of "we will help you".[74] This benevolence ideology is in principle, not unrelated to the civilising mission that informed colonialism in the 17th century by which European nations unilaterally assumed a "God-assigned" responsibility to want to help Africa as illustrated in chapter two. Over the decades after independence, development cooperation has been characterised by paternalism, marked by an asymmetrical relationship that robs Africa of the potential and capacity to chart its own development trajectory.[75] Featuring in the dependency ratio between developed countries and the developing countries under their influence as Girvan points out, is the manifestly incongruous power imbalance that is sustained among others through economic dominance,[76] which is underscored by "donor-dictated conditionalities".[77] In analysing the economic potential and growth rate of emerging economies, especially those in Asia, in comparison with advanced economies, Bilal argues that "[d]eveloping countries do not need to be taught how to grow".[78] Unfortunately, despite pioneering the right to development, Richard Ilorah sees Africa's endemic dependency on foreign aid as a poignant manifestation of inability to survive without aid, which has rather plunged a great number of countries into extreme levels of poverty.[79]

The vicious cycle of paternalism creates a false hope that development in Africa is achievable through foreign assistance, which in effect only ensnares Africa in a debt trap, undermines its autonomy in development policy making

---

73   Todaro, Michael P. & Smith, Stephen C. *Economic Development* (Addison Wesley: Pearson, 2006)115–118; Ngang, Carol C. "Differentiated responsibilities under international law and the right to development paradigm for developing countries" (2017) 11:2 *HR & ILD* 272; Rukare, *supra* note 56, 84; Kirchmeier, *supra* note 8, 14.

74   Bilal, San "The Rise of South-South relations: Development partnerships reconsidered" (2012) *Conference paper – European Centre for Development Policy Management* 1.

75   Brett, Edwin A. "Explaining aid (in)effectiveness The political economy of aid relationships" (2016) *Department of International Development, London School of Economics – Working Paper Series No 16-176* 1-5; Betteraid "Development effectiveness in development cooperation: A rights-based perspective" (2010) *Betteraid* 1.

76   Girvan, Norman "Power imbalances and development knowledge" (2007) *North-South Institute* 5–15; Betteraid, *supra* note 75, 2.

77   Ilorah, Richard "Africa's endemic dependency on foreign aid: A dilemma for the continent" (2011) *ICITI – ISSN: 169412254*–6 & 22–25.

78   Bilal, *supra* note 74, 1–10.

79   Ilorah, *supra* note 77, 1–3.

and the ability to gainfully exploit its immense natural resource endowments and in turn exacerbates the continent's vulnerability to exploitation.[80] Because development cooperation provides foreign stakeholders the platform to patronise developing countries, Africa's irrational dependence on foreign assistance has meant that it cannot legitimately assert the right to development due to the fact that the donor that "pays the piper, determines the tune" in accordance with the aid conditionality principle. I illustrate this claim by moving on to look at some development cooperation prototypes.

2.3 *Cooperation Patterns*

By looking at existing patterns of development cooperation in this section, my purpose is to point out that none of them is designed to achieve the right to development in Africa. There are four identified cooperation patterns within the development cooperation framework, namely; the North-South, South-South, triangular and global partnerships, which as Milani and Muñoz observe have emerged as a result of the struggle for hegemony and legitimacy among competing donor actors.[81] For the purpose of this analysis, the apparently contrasting North-South and South-South patterns are examined to further illustrate the point that development cooperation only provides the opportunity for dominant actors to patronise rather than advance the right to development in Africa.

2.3.1 North-South Cooperation

Traditionally, North-South development cooperation has been understood to refer to the lopsided donor/recipient relationship, where development assistance is made available by affluent developed countries of the North to the impoverished developing countries of the South.[82] North-South cooperation started in the form of a moral responsibility by former colonial masters to carry out "development activities [...] in their overseas territories".[83] Although there is pretence that North-South cooperation is intended to help poor countries, the underlying agenda has always been imperialistic and exploitative.[84] Within

---

80 See Anna, Thomas *et al.* "Real aid: Ending aid dependency" (2011) *ActionAid* 17–20; UNDP *Towards Human Resilience: Sustaining MDG Progress in an Age of Economic Uncertainty* (New York: UN Publication, 2011) 151–152; Ilorah, *supra* note 77, 14–25.

81 Milani & Muñoz, *supra* note 70, 37–38.

82 Rosseel, Peter *et al.* "Approaches to north-south, south-south and north-south-south collaboration: A policy document" (d.n.a) available at: https://lirias.kuleuven.be/bitstream/123456789/229636/1/policy_paper_vlir_uwc_nss.pdf (accessed: 25 April 2016) 11–12.

83 Führer, *supra* note 10, 4.

84 Rosseel *et al.*, *supra* note 82, 12–13.

THE GEOPOLITICS OF DEVELOPMENT COOPERATION   103

the North-South cooperation structure, developing countries are conditioned to become dependent on the life-support of development assistance, which in most cases does not have any long-term objective.[85] Owing to the fact that North-South cooperation is established principally on the provision of development assistance, it gives donor countries the privilege to impose with conditionality their understanding of development on recipient African countries.[86] This often happens notwithstanding that the African perception about development may be diametrically different from that of the donor countries.[87]

As a pre-requisite to the allocation of development aid to Africa, for instance, terms and conditions are often imposed emphasising respect for civil and political rights through good governance and democratisation programmes.[88] Meanwhile, the actual development priorities in Africa as enshrined in the African Charter and ancillary instruments that provide for the right to development relating principally to livelihood security concerns embodied in economic, social and cultural rights are often not given requisite attention by donors.[89] The contents of the Millennium Development Goals (MDGS) and the Sustainable Development Goals (SDGS) support the fact that issues that are central to development are predominantly those of a social, economic and cultural nature.[90] The North-South aid conditionality strategy that principally promotes civil and political rights thus contradicts the African aspirations for development, which establishes that priority be given to the realisation of socio-economic and cultural rights as a guarantee for the enjoyment of civil and political rights.[91]

---

85   As above, 13–14.
86   As above, 13.
87   As above.
88   Mawdsley, *supra* note 70, 634.
89   As above, 635.
90   Six of the MDGS including Goal 1: Eradicate extreme poverty and hunger, Goal 2: Achieve universal primary education, Goal 3: Promote gender equality and empower women, Goal 4: Reduce child mortality, Goal 5: Improve maternal health and Goal 6: Combat HIV/AIDS, malaria and other diseases are all related to socio-economic concerns. Goal 7: Ensure environmental sustainability, deals with environmental issues. And of course, Goal 8: Develop a global partnership for development emphasises the need for cooperation. None of the MDGS deals with civil or political issues, which suggests that they are not as relevant for achieving development as socio-economic issues. Of the 17 SDGS, 8 are directly related to socio-cultural issues, 5 to environmental issues, 2 to economic growth, 1 dwells on peace and security and 1 on development partnership. Basically none of the SDGS deals with civil and political issues.
91   African Charter, *supra* note 25, preamble; AU Commission "Agenda 2063: The Africa we want" (2015) *African Union* Aspiration 1 paras 9-18; Gawanas, Bience "The African Union: Concepts and implementation mechanisms relating to human rights" in Bosl,

In the vain attempt to democratise and to institute good governance to satisfy donor defined standards, aid recipient countries often fail to focus on matters relating to human well-being and livelihood security concerns. Consequently, the provision of development assistance does not translate into better ling standards for the peoples in recipient countries, resulting in the outcry within the donor community about aid ineffectiveness. If development "aid is intended to reduce poverty, or at least improve the welfare and living conditions of the poor" as Oliver Morrissey notes,[92] Olumide Taiwo thinks that such aid needs to be prioritised in accordance with the recipient countries' prerogatives to be able to achieve people-centred development.[93] In this regard, it is not illogical as Esteves and Assunção have argued to label conditionalities attached to development assistance as a means to advance donor interests rather than foster development in the recipient countries.[94] Owing to this shortcoming, the South-South cooperation pattern emerged as an attempt to challenge the North-South *status quo* and promote solidarity among developing countries.

2.3.2 South-South Cooperation

South-South cooperation represents a regrouping of development actors that do not adhere to the OECD-DAC rules and therefore function through operational modalities that are diametrically opposed to the dominant North-South pattern.[95] Basically, South-South cooperation provides the framework within which developing countries make available their expertise and financial support to other developing countries on the basis of mutual benefits rather than just the provision of development assistance.[96] The South-South strategy thus challenges the OECD-DAC practice that distinguishes some countries as donors and others as recipients.[97] As Yun Sun argues, South-South cooperation is more

---

    Anthon & Diescho, Joseph (eds) *Human Rights in Africa: Legal Perspectives on their Protection and Promotion* (Windhoek: Macmillan Education Namibia, 2009) 143.

92   Morrissey, Oliver "Aid effectiveness for growth and development" (2002) *ODI Opinions* 2.

93   Taiwo, Olumide "Improving aid effectiveness for Africa's economic growth" (2011) *Foresight Africa* 16–18.

94   Esteves & Assunção, *supra* note 21, 1781.

95   See Jordan, *supra* note 11.

96   Tortora, Piera "Common ground between south-south and north-south cooperation principles" (2011) *OECD Issues Brief* 1; Zimmermann, Felix & Kimberley, Smith "New partnerships in development co-operation" (2011) 2010:1 *OECD Journal: General Papers* 38; Esteves & Assunção, *supra* note 21, 1784.

97   Zimmermann, *supra* note 96, 43.

often largely transactional and reciprocal in nature[98] than the lop-sided North-South divide. Esteves and Assunção as well as Zimmermann share the view that unlike in the North-South pattern, South-South cooperation emphasises the exchange of technical skills to further the collective self-reliance of developing countries in enhancing their productive capacity to deal with development challenges.[99] According to Fahimul Quadir, the South-South pattern is advantageous to developing countries in the sense that it shifts significantly from policy conditionality-driven development assistance and rather emphasises partnership, entailing a horizontal relationship based on the principles of sovereign equality and mutual interests.[100]

In the light of the divergent approaches, OECD-DAC proponents frown at the unwillingness of South-South actors to impose conditionalities as undermining efforts by North-South donors "to reduce corruption, achieve poverty reduction, and promote human rights".[101] These concerns may be genuine. However, the question is whether the imposition of conditionalities has in effect redressed the issues in question pertaining to development in Africa. South-South partners are united by "a shared experience of colonial exploitation, post-colonial inequality, and present vulnerability to uneven neoliberal globalization, and thus a shared identity with poorer nations".[102] South-South cooperation could to a large extent deal with the issues that hold back developing countries and in effect facilitate the realisation of the right to development to the extent that equitable sharing of the benefits of development is guaranteed.

However, looking at the economic clout of the championing actors of South-South cooperation such as Brazil, Russia, India, China and South Africa (BRICS) emerging countries,[103] it is difficult to resist questioning their underlying motives for exploring the African development space. The one concern is whether as emerging economies these actors are not simply driven by the pursuit of economic expansion, with the aim to impose their economic weight on Africa. Another concern is whether the South-South actors have the potential to support other developing countries, considering that they equally face

---

98 Sun, Yun "Africa in China's foreign policy" (2014) *John L. Thornton China Centre & Africa Growth Initiative* 2.

99 Esteves & Assunção, *supra* note 22, 1779; Zimmermann, *supra* note 96, 43.

100 Quadir, *supra* note 70, 324; Zimmermann, *supra* note 96, 43.

101 Mawdsley, *supra* note 70, 642.

102 As above.

103 Quadir, *supra* note 70, 321–322; De Renzio & Seifert, *supra* note 70, 1864. There are a couple of other developing countries involved in south-south cooperation. The focus on Brazil, China and South Africa is because of their growing interests in Africa.

insurmountable development challenges.[104] These questions do not have straightforward answers. China, in spite of its domestic difficulties dating back to the Cultural Revolution is reported to have since 1955 provided huge amounts of foreign aid to Africa.[105] In the course of this period, it has also managed to uplift millions of Chinese people out of poverty.[106] South Africa on the other hand, in spite of its relatively flourishing economy is yet to satisfactorily deal with the extreme levels of poverty and social inequality at home, but is extending a sizeable amount of assistance to other African countries.[107] With these illustrations, De Siqueira argues that although South-South cooperation is not utterly "sinful", it might not be a "virtuous" project for developing countries to venture into.[108]

While South-South cooperation has on the one hand been recognised as "effective and desirable", the pattern of aid flow among South-South partners has on the other hand been described as unethical. As Mawdsley puts it, South-South partners "appear overwhelmingly motivated by *mere self-interest* rather than *enlightened self-interest*" (emphasis added).[109] Translated literally, it means that the way developing countries project their self-interest in the course of practising development cooperation is "primitive", unlike the "civilised" manner by which developed countries do. Two inferences could be drawn from this. The first is that notwithstanding its form, development cooperation

---

104   De Siqueira, D. Rebens "Brazilian cooperation is not a free lunch: An analysis of the interests contained in the international development cooperation strategy" (2013) 4:1 *Geopolítica(s)* 150. Brazil, China, India and South Africa are known to be the most unequal countries in the world in terms of disparity between the poor and the rich and extensive human rights abuses. A huge proportion of the populations in these countries live in grinding poverty while the largest chunk of the wealth is in the hands of a few highly privileged persons.

105   Sun, *supra* note 98, 3–4.

106   Stahl, Anna K. "Trilateral development cooperation between the European Union, China and Africa: What prospects for South Africa?" (2012) *University of Stellenbosch Centre for Chinese Studies – Discussion Paper No 4* 12; Oyugi, Phoebe "The right to development in Africa: Lessons from China" in Ngang, Carol C.; Kamga, Serges D. & Gumede, Vusi (eds) *Perspectives on the Right to Development* (Pretoria: University of Pretoria Law Press, 2018) 286; Chinese White Paper on the Right to Development "The right to development: China's philosophy, practice and contribution" adopted by China's State Council Information Office on 1 December 2016.

107   Grimm, Sven "South Africa as a development partner in Africa" (2011) *EDC 2020 – Policy Brief* 2; Besharati, Neissan A. "South African Development Partnership Agency (SADPA): Strategic aid or development packages for Africa?" (2013) *SAIIA – Research Report 12* 17–22.

108   De Siqueira, *supra* note 104, 146.

109   Mawdsley, *supra* note 70, 639.

THE GEOPOLITICS OF DEVELOPMENT COOPERATION 107

fundamentally aims to promote a certain self-interest that is unrelated to the advancement of human well-being by which the right to development is defined. The second inference is that developing countries do not have the agency to create development in an *enlightened* manner and, therefore, should not venture into the field of development cooperation where they do not have expertise and do not understand the rules of the game.[110]

It cannot be denied that such sentiments against the South-South cooperation architecture are nursed because the actors do not belong to the OECD-DAC club of imperialist donors and are recalcitrant to profess the OECD-DAC doctrine. It can also not be contested that South-South cooperation does not genuinely practice equal horizontal partnership as it portends to do.[111] It would appear as the current discourse on development cooperation suggests that South-South partnership for development lacks a unified strategy and proper coordination.[112] On this note, it is appropriate to argue that South-South cooperation is yet to prove its potential to achieve the right to development, but has in essence exposed the lapses and weaknesses of the North-South pattern. With this in mind, it is important to also look at multilateralism and the global partnership mechanism.

2.3.3   Multilateralism and Global Partnership

Contemporary international law lays down the principle, as highlighted earlier on that global problems of a socio-economic and cultural or humanitarian nature and in promoting adherence to human rights and fundamental freedoms are to be resolves through international cooperation.[113] International cooperation is, as Arjun Sengupta explains, based on the idea that the reciprocal effect in the pursuit of development policies in today's globalising world obligates states to work together for mutual benefit in the realisation of human right, including in particular, the right to development.[114] The Declaration on the Right to Development indeed, repeatedly emphasises the need for recourse to international cooperation as a mechanism for its realisation.[115] It denotes a multilateral process wherein relevant actors and stakeholders are

---

110   As above, 37.

111   De Siqueira, *supra* note 104, 139.

112   Quadir, *supra* note 70, 324.

113   UN Charter, *supra* note 2, art 1(3), 55 & 56; Declaration on the Right to Development, *supra* note 7, art 3(3) & 4(2); ICESCR, *supra* note 26, art 1(2); Vienna Declaration, *supra* note 45,para I(10).

114   Sengupta 2004, *supra* note 41, 194.

115   Declaration on the Right to Development, *supra* note 7, arts.

required to converge on the basis of global partnership,[116] which has over the last decade, shaped development programming on a universal scale, initially conceived as the Millennium Development Goals (MDGs) and subsequently as the Sustainable Development Goals (SDGs).[117]

The UN High Commission for Human Rights defines global partnerships for development as a multilateral framework wherein nations of the world are obligated to create an enabling environment free from structural impediments that may hinder developing countries accessing opportunities for advancement.[118] Margot Salomon equally sees global partnership in very positive light as envisaged to provide the framework for redressing global development imbalances.[119] For Sengupta, it practically delineates a global compact, which although he says guarantees mutuality of obligation among stakeholders,[120] actually only creates a platform that allows dominant developed countries to dictate global policies and set the pace for development in developing countries. To be mutually beneficial, global partnership ought to operate in accordance with the *jus cogens* principle of sovereign equality of states, which unfortunately has not been the case. Other scholars accordingly observe that for developed countries, global partnership rather provides the opportunity to dominate and exploit, resulting in the structural inequalities that portray Africa and other parts of the world as perpetually fragile and underdeveloped.[121]

Taken literally, the nice-sounding idea of global partnership gives the impression of commonality of purpose, solidarity and a shared commitment to resolving problems that are of a global concern. However, the channeling of development assistance principally towards developing countries with unattainable conditionalities; undermines the sovereignty of the "targeted" countries (most of them in Africa) and thus, limit their capacity to set own development priorities and effectively assume domestic ownership of development processes.

---

116   Sengupta 2004, *supra* note 41, 195.

117   MDG, *supra* note 45, goal 8; SDG, *supra* note 45, goal 17.

118   UN High Commission for Human Rights "The right to development – framework for achieving the MDGs" (2010) *UNOHCHR Infonote/MDGsR2D/15072010*.

119   Salomon, *supra* note 3, 50.

120   Sengupta 2004, *supra* note 41, 196.

121   Alemazung, J. Asongazoh "Post-colonial colonialism: An analysis of international factors and actors marring African socio-economic and political development" (2010) 3:10 *The Journal of Pan African Studies* 70–73; Kirchmeier, Felix; Lüke, Monika & Kalla, Britt *Towards the Implementation of the Right to Development* (Geneva: Friedrich-Ebert-Stiftung, 2008) 7.

THE GEOPOLITICS OF DEVELOPMENT COOPERATION 109

Although Sengupta argues that global partnerships have the advantage of guaranteeing equitable justice in global development policy making,[122] it is not unknown that the global partnership model has not been of much benefit to Africa in spite of the of policies on development assistance and the dispatch of it in substance and absolute quantities to the continent over the decades. It is affirmed in the 2030 global agenda for development that after fifteen years of implementing the MDGs, "progress has been uneven, particularly in Africa".[123] This is probably because of the misconceived approach that prioritises global partnership rather than emphasise recourse to the right to development as an alternative paradigm for development.[124] It might be sensible to see global partnership as a functional mechanism for development, the implementation of which is abused, resulting in questions about the effectiveness of foreign aid in driving development.[125] However, contrary to expectations, until structural imbalances between developed and developing countries are dealt with; global partnership appears not too different from North-South cooperation arrangements and thus, equally poses threats Africa, which is constrained to remain dependent on foreign assistance.

Critically analysing the failure of foreign aid to developing countries, Fabrice Niyonkuru rightly suggests the need to explore alternative models.[126] Perhaps the perception of global partnership as providing the medium where development priorities and the right to development become mutually reinforcing needs to be taken more seriously. The UN High Commission for Human Rights estimates that focusing on the right to development can in reverse; strengthen global partnerships and thus, draws attention to the fact that countries that formulate their development strategies on the basis of the right to development are more likely to achieve greater development gains. Focusing on the right to development infers both the right to sovereignty in setting alternative priorities and the associated duty to formulate development policies that are contextually relevant in redressing perennial development challenges. This is in reality the approach to development that Africa needs to pursue and has in

---

122   Sengupta 2004, *supra* note 41, 194–197.

123   Transforming Our World: The 2030 Agenda for Sustainable Development Resolution A/RES/70/1, adopted by the United Nations General Assembly on 27 September 2015 para 16.

124   Ngang, Carol C. & Kamga, Serges D. "Poverty eradication through global partnerships and the question of the right to development under international law" (2017) 47:3 *Africa Insight* 47–54.

125   Elaya, Moosa "Lack of foreign aid effectiveness in developing countries: Between a hammer and an anvil" (2016) 9:1 *Contemporary Arab Affairs* 87–96.

126   Niyonkuru, Fabrice "Failure of foreign aid in developing countries: A quest for alternatives" (2016) 7:3 *Business & Economics Journal* 231–240.

principle partly done so by giving the right to development legal recognition and protection in the African Charter and ancillary treaty instruments.[127]

While developed countries are expected to reciprocate by acknowledging the right to development as a legally binding obligation, there is no justification why since the adoption of the Declaration on the Right to Development in 1986, with its repeated emphasis on development cooperation, its legal status under international law remains extensively politicised.[128] As Felix Kirchmeier writes, developed countries remain apprehensive that the legal recognition of the right to development would compel them to provide assistance to developing countries as a matter of obligation than as simple charity.[129] Whether the attitude would subsequently change, necessitating developed countries to be guided by the spirit of solidarity embodied in the idea of global partnership and eventually vote in favour of the pending draft convention on the right to development[130] is yet to be ascertained. While the proposed draft convention is still awaiting adoption, a number of European scholars have already out rightly dismissed the necessity of such a convention.[131]

With this analysis, it is important to proceed to test the mechanism of development cooperation from the starting point that the right to development in Africa is not just a claimable entitlement or a quest for assistance but in itself a development paradigm. In other words, it necessitates a closer critical examination of both framework models to determine whether the right to development could indeed, be achieved through development cooperation.

---

127   African Charter, *supra* note 25, arts 1–26; African Youth Charter, *supra* note 54, art 10; Protocol on the Rights of Women in Africa, *supra* note 54, art 19.

128   Marks, S. Philip *The Politics of the Possible: The Way Ahead for the Right To Development* (Geneva: Friedrich Ebert Stiftung, 2011) 3.

129   Kirchmeier, *supra* note 8, 10.

130   Chair Rapporteur; Zamir Akram (Pakistan) Draft Convention on the Right to Development, Human Rights Council Working Group on the Right to Development, A/HRC/WK.2/21/2 of May 2020.

131   Schrijver, Nico "A new Convention on the human right to development: Putting the cart before the horse?" (2020) 38:2 *Neth Qtly of Hum Rts* 84–93; De Feyter, Koen "Right to development: A treaty and its discontents" in Arts, C.J.M.; Tamo, Atabongwung & De Feyter, K. (eds) *UN-Declaration on the Right to Development, 1986–2016: Ways to Promote Further Progress in Practice* (The Hague: T.M.C. Asser Press, 2016) 25; Vandenbogaerde, Arne "The right to development in international human rights law: A call for its dissolution" (2013) 31:2 *Neth Qtly Hum Rts* 187, 203–8.

3   Development Cooperation and the Right to Development

3.1   *Determining the Connection*

Felix Kirchmeier rightly points out that development cooperation ought to be driven by the right to development.[132] The discussion in this section reveals the contrary in the sense that there is in effect no causal relationship between development cooperation and the right to development. This, therefore, begs the question how the right to development is estimated to be achieved through development cooperation. Neither the North-South nor the South-South cooperation patterns examined above demonstrates a direct connection on the basis of which to justify the potential of development cooperation to achieve the right to development. As a pragmatic concept, the right to development can only be achieved when the right holders who are inherently entitled with the right to self-determination to make their own development choices are capable of exercising that right proactively and without constraint.

There might be a legitimate expectation from Africa on the basis of the promises of development assistance envisaged within the framework of development cooperation under international law as a guarantee for the fulfilment of the right to development. However, without a genuine commitment by developed countries to provide such assistance,[133] it is unrealistic to anticipate the right to development to be achieved through development cooperation, unless international law, which is more protective of developed countries, is significantly reformed to achieve global balance. Global balance entails eliminating the policies that perpetuate development injustices and the biased globalisation practices that systematically dispossess the peoples of Africa of the right to self-determination in making their own development choices. Until this is achieved, there is no justification why Africa should embrace development cooperation as a *modus operandi* for development rather than advance the right to development, which requires asserting a legitimate claim against the systems that hold back progress on the continent.[134]

Following the international law principle of *pacta sunt servanda*, which only requires the exercise of good faith, the requirement to assist developing

---

132   Kirchmeier, *supra* note 8, 5.

133   As above, 13.

134   With this explanation, it should be noted that the contrary view to the idea of development cooperation is based on the fact that even were development cooperation is legally binding, it is inappropriate as a modality for implementing the right to development, principally because it undermines the capabilities of the African peoples and disregards the sovereign equality of African states to self-determination.

countries through cooperation is in practice generally only optional and not based on any absolute obligation in terms of specific allocation of responsibilities for which donor countries could be held accountable.[135] With regard to the global partnerships for the achievement of universal benchmarks for development, for instance, Thomas Pogge has expressed doubts about the framing of these global actions to eradicate poverty due to lack of clarity about the roles and responsibilities that states are supposed to play.[136] Without clarity on the actual responsibilities of states, development cooperation remains too vague to be considered a mechanism through which the peoples of Africa could advance legitimate claims for the right to development. The role of development cooperation is thus, not pivotal, but only serves an ancillary purpose as a support mechanism to efforts that aim at the realisation of the right to development. Moreover, development cooperation in the current forms in which it is structured runs contrary to the purpose of the right to development, which is sustained by the principles of self-determination,[137] independent development policy making[138] and domestic ownership of the development process.[139]

To the extent that the right to development is estimated to be achieved through development cooperation; even in the instance where it is guaranteed a status that engenders more than a moral commitment, given the history of foreign domination and the pre-eminence that gives to actual self-determination for Africa, it is argued that development cooperation is unsuited as a development model because of its paternalistic and donor-recipient asymmetrical nature. Without development cooperation, it remains an intrinsic entitlement to the peoples of Africa and a duty for African states to strive for the achievement of the right to development. Otherwise, development cooperation may only become relevant and suitably applicable *sans* its problematic characteristics or only when it is divested of its innate impediments, if at all such divestment can be achieved within the context of the current global arrangement.

---

135   Bunn, Isabella D. "The right to development: Implications for international economic law" (2000) 15:6 *Am U Int'l L Rev* 1453. Bunn highlights that the right to development does not contain any "explicit obligation to provide development assistance". See also Ghandhi, Sandy "Global responsibility for human rights: World poverty and the development of international law by Margot E. Salomon" (2011) 8:1 *Brit Yearbk Int'l L* 333.

136   Pogge, Thomas "The Sustainable Development Goals: Brilliant propaganda?" (2015) *Annals of the University of Bucharest – Political Science Series ISSN 1582-2486* 1.

137   Declaration on the Right to Development, *supra* note 7, art 1(2).

138   As above, art 2(3).

139   See generally Final Draft African Consensus and Position on Development Effectiveness adopted by the African Union in Addis Ababa 30 September 2011.

Although developed countries are required as a matter of obligation under international law to provide development assistance to developing countries, most developed countries contend that they are not compelled by any obligation imposed by the right to development to do so, which they argue, is a duty that developing countries are bound to fulfil.[140] As Kirchmeier has observed, the argument advanced by developed countries hinges on the fear that "the right to development might be perceived as a right to development assistance"[141] and thus, basically threatens the privileged position of dominance that developed countries may not want to relinquish. However, given the requirement envisaged by the Declaration of the Right to development to eliminate obstacles to development that may arise from the unconventional behaviour of developed countries, they are compelled by a negative duty to refrain from actions that may contravene the right to development in Africa.

Pragmatically, the responsibility lies with the peoples of Africa as proponents of the right to development to become more radical in asserting that right, especially with respect to taking adequate measures to ensure its realisation. Article 2(3) of the Declaration on the Right to Development guarantees to every state the duty and the right to formulate appropriate development policies. Within the African context, such policies ought to reflect the legally binding character of the right to development as an assurance of protection against contravention. Beside the increasing fatigue among donor countries on the rationale for the continuous provision of development assistance, Hamilton notes that there is in effect a significant decline in development aid to the extent that its sustainability is uncertain.[142] Without this practical shortcoming, development cooperation still does not become relevant because as underscored in this book, its inappropriateness as a development model for Africa is more fundamental (designed not in a manner to favour development in Africa) than practical. The underlying motives for which donor countries engage in cooperation are often more political and driven by economic growth ambitions than by the people-centred priorities that are embodied in the right to development in Africa, which is principally socio-economic and cultural in nature.[143]

---

140 Kirchmeier, *supra* note 8, 10.

141 As above.

142 Hamilton J. Maxwell "Development cooperation: Creating a public commitment" in Berg, Robert & Gordon, David F. (eds) *Cooperation for International Development: The United States and the Third World in the 1990s* (Boulder: Lynne Rienner Publishers, 1989) 211 213.

143 African Charter, *supra* note 25, art 22(1); UN Charter, *supra* note 2, art 1(3).

114   CHAPTER 3

It makes no sense to promote development cooperation as a mechanism by which to achieve the right to development, knowing that the outcome to anticipate is relatively insignificant. According to Salomon, states are legally accountable for creating global poverty and therefore have the collective obligation through the normative function of the right to development to deal with the resulting injustices and structural imbalances.[144] Her argument is that international law provides the framework for the global community to "assume responsibility for world poverty" and to "eliminate the structural obstacles that impede the realization of basic human rights".[145] She believes that this global responsibility is achievable through international cooperation.[146] However, despite the legal obligations imposed by international law with regard to development cooperation as stipulated in articles 55 and 56 of the UN Charter, the reality as Sandy Ghandhi rightly observes is that "many powerful donor states see development cooperation as "discretionary" rather than as a relevant legal obligation".[147] Thus, without refuting the significant role that development cooperation plays in international development, this book articulates the claim that the deep-seated geopolitical motives behind development cooperation override the motivation to achieve the right to development.

3.2   *Political Nature and the Indeterminate Motives of Cooperation*

The analysis in this section is intended to illustrate with some concrete examples that the right to development in Africa is nowhere near to be achieved through development cooperation. Philip Dann opines that contrary to the framing of development cooperation on the promise of a globalised community that is supposed to operate on the principles of solidarity and fairness, the reality is generally different, consequently posing "seemingly unsolvable problems of global governance in a postcolonial world".[148] My argument draws from this premise and on the fact that donor developed countries often base their choice of countries for cooperation not necessarily to complement Africa's efforts to achieve the right to development as envisaged in article 4(2) of the Declaration on the Right to Development but on the potential of the countries concerned to contribute to the advancement of the donor country's economy.[149] As explained in the following sub-sections; for developed countries,

---

144   Salomon 2008, *supra* note 3, 17.
145   As above, 12.
146   Salomon 2007, *supra* note 46, 109 & 204.
147   Ghandhi, *supra* note 134, 333.
148   Dann, *supra* note 12, 1.
149   Anderssen, *supra* note 29, 10.

THE GEOPOLITICS OF DEVELOPMENT COOPERATION

development cooperation is mostly intended to promote their self-interest and to exert a dominant influence in shaping Africa's development choices.

3.2.1 Self-Interest

Development cooperation might have been established to respond to deep-seated development problems but in reality the reasons why foreign stake-holders initiate and engage in cooperation are predominantly to promote what Mekuria Fikre refers to as "strategic interests" rather than to address the developmental needs in developing countries.[150] Donald Rukare is not far from the point in estimating that development cooperation has in some ways only contributed to maintaining the *status quo* of keeping poor countries in perpetual poverty.[151] This tendency continues to manifest in different forms within the development cooperation framework, whereby donor partners tend to promote their geo-strategic interests rather than aim to enable developing countries to advance beyond their current state of underdevelopment.[152]

The rapidly growing presence of China in Africa for example, has become a subject of great concern and controversy. China's operation in Africa is established within the framework of South-South cooperation, which in theory is based on partnership and mutual benefits.[153] In reality, cooperation often does not reflect what it envisages. In spite of the supposed South-South partnership with Africa, the following excerpts show how China sees Africa in the relationship:

> Politically, China seeks Africa's support for China's 'One China' policy and for its foreign policy agendas in multilateral forums such as the United Nations. Economically, Africa is seen primarily as a source of natural resources and market opportunities to fuel China's domestic growth [...].
>
> China also sees an underlying ideological interest in Africa, as the success of the 'China model' in non-democratic African countries offers

---

150 Faust, Jörg & Ziaja, Sebastian "German aid allocation and partner country selection: Development-orientation, self-interests and path dependency" (2012) *German Development Institute – Discussion Paper 7/2012* 5–6; Alesina, Alberto & Dollar, David "Who gives foreign aid to whom and why?" (2000) 5:1 *Journal of Economic Growth* 33–63; Fikre, *supra* note 48, 262; Hamilton, *supra* note 141, 216; Mawdsley, *supra* note 70, 641.

151 Rukare, *supra* note 56, 47.

152 Esteves & Assunção, *supra* note 21, 1776.

153 Owen, Olly & Melville, Chris "China and Africa: A new era of south-south cooperation" (2005) Open Democracy available at: https://www.opendemocracy.net/en/south _2658jsp/ (accessed: 20 April 2016).

indirect support for China's own political ideology and offers evidence that Western democratic ideals are not universal [...].

Politically, the continent is of small importance to China's foreign policy agenda, with Africa playing a largely supportive role in China's overall international strategy. Rather than being seen as 'key' or a 'priority,' Africa is seen to be part of the 'foundation' on which China's broader strategic ambitions are built (footnote omitted) [...].

Given the general low priority of Africa in China's foreign policy agenda, African issues rarely reach the highest level of foreign policy decision making in the Chinese bureaucratic apparatus.[154]

With such one-sided interests, it is undeniable that aid from China to Africa is designed to promote the goals that China aims to achieve rather than Africa's own development goals. Another example worth noting is Brazil's engagement in Africa within the South-South cooperation framework. In analysing the concentration of Brazil's cooperation programmes in Africa (using the case of Mozambique) and South America, Duarte de Siqueira illustrates that the cooperation is largely driven by the "geopolitical interests" in Brazil's defence policy to control the "Arch of the South Atlantic, where the Blue Amazon and its oil-rich resources are geographically located".[155] Just like China, Brazil as an emerging third-world super-power "wants to gain ground in international decision processes".[156] Many more geopolitical interests of this kind only contribute to the stratification of the international system into cleavages where the states that have the financial muscles shape the policies, make the rules for engagement, arbitrate the game of cooperation and determine the outcome of the development process.[157] Evidently, the outcomes of the development cooperation process have generally not been in favour of recipient developing countries.

---

154 Sun, *supra* note 98, 1–2, see also Houanye, Paulin & Sheng, Sibao "Foreign direct investment in Africa: Securing Chinese investment for lasting development, the case of West Africa" (2012) 3:2 *Review of Business & Finance Studies* 106–107; Wu, Chien-Huei "Beyond European conditionality and Chinese non-interference: Articulating the EU-China-Africa trilateral relations" in Wouters, Jan *et al.* (eds) *China, the European Union and Global Governance* (Cheltenham, UK: Edward Elgar Publishing, 2012) 109.

155 Milani & Muñoz, *supra* note 70, 39; De Siqueira, *supra* note 104, 146–150.

156 De Siqueira, *supra* note 104, 140.

157 Esteves & Assunção, *supra* note 21, 1776–1778.

THE GEOPOLITICS OF DEVELOPMENT COOPERATION

3.2.2 Desire to Dominate

History holds evidence that the imperialistic practices and conflicts that have characterised the past are not unrelated to superpower competition and the quest for global supremacy.[158] Accompanying the need to promote national self-interest is the craving to exercise hegemony over other states. For a long time, this attitude has shaped the field of development cooperation, which Pierre Bourdieu describes as:

> [A] space of structured positions [between] developing and developed countries, or donors and recipients. This dyadic structure, established in the early 1970s, would be kept stable for four decades, consolidating not only donor and recipient positions but also the rules of mobility governing the ways through which one developing country could graduate to become a developed country.[159]

Based on Bourdieu's description of how development cooperation is configured, it is now more than four decades and there is hardly empirical evidence of a developing country that has graduated to the status of a developed country as a result of assistance received through development cooperation. The best that has been achieved during this period has been a re-configuration of what used to be called the "third world" into a different categorisation of states (based on economic strength), now known as; *middle income* and *low income countries* and a further ranking of the low income countries into *fragile states, least developed countries* and *heavily indebted poor countries*.[160] As some form of psychological comfort, the International Monetary Fund (IMF) has in another classification renamed the global divide, which has traditionally been known as developed and developing countries into what is now known as *advanced countries* consisting of some 34 highly industrialised countries and the rest of the 154 countries, which are labelled as *emerging markets* and *developing economies*.[161] These configurations are misleadingly designed to create a

---

158 As above, 1777.

159 Bourdieu, Pierre *Practical Reason: On the Theory of Action* (Stanford: Stanford University Press, 1998) 32; Esteves & Assunção, *supra* note 21, 1777.

160 Alonso, José A.; Glennie, Jonathan & Sumner, Andy "Recipients and contributors: Middle income countries and the future of development cooperation" (2014) available at: http://effectivecooperation.org/wordpress/wp-content/uploads/2014/04/Recipients-and-Contributors-MICs-and-the-future-of-development-cooperat.._.pdf (accessed: 09 April 2016) 5.

161 International Monetary Fund "Proposed new grouping in WEO country classifications: Low-income developing countries" (2014) *IMF Policy Paper* 2.

collective guilt of everlasting underdevelopment and in that way developing countries are locked in a position of continuous subservience.[162]

In contrast to the income per capita criterion that the IMF uses in making the above classifications, Vázquez and Sumner use a more progressive cluster categorisation to describe developing countries based on evolving conceptions about development consisting of: "development as human development; development as economic autonomy; development as political freedom; and development as sustainability".[163] This categorisation enables developing countries to practically focus on expanding capabilities, that is, the means, opportunities or substantive freedoms to advance human functioning in terms of practical outcomes of well-being unlike dependence on patriarchal forms of cooperation that do not guarantee freedoms.[164] The primary motivations why developed countries promote cooperation are not divorced from the imperialistic purposes for which slavery and colonisation were carried out.[165] It is not surprising that issues relating to development in Africa are decided by the OECD-DAC instead of being informed by the actual development priorities on the ground. Owing to the global imbalances that have been created as a result, Africa has remained deeply affected by structural changes that take place within the global framework.[166]

---

162   The World Bank and the IMF acknowledge the fact that development entails well-being and not economic growth. These institutions acknowledge that human development is just a means to achieving human development which is the end. To use economic growth criteria as a basis for their configuration of the world is what I consider fraudulent and misleading. According to another classification by New Economics Foundation (see: Happy Planet Index 2012 Report: available at: http://neweconomics.org/2012/06/happy-planet-index-2012-report/ (accessed: 28 May 2016) based on "happy planet index" criterion, which implies measurement in terms of happiness or well-being, most of the countries that the International Monetary Fund classifies as less development are those that rank top in terms of happiness (well-being).

163   Vázquez, Sergio T. & Sumner, Andy "Beyond low and middle income countries: What if there were five clusters of developing countries?" (2012) *Institute of Development Studies – Working Paper 404* 6 & 14.

164   As above, 6; Sen, *supra* note 62, 18.

165   Führer, *supra* note 10, 8–12. Helmut Führer's historical account on the establishment of OECD-DAC and the Resolution on the Common Aid Effort presents a scenario reminiscent of the Berlin Conference where the decision was taken to partition and colonise Africa. The initiative, which is intended to provide development assistance to developing countries was taken in Europe and America, and involved only highly industrialised countries without consultation or representation of a single developing country in any of the deliberations, decision making or composition of the committees.

166   Linda, Lim Y.C. "The impact of changes in the world economy on developing countries" in Berg, Robert & Gordon, David F. (eds) *Cooperation for International Development: The United States and the Third World in the 1990s* (Boulder: Lynne Rienner Publishers, 1989) 21.

THE GEOPOLITICS OF DEVELOPMENT COOPERATION   119

Mahalu identifies these changes to include the fact that most developing countries have been rendered unable to "exercise full sovereignty over their natural wealth and resources and do not control the prices of their raw materials, nor [do they] have any influence on the prices of imported capital goods".[167] Ahluwalia, Carter and Chenery observe that in spite of the expansion of the world economy, the benefits "have only reached the world's poor [the largest proportion of them in Africa] to a very limited degree".[168] This is due not to any failure on the part of the poor but among other factors to the distributional patterns, which largely exclude the poor from the sphere of economic expansion and material improvements.[169] Besides these systemic impediments, the desire by donor partners to dominate within the development cooperation framework has exposed development prospects in Africa to direct attack by foreign stakeholders.

3.3   *Hurdles to Africa's Development Prospects*
3.3.1   Economic Sabotage
The dawn of the new millennium incited great expectations about Africa's development future, especially revolving around whether Africa is capable of claiming the Twenty First Century.[170] Impressive economic performance across the continent points to the fact that Africa indeed, has the potential to become the centre of development focus.[171] However, the possibility of a sabotage theory cannot be ruled out in the failure to translate the recorded economic growth into right to development gains. Zu Wurong has noted for example, that "the US is not ready for China's rise, nor does it respect China's basic right to development".[172] The same is true for Africa, where the right to development has consistently been sabotaged in many countries by foreign stakeholders.

The boom in export trade during the 1960s ushered in a period of industrial, social and economic transformation that experienced "greater development,

---

167   Mahalu, *supra* note 46, 18.
168   Ahluwalia, Montek S.; Carter, Nicholas G. & Chenery, Hollis B. "Growth and poverty in developing countries" (1979) 6:3 *J Dev't Econ* 299.
169   As above, 299.
170   The World Bank *Can Africa Claim the 21st Century?* (Washington DC: IMF/The World Bank, 2000) 7.
171   UNCTAD *Economic Development in Africa: Catalysing Investment for Transformative Growth in Africa* (New York/Geneva: UN Publication, 2014) 2.
172   Wurong, Zu "Respect for right to development" *China Daily* US [New York, NY] of 28 Feb 2014.

equality and social justice" in Africa.[173] However, the optimism that the trade boom brought soon turned into plunging depression, stagnation, and a debt crisis as most of Africa's development initiatives dramatically ground to a halt.[174] In the absence of an established development model for Africa, the IMF and the World Bank seized the opportunity to introduce the structural adjustment programmes, which was packaged as a recovery strategy but in essence was a vehicle for advancing free market capitalism into Africa.[175] Trusting the expertise of these institutions, African governments quickly embraced their advice to introduce austerity measures, which instead of rescuing the ailing economies rather lured them into a debt trap.[176] By 1990, as Boaduo has observed, many African countries had borrowed much more than they could ever pay off.[177] Left with a deteriorating socio-economic situation and a huge negative balance sheet, the IMF and the World Bank found reason to invade African economies with even more stringent austerity measures.[178]

Some scholars see merit in the SAPS as well-intentioned macro-economic policies that were designed to stimulate economic growth, without which socio-economic development may not be achieved.[179] At face value, the austerity measures seemed like sound structural adjustment strategies. However, Boaduo points out that the primary motive behind the SAPS was to constrain African governments to pay off accumulated debts or surrender their economies to foreign control.[180] The strategy worked and the indebted African governments were compelled to roll back the provision of basic services, to privatise state-owned enterprises (most of which were purchased by foreign conglomerates) and to reduce public expenditures through salary cuts, massive retrenchments and currency devaluation, like the *Communauté Financière d'Afrique* (CFA) Franc that suffered a 104 per cent devaluation in 1994).[181] The

---

173   Boaduo, Nana A.P. "Africa's political, industrial and economic development dilemma in the contemporary era of the African Union" (2008) 2:4 *J Pan Afr Stud* 96.

174   As above, 96.

175   Heidhues, Franz & Obare, Gideon "Lessons from structural adjustment programmes and their effects in Africa" (2011) 50:1 *Qtly J Int'l Agric* 58; Dicklitch, Susan & Howard-Hassmann, Rhoda "Public policy and economic rights in Ghana and Uganda in Hertel, Shareen & Minkler, Lanse (eds) *Economic Rights: Conceptual, Measurement and Policy Issue* (New York: Cambridge University Press, 2007) 327.

176   Bunn, *supra* note 135, 1455–1457; Boaduo, *supra* note 173, 97.

177   Boaduo, *supra* note 173, 97.

178   As above.

179   Dicklitch & Howard-Hassmann, *supra* note 175, 325–327.

180   Boaduo, *supra* note 173, 97.

181   Awung, W.J. & Atanga, Mufor "Economic crisis and multi-party politics in Cameroon" (2011) 5:1 *CJDHR*; Ngwa, A. Kenneth "The baobab tree lives on: Paul Biya and the logic of

SAPs plunged Africa into economic distress of enormous proportions and in spite of the World Bank and the IMF's complicity was instead blamed on poor governance, corruption, political instability and inefficiency in management by the affected African governments.

Without disputing Boaduo's attribution of the failure of the SAPs to the dishonest intentions of the IMF and the World Bank in destabilising African economies,[182] these institutions on the most part barely exploited the vacuum created by the lack of a functional development model, to entangle Africa with attractive loan offers. For Akum, the loan facilities were tailored to look like fine opportunities for economic growth but in essence, turned out to be real threats to socio-economic development.[183] Cameroon for example, like many other African countries was ensnared in a debt trap through the SAPs initiative, which as Akum affirms, has rendered the country permanently dependent on foreign loans in substitution of fiscal revenues.[184] The structure of Cameroon's external debt stands at 50.7 per cent, distributed as follows: World Bank–24.5 per cent, IMF–15.6 per cent, African Development Bank Group–13.1 per cent, Paris Club–12.3 per cent, multilateral donors–20.6 per cent and other official bilateral donors–13.6 per cent.[185] Such a debt profile illustrates that the economy of Cameroon is virtually controlled by foreign stakeholders, thus robbing the country of socio-economic and cultural self-determination. Under these circumstances, it is unlikely that Cameroon would be able to create the enabling domestic environment for asserting the right to development without provoking a coercive reaction from its many creditors.

Where imperial powers have not been successful in restraining the development prospects of African countries through the debt trap, they have employed alternative sabotage strategies, including through coercive economic sanctions. In Zimbabwe for example, sanctions imposed by the European Union (EU) and the US against the Mugabe government's controversial policies have systematically eroded gains in socio-economic and cultural development in that country.[186] Isabella Bunn reminds that the use of unilateral coercive

---

political survival" (2009) *African Studies Department Johns Hopkins SAIS* 5; Boaduo, *supra* note 173, 97–99.

182 Boaduo, *supra* note 173, 98.

183 Akum, Gawum J. "The impact of foreign debt on GDP growth: Cameroon" (Msc thesis, Ritsumeikan Asia Pacific University 2011) 2.

184 As above, 8.

185 International Monetary Fund "Cameroon: Staff report for the 2010 Article IV consultation and debt sustainability analysis" (2010) *IMF Country Report No 10/25 – IMF Washington DC* 36; Akum, *supra* note 164, 8.

186 Ogbonna, Chidiebere C. "Targeted or restrictive: Impact of US and EU sanctions on education and healthcare of Zimbabweans" (2017) 11:3 *African Research Review* 37–39; Masaka,

measures such as the imposition of economic sanctions constitutes an obstacle to the realisation of the right to development.[187] Even with the departure of Mugabe from power, the effects of the economic sanctions remain visible and may take a long time for the right balance to return to Zimbabwe. Apart from economic sabotage, the African development landscape has also been the target of military disruptions.

3.3.2 Military Disruptions

Post-independence Africa has experienced a sequence of *coup d'états* and armed conflicts that have systematically destabilised the continent. The few countries that have not yet plunged into the chaos make up the exception rather than the rule. It is noted that "there have been at least 200 coups across Africa since the 1960s".[188] The proliferation of arms on the continent also triggers curiosity about their origins and the purpose for which they flood the African political landscape. It is not a question of doubt, as Boaduo has pointed out, that instability in Africa has on the most part been orchestrated by mercenaries backed by foreign intelligence agencies as a calculated plan to frustrate Africa's development aspirations.[189] For instance, as Koutonin indicates, of the total number of *coup d'états* that have taken place in Africa, over 61 per cent have happened in francophone Africa, masterminded by France to topple the government of any of the countries that dared to breach the Colonisation Continuation Pact, threaten France's economic interests or challenge French influence and dominance in the country.[190]

France not only uses the military to coerce its African subordinates but has, in exchange for protecting French colonial interests, consistently provided military back-up to some of the longest serving dictators like Paul Biya of

---

Dennis "Paradoxes in the 'sanctions discourse' in Zimbabwe: A critical reflection" (2012) 13:1 *African Studies Monographs* 50–51; Chingono, Heather "Zimbabwe sanctions: An analysis of the 'Lingo' guiding the perceptions of the sanctioners and the sanctionees" (2010) 4:2 *African Journal of Political Science and International Relations* 067.

187   Bunn, *supra* note 135, 1459–1462.

188   Aljazeera "Inside story" Aljazeera News of 18 September 2015.

189   Boaduo, *supra* note 173, 96 & 100.

190   Koutonin, Mamuna R. "14 African countries forced by France to pay colonial tax for the benefits of slavery and colonisation" (2014) *Silicon Africa* available at: http://www.siliconafrica.com/france-colonial-tax/ (accessed: 30 October 2017); Le Vine, Victor T. *Politics in Francophone Africa* (Boulder: Lynne Reinier Publishers, 2004) 2–6. The Colonisation Continuation Pact is a treaty that France (General de Gaulle) signed with its African colonies with the agreement that against the nominal independence that the colonies were granted by the UN, the colonies will remain politically, economically, diplomatically and militarily subservient to French control and domination.

THE GEOPOLITICS OF DEVELOPMENT COOPERATION   123

Cameroon whose stay in power since 1982 is marked by an appalling human rights record.[191] In reaction to the Biya government's indifference to the spiralling conflict resulting from the ruthless crackdown on separatist movements and political opposition, a number of countries including the US and Germany announced the withdrawal of their military support to Cameroon on the grounds of massive human rights violations committed by the government's security forces.[192] While the US and German actions are intended to pressure the Biya regime to end the conflict and to abide by human rights standards, France sees no trouble in reiterating its unremitting military support to Cameroon and more so, conspicuously avoiding to "overly criticize the government's handling of the crisis".[193] The impact of the French continuous military support to Cameroon cannot be underestimated.

Taking cognisance of the detrimental impact of armed conflicts to the realisation of the right to development, the Declaration on the Right to Development suggests reinforcing disarmament efforts and consequently, channel the resources gained through disarmament into comprehensive development initiatives.[194] Sustaining military support to conflict-ridden countries like Cameroon as shown above or perpetrating military assaults like in the case of the North Atlantic Treaty Organisation (NATO) intervention in Libya in 2011, do not only cut back development gains in Africa but also continue to seriously

---

191   Ngang, Carol C. & Kamga, Serges D. " 'O Cameroon, thou cradle of our fathers ...: Land of promise' and the right to development" in Ngang, Carol C.; Kamga Serges D. & Gumede, Vusi (eds) *Perspectives on the Right to Development* (Pretoria: Pretoria University Law Press, 2018) 195–196; Rousselot, Juliette "The impact of French influence on democracy and human rights in Cameroon" (2010) 4:1 *Cameroon Journal on Democracy and Human Rights* 64.

192   Searcey, Dionne; Schmitt, Eric & Gibbons-Neff, Thomas "US reduces military aid to Cameroon over human rights abuses" *The New York Times* 7 February 2019 available at: https://www.nytimes.com/2019/02/07/world/africa/cameroon-military-abuses-united -states-aid.html (accessed: 30 July 2019); Wroughton, Lesley "U. S. halts some Cameroon military assistance over human rights" *Reuters – Washington* 7 February 2019 available at: https://www.washingtonpost.com/world/africa/us-cuts-some-military-assistance-to -cameroon-citing-allegations-of-human-rights-violations/2019/02/06/aeb18052-2a4e -11e9-906e-9d55b6451eb4_story.html (accessed: 30 July 2019); Krippahl, Christina "End of a 'secret' German military mission in Cameroon" *Deutsch Welle* July 2019 available at: https:// www.dw.com/en/end-of-a-secret-german-military-mission-in-cameroon/a-49610889 (accessed: 30 July 2019).

193   Irish, John "France says to continue military cooperation with Cameroon" *Reuters – World News* 7 February 2019 available at: https://uk.reuters.com/article/uk-france-cameroon/ france-says-to-continue-military-cooperation-with-cameroon-idUKKCN1PW1RT (accessed: 30 July 2019).

194   Declaration on the Right to Development, *supra* note 7, art 7.

124 CHAPTER 3

undermine prospects for advancement in living standards on the continent as a whole. While the NATO attack on Libya is explained to have aimed at ousting Qaddafi on account of his human rights abuses, Patrick Terry contends that no concrete evidence of those abuses has ever been presented.[195] On the contrary, Qaddafi raised living standards for the people of Libya to one of the most enviable levels across Africa.[196] While the motive behind the NATO intervention in Libya may not be accurate as Petra indicates, it is incontestable that the use of military force does not advance the right to development by any means. It is worth highlighting that the military expedition in Libya was perpetrated within the context of international law that guarantees the sovereign equality of states, but as Anthony Anghie explains, does not provide sufficient protection to developing countries, which once were (and perhaps still remain) the subjects of domination under the same law.[197]

In spite of the perception with regard to the responsibility to protect as a means to guard against human rights violations,[198] Alan Kuperman observes that a rigorous assessment of the Libyan example reveals a model of failure where the NATO intervention only "increased the duration of Libya's civil war by about six times and its death toll by at least seven times, while also exacerbating human rights abuses, humanitarian suffering, Islamic radicalism, and weapons proliferation in Libya and its neighbors".[199] With regard to the requirement to create an enabling environment for development, Sengupta suggests designing an appropriate programme of action, which he estimates, is a more strategic approach in actualising the right to development.[200] It

---

195   Terry, Patrick C.R. "The Libya intervention: Neither lawful, nor successful" (2015) 48:2 *The Comparative and International Law Journal of Southern Africa* 164.

196   Chengu, Garikai "Libya: From Africa's richest state under Gaddafi to failed state after NATO intervention" (2014) *Global Research* available at: www.globalresearch.ca/libya-from-africas-richest-state-under-gaddafi-to-failed-state-after-nato-intervention/5408740 (accessed: 29 December 2015); Chossudovsky, Michel "Destroying a country's standard of living: What Libya had achieved, what has been destroyed" (2013) *Global Research* available at: www.globalresearch.ca/destroying-a-country-s-standard-of-living-what-libya-had-achieved-what-has-been-destroyed/26686 (accessed: 29 December 2015).

197   Anghie, Anthony *Imperialism, Sovereignty and the Making of International Law* (Cambridge: Cambridge University Press, 2005) 111.

198   Nasu, Hitoshi "The UN Security Council's responsibility and the responsibility to protect" (2011) 15 *Max Planck Yearbook of United Nations Law* 381–382; Rishmawi, Mona "The responsibility to protect and protection of civilians: The human rights story (d.n.a) *Office of the High Commissioner for Human Rights* 91; Evans, Gareth *et al.* "The responsibility to protect" (2001) *International Development Research Centre* 15–18.

199   Kuperman, Alan J. "Lessons from Libya: How not to intervene" Belfer Center for Science and International Affairs, Harvard Kennedy School – Policy Brief, September 2013.

200   Sengupta 2002, *supra* note 3, 860–861.

THE GEOPOLITICS OF DEVELOPMENT COOPERATION

entails as Ibrahim Salama also suggests, adopting a progressive, case-by-case approach to different situations,[201] which by inference necessitates a robust enquiry on how the right to development is conceived to be achieved within the African human rights system.

4 Asserting the Right to Development in Africa

4.1 *Modalities for Realisation*
The modalities for the realisaton of the right to development enshrined in article 22(2) of the African Charter are discussed here in consonance with article 2(3) of the Declaration on the Right to Development, which recognises the right and the duty that states are endowed with to formulate national development policies. It is important to clarify that the right to development as it is formulated in the African Charter does not imply a solicitation for development assistance as it is envisaged at international level, i.e., to be achieved through cooperation with developed countries.[202] Rather, the right to development in Africa is fundamentally an assertion of socio-economic and cultural self-determination, which as stipulated in article 22(2) of the Charter, entails concrete action by African countries in putting the right to development effectively into practice.[203] The Charter makes provision for two possible scenarios. In the first scenario, African countries are required to take individual responsibility while in the second scenario they are required to take collective action to ensure that the right to development is achieved.

4.1.1 Individual State Responsibility
According to Paul Gready, state responsibility is defined in terms of obligations of "*delivery* and *oversight*", meaning that with regard to the right to development, the state has direct responsibilities in making available certain material entitlements as well as an oversight role in ensuring accountability.[204] It is an

---

201   Salama, *supra* note 50, 53.

202   Sengupta 2003, *supra* note 3, 20.

203   Article 22(2) stipulates that "States shall have the duty, individually or collectively, to ensure the exercise of the right to development".

204   Gready, Paul "Rights-based approaches to development: What is the value added?" (2008)18:6 *Development in Practice* 740; see also Van der Have, Nienke "The right to development and state responsibility: Towards idealism without a sense of realism?" (Masters Thesis, University of Amsterdam, 2011) 15–27; Sengupta, Arjun "Realising the right to development" (2000) 31 *Development and Change* 564; Dąbrowska, Anna O. "Legal status of the right to development" (2010) *Haskoli Island University* 7–8.

established principle in international law that the realisation of the right to development remains the primary responsibility of the state. The Declaration on the Right to Development provides that "[s]tates have the primary responsibility for the creation of national and international conditions favourable to the realization of the right to development".[205] The African Charter stipulates as a matter of binding law that "[s]tates shall have the duty, individually [...] to ensure the exercise of the right to development".[206] So, it is first of all a state's obligation to take steps and appropriate measures to ensure well-being and improved livelihood for its peoples before any considerations of engaging with other states for the purpose of achieving the same goal. Because the right to development imposes a legal obligation in Africa, failure to ensure its realisation may raise questions of legal accountability. Accordingly, Koen de Feyter ascertains that an essential feature of the right to development is to create accountability of the duty bearer to the right holders, implying that when the state – being the duty bearer – defaults, it has the obligation to repair the damages that may result from its action or inaction.[207]

A state's responsibility on the right to development extends beyond accountability to the right holders and involves taking protective and preventive measures to insulate right holders against violation by third parties.[208] Consequently, holders of the right to development are empowered to assert claims against the state if the latter fails in its duty. Not only is the state obligated to fulfil the right to development for present generations of its population, it is also required to ensure that the benefits of development are justly and equitably distributed in a manner as to guarantee that future generations will also be able to meet their own development needs.[209] More so, the state may not invoke the lack of development as an excuse to justify the inability to fulfil this mandated duty.[210] All fifty five African states (Morocco not included), have ratified the African Charter, which enshrines the right to development.[211] As state parties to the Charter, the 55 African countries are all legally bound to ensure that the right to development enshrined therein is achieved. This

---

205 Declaration on the Right to Development, *supra* note 7, art 3(1).

206 African Charter, *supra* note 25, art 22(2).

207 De Feyter, *supra* note 3,12.

208 As above, 13.

209 Brundtland, Gro Harlem "Report of the World Commission on Environment and Development: Our common future" (1987) *Brundtland Commission* para 27.

210 Vienna Declaration, *supra* note 45, para I(10).

211 Centre for Human Rights *A Guide to the African Human Rights System: Celebrating 30 Years since the entry into force of the African Charter on Human and Peoples' Rights 1986–2016* (Pretoria: Pretoria University Law Press, 2016) 3.

THE GEOPOLITICS OF DEVELOPMENT COOPERATION 127

includes the commitment that each African state undertakes by adhering to the Charter, to adopt legislative and other measures to give effect to all of the Charter provisions, including the right to development.[212]

African countries have a reputation for treaty ratification, but implementation has remained a daunting problem.[213] This raise concerns relating to compliance with the legal obligations on the right to development. The law on treaties together with the principles that govern international law require states to become committed to the treaties they establish and consequently ensure their application at domestic level.[214] Treaty ratification, as Maluwa has noted, provides at least the first step towards the achievement of the policy goals and objectives enshrined in the treaty.[215] Following the historical development injustices that Africa has suffered, the extensive ratification of the African Charter provides a compelling reason to protect the range of human rights, including the right to development contained therein.[216] Africa's treaty ratification scorecard also indicates the political will expressed by African governments, which needs to be translated into action to ensure that their interactions with the rest of the international community should no longer be conducted like business as usual.[217] It means that treaty ratification must be followed with domestication, in which case monist constitutional regimes allow upon ratification for direct application of a treaty provision as part of domestic law, while dualist systems require a formal procedure of incorporation through parliamentary processes.[218] With regard to domesticating the right to development enshrined in the African Charter, only few African countries have effectively done so.[219]

---

212 African Charter, *supra* note 25, art 1.

213 Maluwa, Tiyanjana "Ratification of African Union treaties by member states: Law, policy and practice" (2012) 13 *Melbourne J Int'l L* 3–4.

214 Brindusa, Marian "The dualist and monist theories: International law's comprehension of these theories" (2007) *Faculty of Economics, Law & Administrative Science University of Târgu-Mureş Romania* 1.

215 Maluwa, *supra* note 213, 9.

216 As above, 10–11.

217 As above, 11.

218 Marian, *supra* note 214, 2–3.

219 Only 6 African countries have so far, domesticated the right to development in the sense that the national constitutions explicitly enshrine the right to development as a constitutional entitlement. These countries include Cameroon, Malawi, the DRC, Ethiopia, Benin and Nigeria. A few other African countries like Uganda, Sao Tome & Principe, Burkina Faso, Zimbabwe and South Africa enshrine a range of socio-economic and cultural rights that could be interpreted to imply the right to development.

128   CHAPTER 3

The scope of this book does not permit an in-depth analysis of the level of achievement of the right to development in different African countries. Only a few have taken legislative measures towards the realisation of the right to development at domestic level. A full discussion of the African constitutions that enshrine the right to development is provided in chapter four. If the realisation of the right to development is to be determined by the extent of its incorporation into domestic law, the conclusion to draw is that progress towards implementation is relatively slow. With the understanding that the obligation to achieve the right to development could be quite arduous to comply with for states individually, especially for the majority of African countries that are burdened by huge development challenges, it is important to explore the option granted by the African Charter to do so collectively.

4.1.2   Shared Responsibility for Concerted Action

The realisation of the right to development in Africa additionally requires the shared responsibility of state parties to the African Charter to take collective action. Although collective action may to some extent be understood to have the same connotation as development cooperation, it actually has a narrower scope in relation to traditional forms of cooperation. Traditional forms of development cooperation, as Anna Stahl has rightly noted are characterised by one-way flows of charitable relief assistance from developed to developing countries.[220] Collective action as it is envisaged for the realisation of the right to development in Africa is based on a responsibility to act with mutual interest to achieve a common purpose.[221] The estimation is that the duty to act collectively not only requires African countries to support each other; they have a collective duty to adopt a common policy, which as it is argued here, does not exclude conceptualising the right to development as a development model.

This is important to consider, because it is evident as pointed out earlier, that the right to development in Africa cannot possibly be achieved through prevailing patterns of development cooperation. The likelihood that it can be accomplished by African countries acting independently, especially faced with the increasing competition among developed countries for global dominance is even more challenging. A number of initiatives hold evidence of the extent

---

220   Stahl, *supra* note 106, 11.

221   See Constitutive Act of the African Union adopted in Lomé Togo on 11 July 2000 art 3(d) provides for example, as one of the objectives of the African Union to "promote and defend African common positions on issues of interest to the continent and its peoples' and art 3(j) "promote sustainable development at the economic, social and cultural levels as well as the integration of African economies".

THE GEOPOLITICS OF DEVELOPMENT COOPERATION

to which African countries are making efforts in collectively dealing with issues relating to development and human rights.[222] One such initiative, referred to as "African common positions", through which policy decisions of major importance are taken by the African Union (AU), provides the framework that could be explored to advance the right to development. African common positions embody some form of "collectivism", which represents an institutional practice within the AU in keeping with one of its primary objectives to "[a]ccelerate the political and socio-economic integration of the continent" and to "[p]romote and defend African common positions on issues of interest to the continent and its peoples".[223]

Important questions to consider are how crucial these common positions are in addressing issues of priority to development and whether they could be used as a means to accelerate African integration in view of the collective obligation to ensure that the right to development is achieved. Tiyanjana Maluwa asserts that through the common position principle, the AU provides a forum through which member states collectively adopt policies and positions on a broad range of issues.[224] The motivation behind one such common position on the Post-2015 Development Agenda is stated in the preamble:

> [t]hat the post-2015 Development Agenda provides a unique opportunity for Africa to reach consensus on common challenges, priorities and aspirations, and to actively participate in the global debate on how to provide a fresh impetus to the MDGs and to examine and devise strategies to address key emerging development issues on the continent in the coming years.[225]

The document emphasises the need for the post-2015 Development Agenda to reaffirm among others "the right to development" and to ensure a "policy space for nationally tailored policies and programmes on the continent".[226] This is strategic not only because the adoption of the common position allows the opportunity to address development concerns collectively, but also because it

---

222   The cooperation initiatives that African countries are engaged in include regional economic blocs such as ECOWAS, SADC, COMESA, ECCAS, EAU and Joint Commissions for Cooperation.

223   AU Constitutive Act, *supra* note 221, art 3(d).

224   Maluwa, *supra* note 213, 2.

225   AU Common Africa Positions on Post-2015 Development Agenda, adopted at the 22nd Ordinary Session of the Assembly of the Union in Addis Ababa, Ethiopia on 31 January 2014.

226   AU Constitutive Act, *supra* note 221, preamble.

provides a unified platform for African countries to influence and shape development policy formulation at the international level. In acknowledging the pro-activeness of the common position initiative, Barry Carin suggests that Africa needs to explore the opportunity strategically to ensure that the post-2015 development agenda is congruent with African priorities.[227]

However, Africa has always been constrained to prioritise foreign interests over its own development prerogatives.[228] Almost all of Francophone Africa for example, despite attaining statehood at independence, has remained under French "modo-colonialism", a system of "compulsory solidarity" known as *Françafrique* established through a French-imposed colonial pact.[229] According to Bradley, attempts to quit by any of the countries trapped in the system have resulted in French backed *coup d'états*, assassinations and economic sabotage.[230] Al Jazeera describes the *Françafrique* connection as "a brutal and nefarious tale of corruption, massacres, dictators supported and progressive leaders murdered, weapon-smuggling, cloak-and-dagger secret services, and spectacular military operations".[231] The system allows France unfettered control over the economy of the African *francophonie* countries, which are compelled to prop up the French economy even while their peoples endure excruciating poverty and underdevelopment.[232] With the understanding that the right to development in Africa has for the most part been compromised through domination, it is unlikely that under the prevailing circumstances, where a large part of the continent is still subject to French colonialism, Africa will be able to advance beyond the status of underdevelopment.

---

227 Carin, Barry "The African Union and the post-2015 development agenda" (2014) *Centre for International Innovation – Policy Brief No 45* 1.

228 See Le Vine, Victor T. *Politics in Francophone Africa* (Boulder: Lynne Rienner Publishers, 2004) 2–6; Moncrieff, Richard "French Relations with Sub-Saharan Africa under President Sarkozy" (2012) *South African Institute of International Affairs – Occasional Paper No 107* 6–7; Koutonin, *supra* note 190; he illustrates how France manipulates its former African colonies made up of some 14 countries to prioritise French interests above their own national interests.

229 Bradley, Penny "The colonial pact: How France sucks the life out of Africa" (2013) *Our World Commentary* available at: https://penniwinkleb.wordpress.com/2013/01/25/the-colonial-pact-how-france-sucks-the-life-out-of-africa/ (accessed: 24 August 2017).

230 Bradley, *supra* note 229.

231 Al Jazeera "The French African connection" (2014) *Al Jazeera* available at: http://www.aljazeera.com/programmes/specialseries/2013/08/201387113131914906.html (accessed: 24 August 2017).

232 Lehmann, Christof "French Africa policy damages African and European economies" (2012) *NSNBC* available at: http://nsnbc.me/2012/10/12/french-africa-policy-damages-african-and-european-economies/ (accessed: 24 August 2017); Bradley, *supra* note, 229.

THE GEOPOLITICS OF DEVELOPMENT COOPERATION

The obligation for collective action to ensure the realisation of the right to development enjoins African countries to direct more attention towards effective integration of the continent as stipulated by the AU Constitutive Act.[233] Such integration will give Africa a stronger voice and sense of purpose in asserting the right to development, especially when engaging in negotiations at the international level. The Abuja Treaty of 1991 has been a progressive move towards bringing the eight existing regional economic blocs into one centrally coordinated African Economic Community (AEC). Unfortunately, the initiative focuses principally on economic integration, omitting the most essential aspects of social and cultural development, which are central to engineering human well-being in Africa. The next section focuses on the context within which the right to development is legitimised in Africa and the normative requirements according to which cooperation may be established.

4.2 *Human Rights and Development Practice*

This section examines the context for exercising the right to development in Africa, which converges at the point of intersection between human rights and development law to set the normative standards for improved well-being and better living standards. According to Alston and Robinson, the process represents an embrace of the values of participation and transparency in formulating policies to ensure the well-being of the poor.[234] The question to consider is how the right to development could rather be explored to regulate the actions of foreign stakeholders within the framework of development cooperation in Africa.

4.2.1 The Law on Human Rights and Development in Africa

The African human rights system has rightly also been described as development law,[235] in the sense that besides protecting human rights it also aims at regulating development practice across the continent. This is explained

---

233 AU Constitutive Act, *supra* note 221, art 3, which lays out the objectives of the African Union makes the following previsions relating to regional integration:
   a) Achieve greater unity and solidarity between the African counties and the peoples of Africa;
   b) Accelerate the political and socio-economic integration of the continent;
   c) Promote sustainable development at the economic, social and cultural levels as well as the integration of African economies.

234 Alston, Philip & Robinson, Mary *Human Rights and Development: Towards Mutual Reinforcement* (New York: Oxford University Press, 2005) 15.

235 Borella, François "Le système juridique de l'Organisation de l'Unité Africaine" (1971) 17 *Annuaire Français de Droit International* 246.

132   CHAPTER 3

by the fact that almost all the treaty instruments that make up the African legal framework combine principles for upholding human rights and the rules according to which development practice is regulated.[236] This has emerged into the unique formulation known as the right to development that envisages the realisation of the composite of human and peoples' rights as the core indicator for gauging development.[237] In spite of arguments denying that there is such a thing as development law,[238] David Kennedy affirms that law constitutes a central aspect of development although it must not usurp the political function of development policy making.[239] With the historical experiences of development injustices, it became necessary in the African constructivist imagination to design a legal system that guarantees justice in development and respect for individual and collective rights. This has practically translated into a register of binding and non-binding continental instruments and domestic legislation that make provision for the right to development in Africa.[240]

Framed in the language of human rights and development, the African legal system is conceptualised to address a broad range of development concerns of an individual and collective nature, including socio-economic and cultural concerns; peace and security concerns; and environmental concerns.[241] Theoretically, the African legal system guarantees the application of human rights law to development practice as a means to protect the impoverished and to ensure the equitable sharing of development gains.[242] It envisages justice to prevail in the development sector, especially where such justice

---

236 See for example AU Constitutive Act, *supra* note 221, arts 3(h), 3(j), 3(k), 4(n).

237 Okafor, Obiora C. "A regional perspective: Article 22 of the African Charter on Human and Peoples' Rights" in UN Human Rights *Realizing the Right to Development: Essays in Commemoration of 25 Years of the United Nations Declaration on the Right to Development* (Geneva: UN Publication, 2013) 375; De Feyter, Koen "The right to development in Africa" (2013) *Law & Development Research Group University of Antwerp* 3; Kirchmeier, *supra* note 8, 9; Gawanas, *supra* note 91, 143–149.

238 Chemillier-Gendreau, Monique "Relations between the ideology of development and development law" in Snyder, Francis G. & Slinn, Peter (eds) *International Law of Development: Comparative Perspectives* (Abingdon: Professional Books, 1987) 58.

239 Kennedy, David "The rule of law as development" in Hatchard, John; Perry-Kessaris, Amanda & Slinn, Peter (eds) *Law and Development – Facing Complexities in the 21st Century: Essays in Honour of Peter Slinn* (Abingdon: Professional Books, 2003) 26.

240 African Charter, *supra* note 25, arts 1–26; AU Constitutive Act, *supra* note 221, art 3; African Youth Charter, *supra* note 54, art 10; Protocol on the Rights of Women in Africa, *supra* note 54, art 19.

241 See African Charter, *supra* note 25, chapter 1, part 1.

242 Gadio, Kalidou "The role of law in development for the African continent from a development agency perspective" *Keynote Speech delivered at the Harvard African Law & Development Conference 17 April 2010* 2–4.

THE GEOPOLITICS OF DEVELOPMENT COOPERATION 133

has been denied through acts of dispossession and subjugation. The African Charter stipulates that "[n]othing shall justify the domination of a people by another",[243] which provides as a guarantee the right and the freedom to make development choices. This principle is affirmed by international law and thus impacts on a broad range of actors including foreign stakeholders whose sometimes excessive influence and uncontrollable behaviour pose a threat to the enjoyment of guaranteed rights. Within this volatile setting, the right to development sets out to play a multifunctional role: as an objective to achieve justice in development;[244] as a means to promote the law on development in Africa;[245] as an instrument to regulate development cooperation practice;[246] and also as an outcome in enabling the enjoyment of well-being and improved livelihood.[247]

The preamble to the African Charter affirms the commitment of member states to "intensify their cooperation and efforts to achieve a better life for the peoples of Africa".[248] Accordingly, the African legal system sets standards that bind all African state parties to the relevant treaties. For foreign stakeholders that are not parties to the African human rights treaties and by implication are not bound by any obligations imposed by those treaties, it remains a concern how they could be compelled to comply with the norms set by the treaty instruments in force. The German Development Institute affirms that development cooperation must be guided by principles, norms, and mechanisms that are legitimate, effective and relevant.[249] However, because foreign stakeholders are often unmindful of the constraints on their actions, it is important to examine the normative requirements for cooperation in relation to the right to development in Africa.

4.2.2 Normative Requirements for Cooperation

4.2.2.1 *Country Ownership of the Development Process*

An important factor to take into consideration is the fact that the peoples of Africa are entitled to exercise the right to development with due regard to their "freedom and identity" as custodians of the African patrimony.[250] This goes

---

243 African Charter, *supra* note 25, art 19; Coleman, Andrew K. *Resolving Claims to Self-Determination: Is there a Role for the International Court of Justice?* (New York: Routledge, 2013) 84–86.
244 AU Constitutive Act, *supra* note 221, art 4(n).
245 As above, art 4(m).
246 As above, art 3(k) & 3(n).
247 As above, art 3(k).
248 African Charter, *supra* note 25, preamble.
249 Janus, Klingebiel & Mahn, *supra* note 23, 1.
250 See African Charter, *supra* note 25, art 22(2).

along with the principle of self-determination that is inherent in the right to development and thus provides the guarantee of effective country ownership of the development process. The Paris Declaration on Aid Effectiveness recognises the idea of country ownership of development programmes, which grants to developing countries the freedom to "exercise effective leadership over their development policies and strategies and co-ordinate development actions".[251] However, it is worth stating that because donor partners provide the funding, it allows them the opportunity to patronise the development processes in developing countries through terms and conditions, which recipient countries are simply constrained to comply with.[252] The trend in Africa has been such that development policies have almost entirely been formulated abroad or has been the subject of extensive external influence.[253]

Country ownership of the development process requires agency and self-determination, which is guaranteed by article 22 of the African Charter that grants entitlement to the peoples of Africa to exercise the right to development. Anthony Giddens' structuration theory, which describes structure and human agency as related and mutually binding, posits that human beings are propelled by a sense of purpose that shapes and directs their actions.[254] The Statement of Common Understanding on the Human Rights-Based Approach to Development Cooperation adopted by UN agencies in 2003 holds that development cooperation should contribute to building the capacity of duty-bearers to meet their obligations as well as of rights-holders in claiming their rights.[255] Granted the context in exercising the right to development, the peoples of Africa have the potential to self-reliantly shape the development future of the continent. Practically, such self-determination has manifested in Libya after the 1969 Revolution, where the state adopted domestic policies that empowered the peoples to participate freely in the development process and to share in the benefits.

---

251 Paris Declaration on Aid Effectiveness and the Accra Agenda for Action (2005/2008) paras 12 & 14; Partnership Agreement between the members of the African, Caribbean and Pacific Group of States and the European Community and its Member States, Cotonou on 23 June 2000 (amended in 2005 & 2010) art 2.

252 Ilorah, *supra* note 77, 4–6 & 22–25; Bilal, *supra* note 74, 12–14.

253 Sun, *supra* note 98, 1.

254 Giddens, Anthony *The Constitution of Society: Outline of the Theory of Structuration* (Cambridge: Polity Press, 1984) 258.

255 OECD "The human rights based approach to development cooperation: Towards a common understanding among the UN Agencies" available at: http://www.oecd.org/derec/finland/43966077.pdf (accessed: 22 April 2015).

Justified by Gidden's theory, the highest standard of living that has ever been recorded in African history could only be made possible through the agency of the state as duty bearer and the peoples of Libya as holders of the right to development. Through the practice of "natural socialism", the Libyan government created the opportunity for sweeping transformation by encouraging the people of Libya to broaden their productive capacity to own and utilise the country's wealth and resources for socio-economic and cultural development.[256] However, the 2011 Arab Spring uprising in Libya illustrates, in accordance with right to development standards that the realisation of one set of human rights at the expense of other human rights, is flawed. More on Libya is discussed in chapter five. Unfortunately, the right to development in Africa does not impose direct legal responsibility on external actors like in the case of the NATO intervention that destabilised Libya in 2011 and brought the country's development gains to ruin. External actions of this nature create the opportunity for the imposition of foreign policies that often do not respond to local realities and therefore, constitute an obstacle to development, which in accordance with the Declaration on the Right to Development ought to be eliminated.[257]

4.2.2.2 *The Duty to Eliminate Obstacles to Development*

To ensure that the right to development does not become a mere abstraction, the duty imposed on state parties to the African Charter to create favourable conditions for its realisation, includes a duty to eliminate existing and perceived obstacles that may hinder the development process. With regards to partnership for development, it entails ensuring that development cooperation does not focus solely on the provision of aid but essentially on ensuring that hindrances to development, especially those that promote injustice, are removed.[258] The first of such obstacles stemming from the development cooperation framework, which promotes development injustice is domination, in reaction to which the African Charter is emphatic in stating that "[n]othing shall justify the domination of a people by another".[259] The need to eliminate

---

256   Deeb, Marius K. & Deeb, Mary-Jane *Libya Since the Revolution: Aspects of Social and Political Development* (New York: Praeger Publishers, 1982) 115–120; Monti-Belkaoui, Janice & Riahi-Belkaoui, Ahmed *Qaddafi: The Man and His Policies* (Aldersrot: Avebury Ashgate Publishing Ltd, 1996) 2; El Fathaly, Omar I. & Palmer, Monte *Political Development and Social Change in Libya* (Toronto: DC Heath and Company, 1980) 23.

257   Declaration on the Right to Development, *supra* note 7, art 5.

258   Olusegun, Olaitan & Aiigbyoye, Oyeniyi "Realising the right to development in Nigeria: An examination of legal barriers and challenges" (2015) 6:1 *J Sust Dev Law & Policy* 156–63; Bunn, *supra* note 135, 1452–1467.

259   African Charter, *supra* note 25, art 19.

foreign domination is justified by the "unquestionable and inalienable right to self-determination", guaranteed by the African Charter.[260] On a softer note, the Declaration on the Right to Development appeals to the moral conscience of the international community; in order to complement the efforts of developing countries, to start by eliminating identified obstacles to development.[261] The Declaration enumerates these obstacles to include human rights violations resulting from discriminatory practices, domination and subjugation, insecurity and dispossession as well as the failure to observe guaranteed human rights.[262] Owing to the principles of universality, interrelatedness and indivisibility, Helen Quane explains the failure to observe human rights to include the situation where civil and political rights are given priority over socio-economic rights.[263]

An important pre-condition for ensuring the exercise and enjoyment of the right to development is peace and security, which in spite of the guarantee on "the right to national and international peace and security",[264] remains an illusion in most parts of Africa. According to Isabelle Roger, the relation between the right to peace and the right to development is of particular importance in the sense that peace constitutes an elementary component of the right to development.[265] Conflicts hinder the realisation of the right to development by destabilising the socio-economic structures that guarantee a decent livelihood.[266] The challenge remains for Africa – if collective action is to become meaningful and instrumental for the right to development to be achieved – that the conflicts that spread across the continent are brought to an end. As a prerequisite for socio-economic development, the AU Constitutive Act obligates state parties to eliminate endemic conflicts that constitute a major impediment to development,[267] in accordance too with the purpose of the UN that aims:

---

260 As above, art 20.

261 Declaration on the Right to Development, *supra* note 7, art 3(3).

262 As above, art 5 & 6(3).

263 Quane, Helen "A further dimension to the interdependence and indivisibility of human rights?: Recent developments concerning the rights of indigenous Peoples" (2012) 25 *Harvard Hum Rts J* 49.

264 African Charter, *supra* note 25, art 23(1).

265 Roger, Isabelle "Le droit au développement comme droit de l'homme: Genèse et concept" (Mémoire Instituts D'Etudes Politiques de Lyon Université Lumière Lyon, 2003) 52–53.

266 Olusegun & Aiigbyoye, *supra* note 258, 161–162.

267 AU Constitutive Act, *supra* note 221, preamble.

[t]o maintain international peace and security, and to that end: *to take effective collective measures* for the prevention and removal of threats to the peace, and for the suppression of acts of aggression or other breaches of the peace, and to bring about by peaceful means, and in conformity with the principles of justice and international law, adjustment or settlement of international disputes or situations which might lead to a breach of the peace (emphasis added).[268]

According to Obechi Ewanfoh, the right to development can only be achieved through development cooperation if the existing obstacles that are generated through development cooperation are eliminated and the development cooperation framework is rationalised to ensure that it does not produce new obstacles.[269]

4.2.2.3   *Obligation to Create an Enabling Environment*

Technically, the right to development in Africa is intended to address concerns relating to the unjust practices that hinder development and therefore stand in the way of the African peoples' right to exercise and enjoy well-being. These practices include the development paradigms imposed by industrialised countries, which often ignite conflicts and are obtained not only at the cost of the peoples' human rights but also at a cost of predatory exploitation and destruction of the natural environment.[270] In accordance with rights-based approaches, the right to development is determined by the fact that it is not the outcome that justifies the process, but the process is supposed to justify the outcome.[271] It implies that it is not just about what, but about how development is achieved. If the process of creating development is wrong, logically, according to rights-based standards the outcome cannot be expected to be right. Thus, the African Charter enjoins state parties to ensure that the development space allows the opportunity and an environment that is enabling enough for the right to development to be achieved.[272]

---

268   UN Charter, *supra* note 2, art 1(1).

269   See Ewanfoh, Obehi P. *Underdevelopment in Africa: My Hands are Clean* (Morrisville: Lulu Press, 2014) 140.

270   Zhenghua, D. "Rights to development and selection in development mode" (2008) *China Hum Rts* 56.

271   Rodney, Walter *How Europe Underdeveloped Africa* (Dar-Es-Salaam: Tanzanian Publishing House, 1973) 1; Sengupta 2004, *supra* note 41, 183–184; Sengupta 2002, *supra* note 3, 848–852.

272   Okafor, Obiora C. " 'Righting' the right to development: A socio-legal analysis of article 22 of the African Charter on Human and Peoples' Rights" in Marks, Stephen P. (ed) *Implementing the Right to Development: The Role of International Law* (Geneva: Friedrich-Ebert-Stiftung,

The need for an enabling environment is not only established by the African Charter but also by international law. It is sustained by a number of provisions of the Declaration on the Right to Development, which require creating favourable conditions for the fulfilment of the right to development.[273] In reaffirming the right to development as an inalienable human right, the Vienna Declaration also emphasises the necessity to create a favourable and equitable environment at the international level for the realisation of the right to development.[274] Thus, an enabling environment forms the foundation for action without which the right to development would remain a pipedream. This said, the follow up question to consider is what an enabling environment could be understood to mean. An enabling environment is described in this context to represent both an ideological and a realistic space within which the right to development can be achieved without undue constraints. In my view, it is ideological in the sense that it denotes the set of principles that must guide development cooperation, and practical in the sense that action must be seen to be taken to ensure the exercise and enjoyment of the right to development.

According to the Declaration on the Right to Development, an enabling environment also entails making national and international conditions favourable for the right to development to be achieved.[275] In this regard, as Melik Özden reiterates, states are charged with the obligation to take legislative and other appropriate measures to ensure that right holders are able to exercise their right to development.[276] The obligation to take other measures is quite broad.[277] In this context, it does not exclude regulating the activities of foreign stakeholders within the framework of development cooperation, which falls within the realm of the right granted to states to formulate policies to

---

2008) 60; Mmari, Amanda "The challenges surrounding the implementation of the right to development in the African Charter on Human and Peoples' Rights in light of the *Endorois* case" (Masters Dissertation, University of Pretoria 2012) 23; Kirchmeier, *supra* note 8, 11; African Charter, *supra* note 25, art 22(2).

273   Declaration on the Right to Development, *supra* note 7, art 3(1); arts 7, 8(1) & 10.

274   Fikre, *supra* note 48,257; Vienna Declaration, *supra* note 45; UN GAOR World Conference on Human Rights 48th Session 22nd Plenary Meeting UN Doc A/CONF 157/23 1993 para 10.

275   Declaration on the Right to Development, *supra* note 7, art 3(1).

276   Özden, Melik "The rights to development" *CETIM Human Rights Programme* 9; see African Charter, *supra* note 26, art 22(2); Declaration on the Right to Development, *supra* note 7, arts 3(2) & 4(1).

277   Ngang, Carol C. "Judicial enforcement of socio-economic rights in South Africa and the separation of powers objection: The obligation to 'take other measures' " (2014) 14:2 *AHRLJ* 672–675.

ensure improved well-being.[278] However, because the right to development is less of an international priority, the necessity to create an enabling environment remains the primary responsibility of developing countries, particularly in Africa where the right to development is legally binding. In accordance, Bertrand Ramcharan thinks that although international action is essential to ensure the effective realisation of the right to development, such action can only build on and complement action at the national and regional levels.[279] Thus, it is a matter of legal obligation for Africa to strive for the necessary enabling environment by compelling foreign stakeholders to comply with the law that guarantees the right to development. This is essentially an inevitable prerequisite for actualising the right to development in Africa. It entails the formulation and implementation of people-centred development policies,[280] and the elimination of the massive and flagrant violations of human rights.[281] It also requires political stability and the redeploying of resources into comprehensive human development efforts,[282] which Paulo notes will create the opportunity for advancement.[283]

It is undeniable that many African states are unable to muster the capacity to fulfil their right to development obligations, and thus will remain dependent on development assistance.[284] However, the circumstances offer the opportunity for such states to influence significantly how development cooperation is conducted in order that development assistance is outcomes-focused to address targeted development priorities that respond to peoples' direct needs. Development cooperation, which is envisaged as the process for realising the right to development, ought to determine the outcome in the form of guaranteeing the attainment of human well-being. In this light, Sengupta points out that an enabling environment requires the international community not only to make provision for development assistance but importantly to create equitable balance as a guarantee of fairness to developing countries within the global system.[285] While Kirchmeier intimates that development cooperation ought to be informed by the concept of the right to development,[286] it

---

278 Declaration on the Right to Development, *supra* note 7, arts 3(2) & 4(1).
279 Ramcharan, Bertrand *The Right to Development in Comparative Law: The Pressing Need for National Implementation* (Cape Town: University of Cape Town, 2010) 6.
280 Declaration on the Right to Development, *supra* note 7, arts 4 & 8(1).
281 As above, arts 5, 3(3) & 6(3).
282 As above, art 7.
283 Paulo, *supra* note 27, 6.
284 As above.
285 Sengupta 2000, *supra* note 204, 571.
286 Kirchmeier, *supra* note 8, 5.

CHAPTER 3

is even more strategic for Africa to part ways with the development cooperation model for development, which pragmatically speaking, exhibits relatively
minimal potential to enable Africa to advance in a comprehensive manner.

4.2.2.4 *Autonomy in Development Policy Formulation*

The realisation of the right to development is contingent on an effective national
development policy framework that is adequately protective and allows the
opportunity for the exercise and enjoyment of well-being and improved livelihood. Accordingly, one of the norms for entering into development cooperation is the obligation to respect the sovereignty of every state in self-reliantly
setting its own development priorities. This is enshrined in the African Charter,
which provides that the peoples of Africa "shall freely determine their political
status and shall pursue their economic and social development *according to
the policy* they have freely chosen" (emphasis added).[287] It is also universally
acknowledged that "[s]tates have the right and the duty to formulate appropriate national development policies that aim at the constant improvement of
the well-being of the entire population and of all individuals".[288]

Development policy-making is not just a duty imposed on African countries;
it is a right that they are entitled to exercise within the framework of development cooperation.[289] The legitimacy in development cooperation with Africa
can only be established by the fact that the policy for implementation is formulated by the African states concerned, which in order to be effective and
relevant must respond to domestic development realities and priorities. Blame
cannot be apportioned elsewhere if African countries fail to take this obligation seriously. The importance for giving attention to development policy making is, as David Kennedy has noted, to ensure equitable redistribution in order
to enable balanced development.[290] Appropriate development policy making
involves making choices among policy alternatives with the aim to achieve
optimal development outcomes.[291] In order to be developmentally relevant,
policy formulation must be attuned to the realities of the socio-economic and
cultural development challenges that Africa is confronted with. It is important
to recognise that the AU has undertaken initiatives, which even though not

---

287 African Charter, *supra* note 25, art 20(1).
288 Declaration on the Right to Development, *supra* note 7, art 2(3).
289 As above, art 3(2). The Declaration states that "States have the right and the duty to for-
     mulate appropriate national development policies that aim at the constant improvement
     of the well-being [...]".
290 Kennedy, *supra* note 239, 18.
291 As above, 19 & 26.

specifically conceived as such, provide framework policy mechanisms through which implementation of the right to could be achieved.

4.2.3 Continental Framework Mechanisms for implementation

4.2.3.1 *New Partnership for Africa's Development/African Union Development Agency*

The formation of the New Partnership for Africa's Development (NEPAD) in 2001 and its subsequent ratification in 2002 as a policy framework "to address Africa's development problems within a new paradigm" inspired hope of a starting point for reshaping Africa's development future.[292] It was eventually also endorsed by African leaders through which they reaffirmed a common vision and shared conviction to rebuild and put their countries back on track from the ruins of the structural adjustment programmes.[293] The NEPAD programme envisages as its primary objective to "eradicate poverty in Africa and place African countries, both individually and collectively, on a path of sustainable growth and development".[294]

NEPAD recognises that "development is a process of empowerment and self-reliance" in respect of which the peoples of Africa are cautioned not to become "wards of benevolent guardians" but the "architects of their own sustained upliftment".[295] Along these lines, Kamga estimates that NEPAD ought to do more for the realisation of the right to development by implementing a rights-based approach to development.[296] On the contrary, its operational strategy, which emphasises reliance on foreign support "marks a radical shift in position" from the aspiration for socio-economic and cultural self-determination, which Appiagyei-Atua contends, Africa has in principle stood for since independence.[297] Along the lines of development cooperation, it is noted that the international community endorses NEPAD as the framework mechanism for

---

292 Murray, Rachel *Human Rights in Africa: From the OAU to the African Union* (Cambridge/ New York: Cambridge University Press, 2004) 266; NEPAD "Historical context: Origins and influences" available at: http://www.nepad.org/history (accessed: 4 December 2016).

293 Littmann, Julia "A human rights approach to the New Partnership for Africa's Development (NEPAD) and the African Peer Review Mechanism (APRM)" (2004) *International Federation for Human Rights* 3.

294 New Partnership for Africa's Development Declaration adopted as a Programme of the AU at the Lusaka Summit at Lusaka, Zambia in July 2001 paras 1, 62 & 67.

295 As above, para 27.

296 Kamga, *supra* note 47, 281.

297 Appiagyei-Atua, Kwado "Bumps on the road: A critique of how Africa got to NEPAD" (2006) 6:2 *AHRLJ* 525.

supporting Africa's development efforts.[298] In this regard, Sengupta estimates that the NEPAD programme represents a "comprehensive partnership" framework for implementing the right to development.[299] This is contradictory in the sense that the patterns of development cooperation that African countries are involved in as discussed earlier in this chapter are opposed to the African conception of the right to development, which conceptually represents the right to self-determination.

As an institutional organ of the AU designated to function as Africa's development agency[300] responsibility is by implication shifted to NEPAD to ensure compliance with the treaty obligations relating to development that states governments have committed to achieve under various instruments. Following the discussion above relating to the right to development dispensation in Africa, a lot is expected of NEPAD in terms of ensuring compliance with right to development standards and in advancing the idea of development as a human right probably through the country-driven peer review processes. By extension, NEPAD has the duty to ensure that interventions by foreign stakeholders do not jeopardise enjoyment of the right to development in Africa. The NEPAD founding instrument only makes mention of the right to development in a very causal manner in paragraph 43. This may be explained by the fact that because its operational modality is tilted more towards development cooperation, the idea of a right to development might not be attractive to potential foreign stakeholders, for the same reason as explained in the preceding paragraph that both approaches to development are conceptually opposed.

Notwithstanding that human rights and socio-economic development are repeatedly mentioned in the NEPAD Declaration and its ancillary instruments,[301] NEPAD's overarching approach to development is generally not human rights-based. Serges Kamga observes that the document is awash with

---

298 Memorandum of Understanding on the African Peer Review Mechanism 2003 para 9; UN General Assembly Declaration on the New Partnership for Africa's Development Resolution A/RES/57/2 of 18 September 2002; UN General Assembly "Final review and appraisal of the United Nations New Agenda for the Development of Africa in the 1990s and support for the New Partnership for Africa's Development" Resolution A/RES/57/7 of 4 November 2002; Urhobo Historical Society "An address by Prime Minister of Great Britain before the Nigerian Parliament, 7 February 2002" available at: http://www.waado.org/NigerDelta/FedGovt/ForeignAffairs/TonyBlair.html (accessed: 3 December 2016); Kamga, *supra* note 47, 108–109.

299 Sengupta, Arjun "Development cooperation and the right to development" (2003) *Copyright©2003 Arjun Sengupta* 19–20.

300 The integration of NEPAD as an organ of the African Union was concluded at the 10th AU Assembly in Addis Ababa in January/February 2008.

301 See Littmann, *supra* note 293, 20–30.

THE GEOPOLITICS OF DEVELOPMENT COOPERATION   143

neoliberal ideologies[302] and consequently, NEPAD has been criticised not only for its neoliberal ideologies but also for promoting structural adjustment policies, which do not reflect African realities.[303] Despite the criticism, while Rachel Murray is of the opinion that NEPAD plays an instrumental role in promoting human rights in Africa,[304] Julia Littmann thinks that "NEPAD seems to put a stronger emphasis on civil and political rights, linking them to the issue of democracy and political governance".[305] Meanwhile, the African Charter highlights the core component of the right to development to be the satisfaction of socio-economic and cultural rights as a guarantee for the enjoyment of civil and political rights.[306]

Although NEPAD's operational approach is designed in favour of "international partnership",[307] accountability is generally required from African governments through the peer review mechanism[308] without an equivalent measure of accountability on the part of foreign stakeholders.[309] The NEPAD Declaration envisages the establishment of "an independent mechanism for assessing donor and recipient country performance".[310] Although such a mechanism could practically serve the purpose of regulating the actions of foreign stakeholders unfortunately, no such accountability mechanism is known to have been established to be able to determine how it operates in reality. As illustrated in the preceding sections of this chapter, it is essential to reiterate that development cooperation is not indispensable for the realisation of the right to development in Africa.

If NEPAD is to accomplish its mandate as Africa's development agency in respect of the African Charter that enshrines and obligates state parties to pay particular attention to the right to development,[311] it would need to redefine its *modus operandi* from the predominantly donor-oriented cooperation model to considering the right to development as the framework model for setting the

---

302   Kamga, *supra* note 47, 97.
303   Bond, Patrick *Fanon's Warning: A Civil Society Reader on the New Partnership for Africa's Development* (Asmara: Africa World Press, 2005) 33; Diamond, Larry "Promoting real reform in Africa" in Gyimah-Boadi, Emmanuel (ed) *Democratic Reform in Africa: The Quality of Progress* (London: Lynne Rienner Publishers, 2004) 277; Kamga, *supra* note 47, 95–96 & 108.
304   Murray, *supra* note 292, 236.
305   Littmann, *supra* note 293, 87.
306   African Charter, *supra* note 25, preamble & art 22(1).
307   Littmann, *supra* note 293, 88.
308   See generally the Memorandum of Understanding on the African Peer Review Mechanism.
309   Dann, *supra* note 12, 1.
310   NEPAD Declaration, *supra* note 294, para 149; Littmann, *supra* note 293, 88.
311   African Charter, *supra* note 25, preamble & art 22.

standards for political conduct that should become acceptable and beneficial for Africa. Interestingly, as part of the institutional reforms at the AU, NEPAD will eventually be transformed into the African Union Development Agency (AUDA) with an expanded mandate to carry out extensive mobilisation of the requisite resources to be able to address Africa's development priorities much more coherently and effectively across the continent.[312] It is not very certain whether AUDA will have to function like other well known international development agencies that operate for the most part to provide development assistance to other, mostly less developed countries.

With regard to the transformation into AUDA, NEPAD Chief Executive Officer is quoted as saying, "[o]ur main focus now as a development agency will be to move to the formulation of development tools that can strengthen the capacity of all African stakeholders to better execute priority development projects".[313] While reference to the *formulation of development tools* and *strengthening the capacity of all African stakeholders* do not seem unambiguous, it is vital to acknowledge that the peoples of Africa constitute the primary stakeholders in setting the pace for their own development and to clearly articulate the fact that an essential tool for strengthening their capacity to drive the development process lies in advancing the right to development, which appears seriously neglected. Faced with the defiant development challenges that Africa continues to grapple with, in order not to replicate the shortcomings of NEPAD, AUDA will as it affirms, need to build into its operational strategy, functional systems that can effectively respond to the socio-economic and cultural development realities highlighted in Agenda 2063.

4.2.3.2 *Agenda 2063 – The Africa We Want*

On the occasion of the 50th Anniversary celebration of the OAU in May 2013, the political leadership in Africa recommitted itself to the pan-African vision of "an integrated, prosperous and peaceful Africa, driven by its own citizens and representing a dynamic force in the international arena", which provided the impetus for the African Union Commission to adopt "Agenda2063: The Africa we want" as an integrated blueprint and a shared strategic framework

---

312 Roby, Christin "Q & A: The African Union Development Agency takes shape" *NEPAD* 4 March 2019 available at: https://www.devex.com/news/q-a-the-african-union-development -agency-takes-shape-94339 (accessed: 26 June 2019); NEPAD "NEPAD's transformation into the African Union Development Agency" available at: http://www.nepad.org/news/ nepads-transformation-african-union-development-agency (accessed: 26 June 2019).

313 Roby, *supra* note 312.

THE GEOPOLITICS OF DEVELOPMENT COOPERATION

instrument for development on the continent in the next fifty years.[314] As part of this noble vision, the document highlights the commitment to address the injustices of the past; referring in principle to the human rights violations and development prejudices that deprived the peoples of Africa of the opportunities and the means to secure a decent standard of living.

The agenda outlines seven prime aspirations for development, which African governments are required to translate into implementable objectives and to incorporate same into their national development plans.[315] The aspirations span the broad spectrum of development challenges that Africa is confronted with and they illustrate that if accurately remedied through the measures and action plans outlined therein, it would enable the peoples of Africa to enjoy a high standard of living, better quality of life and improved well-being. Agenda 2063 broadly envisions an Africa that is liberated from poverty and the structural inequalities that exclude the impoverished peoples from the vast opportunities that abound on the continent. The transformative vision is anticipated to be achieved through mainstreaming democratic governance, universal human rights standards, equity and the rule of law. This operational framework provides the basis for holding African governments to account on their obligations to ensure that the entitlement to well-being and better living standards, which they owe to the peoples of Africa, are fulfilled through adequate people-centred and rights-based development programming.

While the aspirations for better living standards and improved well-being are outlined in the 2063 agenda barely in the form of development objectives, they are in effect human rights entitlements, which impose an obligation on states to provide social protection and to ensure the highest attainable standard of living for their peoples.[316] It entails that every aspect of development programming is geared towards the fulfilment of this ultimate goal and thus, provides justification to the Kigali Declaration in envisioning the realisation of the 2030 and the 2063 agendas for development in Africa through a rights-based approach. However, the elusive reference to human rights in the Agenda 2063 document (without sufficient focus, especially on socio-economic and cultural rights and the right to development) points to a fundamental flaw in the crafting of the African agenda for development.

---

314 AU Commission "Agenda 2063", *supra* note 91, paras 1-4; African Union "50th Anniversary Solemn Declaration" available at: https://au.int/sites/default/files/documents/36205 -doc-50th_anniversary_solemn_declaration_en.pdf (accessed: 24 January 2019).

315 As above, para 75.

316 UN Universal Declaration of Human Rights, UN General Assembly Resolution 217 A(III) adopted on 10 December 1948 art 25; ICESCR, *supra* note 26, art 12(1).

Building on the achievements of the human rights-driven revolution that swept across Africa in the 1990s, resulting in extensive political reforms and the subsequent recognition and protection of a broad range of human rights in the national constitutions of most African countries, Agenda 2063 is supposed to emphasise the pursuit of a rights-based approach to realising the aspirations for development set out therein. Unfortunately, Agenda 2063 does so, if at all, quite insufficiently. The revolution of the 90s largely aimed at re-orientating African governments together with non-state actors towards the path of pursuing development and human rights concurrently with the primary objective to make life better and worth living with dignity for the peoples of Africa. This frame of thinking resuscitated the idea born in the late 6os and early 70s that development is to be claimed as an inherent legal entitlement to be enjoyed by all peoples,[317] which in Africa, has gained recognition and protection as such and consequently imposes a legal obligation for its realisation.

The African Charter enshrines the legal assurance that all the peoples of Africa have a legitimate right to development, which for good reasons is only guaranteed to be claimed by groups of persons and not by individuals.[318] To conceive of development as a human right thus, implies that the peoples of Africa can compel their governments to create development not just as a policy directive that the government may accomplish at its discretion but as a duty owed to the people, which must be fulfilled as a legal obligation.[319] The setting of development objectives and/or aspirations such as is contained in Agenda 2063 must therefore, reflect or be seen to eventually result in the fulfilment of this purpose.

The human rights revolution paved the way for the proliferation of a robust civil society with a purpose to respond to the livelihood sustainability needs of the populations and significantly also, to hold the often-unresponsive African governments to effective accountability on their development and human rights obligations. As part of the evolving African human rights architecture, states governments are required to establish NHRIs with the task to objectively

---

317 Marks, *supra* note 49, 34.

318 African Charter, *supra* note 25, provides in art 22(1) that: "All peoples shall have the right to their economic, social and cultural development with due regard to their freedom and identity and in the equal enjoyment of the common heritage of mankind".

319 African Charter, *supra* note 25, further provides in art 22(2) that: "States shall have the duty, individually or collectively, to ensure the exercise of the right to development". This provision imposes a duty on African governments to create the conditions to ensure that the right to development is achieved, failing which the peoples of Africa are entitled to assert that right from the state and the government would have the obligation to ensure its realisation.

coordinate the duty-bearer obligations of the state and the right-bearer responsibilities of the populations to ensure effective accountability with regard to the promotion, protection and fulfilment of human rights. Like with the global development agenda as indicated above, the African agenda for equally highlights that in envisaging achieving structural transformation, Africa will have capable, "participatory and accountable institutions of governance".[320]

One would anticipate these institutions of governance to include NHRIs. However, in listing the leadership and stakeholder structures earmarked to ensure the implementation, monitoring and evaluation of Agenda 2063, NHRIs are omitted. The mechanisms for implementation listed in Agenda 2063 might have a reputation for sound development practice but lack a dedicated focus on human rights. The Kigali Declaration is then eventually adopted on the heels of Agenda 2063 and it projects NHRIs as an inevitable mechanism for the realisation not only of the African agenda but including also the global agenda for development as it is intended to apply to Africa. With this development geared toward ensuring that these agendas for development practically translate into improved living standards for the peoples of Africa, it is important to take a closer look at the Kigali Declaration and the actual role that it envisages for NHRIs.

4.2.3.3 *Africa Continental Free Trade Area*

It is worth reiterating the shared responsibility for collective action for the realisation of the right to development contained in article 3(1) of the Declaration on the Right to Development and article 22(2) of the African Charter. When the African Charter attributes the duty on state parties to collectively ensure that the peoples of Africa exercise their right to socio-economic and cultural development in freedom and to enjoy the benefits of the common heritage, it essentially implies putting in place functional framework mechanisms such as the recently established Africa Continental Free Trade Area (AfCFTA). As highlighted in chapter two, the AfCFTA is a continental treaty adopted at the 10th Extraordinary Session of the AU Assembly of Heads of State and Government in Kigali, Rwanda on 21 March 2018 establishing a single African market to facilitate the free flow of goods, services and the movement of persons aimed at deepening economic integration of the continent.[321]

---

320   AU Commission "Agenda 2063", *supra* note 91, paras 28, 67 & 74(c).

321   Agreement Establishing the African Continental Free Trade Area adopted by the AU at the 10th Extraordinary Session of the Assembly of Heads of State and Government in Kigali, Rwanda on 21 March 2018 AU Doc TI21086_E arts 2 & 3(a).

148   CHAPTER 3

With the ratification of the treaty in a record period of one year and its entry into force on 30 May 2019, the AfCFTA becomes the largest free trade area in the world, estimated to boost intra-African trade by 52 per cent by the year 2022 and remove trade tariffs on 90 per cent of goods.[322] A free trade area is essentially a protective mechanism against unfettered foreign competition that impedes local productivity. It provides the enabling environment for the nurturing of productive capabilities, allows local economic initiatives to flourish and thus, trigger demand for the ancillary capabilities. A 2017 Policy Brief of the UN Economic Commission for Africa (UNECA) notes that the AfCFTA "present[s] a unique opportunity to bring enhanced growth and increased opportunity to millions of African citizens. The jobs and wealth that can be created through greater and easier intra-African trade have the potential to contribute significantly to eliminating poverty, creating jobs and promoting equality".[323] It is noted that the AfCFTA "has the potential to challenge the age-old dynamic of dependency, and give Africa command over its future".[324]

One crucial factor for the realisation of the right to development is the prerequisite of "full sovereignty over all their natural wealth and resources", enshrined in the African Charter as an entitlement to the common heritage,[325] which unfortunately has been of great benefit to foreign stakeholders and not so much to the peoples of Africa.[326] With an indication to phase out tariffs on 90 per cent of goods exchanged through intra-African trade,[327] a huge proportion of the resources needed to ensure the full realisation of the right to development is guaranteed to remain within the African continent. The

---

322   Cofelice, Andrea "African Continental Free Trade Area: Opportunities and challenges" (2018) xxxi: 3 *De Gruyter – The Federalist Debate* 32; Mumbere, Daniel "AfCFTA agreement to be implemented after Gambia's historic ratification" *AfricaNews* 3 April 2019 available at: https://www.africanews.com/2019/04/03/afcfta-agreement-to-be-implemented-following-gambia-s-historic-ratification// (accessed: 25 April 2019).

323   African Trade Policy Centre (ATPC) & Friedrich-Ebert-Stiftung (FES) "Building a sustainable and inclusive continental free trade area: Nine priority recommendations from a human rights perspective" (2017) *ECA Policy Brief* 1.

324   Van Lennep, Tove "The African Continental Free Trade Area III: Is Africa ready?" (2019) *Helen Suzman Foundation* available at: https://hsf.org.za/publications/hsf-briefs/the-african-continental-free-trade-area-iii-2013-is-africa-ready (accessed: 26 April 2019) 5.

325   Declaration on the Right to Development, *supra* note 7, art 1(2); African Charter, *supra* note 25, art 22(1).

326   In a video footage dated April 2019 (on file with the author), US Secretary of State for Africa, Nagy Tibor observed that "Africa is an incredibly, incredibly rich continent and it seems, so far it has been incredibly rich for colonial powers, for the governments in place; it has not been rich for the peoples who live there".

327   Cofelice, *supra* note 322, 32.

socio-economic benefits (welfare gains) that are envisaged to accrue to the peoples of Africa is according to Andreas Cofelice, "estimated at 16.1 billion dollars, especially favoring women (who currently manage 70% of informal cross-border trade) and young people, who could benefit from new job opportunities".[328] With the expanded opportunities that the continental free market presents, it is accurate to approximate that the AfCFTA provides a suitable framework mechanism through which socio-economic and cultural development can be achieved in Africa.

However, the apparent lack of a people-centred orientation of the AfCFTA (in utter disregard of member states' human rights obligations) implies that equitable redistribution of development gains from trade across the continent is not guaranteed and thus, may end up enriching the haves more and more at the expense of economically fragile African countries and the most vulnerable segments of the African populations. The AfCFTA is innately not conceived with a defined purpose to achieve human rights, including especially the right to development. The treaty makes no mention of the right to development despite its recognition by the political leadership on the continent as instrumental for the realisation of socio-economic and cultural as well as political development.[329] Similar to the NEPAD mechanism, the objectives set out in articles 3 and 4 present the AfCFTA are more neoliberal and market-focused with a noticeable absence of any indication on how the African common market will contribute to addressing the human rights concerns on the continent or to bettering living standards and the well-being of the African peoples. Owing to widespread scepticism about regional integration, trade liberalisation and growing populist anti-trade sentiments around the world, especially with the Brexit experience (Britain's exit from the European Union), it is recommended for Africa to situate human rights at the centre of trade negotiations under the AfCFTA to ensure a sustainable and inclusive free trade area that is equitably beneficial to the peoples of Africa.[330]

While the ECA policy recommendations are well intentioned to set the path for effective implementation, the full accomplishment of the AfCFTA would only be assessed to the extent that member truly commit to ensuring that the peoples of Africa feel a sense of ownership with aspirations to reap the benefits deriving therefrom. It requires as Tove van Lennep indicates, governments to "create enabling conditions for citizens to leverage the opportunities of AfCFTA and mitigate [against] losses".[331] This cautious observation hinges

---

328   As above, 32–33.
329   African Charter, *supra* note 25, preamble para 8, read together with art 22.
330   Cofelice, *supra* note 322, 34; ATPC & FES, *supra* note 323, 1–8.
331   Van Lennep, *supra* note 324, 5.

on the fact that many of Africa's flagship initiatives including for example, the Regional Economic Communities that are looked upon as the building blocs to the AfCFTA have largely not been successful. Van Lennep cites the example of the Southern African Development Community (SADC) that has failed to achieve its purpose owing to nationalistic interests that trump over the over-arching imperative for regional integration.[332] Because African governments are noted for swiftly ratifying treaties without any genuine intention of pro-ceeding to implementation, the signing and ratification of the AfCFTA cannot prematurely be used to count the chicks before they are hatched.

Trusting that the AfCFTA provides a functional mechanism and therefore, satisfies the requirement to create favourable conditions for the realisation of the right to development in Africa, the level of penetration by foreign stake-holders into the continent leaves a crucial question to worry about who the free trade area is likely to benefit more. Genuine commitment by Francophone African countries (least developed on the continent) for instance, may provide the opportunity to rupture the colonial bond entered into with France under the Colonisation Continuation Pact and consequently, allow these countries to gain greater socio-economic and cultural sovereignty and self-determination. The adoption of the ECO as a single currency for member states of the Economic Community of West African States (ECOWAS) as part of the plan to make Africa an integrated continent is an important step towards concretising the AfCFTA.[333] This measure provides opportunity to the eight francophone countries of the ECOWAS region that use the CFA Franc to rupture the French monetary hegemony over these countries. The major concern however, is whether France, with its dominant influence and capacity to coerce (militarily and economically) any of its African colonies that attempts to break the sub-jugation accord, would readily let go of these profitable colonial possessions.

5   Concluding Remarks

The stalemate in development, which according to global categorisation ranks Africa the most underdeveloped part of the world,[334] cannot be attributed

---

332   As above, 2.

333   Mati, Segiru; Civcir, Irfan & Ozdeser, Hüseyin "ECOWAS common currency: How pre-pared are its members?" (2019) 78:308 *Investigación Económica* 90–92; Dewast, Louise "West Africa's eco: What difference would a single currency make?" BBC *Africa, Dakar* available at: https://www.bbc.com/news/world-africa-48882030 (accessed: 6 July 2019).

334   See Bilal, *supra* note 74, 2–12.

THE GEOPOLITICS OF DEVELOPMENT COOPERATION

solely to Africa's failure to advance in a comprehensive manner. The sometimes prejudiced and uncontrollable actions and influences of external actors within the framework of development cooperation have over the decades impacted adversely on the development landscape in Africa. While it is incumbent on African countries to demonstrate genuine commitment to achieving the right to development in respect of the obligations they have undertaken under the African Charter and other instruments, the manner in which foreign stakeholders influence the African development agenda cannot be overlooked. If the right to development is to be achieved through development cooperation as it is envisaged, a shared responsibility is imposed on African states as well as on foreign stakeholders to refrain from actions that may endanger the realisation of that right.

Judged in relation to the fundamental features, it is pointed out that development cooperation is counter-productive to the African conception of the right to development. It is designed to keep Africa perpetually dependent on the benevolence of foreign donors and not necessarily to enable Africa to advance. There only exists a very loose connection between development cooperation as a mechanism for the realisation of the right to development in Africa, which rather constitutes a development model in itself and a suitable alternative to development cooperation. Development cooperation, as it is argued, is driven more by geopolitical motives characterised by the rent-seeking interests of foreign stakeholders and the desire to dominate than by a genuine commitment to assist developing countries in their efforts to achieve the right to development.

The duty to take collective action that obtains from the African Charter enjoins state parties to be more proactive in asserting the right to development in respect of the obligation imposed by the AU Constitutive Act that envisages advancing integration of the African continent. Established within this legal framework, which according to Younkins, is intended to preserve freedom and moral agency, the right to development sets the principle that the pursuit of well-being and improved standard of living must be governed by rules of just conduct in lieu of the arbitrariness often exercised by foreign stakeholders.[335] However, as long as laws remain theoretical they cannot change the circumstances that hinder the exercise of the right to development, which rather demands pragmatic action for its realisation. As illustrated in this chapter,

---

335   See Younkins, Edward W. "The purpose of law and constitutions" (2000) *Le Québécois Libre* No 66 available at: http://www.quebecoislibre.org/000902-11.htm (accessed: 28 December 2015). Younkins explains how the law is supposed to be used to regulate and ameliorate human actions within society.

development cooperation lacks the potential to redress the range of development challenges and therefore unsuited as a development model for Africa. Thus, the argument is reiterated that attention ought to divert towards exploring the right to development as a suitable alternative functional development model in dealing with Africa's development challenges. The next chapter explores the range of instruments that provide the framework for the practical implementation of the right to development in Africa and how that may impact and probably influence thinking about development cooperation as a model for development.

CHAPTER 4

A Dispensation for Socio-economic and Cultural Self-Determination

1   Introduction

This chapter provides a description of the legal context within which develop-ment is envisaged to take place in Africa as a legitimate entitlement as envis-aged by the range of legal instruments that guarantee socio-economic and cultural self-determination to the peoples of Africa in setting their own devel-opment priorities. The analysis stems from the central argument highlighted in the previous two chapters necessitating a shift from development cooper-ation, which as it is argued, only perpetuates subordination to the dominant influence of foreign stakeholders and therefore is unsuited as a development model for Africa. The question then becomes why the right to development cannot be conceived in its own terms as a development model as opposed to envisaging its realisation through development cooperation. As pointed out in chapter three, without concrete action, the principles of law that legitimise development as a human right cannot by themselves, redress the injustices that hinder progress in Africa. Some of these injustices obtain from the fact that despite decolonisation, the development future of most African countries has remained caught up in the systems of industrialised countries.

For instance, since the late 1950s, France has controlled the economic and fiscal policies and is holding the national reserves of fourteen (former) French colonies in the French Central Bank under conditions that prevent these coun-tries from having access to the reserves for development purposes.[1] Although these fourteen francophone countries may be argued not to represent all of Africa, Mahalu points out that most other African countries have also been rendered unable to "exercise full sovereignty over their natural wealth and

---

1   Koutonin, Mawuna R. "14 African countries forced by France to pay colonial tax for the benefits of slavery and colonisation" (2014) *Silicon Africa* available at: http://www.siliconafrica.com/france-colonial-tax/ (accessed: 30 October 2017); Touati, Silvain "French foreign policy in Africa: Between pré-carré and multilateralism" *Chatham House–An Africa Programme Briefing Note* February 2007 2; Le Vine, Victor T. *Politics in Francophone Africa* (Boulder: Lynne Rienner, 2004) 2–6.

© CAROL CHI NGANG, 2022 | DOI:10.1163/9789004467903_005

154   CHAPTER 4

resources and do not control the prices of their raw materials".[2] In spite of guarantees on the basis of the right to self-determination in formulating domestic policies and in exercising sovereign ownership over national wealth and resources as prerequisites for the realisation of the right to development,[3] such circumstances have meant that the right to development in Africa has remained somehow unattainable. Meanwhile, as Stephen Marks observes, the right to development sets universal standards of performance and regulatory functions, which states are required to pursue as an ethical demand reflecting acceptable values and norms of international behaviour.[4]

The illustrations in the previous chapter on how foreign stakeholders have with impunity consistently sabotaged development efforts in Africa, emphasises the need, for Africa is to make significant progress to become more assertive in assuring that the right to development guaranteed to the peoples of Africa can produce anticipated outcomes of well-being and improved standards of living. In accordance with the theory of pragmatism, pursuing the right to development entails the concrete application of the treaty and statutory provisions that enshrine such a right.[5] It means that besides pursuing policy reforms to achieve development, when a violation is alleged, recourse to accountability and remedy processes is guaranteed to ensure that equity and justice become the guiding principles to development practice in Africa. This is anchored in the reading of the right to development in Africa as both a human rights concept and a development paradigm, structured within the law as pointed out in chapter two.

In exploring the extent to which the right to development is guaranteed as a legal entitlement to the peoples of Africa, this chapter is structured as follows: Section 2 examines the framework for implementation with emphasis on the right to development dispensation, which is legitimatised by a range of legal instruments that guarantees to the peoples of Africa entitlement to

---

2   Mahalu, Costa R. "Human rights and development: An African perspective" (2009) 1:1 *Leiden J Int'l L* 18.

3   African Charter on Human and Peoples' Rights adopted in Nairobi, Kenya on 27 June 1981 OAU Doc CAB/LEG/67/3 Rev.5 (1981) arts 20(1), 21(1) & 22(1); International Covenant on Economic, Social and Cultural Rights (ICESCR) adopted on 16 December 1966, 999 UNTS 171 UN Doc A/6316 (1966) art 1(1) & 2(1); Declaration on the Right to Development Resolution A/RES/41/128 adopted by the UN General Assembly on 4 December 1986 arts 1(2) & 2(3).

4   Marks, Stephen P. (ed) *Implementing the Right to Development: The Role of International Law* (Geneva: Friedrich-Ebert-Stiftung, 2008) 8.

5   See Singer, Joseph W. "Property and coercion in federal Indian law: The conflict between critical and complacent pragmatism" (1990) 63:6 *South Calif L Rev* 1821–1822; Radin, Margaret J. "The pragmatist and the feminist" (1990) 63:2 *South Calif L Rev* 1700.

socio-economic and cultural development (2.1), and the associated legal responsibilities deriving from the obligations imposed by the right to development in Africa (2.2). On this account, discussion proceeds in section 3 with the compelling obligation to safeguard the right to development dispensation in Africa in terms of the available enforcement mechanisms (3.1) and also in terms of access to remedy and means of redress (3.2). The chapter concludes with a summary remark in section 4.

2 Framework for Implementation

Following Radin and Singer's theorisation of pragmatism as entailing a results-oriented application of the actual functioning of the law in particular circumstances and within specific contexts,[6] the discussion in this section is intended to identify the range of legal instruments from which the right to development in Africa derives normative force. Unlike within the development cooperation framework where outcomes are unpredictable, the right to development guarantees that through enforcement the rule of law may be applied, justice and equity may prevail and human well-being may consequently be achieved. In view of the commitment to pay particular attention to the right to development necessitating legislative and a broad range of other measures,[7] presupposing a context that is described here as a *right to development dispensation*, the analysis explores to what extent Africa has advanced in this regard.

2.1 *Right to Development Dispensation*

Right to development dispensation refers to the context establish by law in Africa and envisaged to achieve socio-economic and cultural development as a pre-requisite for the enjoyment of civil and political rights. In principle it combines both the political (in terms of policy making) and the legal (in terms of regulation) dimensions for creating development. For the purpose of clarity, the right to development dispensation should be understood as necessitating a combination of the political and the legal commitments in regulating the development processes in Africa as discussed in the subsections that follow.

---

6 See Radin, *supra* note 5, 1700; Singer, *supra* note 5, 1821–1822.

7 African Charter, *supra* note 3 preamble, art 22 & art 1; UN Millennium Declaration Resolution A/55/L.2 adopted by the General Assembly on 8 September 2000 preamble.

2.1.1 Soft Law Provisions on the Right to Development

The soft law instruments that make provision for the right to development embody a moral undertaking by member states of the African Union (AU), which represents an expression of political will absent which consolidated action may not be taken to ensure that development is prioritised as a human right. During the process of adopting the Declaration on the Right to Development in 1986, while the United States (US) voted against and eight European and Asian countries abstained, all African countries voted in favour of the Declaration.[8] The collective response demonstrated a shared conviction of the relevance of the right to development to Africa. At the 1992 Rio Summit, all participating African states voted for the adoption of the Declaration on the Environment and Development, thereby committing to the fulfilment of the right to development contained therein as part of global efforts to achieve sustainable development.[9]

By joining ranks with the rest of the world in adopting the Vienna Declaration, which reaffirms the universality, inalienability and fundamentality of the right to development, all African states commit to ensure its implementation at domestic level so as to meet in an equitable manner the development needs of present and future generations.[10] The political commitment to ensure that the right to development is translated into reality was also unanimously undertaken under the Millennium Declaration by all participating African states, which committed to the domestic implementation of the set of eight time-bound goals intended to achieve socio-economic and cultural development.[11] Joining forces with the rest of the world again in adopting the Durban Declaration in 2001, all participating African states further reaffirmed their solemn commitment to ensure universal respect for all human rights, including the right to development as a necessary step towards eliminating obstacles to development.[12] Relating to specific categories of persons, African states collectively committed under the 2007 Declaration on the Rights of

---

8   Kamga, Serges A.D. "Human rights in Africa: Prospects for the realisation of the right to development under the New Partnership for Africa's Development" (Doctoral Thesis, University of Pretoria, 2011) 147.

9   Rio Declaration on Environment and Development adopted at the UN Conference on Environment and Development Rio de Janeiro 3–14 June 1992 principle 3.

10   Vienna Declaration and Programme of Action adopted by the UN World Conference on Human Rights UN Doc A/CONF.157/24 25 June 1993 paras I(10) & (11).

11   Millennium Declaration, *supra* note 7 paras 11 & 24.

12   Durban Declaration adopted at the World Conference against Racism, Racial Discrimination, Xenophobia and Related Intolerance held in Durban 31 August – 8 September 2001 para 78.

SOCIO-ECONOMIC AND CULTURAL SELF-DETERMINATION

Indigenous Peoples to protect the right to development for indigenous populations in Africa.[13]

As an indication of the commitment to ensure that the promises undertaken at international level become effective at domestic level, similar commitments have been reiterated at the continental level as an auto-reminder to African governments to take the right to development seriously. At the Ministerial Conference on Human Rights held in Mauritius and Kigali, the African Commission requested all member states to adopt adequate strategies to give effect to the right to development.[14] The Grand Bay Declaration calls the attention of member states to the fact that the right to development is universally acknowledged as an inalienable and fundamental human right and therefore must be taken seriously in Africa.[15] The Kigali Declaration further reaffirms that there is indeed a right to development in Africa, which in accordance with the international law requirement for development cooperation, necessitates the support of the international community to ensure its realisation.[16] The Solemn Declaration on Gender Equality also highlights the need to promote and protect the right to development for women and girls in Africa.[17] Owing to resistance in recognising socio-economic and cultural rights, resulting in the exclusion of the majority of African peoples from the entitlement to well-being, governments undertook another solemn commitment under the Pretoria Declaration to ensure the implementation of the full range of human and peoples' rights, including the right to development enshrined in the African Charter.[18] As a follow up to these commitments, the preamble to the Charter on Democracy, Elections and Good Governance underscores the need to promote the right to development.[19] This is based on the acknowledgement in the New Partnership for Africa's Development (NEPAD) Declaration

---

13   UN Declaration on the Rights of Indigenous Peoples Resolution 61/295 adopted by the General Assembly on 13 September 2007 arts 21 & 23.

14   Report of the Meeting of Experts of the First Ministerial Conference on Human Rights in Africa Kigali 5–6 May 2003 EXP/CONF/HRA/RPT(II) para 42.

15   Grand Bay Declaration and Plan of Action adopted by the First OAU Ministerial Conference on Human Rights held in Grand Bay April 1999 para 2.

16   Kigali Declaration adopted by the AU Ministerial Conference on Human Rights in Africa held in Kigali May 2003 para 3.

17   Solemn Declaration on Gender Equality in Africa adopted by the AU Assembly of Heads of State and Government in Addis Ababa July 2004 para 6.

18   Pretoria Declaration on Economic, Social and Cultural Rights in Africa adopted by the African Commission at its 36th Session December 2004 preamble & para 1.

19   African Charter on Democracy, Elections and Governance adopted in Addis Ababa 30 January 2007 preamble.

that "development is impossible in the absence of true democracy, respect for human rights, peace and good governance".[20]

These commitments together with the right to self-determination entitle the peoples of Africa to freely *exercise* the right to development in accordance with the obligation imposed on their respective states to make it possible to do so. By employing the term *exercise* the Charter envisages concrete action in the sense that the political will to do must be accompanied by practical measures as a guarantee that development will be sustained as embodied in this excerpt:

> We affirm that Africa's development is the responsibility of our governments and people. We are now more than before determined to lay a solid foundation for self-reliant human-centred and sustainable development on the basis of social justice and collective self-reliance so as to achieve accelerated structural transformation of our economies.[21]

It is important to note that the realisation of the right to development as it is enshrined in the range of African treaty instruments remains a matter of engaging in policy reforms and therefore, as stated in the introductory part of chapter two, does not raise any legal question. The law becomes implicated when the right to socio-economic and cultural development is threatened or when a violation is established to have been committed. Because this book focuses on interrogating the determinants of development cooperation for the realisation of the right to development, the discussion in this chapter combines the legal and policy dimensions for the reason as shown in the previous chapters that the right to development is conceived to redress endemic injustices and to ensure improvement in the well-being and living standards of the African peoples.

Although the right to development is envisaged to be achieved through cooperation, it is clear from historical evidence that Africa's relationship with foreign stakeholders has more often than not endangered the right to development, necessitating recourse to the law to ensure equity and justice in the development process.[22] This is not to say, as Isabelle Roger rightly asserts that

---

20   New Partnership for Africa's Development (NEPAD) Declaration adopted as a Programme of the AU at the Lusaka Summit (2001) para 79.

21   Speech of the patron of the Thabo Mbeki Foundation, Thabo Mbeki at the "Africa arise summit": University of the Free State Bloemfontein 20 August 2011.

22   Okafor, Obiora C. "A regional perspective: Article 22 of the African Charter on Human and Peoples' Rights" in UN Human Rights *Realizing the Right to Development: Essays in Commemoration of 25 Years of the United Nations Declaration on the Right to Development* (Geneva: UN Publication, 2013) 374; Odinkalu, Chidi A. "Analysis of paralysis or paralysis by

efforts to create development should become completely reliant on the law and legal processes.[23] Arjun Sengupta has cautioned that it is inappropriate to think that the right to development cannot be invoked if it is not legally enforceable.[24] Acceptably, the right to development can more effectively be accomplished through political than judicial processes.[25] However, for the purposes of this book, it is important to emphasise the fact that the right to development dispensation is established by law, which necessitates a scrutiny of the African treaty instruments that enshrine the right to development.

2.1.2 African Treaty Provisions on the Right to Development

One of the preambular convictions on which the African Charter is founded is that it is "essential to pay particular attention to the right to development".[26] The Charter came into force in October 1986 and has to date been ratified by all fifty five AU member states, with the exception of Morocco, which officially is not a member state of the AU.[27] As Chinedu Okafor rightly observes, the African Charter remains the pioneer treaty instrument to give the right to development the force of positive law with binding effect.[28] Accordingly, it sets obligatory standards that state parties are duty-bound to comply with.[29] This is explained by 1) the commitment to eradicate foreign domination that has impoverished and dispossessed the African peoples of the capabilities to shape their own development future,[30] 2) the need to further the struggles for

---

     analysis?: Implementing economic, social, and cultural rights under the African Charter on Human and Peoples' Rights" (2001) 23:2 *Hum Rts Qtly* 347; An agenda for development: Report of the Secretary-General (A/48/935) para 3.

23   Roger, Isabelle "Le droit au développement comme droit de l'homme: Genèse et concept" (Mémoire, Instituts D'Etudes Politiques de Lyon, 2003) 9.

24   Sengupta, Arjun "On the theory and practice of the right to development" (2002) 24:4 *Hum Rts Qtly* 859–860.

25   Sengupta 2002, *supra* note 24, 860.

26   African Charter, *supra* note 3, preamble.

27   Centre for Human Rights *A Guide to the African Human Rights System: Celebrating 30 Years since the entry into force of the African Charter on Human and Peoples' Rights 1986–2016* (Pretoria: Pretoria University Law Press, 2016) 3.

28   Okafor, Obiora C. " 'Righting' the right to development: A socio-legal analysis of article 22 of the African Charter on Human and Peoples' Rights" in Marks, Stephen P. (ed) *Implementing the Right to Development: The Role of International Law* (Geneva: Friedrich-Ebert-Stiftung, 2008) 52.

29   Kamga, Serges A.D. "The right to development in the African human rights system: The *Endorois* case" (2011) 44:2 *De Jure* 386.

30   Eckel, Jan "Human rights and decolonization: New perspectives and open questions" (2010) *Essay-Reviews* 111.

political independence, human dignity and economic emancipation,[31] and 3), the necessity to redress the effects of global coloniality that impacts negatively on the human condition in Africa.[32]

While the African Charter remains the most authoritative normative instrument on the protection of the right to development in Africa, other ancillary instruments (discussed below) also enshrine the right to development, specifically to certain groups of persons,[33] as well as the AU Constitutive Act, which as a framework of laws and principles that govern Africa, paves the direction for human and peoples' rights protection within the continent.[34]

2.1.2.1 *African Charter – Article 22*

The African Charter remains the pioneer treaty instrument that "sanctions the right to development as a human right".[35] Among the continuum of human and peoples' rights recognised and protected by the Charter is the article 22 provision on the right to development, which as Bience Gawanas reiterates, deserves particular attention.[36] The right to development needs prioritising because as a composite of all human rights, it constitutes the mechanism by which justice may be established to protect the African peoples from continuous development injustices. The preamble to the Charter highlights that the right to development provides the opportunity for safeguarding not only socio-economic and cultural entitlements but also civil and political liberties. Accordingly, although article 22 focuses on socio-economic and cultural development because of its relevance in guaranteeing sustainable livelihood in Africa, it does not exclude the reading of civil and political development into the same provision.

---

31   Constitutive Act of the African Union adopted in Lomé Togo on 11 July 2000 art 3.

32   Haüsermann, Julia "A human rights approach to development: Some practical implications for WaterAid's work" (1999) *Rights & Humanity* 20.

33   African Youth Charter adopted in Banjul The Gambia on 2 July 2006 art 10; Protocol to the African Charter on Human and Peoples' Rights on the Rights of Women in Africa adopted in Maputo Mozambique on 11 July 2003 art 19.

34   See AU Constitutive Act, *supra* note 31.

35   Resolution on the African Commission on Human and Peoples' Rights 29th Ordinary Session of the Assembly of Heads of States and Governments of the Organisation of African Unity Cairo Egypt 28–30 June 1993; Murray, Rachel *Human Rights in Africa: From the OAU to the African Union* (Cambridge: Cambridge University Press, 2004) 241.

36   Gawanas, Bience "The African Union: Concepts and implementation mechanisms relating to human rights" in Bosl, Anton & Diescho, Joseph (eds) *Human Rights in Africa: Legal Perspectives on their Protection and Promotion* (Windhoek: Macmillan Education Namibia, 2009) 136.

SOCIO-ECONOMIC AND CULTURAL SELF-DETERMINATION

Civil and political development has an important role to play in guaranteeing effective governance, the rule of law as well as equity and justice for the realisation of the right to development. A fuller understanding of the entitlements that article 22 guarantees and the obligations that it imposes needs to be situated within the broader context of the range of human and peoples' rights contained in the Charter and associated human rights instruments. As such, civil and political development could be read into article 22, deduced from the assurance that the right to development must be exercised "with due regard to [the peoples'] freedom and dignity". This could be understood to refer to the liberties that permit the African peoples to enjoy improved well-being with dignity. The preamble also assures that when socio-economic and cultural rights are fulfilled, the enjoyment of civil and political rights is accordingly guaranteed. This may further be explained by the fact that the Charter elaborately protects the totality of human and peoples' rights without dissociating them into generations of rights.[37]

Owing to its composite nature, the right to development in Africa cannot be interpreted to focus exclusively on the achievement of economic, social and cultural development. Depending on the circumstances, failure to achieve socio-economic and cultural development may also mean deprivation of the liberty to enjoy civil and political rights, which would directly imply, in keeping with Amartya Sen's conception of development as freedom, a denial of the freedom to enjoy the right to development.[38] Development in this instance, according to Sen, is conceptualised as a process of expanding the real human freedoms that people enjoy, the actual determinants of which are the socio-economic and cultural arrangements in society, in combination with the exercise of civil and political rights.[39]

The African Charter identifies peoples as the primary beneficiaries of the right to development and conveys the fact that socio-economic and cultural development is a collective right that they are entitled to exercise and enjoyed in freedom and dignity.[40] The Charter further attributes to the right

---

37 Human rights are generally classified into three generations, namely; the first generation consisting of civil and political rights, the second generation consisting of socio-economic and cultural rights and the third generation consisting of solidarity or group rights.

38 Sen, Amartya *Development As Freedom* (Oxford: Oxford University Press, 1999) 15–16; see also Quane, Helen "A further dimension to the interdependence and indivisibility of human rights?: Recent developments concerning the rights of indigenous Peoples" (2012) 25:1 *Harvard Hum Rts J* 49.

39 Sen, *supra* note 38, 13–18.

40 African Charter, *supra* note 3, art 22(1).

162   CHAPTER 4

to development an uncommon component, which includes "the equal enjoyment of the common heritage".[41] The "common heritage" principle is understood in international law as establishing the rule that certain resources are
common assets of communal ownership to be utilised for the mutual benefit of present as well as future generations.[42] The common heritage principle
embodies the idea of sovereignty over natural wealth and resources as stated
in the Declaration on the Right to Development.[43] Associating the common
heritage principle to the right to development implies that Africa's resources
constitute a communal legacy that must be distributed equitably for the collective benefit of all the peoples of Africa.[44]

From this viewpoint, article 22 would be interpreted to mean that the right
to development imposes an obligation to manage and redistribute Africa's
wealth and resources sustainably for the benefit of the continent's present
and future generations. This explains why article 22(2) enjoins state parties to
individually or collectively ensure that the right to development is achieved.
Paradoxically, the African resource-base has over the decades suffered wanton
and abusive exploitation to serve private and especially imperialist interests
while the standard of living of the African peoples continues to deteriorate.
This supports the argument in favour of diverting focus from development
cooperation to conceptualising the right to development as a development
model to ensure that Africa's resource potential is judiciously utilised to the
benefit of the African peoples. It is worth noting that article 22 does not make
provision for recourse to international cooperation for the realisation of the
right to development, apparently as a precautionary measure against foreign
domination, which the African Charter denounces.[45] Owing to the need to pay

41   As above.
42   Larschan, Bradley & Brennan, Bonnie C. "The common heritage of mankind principle
      in international law" (1983) 21:2 *Columbia J Trans L* 305–312; Noyes, John "The common
      heritage of mankind: Past, present and future" (2012) 40:1–3 *Denver J Int'l L & Pol* 449–450;
      Shackelford, Scott J. "The tragedy of the common heritage of mankind" (2007) 27 *Stanford
      Envt'l L J* 102–104; Wolfrum, Rüdiger "The principle of the common heritage of mankind"
      (1983) *Max-Planck-Institutfür Ausländisches Öffentliches Recht und Völkerrecht* 313; Taylor,
      Prue "The common heritage of mankind: A bold doctrine kept within strict boundaries"
      available at: http://wealthofthecommons.org/essay/common-heritage-mankind-bold
      -doctrine-kept-within-strict-boundaries (accessed: 24 April 2015).
43   Declaration on the Right to Development, *supra* note 3, art 1(2).
44   Roe, Dilys; Nelson, Fred & Sandbrook, C. *Communities as Resource Management
      Institutions: Impact, Experiences and New Directions* (London: International Institute for
      Environment and Development, 2009) 5–12.
45   African Charter, *supra* note 3, arts 19. Article 19 stipulates that "[a]ll peoples shall be equal;
      they shall enjoy the same respect and shall have the same rights. Nothing shall justify the
      domination of a people by another".

SOCIO-ECONOMIC AND CULTURAL SELF-DETERMINATION 163

attention to the right to development in Africa, if justice in development is to prevail, legal action must proceed where a violation is alleged. This is guaranteed in principle by the fact that access to judicial remedies is envisaged under the measures of safeguard and procedural rules provided for by the Charter,[46] although this is yet to become actual practice in law.

2.1.2.2 *Protocol on the Rights of Women in Africa – Article 19*

It is acknowledged that women make up the cornerstone for development in Africa.[47] Consequently, the Protocol on the Rights of Women gives specific recognition to women's right to sustainable development as a justiciable entitlement.[48] It states that:

> Women shall have the right to fully enjoy their right to sustainable development, in respect of which state parties are required to take appropriate measures to introduce gender perspectives in national development planning, ensure the active participation of women in the development process and in the sharing of the benefits of development.[49]

The binding nature of the Protocol imposes legal obligations on state parties to ensure through all appropriate measures that the standards for sustainable development guaranteed to all the women of Africa are adequately captured in national development policies and programmes as a guarantee of they would effectively be realised. It entails gender-responsive action to ensure improvement in the well-being of African women, importantly because they bear the brunt of development injustices due to their subjugated roles in the largely patriarchal African societies.[50] The entitlement to sustainable development literally means that present and future generations of African women can henceforth enjoy better living standards.

Owing to African women's marginalised status, the standards established for the realisation of their right to sustainable development entail their active

---

46 African Charter, *supra* note 3, arts 30 & 46–61.

47 OECD "Women in Africa" available at: http://www.oecd.org/dev/poverty/womeninafrica .htm (accessed: 3 July 2016).

48 Protocol on the Rights of Women, *supra* note 33, art 19.

49 As above, art 19.

50 Meena, Ruth "Women and sustainable development" available at: http:// www.un-ngls.org/orf/documents/publications.en/voices.africa/number5/vfa5.07.htm (accessed: 16 December 2017); Assefa, A. Getachew "The impact of the African Charter on Human and Peoples' Rights and the Protocol on the Rights of Women on the South African judiciary" (Masters Dissertation, University of Western Cape, 2011) 16–17.

contribution to and equitable sharing of the benefits deriving from the development process, leveraging their agency and leadership and an enabling gender-equitable framework for development.[51] Gender equality and women's empowerment are central to economic and human development in every country, not just in terms of integrating women into the development process but in ensuring that they influence the broader development agenda.[52] It is more so, because, inequalities and unjust discriminatory practices inhibit development not only for women, but for society as a whole.[53] The right to sustainable development provides a more definitive and expanded scope for achieving gender equality, which in itself is fundamentally abstract and lacks specificity as to how it is envisaged to add value to the living standards of women in Africa. It guarantees that the development challenges that impact on women are approached not only from a gender point of view but importantly from the point of view of the opportunities for development that are entitled to all peoples without gender considerations.

Although development cooperation, which constitutes one of the focal points of this book, may not have a direct bearing on the women of Africa, inequalities that are generated and sustained through the processes of development cooperation affect African women negatively and are thus anathema to their right to sustainable development. According to Harcourt, the inequalities that impede women's rights to sustainable development can only be redressed through concrete measures that promote gender equality and women's rights in all their dimensions as a prerequisite for achieving sustainable development outcomes for Africa.[54] It involves tackling global inequalities perpetuated through development cooperation and the discriminatory practices engrained in the patriarchal cultures in African societies that hinder the advancement of women.[55] As a treaty provision, the right to sustainable development

---

51 UN Women "The future women want: A vision of sustainable development for all" (2012) *UN Women* 37–38.

52 UN Human Rights "The right to development and gender" *Information Note* 1.

53 UNOHCHR "TST issues brief: Human rights including the right to development" *Joint Issue Brief* available at: https://sustainabledevelopment.un.org/content/documents/2391TST%20Human%20Rights%20Issues%20Brief_FINAL.pdf (accessed: 20 October 2016).

54 Harcourt, Wendy "Gender equality and development effectiveness" (2011) *Open Forum for CSO Development Effective* 3; Arbour, Louise "Using human rights to reduce poverty" in Ingram, Joseph K. & Freestone, David (eds) *Human Rights and Development* (Washington DC: World Bank Institute, 2006) 6; Declaration on the Right to Development, *supra* note 3, art 8(1).

55 Harcourt, *supra* note 54, 3; Istanbul Principles for CSO Development Effectiveness adopted by the First Global Assembly of the Open Forum (2010) principle 2.

SOCIO-ECONOMIC AND CULTURAL SELF-DETERMINATION 165

empowers African women with the liberty to demand accountability when the composite of rights which they are legitimately entitled to is threatened.

2.1.2.3 African Youth Charter – Article 10

Constituting over 60 per cent of the African population, the Africa's youth population is recognised as the most important pillar for development[56] and thus are granted special protection under the African Youth Charter. Besides dealing generally with matters of youth empowerment the African Youth Charter also recognises their right to development.[57] As a legally binding document, the Charter imposes an obligation on state parties to create the possibilities for expanded opportunities for development for all the youths of Africa.[58] The provision on the right to development particularly underscores the fact that state parties must create the conditions necessary for the youth of Africa to exercise without constraint their right to development.[59] The AU highlights that:

> Member States under the Charter are obliged to develop and implement comprehensive, integrated and cross-sectoral Youth Policies and programs with the active involvement of young people. Such policy and program development process needs to be underpinned by the mainstreaming of youth perspectives into broader development goals and priorities, and investing in a meaningful participation and contribution of young people towards Africa's progress and sustenance of current gains.[60]

To achieve this objective requires implementing the Youth Charter provision on the right to development at the domestic level. However, on account of the need for active and meaningful participation in the development process, which demands maximum levels of proficiency to yield desirable outcomes, it

---

56 African Union "African youth decade 2009–2018 plan of action: Accelerating youth empowerment for sustainable development" (2011) *African Union* vii-viii.

57 African Youth Charter, *supra* note 33, art 10, stipulates that:
   1) Every young person shall have the right to social, economic, political and cultural development with due regard to their freedom and identity and in equal enjoyment of the common heritage of mankind.
   2) State parties shall encourage youth organisations to lead youth programmes and to ensure the exercise of the right to development.

58 African Union "African Youth Charter: A framework defining Africa's youth agenda!" available at: http://africa-youth.org/charter (accessed: 13 October 2016); African Union 2011, *supra* note 56, 1.

59 African Youth Charter, *supra* note 33, art 10(1) & (2). See also art 11 on youth participation.

60 African Union 2011, *supra* note 56, 1.

would have been more reasonable if the provision on the right to development in the Youth Charter clearly defined and placed a firm emphasis on the capabilities and skills-set that the youths of Africa should strive to acquire as a guarantee of their productive contribution to actualising the right to development. The Charter rather only talks of encouraging youth organisations to lead youth programmes, which is quite ambiguous and provides no clarity with regard to what the youth organisations and programmes should aim to achieve, and the corresponding capabilities needed to accomplish that purpose.

Given that Africa's development future lies in the hands of the youth, as a first step, ratification and domestication of the Youth Charter is fundamental to ensuring that they are given the opportunity to exercise the right to development as well as the legitimacy to assert claims when the range of entitlements pertaining to that right are threatened or violated.[61] As of June 2019, thirty nine countries have ratified the Youth Charter,[62] which means the right to development among other entitlements guaranteed to the youth may only be enforced by those states that have established their commitment to be bound by the Charter. In spite of this impediment, in the event of a contravention a claim may equally be brought under the umbrella protection provided by article 22 of the African Charter, which has widely been ratified and guarantees the right to development to all the peoples of Africa, including the youths.

While it is important not to ignore the legal angle in certifying enforcement of the right to development for the youths of Africa, it is even more crucial to ensure that domestic governance mechanisms are sufficiently incorporated with systems that equip the youths with the capabilities to contribute productively people-centred development outcomes.

2.1.2.4   *African Union Constitutive Act*

As Hansungule has noted, the adoption of the AU Constitutive Act marked "a major turning point in the quest for development, justice, human rights, the rule of law and good governance" in Africa.[63] Although the Constitutive Act does not expressly enshrine the right to development, it constitutes the basis on which the AU formulates its institutional focus in mainstreaming human

---

61   African Union, *supra* note 58; African Union 2011, *supra* note 56, 1.

62   African Union "List of countries which have signed, ratified/acceded to the African Youth Charter" available at: https://au.int/sites/default/files/treaties/7789-sl-AFRICAN%20 YOUTH%20CHARTER.pdf (accessed: 29 December 2020).

63   Hansungule, Michelo "African courts and the African Commission on Human and Peoples' Rights" in Bosl, Anton & Diescho, Joseph (eds) *Human Rights in Africa–Legal Perspectives on their Protection and Promotion* (Windhoek: Macmillan Education Namibia, 2009) 234.

SOCIO-ECONOMIC AND CULTURAL SELF-DETERMINATION 167

and peoples' rights into development programming.[64] Having attained full ratification, as a constitutive instrument that binds all African states by virtue of membership in the AU, the Act sets the standards for human rights protection and therefore has a normative impact in advancing the right to development in Africa.[65]

The preamble to the Constitutive Act affirms a common identity among African states as a unique framework for collective action in confronting the challenges posed by globalisation, which in conformity with article 22(2) of the African Charter, lays the foundation for collective action for the realisation of the right to development.[66] Additionally, with regard to achieving balanced development, essentially through the pursuit of social justice and the protection of human rights, the Act makes provision for enforcement and access to justice through the African Court,[67] which together with other enforcement mechanisms discussed later, is crucial for protecting the right to development dispensation in Africa.

2.1.3 Constitutional Guarantees

2.1.3.1 *Entrenched Provisions*

Following the recognition and protection of the right to development in the African Charter and ancillary instruments, a number of African countries have proceeded to enshrine the right in their domestic constitutions. Long before the adoption of the African Charter, the preamble to the 1972 Constitution of Cameroon already provided for the right to development. Article 65 stipulates that the preamble forms an integral part of the Constitution, implying that the right to development in Cameroon is established as legally enforceable.[68] A close reading of the right to development in the Constitution of Cameroon indicates that it is not just a claimable entitlement but in effect a development paradigm that the government envisages to pursue to ensure the well-being of its citizens. It underscores the principles of sovereignty, self-determination and as Kamga reiterates, reliance on the country's natural resources as prerequisites for improving the standard of living in the country.[69] Thus, the right to development in Cameroon can be applied not only as a positive right but

---

64   Gawanas, *supra* note 36, 155.
65   Nmehielle, Vincent O. "Development of the African human rights system in the last decade" (2004) 11:3 *Hum Rts Brief* 6.
66   Constitutive Act, *supra* note 31, art 3(j) & (k).
67   Constitutive Act, *supra* note 31, art 18; Hansungule, *supra* note 63, 234.
68   Kamga, *supra* note 8, 204.
69   As above.

also a guiding principle to inform interpretation of the law and development policy making.

Apart from Cameroon, the Constitution of Malawi also provides for the right to development, formulated as an individual and a collective right, implying that it can be claimed by individuals as well as by groups of people within the country.[70] Unlike the African Charter, the Malawian Constitution includes specific categories of beneficiaries, namely women, children and persons with disabilities to whom consideration must be given in view of achieving the right to development.[71] To this end, Kamchedzera and Banda point out that the Malawian government is, as a matter of constitutional obligation, required to take policy and legislative measures to promote the welfare of the people as an indicator of the country's state of human development.[72] Conceived in terms of a development paradigm, the right to development provides the framework for policy reforms by which the government of Malawi could ensure improved standard of living for its people. In contravention of this, as Kamchedzera and Banda further observe, the people of Malawi have practically been deprived of this fundamental right, which has resulted in deterioration in living standards.[73] Accordingly, the peoples of Malawi are entitled to lay claim on the right to development against the state as a constitutional right although this is yet to become a subject of litigation.

The Constitution of the Democratic Republic of Congo (DRC), which has emerged as one of Africa's most progressive in recent times also enshrines the right to development as a constitutional entitlement.[74] It provides that all Congolese people are entitled to benefit from the country's wealth, which the state is obligated to distribute equitably as a guarantee for the enjoyment of the right to development.[75] In spite of this constitutional guarantee and the affluence of mineral and other natural resource deposits, the DRC has not only remained poverty-stricken and underdeveloped, it represents a good example of a state where the people have no sovereign control over their natural resources, lest to talk of redistributing the resources equitably. The DRC is said to be one of the richest countries in the world in terms of natural resource

---

70   Constitution of the Republic of Malawi 1994 art 30.

71   See Heyns & Killander, *supra* note 62, 430 (Malawi ratified the African Charter on 17 November 1989); Constitution of Malawi, *supra* note 71, art 30.

72   Kamchedzera, Garton & Banda, Chikosa U. "The right to development, the quality of rural life and the performance of legislative duties during Malawi's first five years of multiparty politics" (2002) *Research Dissemination Seminar Number Law/2001–2002/001* 1.

73   Kamchedzera & Banda, *supra* note 72, 35–37.

74   Constitution of the Democratic Republic of Congo (DRC) 1996 art 58.

75   Constitution of the DRC, *supra* note 74, art 58.

endowment but has consistently ranked among the most impoverished/least developed with its people languishing in excruciating poverty meanwhile, for decades its resources have been the source of violent conflicts fuelled and perpetuated by foreign extractive multinationals.[76]

Elsewhere on the African continent, the Ethiopian Constitution explicitly enshrines the right to development with an even broader dimension with regard to collectives that are entitled to assert such a right, which include "each Nation, Nationality and People in Ethiopia".[77] The Constitution clearly attributes to all of these constituted communities in Ethiopia the right to "improved living standards", "sustainable development" and "participation in national development" which they are guaranteed to assert and to enjoy as a constitutional entitlement.[78]

Unlike the above cited examples where the constitutions explicitly enshrine the right to development as stand-alone provisions, a few other constitutions provide for the direct application of the provisions of the African Charter as part of domestic law. In Benin, the Constitution allows for direct domestic enforcement of the African Charter, which the state ratified in 1986 and thus incorporated it into domestic law.[79] It provides in article 7 that the rights and duties proclaimed and guaranteed by the Charter constitute an integral part of the Constitution and of Beninese law. These measures provide the assurance that article 22 of the Charter has the same normative force and is legally binding as domestic law, meaning that the people of Benin can legitimately assert the right to development before domestic courts, which would then be required to apply article 22 of the African Charter in adjudicating such a claim.

The Federal Republic of Nigeria has also, through an Act of Parliament domesticated the African Charter to the effect that all the rights contained therein can be invoked in Nigerian courts as part of domestic law.[80] The

---

76　Carpenter, Louisa "Conflict minerals in the Congo: Blood minerals and Africa's underreported first world war" (2012) *Suffolk University – Working Paper* 1–25.

77　Constitution of the Federal Republic of Ethiopia 1994 art 43.

78　As above.

79　Constitution of the Republic of Benin 1990 art 7.

80　African Charter on Human and Peoples' Rights (Ratification and Enforcement) Act No 2 of 1983 – Laws of the Federal Republic of Nigeria on the Enforcement of provisions of African Charter on Human and Peoples' Rights; In the SERAC case at para 41, the African Commission acknowledged the fact that Nigeria has incorporated the African Charter into domestic law, meaning that article 22 of the Charter is directly applicable in Nigeria as a justiciable right and therefore can be invoked by the peoples of Nigeria before the local courts and the courts have the jurisdiction to adjudicate upon and award remedies accordingly.

170   CHAPTER 4

domestication Act actually presents the African Charter as having an overarching status over domestic law within the Nigerian legal system. The Nigerian Supreme Court affirmed this stance in the *Abacha v Fawehinmi* case in which it held that the provisions of the African Charter constitute an integral part of domestic law and therefore, must be enforced by all courts in Nigeria.[81] The Court further explained that in the event of a conflict between the African Charter and a domestic statute, the provisions of the Charter shall prevail over those of the domestic statue based on the reasoning that domestic legislation cannot be seen to breach an international obligation.[82]

2.1.3.2   *Implicit Guarantees*

Following narratives that attribute to provisions of international human rights treaties interpretations that imply the right to development,[83] a number of constitutions in Africa do not explicitly enshrine the right to development but contain provisions that could purposively be read as implying the right to development. Examples include the Constitution of Uganda, which provides for the right to development in a rather cursory manner; not explicitly enshrined on par with other human rights contained in the Constitution but as a directive principle of state policy to be determined and pursued at the discretion of the government.[84] Except where otherwise stated, preambles and directive principles as some scholars have observed, generally do not carry the same normative force as the rights-proclaiming provisions of a constitution.[85] They are often considered only as aspirational goals intended to guide

---

81   *Abacha v Fawehinmi* (2000) FWLR (Pt.4) paras 553 & 586.

82   As above, 586.

83   See Ware, Anthony "Human rights and the right to development: Insights into the Myanmar government's response to rights allegations" (2010) *18th Biennial Conference of the Asian Studies Association of Australia* 3; Kirchmeier, Felix "The right to development– where do we stand?: State of the debate on the right to development" (2006) *Friedrich Ebert Stiftung – Occasional Paper No 23* 6–8; Johnson, Glen M. "The contributions of Eleanor and Franklin Roosevelt to the development of international protection for human rights (1987) 9:1 *Hum Rts Qtly* 36; Alston, Philip "Making space for new human rights: The case of the right to development" (1988) 1 *Hum Rts Yearbk* 5–6.

84   Constitution of the Republic of Uganda 1995 as amended in 2005, national objectives and directive principles of state policy objective ix.

85   Sanni, Abiola "Fundamental Rights Enforcement Procedure Rules 2009 as a tool for the enforcement of the African Charter on Human and Peoples' Rights in Nigeria: The need for far-reaching reform" (2011) 11:2 *AHRLJ* 511; Cissé, Hassane *et al.* (eds) *The World Bank Legal Review Volume 5: Fostering Development through Opportunity, Inclusion and Equity* (Washington, DC: The World Bank, 2014) 572; Chiviru, Theophilous "Socio-economic rights in Zimbabwe's new Constitution" (2014) 36:1 *Strategic Review for Southern Africa* 111.

SOCIO-ECONOMIC AND CULTURAL SELF-DETERMINATION   171

government action in the formulation of policies and therefore, are in most instances not considered justiciable. However, Rukare has made clear that the Ugandan Constitution of 1995 as amended contains a new provision that basically translates the national objectives into justiciable obligations.[86] It means that although the right to development in the Ugandan Constitution is formulated as a directive principle, in effect it has the same force of law as the other human rights provisions and therefore can stand up for adjudication before a domestic court of law.

Other African countries enshrine a broad range of economic, social and cultural rights, the realisation of which, taking from the formulation in article 22(1) of the African Charter may be interpreted to amount to an implicit recognition of the right to development. To cite a few examples, the Constitution of Sao Tome and Principe provides for the rights to work, social security, housing, health care, education and culture.[87] The Constitution of Burkina Faso makes provision for the right of ownership over the country's natural wealth and resources, which must be utilised for ameliorating living standards, and for advancing the rights to education, social security, housing and culture, decent work, and health care.[88] In Zimbabwe, the 2013 Constitution enshrines a provision on national development, which in its convoluted formulation is required to be interpreted as giving rise to the right to development.[89] It states that: "Measures referred to in this section must protect and enhance the right of people, particularly women, to equal opportunity in development".[90] In spite of this guarantee, the reality does not show evidence of an effective right to development practice.[91] The Constitution also enshrines the rights to education, health care, food and water among other socio-economic rights, which however are only recognised as national objectives of state policy.[92]

The Constitution of South Africa contains a comprehensive bill of rights, which besides the range of civil and political rights guarantees, incorporates

---

86   Rukare, Donald "The role of development assistance in the promotion and protection of human rights in Uganda" (Doctoral Thesis, University of Pretoria 2011) 122–123.

87   Sao Tome & Principe's Constitution of 1975 with amendments through 1990 arts 41, 43, 48, 49, 54 & 55.

88   Burkina Faso's Constitution of 1991 with amendments through 2012 arts 14, 18, 19 & 26.

89   Constitution of Zimbabwe Amendment Act No 20 of 2013 sect 13.

90   As above, sect 13(3).

91   See Moyo, Khulekani "Implementing the right to development at the domestic level: A critique of the Zimbabwean Constitution of 2013" in Ngang, Carol C., Kamga, Serges D. & Gumede, Vusi (eds) *Perspectives on the Right to Development* (Pretoria: Pretoria University Law Press, 2018) 255–272.

92   As above, sects 75, 76 & 77; Chiviru, *supra* note 85,112–113.

172   CHAPTER 4

a continuum of livelihood sustainability socio-economic entitlements, which
are envisaged to lead to broad scale transformation of the largely unequal
post-apartheid society.[93] The socio-economic rights provisions could through
a creative interpretation be understood as Shadrack Gutto rightly argues, to
imply that the right to development is implied in the South African constitutional order.[94] This is underscored by the fact that South Africa has ratified the
African Charter and is bound by the right to development enshrined therein,
which the domestic courts are enjoined to apply in order to promote the values
of socio-economic development within the country.[95] Relating to the collective nature that is attributed to the right to development, although the socio-
economic rights in the South African Constitution are mostly individualistic in
nature, they have often been claimed through public interest litigation involving large numbers of individual right holders.[96] Anna-Lena Wolf has described
such an approach as "juridification of the right to development", applied as
a legal argument for the protection of minority and marginalised groups.[97]
Illustrating with the practice of judicial activism in Indian, Wolf explains how
the right to development is interpreted as part of article 21 on the right to life in
the Indian Constitution.[98] Accordingly, a purposive reading of article 39(1)(b)
requiring South African courts to consider international law when interpreting
the bill of rights implies that article 22 of the African Charter could be invoked
to justify application of the right to development in South Africa.

For the states that have ratified the African Charter and also enshrined
socio-economic and cultural rights in their national constitutions, the implicit
constitutional guarantees could be read together with article 22 of the Charter

---

93   Constitution of the Republic of South Africa 1996 sects 26, 27, 29 & 31.
94   Gutto, Shadrack "The right to development: An implied right in South Africa's consti-
      tutional order" in SAHRC *Reflections on Democracy and Human Rights: A Decade of the
      South African Constitution (Act 108 of 1996)* (Cape Town: South African Human Rights
      Commission, 2006) 109–118; see also the First Periodic Report of South Africa to the
      African Commission 38th Ordinary Session 2005 para 325.
95   See Heyns & Killander, *supra* note 62, 430 (South Africa ratified the African Charter on 9
      July 1996); Constitution of South Africa, *supra* note 89, sect 39(1).
96   See for example *Abahlali baseMjondolo Movement SA & Another v Premier of the Province
      of KwaZulu-Natal & Others* 2010 (2) BCLR 99(CC); *Minister of Health & Others v Treatment
      Action Campaign & Others* (1) 2002 10 BLCR 1033 (CC); *Schubart Park & Others v City of
      Tshwane & Another* CCT 23/12 [2012] ZACC 26; *Government of the Republic of South Africa
      v Grootboom & Others* 2000 11 BLCR 1169 (CC); *President of the Republic of South Africa v
      Modderklip Boerdery (Pty) Ltd* 2005 (5) SA 3 (CC).
97   Wolf, Anna-Lena "Juridification of the right to development in India" (2016) 49 *Verfassung
      und Recht in Übersee* VRÜ 184–185.
98   As above.

to impose a legally enforceable right to development at domestic level as mandated by the Charter.[99] This is particularly significant for Africa, to ensure that development is achieved with equity and justice as Sengupta has noted.[100] It is relevant to do so for reasons that the right to that process is recognised as an entitlement to self-determination, which as an essential component in culminating the process of decolonisation and in dissociating from the injustices of imperial domination, it is imperative for Africa to achieve.[101] However, if the commitments undertaken under the various instruments that establish the right to development dispensation as illustrated above are to translate into practice, it is likely to significantly shift the goal-posts within the cooperation framework for development in favour of actual self-determination for Africa. This is further explained in the next section.

2.2 Entitlement to Self-Determination

It is established that the right to development is indeed inbuilt in the right to self-determination, which guarantees the liberty to seek not only political freedoms but importantly to pursue socio-economic and cultural development without restraint.[102] By implication, the right to development can be achieved by asserting the right to self-determination, which is guaranteed to the peoples of Africa as a non-negotiable entitlement that cannot be traded off. The African

---

99   African Charter, *supra* note 3, art 56(6).
100 Sengupta, Arjun "Right to development as a human right" (2001) 36:27 *Econ & Pol Wkly* 2534.
101 Kiwanuka, Richard "The meaning of 'people' in the African Charter on Human and Peoples' Rights" (1988) 82:1 *Am J Int'l L* 95.
102 Charter of the United Nations adopted in San Francisco on 26 June 1945 art 1(2) & 55; Declaration on the Right to Development, *supra* note 3, art 1(2); Vienna Declaration, *supra* note 10, para 1(2); Kamga, *supra* note 8, 131–132; Declaration on the Granting of Independence to Colonial Countries and Peoples adopted by General Assembly Resolution 1514 (XV) 14 December 1960; common art 1 of the ICESCR, *supra* note 3; the International Covenant on Civil and Political Rights (ICCPR) adopted by Gen Ass Res 2200A (XXI) 1966; Declaration on Principles of International Law concerning Friendly Relations and Co-operation among States in accordance with the Charter of the United Nations Resolution 2625 (XXV) adopted by the General Assembly on a Report from the Sixth Committee (A/8082) on 24 October 1970; Declaration on Social Progress and Development adopted by Gen Ass Res 2542 (XXIV) 11 December 1969; Anghie, Anthony "Whose utopia?: Human rights, development and the third world" (2013) 22:1 *Qui Parle: Critical Humanities and Social Sciences* 66; Oloka-Onyango, Joe "Heretical reflections on the right to self-determination: Prospects and problems for a democratic global future in the new millennium" (1999) 15:1 *Am U Int'l L Rev* 166; Udombana, Nsongurua J. "The third world and the right to development: Agenda for the next millennium" (2000) 22:3 *Hum Rts Qtly* 769–770.

Charter provides that the peoples of Africa shall have the "unquestionable and inalienable right to self-determination" and the liberty to assert to determine their political status and to pursue their socio-economic and cultural development in a manner that is apposite to the policies they have freely chosen.[103] As highlighted in chapter two, the right to self-determination provided the opportunity for the attainment of absolute sovereignty, but unfortunately, at the collapse of the colonial project, African states were granted only nominal political independence without socio-economic and cultural autonomy.[104]

Independence allowed the peoples of Africa a free hand over governance, whereas the succeeding neo-colonial dispensation created gaps through which the colonial entrepreneurs retained their exploitative grip on African economies and other aspects of socio-cultural life.[105] Following Amartya Sen's theorisation of development as freedom,[106] it is worth noting that asserting the right to socio-economic and cultural self-determination is central to achieving full autonomy, which the peoples of African were dispossessed of at independence. Development as freedom as implied by the capabilities theory means that with freedom, which according to Bedjaoui is justified by the independence of nations,[107] African countries ought to be able to create the conditions for their peoples to exercise the right to development by performing the human functioning that is necessary to achieve anticipated outcomes of well-being.[108] Besides that, because the right to development in Africa is established by law, its realisation requires as a preliminary measure, compliance with the standards set within the content of the right to development dispensation in Africa.

2.2.1 The Rule of Law

Besides the moral imperative to make the right to development a reality, a binding obligation is attributed to African states to ensure that this is done in accordance with the law.[109] The rule of law guarantees that the peoples

---

103 African Charter, *supra* note 3, art 20(1).

104 Özden, Melik & Golay, Christophe "The right of peoples to self-determination and to permanent sovereignty over their natural resources seen from a human rights perspective" (2010) *CETIM* 1.

105 Ngang, Carol C. "Differentiated responsibilities under international law and the right to development paradigm for developing countries" (2017) 11:2 *HR & ILD* 274.

106 Sen, *supra* note 38, 87–95.

107 Bedjaoui, Mohammed "Some unorthodox reflections on the 'right to development'" in Snyder, Francis G. & Slinn, Peter (eds) *International Law of Development: Comparative Perspectives* (Abingdon: Professional Books, 1987) 93–94.

108 See Sen, *supra* note 38, 95.

109 See African Charter on Democracy, *supra* note 19, art 4(1).

SOCIO-ECONOMIC AND CULTURAL SELF-DETERMINATION 175

of Africa can hold the state to legal accountability and the state can in turn exercise its obligation to regulate the actions of non-state actors to ensure the constant improvement in standard of living, devoid of undue external influences that may prejudice the well-being of the African peoples. For the reason that slavery and colonialism exposed Africa to abuse and exploitation and that such imperialistic practices remain prevalent, compliance with the law in this context includes ensuring that development cooperation, which is by nature paternalistic and therefore problematic to the realisation of the right to development in Africa, is effectively regulated by law. It requires that development cooperation as it is envisaged in the UN Charter is pursued with due respect for the principles of sovereign equality and self-determination of states.[110]

According to Isabella Bunn, the rule of law constitutes a major guiding principle in the advancement of the right to development (although not necessarily achievable only through judicial processes) and as such, to act outside the law undermines this principle.[111] The rule of law entails compliance with the treaties, domestic legislation and other relevant instruments that enshrine the right to development and, therefore, impose obligations to adequately regulate the activities of foreign stakeholders operating within the right to development dispensation in Africa. By this is meant that the right to development creates a primary legal duty that directly implicates the states that have ratified the Charter and are thus, bound by it. When these states default in their obligations on the right to development, they are directly accountable for their actions or inactions. Additionally, Africa has over the decades been the subject of imperial domination, resulting in unjust practices that impede development on the continent. In this light, the need to deal with such injustices imposes a greater obligation on state parties to the African Charter and ancillary instruments to become even more radical in asserting the right to development as a policy tool by which to protect the peoples of Africa against the excesses that foreign stakeholders often commit with impunity.

This scenario provides the basis for formulating domestic legislation and national development policies that are informed by the right to development governance (discussed in chapter five) as a standard-setting paradigm by which to regulate cooperation agreements and the activities of foreign stakeholders. As David Kennedy notes, the "[r]enewed interest to bring law to bear in the struggle for development offers an opportunity to contest the

---

110   See UN Charter, *supra* note 102, arts 55 & 56.
111   Bunn, Isabella D. "The right to development: Implications for international economic law" (2000) 15:6 *Am U Int'l L Rev* 1460.

distributive choices and market alternatives of development policy-making",[112] which is still largely determined by foreign stakeholders. The economic and political systems of developing countries, as Kennedy further asserts differ from those of developed societies "in ways which encourage *attention to particular legal arrangements* rather than universal economic and political theories" (emphasis added).[113] In accordance, D'Hollander, Marx and Wouters observe that cooperation agreements and international development policy statements have increasingly mainstreamed human rights as a crucial factor in poverty reduction initiatives in developing countries.[114]

Unfortunately, this has not translated into practice, due on the most part to the imbalances and development injustices generated by the global system, which as Cristina Diez identifies, include the financial systems that developed countries operate and the trade agreements that they broker.[115] Attempts, for instance, through the campaign for a New International Economic Order (NIEO) championed by Africa in the 1970s, with the hope to achieve equitable balance within the global system met with substantial resistance by industrialised countries.[116] Considering the excessive, and sometimes abusive influence of foreign stakeholders in the course of their operations in Africa, it is relevant to look at the extent of legal responsibility they may incur for contravening the right to development.

2.2.2   Associated Legal Responsibilities

This section relates to the question of legal responsibility for enforcing the right to development in Africa as a justiciable entitlement and on the basis that impunity ought to be redressed as a prerequisite for genuine sustainable development to take place in Africa.[117] The law envisages not only practical implementation of the right to development as a remedy to the development

---

112   Kennedy, David "The 'rule of law' as development" in Hatchard, John & Perry-Kessaris, Amanda (eds) *Law and Development: Facing Complexities in the 21st Century* (Oregon: Cavendish Publishing Ltd, 2003) 17.

113   As above, 18.

114   D'Hollander, David; Marx, Axel & Wouters, Jan "Integrating human rights in development policy: Mapping donor strategies and practices" (2013) *Leuven Centre for Global Governance Studies – Working Paper No 108* 14.

115   Diez, Cristina "Policy brief and proposals: Common but differentiated responsibilities" (2014) *International Movement ATD Fourth World* 3.

116   Nagan, Winston "The right to development: Importance of human and social capital as human rights issues" (2013) 1:6 *Cadmus Journal* 29; Bunn, *supra* note 112, 1431.

117   Manby, Bronwen "The African Union, NEPAD and human rights: The missing agenda" (2004) 26:4 *Hum Rts Qtly* 1005.

SOCIO-ECONOMIC AND CULTURAL SELF-DETERMINATION   177

challenges that inhibit the enjoyment of a better standard of living,[118] the African Charter actually imposes a duty on state parties to ensure that development is achieved with fairness at the domestic level by ensuring equitable sharing of development gains.[119]

2.2.2.1 Domestic Responsibilities

As established by international law, issues pertaining to human rights remain the primary responsibility of states.[120] The obligation of African states in ensuring the realisation of the right to development is innately not problematic in the sense that the law obligates them to do so. The obligation invokes the positive duties to protect, to promote and to fulfil, which compels state parties to ensure that the peoples of Africa freely exercise their right to socio-economic and cultural development. The duty to protect obliges state parties to take legislative and other measures to safeguard against actions that may contravene the right to development, which entails regulating the activities of non-state actors and accordingly, provision is made for remedial action when a violation is established.[121] When a state defaults in this regard, it assumes a double legal responsibility for its own actions as well as for the actions of the non-state actors that it fails to regulate.[122] The duty to promote enjoins the state to ensure that conditions are made favourable for exercising the right to development.[123] The duty to fulfil creates positive expectations obligating

---

118   Declaration on the Right to Development, *supra* note 3, art 5.

119   African Charter, *supra* note 3, art 22; Declaration on the Right to Development, *supra* note 3, arts 4 & 8. These provisions stipulate that states have the duty to undertake all necessary measures, including the formulation of policies for the realisation of the right to development. The obligation does not exclude taking measures to ensure respect for the right to development as well as assuming legal responsibility when the right to development is violated.

120   Commission on Human rights, Sub-commission on the promotion and protection of human rights 55th Session Agenda Item 4 Distr General E/CN.4/Sub.2/2003/12/Rev 2 26th August 2003.

121   Frankovits, André "Rules to live by: The human rights approach to development" (2002) 17 *PRAXIS-The Fletcher J Dev't Stud* 9; Chirwa, Danwood M. "Toward revitalizing economic, social and cultural rights in Africa: *Social and Economic Rights Action Centre and the Centre for Economic and Social Rights v. Nigeria*" (2002) 10:1 *Hum Rts Brief* 16; *Social and Economic Rights Action Centre (SERAC) & Another v Nigeria* Comm 155/96 (2001) AHRLR 60 (ACHPR 2001) para 46; African Charter, *supra* note 3, art 1; Okafor 2008, *supra* note 28, 60; Maastricht Principles on Extraterritorial Obligations of States in the area of Economic, Social and Cultural Rights adopted by the International Commission of Jurists on 28 September 2011 para 27.

122   See *SERAC, supra* note 121, paras 70-72.

123   Chirwa 2002, *supra* note 121, 16; Frankovits, *supra* note 121, 9.

178 CHAPTER 4

state parties to take concrete action or to make substantial efforts towards the realisation of the right to development.[124] It entails measures to ensure that substantive development is achieved through the provision of goods and services to satisfy requirements for an improved standard of living.

Following the standards of human rights law and the obligations imposed by the legal instruments discussed above, it is the incontestable duty of African states to ensure that these duties are accomplished at domestic level, not excluding the obligation to remedy violations perpetuated either by the state or by non-state actors.[125] The African Commission established in the *SERAC* case that the full enjoyment of some rights requires the state to take concerted action consisting of more than one of the above-mentioned duties.[126] The Maastricht Guidelines hold that a violation can occur through the direct action of the state or other entities that are insufficiently regulated by the state.[127] On the basis of this principle, the African Commission held that because the Nigerian government failed to regulate the activities of Shell Corporation, it was accordingly, liable to remedy the human rights violations resulting therefrom.[128]

States are therefore, by default, bound by the duty to protect human rights, including against violations committed by non-state actors, which means that when they fail in this obligation they are directly accountable. The state would be considered to contravene its obligations under the Charter by engaging in wrongful action or by failing to regulate interventions that turn out to be detrimental to entrenched rights.[129] By this, an even greater duty is imposed on African states to not only take legislative but also regulatory measures to ensure that the right to development is not violated by foreign stakeholders and non-state actors, which have continued to do so with impunity. In respect of the Constitutive Act of the African Union that enshrines as one of its principles to reject impunity on the continent,[130] there is no reason why liability cannot be imputed to foreign stakeholders that contravene the right to development in Africa.

---

124 Frankovits, *supra* note 121, 9; Chirwa 2002, *supra* note 121, 16.
125 See *SERAC* case, *supra* note 121, paras 57-72; Maastricht Guidelines on Violations of Economic, Social and Cultural Rights adopted by the International Commission of Jurists 26 January 1997 para 12.
126 *SERAC* case, *supra* note 121, para 48; Chirwa 2002, *supra* note 121, 16.
127 Maastricht Guidelines, *supra* note 125, para 14.
128 *SERAC* case, *supra* note 121, paras 43-72; Kamga, *supra* note 29, 387.
129 Chirwa 2002, *supra* note 121, 16.
130 AU Constitutive Act, *supra* note 32, art 5(o).

SOCIO-ECONOMIC AND CULTURAL SELF-DETERMINATION 179

As a general principle of human rights law, states have the duty to regulate the actions of non-state actors to ensure that they do not violate established rights within their domestic jurisdiction. This is embodied in the duty to protect, which in accordance with the African Charter enjoins state parties to "adopt legislative and other measures" to guard against possible contraventions.[131] As part of the duty to protect, adopting domestic legislation on the right to development requires states, as a matter of necessity, to impose obligations necessitating foreign stakeholders to abide by human rights standards. This proposition obtains from the fact that their activities in Africa are known to have a severe negative bearing on the enjoyment of human rights, implying that they equally do incur liabilities as explained below.

2.2.2.2   *Liability for Foreign Stakeholders and Non-state Actors*

With regard to the excessive influence of foreign stakeholders and non-state actors, which often dwarfs the role of most African states in protecting human rights,[132] it is of essence to look into the question of the liability of these entities, especially when their actions contravene the right to development in Africa. The on-going debate with regard to the human rights obligations of non-state actors[133] is according to Svensson-McCarthy, still very much in its formative stages and thus may only be considered as *lex ferenda* (the law as it is supposed to be).[134] Conversely, for D'Aspremont *et al.,* the actual concern is no longer whether non-state actors have obligations, or should bear legal responsibility but rather how they should be held legally accountable for wrongful behaviour or when their actions produce harmful outcomes.[135]

---

131   African Charter, *supra* note 3, art 1; Frankovits, *supra* note 121, 16; SERAC case, *supra* note 121, para 46.

132   Chirwa, Danwood M. "In search of philosophical justifications and suitable models for the horizontal application of human rights" (2008) 8:2 *AHRLJ* 294–295.

133   See for example Ronen, Yaël "Human rights obligations of territorial non-state actors" (2013) 46:1 *Cornell Int'l L J* 21–50; Clapman, Andrew *The Human Rights Obligations of Non-State Actors* (New York: Oxford University Press, 2006) 25–58; Danailov, Silvia "The accountability of non-state actors for human rights violations: The special case of transnational corporations" (1998) *Law and Development* 1–74; Cassel, Douglass "Corporate initiatives: A second human rights revolution?" (1996) 19:5 *Fordham Int'l L J* 1963; Clapman, Andrew "The privatisation of human rights" (1995) Launce Issue *Eur Hum Rts L Rev* 20.

134   Svensson-McCarthy, Anna-Lena *Human Rights in the Administration of Justice: A Manual on Human Rights for Judges, Prosecutors and Lawyers* (New York/Geneva: UN Publication, 2003) 19.

135   D'Aspremont, Jean *et al.* "Sharing responsibility between non-state actors and states in international law: Introduction" (2015) 62:1 *Neth Int'l L Rev* 50.

The Universal Declaration of Human Rights (UDHR) envisages that "human rights should be protected by the rule of law", requiring recognition and observance not only by states but also by *every organ of society*" (emphasis added).[136] This seems necessarily to imply that rule of law prohibits states as well as non-state actors from acting in violation of universally recognised human rights. An organ of society would be understood to include foreign stakeholders, which as "global actors, exert considerable influence on the realisation of economic, social and cultural rights across the world", and should as underscored by the Maastricht Principle be required to abide by universal human rights standards.[137] A number of non-binding instruments have emerged in this regard, providing guidelines on regulating non-state actors and the extraterritorial activities of foreign stakeholders.[138] However, in the absence of any legally binding instrument under international law compelling non-state actors to abide by human rights standards, these actors remain insulated from accountability, which poses a challenge to the effective realisation of the right to development in Africa.

The Maastricht Principles establish that the responsibility of foreign stakeholders derives from "obligations of a global character" that are set out in the UN Charter and human rights instruments to "take action, separately, and jointly through international cooperation" for the realisation of human rights.[139] It includes among others the obligation to refrain from causing harm,[140] applicable in any situation over which foreign stakeholders exercise authority or effective control, "whether or not such control is exercised in accordance with international law".[141] Where a foreign stakeholder is not a subject of international law *per se*, its responsibility resulting from conduct that infringes on human rights becomes attributable to the state that has the

---

136 UN Universal Declaration of Human Rights adopted by General Assembly Resolution 217 A(III) of 10 December 1948 preamble.

137 Maastricht Principles, *supra* note 121, preamble.

138 Nkonge, Christine G. "The right to development under international law: Reflections from the European Union and Nigeria" (Masters Dissertation Central European University2014) 55–65. The instruments in question include; OECD Convention on Combating Bribery of Foreign Public Officials in International Business Transactions and Related Documents 2011; United States Alien Tort Act 1789; UN Guiding Principles on Business and Human Rights: Implementing the United Nations "protect, respect and remedy" Framework adopted by the UN Human Rights Council UN Doc A/HRC/17/L17/31 (2011); ILO's Tripartite Declaration of Principles concerning Multinational Enterprises and Social Policy 2006; Maastricht Principles, *supra* note 121, paras 1-44.

139 Maastricht Principles, *supra* note 121, para 8(b).

140 As above, para 13.

141 As above, para 9(a).

SOCIO-ECONOMIC AND CULTURAL SELF-DETERMINATION   181

obligation to regulate its activities.[142] However, in respect of the violations approach in adjudicating human rights,[143] and the discourse in favour of holding non-state actors legally accountable,[144] Skogly as well as Jean D'Aspremont *et al.* argue that when a violation is alleged involving a foreign stakeholder, legal action should be brought jointly against the state concerned and the foreign stakeholder that perpetrates the violation.[145]

It is worth noting that this would be possible only to the extent that domestic remedies relating to the right to development are available in a specific country. It makes the duty to protect through creating domestic laws that allow joint legal action against the state and foreign stakeholders much more imperative. In this instance, according to the established law of the state concerned, legal action would be permissible in domestic courts, jointly against the state and a foreign corporation, for example that contravenes the right to development within that jurisdiction. Unfortunately, the prevailing context under general international law is yet to allow legal action against non-parties to the treaties that impose obligations for the respect and protection of human rights. Beyond the jurisdiction of the state and domestic law, legal action can only be taken against the state and not against a foreign stakeholder that colludes with the state in contravening the right to development. If Africa is to advance beyond the external pressures exerted by foreign stakeholders, states governments are obligated to proactively assert the right to self-determination in taking appropriate legislative and other measures to protect the right to development.

3   Safeguard Measures

Attention is drawn to the fact that Africa has not only extensively recognised and provided legal protection to the right to development in various instruments; it has indeed also put in place institutional enforcement mechanisms to give effect to the provisions on the right to development as an assurance that victims of violations can legitimately seek redress.[146] These mechanisms,

---

142   As above, paras 12, 24 & 25.

143   Odinkalu, *supra* note 22, 239; Chirwa 2002, *supra* note 121, 15.

144   Chirwa 2002, *supra* note 121, 15; Skinner, Gwynne *et al. The Third Pillar: Access to Judicial Remedies for Human Rights Violations by Transnational Business* (International Corporate Accountability Roundtable, CORE & European Coalition for Corporate Justice, 2013) 4–5.

145   Skogly, Sigrun I. "Global responsibility for human rights" (2009) 29:4 *Oxf J Leg Stud* 832–845; D'Aspremont *et al., supra* note 135, 49–67.

146   Hansungule, *supra* note 63, 233.

which at the continental level include the African Commission and the African Court[147] and at the national levels the range of domestic courts, are mandated to interpret the law and to dispense justice by offering the platform where claims relating to the right to development could be made and adjudicated upon and remedies crafted appropriately. Before moving on to examine the functioning of these mechanisms it is essential, particularly in relation to the behaviour of foreign stakeholders and non-state actors, to first look at the duty incumbent on Africa states to protect the right to development from inappropriate incursion.

3.1   *The Duty to Protect*

Human rights law generally requires as a matter of obligation, besides the duties to respect and to fulfil, for the state to protect its people against potential threats or actual violation of universally recognised human rights. In effect, within the context of Africa, state parties to the African Charter commit in respect of article 1, to "undertake to adopt legislative or other measures" to convert the abstract rights contained therein into substantive entitlements. With evidence of the historical injustices committed against the peoples of Africa as discussed in chapter two, which resulted in the birth of the right to development, a reading of article 1 in consonance with article 22 of the African Charter compels state parties to protect the peoples of Africa against continuous external/foreign domination and exploitation. Danwood Chirwa defines the duty to protect as including the obligation imposed on states to prevent violations that may be committed by individuals or non-state actors.[148] Felix Kirchmeier affirms that because human rights can be violated not only by the state but also by private and non-state actors, the state has a core obligation to protect its peoples from the violations that may be committed by private persons and non-state entities.[149] It requires state parties, in addition to ratifying the African Charter, to proceed, as a matter of legal obligation to domesticate the provision on the right to development by taking adequate legislative and/ or other measures at the national level to ensure the requisite protection to their peoples.

---

147   The African Commission is established by art 30 of the Charter as a measure of safeguard within the African Union to promote human and peoples' rights and ensure their protection in Africa while the African Court is established by additional Protocol to the African Charter adopted on 10 June 1998.

148   Chirwa 2002, *supra* note 121, 17.

149   Kirchmeier, *supra* note 83, 12.

According to Mohammed Bedjaoui, the right to development imposes an *erga omnes* obligation as *a jus cogens* permitting no exception in so far as states obligations are concerned.[150] This is established by case law where, by finding the Kenyan government in violation in the *Endorois* and *Ogiek community* cases (discussed in details below), the African Commission and the African Court respectively underscore the duty of the state to protect, implying an absolute obligation to make conditions favourable to ensure the effective exercise of the right to development.[151] With regard to taking legislative measures at the domestic level, as required by article 1 of the Charter, a handful of countries have indeed, as highlighted earlier in this chapter, explicitly enshrined the right to development in their national constitutions. This is a significant positive step, which guarantees that the states concerned are duty bound by their treaty obligations at the continental level but crucially also by their constitutional obligations at the domestic level to ensure that the people feel protected to set their own development priorities and to drive the development processes.[152]

The duty imputed on states to protect involves, according to a 2010 report in this regard published by the South African Institute for Advanced Constitutional, Public, Human Rights and International Law (SAIFAC), "a consideration of the state's obligations to ensure that third parties, including corporations, do not violate or assist in the violation of the rights in the charter".[153] Providing protection to the peoples of Africa under the regime of the right to development, guarantees that violations of the range of socio-economic and cultural rights as well as civil and political rights can significantly be curbed. However, contrary to the acknowledgement by African state parties as stipulated in the preamble to the Charter, to give the right to development utmost priority, response in this regard has remain comparatively sluggish. Except for additional doctrinaire recognition of the right to development under further declarations and development agendas, which by their nature do not impose any absolute obligations, there is only little evidence, including in the form of

---

150 Bedjaoui, *supra* note 107, 69–86.
151 See Ozoemena, Rita & Hansungule, Michelo "Development as a right in Africa: Changing attitude for the realisation of women's substantive citizenship" (2014) 18 *Law, Democracy and Development* 230; *Centre for Minority Rights Development (Kenya) & Minority Rights Group International on Behalf of Endorois Welfare Council v Kenya* Comm 276/2003 (2009) AHRLR 75 (ACHPR 2009) paras 269-298; *African Commission on Human and Peoples' Rights (Ogiek Community) v Republic of Kenya* (2017) Appl No 006/2012 paras 201-217.
152 *Ogiek Community* case, *supra* note 151, para 212-217.
153 SAIFAC "The state duty to protect, corporate obligations and extra-territorial application in the African regional human rights system" (2010) *SAIFAC* 15.

184   CHAPTER 4

established enforcement mechanisms as a practical measure in guaranteeing protection to the peoples of Africa.

3.2   *Enforcement Mechanisms*

3.2.1   African Commission on Human and Peoples' Rights

The African Commission, as a monitoring mechanism established by the African Charter is bestowed with a two-fold mandate: to promote and to protect human and peoples' rights in Africa.[154] It monitors state parties' compliance with the Charter in ensuring state reporting and adjudicating complaints in accordance with laid down rules of procedure.[155] The mandate to promote represents a less compelling duty, necessitating the Commission to compile states reports on the measures undertaken to implement the Charter provisions; to carry out focused research and to ensure appropriate dissemination of the findings; to encourage the establishment of domestic institutional frameworks; and to provide adequate advice and recommendations to governments.[156] Additionally, the Commission is required to formulate legal standards to guide governments in adopting legislation and policies to ensure effective implementation of the Charter provisions at domestic level.[157]

Of more interest is the Commission's protective mandate, which deserves to be explored more to ensure effective protection of the right to development guaranteed to the peoples of Africa. The Commissions protective mandate is designed to follow applicable principles of law through a complaint procedure.[158] It means that the Commission functions on the basis of complaints brought to its attention by victims of violation or their legal representatives. As Chidi Odinkalu has noted, the Commission's protective mandate follows the "violations approach" through which real-life situations and specific allegations are dealt with.[159] The protective mandate requires first and foremost for the Commission to ensure that precautionary measures are in place to pre-empt violations. When a violation is alleged, the Commission is required to provide appropriate redress by carrying out preliminary investigations and deciding on admissibility of complaints prior to adjudication.[160]

---

154   Benedek, Wolfgang *et al. The Role of Regional Human Rights Mechanisms* (Brussels: European Parliament, 2010) 70; African Charter, *supra* note 3, arts 30 & 45.

155   Heyns, Christof "The African human rights system: In need of reforms?" (2001) 2 *AHRLJ* 155; African Charter, *supra* note 3, art 45.

156   See African Charter, *supra* note 3, art 45(1)(a).

157   As above, art 45(1)(b) & (c).

158   As above, arts 46-62.

159   Odinkalu, *supra* note 22, 239; Chirwa 2002, *supra* note 121, 15.

160   African Charter, *supra* note 3, arts 46-59.

SOCIO-ECONOMIC AND CULTURAL SELF-DETERMINATION   185

The jurisdiction of the African Commission in dealing with cases involving state parties under the right to development dispensation in Africa is not an issue for debate. The Commission has indeed through its nascent jurisprudence established competence in adjudicating on the right to development, illustrated by a number of cases, some of which are discussed below. Although a number of scholars have advanced convincing arguments relating to the fact that non-state parties have an obligation to respect human rights,[161] the question of jurisdiction where they could be held accountable, remains unsettled. Consequently, the peoples of Africa can only increasingly explore the litigation avenues through the African Commission, which may ultimately influence domestic legal reforms to ensure adequate protection of the right to development. For instance, it is reported that the landmark *Endorois* decision has had a huge positive impact in shaping constitutional reforms in Kenya, where greater protection was eventually granted to minority groups unlike was the situation before the case.[162]

3.2.2   African Court on Human and Peoples' Rights

The African Court on Human and Peoples' Rights is created by an additional Protocol to the African Charter "with the authority to issue legally binding and enforceable decisions" to complement and reinforce the protective mandate of the African Commission.[163] According to Christof Heyns, "[t]he ultimate test for any legal system that purports to deal with human rights is the difference it makes to the lives of people".[164] Comparing it by analogy to the European and inter-American human rights systems, Heyns points out that the African Court is charged with the vital role to effect transformation in Africa.[165] Unlike the

---

161   Chirwa 2008, *supra* note 132, 303–311; Ronen, *supra* note 133,21–50; Clapman, *supra* note 133, 25–58; Danailov, *supra* note 133, 1–74; Cassel, *supra* note 133, 1963; Clapman, *supra* note 133, 20; D'Aspremont *et al.*, *supra* note 135, 49–67.

162   Rutin, Yobo "A call to re-evaluate the status of minority and indigenous rights in Kenya: Decision on the Endorois communication before the African Commission on Human and Peoples' Rights" (2010) *Centre for Minority Rights Development* 2.

163   Protocol to the African Charter on Human and Peoples' Rights on the Establishment of an African Court on Human and Peoples' Rights 1998 art 2. The Protocol entered into force on 25 January 2004. The Protocol on the Statute of the African Court of Justice and Human Rights was further adopted at Sharm el-Sheikh Egypt on 1 July 2008; Benedek *et al.*, *supra* note 154, 70.

164   Heyns, *supra* note 155, 156.

165   As above, 166.

relatively weak Commission, the African Court provides assurance for more effective protection of human and peoples' rights.[166]

The Court is in effect established with a wide mandate of jurisdiction to interpret, adjudicate and issue binding rulings on questions of human and peoples' rights.[167] In exercising these functions, the Court passed judgment in the *Ogiek Community* case in 2017 in which it found the Kenyan government in violation of provisions of the Charter, including article 22 on the right to development.[168] This seminal judgment not only upholds the African Commission's decision in the *Endorois* case in affirming the justiciability of the right to development, it also underscores states'' overarching duty to protect as discussed above. In this regard, despite evidence of some enacted legislation by the Kenyan government to ensure the enjoyment of rights in greater freedom, the Court held that those measures do not sufficiently guarantee protection to the Ogiek community.[169] More so, without evidence of haven "taken other measures" as stated in article 1 of the Charter, the Court further found the Kenyan government in violation of its obligation to protect the Ogiek community.[170]

Traditionally, human rights law has been narrowly interpreted as imposing obligations only on states.[171] According to this *lex lata* interpretation, the International Justice Resource Centre underscores the fact that under regional human rights systems "only [s]tates may be held accountable for human rights violations".[172] This current state of the law constitutes a major obstacle to redressing violations of the right to development effectively. In accord with Sigrun Skogly's view, it is argued because of the dominant bearing of their actions on human livelihood, international organisations and multinational corporations should equally be held accountable for human rights violations.[173] Indeed, as Yaël Ronen also rightly puts it, there is "nothing in human rights theory that precludes the imposition of legal obligations on actors other

---

166 Udombana, Nsongurua J. "A harmony or a cacophony? The music of integration in the African treaty and the New Partnership for Africa's Development" (2002) 13:1 *Indiana & Comp L Rev* 46.

167 Protocol on the African Human Rights Court, *supra* note 163, arts 3, 7 & 28; see also Rules of Court 2010 rules, rules 26 & 61; Benedek *et al.*, *supra* note 154, 70.

168 *Ogiek Community* case, *supra* note 151, paras 202-217.

169 As above, para 216.

170 As above, para 217.

171 Gunduz, Canan "Human rights and development: The World Bank's need for a consistent approach" (2004) *Development Studies Institute – Working Paper Series No 04-49* 5.

172 International Justice Resource Centre "Regional systems" available at: http://www.ijrcenter.org/regional/ (accessed: 8 September 2017).

173 Skogly, Sigrun *The Human Rights Obligations of the World Bank and the IMF* (London: Cavendish Publishing, 2001) 50.

than states", which he argues are hardly the only entities that are likely to violate human rights.[174] In addition, the UDHR, which constitutes the foundational instrument of human rights law, envisages that human rights obligations may be imputed to non-state actors.[175] Nevertheless, there are no functional mechanisms under international law through which to enforce human rights norms such as the right to development against non-state actors, except indirectly through domestic laws, which Benedek Wolfgang *et al.* say, have a greater propensity for enforcement through domestic mechanisms, which are more likely to have binding force.[176]

Potentially, the African Court on Human and People's Rights may eventually be replaced by the hybrid African Court of Justice and Human Rights, envisaged to become operational when the requisite number of ratifications is achieved.[177] When the Court ultimately becomes functional, besides dealing with "any question of international law",[178] it is envisaged in accordance with the Malabo Protocol to have an even broader jurisdiction, including criminal jurisdiction in dealing with the corporate liability of multinational corporations operating in Africa.[179]

3.2.3 Domestic Courts of First Instance

With regard to adjudicating cases relating to the right to development in Africa, by stating as one of the admissibility criteria that communications can only be received by the African Commission after complainants must have exhausted local remedies, the African Charter makes clear that domestic courts constitute jurisdictions of first instance.[180] Additionally, the first instance jurisdiction of domestic courts provides the basis for accessing higher jurisdictions such as the African Commission and the African Court. The Charter enshrines the principle that access to the African Commission can only be sanctioned on the basis of the exhaustion of local remedies, unless it is obvious that such remedies do not exist or are inaccessible or ineffective.[181] The procedural

---

174   Ronen, *supra* note 133, 21.
175   Universal Declaration, *supra* note 136, preamble.
176   See Benedek *et al.*, *supra* note 154, 6–7.
177   Protocol on the African Court of Justice and Human Rights, *supra* note 163. The entry into force of the Protocol requires 15 ratifications (art 9). As of date only 5 state parties have complied with ratification.
178   Protocol on the African Court of Justice and Human Rights, *supra* note 163, art 28(d) & (g).
179   Protocol on Amendments to the Protocol on the Statute of the African Court of Justice and Human Rights adopted in Malabo, Equatorial Guinea on 27 June 2014.
180   African Charter, *supra* note 3, para 50 & 56(5).
181   Odinkalu, *supra* note 22, 227; African Charter, *supra* note 3, para 50 & 56(5).

requirement to exhaust local remedies as a prerequisite for admissibility of complaints before the Commission affirms the fact that domestic courts have the first instance jurisdiction to adjudicate on the right to development.

It implies in principle that the domestic law of the state in which a violation is alleged is designated as the applicable law.[182] In this instance, although the state might not have incorporated the right to development into national law, domestic courts, especially in a monist system may not be precluded from invoking the African Charter on the basis of the state's binding commitment to the Charter deriving from ratification. In the *SERAC* case (discussed in detail below) it was held that the requirement to exhaust local remedies is intended first to give domestic courts an opportunity to decide upon cases before they are brought to an international forum and by so doing avoid contradictory judgements at the national and international levels;[183] second, to allow domestic courts to bring to the attention of the government allegations of violation so that the state may have the opportunity to remedy such violations before being called to account by an international tribunal;[184] and third, to ensure that the Commission does not become a tribunal of first instance for cases for which an effective domestic remedy exists.[185] The Commission explained the requirement for the exhaustion of local remedies as implying an obligation to ensure that domestic remedies are not only available but also free of impediments, effective in offering prospects of success and also sufficient in redressing a complaint.[186]

This explains why, in respect of the preambular commitment to pay particular attention to the right to development, it is absolutely required of all state parties to the African Charter to do the domestication ritual not only on account of achieving the right to development at the domestic level but also to ensure that it becomes evenly enforceable across the continent. Failure to do this amounts to abdication of treaty obligations.[187] The rationale for domestication stems from the fact that the right to development provides a consolidated basis for formulating national policies, increases the negotiating capacity of African states *vis-à-vis* foreign stakeholders on important questions relating to

---

182 Skinner *et al.*, *supra* note144, 8.

183 *SERAC* case, *supra* note 121, para 37.

184 As above, para 38.

185 As above, para 39.

186 Odinkalu, *supra* note 22, 237.

187 Ngang, Carol C. "Transgression of human rights in humanitarian emergencies: The case of Somali refugees in Kenya and Zimbabwean asylum-seekers in South Africa" (2015) *Journal of Humanitarian Assistance* 8–9.

development in Africa,[188] allows the peoples of Africa the freedom to exercise their right to development and promotes the liberty to enjoy well-being deriving from the equitable distribution of the benefits of development.[189]

With the liabilities attributable to foreign stakeholders as discussed above, the concern is whether domestic courts have jurisdiction against foreign stakeholders when their actions contravene the right to development within the state? Following Chirwa's argument that African conceptions of human rights impute obligations to non-state actors,[190] it is rational to posit that domestic courts provide the most appropriate jurisdictions for holding these actors accountable for wrongful action on account of the legally binding nature of the decisions of the courts.[191] The South African Constitution for instance, makes provision to the effect that human rights apply vertically as well as horizontal, meaning that domestic courts have jurisdiction not only over the state but equally over non-states actors.[192] This can be achieved either indirectly by invoking human rights through private law litigation or directly by invoking the violation of an entrenched constitutional right, especially based on the "nature of the right, the nature of the duty, the extent of the violation, the nature of the non-state actor, and the relationship between the non-state actor and the victim[s]".[193] The latter approach could be more strategic for claiming the right to development at domestic level if such a provision has been enshrined in the national constitution as a claimable entitlement like in the case of Cameroon, Malawi, the DRC and Ethiopia among others as highlighted earlier. It further justifies the need for African countries to strengthen their domestic laws to ensure that they provide sufficient guarantees to hold non-state actors and foreign stakeholders accountable when their actions contravene right to development standards.

Although the first instance jurisdiction of domestic courts provides the basis for accessing higher jurisdictions as aforementioned, the challenge with regard to cases involving foreign stakeholders is that it might not be possible to go beyond the jurisdiction of domestic courts. This is because the law in its practical application does not provide jurisdiction to regional enforcement mechanisms over external actors that are not parties to regional treaties. It is to be noted that in some instances, particularly concerning inter-state

---

188   Roger, *supra* note 23, 8.

189   Declaration on the Right to Development, *supra* note 3, art 2(3).

190   Chirwa 2008, *supra* note 132, 303.

191   See Benedek *et al.*, *supra* note 154, 6–7.

192   Constitution of South Africa, *supra* note 93, sects 8 & 39; Chirwa 2008, *supra* note 132, 299.

193   Chirwa 2008, *supra* note 132, 308–310.

communications, the requirement to exhaust local remedies as pre-condition for admissibility may not apply. Such is the ruling on admissibility that the African Commission made in the DRC case (discussed below).[194]

3.2.4   National Human Rights Institutions

Considering that the right to development may not only be achieved through the courts and lengthy judicial processes, non-adversarial mechanisms such as national human rights institutions (NHRIs) provide alternative remedy mechanisms, especially to victims of violation who may not want to pursue the path of the law.[195] The Office of the UN High Commissioner for Human Rights describe NHRIs as entities created and funded by the state and forming an integral part of the state apparatus, having a statutory mandate to protect and promote human rights, including a core function authorised by the state to investigate allegations of human rights violations.[196] In 2017 the Network of African National Human Rights Institutions (NANHRI) adopted the Kigali Declaration and Plan of Action, which envisages among others the role of NHRIs in implementing the Sustainable Development Goals and the 2063 African agenda for development at the national level through a human rights-based approach.[197] It is important to highlight that the Kigali Declaration is just a guideline instrument for NHRIs and has no binding effect on any African state government.

As part of the responsibility to promote a human rights-based approach to development, the Declaration adds that NHRIs are required to provide advice to the state, rights-holders and other actors, including by assessing the impact of laws, policies, programmes, national development plans, administrative practices and budgets on the realisation of human rights for all.[198] It also requires NHRIs to facilitate access to justice and provide appropriate redress and remedy for those who experience abuse and violations, including by handling complaints relating to the contravention of rights in the process of development.[199] The argument is made in chapter two that the right to development

---

194   *Democratic Republic of Congo v Burundi, Rwanda & Uganda* (2004) AHRLR 19 (ACHPR 2003) para 63.

195   Maastricht Principles, *supra* note 121, para 40.

196   UN Human Rights *National Human Rights Institutions: History, Principles, Roles and Responsibilities* (New York/Geneva: UN Publication, 2010) 13 &16.

197   Kigali Declaration and Plan of Action on the 2030 Agenda for Sustainable Development and the African Agenda 2063 and the role of National Human Rights Institutions adopted by the Network of African National Human Rights Institutions in Kigali, Rwanda on 9 November 2017 para 11.

198   As above, para 15.

199   As above.

was originally not envisioned to pitch the peoples of Africa in confrontational court battles or activism against their governments but rather as a governance paradigm that is supposed to guide the states in the pursuit of their human rights and development obligations. Instead of the instance where the peoples of Africa have to consistently seek protection through the courts, it is argued that more and more efforts rather need to be invested in promoting the right to development as a model for governance.

The promotion mandate requires NHRIS to serve as useful link in synchronising states' obligations and the aspirations of their populations through informational initiatives to create awareness on the relevance of the right to development in ensuring the realisation of the full range of socio-economic and cultural as well as civil and political rights.[200] The promotion mandate entails ensuring that human rights are respected, protected and fulfilled and essentially that states comply with their obligations under the international and regional treaties they have ratified and the domestic laws they have adopted. The strategic role of NHRIS is vital for instance, in making recommendations to various state organs and authorities for the purpose of shaping the policy direction towards implementation of the right to development as a means to ensure that human rights and development (human well-being) are achieved simultaneously.

Interestingly, the NHRI in Africa have not given sufficient attention or demonstrated the zeal to promote the right to development as they do for other human rights. Because NHRIS are created and mandated by the state, the circumstances under which they operate – under repressive and authoritarian regimes in Africa – raises vital concerns with regard to their efficiency, technical capacity and autonomy in demanding accountability from the governments that create them and more so, whether they actually have any impact in advancing human rights.[201] Apart from broadly playing a human rights custodian role, there is no documented evidence, particularly from those countries that have enshrined the right to development in their national constitutions to show how and to what extent NHRIS promote or provide the platform for its realisation. In the absence of NHRIS playing an active role in promoting the right to development or in enabling the enforcement of legitimate claims

---

200   As above, 21–22 (stating the promotion mandate of NHRIS).
201   Jensen, Stephen; Corkery, Allison & Donald, Kate "Realising rights through the Sustainable Development Goals: The role of national human rights institutions" (2015) *Briefing Paper – Danish Institute for Human Rights & Centre for Economic and Social Rights* 6; Lagoutte, Stéphanie; Kristiansen, Annali & Thonbo, Lisbeth A.N. "Review of literature on national human rights institutions" (2006) *The Danish Institute for Human Rights* 2–3.

192   CHAPTER 4

at the domestic level, victims of violation like in the *Endorois* and the *Ogiek Community* cases have had to pursue their claims through the African human rights system, essentially with the help of non-governmental organisations, necessitating an enquiry into the aspect of access to justice and means of redress.

3.3   *Access to Justice and Means of Redress*
3.3.1   Procedural Considerations

Where due process of the law becomes unavoidable in order to guarantee adequate protection, judicial remedy mechanisms must also be made available and accessible. The existence of domestic courts, particularly in the countries where the right to development has been domesticated, as well as the African Commission and the African Court provide assurance that redress could be sought when a threat or violation of the right to development is alleged to have been committed. Two important questions need to be considered: First, how is access to justice guaranteed to victims of violation? Second, who can bring a complaint alleging a violation of the right to development?

Generally, access to domestic enforcement mechanisms is determined by the domestic law of the state concerned. For instance, the South African Constitution makes provision for generous procedural measures that allow for individual actions as well as representative and public interest actions on behalf of persons to whom access to justice is limited by circumstances beyond their own making.[202] Although as Okogbule argues that redistributive justice is not feasible without access to remedy,[203] the inability to access the courts and to navigate the legal processes owing for example, to the lack of independence of the judiciary in most domestic jurisdictions in Africa explains why litigating the right to development at domestic level might be particularly challenging and therefore also limits access to higher enforcement mechanisms.[204]

---

202   South African Constitution, *supra* note 93, sects 34 & 38.

203   Okogbule, Nlerum S. "Access to justice and human rights protection in Nigeria: Problems and prospects" (2005) 2:3 SUR – *Int'l J Hum Rts* 94–97.

204   See for example, the *Bakweri Land Claims Committee v Cameroon* (2004) AHRLR 43 (ACHPR 2004) paras 28-37 in which the complainants averred political influence over the judiciary and the legal processes in Cameroon as a hindrance to effective domestic remedy. Although the complainants showed prove of seeking redress through political processes, the African Commission refused to entertain their complaint for failing to satisfy the requirement to exhaust local domestic remedies. It begs the question what constitutes domestic remedy? Whether domestic remedy only constitutes legal action? What if the complainants had found redress through the political processes they engaged, would that not have resolved the problem?

With regards to access to the African Commission for remedy, the Charter makes provision for inter-state and other communications that must comply with laid down admissibility criteria.[205] Quite explicitly, inter-state communication refers to a complaint that one state party to the African Charter may bring against another like in the DRC case against Burundi, Uganda and Rwanda.[206] The inference as highlighted in article 2(3) of the Declaration of the Right to Development is that a state is entitled to claim the right to development. With the understanding that the right to development in Africa is guaranteed to collectives and not to individuals, "other communications" would be interpreted to include complaints that may be brought by groups of persons. The Commission's jurisprudence on the right to development illustrates that access to remedy on the grounds of an alleged violation of the right to development is possible through representative action or public interest litigation in the form of legal representation and *amicus curiae* interventions by individuals and civil society organisations on behalf of the peoples concerned.[207] Owing to logistical difficulties, litigating the right to development on behalf of a collective can ensure redress to a large number of victims[208] who might otherwise not have the opportunity to seek justice individually because of the costly and lengthy processes involved.[209]

Unlike the African Commission, access to the African Court is allowed to state parties and accredited non-governmental organisations as well as to individuals whose states have duly recognised the competence of the court.[210] Under the prevailing circumstances, with the high-handedness under which the African peoples are governed, the burden that victims bear to prove their case in most instances makes it difficult to litigate the right to development against the state.[211] The Protocol on the African Human Rights Court makes provision to the effect that when a violation of the right to development is alleged, the state has right of access to the Court to seek redress.[212]

---

205 African Charter, *supra* note 3, arts 47 & 55.

206 See generally DRC case, *supra* note 194.

207 See Ngang, Carol C. "Socio-economic rights litigation: A potential strategy in the struggle for social justice in South Africa" (Masters Dissertation, University of Pretoria, 2013)49.

208 Skinner *et al.*, *supra* note 144, 11.

209 Skinner *et al.*, *supra* note 144, 9; The *Endorois* litigation was instituted by the Centre for Minority Rights Development (CEMIRIDE) and Minority Rights Group International on behalf of the Endorois community, while the *Kevin Gumne* case was brought by 14 individuals on behalf of the peoples of Southern Cameroon.

210 Protocol on the African Human Rights Court, *supra* note 163, art 5.

211 Skinner *et al.*, *supra* note 144, 8.

212 Protocol on the African Human Rights Court, *supra* note 163, art 5(d).

194 CHAPTER 4

3.3.2 Litigation

The right to development has been the subject of litigation in a good number of cases that have dealt comprehensively with legitimate claims on the concept of a human right to socio-economic and cultural development enshrined in the African Charter. This section analysis the following four cases that have been adjudicated by the African Commission and the African Court with the aim to illustrate how and to what extent the right to development in its legal nature as a justiciable human right as discussed in chapter two, is enforceable through litigation. Further to this, the nature of remedies that could be anticipated as a result of asserting the right to development is also examined. The SERAC case is used to show the involvement of a foreign stakeholder in the violations committed against an African (the Ogoni) people.

3.3.2.1 *Social and Economic Rights Action Centre (SERAC) Case*

In 2001, the African Commission issued a milestone ruling in the matter *Social and Economic Rights Action Centre & Another v Nigeria*, which is commonly known as the SERAC case.[213] The case, which dealt with the after effects of environmental degradation caused by Shell Corporation in the Niger Delta region of Nigeria, highlights the important role that African states are obligated to play in protecting the human and peoples' rights enshrined in the African Charter.[214] The litigation originated from the uncontrolled abusive exploitation of crude oil by Shell Corporation in complicity with the Nigerian government in Ogoniland, resulting in massive oil spills that caused severe damage to the environment and therefore adversely affected the livelihood of the Ogoni people. The complaint against the Nigerian government was brought to the African Commission by the Social and Economic Rights Action Centre and the Centre for Economic and Social Rights on behalf of the Ogoni community, alleging violation of a range of socio-economic and environmental rights protected by the African Charter.[215]

Although the alleged violations resulted principally from the operations of Shell Corporation (a non-state actor), it is important to point out as the African Commission noted that Nigeria has ratified and domesticated the African Charter and is thus obligated to comply with the human and peoples' rights provisions contained therein.[216] This creates a legal obligation, which

---

213 SERAC case, *supra* note 121.
214 Kamga, Serges A.D. & Fombad, Charles M. "A critical review of the jurisprudence of the African Commission on the right to development" (2013) 57:2 *Journal of African Law* 14; SERAC case, *supra* note 121, para 57.
215 SERAC case, *supra* note 121, paras 43 & 70.
216 As above, para 41.

SOCIO-ECONOMIC AND CULTURAL SELF-DETERMINATION

Svensson-McCarthy describes as a "*third-party effect*" by which states may incur responsibility for failing to take reasonable action to prevent non-state actors from carrying out acts or engaging in practices that violate human rights, or for failing to "provide adequate protection against such violations under domestic law".[217] In contravention of these standards, the government colluded with Shell Corporation in "the destruction of the Ogoniland" through the abusive exploitation of the people's oil wealth and therefore failed in its duty to exercise due diligence in preventing the violation of established human rights.[218]

The African Commission has rightly been criticised for inconsistency in its adjudication approach.[219] For instance, while the Commission established in the DRC case that the violation of the Congolese peoples' right to dispose of their wealth and natural resources occasioned the violation of the right to development,[220] it failed to apply the same standard in the SERAC case. The Commission found that by failing to adequately protect the Ogoni people, thus allowing a non-state entity to act "freely and with impunity", the Nigerian government acted in violation of its obligations under the African Charter.[221] Although the complaint was not instituted as a right to development litigation *per se*, Kamga and Fombad argue that all the rights alleged to have been violated constitute the building blocks of the right to development, necessitating the Commission to have summarised them into a violation of the right to development.[222] Through a creative interpretation of the law, the Commission established a violation of the right to shelter even though such a provision is not enshrined in the African Charter.[223] It further acknowledged that by violating the right to food, the Nigerian government in complicity with Shell Corporation violated the right to development.[224] Based on these

---

217   Svensson-McCarthy, *supra* note 134, 17; SERAC case, *supra* note 121, para 57.

218   SERAC case, *supra* note 121, para 58; Chirwa 2008, *supra* note 132, 305–306.

219   Olowu, Dejo *An Integrative Rights-Based Approach to Human Development in Africa* (Pretoria: Pretoria University Law Press, 2009) 154; Kamga, *supra* note 29, 391; Yeshanew, Sisay A. "Approaches to the justiciability of economic, social and cultural rights in the jurisprudence of the African Commission on Human and Peoples' Rights: Progress and perspectives" (2011) 11:2 *AHRLJ* 339–340.

220   DRC case, *supra* note 194, para 95.

221   SERAC case, *supra* note 121, paras 57 & 70.

222   Kamga & Fombad, *supra* note 214, 18.

223   SERAC case, *supra* note 121, para 60; Kamga & Fombad, *supra* note 214, 18.

224   SERAC case, *supra* note 121, para 64.

interpretations, it would have been appropriate to pronounce on a violation of the right to development but as Kamga remarks, the Commission avoided doing so.[225]

Considering the relevance of the right to development as a vital instrument by which to establish justice in development within Africa, the Commission might not have been wrong in taking an activist position by explicitly compelling the Nigerian government to cause Shell Corporation to repair the damages it had caused. This is explained by the fact that many multinational corporations like Shell have become so powerful that most states have increasingly lost the capacity to regulate their actions.[226] Accordingly, "[w]here a non-state actor has the capacity to redress the violation itself, it does not make sense to hold the state alone responsible".[227] As Ronen also argues, "to insist solely on the governmental obligations obscures the true nature of the violation; reinforces the corporation's impunity and thus also generates a dangerous sense of impunity for non-state actors that contravene guaranteed rights".[228] However, because of the limitations of the law that insulates non-state actors, such a determination cannot be made under the present dispensation.

3.3.2.2 *Democratic Republic of Congo (DRC) Case*

This case, which is often referred to as the DRC case is the first inter-state communication in which the DRC alleged grave and massive violations of provisions of the African Charter committed in the eastern provinces of the country by the armed forces of Burundi, Rwanda and Uganda.[229] On the merits of the case, the African Commission found the respondent states in violation of a number of rights including the right to development.[230] The Commission applied an expanded interpretation of what would constitute a violation of the right to socio-economic and cultural development. Relating to cultural

---

225   Kamga, *supra* note 29, 389; SERAC case, *supra* note 1221, para 64. In adjudicating the SERAC case the African Commission pointed out that there was in effect a violation of the right to development which the complainants should have evoked but failed to do so.

226   Chirwa, Danwood M. "The doctrine of state responsibility as a potential means of making private actors accountable for human rights" (2004) 5:1 *Melbourne J Int'l L* 26–28 & 33–35; Chirwa 2008, *supra* note 132, 306.

227   Chirwa 2008, *supra* note 132, 307.

228   Ronen, *supra* note 133, 54.

229   DRC case, *supra* note 194, para 2 & 69.

230   As above, para 95; Kwame, Asare L.P. "The justiciability of the right to development in Ghana: Mirage or possibility?" (2016) 1:1 *Strathmore Law Review* 87–88; Sceats, Sonya "Africa's new human rights court: Whistling in the wind?" (2009) *Chatham House–Briefing Paper* 8; Oduwole, Olajumoke "International law and the right to development: A pragmatic approach for Africa" (2014) *International Institute of Social Studies* 15.

development, the Commission established a violation of the Congolese peoples' right to cultural development resulting from the indiscriminate dumping and indecent burial of the massacred Congolese people, which it considered "an affront on the noble virtues of the African historical tradition and values".[231] By this novel interpretation, an attack on peoples' values and virtues would be conceived to constitute a violation of the right to development enshrined in the Charter.

The Commission further found the illegal exploitation and pillaging by Burundi, Rwanda and Uganda as a contravention of the Congolese peoples' right to ownership of their wealth and natural resources as enshrined in article 21 of the Charter.[232] The right to ownership over wealth and natural resources is not expressly stated as a component of article 22 of the Charter but as explicitly stipulated by the Constitution of the DRC and as Kamga and Fombad also rightly indicate, it is associated with the realisation of the right to development.[233] As a justification for linking associated rights to the right to development, the African Commission held that:

> The deprivation of the right of the people of the Democratic Republic of Congo, [...] to freely dispose of their wealth and natural resources, has also occasioned another violation – their right to their economic, social and cultural development and of the general duty of states to individually or collectively ensure the exercise of the right to development, guaranteed under article 22 of the African Charter.[234]

The Commission found Burundi, Rwanda and Uganda in violation of the right to development among others and drew their attention to the need to abide by their treaty obligations under the African Charter as well as under general international law.[235] In terms of remedy, the Commission recommended the respondent states to pay *adequate reparation* to the DRC on behalf of the dispossessed Congolese people.[236] While the Commission's ruling constitutes an important step in advancing the right to development, the abstract nature of the remedy it granted leaves much to be desired in terms of anticipating adequate protection on the right to development through litigation. It would have

---

231   DRC case, *supra* note 194, para 87; Kamga & Fombad, *supra* note 214, 11.
232   Kamga & Fombad, *supra* note 214, 11–12; DRC case, *supra* note 194, para 94-95.
233   Constitution of the DRC, *supra* note 75, art 58; Kamga & Fombad, *supra* note 214, 12.
234   DRC case, *supra* note 194, para 95.
235   Kamga & Fombad, *supra* note 214, 11; DRC case, *supra* note 194, para 95.
236   DRC case, *supra* note 194, para 98.

been more appropriate for the Commission to be a bit more precise as to the nature of reparation for the damages incurred by the victims.

Foreign stakeholders, especially extractive industry multinational corporations are known to be actively involved in similar practices of looting and exploitation of "conflict minerals" in the DRC,[237] which, as the African Commission acknowledged in the *DRC* litigation, occasioned a violation of the right to development.[238] However, no known legal action has been taken against those corporations conceivably because they are not bound by the African Charter that proscribes wrongful behaviour that violates the right to development guaranteed to the peoples of Africa. The Commission ruled against Burundi, Rwanda and Uganda because in effect as state parties to the Charter, they bear direct legal responsibility for their actions which contravened provisions of the Charter. In the *SERAC* litigation, although Shell Corporation's reckless exploitation and deprivation of the Ogoni peoples' right to dispose freely of their wealth and resources came out evidently, the government of Nigeria shouldered the legal responsibility that should have been shared with Shell Corporation. One would wonder whether such a legal bias in favour of foreign stakeholders does not condone impunity.

3.3.2.3   *Endorois Case*

The *Centre for Minority Rights Development & Another v Kenya* case generally referred to as the *Endorois* case remains one of the most celebrated of the African human rights jurisprudence on the right to development as a legally enforceable entitlement.[239] The complaint was filed on behalf of the Endorois community by the Centre for Minority Rights Development and Minority Rights Group International, with *amicus curiae* submissions made by the Centre on Housing Rights and Evictions.[240] The complainants alleged violations of a range of human and peoples' rights perpetuated by the Kenyan government against the indigenous Endorois community.[241] The violations involved the forcible and arbitrary removal of the Endorois peoples from ancestral land that they have inhabited from time immemorial,[242] resulting in disruptions of their

---

237   Petitjean, Olivier "Perenco in the Democratic Republic of Congo: When oil makes the poor poorer" (2014) Multinationals Observatory available at: http://multinationales.org/Perenco-in-the-Democratic-Republic (accessed: 28 October 2016); Report of the Panel of Experts on the Illegal Exploitation of the Natural Resources and other Forms of Wealth of the Democratic Republic of Congo 12 April 2001 UN Doc S/2001/357 6–7.

238   *DRC* case, *supra* note 194, paras 92-95.

239   *Endorois* case, *supra* note 151.

240   As above, para 1.

241   As above, para 144.

242   As above, paras 2-6 & 144.

established functional indigenous systems, patterns of existence, collective well-being and and prospects for sustainable development.[243]

The Endorois are a semi-nomadic community who, from time immemorial had established a sustainable pastoral economy and practiced a cultural lifestyle that intimately connects them to the land in the locality of Lake Bogoria in central Kenya.[244] In their customary understanding of land ownership, they assume exclusive entitlement by right of ancestry to the land in the Lake Bogoria region, which they have accordingly utilised for habitation, cultural practices and ancestral worship.[245] The land in question was expropriated by the Kenyan government in 1973 for the development of a wildlife reserve to boost the tourism industry.[246] The Endorois people were consequently evicted and relocated to an unproductive area and granted only sporadic access to the sites central to their spiritual beliefs.[247]

Promises by the Kenyan government to provide compensation and an equitable share of the proceeds from the conservation project were never fulfilled.[248] The community was further denied access to their ancestral shrines and therefore completely severed from the spiritual and cultural practices that they valued and identified with as a community.[249] After several unsuccessful attempts to secure compensation the Endorois community launched a first instance action against the Kenyan government at the Nakuru High Court.[250] Justice was however, denied as the Court dismissed the Endorois claims without investigating the broader underlying issues.[251] The complainants therefore, approached the African Commission to seek restitution of the Endorois ancestral land and compensation for wrongful displacement.[252]

---

243   As above, paras 144.
244   Kavilu, Shadrack "Indigenous Endorois call for implementation of African Commission ruling on their ancestral land" available at: http://www.galdu.org/web/index.php?odas=5087 (accessed: 12 June 2015).
245   *Endorois* case, *supra* note 151, paras 72-73 & 87.
246   Sing'Oei, Kori "Engaging the leviathan: National development, corporate globalisation and the Endorois quest to recover their herding grounds" in Henrard, Kristin (ed) *The Interrelation between the Right to Identity of Minorities and their Socio-Economic Participation* (Leiden/Boston: Martinus Nijhoff Publishers, 2013) 375.
247   Williams, Rhodri C. "The African Commission "*Endorois* case" – Toward a global doctrine of customary tenure?" available at: http://terraonullius.wordpress.com/2010/02/17/the-african-commission-endorois-case-toward-a-global-doctrine-of-customary-tenure/ (accessed: 2 June 2015).
248   Williams, *supra* note 247.
249   *Endorois* case, *supra* note 151, paras 115 & 124.
250   As above, para 2.
251   Sing'Oei, *supra* note 246, 386.
252   Rutin, *supra* note 162, 1.

The complainants raised a number of arguments in substantiation of the allegations they advanced, including in particular, argument that the Endorois peoples' right to development had been violated as a result of the Kenyan government's failure to involve the community adequately in the development process or to ensure sustained improvement of the community's well-being.[253] They argued that the Kenyan government's decision to force the Endorois peoples to give away their land for the development of a game reserve deprived the community of the opportunity to make a choice, which directly contradicts the component elements of the right to development that entitles peoples to be actively involved, to participate meaningfully in and to benefit equitably from the development process.[254] The complainants further argued that the forceful expropriation of the Endorois ancestral land deprived them of the right to self-determination and the right to dispose of their natural resources as the community would have wished.[255] Lastly, the complainants argued that by failing to embrace a rights-based approach to economic growth, the Kenyan government systematically excluded the Endorois from partaking in the benefits of development and by so doing, impacted negatively on the economic, social and cultural development of the people as a community.[256]

In adjudicating the matter, the African Commission addressed a number of concerns relating to the right to development as a collective entitlement enforceable through judicial processes. Importantly, the Commission helped to clarify the contested concept of "peoples" as holders of the right to development. It ascertained that there is no clear-cut definition of the concept of peoples but in the context of the African Charter it is closely associated with collective rights.[257] The Commission went on to explain the characteristics by which peoples are identified. This includes a common ancestry, self-identification, cultural homogeneity, linguistic unity, religious and ideological affinities, territorial connection and a common economic life or other bonds of common interest.[258] Thus the Commission acknowledged the Endorois community as constituting a *people*, "a status that entitles them to benefit from provisions of the African Charter that protect collective rights".[259] On the basis

---

253 *Endorois* case, *supra* note 151, para 125.
254 As above, paras 126-127; Declaration on the Right to Development, *supra* note 3, arts 1(1), 2(1) & 2(3).
255 As above, paras 126-127.
256 As above, para 125.
257 As above, para 149.
258 As above, para 150-151.
259 As above, para 162; see also *Kevin Mgwanga Gumne & others v Cameroon* Comm 266/2003 (2009) AHRLR 9 (ACHPR 2009) para 179.

SOCIO-ECONOMIC AND CULTURAL SELF-DETERMINATION 201

of this clarification, the African Commission established that the Endorois constitute a people entitled to assert the right to development enshrined in the African Charter.

Besides highlighting some of the core components that are discussed in chapter two, the African Commission had the opportunity to expatiate on the meaning of the right to development in even more concrete terms. It established that the right to development does not imply dependency but an emancipating process that emphasises the importance of choice and the liberty of action in view of the attainment of human well-being.[260] Closely related to the requirement of meaningful participation the *Endorois* decision conveys the fact that it is not economic growth or the welfare of the state economy that matters but peoples' well-being more than anything else. Of course, the wildlife project envisaged by the Kenyan government has potential to fetch huge sums of foreign currency to boost the economy. However, following Sengupta's logic that the right to development would improve if at least one right is improved and none is violated;[261] it can be argued that the wildlife project could only have be considered to advance the right to development if measures were taken to ensure that the lives of the affected peoples simultaneously improved in the process. In essence, the *Endorois* decision promotes and encourages the kind of development that enhances rather than diminishes the choices and capabilities of local communities.[262]

As stated earlier, the article 22 provision of the African Charter is not a stand-alone provision. It is interrelated with other provisions of the Charter, which highlight elements of the right to development. In this regard, the determination made by the African Commission relating to article 17(2) and (3) on the right to culture as an integral part of the right to development is examined. The Commission held that by restricting access to the Endorois ancestral land, the Kenyan government not only denied the community the right to exercise their integrated culture and ancestral spirituality but also deprived them of the right to collective well-being.[263] Accordingly, the decision was reached that the Kenyan government violated article 22 of the African Charter and thus a wide range of remedies were granted to the complainants, including *inter alia* restitution of the Endorois ancestral land, unrestricted access to their cultural and spiritual sites and grazing places, adequate compensation for the damages suffered and equitable sharing in the benefits deriving from the wildlife reserve.[264]

---

260 *Endorois* case, *supra* note 151, para 283; Sing'Oei, *supra* note 246, 395.
261 Sengupta, Arjun "The human right to development" (2004) 32:2 *Oxf Dev't Stud* 183.
262 Sing'Oei, *supra* note 246, 395.
263 *Endorois, supra* note 151, paras 248-250.
264 As above, para 298.

202   CHAPTER 4

Although restitution of the land in question and the payment of damages has not taken place as the Commission ruled, the decision nevertheless reiterates the fact in law that the right of ownership over natural resources belongs to the peoples and not the state and thus, also sets the rule that colonial-style invasion and land grabbing, including by the state is unlawful.

3.3.2.4   *Ogiek Community Case*

The landmark judgment in the *African Commission on Human and Peoples' Rights v The Republic of Kenya* case passed in 2017 is recorded as the first right to development litigation adjudicated by the African Court.[265] It is commonly referred to as the *Ogiek Community* case in the sense that the litigation was instituted by the African Commission on behalf of the Ogiek community of Kenya. The Ogiek people are the most vulnerable and marginalised nomadic hunter gatherer indigenous community with a population size of between 20 000 to 30 000 living in the Mau forest of central Kenya, which they have inhabited for centuries prior to the coming of other settlers and thus, have developed a sentimental attachment to the forest.[266] In spite of their ancestral bond to the forest, the Ogiek people have, dating back to the colonial period, been alienated and denied access to the forest habitat, which they have preserved covetously as the principal source of livelihood and survival.

Following a series of systematic injustices perpetuated by the Kenyan government against the Ogiek peoples through repeated arbitrary evictions without consultation or compensation, a complaint was initiated at the African Commission by three Kenyan based non-governmental organisations following a 30 days eviction notice issued by the Kenyan government in 2009 compelling the Ogiek and other inhabitants to vacate the Mau forest and make way for its conservation as a water catchment area.[267] Convinced that the allegations against the Kenyan government evinced serious and massive violations of several provisions, including article 22 of the African Charter, the

---

265   *Ogiek Community* case, *supra* note 151.

266   Sang, Joseph K. "Case study 3 – Kenya: The Ogiek of Mau forest" (2001) 114–118; Claridge, Lucy "Litigation as a tool for community empowerment: The case of Kenya's Ogiek" (2018) 11:1 *Erasmus Law Review* 57; Minority Rights Group International "African Commission of Human and Peoples' Rights vs Kenya (The "Ogiek Case" *Factfile – Justice for the Ogiek* 26 May 2017 1; *Ogiek Community* case, *supra* note 151, para 6.

267   *Ogiek Community* case, *supra* note 151, para 3 & 8; Ogiek Peoples' Development Programme "Facts about Ogiek Case at the African Court and its Ruling: *Case No 006/2012: African Commission on Human and Peoples' Rights (ACHPR) versus Republic of Kenya*" (d.n.a) 3.

SOCIO-ECONOMIC AND CULTURAL SELF-DETERMINATION   203

Commission seized the African Court pursuant to art 5(1)(a) of the Protocol establishing the Court.[268]

Perceiving a "situation of extreme gravity and urgency, as well as a risk of irreparable harm to the Ogiek", the Court issued an order for provisional measures, which the Kenyan government ignored and carried on with the evictions accompanied by police harassment and intimidation.[269] The Court also failed to get the parties to agree on an amicable settlement following overwhelming evidence against the Kenyan government.[270] Lucy Claridge notes that the critical failure by the Kenyan government to consult with or seek consent from the Ogiek community about their shared cultural, economic and social life within the Mau forest resulted in a violation of the Ogiek peoples' right to development protected by article 22 of the African Charter.[271] The Charter states: "All *peoples* shall have the right to their economic, social and cultural development with due regard to their freedom and *identity* and in the *equal enjoyment of the common heritage* of mankind" (emphasis added).[272] On the question of peoples and the contested identity of the Ogiek, the Court recognised that they are indeed, a distinct indigenous community in Kenya and because of their vulnerability and the historical disadvantage they have experienced; deserve special protection under the law.[273]

The Court accordingly found that the Kenyan government effectively contravened the several provisions (except article 4) alleged by the applicant. In its assessment of article 22, the Court made allusion to article 21 of the African Charter and to article 23 of the UN Declaration on the Rights of Indigenous Peoples in pronouncing on the violation of the right to development. By this, the Court established that as an indigenous people, the Ogiek community are entitled to determine their development priorities and strategies, to actively engage in the planning and implementation of the socio-economic and cultural development programmes that affected them, and in the administration of those programmes through their own indigenous institutions. The Court held that by evicting the Ogiek people from the Mau forest without effective consultation and also by not actively involving them in the planning of

---

268   *Ogiek Community* case, *supra* note 151, paras 1, 6-10, 58-61 & 101; Claridge, *supra* note 265, 57; Ogiek Peoples' Development Programme, *supra* note 267, 3.

269   Order for Provisional Measures available at: http://en.african-court.org/images/Cases/ Orders/006-2012-ORDER__of_Provisional_Measures-_African_Union_v._Kenya.pdf (accessed: 2 April 2019); *Ogiek Community* case, *supra* note 151, paras 16-18.

270   *Ogiek Community* case, *supra* note 151, paras 31-39; Claridge, *supra* note 266, 58.

271   Claridge, *supra* note 266, 59.

272   African Charter, *supra* note 3, art 22(1).

273   *Ogiek Community* case, *supra* note 151, paras 105-112; Claridge, *supra* note 266, 57–58.

204   CHAPTER 4

development programmes and activities within their community, the Kenyan government violated their right to development.[274]

This milestone judgment of the African Court is of great import to the Ogiek Community[275] and significantly also in advancing the jurisprudence of the African human rights system in adjudicating on the right to development and in providing insight into what the right promises in actual terms. The judgment elucidates on the meaning of "all peoples" contained in article 22 of the African Charter, which in effect means *all peoples*, including especially the vulnerable and most marginalised of indigenous peoples. By inference, the judgment reiterates the guarantee that the right to socio-economic and cultural development cannot be substituted with or subsumed to the governments' prerogatives for development. Over and above all, the judgment sets the record straight with regard to the persistent contention between the state and the peoples of Africa over natural resource ownership.

In addition to making an order for the applicant to file submissions on reparations for a reserved ruling, the Court ordered the Kenyan government to "take all appropriate measures within a reasonable time frame to remedy all the violations established and to inform the Court of the measures taken within six (06) months from the date of this Judgment".[276] Unlike the nonbinding rulings of the African Commission in the previous cases, the *Ogiek Community* judgment of the African Court is legally binding and has the force of law, which imposes an obligation on the Kenyan government for its enforcement. Faced with conflicting politicised interests of different stakeholders over the Mau forest as San Joseph draws attention to,[277] the question to ask is whether the government of Kenya would choose to compromise its interests and development choices in favour of justice for the Ogiek community. The Kenyan government has only to a minimal extent, demonstrated compliance with the Court's ruling by establishing a Task Force charged with enforcement of the judgment.

Interestingly however, in spite of the Court's clear findings that the Ogiek were not adequately consulted or their prior informed consent obtained prior to the evictions and that they are not actively involved in matters relating to their well-being and the development of their community, Claridge notes that

---

274   *Ogiek Community* case, *supra* note 151, paras 207-211.
275   Claridge, *supra* note 266, 66; Minority Rights Group International, *supra* note 266, 1.
276   *Ogiek Community* case, *supra* note 151, paras 226(iv).
277   Sang, *supra* note 266, 129–131; see also Chabeda-Barthe, Jemaiyo & Haller, Tobias "Resilience of traditional livelihood approaches despite forest grabbing: Ogiek to the West of Mau forest, Uasin Gishu county" (2018) 7:140 *Land MDPI Journal* 2.

SOCIO-ECONOMIC AND CULTURAL SELF-DETERMINATION

the composition of the Task Force neither includes Ogiek representatives nor does its operational processes reflect the needs or wishes of the Ogiek community.[278] It would seem as can be deduced from the non compliance with the Court's order for provisional measures and the proposition for amicable settlement that deference to the Kenyan government for enforcement of the final judgment, not excluding through a political solution, will not favour the Ogiek people who like other indigenous communities in Kenya, are generally excluded from mainstream politics in the country. Otherwise, there is no clarity on what the Court implies in its judgment by requiring the Kenyan government "to take all appropriate measures within a reasonable time frame". An order of this kind renders the nature of remedies that can be expected from jurisprudence on the right to development convoluted as explained in the next section.

3.3.3 Nature of Remedies

In the event that legal action becomes inevitable as a result of violation of an entrenched right, justice demands offenders of the law to be held accountable and that a remedy is granted to the victims.[279] In principle, the Covenant on Civil and Political Rights binds state parties with the obligation to ensure that effective remedy is available and accessible to victims of a violation.[280] In this regard, the Principles and Guidelines on the Right to Fair Trial provide that the right to effective remedy entails among others; "1) access to justice; 2) reparation for the harm suffered".[281] When the right to development is violated victims are entitled to effective remedies as supported by international law.[282] The Maastricht Principles additionally stipulate that for:

> [r]emedies, to be effective, [they] must be capable of leading to a prompt, thorough and impartial investigation; cessation of the violation if it is ongoing; and adequate reparation, including, as necessary, restitution, compensation, satisfaction, rehabilitation and guarantees of non repetition. To avoid irreparable harm, interim measures must be available and

---

278 Minority Rights Group "Kenyan government Task Force to implement African Court's Ogiek judgment deeply flawed, MRG and OPDP say" *Relief Web* 13 November 2017 available at: https://reliefweb.int/report/kenya/kenyan-government-task-force-implement-african-court-s-ogiek-judgment-deeply-flawed-mrg (accessed: 4 April 2019).

279 Van Boven, Theo "Human rights and rights of Peoples" (1995) 6:1 *European J Int'l L* 462.

280 ICCPR, *supra* note 102, art 2(3)(a).

281 Principles and Guidelines on the Right to a Fair Trial and Legal Assistance in Africa 2003 para C(b)(1)&(2).

282 Van Boven, *supra* note 279,475; Skinner *et al.*, *supra* note 144, 1.

> States must respect the indication of interim measures by a competent judicial or quasi-judicial body.[283]

The African Charter envisages three types of remedies that are likely to redress violations of the right to development, which include reparation of damages, interdict and provisional measures. In the event of spoliation, the Charter provides for the right to "lawful recovery" or restitution and the right to "adequate compensation".[284] By inference, the Charter sets the rule that remedy for damages suffered as a result of a violation is not a privilege but a claimable right. In principle, lawful recovery or restitution applies in the case where a people have been dispossessed of some recoverable tangible thing like in the instance of land dispossession discussed in the *Endorois* and *Ogiek Community* cases, the value of which is indispensable for the achievement of substantive development. Lawful recovery also means that the dispossessed peoples are legitimately entitled to get back what they have been deprived of and the offender is compelled to restore same. In the instance where the damage incurred includes or is of an intangible nature, justice demands the payment of adequate compensation to the effect that the remedy must be proportionate to the damage suffered.

When a violation of the right to development, involving the actual perpetration of an act or a threat happens, an interdict may be more effective in ensuring respect for the negative obligation to refrain from actions that have the potential to cause harm. Otherwise, a threat or actual violation of the right to development may also be remedied through the granting of a provisional measure, requiring a discontinuation of a harmful action from degenerating into further harm. To this end, the African Court issued a provisional order to halt the eviction of the Ogiek community from the Mau forest, which as discussed above, the Kenyan government contemptuously ignored. As stipulated in the Rules of Procedure, the African Commission may in matters of emergency involving "serious or massive human rights violations", or a situation that "presents the danger of irreparable harm or requires urgent action to avoid irreparable damage", order for provisional measures.[285] The enforcement of provisional measures may not directly result in the realisation of the right in question but is intended to prevent harm or from causing a regression in the enjoyment of existing rights.

---

283   Maastricht Principles, *supra* note 121, para 38.
284   African Charter, *supra* note 3, art 21(2).
285   Rules of Procedure of the African Commission on Human and Peoples' Rights 2010 rules 79 & 80.

SOCIO-ECONOMIC AND CULTURAL SELF-DETERMINATION 207

In terms of redress, drawing from the cases discussed above, Odinkalu observes that the African Commission's (and recently, the African Court's) remedial measures have not been sufficiently explicit.[286] The law is supposed to provide clarity and exactitude and not leave room for doubt and uncertainty. For instance, although the African Commission rightly ordered for the payment of adequate compensation in the *SERAC, DRC* and *Endorois* cases,[287] it is unclear what adequate compensation actually amounts to. The African Court's order for the Kenyan government "to take all appropriate measures within a reasonable time"[288] is equally quite vague, which leaves the respondent states with the discretion to determine what they would consider to be adequate compensation or appropriate measures. With regard to granting an interdict, in the *DRC* case the African Commission ordered the governments of Burundi, Rwanda and Uganda to stop their military operations and withdraw their troops from the DRC, which it is noted they immediately complied with.[289] Similarly, in the *SERAC* litigation, the decision of the African Commission also contained an interdict requiring the Nigerian government to stop all attacks on the Ogoni people.[290] However, despite acknowledging the deplorable degradation of the environment within the Ogoni community as a result of Shell's evidently direct abusive exploitation, which "devastatingly affect[ed] the well-being of the Ogonis",[291] by not providing a remedy to stop Shell's harmful activities, the Commission failed to do justice to the Ogoni people.

The Principles and Guidelines on the Right to Fair Trial further make clear that the "granting of amnesty to absolve perpetrators of human rights violation from accountability violates the right of victims to an effective remedy".[292] For instance, if a violation is established to have been committed by a foreign stakeholder like in the *SERAC* case in which the African Commission acknowledged the violations perpetrated by Shell Corporation,[293] and the legal responsibility is shifted to the Nigerian government for not regulating the activities of the former, the likelihood that the state would remedy the damages is minimal.

---

286 Odinkalu, *supra* note 22, 242.

287 *SERAC* case, *supra* note 121, para 71; *Endorois* case, *supra* note 151, para 298(c); *DRC* case, *supra* note 194, para 98.

288 *Ogiek Community* case, *supra* note 151, para 227(iii) – on the merits.

289 *DRC* case, *supra* note 194, para 98.

290 *SERAC* case, *supra* note 121, para 71.

291 As above, para 58; Amao, Olufemi "The African regional human rights system and multinational corporations: Strengthening the host state responsibility for control of multinational corporations" (2008) 12:5 *Int'l Journal for Hum Rts* 771.

292 Principles and Guidelines on the Right to a Fair Trial, *supra* note 281, para C(d).

293 See *SERAC* case, *supra* note 121, para 57-72.

Meanwhile, if the actual perpetrator of the violation is brought to account, the chances are high that remedy would be effective. Thus, while the UN Guiding Principles ascertains that victims of rights violation resulting from the actions of non-state actors are entitled to effective judicial remedy,[294] enforcement remains problematic owing to the shortcomings examined below.

3.4 *Critique of the Regime of Protection*

3.4.1 Extraterritoriality and the Constraints of International Law

The legal basis of extraterritoriality for the realisation of the right to development or better still for the realisation of socio-economic and cultural rights has been explored extensively.[295] Henry Shue for instance, makes clear that "where the state with the primary duty to protect rights fails – for lack of will or capacity – to fulfil its duty, some other agent at least sometimes must step in and provide the missing protection".[296] This has mainly been conceived from a perspective of need, entailing the provision of development assistance to satisfy those needs.[297] However, as Thomas Pogge contends, effective remedy is not to be found in charity-based assistance but rather in an obligation to redress the harm inflicted on the poor, particularly those in Africa through the established unjust global system.[298] This notwithstanding, the perpetrators of

---

294 UN Guiding Principles on Business and Human Rights, *supra* note 138, paras 25-28.

295 De Schuter, Olivier *et al.* "Commentary to the Maastricht Principles on Extraterritorial Obligations of States in the Area of Economic, Social and Cultural Rights" (2012) 34 *Hum Rts Qtly* 1084–1169; Ooms, Gorik & Hammonds, Rachel "Global constitutionalism, responsibility to protect, and extra-territorial obligations to realise the right to health: time to overcome the double standard (once again)" (2014) 13:68 *Int'l Journal for Equity in Health* 2–4; Maastricht Principles, *supra* note 122, paras 1-44; Skogly, Sigrun I. "Extra-national obligations towards economic and social rights" (2002) *International Council on Human Rights Policy* 1–24.

296 Shue, Henry *Basic Rights: Subsistence, Affluence, and U.S. Foreign Policy* (2nd Edn, Princeton: Princeton University Press, 1996) 176–177.

297 Sengupta 2002, *supra* note 25, 880; De Feyter, Koen "Towards a framework convention on the right to development" (2013) *Friedrich Ebert Stiftung* 17; Salomon, Margot E. "Legal cosmopolitanism and the normative contribution of the right to development" in Marks, Stephen P. (ed) *Implementing the Right to Development: The Role of International Law* (Geneva: Friedrich-Ebert-Stiftung, 2008) 17; Sengupta, Arjun "Development cooperation and the right to development" (2003) *Copyright©2003 Arjun Sengupta* 20; Siitonen, Lauri "Political theories of development cooperation: A study of theories of international cooperation" (1990) *UN University WIDER* 15–16; Arts, Karin & Tamo, Atabongawung "The right to development in international law: New momentum thirty years down the line?" (2016) 63:3 *Neth Int'l L Rev* 239–242; Hausermann, *supra* note 32, 5.

298 Pogge, Thomas W. "Severe poverty as human rights violation" (2003) UNESCO *Poverty Project* 35.

SOCIO-ECONOMIC AND CULTURAL SELF-DETERMINATION

these injustices have remained reticent about a legal obligation to repair the damages that their actions have caused in developing countries.[299] Despite the observation that regional human rights enforcement mechanisms provide the cornerstones for the effective protection of universally recognised human rights,[300] it is noted that foreign stakeholders are generally not accountable to regional enforcement mechanisms.[301] The European and the Inter-American Conventions on Human Rights explicitly limit the enforcement of guaranteed rights within the jurisdiction of the ratifying states.[302] Contrary to Skogly's claim that the "African Charter [...] does not contain any specific jurisdictional or territorial limitation",[303] article 47 of the African Charter allows any state party that has good reason to believe that another state party has violated the provisions of the Charter to make a complaint. It is clear that a complaint can only be made against a state party and not against a non-state party to the Charter. The Maastricht Principles indeed confirm the fact that violations committed by non-state actors are directly attributed to the state, which has the responsibility to regulate the activities of the non-state actors.[304]

Not until the law has actually changed in favour of holding non-state actors and foreign stakeholders directly accountable for human rights offences, they remain insulated and may continue to contravene the right to development with impunity. In line with the argument advanced by Jean D'Aspremont *et al.* with regard to how non-state actors could be held accountable for wrongful actions,[305] the opinion articulated here is that international law is supposed to have a primary role to play in giving effect to the extraterritorial obligations of foreign stakeholders. However, it is important to note that human rights treaties have separate monitoring mechanism with specific enforcement procedures.[306] Unfortunately, there is yet no international treaty and therefore no

---

299 Kirchmeier, *supra* note 83, 11; Oduwole, *supra* note 230, 8.

300 Benedek *et al.*, *supra* note 154, 5.

301 See Gunduz, *supra* note 171, 5; International Justice Resource Centre, *supra* note 172.

302 Compare common articles 1 of the European Convention on Human Rights, the American Convention on Human rights and the African Charter on the obligations of the state parties to these treaties with regard to the realisation of the human rights provisions of the treaties.

303 Skogly, Sigrun I. "Extraterritoriality: Universal human rights without universal obligations?" (d.n.a.) *Lancaster University UK* 18–19; Compare common articles 1 of the European Convention on Human Rights, the American Convention on Human rights and the African Charter on the obligations of the state parties to these treaties with regard to the realisation of the human rights provisions of the treaties.

304 Maastricht Principles, *supra* note 121, para 12.

305 D'Aspremont *et al.*, *supra* note 135, 50.

306 Benedek *et al.*, *supra* note 154, 6–7; Svensson-McCarthy, *supra* note 134, 28–29.

universal monitoring mechanism on the right to development. International law has developed over time principally as a framework of principles to regulate relations between states and to protect human rights but has only recently begun to look into the behaviour of non-state actors in this regard.[307] Regarding the advancement of human rights, the aim has been to improve human well-being, which as Sengupta posits constitutes "the objective of development".[308]

Although non-state actors are known to be involved in global development processes and their actions have had huge negative impact on the basic human rights of local peoples around the world, international law only compels states, as Steiner and Alston point out, to: a) respect the human rights of the peoples of other states, b) create institutional mechanisms for realisation, c) protect human rights and prevent violations, d) provide goods and services to ensure the fulfilment of human rights, and most importantly, e) promote human rights.[309] The application of international law mostly depends on the toothless *pacta sunt servanda* principle to act in good faith, which as Steven Reinhold argues, only serves the purpose of "limiting state sovereignty that is inherent in international law".[310] Developed countries have often taken advantage of the lacuna in the *stricto sensu* application of international law to engineer chaos and destruction in developing countries under the pretext of humanitarian interventions to protect human rights.[311]

In the face of divergent perspectives on international law as a law of general application according to D'Amato[312] as opposed to McDougal, Lasswell and Chen who are unconvinced that international law actually constitutes law,[313] Anghie points out that international law was conceived by and exists essentially for "civilised nations".[314] In line with Anghie's view, the argument advanced in this section is informed by a subjective perception of international law as an

---

307 Manby, Bronwen "Shell in Nigeria: Corporate social responsibility and the Ogoni crisis" (2000) *Carnegie Council on Ethics and International Affairs – Case Study No 20* 2; Skogly 2002, *supra* note 295, 1–8.

308 Sengupta 2002, *supra* note 24, 843.

309 Steiner, Henry J. & Alston, Philip *International Human Rights in Context: Law, Politics, Morals* (3rd Edn, New York: Oxford University Press, 2000) 182–84. Sengupta 2002, *supra* note 24, 856.

310 Reinhold, Steven "Good faith in international law" (2013) 2:1 *UCL Journal of Law and Jurisprudence* 41.

311 D'Amato, Anthony "Is international law really law?" (1985) 79 *North-Western Law Review* 1298.

312 As above, 1293–1310.

313 McDougal, Myres; Lasswell, Harold & Chen, Lung-Chu *Human Rights and World Public Order* (Yale: Yale University Press, 1980) 161–363.

314 Anghie, *supra* note 102, 52.

instrument of protection for western industrialised countries and not necessarily for developing countries, particularly those in Africa. In spite of the guarantees contained in the Declaration on the Right to Development, its soft law nature as an instrument of international law makes it an ineffective tool to rely on for the protection of the right to development in Africa. In the absence of any provision for legal accountability in the event of a wrongful action and by promoting development cooperation as a means for the realisation of the right to development, the Declaration on the Right to Development appears more as an instrument for patronage than as a safeguard mechanism for protection.

3.4.2   Inadequacies within the African Human Rights System

While the next chapter highlights the fact that the right to development imposes an obligation for policy making as a means to translate the abstract provisions enshrined in different instruments into practical reality, it is important to highlight here that doing so implies an overriding duty to assert the entitlement to self-determination both at the continental and domestic levels. In spite of arguments to the contrary,[315] the preceding analysis demonstrates that the right to development is not just a legal theory, it is indeed justiciable and legally enforceable in the sense that legitimate claims have effectively been adjudicated upon by competent jurisdictions.[316] In essence, the right to development in Africa sets standards for seeking protection, the weaponry for asserting claims and the tool for crafting judicial remedies in the event that a threat or actual violation is established to have been committed. However, despite evidence of the harmful practices that have compromised or held back development in Africa, and in spite of the guarantees contained in the treaty instruments and domestic constitutions that enshrine the right to development as illustrated earlier, the general framework of law in Africa does not

---

315   Rosas, Allan "The right to development" in Eide, Asbjørn; Krausus, Catherina & Rosas, Allan (eds) *Economic Social and Cultural Rights* (Dordrecht: Martinus Nijhoff Publishers, 2001) 251; Bello, Emmanuel "Article 22 of the African Charter on Human and Peoples' Rights" in Bello, Emmanuel & Ajibola, Bola (eds) *Essays in Honour of Judge Taslim Olawale Elias* (Dordrecht: Nijhoff Publishers, 1992) 462; Shivji, Issa *The Concept of Human Rights in Africa* (London: African Books Collective, 1989) 82; Ghai, Yash "Whose human right to development?" (1989) *Commonwealth Secretariat Occasional Papers* 124; Donnelly, Jack "In search of the unicorn: The jurisprudence and politics on the right to development" (1985) 15:3 *Cal W Int'l L J* 473.

316   Yeshanew, *supra* note 219,320; Browning, Rebecca "The right to development in Africa: An emerging jurisprudence?" (2011) *Kenya Law* 10; Dąbrowska, Anna O. "Legal status of the right to development" (2010) *Haskoli Island University* 8.

make provision for holding foreign stakeholders and other non-state actors legally accountable for wrongful action.

In a nutshell, transgression of the right to development in Africa may happen when states fail in their positive duties to fulfil or to prevent violations that may be committed by non-state third parties. Contraventions may also occur when states and non-state actors fail in their negative duties to refrain from actions that may impact negatively on the right to development. In the instance where a violation resulting from the conduct of a foreign stakeholder "constitutes a crime under international law", the Maastricht Principles stipulates that the matter may lawfully be referred to "an appropriate jurisdiction" for adjudication.[317] It begs for explanation what is envisaged as appropriate jurisdiction, considering that foreign stakeholders are not parties to the African human rights treaties and therefore are neither bound by those treaties nor are they subject to the treaty enforcement mechanisms. Thus, in spite of the liability that non-state actors and foreign stakeholders may incur, the actual functioning of the law as it is (*lex lata*), attributes responsibility primarily to the state to remedy violations of the right to development.

Otherwise, as a legally enforceable entitlement the right to development in Africa engenders, as a host of scholars have noted, a combination of positive and negative duties that enjoin state parties to the African Charter and its ancillary instruments to respect, protect, promote and fulfil the right.[318] The African treaty instruments do not impose any binding obligations on foreign stakeholders, which explains why developed countries have argued against and out-right denied any legal commitment relating to implementing the right to development in developing countries,[319] but would rather only do so through development cooperation. Because the right to development is envisaged to result in the constant improvement in human well-being,[320] cooperation ought to envisage not only the provision of development assistance but also an obligation of non-violation to ensure that development gains are not eroded.[321] This is often not the case as the framework of development cooperation generally does not impose such restraints, which in effect is most relevant

---

317 Maastricht Principles, *supra* note 121, para 25(e).

318 Chirwa 2002, *supra* note 121,16; Maastricht Guidelines, *supra* note 125, para 6; Okafor 2008, *supra* note 28, 61; Shue, *supra* note 276, 52.

319 Oduwole, *supra* note 230,8; Kirchmeier, *supra* note 83, 11.

320 Declaration on the Right to Development, *supra* note 3, art 2(3).

321 Mmari, Amanda "The challenges surrounding the implementation of the right to development in the African Charter on Human and Peoples' Rights in light of the *Endorois* case" (Masters Dissertation, University of Pretoria, 2012) 24; Okafor 2008, *supra* note 28, 61.

SOCIO-ECONOMIC AND CULTURAL SELF-DETERMINATION   213

in order to ensure progress in Africa. Although the African Union Constitutive Act highlights the need to encourage international cooperation,[322] the actual problem Africa is confronted with cannot be redressed through soliciting development assistance but by setting out a model by which to confront the range of issues that contribute to sustaining low standards of living across the continent.

Thus, with regard to safeguarding the right to development dispensation from on-going imperialistic practices, it is important to highlight the negative obligation not to hinder the enjoyment of the collective right to development guaranteed to the peoples of Africa.[323] According to Thomas Pogge, the negative obligation entails a duty not to harm or to avert harm that present actions may generate in the future.[324] For Skogly, the negative obligation compels states to respect human rights not only of their own citizens but also of the peoples in other countries who might be affected by their activities.[325] Accordingly, foreseeable harm must be avoided, which demands restrained action or behaviour that may infringe on or jeopardise the liberty of action to freely exercise the right to development.[326] If the right to development in Africa is to be achieved, actions that are foreseeable to adversely affect the human person or to violate other fundamental human rights must be avoided or prevented.[327] Such avoidable actions include development injustices in the form of "colonialism, foreign domination and occupation, aggression, foreign interference and threats against national sovereignty, [...] threats of war and refusal to recognize the fundamental right of peoples to self-determination".[328]

While the African Court on Human and Peoples' Rights or the African Court of Justice and Human Rights when it eventually replaces the former is anticipated to become fully operational, the African Commission remains the most active enforcement mechanism on issues of human and peoples' rights with

---

322   AU Constitutive Act, *supra* note 31, art 3(e).
323   N'Sengha, Mutombo N. "The African Charter on Human and Peoples' Rights: An African contribution to the project of global ethic" available at: http://globalethic.org/Center/mutombo1.htm (accessed: 17 April 2015).
324   Pogge, Thomas "Real world justice" (2005) 9:1/2 *The Journal of Ethics* 34; Pogge, Thomas *World Poverty and Human Rights: Cosmopolitan Responsibilities and Reforms* (Cambridge: Polity Press, 2002) 67, 145 & 172.
325   Skogly d.n.a, *supra* note 303, 4.
326   Eide, Asbjørn "Realisation of social and economic rights and the minimum threshold approach" (1989) 1:2 *Hum Rts LJ* 10; Chirwa 2002, *supra* note 121, 16; Frankovits, *supra* note 121, 9; *SERAC* case, *supra* note 121, para 45; see also Skogly d.n.a, *supra* note 303, 8–9.
327   Sengupta 2004, *supra* note 261, 193.
328   Declaration on the Right to Development, *supra* note 3, art 5.

an established jurisprudence on the right to development. The Commission's complaints procedure provides assurance that a violation of the right to development can be redressed through litigation.[329] However, although the African Charter imposes binding obligations and mandates the Commission as a measure of safeguard to interpret and apply the principles of the law through adjudication in specific cases, the mandate of the Commission has been construed rather too narrowly to mean that its decisions do not have the force of law. It is noted that the Commission has itself increasingly articulated the view that its findings and decisions have a binding character.[330] As provided for by article 45(2) and (3) when the Commission engages in its protective function to interpret the law, it constitutes itself as a tribunal. Because the Charter is legally binding, the decisions of the Commission create precedent to give practical effect to the principles of law and therefore, are supposed to also have enforceable effect deriving from the legal obligations imposed by the Charter.

However, the Commission's decisions have been seen principally as mere recommendations without binding force and therefore may only be enforced at the discretion of the states concerned, which of course, a host of scholars have dismissed as unreasonable.[331] It is argued that the Commission's decisions are not devoid of legal effect and unenforceable. In effect, the Principles and Guidelines on the Right to a Fair Trial provide that "any remedy granted shall be enforced by competent authorities" and that "any state body against which a judicial order or other remedy has been granted shall comply fully with such an order or remedy".[332] Once the Commission has rendered its ruling, it is left

---

329 Frankovits, *supra* note 121, 10.

330 Inman, Derek *et al.* "The (un)willingness to implement the recommendations of the African Commission on Human and Peoples' Rights: Revisiting the *Endorois* and the *Mamboleo* decisions" (2018) 2 *African Human Rights Yearbook* 403.

331 Odinkalu, Chidi A. "The individual complaints procedure of the African Commission on Human and Peoples. Rights: A preliminary assessment" (1998) 8 *Transnational Law & Contemporary Problems* 398; Naldi, Gino & Magliveras, Konstantinos "Reinforcing the African system of human rights: The Protocol on the establishment of a regional Court of Human and Peoples' Rights" (1998) 16:4 *Neth Qtly Hum Rts* 432; Welch Jr, Claude E. "The African Charter and freedom of expression in Africa" (1998) 4 *Buff Hum Rts L Rev* 113–115; Murray, Rachel "Decisions by the African Commission on Human and Peoples. Rights on individual communications under the African Charter on Human and Peoples' Rights" (1997) 46:2 *Int'l & Comp L Q* 413; Kodjo, Edem "The African Charter on Human and Peoples' Rights" (1990) 11 *Hum Rts L J* 280; Benedek, Wolfgang "The African Charter and Commission on Human and Peoples' Rights: How to make it more effective" (1993) 11:1 *Neth Qtly Hum Rts* 31; Robertson, Geoffrey *Crimes against Humanity: The Struggle for Global Justice* (London: Penguin Adult, 2000) 62–64.

332 Principles & Guidelines on the Right to a Fair Trial, *supra* note 281, para C(c)(3) & (4).

for the relevant national authorities to proceed with ensuring that the law is complied with and that damages suffered by victims are effectively remedied. Compliance with the law deriving from article 22 of the African Charter entails an enabling domestic environment that does not condone impunity; one that allows for substantive development to be achieved and for justice in development to prevail.

By deferring enforcement of its decisions, the Commission is in effect throwing back legal responsibility to state parties to exercise the right to sovereignty by complying in good faith with the legal commitments they have freely undertaken under the African Charter and other human rights instruments. In respect of the negative duty that the right to development imposes, African governments have a primary obligation to ensure that the right to development guaranteed to the peoples of Africa is not violated. It is important that when the right to development is contravened either by state parties or by non-state parties, including foreign stakeholders, justice is sought as a guarantee to safeguarding the right to development dispensation in Africa. Practically, this can only be achieved through effective legislative and regulatory policy measures that impose constraints on the often-uncontainable actions of foreign stakeholders. A serious shortcoming in this regard is that most African countries are yet to domesticate the right to development, which they have committed to under the African Charter. As a result, the African continent has remained at the mercy of powerful external actors, as the AU Commission has rightly observed.[333] Meanwhile, judging from the analysis in this chapter, significant progress is possible in Africa, which entails advancing the right to development not only as a claimable entitlement but decisively also as a development paradigm.

4 Concluding Remarks

While it is true that developing countries need to align their national development policies with the realities of a global economy that is largely shaped and dominated by western capitalist paradigms,[334] the fact cannot be ignored that global realities will not always be endured when the scales of justice remain tilted in favour of the exploitative attitude of foreign stakeholders in their

---

333 African Union Commission "Agenda 2063: The Africa we want" (2015) *African Union* para 59.

334 Monti-Belkaoui, Janice & Riahi-Belkaoui, Ahmed *Qaddafi: The Man and His Policies* (Aldersrot: Avebury Ashgate Publishing Ltd, 1996) 268.

relations with Africa. Global realities include the fact that the peoples of Africa are not condemned to subordination. It entails foreign stakeholders to respect international human rights law, which guarantees that the peoples of Africa are legitimately entitled to make their own development choices as a matter of right. The exercise of this right has practically manifested through the recognition and protection of the right to development in a range of legal instruments that together define the right to development dispensation in compliance with the conviction established in the preamble to the African Charter to prioritise the right to development.

Of significance is the fact that the right to development dispensation guarantees to the peoples of Africa entitlement to actual self-determination and in relation attribute responsibilities to African states to ensure its protection and fulfilment as well as liabilities to foreign stakeholders when their actions contravene the right to development in Africa. Following Amartya Sen's theorisation of development as freedom,[335] it is worth noting that having gained political independence, it is important to envisage the right to development as a legitimate platform on which to advance the crusade for socio-economic and cultural emancipation in the same manner that the right to self-determination facilitated the achievement of independence. To aspire for the kind of freedom that Sen envisages as development as implied by the capabilities theory means that with freedom, which according to Bedjaoui is justified by the independence of nations,[336] Africa ought to be able to create the conditions for its peoples to exercise the right to development by performing the human functioning necessary to achieve anticipated outcomes of well-being.[337] Asserting the right to self-determination in Africa represents not only the right to achieve socio-economic and cultural development but essentially, as part of that process, to seek to be liberated from external domination and to claim as a matter of right, sovereign ownership over the resources that are indispensable to achieve the right to development.[338]

In spite of the extensive commitments to make the right to development a reality, actual implementation remains problematic due largely to the fact that most of Africa is still subject to foreign domination that jeopardises the enabling environment for exercising that right. Notwithstanding the available enforcement mechanisms at the continental and domestic levels and the

---

335 Sen, *supra* note 38, 87–95.

336 Bedjaoui, *supra* note 107, 93–94.

337 See Sen, *supra* note 38, 87–95.

338 African Charter, *supra* note 3, art 20(2); Declaration on the Right to Development, *supra* note 3, arts 1(2) & 5.

means of redress through litigation, the regime of protection under the right to development dispensation remains noticeably insubstantial, especially with regard to holding foreign stakeholders accountable for wrongful actions that contravene the right to development guaranteed to the peoples of Africa. Because of the imperative to achieve justice and equity in development, part of the discussion in this chapter has dwelled on aspects of legal enforcement. However, it is worth acknowledging that the right to development cannot be achieved solely through legal processes, but essentially also through policy reforms. This imposes an even bigger responsibility on Africa, as part of the commitment under the African Charter to create the conditions for greater autonomy and self-determination as opposed to the endemic dependence on foreign assistance as a model for development.[339] It entails ensuring more concrete initiatives to deepen the integration that has begun among African countries and therefore also an enquiry into how the right to development could, in its formulation as a development paradigm, be conceptualised as a framework model suitable for accelerating Africa's development prospects. The next chapter looks at how the right to development governance could be conceptualised to apply in redressing the development challenges in Africa.

---

339 Ilorah, Richard "Africa's endemic dependency on foreign aid: A dilemma for the continent" (2011) *ICITI – ISSN: 16941225* 13; Bilal, San "The rise of South-South relations: Development partnerships reconsidered" (2012) *Conference Paper – European Centre for Development Policy Management* 1–3.

CHAPTER 5

Right to Development Governance for Africa

1 Introduction

This chapter illustrates how the right to development could be conceptualised as a suitable alternative to development cooperation owing to its formulation as an expression of self-determination against foreign domination and imperialistic neo-colonial practices. This is informed by the fact as stated in the introductory section of chapter one that Africa's retarded development is caused not by the need for development assistance but in essence by the lack of a functional model to drive development processes on the continent. Of interest in this regard is the reality that the right to development, which is embodied in the right to self-determination, creates the opportunity for independent policy formulation that may significantly shape development processes and of course, the manner too in which development cooperation is practiced in Africa.[1] The proposition to reject development cooperation as a mechanism for the realisation of the right to development is made with reference to Achille Mbembe's decolonial perception, which as he posits, entails getting rid of the pre-existing models of coloniality and not use them as paradigms.[2]

Accordingly, state action and development programming ought to be informed and guided by the right to development paradigm, which as it is argued, is an appropriate development model for Africa, and therefore, needs to be conceptualised as such, as illustrated later in this chapter. As a pragmatic concept, the right to development holds the promise to remodel the imperialistic tendencies that continue to inform developed countries' actions, which the peoples of Africa have manifestly or inexplicitly contested. It is important to clarify that as a human right, the right to development binds state parties with the duty to ensure its realisation. Meanwhile, development cooperation

---

1   See African Charter on Human and Peoples' Rights adopted in Nairobi, Kenya on 27 June 1981 OAU Doc CAB/LEG/67/3 Rev.5 (1981) arts 22(2) & 20(1); Declaration on the Right to Development Resolution A/RES/41/128 adopted by the UN General Assembly on 4 December 1986 arts 1(2) & 2(3).

2   Mbembe, Achille "Decolonizing knowledge and the question of the archive" (2015) available at: http://wiser.wits.ac.za/system/files/Achille%20Mbembe%20%20Decolonizing%20 Knowledge%20and%20the%20Question%20of%20the%20Archive.pdf (accessed: 26 April 2018) 8–14.

© CAROL CHI NGANG, 2022 | DOI:10.1163/9789004467903_006

is generally not informed by any obligation to achieve a human right to development but rather by foreign policy considerations characterised by the pursuit of self-interest.[3] In spite of the right to development dispensation that has been established in Africa as illustrated in the previous chapter, implementation as De Feyter rightly observes, is a problem.[4] In examining the challenges involved in implementing the right to development, it is shown in this chapter where the constraints lie and in effect, why it is important to prioritise the right to development over development cooperation.

The idea to have recourse to development cooperation as a mechanism for the realisation of the right to development stems from the assumption that developing countries need the assistance of developed countries to achieve comprehensive development.[5] The Declaration on the Right to Development stipulates in article 4(2) that sustained action is required, by making the "appropriate means and facilities" available through international cooperation to accelerate "comprehensive" development in developing countries. In relation, global actions in the form of the Millennium Development Goals (MDGs) and the Sustainable Development Goals (SDGs) among others have consistently emphasised the need for global partnerships as a means to complement the efforts of developing countries. This is counter-productive and of course, constitutes a limiting factor to developing countries' capacity for advancement in a self-sustainable manner.[6]

On the contrary, reflecting the view of the United Nations (UN) Working Group on the Right to Development, Ibrahim Salama draws attention to the fact that the right to development does not guarantee a right to lay claim to the wealth and resources of other countries and thus, international commitments to support the efforts of developing countries can only be accomplished on a voluntary basis.[7] Accordingly, developed countries have argued against

---

3   See Mawdsley, Emma "Human rights and south-south development cooperation: Reflections on the 'rising powers' as international development actors" (2014) 36:3 *Hum Rts Qtly* 641. Hamilton J. Maxwell "Development cooperation: Creating a public commitment" in Berg, Robert & Gordon, David F. (eds) *Cooperation for International Development: The United States and the Third World in the 1990s* (Boulder: Lynne Rienner Publishers, 1989) 216.

4   De Feyter, Koen "The right to development in Africa" (2013) *Law and Development, University of Antwerp* 7.

5   Bilal, San "The Rise of South-South relations: Development partnerships reconsidered" (2012) *Conference Paper – European Centre for Development Policy Management* 1; Declaration on the Right to Development, *supra* note 1, art 4(2).

6   Ngang, Carol C. "Differentiated responsibility under international law and the right to development paradigm for developing countries" (2017) 11:2 *HR & ILD* 280–281.

7   Salama, Ibrahim "The right to development: Towards a new approach?" (2005) *Perceptions* 58; see also Donnelly, Jack "In search of the unicorn: The jurisprudence and politics on the right to development" (1985) 15:3 *Calif West Int'l LJ* 509.

the idea of framing development as a human rights entitlement with binding extraterritorial obligations, as inherently flawed.[8] This notwithstanding, Bonny Ibhawoh observes that many of the actions of developed countries that undermine the full realisation of the right to development have remained immune to criticism.[9] This is problematic, because as noted, the excessive influence exercised by foreign stakeholders in their extraterritorial activities threatens and in most cases, actually violate socio-economic and cultural rights in developing countries, which by implication necessitates legal responsibility.[10]

With regard to parties to the right to development dispensation in Africa, the procedures for seeking remedy before the African Commission and the African Court have accordingly been laid down for immediate application when a violation is alleged.[11] The principal concern is whether legal responsibility is equally imputed to foreign stakeholders when they contravene the right to development in Africa. Unfortunately, as a standard principle on the law of treaties, foreign stakeholders cannot be held accountable under treaty instruments that they are not party to and therefore are not bound to comply with. Thus, the legal obligations imposed by the right to development in Africa only apply to state parties to the African Charter and not to foreign stakeholders that are not party to the Charter. Following the recognition as contained in the preamble to the African Charter for the pursuit of justice as one of the primary objectives for the achievement of the legitimate aspirations of the African peoples,[12] the responsibility is imputed to Africa to ensure protection of the right to development enshrined therein for all its peoples. This responsibility includes, as the African Commission acknowledges in the *Social and Economic Rights Action Centre* (*SERAC*) case, regulating the activities of foreign stakeholders and non-state actors to ensure that their actions do not infringe

---

8 Ibhawoh, Bonny "The right to development: The politics and polemics of power and resistance" (2011) 33:1 *Hum Rts Qtly* 97; Kirchmeier, Felix "The right to development– where do we stand?: State of the debate on the right to development" (2006) *Friedrich Ebert Stiftung – Occasional Paper No 23* 13–14; Donnelly, *supra* note 7, 509.

9 Ibhawoh, *supra* note 8, 100.

10 Maastricht Principles on Extraterritorial Obligations of States in the area of Economic, Social and Cultural Rights adopted by the International Commission of Jurists on 28 September 2011 preamble.

11 see also Rules of Procedure of the African Commission on Human and Peoples' Rights 2010 rules 83–113; Protocol to the African Charter on Human and Peoples' Rights on the establishment of an African Court on Human and Peoples' Rights adopted in Addis Ababa Ethiopia on 10 June 1998 arts 3-10; see also Rules of Court 2010 rules 26–73; African Charter, *supra* note 1, arts 46-61.

12 African Charter, *supra* note 1, preamble para 2.

RIGHT TO DEVELOPMENT GOVERNANCE FOR AFRICA

on guaranteed rights.[13] This concern draws from the fact that paternalistic practices remain a major setback to development in Africa. Consequently, for the situation to change, the focus in right to development studies should be on creating real self-determination for Africa. How this could be achieved is the determination that this chapter seeks to make.

The chapter is structured as follows: Section 2 explores the incongruities and the complex dynamics that prevail in Africa. Section 3 looks at the envisaged right to development regulatory mechanisms, with focus on the frameworks for development policy making in (3.1), the implications for ineffective implementation in (3.2) and the justification for a shift in paradigm in (3.3). On this account, the chapter proceeds to portray in section 4 the right to development as an alternative development model for Africa, describes as the right to development governance, with emphasis on its conceptual formulation in (4.1) and the operational considerations, especially with regard to contraventions in (4.2). The chapter concludes with a summary of the main highlights in section 5.

2 Incongruities and the Complex Dynamics in Africa

While the right to development is envisaged to be achieved as a collective entitlement to the benefit of all the peoples of Africa, it is noteworthy to acknowledge that Africa is not a homogenous entity. However, with regard to questions relating to development, the continent is indeed united by a common characteristic – the prevalence of poverty among other development challenges – that impact on and constrain the full realisation of the right to development. The continent of Africa is made up of 55 sovereign states with diversified realities. Colonial histories and the post-independence experiences of African countries differ greatly to the extent that while some of these countries acquired full sovereignty at independence; others, as explained later below, cherished to preserve the colonial bond of dependency, which to date has been difficult to severe. In justification of the dependency theory, Africa has generally been portrayed as inherently lacking of the resource potential to create development.[14] Strangely, the same Africa has over the centuries, dating

---

13   *Social and Economic Rights Action Centre (SERAC) & Another v Nigeria* Comm 155/96 (2001) AHRLR 60 (ACHPR 2001) para 57.

14   OECD "Foreign direct investment for development: Maximising benefits, minimising costs" (2002) *Organisation for Economic Co-Operation and Development* 8; Blanton, Shannon L. & Blanton, Robert G. "What attracts foreign investors? An examination of human rights and foreign direct investment" (2007) 69:1 *The Journal of Politics* 145.

back to the days of slavery and colonialism, been the primary source of man power and raw materials, which have gratuitously been extracted from the continent to build and fuel the economies of western industrialised countries and continues to be extracted by present day economic giants like China.[15] With regard to the potential for self-sustainability as opposed to dependency on development assistance as explained in the previous chapters, it is worth acknowledging that while some African countries are exceedingly rich in natural resource endowments, others are undeniably so disadvantaged that they have to persistently reach out to developed countries for help.

Controversially, the resource availability requirement which the realisation of socio-economic and cultural rights (and by implication the right to development) is subjected to as stated in article 2(1) of the Covenant on Economic, Social and Cultural Rights does not seem to hold true for Africa. Africa is by far the richest continent in the world in terms of mineral deposits and other natural wealth.[16] The availability of these resources has practically not translated into the realisation of socio-economic and cultural rights or better still into improved standards of living but literally into extreme levels of poverty. The Democratic Republic of Congo (DRC) for example, is apparently the richest country in Africa and probably also in the world, with extensive deposits of gold, diamond, coltan, copper, manganese, tin, uranium, a sprawling tropical equatorial rainforest with an expansive biodiversity and rare species of flora and fauna and the aquatic resources of the River Congo.[17] On the contrary, the

---

15 Cheung, Yin-Wong *et al.* "China's outward direct investment in Africa" (2012) 20:2 *Review of International Economics* 201–220; Kolstad, Ivar & Wiig, Arne "Better the devil you know? Chinese foreign direct investment in Africa" (2011) 12:1 *Journal of African Business* 34; Sanfilippo, Marco "Chinese FDI to Africa: What is the nexus with foreign economic cooperation?" (2010) 22:1 *African Development Review* 600–601; Biggeri, Mario & Sanfilippo, Marco "Understanding China's move into Africa: An empirical analysis" (2009) 7:1 *Journal of Chinese Economic and Business Studies* 32; Asiedu, Elizabeth "Foreign direct investment in Africa: The role of natural resources, market size, government policy, institutions and political instability" (2006) 29:1 *World Economy* 66–67; Busse, Mathias; Erdogan, Caren & Mülhen, Henning "China's impact on Africa: The role of trade and FDI" (2016) 69:2 *Kyklos – International Review for Social Sciences* 242.

16 Tamasang, Christopher F. "Illicit financial flows and the regulatory framework for mineral exploitation arrangements in Cameroon" (2017) *Trust Africa – Illicit Financial Flows Research Series* 1.

17 Herdeschee, Johannes; Kaiser, Kai-Alexander & Samba, D. Mukoko *Resilience of an African Giant: Boosting Growth and Development in the Democratic Republic of Congo* (Washington DC: The World Bank, 2012) 13–14; Kors, Joshua "Blood mineral" (2010) 9:95 *Current Science* 10–12; Carpenter, Louisa "Conflict minerals in the Congo: Blood minerals and Africa's under-reported first world war" *Suffolk University Working Paper*, 2 April 2012 2–4; Inter Press Service "DRC: Minerals flow abroad" (2006) *Africa Research Bulletin* 1704;

RIGHT TO DEVELOPMENT GOVERNANCE FOR AFRICA 223

country's population of over 77 million is heavily impoverished, with an average per capita growth rate of -1.1 per cent[18] and a global human development ranking at 176th position out of 189 countries.[19]

Incidentally, although the African Charter guarantees that the right to development is to be enjoyed by all the peoples of Africa, there are glaring disparities in terms of uneven access to the natural resources (common heritage) required to create development. It implies too that opportunities for development are not fairly distributed and thus, implementation of the right to development in Africa cannot be expected to be absolute. The disparities are even more pronounced when the question of "all peoples" is examined more closely; composed of varying population groupings with diverse value systems and development expectations. Africa's youth population is the largest and most vibrant around the world, but its productive capabilities is yet to be sufficiently explored to maximise prospects for advancing development on the continent. Although women too make up over 50 per cent of the African population; constituting a potential driving force for development, they have remained one of the most disadvantaged with respect to access to opportunities for development.

Across all of Africa, indigenous communities are also seriously marginalised in spite of the fact that most of the natural resources required to facilitate the realisation of the right to development are situated within their ancestral lands. Owing to mainstream perceptions about indigenous peoples, they are generally excluded from participating in, contributing to or sharing in the benefits of development. They are by law entitled to first ownership rights over their natural resources and consequently are supposed to have a leveraging decision making power regarding the exploitation or disposal of those resources for development.[20] Owing to conflicting claims over resource ownership, especially with the state, indigenous communities have had to embark on extensive campaigns to gain legal recognition of their proprietary rights over the resources that naturally belong to them.[21] Legal recognition of these rights

---

Khadija, Sharife "DR Congo: The heavy price of the world's high-tech" *New African* (May 2008) 27.

18 Radelet, Steven "Emerging Africa: How 17 countries are leading the way" *Centre for Global Development – Policy Brief* September 2010.

19 UNDP "Human development reports: 2018 statistical update" *United Nations Development Programme* available at: http://hdr.undp.org/en/2018-update (accessed: 3 April 2019).

20 Declaration on the Rights of Indigenous Peoples Resolution 61/295 adopted by the UN General Assembly on 13 September 2007.

21 Cultural Survival and the Indigenous Peoples' Caucus "Our land, our identity, our freedom" (2007) 5:2 *Cultural Survival Voices*; Alwyn, Josh "Land and resources" (2006) 30:4 *Cultural Survival Quarterly*; UN Special Rapporteur on the situation of human rights and

would mean that in the instance where resources have to be exploited for economic purposes, first priority in the redistribution of development gains ought to be given to the communities where the resources are extracted in satisfaction of the African Charter provision, which states that the disposal of natural resources shall be done in the exclusive interest of the people who shall not be deprived of that right.[22] On the contrary, the number of litigation involving indigenous claims to their ancestral lands and the natural resources found thereon explain that the question of resource ownership remains a major issue that still needs to be resolved.

In spite of these incongruities and diversified realities, Africa remains united by a common denominator of human rights and development challenges, which is justified by the several concerted efforts in the form of continental and global development programmes that have aimed at redressing these challenges. Despite consolidating individual state sovereignty for over half a century after decolonisation, Africa is currently at the verge of a critical turning point, with renewed commitment and determination to forge a more unified front intended to achieve structural transformation, inclusive growth and sustainable development as outlined in the 2063 agenda for development.[23] Over the last decade, a growing number of African countries like Botswana, Rwanda, Kenya and a host of others have experienced sustained levels of economic growth, and positive movements on a number of human development indicators.[24] It is reported that African economies are currently growing at an average annual gross domestic product (GDP) rate of 4 per cent across the continent and this figure is estimated to increase approximately three-fold by 2030 and seven-fold by 2050.[25] However, with a largely unregulated development and investment space, the blind pursuit of foreign direct investment (FDI) by African governments, which has attracted an increasing encroachment of Chinese companies among other foreign stakeholders into every sector of African society, including the informal, it is unclear what proportion of the growth statistics pertains to the peoples of Africa.

---

fundamental freedoms of indigenous peoples. Report to the Fourth Session of the UN Human Rights Council, 27 February 2007.

22   African Charter, *supra* note 1, art 21(1).

23   African Union Commission "Agenda 2063: The Africa we want" (2015) *African Union* para 66(b).

24   As above, para 66(b).

25   International Renewable Energy Agency "Africa's renewable future: The path to sustainable growth" (2013) *International Renewable Energy Agency* 5.

Contrary to the understanding that development is intended to better the livelihood circumstances of the human person, while Africa is reported to have experienced economic development calculated in growth rates, living standards have not improved for the large majority of the African peoples and thus, progress in meeting the range of human development targets remains elusive.[26] African countries remain classified either as least developed, extremely poor or heavily indebted; meaning that the incidence of poverty overrides the extent to which economic growth can be expected to redress the setbacks to development on the continent. Because the context demands a more harmonised approach to development, it provides justification to examine the regulatory mechanisms through which the right to development is envisaged to be actualised.

3 Right to Development Regulatory Mechanisms

This section looks at the right to development regulatory mechanisms with the aim to determine the structural and policy dimensions within which the right to development is envisaged to evolve as a development paradigm for engineering transformation in Africa. As indicated in the introductory section above, the right to development by nature imposes an obligation for development policy formulation to ensure its realisation, which requires a scrutiny of the relevant entities at the continental and country levels that are mandated to regulate the realisation of the right to development in Africa. This is illustrated through a cursory analysis of the African Union (AU) and a country analysis of Cameroon, Qadaffi's Libya, post-apartheid South Africa, Ethiopia and Nigeria, selected randomly from each of the major regional economic blocs on the continent. While three of these countries have domesticated the right to development, the two others are yet to do so and thus, all five countries are juxtaposed to show how and to what extent the right to development is taken seriously by African countries.

---

26 Beegle, Kathleen *et al. Poverty in a Rising Africa* (Washington DC: International Bank for Reconstruction and Development/The World Bank, 2016) xi-xii; Sako, Soumana & Ogiogio, Genevesi "Africa: Major development challenges and their capacity building dimensions" (2002) *The African Capacity Building Foundation – Occasional Paper No 1* 3–4; Jibril, Ali A. "The right to development in Ethiopia" in Brems, Eva; Van dee Beken, Christopher & Abay, Yimer, S. (eds) *Human Rights and Development: Legal Perspectives from and for Ethiopia* (Leiden: Brill/Nijhoff, 2015) 70; Kiely, Ray "The crisis of development" in Kiely, Ray & Marflect, Phil (eds) *Globalisation and the Third World* (London/New York: Routledge, 1998) 24.

226   CHAPTER 5

The choice of countries is motivated by three foremost reasons: The first reason is that all five countries have ratified the African Charter and therefore, are bound to ensure domestic implementation of the right to development enshrined therein.[27] Cameroon for instance, has an even bigger commitment owing to the fact that it is the pioneer country to enshrine the right to development in the 1972 Constitution, which has since then remained a provision in amended versions of the Constitution. Second, because in accordance with the provisions of the African Charter and the Declaration on the Right to Development, the right to development is supposed to provide policy direction in national development planning for these countries among others.[28] Third, because as a paradigm for development suited to Africa, the right to development is expected to inform and guide development processes across the continent and therefore also regulate relations with foreign stakeholders as Felix Kirchmeier rightly points out.[29]

The focus on these five countries does not imply any kind of an empirical analysis but a simple theoretical assessment of their commitment under the African Charter and the extent of realisation of the right to development contained therein. The analysis also aims to illustrate in some of the instances how development cooperation and the actions of foreign stakeholders impact negatively on the realisation of the right to development. In the case of Cameroon, Ethiopia and Nigeria (considered as bad examples) the analysis illustrates how in spite of constitutional provisions on the right to development, implementation remains constrained. Meanwhile, with Libya under Qadaffi's reign and post-apartheid South Africa (taken as good practice examples), it is shown how in the absence of explicit constitutional provisions, the systems in place allow for improved living standards, which arguably sum up to the realisation of the right to development.

3.1. *Mandated Entities for Development Policy Making*

3.1.1 African Union (AU)

With respect to the commitment under the African Charter that compels state parties to take collective action to ensure the realisation of the right to development as pointed out in the previous chapters, one would imagine the AU to provide the institutional platform or forum for such concerted action to take

---

27   Heyns, Christof & Killander, Magnus (eds) *Compendium of Key Human Rights Documents of the African Union* (Pretoria: Pretoria University Law Press, 2016) 429–430.

28   African Charter, *supra* note 1, preamble & arts 22 read together with art 1; Declaration on the Right to Development, *supra* note 1, art 2(3).

29   Kirchmeier, *supra* note 8, 5.

place. However, in spite of the treaty guarantees on the right to development in Africa, the AU Commission recognises that Africa remains exposed to "continued external influence".[30] Even as it is important to come to the self-realisation that the continent of Africa remains vulnerable and exposed to continuous foreign exploitation, a more pressing concern is whether there is an equivalent recognition of the absence of an operational model for development. It is my view that the development context would have experienced significant transformation if, as stipulated in the preamble to the African Charter, the right to development were taken seriously, probably as an interpretative guide to policy making and development programming. This provides reason to examine the institutional role of the AU as custodian of the treaty instruments that enshrine the right to development in Africa.

The AU succeeded the Organisation for African Unity (OAU) as a standard setting supra-national entity, meaning that it has the duty to set policy standards on the right to development applicable to all its member states.[31] However, as Rachel Murray rightly observes, the AU's standard setting function "has not been backed up in practice with a clear enforcement mechanism".[32] However, because the right to development in Africa also provides the option for its realisation by individual member states of the AU, it is important to do an analysis of some of these states to determine the extent of the realisation of the right to development at the domestic level.

3.1.2   States Governments – Selected Country Analysis

Given that all African countries have ratified the African Charter and are legally bound to ensure domestic implementation of the right to development enshrined therein, a country-by-country assessment is definitely necessary to determine to what extent this has been achieved. However, because such an extensive analysis is not feasible within the scope of this book, only five randomly selected countries are examined, namely; Cameroon, Libya under Qaddafi's rule, post-apartheid South Africa, Ethiopia and Nigeria. The purpose is to explain the nature of the constraints involved in implementing the right to development in these countries and by implication in Africa as a whole. In so doing, justification is provided on the need to seriously rethink Africa's dependence on development assistance and in relation, to consider redefining

---

30   AU Commission "Agenda 2063", *supra* note 23, para 59.

31   See Constitutive Act of the African Union adopted in Lomé, Togo on 11 July 2000 preamble & art 3.

32   Murray, Rachel *Human Rights in Africa: From the OAU to the African Union* (Cambridge: Cambridge University Press, 2004) 264.

228   CHAPTER 5

and remodelling development on the continent from the perspective and within the framework of the right to development governance.

3.1.2.1   *Cameroon*

Prior to independence, Cameroon was administered under UN trusteeship by the French and the British.[33] Upon independence, the 1972 Constitution of Cameroon became the pioneer legal instrument to afford statutory recognition to the right to development, framed in the form of a national resolve to utilise the country's natural resources for the well-being of the entire population as highlighted in chapter two. As would be noticed, the right to development in Cameroon is formulated not just as a claimable entitlement but indeed as a post-independence model for development underscored by the principles of sovereignty, self-determination and as Kamga reiterates, self-reliance on the country's natural resources, which the government envisaged to utilise adequately in raising living standards for the peoples of Cameroon.[34] In view of achieving this objective, the government initiated a progressive policy of "balanced development, and planned liberalism".[35] However, following a range of "cooperation accords" that Cameroon concluded with France prior to independence,[36] the policy reforms that the Cameroon government

---

33   Nfi, Joseph L. *The Reunification Debate in British Southern Cameroons: The Role of French Cameroon Immigrants* (Bamenda: Langaa Publishing, 2014) 339–349; Ndahinda, Felix M. "Peoples' rights, indigenous rights and interpretative ambiguities in decisions of the African Commission on Human and Peoples' Rights" (2016) 16:1 *AHRLJ* 44–48. For an ample account of the Anglophone/Francophone problem see also Awasom, Nicodemus F. "Negotiating federalism: How ready were Cameroonian leaders before the February 1961 United Nations Plebiscites?" (2002) 36:3 *Canadian J Afri Stud* 425; Anyefru, Emmanuel "Paradoxes of internationalisation of the Anglophone problem in Cameroon" (2010) 28:1 *J Contemp Afri Stud* 85.

34   Kamga, Serges A.D. "Human rights in Africa: Prospects for the realisation of the right to development under the New Partnership for Africa's Development" (Doctoral Thesis, University of Pretoria 2011)204.

35   Awung. W.J. & Atanga, Mufor "Economic crisis and multi-party politics in Cameroon" (2011) 5:1 *CJDHR* 102.

36   Ogunmola, Dele "Redesigning cooperation: The eschatology of Franco-African relations" (2009) 19:3 *J Soc Sci* 233–242; Touati, Sylvain "French foreign policy in Africa: Between pré-carré and multilateralism" *Chatham House – An Africa Programme Briefing Note* February 2007 2; Feuer, Guy "La révision des accords de coopération Franco-Africains et Franco-Malgaches" (1973) *Annuaire Français de Droit International* 720–739; Koutonin, Mauna R. "14 African countries forced by France to pay colonial tax for the benefits of slavery and colonisation" (2014) *Silicon Africa* available at: http://www.siliconafrica.com/france-colonial-tax/ (accessed: 30 October 2017); Le Vine, Victor T. *Politics in Francophone Africa* (Boulder: Lynne Rienner, 2004) 2–6.

RIGHT TO DEVELOPMENT GOVERNANCE FOR AFRICA

intended to embark on were unfortunately quickly replaced with institution-alised "patrimonialism, personality cult[ism][...] [and] bureaucratic and polit-ical corruption" with the associated "negative consequence on the country's development".[37]

Although Cameroon subsequently ratified the African Charter in 1989 among other regional instruments that enshrine the right to development and is thus, legally bound to ensure its realisation, as Rousselot rightly observes, the country is on record for serious human rights abuses (the right to development inclusive) and deprivation of fundamental freedoms that undermine its development.[38] Based on constitutional recognition and following a political statement made by President Biya at the UN summit in 2001 that the government of Cameroon takes the right to development seriously,[39] the situation in the country does not give the impression that it actually does. The end of colonial rule saw most colonial powers taking a complete hands-off approach to their territorial possessions in the colonies. However, for Francophone Africa, decolonisation rather marked a re-invention of imperial relations with France in what has come to be known as *Françafrique*.[40] Compliance with the secretive cooperation accords, which Moncrieff says, defy standard interpretations of cooperation,[41] has meant that the constitutional guarantee of the right to development in Cameroon is stifled by the nature of Franco-Cameroon relations, described by Peter Uvin as a "private pres-idential matter beyond democratic scrutiny".[42] The cooperation accords ensured a nominal kind of independence for Cameroon that would not upset French eco-nomic interests in the country, and thus allowed the latter greater benefit at the expense of the well-being of the Cameroonian people.[43]

With regard to the obligations imposed on states to respect human rights extraterritorially,[44] although France purports to promote rights-based

---

37   Awung & Atanga, *supra* note 35,102.
38   Rousselot, Juliette "The impact of French influence on democracy and human rights in Cameroon" (2010) 4:1 *CJDHR* 61–62.
39   See Kamga, *supra* note 34, 204.
40   Benneyworth, I.J. "The ongoing relationship between France and its former African colo-nies" *E-International Relations* of 11 June 2011 1–6.
41   Moncrieff, Richard "French relations with Sub-Saharan Africa under President Sarkozy" (2012) *South African Institute of International Affairs* 6–7.
42   Uvin, Peter "On high moral ground: The incorporation of human rights by the develop-ment enterprise" (2002) XVII *The Fletcher Journal of Development Studies* 5.
43   Konings, Piet & Nyamnjoh, Francis B. *Negotiating an Anglophone Identity: A Study of the Politics of Recognition and Representation in Cameroon* (Leiden/Boston: Koninklijke Brill NV, 2003) 4; Rousselot, *supra* note 38, 60.
44   Skogly, Sigrun I. "Extra-national obligations towards economic and social rights" (2002) *International Council on Human Rights Policy* 7–34.

230   CHAPTER 5

approaches to development,[45] its relations with Cameroon, established in accordance with the cooperation accords entered into in 1959, is not based on any considerations for development as a human right. As Rousselot has written, the colonial bond between France and Cameroon remains unbroken, because of "the economic benefits that Cameroon represents for France".[46] Accordingly, since independence France has maintained unfettered control over Cameroon's natural resources and in shaping its domestic policies to ensure they do not run contrary to French interests,[47] with little or no regard as to whether such interests are compatible with those of the people of Cameroon.[48] Although France has since independence remained the leading development cooperation partner to Cameroon,[49] it has used this as a means to foster its colonial continuation policies in contravention of the right to development and other human rights guaranteed to the people of Cameroon.[50]

Such colonial allegiance to France constitutes a major constraining factor to the realisation of the right to development in Cameroon in the sense that it limits Cameroon's potential to adopt appropriate domestic policies to advance that right to development. This is explained in part by popular uprisings that have erupted in Cameroon and how France has directly intervened to suppress legitimate demands for change.[51] For instance, a booming Cameroonian economy that kicked off after independence with an annual growth rate of 6–7 per cent, which was considered an economic success story in sub-Saharan Africa, dramatically collapsed in 1985 as a result of an economic crisis that aggravated the poverty situation.[52] The government's failure to deal with the crisis frustrated aspirations for advancement, which led to popular demands for multiparty politics in the wave of democratisation that hit the country in

---

45   See generally French Ministry of Foreign Affairs "Post-2015 Agenda on development: French position paper prepared with civil society" (2013) *Directorate-General of Global Affairs, Development and Partnerships – Working Document* 1–21.

46   Rousselot, *supra* note 38, 64.

47   As above, 64.

48   Amuwo, Kunle "France and the economic integration project in Francophone Africa" (1999) 4:1 *Afr J Pol Sc* 4.

49   OECD *OECD Development Cooperation Peer Reviews: France 2013* (France: Organisation for Economic Cooperation and Development Publishing, 2014) 118.

50   Rousselot, *supra* note 38, 61–62.

51   Konings, Piet & Nyamnjoh, Francis B. "The Anglophone problem in Cameroon" (1997) 35:2 *The Journal of Modern African* 222; Fearon, James & Laitin, David "Cameroon" (d.n.a.) *Standford University* 1–25;Rousselot, *supra* note 38, 66.

52   MINEPAT "Cameroon Vision 2035: Working paper" (2009) *Republic of Cameroon* ix; Awung & Atanga, *supra* note 35, 95; Konings & Nyamnjoh 2003, *supra* note 43, 6–8.

the early 90s.[53] Orchestrated by a radical opposition movement, the political turmoil lasted several months, with massive civil disobedience characterised by a "ghost city" campaign that witnessed among others, the boycott of French goods and services, the grounding of business activities, and refusal to pay taxes and utility bills, which almost brought the nation to a stand-still.[54] In a desperate effort to stabilise the economy, the government resorted to donor assistance, which unfortunately failed.[55] The situation was exacerbated with the introduction of the World Bank and International Monetary Fund (IMF) imposed structural adjustment austerity measures, which resulted in currency devaluation of the *Communauté Financière d'Afrique* (CFA) Franc,[56] discontinuation of development projects and deepening poverty as living conditions plummeted.[57]

The nation-wide anti-government protests posed a real threat to French economic interests. In the heat of the political turmoil, President Francois Mitterrand issued a policy statement at the La Baule *Françafrique* summit, pledging unflinching support for democratisation in Africa.[58] However, because of fears of losing control over Cameroon to the radical opposition, the French government rather increased its Official Development Assistance (ODA) to the government in power by FF335 million (approximately USD55.7 million) within the period of two years, coupled with the granting of debt relief in 1992.[59] Thus, the Biya regime backed by French support, used militarised operational commands in a prolonged state of emergency to thwart popular demands for change and thus held the country's development prospects at bay.[60] The turn of events, which ended up in the suppression of the anti-French opposition leaves the conclusion that the increase in French assistance to Cameroon was actually not intended to support the democratisation process but to retain the Biya regime in power in return for protecting French economic interests.[61] Another popular uprising in February 2008 triggered by increasing prices of foodstuff and other basic commodities and aimed to achieve improved living

---

53   Awung & Atanga, *supra* note 35, 95; Konings & Nyamnjoh 2003, *supra* note 43, 8.
54   Konings & Nyamnjoh 1997, *supra* note 51, 215–216 & 222; Awung & Atanga, *supra* note 35,116.
55   MINEPAT, *supra* note 52, ix.
56   Ngwa, A. Kenneth "The baobab tree lives on: Paul Biya and the logic of political survival" (2009) *African Studies Department Johns Hopkins SAIS* 4.
57   MINEPAT, *supra* note 52, ix.
58   Ngwa, *supra* note 56, 6; Rousselot, *supra* note 38, 68.
59   Rousselot, *supra* note 38, 68.
60   Rousselot, *supra* note 38, 68–69; Ngwa, *supra* note 56, 8–10.
61   Rousselot, *supra* note 38, 69.

conditions, was also ruthlessly suppressed by the government, with the support of the resident French military in the country.[62] Contrary to article 7 of the Declaration on the Right to Development, which encourages the conversion of funds spent on arms into development efforts, France rather promotes the use of arms against aspirations for development in Cameroon.

The Constitution of Cameroon and the African Charter recognise the importance of a country's wealth and resources as requisite for improved livelihood.[63] There is no denying that as a "former" colonial master, France remains Cameroon's leading development cooperation partner, providing a net ODA of USD202 million in 2011 alone according to the Organisation for Economic Cooperation and Development (OECD).[64] Paradoxically, the standard of living in Cameroon remains unacceptably low, ranking at 151st out of 189 on the human development index.[65] As Arjun Sengupta has underscored, the right to development entails equality, which includes equality of opportunity, of access to resources, of participation in the development process and also in the equitable distribution of development gains.[66] In spite of these guarantees, the peoples of Cameroon have through the complicity of the Franco-Cameroon policy of subjugation been denied enjoyment of the right to development guaranteed to them by the Constitution of Cameroon and the African Charter. Because France is not necessarily bound by these instruments, the duty remains that of Cameroon as a sovereign state to concretely prioritise the right to development, which could in effect, dramatically change the *status quo* and power dynamics in Franco-Cameroon relations.

Cameroon's lack of commitment in protecting the right to development has been the subject of litigation in the *Bakweri Lands Claim* and *Kevin Gumne* cases.[67] The *Bakweri Lands Claim* case, in which the complainants alleged the expropriation of their historic lands as constituting a violation of their right

---

62 As above, 70.

63 Constitution of the Republic of Cameroon 1998 preamble; African Charter, *supra* note 1, art 21.

64 OECD 2014, *supra* note 49, 118; Mbangsi, Chi "Cameroon/France: Does Cameroon benefit from special relationship?" (2013) *Iroko Africa* available at: http://irokoheritage.com/2013/08/22/cameroon-special-relationship-with-france-a-benefit/ (accessed: 5 September 2017).

65 UNDP "Human Development Report 2013: Cameroon" (2013) *UNDP* 2; UNDP "2018 statistical update", *supra* note 19.

66 Sengupta, Arjun "On the theory and practice of the right to development" (2002) 24:4 *Hum Rts Qtly* 849.

67 *Bakweri Land Claims Committee v Cameroon* Comm 260/2002 AHRLR (2004) 43; *Kevin Mgwanga Gumne & Others v Cameroon* (2009) AHRLR 9 (ACHPR 2009) paras 205 & 206.

to development protected by the African Charter was the first right to development claim to be brought before the African Commission.[68] However, the complaint failed the admissibility test for failing to satisfy the requirement of exhausting local remedies and therefore, the Commission did not get a chance to pronounce on the merits.[69] In the *Kevin Gumne* case, the English-speaking people of Cameroon alleged marginalising treatment by the predominantly French-speaking part of the country amounting to violation of a range of provisions of the African Charter, including the right to development.[70] Quite controversially, the African Commission acknowledged evidence of discriminatory treatment of the English-speaking population perpetrated by the respondent state[71] but failed to establish a violation of the right to development resulting from such discriminatory practices. The Commission thus squandered the opportunity to uphold the right to development guaranteed to the peoples of Cameroon and therefore also, the opportunity to compel Cameroon as a state to take its constitutional and treaty obligations on the right to development seriously.[72]

It is uncertain that the Vision 2035 development plan, in which the government envisages to reconsider its development processes,[73] would be achieved under the present cooperation arrangement with France. Dependency theorists posit that developing countries can only advance by breaking their links with developed countries.[74] Following this logic, if Cameroon is to fulfil its obligations on the right to development, the lopsided relations with France

---

68   Kamga, Serges A.D. & Fombad, Charles M. "A critical review of the jurisprudence of the African Commission on the right to development" (2013) 57:2 *J African Law* 10; Okafor, Obiora C. "A regional perspective: Article 22 of the African Charter on Human and Peoples' Rights" in UN Human Rights (eds) *Realising the Right to Development: Essays in Commemoration of 25 Years of the United Nations Declaration on the Right to Development* (Geneva: UN Publication, 2013) 376.

69   Okafor 2013, *supra* note 68, 376.

70   *Kevin Gumne, supra* note 67, paras 1-19.

71   As above, paras 100 & 215(1)(1).

72   For example, none of the recommendations made by the African Commission in para 215 of the *Gumne* case have been respected by the government of Cameroon, defendant in the litigation. This has resulted in the lethal conflict that sparked off in the country in October 2016, where, because of the continuous marginalisation, subjugation and forced assimilation, the people of the Northwest and Southwest regions (historically known as Southern Cameroons) who constituted the complainants in the case rose up again to claim the right to sovereign statehood based on the "unquestionable and inalienable right to self-determination" guaranteed by article 20 of the African Charter.

73   MINDEPAT, *supra* note 52, ix.

74   Singh, Katar *Rural Development: Principles, Policies and Management* (New Delhi: SAGE Publications, 2003) 63.

234 CHAPTER 5

need to be ruptured to a great extent. It requires France to give up most of the privileges that it currently enjoys, to ensure a shift in the balance of power in favour of greater autonomy for Cameroon in matters of domestic policy formulation. Of course, as Kunle Amuwo rightly observes, "France is hard put to close shop in Africa", a sentiment that has been reiterated by French Heads of States ruling out the possibility of abandoning their colonial possessions in Africa.[75] Similar feelings have also been expressed by francophone African leaders who see cooperation with France as indispensable for the survival of their countries.[76]

Considered in relation to the right to development standards discussed in chapter two, the nature of Franco-Cameroon relations is designed such that in spite of the right and the duty granted to states to formulate policies to uphold the right to development, Cameroon is unable to adopt any such policies that would jeopardise relations with France. With the understanding that the right to development demands action, and with evidence that it may not possibly be achieved through policy reforms or litigation the subjugated peoples are left as alternative remedy only with radical activism, probably on the basis of the right to self-determination, which Udombana asserts is of the same nature as the right to development.[77] Otherwise, this analysis has aimed to demonstrate how development cooperation negatively impacts on the realisation of the right to development in Cameroon, and thus justifies the need for a shift in paradigm to considering the right to development as a model for development as illustrated later.

3.1.2.2   *Libya under Qaddafi's Reign*

The following historical narrative explains the context within which socio-economic and cultural transformation took place in Libya, which is explained here as relating to the realisation of the right to development. Present-day Libya has at different stages throughout its history suffered conquest, subjugation and humiliation[78] as well as invasion by European

---

75   Amuwo, *supra* note 48, 2–4.

76   As above 59 2; the late President Omar Bongo of Gabon is quoted to have remarked that "France without Gabon is like a car without petrol, Gabon without France is analogous to a car without a driver", while Cameroonian President Paul Biya is remembered for his unapologetic public statement in which he declared himself the "best pupil" of the then French President Francois Mitterrand.

77   Udombana, Nsongurua J. "The third world and the right to development: Agenda for the next millennium" (2000) 22:3 *Hum Rts Qtly* 770.

78   Monti-Belkaoui, Janice & Riahi-Belkaoui, Ahmed *Qaddafi: The Man and His Policies* (Aldersrot: Avebury Ashgate Publishing Ltd, 1996) 2; El Fathaly, Omar I. & Palmer, Monte

RIGHT TO DEVELOPMENT GOVERNANCE FOR AFRICA

powers.[79] Before the UN resolution that granted Libya independence in 1951,[80] as El Fathaly and Monte Palmer have noted, Libya by every indication ranked poorest on the development scale.[81] However, with the discovery and commercial production of oil in 1959, the Senussi Monarchy that was established at independence under Mohammed Idris, in spite of its political weaknesses, managed to transform the country that initially "lacked people, skills, resources and even much hope [...] into a wealthy little state with enviable expectations".[82]

Unmindful of the suppression that Libya endured under foreign invasion, Idris established his reign on a "stubborn loyalty" to western powers whose primary interest was the thirst for Libyan oil, much to the annoyance of the Libyan people who yearned for total liberation from the "yoke of imperialism".[83] Mohammed Idris' indebtedness and allegiance to the former colonisers led to many concessions that virtually traded off Libya's autonomy.[84] Coupled with corruption and looting, the opulence that the oil economy brought to Libya saw very little trickling down to the rest of the population.[85] This scenario is not unlike the post-independence difficulties that other African countries faced in the 1960s, which is attributed to the fact that independence was achieved without an operational model for development. Taking advantage of widespread anti-imperialist sentiments, Muammar Qaddafi masterminded the overthrow of Idris in 1969,[86] in a bloodless *coup d'état* that was welcomed across Libya with spontaneous popular support.[87]

In response to popular will and the interest of Libyan society, radical socio-economic and cultural reforms, including drastic reduction in rents to encourage property ownership, doubling of the minimum wage and nationalisation of foreign banks were introduce to purge the country of colonial exploitation

---

     Political Development and Social Change in Libya (Toronto: DC Heath and Company, 1980) 15.

79   Sklare, Aly "Libya: Struggle for independence" available at: http://hj2009per4libya.weebly .com/struggle-for-independence.html (accessed: 10 July 2016); Monti-Belkaoui & Riahi-Belkaoui, *supra* note 78, 3–4.

80   Wright, John *A History of Libya* (London: Hurst & Company, 2010) 175.

81   El Fathaly & Palmer, *supra* note 78, 1.

82   Wright, *supra* note 80, 177.

83   Monti-Belkaoui & Riahi-Belkaoui, *supra* note 78, 6–7; Wright, *supra* note 80, 179–184.

84   Wright, *supra* note 80, 182; Monti-Belkaoui & Riahi-Belkaoui, *supra* note 78, 5.

85   Monti-Belkaoui & Riahi-Belkaoui, *supra* note 78, 8; El Fathaly & Palmer, *supra* note 78, 37–38.

86   Wright, *supra* note 80, 181; Monti-Belkaoui & Riahi-Belkaoui, *supra* note 78, 9.

87   El Fathaly & Palmer, *supra* note 78, 41.

236 CHAPTER 5

and ensure prosperity for the Libyan peoples.[88] Although Libya only ratified the African Charter in July 1986,[89] Qaddafi's governing ideology of "post colonial third world development" signalled a pursuit of the right to well-being and improved living standards,[90] which is not unconnected to the concept of the right to development. However, because Qaddafi's policies clashed with western conceptions of development, his revolutionary policies met with fierce criticism.[91] Considering that there is no unique model for development, it is of interest to note how the policies of the Libyan government contributed to advancing the right to development in Libya.

To begin with, it is argued that Libya did not need to pursue western conceptions of economic development underlined by the accumulation of wealth in the hands of a few while the reality on the ground necessitated socialist redistribution of the country's wealth among the impoverished masses. Although not specifically formulated to respond to the right to development, it is possible to argue that the government's policies significantly complied with right to development standards, in respect of which the quality of life of the Libyan people is recorded to have improved dramatically.[92] Because of the oil wealth, Libya was capable of adopting and sustaining a radical self-reliant development policy without which, like many other African countries, it might have remained under foreign exploitation. This supports Amartya Sen's theory of development as freedom, which implies that when granted complete freedom from imperial domination the people are capable of self-sustainably shaping their own development trajectory.[93] Unfortunately, such freedom was not absolute in Libya, where despite enjoying the highest standard of living in Africa according to the United Nations Development Programme (UNDP) human development ranking, Qaddafi's repressive leadership generally deprived the Libyan people of basic human rights.

The Declaration on the Right to Development requires state parties to formulate national development policies to ensure sustained livelihood and well-being through meaningful participation and the equitable redistribution of the benefits deriving from the development process.[94] As

---

88   Monti-Belkaoui & Riahi-Belkaoui, *supra* note 78, 11; Deeb, Marius K. & Deeb, Mary J. *Libya since the Revolution: Aspects of Social and Political Development* (New York: Praeger Publishers, 1982) 116–117.

89   Heyns & Killander, *supra* note 27, 504.

90   Monti-Belkaoui & Riahi-Belkaoui, *supra* note 78, 14.

91   Sicker, Martin *The Making of a Pariah State: The Adventurist Politics of Muammar Qaddafi* (Westport: Praeger, 1987) 21–22; Monti-Belkaoui & Riahi-Belkaoui, *supra* note 78, 15.

92   Monti-Belkaoui & Riahi-Belkaoui, *supra* note 78, 15.

93   See Sen, Armatya *Development as Freedom* (Oxford: Oxford University Press, 1999) 87–95.

94   Declaration on the Right to Development, *supra* note 1, para 2(3).

RIGHT TO DEVELOPMENT GOVERNANCE FOR AFRICA

universally acknowledged, the right to development incorporates the right to self-determination, which implies asserting sovereign ownership over domestic natural wealth and resources.[95] In contrast to the practice of caution that has held back development in most African countries, Qaddafi confronted imperialism head-on, notably in formulating domestic policies which foreign stakeholders were obliged to comply with. It is noted that United Sates (US) President Nixon was constrained by these measures to compromise on his foreign policy to employ force and repression on Libya and rather opted to negotiate on business terms with Qaddafi, who held the trump card – Libyan oil.[96] Like Libya, the rest of Africa is endowed with valued resources which place the continent at a geostrategic advantage over foreign stakeholders. As a pre-requisite to achieving the right to development, African governments are obligated as stipulated by the African Charter to "eliminate all forms of foreign economic exploitation",[97] which Libya succeeded in doing.

Libya thus debunked the myth that Africa's development agenda can only be determined by foreign powers, whereas international law recognises the sovereignty of every state to shape its own development policies. By adopting policies that favoured fair redistribution of the country's resources to ensure better quality of life, Libya demonstrated that the right to development is achievable in Africa. It goes beyond theorising political ideologies[98] and necessitates "a highly pragmatic, nondoctrinaire approach to major national issues".[99] It seems as Vandenbogaerde has noted that states are often not comfortable with framing their domestic policies in light of the right to development.[100] This is evident in their promptness to compromise state sovereignty and the right to independent policy formulation in favour of foreign interests.[101] In spite of their avowed commitments to ensure the realisation of the right to development, African governments are "yet to move adequately from the abstract to the concrete", to get out of the theoretical sphere into the domain of "development in action".[102] Having experienced colonialism, Qaddafi nursed a deep

---

95   As above, para 1(2).

96   Monti-Belkaoui & Riahi-Belkaoui, *supra* note 78, 11.

97   African Charter, *supra* note 1, art 21(5).

98   Deeb & Deeb, *supra* note 88, 115.

99   Amir, Shimeon *Israel's Development Cooperation with Africa, Asia and Latin America* (New York: Praeger Publishers, 1974) 2.

100 Vandenbogaerde, Arne "The right to development in international human rights Law: A call for its dissolution" (2013) 31:2 *Neth Qtly Hum Rts* 202.

101 See for example, the illustration on Cameroon.

102 Amir, *supra* note 99, 5 & 1.

resentment against imperialism and exploitation.[103] Although his revolutionary foreign expeditions brought him into the bad books of international politics, he is credited for putting an end to foreign domination in Libya, at least during his time in power.[104]

Poor domestic political organisation no doubt created bureaucratic challenges that threatened the government's ability to deal with the increased socio-economic demands from the masses.[105] Nonetheless, before the North Atlantic Treaty Organisation's (NATO) supposed humanitarian intervention, the people of Libya enjoyed a standard of living that rated the highest in Africa. Libya's per capita income ranked as one of the highest in the world, access to socio-economic amenities such as education, health care and housing was free, the people enjoy a life expectancy of 74 years and in spite of several years of imposed economic sanctions the country survived on an absolutely debt-free economic balance sheet.[106] According to Monti-Belkaoui and Riahi-Belkaoui, women in Libya enjoyed extensive protection of human rights, unlike in most other Arab countries in Africa and the middle-east,[107] a view which unfortunately is not universally accepted, owing especially to Qaddafi's repressive leadership and appalling human rights record.

Despite the high standard of living and the enjoyment of a wide range of socio-economic and cultural rights, the people of Libya were reportedly deprived of many civil and political rights, constituting a serious constraint to the full realisation of the right to development in that country. The situation is exacerbated following the revolution that ushered-in the National Transition Council, which Monti-Belkaoui and Riahi-Belkaoui, create uncertainty as to whether the high standard of living that the people once enjoyed will ever be restored.[108] Many of the constitutional guarantees that enabled the Libyan peoples to live a lifestyle incomparable with the rest of Africa have been scrapped by the National Transition Council. Compare for example, the

---

103   Monti-Belkaoui & Riahi-Belkaoui, *supra* note 78, 18.

104   Wright, *supra* note 80, 202–204.

105   El Fathaly & Palmer, *supra* note 78, 7–8; Wright, *supra* note 80, 228.

106   Chengu, Garikai "Libya: From Africa's richest state under Gaddafi to failed state after NATO intervention" (2014) *Global Research* available at: www.globalresearch.ca/libya-from-africas-richest-state-under-gaddafi-to-failed-state-after-nato-intervention/5408740 (accessed: 29 December 2015); Chossudovsky, Michel "Destroying a country's standard of living: What Libya had achieved, what has been destroyed" (2013) *Global Research* available at: www.globalresearch.ca/destroying-a-country-s-standard-of-living-what-libya-had-achieved-what-has-been-destroyed/26686 (accessed: 29 December 2015).

107   Monti-Belkaoui & Riahi-Belkaoui, *supra* note 78, 268.

108   As above, 18.

RIGHT TO DEVELOPMENT GOVERNANCE FOR AFRICA

radical promise contained in the preamble to the 1969 Libyan Constitution and the aspirational undertone contained in the preamble to the 2011 Constitution, which stipulate respectively as follows:

> The Revolutionary Command Council, in the name of the Arab people in Libya, who pledged to restore their freedom, enjoy the wealth of their land, live in a society in which every loyal citizen has the right to prosperity and well-being, who are determined to break the restraints which impede their growth and their development, [...] who understand fully that the alliance of reaction and imperialism is responsible for their underdevelopment despite the abundance of their natural resources.[109]

> Based on the legitimacy of [the 17 February 2011] revolution, and in response to the desire of the Libyan people and their aspirations for achieving democracy and promoting the principles of political pluralism and statehood based on institutions, and aspiring to a society enjoying stability, tranquillity and justice which develop through science and culture, achieves prosperity and sanitary well-being and works on educating the future generations in the spirit of Islam and love of the good and of the country.[110]

It is important to note the regression from the authoritative nature of the rights to well-being in the 1969 Constitution and the cursory manner in which rights envisaging a reasonable standard of living are crafted in the 2011 Constitution, which provide respectively as follows:

> Work in the Libyan Arab Republic is a right, a duty, and an honour for earnable-bodied citizen [...]
> The state will endeavour to liberate the national economy from dependence and foreign influence, and to turn it into a productive national economy, based on public ownership by the Libyan people and on private ownership by individual citizens [...].
> Education is a right and a duty for all Libyans [...].
> Health care is a right guaranteed by the State through the creation of hospitals and health establishments in accordance with the law.[111]

---

109   Libya Constitution 1969 preamble.
110   Libya's Constitution of 2011 preamble.
111   Libya Constitution 1969, *supra* note 109, arts 4, 7, 14 & 15.

240   CHAPTER 5

As opposed to -

> The state shall ensure equal opportunity and strive to guarantee a proper
> standard of living, the right to work, education medical care and social secu-
> rity to every citizen [...]. It shall guarantee the just distribution of national
> wealth among citizens and among the different cities and regions of the
> State.[112]

The above extracts illustrate that the present constitutional dispensation under
the National Transition Council does not guarantee the enabling environment
within which the right to development, which the peoples of Libya had enjoyed
for over 40 years may ever again be exercised. This notwithstanding, the new
Libya remains legally bound by its treaty obligations under the African Charter
to ensure that development in the country is achieved with equity and justice.
Consequently, if present-day Libya is to regain its position on the human development index, it would need to proactively assert the right to development guaranteed by the African Charter rather than surrender the rebuilding of the country to
foreign stakeholders.

Unlike in the case of Cameroon, the analysis on Libya has aimed to show how
the country successfully established a post-colonial right to development dispensation through actual self-determination in domestic policy formulation, which
however, has been brought to ruin by foreign stakeholders. Like Libya, South
Africa equally managed its post-apartheid transition through a robust responsive
democratic dispensation that allows for a purposive reading of the right to development within the domestic constitutional order.

3.1.2.3   *Post-apartheid South Africa*

Apart from a creative and purposive reading of the provisions of the bill of
rights in the South African Constitution, the right to development is not
enshrined in the Constitution, which however, is hailed as one of the most
progressive in the world owing to its generous guarantee of an extensive range
of civil and political, socio-economic, community as well as environmental
rights.[113] The drafters of the Constitution are said to have drawn inspiration
heavily from the Constitutions of Canada and Germany among others, which
greatly influenced the formulation of the provisions of the bill of rights.[114] In

---

112   Libya's Constitution 2011, *supra* note 110, art 8.

113   Constitution of the Republic of South Africa 1996 sects 9–31 on the bill of rights.

114   Davis, Dennis M. "Constitutional burrowing: The influence of legal culture and legal
        history in the reconstruction of comparative influence – the South African experience"

the same year, 1996 that the Constitution was adopted, South Africa also ratified the African Charter in July 1996 and by implication became bound by the human and peoples' rights provisions contained therein.

Although the African Charter enshrines a continuum of human and peoples' rights that are framed to reflect the realities on the continent, it seems that the South African Constitution did not draw much inspiration and conceptual lessons from it. Consequently, most of the collective rights, including especially the right to development, which as Sedar Senghor emphasised, are of "particular importance" to Africa,[115] missed to be captured in the South African Constitution. This notwithstanding, the entire transformative constitutional dispensation has correctly been interpreted to provide the context for the realisation of the right to development[116] even much more than in the case of the DRC, Ethiopia and Malawi where the right is clearly guaranteed constitutional protection. Neither the Vision 2030 National Development Plan adopted in 2011[117] nor any other domestic development policy instrument makes any mention of the right to development guaranteed to the peoples of South Africa.

However, in submitting its first periodic report to the African Commission in 2005 and the 2015 combined report under the African Charter on Human and Peoples' Rights and the Protocol to the African Charter on the Rights of Women in Africa on the extent of realisation of the human and peoples' rights provisions contained in these instruments, the South African government reported haven complied with the right to development enshrined in article 22 of the African Charter.[118] The right to development imposes an obligation

---

(2003) 1:2 *I.CON* 185–188; Sarkin, Jeremy "The effect of constitutional borrowings on the drafting of South Africa's bill of rights and interpretation of human rights provisions" (1998) 1:2 *Journal of Constitutional Law* 176–204.

115 See the African Commission's ruling in the *Kevin Gumne* case, *supra* note 67, para 173.

116 Ngang, Carol C. "Radical transformation and a reading of the right to development in the South African constitutional order" (2019) 35:1 *South African Journal on Human Rights* 25–49; Shai, Isaac "The right to development, transformative constitutionalism and radical transformation in South Africa: Postcolonial and decolonial reflections" (2019) 19:1 *African Human Rights Law Journal* 494–509;Gutto, Shadrack "The right to development: An implied right in South Africa's constitutional order" in SAHRC *Reflections on Democracy and Human Rights: A Decade of the South African Constitution (Act 108 of 1996)* (Cape Town: South African Human Rights Commission, 2006) 109–118; First Periodic Report of South Africa to the African Commission 38th Ordinary Session 2005 para 325.

117 South African National Planning Commission "National Development Plan: Vision for 2013" adopted on 11 November 2011.

118 First Periodic Report of South Africa to the African Commission 38th Ordinary Session 2005 para 325, Combined Second Periodic Report under the African Charter on Human

242   CHAPTER 5

not just for the realisation of socio-economic and cultural rights but also for
the institutionalisation of equality, legality and legitimacy in asserting equity
and justice in the development process. Accordingly, Sandra Liebenberg
affirms that the South African Constitution imposes an overwhelming obligation on the state to adhere to the provisions in the bill of rights.[119] It also
imposes an obligation to consider international law when interpreting the
bill of rights, which does not deny the existence of other rights and freedoms
enshrined in other instruments, including the right to development in the
African Charter.[120]

Indeed, the post-apartheid transformative constitutional dispensation constituting a number of robust institutional mechanisms such as the
Constitutional Court and the Office of the Public Protector among others, have
been able to cause the government to adhere to its human rights, especially
socio-economic rights obligations. These measures have facilitated transformation for a large number of previously disadvantaged black South Africans
even though the proportion of those that have experience improvement in
living standards remains relatively minimal. Even though it is important to
explicitly incorporate the right to development as a standalone provision in
domestic law, the South African experience illustrates that such a measure is
not an inevitable prerequisite to guarantee implementation. Contrary to the
case of Ethiopia, discussed below, besides taking legislative measure in respect
of article 1 of the African Charter, state parties are required to go a bit further
to put in place functional mechanisms to ensure that the right to development
practically becomes beneficial to the peoples to whom it is guaranteed.

3.1.2.4   *Ethiopia*

As indicated in the previous chapter, Ethiopia is one of the African countries
that has domesticated and explicitly enshrined the right to development in its
constitution, implying that the entitlement to development is recognised and
protected as an integral part of the supreme law of the country. In connection
to recognising the right to development as a central part of the domestic legal
framework in Ethiopia, the Constitution adds that "[a]ll international agreements ratified by Ethiopia are an integral part of the law of the land", which

---

      and Peoples' Rights and Initial Report under the Protocol to the African Charter on the
      Rights of Women in Africa 2015 paras 485-487.
119   Liebenberg, Sandra "Adjudicating social rights under a transformative constitution" in
      Langford, Malcolm (ed) *Social Rights Jurisprudence: Emerging Trend in International and
      Comparative Law* (Cambridge: Cambridge University Press, 2009) 77.
120   Constitution of South Africa, *supra* note 113, sect 39(1)(b) & (3).

RIGHT TO DEVELOPMENT GOVERNANCE FOR AFRICA

means that the right to development enshrined in the African Charter which Ethiopia ratified in 1998 applies directly and has the same force of law as domestic law.[121] However, unlike the African Charter, the Ethiopian Constitution is a bit more precise in its conceptualisation of the right to development; what it aims to achieve, how it intends to achieve that goal and the implication for its relations with foreign stakeholders within the framework of international cooperation. It provides that:

1. The Peoples of Ethiopia as a whole, and each Nation, Nationality and People in Ethiopia in particular have the right to improved living standards and to sustainable development.
2. Nationals have the right to participate in national development and, in particular, to be consulted with respect to policies and projects affecting their community.
3. All international agreements and relations concluded, established or conducted by the State shall protect and ensure Ethiopia's right to sustainable development.
4. The basic aim of development activities shall be to enhance the capacity of citizens for development and to meet their basic needs.[122]

Yonas Sisay explains that improved living standards literally refers to "the average level of well-being of peoples in a particular country", which is granted to be enjoyed by the peoples of Ethiopia as a constitutional entitlement.[123] Practically, it guarantees entitlement to the most essential material possessions necessary for sustaining life, the development of human productive capabilities as well as the eradication of poverty among other obstacles that hinder development. The otherwise ambiguous concept of sustainable development has generally been explained to embody the idea of social justice and intergenerational equity, which in this context entitles present generations of Ethiopian peoples to aspire for the highest attainable standard of well-being without compromising the rights reserved to future generations to eventually also meet their own development needs. The right to participation provides in principle that the peoples of Ethiopia would actively, freely and meaningfully

---

121   Constitution of the Federal Republic of Ethiopia 1994 art 9(4).

122   As above, art 43.

123   Sisay, Yonas T. "Human rights and development in Ethiopia: Taking the constitutional right to development seriously" in Ngang, Carol C. & Kamga Serges D. (eds) *Insights into Policies and Practices on the Right to Development* (London/New York: Rowman & Littlefield International, 2020) 17.

244 CHAPTER 5

be involved in the framing and implementation of development policies and programmes and in the equitable sharing of development gains.[124]

In addition to defining the right to development in specific terms as comprising the three component elements above, the Ethiopian Constitution also makes provision for a range of civil and political (and democratic) as well as socio-economic and cultural rights, which in accord with the Declaration on the Right to Development and article 22 of the African Charter, sum up into the composite entitlement to development that envisages the constant improvement in living standards for the Ethiopian peoples. This is guaranteed to be achieved in a sustainable manner and with due regard to the fact that only the peoples of Ethiopia have the potential to shape their own development processes in a productive manner.

Historically, Ethiopia has been a poor country, noted for extensive famines and draughts, which amplify poverty levels in the country and also directly impact on living standards in many ways. By giving constitutional recognition and protection of the right to development suggests, as the wording of article 43 indicates that living standards and sustainable development are ascertained to be achieved. It also suggests as a matter of legal obligation that the government will adopt the kind of radical domestic policies to facilitate the attainment of this development goal, which is guaranteed to be enjoyed as a right by all the peoples, nations and nationalities in Ethiopia. On the contrary, and as a matter of fact, in 25 years (a quarter of a century) since the adoption of the Ethiopian Constitution in 1994, the drive to achieve improved living standards and sustainable development is yet to become standard practice in the country.

Ethiopian has since the 1990s, following the UNDP human development criteria for measuring development, consistently ranked among the least developed countries in the world; currently occupying the 173rd position on the human development index out of 189, just a bit better than 16 other countries in the world. The Ethiopian example illustrates that it does not just suffice to enshrine the right to development into domestic law. Importantly, if this constitutional provision is to practically translate into better living standards and

---

124   Osmani, Siddiq R. "The human rights-based approach to development in the era of globalization" in UN Human Rights (ed) *Realizing the Right to Development: Essays in Commemoration of 25 Years of the United Nations Declaration on the Right to Development* (Geneva: UN Publication, 2013) 122; Cornwall, Andrea "Unpacking 'participation': Models, meanings and practices" (2008) 43:3 *Community Development Journal* 278; Crocker, David "Deliberative participation in local development" (2007) 8:3 *Journal of Human Development* 432.

sustainable development, the national development policy framework must indeed, reflect the enabling environment for that entitlement to be exercised and enjoyed.

The requisite enabling environment entails that the domestic policy framework must ensure that cooperation with foreign stakeholders does not adversely affect the realisation of the right to sustainable development. It further states that national development planning must be designed to advance the capabilities of the peoples of Ethiopia (in terms of participation) to contribute productively to sustainable development in the country and in that process, also satisfy their livelihood needs for improved living standards.

Although the constitutional right to development is understood as a composite entitlement comprising the rights to improved living standards, sustainable development and participation in national development, some scholars contend that it remains predominantly unclear what the realisation of these guarantees practically entail.[125] Sisay contends that the politicised policy framework in Ethiopia, which is driven by a controversial ideology of revolutionary democracy, a ruling party dominated state, conflict in the understanding of collective and individual rights, the creed of a developmental state and lack of credible accountability does not provide assurance that the right to development enshrined in the Constitution would be achieved.

It does not suffice to have the right to development enshrined as a constitutional entitlement.[126] What is most important as the examples of Libya and South Africa illustrate, is an enabling people-centred pro-poor policy framework that allows for socio-economic and cultural development (amounting to improved living standards, sustainable development and participation in government, in the case of Ethiopia) to be achieved. Abdi Ali highlights that article 13(2) of the Ethiopian Constitution require the constitutional right to development to be interpreted in conformity with the African Charter among other international human rights instruments.[127] However, contrary to the stipulation in article 1 of the African Charter in respect of which state parties commit to adopt legislative and other measures to give effect to the provisions of the Charter, Woldemichael intimates that the government of Ethiopia is yet to put in place a comprehensive legislation clarifying the content and application of the right to development enshrined in the domestic constitution.[128]

---

125 Woldemichael, Zelalem S. "The right to development under the Constitution of the Federal Democratic Republic of Ethiopia: Some reflections" (d.n.a) PROLAW *Student Journal of Rule of Law for Development* 3; Jibril, *Supra* note 26, 69.

126 Sisay, *supra* note 123.

127 Jibril, *supra* note 26, 69.

128 Woldemichael, *supra* note 125, 17; Sisay, *supra* note 123.

246   CHAPTER 5

There has also not been any legal claim before the courts of Ethiopia on the right to development guaranteed by the Constitution.[129]

3.1.2.5   *Nigeria*

As already highlighted in chapter four, the Constitution of Nigeria does not enshrine the right to development. Unlike older versions of the Nigerian Constitution, the one adopted in 1979 as subsequently amended in 1999 only came a bit close by making provision for a socio-economic rights regime in the form of national objectives and directive principles of state policy.[130] National objectives and directive principles are by nature (except explicitly stated) not justiciable, enforceable or subject to judicial review; generally only intended to inform the formulation of laws and policies[131] and applicable only at the discretion of the government.

Following Nigeria's ratification of the African Charter in June 1983 by an Act of Parliament,[132] the international law principle of treaty ratification required the government to proceed to domesticate the Charter into national law. This did not immediately happen until 2004 when the domestication of the Charter took place.[133] Accordingly, the right to development enshrined in the Charter, acquired the status of a claimable and enforceable entitlement within the Nigerian legal framework. Jurisprudence confirms that the provisions of the African Charter, including article 22 on the right to socio-economic and cultural development are directly applicable in Nigeria and consequently, can legitimately be claimed through the courts[134] or otherwise through political activism and the government of Nigeria would have the obligation to respond to such claims. This assurance has however, remained a matter of principle with no evidence of any actual legal or political action that has been undertaken in Nigeria with regard to asserting the right to development. Even though the African Commission on Human and Peoples' Rights held in paragraph 64 of the *SERAC* case that a violation of the right to food occasioned a violation

---

129   Jibril, *supra* note 125, 69.

130   Constitution of the Federal Republic of Nigeria (Promulgation) Act 24 of 1999 Cap C23 Vol 3 (LFN 2004 Revised) chap 2.

131   De Villiers, Bertus "Directive principles of state policy and fundamental rights: The Indian experience" (1992) 8:1 *South African Journal on Human Rights* 34.

132   African Charter on Human and Peoples' Rights Ratification and Enforcement Act No 2 of 1983.

133   Laws of the Federation of Nigeria 2004 on the Enforcement of provisions of the Charter on Human and Peoples' Rights Cap.A9 of 2004.

134   *Abacha v Fawehinmi* (2000) FWLR (Pt.4) paras 553 & 586; *SERAC* case, *supra* note 13, para 41.

of the right to development, it is important to note that the Ogoni community actually did not allege a violation of the right to development their complaint.

It is rational to anticipate that following the ratification and domestication of the African Charter by the Nigerian government two years after the Charter was adopted in 1981; implementation of the right to development enshrined therein would have become a defining factor in the country's development efforts. Unfortunately, this has not the case, especially owing to the fact that the governance system and policy framework during the fifteen years of military rule did not provide the requisite enabling enough to ensure that the peoples of Nigeria could assert entitlement to socio-economic and cultural development among other rights guaranteed by the African Charter. A National Action Plan for the Promotion and Protection of Human Rights initially adopted in 2009 is currently in force for an extended five-year period from 2017 to 2021.[135] In addition to enforcing the African Charter at the domestic level in Nigeria, the National Action, which recognises the government's role as the primary duty bearer, provides a suitable policy framework to ensure the implementation of the right to development.

The National Development Plan highlights the government's commitment to "improve the quality of life of all citizens, free the potential of every person in Nigeria and respect, protect, promote and fulfil all political, civil, social, economic and cultural rights".[136] In view of achieving this objective, Eric Ojo notes that the Nigerian government has proceeded to complement the National Action Plan with ancillary poverty eradication and development related strategic programmes, including the National Poverty Alleviation Programme, the National Economic Empowerment and Development Strategy, the State Economic Empowerment and Development Strategy and the Federal Capital Territory Economic Empowerment and Development Strategy among others.[137] These measures notwithstanding, the realisation of the right to development in Nigeria remains far-fetched owing to a combination of constraints,

---

135 Anon "NHRC reviews national action plan for promotion, protection of human rights" *Metrowatch* 12 March 2015 http://metrowatchonline.com/nhrc-reviews-national-action-plan-for-promotion-protection-of-human-rights/ (accessed: 6 June 2018); Nigeria's 6th Periodic Country Report: 2015–2016 on Implementation of the African Charter on Human and Peoples' Rights in Nigeria, Federal Ministry of Justice August 2017; National Action Plan for the Promotion & Protection of Human Rights in Nigeria (2009–2013).

136 Nigeria's National Action Plan, *supra* note 135.

137 Ojo, Eric "Making the right to development a reality in Nigeria: Policies, strategies, targets and challenges" in Ngang, Carol C. & Kamga, Serges D. (eds) *Insights into Policies and Practices on the Right to Development* (London/New York: Rowman & Littlefield International, 2020) 109–110.

which basically amount to lack of implementation resulting from inconsistencies in government actions, the influence of foreign stakeholders and endemic corruption among others rather than the absence of feasible plans.[138]

3.2 Implication for Ineffective Implementation

By ratifying the African Charter, which 53 of the 55 African countries have accomplished, state parties have only partially demonstrated the commitment to make the right to development a reality, necessitating a closer examination of what ineffective implementation would imply for Africa. On account of the understanding that the right to development aims ultimately at improving living standards and the well-being of the human person, the reality with regard to ineffective implementation indicates that aspirations for improved well-being and better living standards in Africa may not be attained or probably only at a very slow pace.[139] Drawing from the analysis on the institutional role of the AU and of the five countries discussed above, the fact that they have not fully complied with their obligations under the African Charter compromises the legitimate expectations that flow from the entitlements contained in article 22 of the Charter.

To falter in the duty to implement the right to development implies that the development injustices, foreign domination, economic exploitation, livelihood sustainability challenges and the policy choices that generate and sustain impoverishment among other governance constraints will persist in shaping living standards for the peoples of Africa, which generally reflects in extreme levels of poverty. Taking the right to development as a model for the eradication of poverty,[140] effective domestic implementation for example,

---

138   Eneh, Onyenekenwa C. "Failed development vision, political leadership and Nigeria's underdevelopment: A critique" (2011) 1:1 *Asian Journal of Rural Development* 63–69; Makinde, Taiwo "Problems of policy implementation in developing nations: The Nigerian experience" (2005) 11:1 *Journal of Social Science* 63–69; Egwemi, Victor "Corruption and corrupt practices in Nigeria: An agenda for taming the monster" (2012) 14:3 *Journal of Sustainable Development in Africa* 72; Ogbu, Osita N. "Combating corruption in Nigeria: A critical appraisal of the laws, institutions and the political will" (2010) 14:1 *Annual Survey of International and Comparative Law* 99.

139   Ngang, Carol C. "The right to development in Africa: Implications of its ineffective implementation to prospects for development on the continent" in Kamga, Serges D. (ed) *The Right to Development in Africa: Issues, Constraints and Prospects* (Austin, TX: Pan-African Press 2020) 151–172.

140   Mazur, Robert E. "Realization or deprivation of the right to development under globalization? Debt, structural adjustment, and poverty reduction programs" (2004) 60:1 *Geo Journal* 61–71; Perry, Robin "Preserving discursive spaces to promote human rights: Poverty reduction strategy, human rights and development discourse" (2011) 7:1 *Journal of Sustainable Development Law & Policy* 80–86; Wang, Xigen "Eradicating

RIGHT TO DEVELOPMENT GOVERNANCE FOR AFRICA

through expanded exposure to egalitarian opportunities in making development choices, genuine redistributive measures and the active and meaningful participation of the African peoples in the processes for development would arguably upset the associated obstacles that set the bar for living standards in Africa unacceptably low.

The extreme levels of poverty that prevail in Africa, which besides posing a threat to livelihood security and survival also robs the peoples of Africa of the resilience in seeking to get out of poverty is a direct outcome of the ineffective implementation of the right to development.[141] Former UN High Commissioner for Human Rights, puts this succinctly in stating that "[i]t's not an act of nature that leaves more than one billion people around the world locked in the jaws of poverty. It's a result of the denial of their fundamental human right to development".[142] By inference, ineffective implementation of the right to development means that levels of extreme poverty in Africa is not likely to change and therefore, also suggesting that the impoverished will remain unfairly disfavoured.[143]

As a practical illustration, Nigeria (overtaking India in 2018) is reported to be the country with the largest number of people (an estimated 87 million, almost half of the country's population) living in extreme poverty.[144] It is worth noting that Nigeria has the largest population of an estimated 1.8 million people on the entire continent and despite also ranking as Africa's largest economy and leading producer of crude oil, Bukola Adebayo reports that the country "has struggled to translate its resource wealth into rising living

---

poverty and the role of the right to development" (2017) *Human Rights Institute of Wuhan University, China – Recommendation for the 18th Session of UN Working Group on the Right to Development* 1–4.

141   See Ngang, Carol C. & Kamga, Serges D. "Poverty eradication through global partnerships and the question of the right to development under international law" (2017) 47:3 *African Insight* 41–46.

142   UN "25th Anniversary of the Declaration on the Right to Development" *Declaration on the Right to Development at 25* available at: www.un.org/en/events/righttodevelopment/ (accessed: 28 April 2019).

143   See the Brooking Institute report on the world poverty clock by Golubski, Christina "Africa in focus: Africa and the world poverty clock" *Brooking Institute* 18 May 2017 available at: https://www.brookings.edu/blog/africa-in-focus/2017/05/18/africa-and-the-world -poverty-clock/ (accessed: 28 April 2019). The report points out that more and more people, especially in Africa are falling into extreme poverty than are escaping it, which makes it harder for the continent to get out of the poverty bracket.

144   Adebayo, Bukola "Nigeria overtakes India in extreme poverty ranking" cnn (Lagos, June 2018) available at: https://edition.cnn.com/2018/06/26/africa/nigeria-overtakes-india -extreme-poverty-intl/index.html (accessed: 28 April 2019).

standards".[145] Accordingly, on account of Nigeria's commitments on the right to development under the African Charter as well as under domestic law, the absence of effective implementation means that the 87 million impoverished Nigerians are not trapped in extreme poverty by fate or by choice but because they are deprived of equal opportunities and equitable redistribution of the country's development gains as a Adebayo explains.[146]

Ethiopia is Africa's second most populous country after Nigeria, with a population size of 1.4 million among which, 24 million are living in excruciating poverty. Ethiopia has recently also emerged as one of Africa's investment destinations of choice, with an impressive economic growth rate of 4.1 per cent.[147] As one of the few African countries that have given domestic legal recognition and protection on the right to development but without effective implementation as illustrated earlier, it is left to be seen how and to what extent the country could potentially translate its economic growth performance to the benefit of the 24 million Ethiopians that are currently locked in the extreme poverty bracket. In spite of the DRC's enormous natural wealth and resources, of the population of 77 million people, 61 million (about 75 per cent of the entire population) is extremely poor.

Notwithstanding that the extreme levels of poverty as illustrated with the examples of Nigeria, Ethiopia and the DRC as discussed above could be redressed through prioritising the right to development, African countries generally seem to think that the solution to their development problems can only be found by turning to other countries for assistance. This is evident in the obvious failure to learn from previous experience in the futile dependency on countries of the West for assistance. There is apparently no justification in the shift from the West towards China for development financing within the supposedly mutually beneficial China-Africa South-South cooperation framework considering the huge shady debts that continue to pile up on Africa as a result. Among the African countries with the largest share of Chinese debts as of October 2018; the DRC owes a total of USD3.4 billion, Nigeria owes USD4.8 billion while Ethiopia owes a colossal sum of USD13.5 billion.[148] With these figures, it is unclear whether Africa's increasing dependence on China for development financing is intended to redress the problem of extreme poverty or to

---

145   As above.

146   As above.

147   Radelet, *supra* note 18.

148   The African Exponent "The top ten African countries with the largest Chinese debt" 2 October 2018 available at: https://www.africanexponent.com/post/9183-here-are-the-top-ten-countries-in-africa-bearing-the-largest-chinese-debt (accessed: 24 October 2018).

aggravate it. Admittedly, the AU Commission is right in stating that the entire continent remains exposed to the excessive influence of foreign stakeholders,[149] providing justification to consider a substitute approach in the pursuit of aspirations for development in Africa as explained in the next section.

3.3 On the Decoloniality of Thought in Development Programming

It is essential to reiterate the decolonial arguments in favour of imagining and of course, creating possible new futures for Africa, requiring a radical uncoupling from contemporary engagements, which only have the advantage of conformism with global norms.[150] Joel Modiri convincingly argues that alternative outcomes to legal problems are possible through different conceptions of law and legal reasoning.[151] Asserting the right to development from this point of view allows seeing Africa in light of the aspiration for socio-economic and cultural sovereignty. Based on the understanding that circumstances necessitating the realisation of the right to development globally are not unique, Ibrahim Salama submits that the only way to surmount the conceptual problematic and legalistic debate on the scope of obligations is to adopt a case-by-case approach to different situations.[152] Such differentiation is informed by the understanding that the right to development provides the opportunity to choose between alternatives in development planning and policy making. Defining the specific outcomes that development is intended to achieve is strategic to determining the approach and the processes to follow in achieving those outcomes, which explains the justification for a shift in development thinking. To anticipate the kind of development outcomes as well as the model and the processes to attain that purpose necessitates contrasting the analysis in this section with the insufficiencies in existing cooperation approaches to development in Africa.

3.3.1 Insufficiency in Development Cooperation Approaches

3.3.1.1 Charity Approach

It may be necessary to commence the discussion in this subsection by asking whether development as a process and the right to development as an entitlement to that process, could be achieved through charity. This question arises from the fact as illustrated in chapter three that the concept of development

---

149 AU Commission "Agenda 2063", *supra* note 23, para 58.
150 Ndlovu-Gatsheni, Sabelo J. "Global coloniality and the challenges of creating African futures" (2014) 36:2 *Strategic Review for Southern Africa* 181–202.
151 Modiri, Joel "The crisis in legal education" (2014) 46:3 *Acta Academica* 12.
152 Salama, *supra* note 7, 53.

cooperation has been narrowed down to the provision of aid rather than genuine partnership based on sovereign equality. This has meant that development cooperation is just a matter of charity, denoting some act of benevolence that involves extending a helping hand to the "needy".[153] The charity approach to driving development in Africa thus, represents a dependency-based relationship between the donor community at the giving end and African countries at the receiving end.[154] In this instance, the provision of development assistance is informed by compassion, which is motivated more by the political discretion of donor countries than by the developmental priorities of developing countries.[155] It is anchored on the assumption that Africa needs help rather than that the people are entitled to the right to development.[156]

On the contrary, Mesenbet Tadeg argues that the right to development imposes a compelling obligation that cannot be reduced to charity.[157] Charity-based assistance provides little to Africa in terms of human development in the sense that it is offered like a "gift horse", with the "beggar has no choice" attitude, which generates dependency rather than promotes the right to development. The development challenges that Africa is confronted with are generally not caused by lack of material resources but by development injustices, which cannot be redressed through charity assistance. For instance, although conceptualised as development aid, French assistance to Cameroon as has been indicated earlier is generally not intended to meet the exigencies of the Cameroonian people but promote French interest in the country.[158]

In the landmark *Endorois* litigation that dealt comprehensively with the concept of the right to development as a legally enforceable entitlement, the African Commission established that the right to development does not imply dependency but represents an emancipating process that emphasises the

---

153 Rukare, Donald "The role of development assistance in the promotion and protection of human rights in Uganda" (Doctoral Thesis, University of Pretoria 2011) 84.

154 Todaro, Michael P. & Smith, Stephen C. *Economic Development* (London: Pinter Publishers, 2006)115–118; Ngang 2017, *supra* note 6, 272–282; Rukare, *supra* note 151, 84; Kirchmeier, *supra* note 8, 14.

155 Ilorah, Richard "Africa's endemic dependency on foreign aid: A dilemma for the continent" (2011) *ICITI – ISSN: 1694122513*.

156 Bilal, *supra* note 5, 1.

157 Tadeg, Mesenbet A. "Reflections on the right to development: Challenges and prospects" (2010) 10:2 *AHRLJ* 329.

158 Emmanuel, Nicholas G. "With a friend like this [...]: Shielding Cameroon from democratisation" (2013) 48:2 *Journal of Asian & African Studies* 145–160; Rousselot, *supra* note 38, 68–69; Ngwa, *supra* note 56, 8–10.

importance of choice and liberty of action in achieving human well-being.[159] This jurisprudential interpretation makes clear that the right to development cannot be achieved through charitable assistance and therefore sets the parameters on which development cooperation should not be accepted in Africa, based particularly on the fact that the peoples of Africa are guaranteed the freedom to make their own development choices. Informed by the capability model in dealing with issues relating to development and human rights, the right to development represents a moral commitment to achieve a better standard of living.[160] It entails activating human capabilities as a guarantee for the constant improvement of well-being and not charity, which has become the underlying modality of development cooperation.[161]

In concurrence with Richard Ilorah, "[c]ountries that are less dependent on foreign aid are more likely to follow their own 'home-grown' development routes, both politically and economically".[162] From this analysis, it is argued that the charity approach does not offer a realistic functional modality to ensure that the right to development is achieved, which supports my argumentation in favour of rejecting development cooperation in favour of the right to development as the suitable development paradigm for Africa. However, because some scholars think that the right to development is achievable through a claims approach as a viable alternative to the charity approach,[163] it

---

159 Sing'Oei, Kori "Engaging the leviathan: National development, corporate globalisation and the Endorois quest to recover their herding grounds" in Henrard, Kristin (ed) *The Interrelation between the Right to Identity of Minorities and their Socio-Economic Participation* (Leiden/Boston: Martinus Nijhoff Publishers, 2013) 395; *Centre for Minority Rights Development (Kenya) and Minority Rights Group International on behalf of Endorois Welfare Council v Kenya* Comm 276/2003 (2009) AHRLR 75 (ACHPR 2009) para 283.

160 Nussbaum, Martha C. *Creating Capabilities: The Human Development Approach* (Cambridge/Massachusetts/London: Harvard University Press, 2011) 33–34.

161 The Declaration on the Right to Development stipulates in art 4(2) that "States have the duty to cooperate with each other in ensuring development and eliminating obstacles to development", art 3(3). It further states that "effective international cooperation is essential in providing these countries with appropriate means and facilities to foster their comprehensive development".

162 Grabowski, Richard "Political development, agriculture, and ethnic divisions: An African perspective" (2006)18:2 *African Development Review* 163–182; Ilorah, *supra* note 155, 3.

163 Golay, Christophe; Biglino, Irene & Truscan, Ivona "The contribution of the UN Special Procedures to the human rights and development dialogue" (2012) 7:17 *SUR – Int'l J Hum Rts* 21; Uvin, Peter *Human Rights and Development* (Bloomfield: Kumarian Press, 2004) 129; Grover, Anand "Report of the Special Rapporteur on the right of everyone to the enjoyment of the highest attainable standard of physical and mental health" (2011) *UN A/HRC/ 17/25* 49.

254   CHAPTER 5

makes sense to test the potential of the claims approach to achieve the right to
development in Africa.

3.3.1.2   *Claims Approach*

The claims approach denotes a situation where African countries may be
required to demand reparation for damages resulting from the actions of foreign stakeholders, including reparations for the ills of slavery and colonialism.
Ramona Biholar makes a strong argument for righting the historical wrongs of
slavery, genocide, colonialism and apartheid among others that continue to
impact on the present through asserting the right to development as a means
to achieve restorative justice.[164] In Golub, Mahoney and Harlow's conception,
they posit that intergenerational equity should not aim solely at the welfare of
future generations, but most also seek to redress historical injustices suffered
by past generations, particularly those that have a replicating effect on present
generations.[165]

The Durban Declaration acknowledges that these "historical injustices
have undeniably contributed to the poverty, underdevelopment, marginalisation, social exclusion, economic disparities, instability and insecurity that
affect many people in different parts of the world, in particular in developing countries".[166] The Programme of Activities for the Implementation of the
International Decade for People of African Descent broadly emphasises the
need for reparative justice against historical wrongs inflicted on the peoples of
Africa.[167] The suggested means by which reparation is envisaged to be achieved
"within the framework of a new partnership based on the spirit of solidarity
and mutual respect"[168] leaves doubts about the authenticity to achieve reparative justice.

The claims approach equally represents the instance where the peoples
of Africa may be justified to demand development assistance as a matter of

---

164   Biholar, Ramona "Imagining Caribbean development: The right to development and rep-
      arations nexus" in Ngang, Carol C., Kamga, Serges D. & Gumede, Vusi (eds) *Perspectives on
      the Right to Development* (Pretoria: Pretoria University Law Press, 2018) 326–344.
165   Golub, Aaron; Mahoney, Maren & Harlow, John "Sustainability and intergenerational
      equity: Do past injustices matter?" (2013) 8:2 *Sustainable Science* 269–271.
166   Durban Declaration and Programme of Action adopted at the World Conference against
      Racism, Racial Discrimination, Xenophobia and Related Intolerance, Durban, South
      Africa on 8 September 2001 paras 158.
167   Programme of Activities for the Implementation of the International Decade for People
      of African Descent Resolution A/RES/69/16 adopted by the UN General Assembly on 18
      November 2014 para 17(i).
168   Durban Declaration and Programme of Action, *supra* note 166, para 158.

RIGHT TO DEVELOPMENT GOVERNANCE FOR AFRICA

right, deriving from the expectation that such assistance has been promised and therefore, can legitimately be conceived as a claimable entitlement. In this regard, Sengupta holds the view that when developing countries are unable to create the conditions necessary for exercising the right to development; they have the right to claim assistance from the international community.[169] While this is theoretically possible, there are no established mechanisms through which claims to development assistance could effectively be made. The likelihood to achieve the right to development through the claims approach leaves unanswered questions to which a response is attempted by looking at the commitments undertaken by developed countries to provide assistance to developing countries.

Developed countries have formally undertaken the commitment to provide 0.7 per cent of their GDP as overseas development assistance to developing countries.[170] Available information in this regard illustrates that only a few, mostly Scandinavian countries have actually met the target.[171] Sweden is said to have reached the target in 1974 followed by the Netherlands in 1975 and then Norway and Demark in 1976 and 1978 respectively, and have since then consistently honoured their commitments.[172] Finland is said to have achieved the target once in 1999 while Luxemburg did so in 2000 and has since also remained consistent.[173] Thus in total, only five countries have kept the commitment, while it is stated that the weighted ODA average to developing countries has never exceeded 0.4 per cent of the national income of donor countries,[174] implying that the target has never fully been met. With the global financial crisis and enduring austerity, Moody observes that there is increasing disquiet among European donors whether they should continue to set aside the promised 0.7 per cent of their national income to assist developing countries.[175]

---

169   Sengupta, Arjun "The human right to development" (2004) 32:2 *Oxf Dev't Stud* 186.

170   Monterrey Consensus of the International Conference on Financing for Development adopted at the International Conference on Financing for Development, Monterrey Mexico *United Nations* 2002 para 42; United Nations Resolution 2626 (1970) *The International Development Strategy for the Second United Nations Development Decade*.

171   OECD "History of the 0.7% ODA target" (2010) *Original Text from DAC Journal* (2002) 3:4 III-9–III-11 revised June 2010; Sengupta 2004, *supra* note 169, 195.

172   OECD 2010, *supra* note 171, 10.

173   As above.

174   As above, 11.

175   Moody, Andrew "China has changed discourse on Africa: Africa Programme Head at Chatham House keen to forge links with Chinese institutions" *China Daily-Africa Weekly* 10–16 July 201532.

Before it has actually come to the decision to terminate the provision of development assistance, it is possible to argue in accordance with the obligations imposed by articles 55 and 56 of the UN Charter that Africa is legally entitled to the 0.7 per cent GDP quota promised by developed countries. However, in the absence of a claim mechanism, it is difficult to comprehend how a claim on such assistance can be achieved, which makes the claims approach functionally problematic.[176] This notwithstanding, it is argued that the right to development is in effect not necessarily about the shipment of development assistance from the haves in developed countries to the have-nots in Africa but an expression of self-determination. The failure to fulfil the promise to provide development assistance is not likely to violate the right to development, just like the right to development is also unlikely to diminish as a result of the absence of development assistance.[177] It is uncertain that any African country can succeed with a claim on the violation of the right to development on the grounds of the failure by developed countries to make available the promised 0.7 per cent quota of their GDP. Even so, in the absence of a suitable model for development, whether the 0.7 per cent quota is fulfilled in its entirety is immaterial and therefore renders the claims approach irrelevant as an operational model for development in Africa.

In addition to the setbacks to development resulting from development cooperation as shown in chapter three, the insufficiencies in the cooperation approaches discussed above provide reason to look at some additional major hurdles that Africa continues to grapple with.

3.3.2 Some Major Impediments

3.3.2.1 *Contradictions of Good Governance*

As discussed throughout this book, the right to development has evolved for genuine reasons in the course of Africa's development history as an alternative model to colonial paradigms and imperialistic practices. In commemorating 50 years of independence, the AU Commission adopted a consolidated roadmap for development that provides a policy framework to harmonise national and regional efforts intended to achieve radical transformation through optimal use of the continent's resources to the benefit of the African peoples.[178] Although the transformation agenda is envisaged to be achieved through "self-reliance", "self-determination" and "people-centred governance",[179] Africa has

---

176 See Rukare, *supra* note 153, 91–93.
177 Sengupta 2002, *supra* note 66, 877.
178 AU Commission "Agenda 2063", *supra* note 23, paras 9-18.
179 As above, para 19.

RIGHT TO DEVELOPMENT GOVERNANCE FOR AFRICA

rather embraced the good governance ideology as a tool for development policymaking.[180] As promising as it appears, the agenda for development leaves unanswered questions relating to the right to development enshrined in the African Charter and ancillary treaty instruments[181] and, thus, also begs the question, why good governance in Africa?

Good governance embodies a broad range of issues which summarily imply the "the responsible use of political authority to manage a nation's affairs".[182] Understood in this light, the good governance ideology poses no issue for contention. However, as a concept which many scholars rightly identify as an IMF/World Bank invention that came into use following the failure of the structural adjustment programmes in the 1990s,[183] its application in Africa becomes problematic. Questioning the good governance concept is thus, intended to illustrate its dficiency as a model for development in Africa. A comprehensive understanding of this deficiency entails a scrutiny of how the structural adjustment programmes (SAPs) that gave birth to good governance adversely impacted on development in Africa and the risk that it may still do so. Following the collapse of commodity prices and the resulting economic crisis in the 1970s, the structural adjustment programmes were introduced as an economic recovery programme through which "conditional lending" was provided to African countries.[184] Although the SAPs appeared like sound economic policies, they were in effect a vehicle for driving free market capitalism into Africa. Countries targeted for debt relief were obligated to adjust their economic policies in favour of trade liberalisation; privatisation of state-owned enterprises; reductions in public expenditures through salary cuts and retrenchments of public service functionaries; closing down of state marketing boards;

---

180   As above, para 27.
181   Ngang, Carol C. "Towards a right-to-development governance in Africa" (2018) 17:1 *Journal of Human Rights* 107.
182   Dias, Clarence J. & Gillies, David *Human Rights, Democracy, and Development* (Montreal: The International Centre for Human Rights and Democratic Development, 1993) 10; Udombana, Nsongurua J. "Articulating the right to democratic governance in Africa" (2003) 24:4 *Michigan Journal of International Law* 1231.
183   Maldonado, Nelson "The World Bank's evolving concept of good governance and its impact on human rights" (2010) *Doctoral Workshop Stockholm Sweden 29–30 May 2010* 4; Ake, Claude *Democracy and Development in Africa* (Oxford: Oxford University Press, 1996) 32–40; Manzo, Kate "Africa in the rise of rights-based development" (2003) 34:4 *Geoforum* 444; Leftwich, Adrian *States of Development: On the Primacy of Politics in Development* (Cambridge: Polity Press, 2000) 116; Uvin 2002, *supra* note 42, 4–6.
184   Thomson, Alex *An Introduction to African Politics* (3rd Edn, New York: Taylor & Francis, 2010) 197; Were, Anzetse "Debt trap? Chinese loans and Africa's development options" (2008) *South Africa Institute of International Affairs – Policy Insights 66* 5.

258   CHAPTER 5

instituting export-driven agricultural reforms; undertaking currency devaluation; and implementation of fiscal austerity measures.[185]

According to Dicklitch and Howard-Hassmann, the macro-economic policies that informed the SAPs were intended to release the productive capacity of the African peoples and thus stimulate economic growth, without which as they claim, socio-economic rights would not be achieved.[186] On the contrary, Abouharb and Cingranelli argue that respect for human rights constitutes the pre-requisite for equitable economic growth, meaning that structural adjustment could only have been achieved to the extent that human rights, particularly socio-economic and cultural rights were respected.[187] In spite of the institutional commitment of the IMF and World Bank to ensure that human rights are not violated in the course of their operations, implementation of the SAPs significantly infringed on the socio-economic and cultural rights of the peoples of Africa, causing "overall economic failure" with "destructive social consequences".[188] Dismissing claims about the successful implementation of structural adjustment in Ghana, Odutayo argues that the structural adjustment policies failed in their intended objectives to alleviate poverty, improve living conditions, or promote economic growth but instead created the opportunity for the wanton exploitation of the country's resources.[189] Kingston *et al.* point out that in Uganda, structural adjustment took the form of trade liberalisation and privatisation, which disproportionately benefitted foreign stakeholders who purchased most of the privatised public enterprises, as opposed to the Ugandan people.[190] In Kenya also, Joseph Rono points out how the implementation of structural adjustment as a policy tool to accelerate economic growth

---

185   Heidhues, Franz & Obare, Gideon "Lessons from structural adjustment programmes and their effects in Africa" (2011) 50:1 *Qtly J Int'l Agric* 58; Dicklitch, Susan & Howard-Hassmann, Rhoda "Public policy and economic rights in Ghana and Uganda" in Hertel, Shareen & Minkler, Lanse (eds) *Economic Rights: Conceptual, Measurement and Policy Issue* (New York: Cambridge University Press, 2007) 327; Were, *supra* note 184, 5.

186   Dicklitch & Howard-Hassmann, *supra* note 185, 325–327.

187   Abouharb, M. Rodwan & Cingranelli, David *Human Rights and Structural Adjustment* (New York: Cambridge University Press, 2007) 40.

188   Anghie, Anthony "Whose utopia?: Human rights, development and the third world" (2013) 22:1 *Qui Parle: Critical Humanities and Social Sciences* 75; Logan, Fraser "Did structural adjustment programmes assist African development?" *E-International Relations* 13 January 2015 1–6; Abouharb & Cingranelli, *supra* note 187, 40.

189   Odutayo, Aramide "Conditional development: Ghana crippled by structural adjustment programmes" – *E-International Relations* 1 March 2015 1–11.

190   Kingston, Kato G. "The impacts of the World Bank and IMF structural adjustment programmes on Africa: The case study of Cote D'Ivoire, Senegal, Uganda and Zimbabwe" (2011) 1:2 *Sasha J Pol & Strat Stud* 121.

instead resulted in "the marginalisation of the poor", principally because the programmes were ill-conceived in a manner that ignored existing social structures and aspects related to human development.[191]

Originating from this background, the central premise underlying the good governance model obtains from the idea that the SAPs failed not necessarily because they were ill-conceived but supposedly because of the incompetence of African governments in managing their economies.[192] Good governance was thus introduced as a model to remedy the failures by improving the "institutional performance" of the state as a pre-condition for securing further loans from the World Bank.[193] The focus on good governance is justified by neoliberal claims that "better governance promotes economic development".[194] Among the main components that Rachel Gisselquist identifies as making up the concept of good governance, the issue of human development, which constitutes Africa's major development challenge, is unfortunately not included. This raises concerns as to the relevance of good governance as a development model for Africa, which as Gisselquist rightly contends, is not a useful concept for development analysis.[195] Although good governance makes mention of human rights, the Lawyers' Committee for Human Rights (now Human Rights First) argues that "[t]he governance debate looks to human rights not for their intrinsic value but for their instrumental role in creating an environment in which effective and sustainable economic development can occur".[196]

As stated above, good governance is more focused on the institutional performance of the state than the more pressing problem of human capabilities development. The concept of right to development on the other hand encourages meaningful participation and therefore places the power of development decision making in the hands of the people, whereas, good governance systematically excludes large segments of the African population from the development process.[197] Unlike good governance, which approaches the African problem from a foreign standpoint, the right to development paradigm envisages the formulation of appropriate development policies that are suited to African

---

191   Rono, Joseph "The impact of the structural adjustment programmes on Kenyan society" (2002) 17:1 *Journal on Social Development in Africa* 81–98.

192   Ngang 2018, *supra* note 181, 116.

193   Maldonado, *supra* note 183, 5–10.

194   Gisselquist, Rachel M. "Good governance as a concept and why this matters for development policy" (2012) *UNU-WIDER* 1–3.

195   As above, 2.

196   Lawyers' Committee for Human Rights *The World Bank: Governance and Human Rights* (2nd Edn, New York: Lawyers' Committee for Human Rights, 1995) 61.

197   Ngang 2018, *supra* note 181, 116.

realities.[198] Democratisation, political reforms and institutional performance, which constitute good governance priority areas, are in effect of little livelihood value to the millions of African peoples who do not have an education, a roof over their heads and cannot afford sufficient food.[199] The right to development also envisages relieving Africa of dependency on development assistance and the associated debt burden, and in turn compels African governments to explore domestic sources of economic potential.

In resonance with the capabilities theory as a test to Africa's ability to achieve the right to development, it is certain that the continent is endowed with the potential to facilitate a sustainable management of the economy.[200] With an appropriate right to development policy framework, Africa is capable of redressing the myriad of development challenges on the continent much more than through the good governance model, which as indicated earlier, is an imported model of the same patronising nature as development cooperation. Good governance, understood in the context in which it was introduced by the IMF and the World Bank as already explained, descends from the problem of a naive political leadership that is persistently in search for new frontiers of domination in the quest for development assistance.

3.3.2.2   *Africa's Persistent Search for New Frontiers of Assistance*

Unless there is a decisive remarkable shift in development thinking as illustrated earlier, it seems that Africa's development challenges will continue to be amplified by the inordinate dependence on global standards with the hope to find solutions to the recurrent problems on the continent. In the backdrop of Africa's inopportune experiences with slavery and colonialism, its persistent search for new frontiers of assistance demonstrates an unfortunate lack of visionary leadership, which virtually translates into an obdurate resistance

---

198   Corrigan, Terrence "Socio-economic problems facing Africa: Insights from six APRM country review reports" (2009) *SAIIA Occasional Paper No 34* 8. Research conducted by Corrigan indicates that the central issues that need addressing in order to accelerate development in Africa are more of a socio-economic and cultural character.

199   Gauri, Varun & Brinks, Daniel (eds) *Courting Social Justice: Judicial Enforcement of Social and Economic Rights in the Developing World* (New York: Cambridge University Press, 2008) vii.

200   Ayittey, George B.N. "Can foreign aid reduce poverty?: No" in Haas, Peter M. & Hird, John A. (eds) *Controversies in Globalisation: Contending Approaches to International Relations* (New Delhi: SAGE Publishing, 2009) 88–89; Boaduo, Nana A.P. "Africa's political, industrial and economic development dilemma in the contemporary era of the African Union" (2008) 2:4 *J Pan Afr Stud* 93; Moyo, Dambisa "Why foreign aid is hurting Africa" (2009) *The Wall Street Journal* available at: http://www.wsj.com/articles/SB123758895999200083 (accessed: 6 December 2017).

RIGHT TO DEVELOPMENT GOVERNANCE FOR AFRICA

to decolonial thinking. It is worth restating that the leadership that ushered Africa into independence failed to align the purpose of decolonisation with a sustainable development trajectory for the continent.[201] The prevailing context presents greater worries where the contemporary leadership appears stuck in between the pressing obligation to do away with the legacies of colonial underdevelopment and the difficult task of having to rupture global norms that articulate the reasoning that there are no alternative remedies to Africa's development setbacks except those prescribed by foreign stakeholders.

Africa's dramatic drift from dependency on the West towards a growing but questionable asymmetrical relationship with China tells the story. It is reported that the largest proportion of Africa's debts is from China.[202] Many African countries are heavily indebted to China to the total tune of over 83 billion Dollars.[203] At the 2018 Beijing Forum for China-Africa Cooperation (FOCAC), Chinese President Xi Jinping announced a further USD60 billion earmarked for development financing for Africa.[204] The figures are certainly tempting to resist, especially with the forged acceptance that Africa cannot sustain itself. Ethiopia is one of China's investment destinations of choice, a relationship that has elevated Ethiopia to one of the leading emerging economies in Africa.[205] Interestingly, Ethiopia's USD13.5 billion debt to China is just slightly lower than the country's annual budget of USD13.9 billion for the fiscal year 2017/2018.[206] This raises eyebrows regarding the country's sovereignty and ability to self-sustain in accordance with the constitutional obligation to ensure improved living standards, sustainable development and the participation of the Ethiopian peoples in national development.[207]

With the shadiness that underlines the contracting of these debts from China, there is good reason to question the shrewdness in development thinking among Africa's political leadership. Contrary to seventh aspiration

---

201 Khensane, Hlongwane "Transformative leadership in Africa: Thabo Mbeki and Africa's development agenda" (Masters Dissertation, University of the Witwatersrand, 2010) 3–7.
202 Were, *supra* note 184, 7.
203 The African Exponent, *supra* note 148.
204 Financial Express "China's Xi Jinping offers $60 billion Africa aid, says 'no strings attached'" 3 September 2018 available at: https://www.financialexpress.com/world-news/chinas-xi-jinping-offers-60-billion-africa-aid-says-no-strings-attached/1301355/ (accessed: 24 October 2018).
205 Radelet, *supra* note 18.
206 Alfa, Shaban A.R. "Ethiopia parliament passes $13bn budget after World Bank, IMF praise" *Reuters – Africa News* 8 July 2017 available at: https://www.africanews.com/2017/07/08/ethiopia-parliament-passes-13bn-budget-after-world-bank-imf-praise// (accessed: 22 April 2019).
207 Constitution of Ethiopia, *supra* note 121, art 43(1) & (2).

of Agenda 2063 that says Africa is poised to become an "influential global player", it is incomprehensible that the political leadership thinks that the realisation of that goal requires burrowing from China. Notwithstanding the fine arguments in justification of China's contribution to development financing in Africa, Agenda 2063 clearly highlights the dangers of "continued external interference" and in essence the urgency to curb dependency on aid and to reduce unsustainable levels of debts.[208] Although sustained action, including the provision of development assistance is envisaged within the framework of development cooperation as a means to complement the efforts of developing countries, the core essence of the right to development negates the justification of incurring debts to finance development. The right to development emphasises the need to remove obstacles to development, not excluding the debt burden that has stalled progress in Africa over the decades.

While Africa's constant search for assistance stems directly from an unfocused leadership, it is not of no much importance at this stage to delve into the complexity of the different leadership theories and its various characteristics, which has been the subject of extensive scholarship[209] to illustrate where African leadership has missed the path for development. However, contrary to the "Africa rising" narrative that gives the feeling of some degree of change happening and a few exceptions of committed leadership in driving that process, the one thing that stands out clearly is that genuine political leadership has generally eluded Africa.[210] This is mirrored in the many facets against which

---

208 AU Commission "Agenda 2063", *supra* note 23, paras 59 & 72(o).

209 For some general reading on leadership, see Cooper, J. Fenimore & Nirenberg, John *Leadership Effectiveness* (Encyclopaedia of Leadership Edition 5, Thousand Oaks, CA: Sage, 2012); Bass, Bernard M. *Leadership and Performance Beyond Expectations* (New York: Free Press, 1985); Kuada, John "Culture and leadership in Africa: A conceptual model and research agenda" (2010) 1:1 *African Journal of Economic and Management Studies* 9–24; Nikezic, Srdan; Purić, Sveto & Purić, Jelena "Transactional and transformative leadership: Development through changes" (2012) 6:3 *International Journal for Quality Research* 285–296; Odumeru, James A. & Ifeanyi, G. Ogbonna "Transformative vs transactional leadership theories: Evidence in literature" (2013) 1:2 *International Review of Management and Business Research* 355–361; Rowold, Jens & Schlotz, Wolff "Transformative and transactional leadership and followers' chronic stress" (2009) 9 *Kravis Leadership Institute – Leadership Review* 35–48; Sinclair, Amanda "Leadership for the disillusioned" (2007) 3:1 *The Melbourne Review* 65–71.

210 Manfred, F.R. Kets de Vries; Sexton, Jennifer and Parker Allen III, B. "Destructive and transformative leadership in Africa" (2016) 2:2 *Africa Journal of Management* 166–187; Gonye, Jairos & Moyo, Thamsanqa "African nationalist transformative leaders: Opportunities, possibilities and pitfalls in African fiction and politics" (2013) 5:6 *Journal of African Studies and Development* 126; Afegbua, Salami I. & Adejuwon, Kehinde D. "The challenges of leadership and governance in Africa" (2012)2:9 *International Journal of Academic*

leadership is tested, including: economic performance, democratisation, governance, living standards and poverty levels among others. It is worth reemphasising that Africa's political leadership owes an obligation to find practical solutions to these challenges.

3.3.3 The Obligation to Fulfil

The African Charter imposes an obligation on state parties to fulfil the right to socio-economic and cultural development, which is guaranteed as an absolute entitlement to all the peoples of Africa. Felix Kirchmeier notes that because the obligation to fulfil is mostly associated with socio-economic and cultural rights, states are obligated to put in place an appropriate legislative framework to enable the realisation of these entitlements.[211] It compels state parties to utilise state resources (the common heritage) to provide the material things; adequate housing, sufficient food, quality education, affordable healthcare, and social assistance for example, that are needed to satisfy the realisation of socio-economic and cultural rights and consequently contribute to the highest attainable standards of living. Where the provision of these material things is practically not possible, state parties are enjoined as implied in article 22(2) of the African Charter, to create an enabling environment (through appropriate legislative, policy and *other* measures) and provide favourable conditions (through equitable redistribution of the common heritage) that allow the peoples of Africa to create well-being for themselves.

The obligation to fulfil in the second instance requires that the measures taken by the state should not be "qualified or limited by other considerations, but entails such steps to be deliberate, concrete and clearly targeted towards [the] realisation"[212] of the socio-economic and cultural entitlements guaranteed to the peoples of Africa. Defining the actual contents of socio-economic and cultural rights has been one of the problematics that has fuelled the controversy surrounding the right to development. The obligation to fulfil, necessitating taking appropriate measures may simply require the state to give content to what would amount to socio-economic and cultural development. It entails looking at the livelihood circumstances of the impoverished peoples of

---

    Research in Business and Social Sciences 149–151; Van Wyk, Jo-Ansie "Political leaders in Africa: Presidents, patrons or profiteers?" (2007) *Accord Occasional Paper Series* 1–38.

211   Kirchmeier, *supra* note 8, 12.

212   Ngang, Carol C. "Judicial enforcement of socio-economic rights in South Africa and the separation of powers objection: The obligation to take other measures" (2014) 14:2 *AHRLJ* 672; ESCR Committee General Comment 3, the nature of state parties' obligations UN Doc HRI/GEN/1/Rev.6 14 (2003) para 2.

Africa and matching those circumstances with their expectations for the highest attainable standard of living. The measures taken by the state must, on the one hand, literally translate into improved well-being and better living standards for the impoverished and on the other hand, guarantee that state action or the activities of non-state actors do not hinder or infringe on these aspirations and the associated entitlements to socio-economic and cultural development.

Accordingly, when a threat or actual violation of the right to development becomes the subject of litigation as in the SERAC, DRC, *Endorois and Ogiek Community* cases discussed in chapter four, the "result of positive adjudication should equally amount to entitlement to the same material things promised by the right in question"[213] or at minimum, prevent further violation. The judgment by the African Court in the *Ogiek Community* case imposes an imperative for enforcement to ensure that the positive ruling enables the indigenous Ogiek Community to reclaim the ancestral lands that there were dispossessed of by the Kenyan government. The obligation to fulfil requires accurately defining the tangible contents of the right to development on the one hand and creating an enabling environment for its realisation on the other hand. The right to development would be said to have been achieved when living conditions have been standardised or at least when the requisite systems have been put in place to ensure genuine equality of opportunity for all the peoples of Africa. It mandates states governments in Africa to take such actions and policy measures that would practically translate into anticipated levels of human well-being and better standards of living that the effective realisation of the right to development would amount to.

3.3.4 The Right to Development as a Tool for Policy Making
In line with the international law principle that guarantees state sovereignty, the Declaration on the Right to Development entitles states with the right and the duty to formulate national development policies to ensure improved well-being for their peoples.[214] This is also highlighted by the fact that the right to development derives from the right to self-determination,[215] which according to the African Charter requires the peoples of Africa "to freely determine their political status" and to "pursue their economic and social development according to the policy they have freely chosen".[216] Incidentally, the right to development is conceived as one of the rights-based alternative approaches to

---

213 Ngang 2014, *supra* note 212, 674.
214 Declaration on the Right to Development, *supra* note 1, art 2(3).
215 Anghie, *supra* note 188,66; Udombana, *supra* note 77, 769–770.
216 African Charter, *supra* note 1, art 20(1).

economic growth models to development that has gained currency in recent years.[217] It represents a policy mechanism that is informed not solely by the pursuit of economic growth objectives but simultaneously by aspirations to maximise well-being and thus envisages a framework for accountability against abuse, injustice and impunity within which the peoples of Africa can seek new ways of advancing their productive capabilities. As a policy mechanism, the right to development envisages both legislative and regulatory measures to protect the African patrimony from the abusive exploitation by foreign stakeholders, a development process that is people-driven and an integrated system that guarantees equitable distribution of development gains.

However, faced with intensifying global inequalities, the challenge remains whether Africa is capable of fulfilling the duty to establish a policy framework for development of the sort.[218] The relevance of such a context-specific policy structure is explained by the absence of an African model for development in spite of the growing global quest for innovative models to replace outdated conventional paradigms.[219] Despite pioneering the right to development as a safeguard against injustice and impunity, it seems that Africa has lost track of its bearing to the prevailing circumstances on the continent. For instance, in adopting the ambitious 2063 agenda for development as a roadmap for "structural transformation" across the continent,[220] the African Union Commission failed to specify the applicable model by which to deal concretely with the development aspirations contained in the document.

While Agenda 2063 makes mention of an African model for development and transformation,[221] it does not state in accurate terms what that model is and how it envisages driving the roadmap for development to effective realisation. It is estimated that the envisaged African model ought to be anchored on the concept of the right to development as a policy tool for addressing the continent's development challenges, including those resulting from external factors such as the overbearing influence of foreign stakeholders in the course

---

217   UN Human Rights (eds) *Realizing the Right to Development: Essays in Commemoration of 25 Years of the United Nations Declaration on the Right to Development* (Geneva: UN Publication, 2013) 495; Nagan, Winston P. "The right to development: Importance of human and social capital as human rights issues" (2013) 1:6 *Cadmus Journal* 30; Ibhawoh, *supra* note 8, 103; Udombana, *supra* note 77, 762.

218   Šlaus, Ivo & Jacobs, Garry "In search of a new paradigm for global development" (2013) 1:6 *Cadmus Journal* 2–3; The World Bank *Can Africa Claim the 21st Century?* (Washington DC: International Bank for Reconstruction and Development/The World Bank, 2000) 7.

219   Šlaus & Jacobs, *supra* note 218, 4–5.

220   AU Commission "Agenda 2063", *supra* note 23, paras 47-58.

221   As above, para 74(e) & (h).

of their operations.[222] With evidence of the development injustices perpetuated by external actors as illustrated in the previous chapters, the case is made for a radical shift in development thinking in Africa towards greater focus on the right to development as a home-grown model, which as proposed could be conceptualised as *right to development governance*.

4 Right to Development Governance

This section explores in greater detail the dimension of the right to development as a development paradigm as highlighted in chapter two. In doing so, the sub-sections that follow describe what the right to development governance represents in theory. The justification for having such a model is further presented alongside what its implementation entails in practical terms. Governance, as it is used in context with the right to development is expressed in terms of the processes, the actions, the systems and the institutions, which as Mark Rutgers explains, work together in ensuring the "attainment of socially desired ends within a state".[223]

4.1 *Conceptual Formulation*

4.1.1 Definition and Justification for the Model

In looking at why some countries fair better in terms of capabilities for development than others, Fagerberg and Srholec posit that "what matters most for growth and development is a well-functioning innovation system and the quality of governance".[224] The requisite functioning innovation system and quality of governance for Africa would be understood as one that responds to the socio-economic and cultural development exigencies on the ground. The right to development governance is conceived in this light and defined as an integrated rights-based development model, grounded in popular participation and the liberty of action in advancing human capabilities for the sustainable management of Africa's resources, and the propagation of the African identity and value systems within a legal framework that guarantees

---

222 AU Commission "Agenda 2063", *supra* note 23, para 59. The AU Commission acknowledges that African development space remains threatened by external influences and proposes (para 74) to address the problem by having recourse to an African model but does not explicitly state what the African model is.

223 Rutgers, Mark R. "The purpose of the state" (2008) 30:3 *Administrative Theory & Praxis* 353.

224 Fagerbergm, Jan & Srholec, Martin "The role of 'capabilities' in development: Why some countries manage to catch up while others stay poor" (2008) *DIME Working Paper 2007.8* 3.

genuine accountability and equitable redistribution for improved well-being. Africa's all time record low human development indicators across all dimensions of measurement remains a major challenge despite significant gains in economic development. To address this challenge requires a development model that straightforwardly deals with the socio-economic and cultural realities in Africa. While the component ideas that make up the proposed right to development governance may not entirely be new, naming the concept as a home-grown model for Africa can significantly shape the manner in which development is conceived and prioritised as a human right and the manner too in which implementation could be achieved.

In effect, the right to development governance represents an assertion of self-determination to be allowed the opportunity to advance beyond the circumstances that Africa is presently confronted with, which as indicated, is largely due to over-dependence on development cooperation as a model for development.[225] By advancing the argument for the right to development governance, it envisages an operational paradigm of a similar nature like the "social state principle" used in German constitutional law as an interpretative guide to applying the law and to policy making.[226] Its application within the context of the right to development dispensation in Africa demands on the one hand an affirmation of the potential to take positive action in translating abstract principles into effective measures for implementation[227] and on the other hand, serves as the kind of policy tool envisaged in article 2(3) of the Declaration on the Right to Development.

Akinola Aguda highlights the relevance of the right to development in Africa by stating that every African government that has concern for its people, "must accord [priority to] the right to development in its governance of the country".[228] The proposed model derives from the generic concept of the right to development and therefore, as a home-grown model has potential to respond to the socio-economic and cultural realities in Africa. It imports conceptual ideas from good governance, which has no doubt engineered political accountability, public sector reforms and democratisation, yet lacks the

---

225   Ilorah, *supra* note 155, 1–36; Grabowski, *supra* note 162,163–182; Ayittey 2009, *supra* note 200, 89.

226   King, Jeff "Social rights, constitutionalism, and the German social state principle" (2014) 1:3 *Revista Electrónica De Direito Público* 13–14; Karpen, Ulrich "Effectuating the constitution: Constitutional law in view of economic and social progress" (2012) *Law Faculty, University of Hamburg* 10–11.

227   See Amir, *supra* note 99, 2.

228   Aguda, T. Akinola *Human Rights and the Right to Development in Africa* (Lagos: Nigerian Institute of International Affairs, 1989) 25.

potential to redress the range of development challenges because of its more institutional focus on the state as the primary driver of national development. This is not intended to discount the role of the state, which as a duty bearer and holder of the right to development, constitutes as Rachel Murray highlights, "an essential first, if not the most, important step in the transition to sustainable development".[229]

However, it is contradictory to favour the development of the state over human development and expect to achieve people-centred sustainable development as envisaged in the 2063 agenda for development in Africa.[230] The right to development governance model proposes the basis for advancing the human potential through appropriate policies that respond to the realities of the largest majority of African peoples. As Winston Nagan has observed, the right to development approach demonstrates that development must be understood in terms of an all-inclusive value system as embodied in the concept of human rights and not simply in terms of the accumulation of wealth.[231] The right to development governance thus represents an integrated, inclusive and holistic model with the potential to address Africa's development challenges by incorporating socio-economic and cultural concerns and political governance into development programming. It is underlined by the fact that a system change entailing capabilities development, institutional strengthening, structural innovation, economic growth, social transformation and cultural reawakening can only be achieved by a politically liberated and socio-economically empowered people.[232]

The following six reasons explain the rationale for the proposition to redirect focus from development cooperation to the right to development governance as a model to drive radical transformation in Africa: First, African governments owe the obligation to ensure that the stage is set for development to be achieved as a collective entitlement as guaranteed by the African Charter and associated instruments.[233] Second, owing to deep-rooted governance malpractices African governments equally owe the duty to become accountable in terms of "respect for democratic principles, human rights, the rule of law and good governance".[234] Third, the peoples of Africa are lawfully entitled to

---

229   Murray, *supra* note 32, 242.
230   AU Commission "Agenda 2063", *supra* note 23, paras 66(e) & 67.
231   Nagan, *supra* note 217, 34.
232   AU Commission "Agenda 2063", *supra* note 23, paras 47-58.
233   African Charter, *supra* note 1, arts 20 (1) & 22; Declaration on the Right to Development, *supra* note 1, art 1(2).
234   AU Constitutive Act, *supra* note 31, art 4(m); AU Commission "Agenda 2063", *supra* note 23, paras 27 & 74(c); Aguda, *supra* note 225, 25.

RIGHT TO DEVELOPMENT GOVERNANCE FOR AFRICA   269

freely and actively engage in determining their own well-being and to participate meaningfully in shaping Africa's development future.[235] Fourth, owing to
historical experiences and present-day realities, Africa's framework for development described in the previous chapter as a right to development dispensation, necessitates an implementation model that is equally established on
legality to combat impunity by upholding justice and equity in the development process.[236] Fifth, African governments are enjoined by their entitlement
to self-determination and sovereign equality, to assert their autonomy against
foreign domination.[237] Lastly, that development gains are equitably redistributed to ensure improved well-being and better conditions for the African peoples.[238] Drawing inspiration from the text of the law, the African Charter for
Popular Participation acknowledges with conviction that:

> [T]he crisis currently engulfing Africa, is not only an economic crisis but
> also a human, legal, political and social crisis. It is a crisis of unprece-
> dented and unacceptable proportions manifested [...] glaringly in the
> suffering, hardship and impoverishment of the vast majority of African
> people [...].[239]

If human development is acknowledged to be Africa's major setback, right
judgment would necessitate pursuing models that focus on developing the
continent's human potential rather than models that consider the African
peoples only as passive recipients of charity-based development assistance
from foreign donors.[240] The Charter for Popular Participation underscores the

---

235   Constitutive Act, *supra* note 31, arts 3(g) & 4(c); AU Commission "Agenda 2063", *supra*
       note 23, para 74(c); see also Perry, Robin "Preserving discursive spaces to promote human
       rights: Poverty reduction strategy, human rights and development discourse" (2011) 7:1
       McGills Int'l J Sust Dev't L & Policy 76.
236   See UN Human Rights, *supra* note 217, 495; Nagan, *supra* note 217, 30; Ibhawoh, *supra* note
       8, 103; Udombana, *supra* note 77, 762; Sengupta 2002, *supra* note 66,846.
237   African Charter, *supra* note 1, arts 20(1) & 22; Constitutive Act, *supra* note 31, art 3(i);
       Declaration on the Right to Development, *supra* note 1, art 1(2); AU Commission "Agenda
       2063", *supra* note 23, paras 19, 59, 61 & 72(n).
238   African Charter, *supra* note 1, art 22(1) stipulates that: "All peoples shall have the right
       to their economic, social and cultural development with due regard to their freedom
       and identity and in the equal enjoyment of *the common heritage of mankind*" (emphasis
       added); see also Sengupta 2004, *supra* note 169, 187–188.
239   African Charter for Popular Participation in Development and Transformation adopted in
       Arusha, Tanzania 1990 art 6.
240   See AU Commission "Agenda 2063", *supra* note 24, para 72(o). As part of the commit-
       ment to speed up action for the realisation of the African agenda for development,
       the AU Assembly of Heads of State and Government agree to curb dependency on aid.

fact that development policy-making must align with peoples' aspirations and incorporate rather than alienate African values systems.[241] It requires a "development approach rooted in popular initiatives and self-reliant efforts"[242] devoid of preventable constraints and unwarranted external pressures[243] such as those perpetuated by foreign stakeholders in Africa.

Relating to why a development model should be lodged within the framework of the law, the South African experience is used to illustrate the need for subjugated peoples to have recourse to legal protection as an assurance for improved well-being. In designating South Africa's governance and development model of "transformative constitutionalism", Karl Klare posits that the process of transformation must be guided by law.[244] Unlike many other African countries that plunged into chaos after independence, transformation in post-apartheid South Africa has been relatively sustainable. This may be attributed to the fact that the transition to democracy in South Africa was negotiated and established on a legal (constitutional) foundation as a safeguard against impunity and the injustices of a past that was characterised by gross human rights

---

African leaders, including for example, President Uhuru Kenyatta of Kenya, President Paul Kagame of Rwanda, former President Thabo Mbeki of South Africa and Nana Akufo-Addo during the 2017 EU-Africa Summit, among others, have repeatedly made public statements calling for an end to dependency on foreign aid. In a TED Talk presentation dated April 2019, President, Julius Maada Bio of Sierra Leone in articulating his strategy and approach to development, observed that his country has received development assistance for 58 years but remains poor. See also Marshall Plan Project Group, BMZ "Africa and Europe – A New Partnership for Development, Peace and a Better Future" (2017) *German Federal Ministry for Economic Cooperation and Development (BMZ)* 4.

241   African Charter for Popular Participation, *supra* note 239, art 23(a)(1); *Endorois* case, *supra* note 159, para 291.

242   African Charter for Popular Participation, *supra* note 239, art 4(b); AU Commission "Agenda 2063", *supra* note 23, para 19.

243   AU Commission "Agenda 2063", *supra* note 23, para 59.

244   Klare, Klare "Legal culture and transformative constitutionalism" (1998) 14 *SAJHR* 150. For a comprehensive account of transformative constitutionalism, see also Langa, Pius "Transformative constitutionalism" (2009) *Prestige Lecture Stellenbosch University* 2; Sibanda, Sanele "Not purpose-made! Transformative constitutionalism, post-independence constitutionalism and the struggle to eradicate poverty" (2011) 22:3 *Stell L Rev* 482–500; Rosa, Solange "Transformative constitutionalism in a democratic developmental state" (2011) 22:3 *Stell L Rev* 452–565; Van Marle, Karin "Transformative constitutionalism as/and critique" (2009) 20:2 *Stell L Rev* 286; Roux, Theunis "Transformative constitutionalism and the best interpretation of the South African Constitution: Distinction without difference" (2009) 20:2 *Stell L Rev* 258; Pieterse, Marius "What do we mean when we talk about transformative constitutionalism?" (2005) 20:1 *SA Pub L* 155.

violations and the legacy of poverty and inequalities created by the apartheid system.[245]

On account of the development injustices resulting from slavery and colonialism, post-colonial Africa is undeniably in need of an alternative development model established within a legal framework in the form of a collective recognition of the right to development. Outlining a development agenda as has been done under Agenda 2063 is an expression of political good will; making clear that the realisation of that agenda is owed to the peoples of Africa as a legal entitlement as guaranteed by the African Charter is crucial. However, in the absence of a functional model, efforts to actualise the ambitious development agenda may not be achieved as the continent remains exposed to the imperial influence of foreign stakeholders.[246] It begs the question why Africa continues to rely on development cooperation while it has the requisite capacity to advance the right to development governance as a substitute to development cooperation. On this note, it is important to highlight some guidelines requirement for implementing the right to development governance.

4.1.2 Functional Requirements

For the right to development governance model to be achieved, four requirements deduced from the conceptual nature of the right to development need to be met: requirements of purpose, conduct, process and outcome. The requirement of purpose requires the peoples of Africa as stipulated in legal and policy instruments to meaningfully engage with the state in defining national development priorities. African governments must marshal the political will, in turn, to recognise the right to development as both a moral and legal obligation that they owe to the peoples of Africa in ensuring their improved well-being. It also entails the concrete allocation of rights and liberties to the peoples of Africa in asserting their entitlement to socio-economic and cultural development. The formulation of national development policies must, therefore, primarily be informed by the obligation purpose.

The requirement of conduct defines and regulates the behavioural patterns within the context of the right to development dispensation in Africa, which as contained in the relevant instruments, entails eliminating exogenous as well as endogenous obstacles to development, including massive human rights

---

245 See *Ex Parte Chairperson of the Constitutional Assembly: In re Certification of the Constitution of the Republic of South Africa* 1996(4) SA 744 (CC) para 5.

246 African Charter, *supra* note 1, arts 20(1) & 22; Constitutive Act, *supra* note 31, art 3(i); Declaration on the Right to Development, *supra* note 1, art 1(2); AU Commission "Agenda 2063", *supra* note 23, paras 19, 59, 61 & 72(n).

272 CHAPTER 5

violations, endemic corruption and the persistent abuse of state power, which cumulatively hinder progress on the continent.[247] It structures relationships of transparency and accountability through which every actor within the right to development dispensation in Africa is enjoined to ensure that development is achieved without compromising the enjoyment of human rights. While the aspiration for a unified Africa as envisaged by the AU Commission can only be achieved over the long term,[248] the requirement of conduct necessitates that in the meantime, domestic arrangements are made to safeguard the right to development both as a claimable entitlement by which to hold the state to greater levels of responsiveness and accountability and also as a development model to serve as an interpretative guide to the law, policy making and development programming.[249] As indicated in chapter four, a number of African countries have enshrined the right to development as a domestic constitutional entitlement, including provisions that could be interpreted purposively to imply the right to development like in the case of South Africa.[250] In accordance with the obligation to engage in collective action, the rest of Africa is enjoined to provide domestic guarantees on the right to development as a means of reinforcing the right to development dispensation in Africa.

The requirement of process necessitates the pursuit of people-centered and rights-based approaches to development, primarily because the fulfilment of human rights and the development of human capabilities remain major challenges to development in Africa. It entails forging a system of legality to enure that in the process of creating development, human rights, particularly the right to development are not violated. This is illustrated by the *Endorois* case, which established the precedent that development cannot be carried out

---

247 Declaration on the Right to Development, *supra* note 1, art 5; Convention on Preventing and Combating Corruption adopted in Maputo on 11 July 2003 art 3; Kar, Dev & Cartwright-Smith, Devon "Illicit financial flows from Africa: Hidden resource for development" (d.n.a) *Global Financial Integrity* 5–6; Reuter, Peters "Illicit financial flows and governance; The importance of disintegration" (2017) *The World Bank – World Development Report Background Paper;* see also Ayogu, Melvin D. & Gbadebo-Smith, Folarin "Governance and illicit financial flows" (2014) *Political Economy Research Institute – Working Paper Series No 366* 1–36; Corruption Watch "Mbeki: Illicit financial flows crippling the continent" (2015) *Corruption Watch* available at: http://www.corruptionwatch.org.za/mbeki-illicit -financial-flows-crippling-the-continent/ (accessed: 12 September 2017); Transparency International "Corruption on the rise in Africa poll as governments seen failing to stop it" (2015) available at: http://www.transparency.org/news/pressrelease/corruption_on_the _rise_in_africa_poll_as_governments_seen_failing_to_stop_i (accessed: 4 May 2017).
248 AU Commission "Agenda 2063", *supra* note 23, para 20.
249 See King, *supra* note 226, 13–14; Karpen, *supra* note 226, 10–11.
250 Gutto, *supra* note 116, 109–118.

in contravention of the right to development.[251] In adjudicating the case, the African Commission held that the right to development is in effect an emancipating process that emphasises the importance of choice and liberty of action for the achievement of well-being.[252] In finding the Kenyan government in contravention of the right to development, the African Commission conveyed the fact that human well-being must precede economic growth and the welfare of the state economy. Although restitution of the land in question and the payment of damages is yet to be effected as the Commission ruled, the decision however, sets the sandard that colonial-style invasion and land grabbing (of indigenous territories) is unlawful.

Finally, the requirement of specific forms of outcome is rooted in the principle of equitable distribution, which constitutes an important component of the right to development.[253] Outcome requirements ensure that specific material or abstract entitlements could be anticipated from the development process, either through policy measures to guide implementation in the development process or through judicial processes when a violation is established. Article 22(1) of the African Charter requires that the gains from development be shared; hence, the peoples of Africa legitimately should be able to expect to enjoy on an equitable basis the communal resources pertaining to the African patrimony. Agenda 2063 lays out the policy framework at the continental level for translating the abstract principles of law enshrined in the African Charter, but unfortunately does not define the model for its realisation.

In response to the global search for an innovative development paradigm owing to the failure of prevailing models in dealing with the challenges that confront humanity,[254] Nagan suggests that with proper clarification, the right to development could effectively be conceptualised as "a new global economic paradigm".[255] While the quest for a new paradigm is important for the global economy, it is even more relevant to Africa. If the right to development governance as described above finds resonance with the 2063 policy agenda for transformation, it is likely to significantly shift the goalposts and therefore place Africa at a comparative advantage as an influential actor as highlighted in Agenda 2063.[256] It would mean the attainment of self-determination for Africa in shaping its development priorities in accordance with local realities

---

251 *Endorois* case, *supra* note 158, paras 72-73 & 283.
252 Sing'Oei, *supra* note 159,395.
253 Sengupta 2004, *supra* note 169, 187–188.
254 Nagan, *supra* note 217, 30; Šlaus & Jacobs, *supra* note 218, 1–2.
255 Nagan, *supra* note 217, 30.
256 AU Commission "Agenda 2063", *supra* note 23, paras 59-63.

274   CHAPTER 5

and not otherwise, where development policy choices have frequently been determined by foreign stakeholders. Such an arrangement is of primary importance in setting the attainable standards for development that should become binding under the right to development dispensation in Africa. Of interest is whether Africa has the capacity to make it possible.

4.1.3   Capacity to Fulfil

In looking at the capacity to fulfil, this section demonstrates to what extent the right to development or better still the right to development governance could be achieved. Obtaining from the legal dimensions of the right to development as a human right concept and its developmental dimension as a development paradigm, the capacity to fulfil can appropriately be summarised into the legal capacity and the resource capacity.

4.1.3.1   *Legal Capacity*

The office of the UN Office of the High Commissioner for Human Rights (UNO-HCHR) defines legal capacity as "the capacity and power to exercise rights and undertake obligations [...] without assistance or representation by a third party".[257] It presupposes the capability to be a potential holder of rights and obligations, implying the capacity to exercise those rights and the duty to initiate, to modify or terminate legal relationships.[258] The UNHOCHR further indicates that legal capacity constitutes an important aspect relating to the sovereignty of states without which peoples "would be subject to injustice and injury without legal remedy".[259] For instance, the granting of independence to Africa has meant autonomy only to the extent that the decolonised peoples can freely make political choices while the power of socio-economic policy-making is largely retained in the hands of the colonial masters. The right to development as Richard Kiwanuka has noted, culminates the process of dissociating from the injustices of imperial domination and as a result, affirms the socio-economic and cultural autonomy of African states *vis-à-vis* advanced societies.[260] The legal capacity that the right to development bestows thus broadly defines the autonomy that enables African states to engage with other

---

257   UN Office of the High Commissioner for Human Rights (UNOHCHR) "Legal capacity" *Background Conference Document – Office of the United Nations High Commissioner for Human Rights* 4.

258   As above, 13.

259   As above.

260   Kiwanuka, Richard "The meaning of 'people' in the African Charter on Human and Peoples' Rights" (1988) 82:1 *Am J Int'l L* 95.

states as subjects of international law on the basis of sovereign equality. It entails the liberty to assert the right to development based on the authority conferred by law in order that the outcomes of such actions may impose binding obligations, including on third parties.

The legal capacity conferred on the peoples of Africa to achieve the right to development is accompanied by the capability to determine what development entails in their situation and by extension to shape the African development agenda accordingly. It entails also the capability to discern the nature of development cooperation that is appropriate for Africa, and be able to seek remedy when the right to development is contravened or threatened. It has earlier been stated that the right to development empowers African states with the legitimacy to formulate appropriate development policies to ensure well-being and improved living standards for the populations.[261] Although African countries are individually recognised as sovereign states, they are enjoined by their obligations under the African Charter to jointly assert the right to development, which in my view constitutes an instrument for leverage and a collective bargaining strategy to forge negotiations at international fora and to broker cooperation agreements for development in Africa's favour.

With the understanding that implementation of the African Charter can most effectively take place at domestic level, states are enjoined to undertake necessary measures, including adopting domestic legislation,[262] to reinforce their legal capability in asserting the right to development. In the same manner that legal capacity is bestowed on the peoples of Africa to exercise the right to development, legal capacity also provides leverage to African states to protect their peoples when their entitlement to development is threatened or violated. State parties are required to demonstrate the legal capacity to access the African Commission through compliance with the admissibility criteria.[263] In the DRC case for example, the government of the Congo exercised its legal capacity as a state party to the Charter by filing a communication against Burundi, Rwanda and Uganda in which the African Commission established among others a violation of the right to development.[264]

---

261 Declaration on the Right to Development, *supra* note 1, art 2(3).
262 As above, art 8.
263 African Charter, *supra* note 1, arts 47-49.
264 *Democratic Republic of Congo v Burundi, Rwanda and Uganda* (2004) AHRLR 19 (ACHPR 2003) para 87, Kwame, Asare L.P. "The justiciability of the right to development in Ghana: Mirage or possibility?" (2016) 1:1 *Strathmore Law Review* 87–88; Oduwole, Olajumoke "International law and the right to development: A pragmatic approach for Africa" (2014) *International Institute of Social Studies* 15; Sceats, Sonya "Africa's new human rights court: Whistling in the wind?" (2009) *Chatham House – Briefing Paper* 8.

276   CHAPTER 5

4.1.3.2   *Resource Potential*
In terms of substantive development, the obligation that the right to development imposes for its realisation is predominantly positive in nature, requiring
dependence on or the mobilisation of enormous resources, which developing
countries are often, presumed to be unable to muster. Incidentally, the global
arrangement has been designed such that developing countries are required to
remain dependent on developed countries for assistance.[265] Such an arrangement derives from the perception that developing countries are incapable
of self-sustainably mobilising the requisite resources to meet their human
rights obligations. The result, as George Ayittey points out, "has been hopeless
dependency on foreign aid".[266] While Jeffrey Sachs argues in favour of foreign
aid as a tool for assisting developing countries,[267] other scholars argue to the
contrary that Africa really does not have need for foreign aid for the reasons
that the resources required for development are located in Africa.[268] Nana
Boaduo thinks that the "habit of begging and borrowing [...] should be abandoned" because "Africa has the potential to stand on its own feet to initiate
its industrial and economic development agenda".[269] However, on a balance
of probabilities, Anup Shah estimates that "[w]hile the reliance on aid is not
a good strategy for poor countries at any time; some [African countries] have
little choice in the short term".[270]

---

265   International Covenant on Economic, Social and Cultural Rights adopted by Gen Ass Res
       2200A (XXI) of 16 December 1966 art 2(1); Declaration on the Right to Development, *supra*
       note 1, art 4(2); United Nations Millennium Declaration Resolution A/55/L.2 adopted by
       the United Nations General Assembly on 8 September 2000 (Millennium Development
       Goal) goal 8.
266   Ayittey 2009, *supra* note 200, 89; Kwame, Akonor "Foreign aid to Africa: A hollow hope?"
       (2008) 40:4 *International Law and Politics* 1074.
267   Sachs, Jeffrey "Can foreign aid reduce poverty?: Yes" in Haas, Peter M. & Hird, John A. (eds)
       Controversies in Globalisation: Contending Approaches to International Relations (New
       Delhi: SAGE Publishing, 2009) 72–88.
268   Ayittey 2009, *supra* note 200, 88–89; Moyo, *supra* note 200; Were, *supra* note 184, 1–13;
       Ayodele, Thomson; Nolutshungu Temba A., & Sunwabe Charles K. "Perspectives on
       aid: Foreign assistance will not pull Africa out of poverty" (2005) *African Cato Institute
       Economic Development Bulletin No 2 of 14 September 2005* 1; Siyum, Negussie "Why Africa
       remains underdeveloped despite its potential? Which theory can help Africa to develop?"
       (2018) 1:2 *Open Access Biostatistics & Bioinformatics* 1–2; Kumar, Mahendra "Arguments for
       and against foreign aid" available at: http://www.economicsdiscussion.net/foreign-aid/
       arguments/arguments-for-and-against-foreign-aid/11838 (accessed: 6 September 2017).
269   Boaduo, *supra* note 200, 93.
270   Shar, Anup "Foreign aid for development assistance" (2014) *Global Issues* available at:
       http://www.globalissues.org/article/35/foreign-aid-development-assistance (accessed: 6
       September 2017); Ayittey, *supra* note 200, 72–88.

RIGHT TO DEVELOPMENT GOVERNANCE FOR AFRICA

It is argued in the previous chapter that development cooperation, especially when it only involves the provision of development assistance is not indispensable for the realisation of the right to development in Africa. The question therefore is whether without the assistance that is made available through cooperation, Africa has the resource potential to self-reliantly achieve the right to development? To give a straightforward answer to this question may not provide an accurate assessment of Africa's resource potential. In respond to the question two instances are alluded to where on the one hand, Libya survived economic sanctions imposed by the US in the period between 1980 and 1992 as well as by the international community in the period between 1992 to 2003[271] and on the other hand, where although rated as a developed country, France is able to survive economically only at the expense of its African colonies.[272]

Following Qaddafi's extremism against imperialism which threatened the hegemony of the western world, the international community jointly authorised punitive economic sanctions and diplomatic isolation on Libya in 1986. Economic sanctions are generally intended to paralyse or destabilise the economic base of a target country with the aim to constrain the country to submit to international pressure.[273] This is usually achieved through the withdrawal of foreign assistance, the imposition of trade and arms embargoes, the freezing of foreign assets as well as diplomatic isolation.[274] In spite of these measures imposed on Libya, the country not only survived the international pressure but surprisingly never got entangled in any foreign debts. Instead, the economy faired exceedingly well while the standard of living for the Libyan people is established to have increased steadily over the years from 0.741 in 2005 to 0.760 in 2011 according to the UNDP human development index.[275] Owing to

---

271 Nephew, Richard "Libya: Sanctions removal done right – A review of the Libyan sanctions experience, 1980–2006" (2018) *Centre on Global Energy Policy* 9–15; Global Policy Centre, "Libya" available at: https://archive.globalpolicy.org/security/sanction/libya/indxirlb.htm (accessed: 30 October 2018).

272 Bart-Williams, Mallence "Change your channel" *TED Talk Berlin* (2015) available at: https://www.youtube.com/watch?v=_pvNp9gHjfk (accessed: 30 October 2018); Koutonin, *supra* note 36.

273 Hurungo, James "An inquiry into how Rhodesia managed to survive under economic sanctions: Lessons for the Zimbabwe government" (2010) *Trane and Development Centre – Discussion Paper* 8.

274 Mlambo, Alois S. *A History of Zimbabwe* (New York: Cambridge University Press, 2014) 36–44; Hurungo, *supra* note 273, 4–7.

275 Libya 360° Archive "Libya: UN HDI country profile" available at: https://libyadiary.wordpress.com/2011/03/05/libya-un-hdi-country-profile/ (accessed: 28 July 2016).

its abundant oil wealth, the sanctions only constrained Libya to explore internal strengths and opportunities to overcome weaknesses and threats posed by the international community.

It often does not add up that Africa is said to lack the resources needed for development yet, from time immemorial, it has supplied basically all the resources needed to feed the capitalist economies of developed countries. For instances, France is reported to be the largest provider of development assistance to its African colonies.[276] However, as contrary evidence has it, the French economy is confirmed to be sustained by the wealth that it takes "illegally" from some fourteen African countries.[277] France is reported to extract an estimated USD500 billion from Africa annually in the form of "colonial taxes" which its *Françafrique* subordinates are obligated to pay to France in respect of the terms of the Colonisation Continuation Pact.[278] This amount is more than the total sum of USD400 billion in the form of official development assistance (ODA), which the Organisation for Economic Cooperation and Development (OEDC) reports has been disbursed to the whole of Africa in the period from 1960 to 1997.[279] Former French Presidents, Francoise Mitterrand is said to have stated in 1957 that "without Africa, France will have no history in the 21st Century" while in 2008, Jacque Chirac confessed in a television interview that if all the wealth that France has accumulated through the exploitation of Africa were to be returned, France would descend to the level of a third world country.[280]

Contrary to the perception that Africa is incapable of self-sustained development and therefore, must look to developed countries for assistance, these illustrations justify the fact that Africa can, based on its resource potential, achieve the right to development without necessarily relying on foreign assistance. It is evident that Africa's natural wealth is not evenly distributed and thus the resource capacity for the realisation of the right to development may not apply uniformly. However, while a few African countries may be resource-deficient, Africa as a whole is largely endowed with huge mineral reserves alongside aquatic, flora and fauna resources, which make it even more imperative for

---

276   See generally OECD 2014, *supra* note 49.
277   Le Vine, *supra* note 36, 2–6; Koutonin, *supra* note 36.
278   World Bulletin News Desk "French colonial tax still enforce for Africa" *World Bulletin* available at: https://www.worldbulletin.net (accessed: 31 October 2018).
279   Ayittey, George B.N. "Why Africa is poor" in Morris, Julian (ed) *Sustainable Development: Promoting Progress or Perpetuating Poverty?* (London: Profile Books, 2002) 11.
280   Bart-Williams, *supra* note 272, Koutonin, *supra* note 36.

RIGHT TO DEVELOPMENT GOVERNANCE FOR AFRICA

consolidated action among African countries to ensure equitable redistribution of the common heritage of the African patrimony as a prerequisite for the realisation of the right to development as envisaged by the African Charter.[281] As long as Africa carries on with the habit of hand-stretching for assistance, it would never be able to make use of its enormous resources, which developed countries continue to exploit to feed their industrialised economies. Asserting the right to development in Africa entails rejecting dependency on development assistance, which provides good reason to productively utilise the continent's resources to the benefit of the African people.[282] Otherwise, making the right to development governance a reality also requires giving consideration to contraventions that may be committed.

4.2 *Operational Considerations*

4.2.1 Collective Socio-economic and Cultural Freedoms

To implement the right to development governance as a model for development in Africa requires first and foremost, measures that concretely guarantee the full enjoyment of basic freedoms. The 1990 UNDP Human Development Report clearly states that human freedom is crucial for the attainment of any development objective.[283] The right to development generally provides the framework within which these *freedoms* can be achieved in their entirety.[284] The African Charter states that the right to economic, social and cultural development can only be achieved with due regard to the *freedom* and identity of the peoples of Africa.[285] Amartya Sen has in his theorisation of *Development as Freedom*, extensively explored the instrumental role that freedoms play in the attainment of development objective.[286] Mark Rutgers posits that freedom is not a goal that can be pursued on an individual basis but can only be achieved collectively.[287] By inference, for development to be achieved demands the broadest range of collective freedoms, which must literally contribute to facilitating the processes and expanding opportunities for development.

---

281 African Charter, *supra* note 1, art 22(2).
282 Declaration on the Right to Development, *supra* note 1, art 1(2); African Charter, *supra* note 1, art 21; see also Ayittey 2009, *supra* note 200, 88–89; Moyo, *supra* note 200; AU Commission "Agenda 2063", *supra* note 23, para 72(o).
283 United Nations Development Programme *Human Development Report 1990* (New York: Oxford University Press, 1990), 1; see generally also, Sen, *Supra* note 93.
284 Declaration on the Right to Development, *supra* note 1, art 1(1).
285 African Charter, *supra* note 1, art 22(1).
286 See Sen, *supra* note 93, 14–15.
287 Rutgers, *supra* note 223, 352.

280 CHAPTER 5

The preamble to the African Charter draws attention to the fact that the freedoms that are of relevance in facilitating the processes for development in Africa are those of a socio-economic and cultural nature without which political liberties may amount to no great value to the well-being of the African peoples. Contrary to the existing realities where political liberties are given central place in governance, in the face of the recurrent development contradictions that prevail in Africa, the right to development governance require that attention should rather be directed towards the pursuit of socio-economic and cultural freedoms as a means to unleash the potential of the peoples of Africa. Along these lines, Sen contends that impoverishment cannot justifiably be measured by the income barometer but rather in terms of the deprivation of human capabilities.[288] Understood in this light, the right to development governance provides justification for the development framework in Africa to focus on eliminating the obstacles (unfreedoms) that limit socio-economic and cultural opportunities for the peoples of Africa.

The obstacles envisaged here include those generated by the patronising nature of development cooperation, necessitating preventive measures to forestall setbacks in applying the right to development governance as a development model for Africa. Given that development cooperation sometimes allows external actors excessive control over development processes in Africa, prevention suggests taking pre-emptive measures to avert foreseeable actions resulting from their operations that may contravene the right to development. It requires African states governments as a matter of obligation to take appropriate legislative and other measures to regulate the framework for development in a manner that does not limit socio-economic and cultural freedoms or deprive the peoples of Africa of opportunities for development.[289] Without undermining the goodwill of the donor community in seeking to assist developing countries in their development efforts, rights-based standards require development cooperation to be exercised with "due diligence" and "global standards of care" in respect of the duty to prevent human rights violations.[290] The universal approach in this regard is underscored by the obligation to create better conditions for every human person.[291]

---

288   Sen, *supra* note 93, 17.
289   African Charter, *supra* note 1, art 1; UN Human Rights *Guiding Principles on Business and Human Rights: Implementing the United Nations "Protect, Respect and Remedy" Framework* (New York/Geneva: United Nations, 2011) 16–17.
290   Salomon, Margot E. *Global Responsibility for Human Rights: World Poverty and the Development of International Law* (Oxford: Oxford University Press, 2007) 186; Skogly, Sigrun I. "Global responsibility for human rights" (2009) 29:4 *Oxf J Leg Stud* 829.
291   Skogly 2009, *supra* note 290, 829.

RIGHT TO DEVELOPMENT GOVERNANCE FOR AFRICA

A default to these standards subjects the defaulting party to international reproach, which is often accompanied by military intervention or economic sanctions on humanitarian grounds with the intention of remedying an appalling human rights situation. Of concern is when these sanctions contribute to making the human rights situation worse. For instance, economic sanctions imposed by the US and the European Union (EU) on Zimbabwe for a period of over fifteen years are reported to have inflicted acute socio-economic hardship on the people of Zimbabwe.[292] The sanctions, which included the withdrawal of development assistance, financial prohibitions, travel bans, arms embargoes, commodity boycotts, freezing of foreign assets and diplomatic isolation, have had a devastating impact on the entire population rather than the Zimbabwe African National Union–Patriotic Front (ZANU-PF) political leadership that constituted the primary target.[293] As a result, the country that once was known as the "breadbasket of Africa" has been reduced to a famished land, where an "estimated 4 million rural poor suffer from food shortages".[294] While the sanctions were imposed in response to the deceased Robert Mugabe's controversial land reform policies,[295] the effects were far-reaching and contributed to worsening the human rights situation in the country.[296] Socio-economic and cultural freedoms were thus, systematically limited, which caused a massive influx of hundreds of thousands of Zimbabweans into South Africa to seek better living conditions.[297]

---

292   Ogbonna, Chidiebere C. "Targeted or Restrictive: Impact of U.S. and EU Sanctions on Education and Healthcare of Zimbabweans" (2017) 11:3 *African Research Review* 37–39; Masaka, Dennis "Paradoxes in the 'sanctions discourse' in Zimbabwe: A critical reflection" (2012) 13:1 *African Studies Monographs* 50–51; Chingono, Heather "Zimbabwe sanctions: An analysis of the 'Lingo' guiding the perceptions of the sanctioners and the sanctionees" (2010) 4:2 *African Journal of Political Science and International Relations* 067.

293   Mlambo, *supra* note 274, 246–247.

294   Peta, Basildon "Regime has turned 'breadbasket of Africa' into famished land" (2005) *The Independent – UK* available at: www.rense.com/general64/mugg.htm (accessed: 15 November 2014); Mlambo, *supra* note 274, 231 & 237.

295   Thabani, Nyoni "The curse is real in Zimbabwe: Economic sanctions must go!" (2009) *MPRA Paper No 96911* 1–14.

296   Holman, Michael "Sanctions have been counterproductive in Zimbabwe" *The New York Times* 21 November 2013 available at: http://www.nytimes.com/roomfordebate/2013/11/19/sanctions-successes-and-failures/sanctions-have-been-counterproductive-in-zimbabwe (accessed: 5 September 2016); Alston, Philip "International trade as an instrument of positive human rights policy"(1982) 4:2 *Hum Rts Qtly* 168 relating to the effectiveness of sanctions as a means by which to punish or to compel compliance with international legal norms.

297   Ngang, Carol C. "Transgression of human rights in humanitarian emergencies: The case of Somali refugees in Kenya and Zimbabwean asylum seekers in South Africa" (2015) *The Journal of Humanitarian Assistance* 4.

282   CHAPTER 5

The Maastricht Principles make clear that it is wrong to impose embargoes and economic sanctions that would result in impairing the enjoyment of socio-economic and cultural rights.[298] Where such measures become necessary in order to fulfil international obligations, measures must be taken to ensure that human rights standards are fully respected.[299] It begs the question to what extent the international community takes the right to development seriously when interventions under the pretext of the responsibility to protect are carried out against a human rights defaulting country, considering such interventions may also aggravate the human rights situation.[300] To the best of understanding, no intervention purporting to protect human rights is justified if such an intervention renders the human rights situation worse than it would be without the intervention.[301] This point is made to justify the fact that if appropriate attention is given to the right to development, circumstances of this nature could be prevented. The prevention approach thus offers a pragmatic option for actualising the right to development in terms of guaranteeing protection against violation, including by the state which is obligated to regulate the actions of foreign stakeholders.[302] As a practical measure, a state party to the African Charter may seek remedy on behalf of its people in accordance with article 5(1)(d) of the Protocol on the African Human Rights Court,

---

298   Maastricht Principles, *supra* note 10, para 22; see also Bunn, Isabella D. "The right to development: Implications for international economic law" (2000) 15:6 *Am U Int'l L Rev* 1460.

299   Maastricht Principles, *supra* note 10, para 22.

300   Francioni, Francesco & Bakker, Christine "Responsibility to protect, humanitarian intervention and human rights: Lessons from Libya to Mali" (2013) *Transworld – Working Paper* 15 1–20. The authors argue that the NATO assault on Libya in 2011 supposedly under the pretext of the responsibility to protect was unjustified in the sense that the operation was actually not intended to protect the Libyan people against human rights violations but to effect a regime change in Libya with the resulting negative impact that the operation has left on the human rights situation in the country.

301   See Rishmawi, Mona "The responsibility to protect and protection of civilians: The human rights story" (d.n.a) *Office of the High Commissioner for Human Rights* 91. Rishmawi points out that responsibility to protect operations must be informed by the "requirement that the obligations for the protection of fundamental human rights are not affected" entailing the duty to prevent, to protect and to respect established rights.

302   See D'Aspremont, Jean *et al.* "Sharing responsibility between non-state actors and states in international law: Introduction" (2015) 62:1 *Neth Int'l L Rev* 49–67; Ronen, Yaël "Human rights obligations of territorial non-state actors" (2013) 46:1 *Cornell Int'l LJ* 21–50; Clapman, Andrew *The Human Rights Obligations of Non-State Actors* (New York: Oxford University Press, 2006) 25–58; Danailov, Silvia "The accountability of non-state actors for human rights violations: The special case of transnational corporations" (1998) *Law and Development* 1–74; Cassel, Douglass "Corporate initiatives: A second human rights revolution?" (1996) 19:5 *Fordham Int'l LJ* 1963.

which grants access to the "state party whose citizen is the victim of a human rights violation", to bring a case to the Court even though only against another state party.

4.2.2 Non-regression in the Enjoyment of Existing Rights

A fundamental attribute of the right to development is the fact that it must inevitably lead to the constant improvement of human well-being, which provides reasons to aim at eliminating the possibility of a regression or deprivation in the exercise and enjoyment of that right.[303] When prevention fails and a violation takes place, it necessitates a remedy to ensure that the ultimate goal of increasingly improving the human condition is retained. To halt that process would amount to a violation of the right to development, necessitating an explanation of what will constitute a violation. The right to development in Africa involves an entitlement to self-determination in setting development priorities freely, without external interference or economic coercion.[304] It involves the right to formulate development policies that aim at constantly improving human well-being, guaranteeing freedoms, expanding opportunities and choices and advancing capabilities.[305] It also entails non-regression in the enjoyment of existing rights as the African Commission affirmed in the *Endorois* case.[306] In addition to the right to development, the African Charter makes provision for the rights to self-determination and freedom from domination.[307] In sum, these guarantees demand appropriate domestic laws to regulate actions that may contravene the right to development.

Thus, the right to development in Africa would be violated when peoples' entitlement to sustained livelihood is not respected and protected, when the liberty to choose between development alternatives is denied and/or when the right to formulate national development policies is hijacked by dominant political or economic forces. The right to development will also be violated under any circumstance that leads to a regression in the enjoyment of well-being and standard of living that is valued by the peoples of Africa to whom the right to development is guaranteed. In the *Endorois* and *Ogiek Community*

---

303 Declaration on the Right to Development, *supra* note 1, art 2(3); Sengupta 2004, *supra* note 169, 184.

304 Van der Have, Nienke S. "The right to development and state responsibility: Can states be held to account?" (2013) *Amsterdam Centre for International Law – SHARES Research Paper* 23 4.

305 Declaration on the Right to Development, *supra* note 1, arts 2(3) & 10.

306 As above, art 2(3); *Endorois* case, *supra* note 157, para 294.

307 African Charter, *supra* note 1, arts 19 & 20(1).

cases for instance, the African Commission and the African Court, respectively held that by evicting the indigenous communities from their ancestral lands (significantly affecting their well-being), the Kenyan government violated their right to socio-economic and cultural development.[308]

The violations approach thus, entails the right to seek a remedy when a threat to or a violation of the right to development is established. Incidentally, both rulings highlight the fact that the lack of proper consultation and meaningful participation in decisions affecting their well-being, denial of the opportunity to make a choice or to exercise "liberty of action", the use of coercion and intimidation in the development process and exclusion from sharing in development gains violates the right to development.[309] In the *Ogiek Community* and *Endorois* cases, the African Court and the Commission respectively found that by restricting the Ogiek and the Endorois peoples from access to their ancestral lands and traditional place of habitation, they were virtually deprived of the right to the constant improvement in their well-being.[310]

On the contrary, the failure to provide development assistance – the basis on which development cooperation is largely structured – might not necessarily amount to a violation of the right to development, especially if such failure does not affect human well-being in any negative way. As stated above, a fundamental factor in advancing the right to development in Africa is to ensure that peoples' freedoms are not denied, that human capabilities are not diminished and that they are not dispossessed of the potential to contribute to development. The Maastricht Principles provide that global actors are obligated to respect, to protect and to fulfil human rights extraterritorially.[311] This notwithstanding, the globalisation practice has created the scenario where states' domestic policies and practices are controlled more by external actors than by the peoples of Africa, consequently affecting the human rights situation, particularly with regard to socio-economic and cultural development in most developing countries.[312]

When foreign stakeholders fail in their extraterritorial human rights obligations, they are by law – although so far just in principle – responsible for their

---

308 *Endorois* case, *supra* note 159, para 294; *African Commission on Human and Peoples' Rights (Ogiek Community) v Republic of Kenya* (2017) Appl No 006/2012 paras 210-211.

309 *Ogiek Community* case, *supra* note 308, para 210; *Endorois* case, *supra* note 159, para 269-298.

310 *Endorois* case, *supra* note 159, para 144; *Ogiek Community* case, *supra* note 308, paras 210 & 216.

311 Maastricht Principles, *supra* note 10, para 3.

312 Sengupta 2004, *supra* note 169, 194.

actions.[313] However, because of the overbearing influence that foreign stake-holders enjoy, they have often contravened the right to development in Africa with impunity, which begs the question why they remain insulated from legal action. Through the imposed SAPs for example, the World Bank and the IMF helped to wreck the economies of many African countries, and by so doing, transgressed article 22 of African Charter.[314] However, as external actors (not party to the Charter) these institutions cannot be held accountable under the African human rights system that provides no latitude for legal action against non-state entities.[315]

A regression in the enjoyment of existing rights and freedoms or in an established and valued standard of well-being would amount to a violation of the right to development.[316] For instance, before the supposedly humanitarian NATO intervention in 2011, the peoples of Libya enjoyed a standard of living that rated the highest in Africa, with one of the highest per capita incomes in the world, free access to socio-economic amenities, life expectancy of 74 years, a completely debt-free economy[317] and respect for women's rights unlike in most Arab countries.[318] The NATO intervention caused the dismantling of the socio-economic gains achieved over a period of forty years and as a result, Michel Chossudovsky estimates that the country is certain to be dragged into an endless debt trap under a possible World Bank and IMF post-war reconstruction programme.[319] Under the circumstances, it is unlikely that the peoples of Libya will ever be able to enjoy the same standard of living that they have previously been entitled to under Qadaffi's regime.

In essence, to ensure the actualisation of the right to development governance within the context of the right to development dispensation in Africa, it is crucial to factor in how violations of the right to development may effectively

---

313   See generally the UN Human Rights *Guiding Principles on Business and Human Rights*, *supra* note 288; see also chapter four for a detail analysis on the liability of foreign stake-holders on violations of the right to development in Africa.

314   Zattler, Jürgen "The effects of structural adjustment programmes" (1989) 24:6 *Verlag Weltarchiv* 282–285; Ismi, Asad "Impoverishing a continent: The World Bank and the IMF in Africa" (2004) *Canadian Centre for Policy Alternatives* 8–10; Lopes, Carlos "Structural adjustment policies and Africa: A reply to Shantayanan Devarajan" *Think Africa Press of 15 November 2013* available at: http://allafrica.com/stories/201311252050.html (accessed: 5 September 2016).

315   See Viljoen, Frans *International human rights law in Africa* (London: Oxford University Press, 2012) 300–302.

316   Skogly 2002, *supra* note 44,8.

317   Chengu, *supra* note 106; Chossudovsky, *supra* note 106.

318   Monti-Belkaoui & Riahi-Belkaoui, *supra* note 78, 268.

319   Chossudovsky, *supra* note 106.

be remedied as a guarantee for the constant improvement in the living standard of the African peoples. In this way foreign stakeholders, as the Maastricht Guidelines stipulate may be compelled to respect human rights in the jurisdictions where they exercise influence.[320] As underscored by the UN Commission on Human Rights, a rights-based approach to development cooperation would ensure that development assistance is properly targeted to ensure that all parties to the development process are equally accountable.[321] This is still largely problematic, possibly because of the lack of appropriate avenues for redressing violations committed by foreign stakeholders when they interfere with the enjoyment of the rights enshrined in the African Charter.[322]

The provisions of the African Charter highlight the same human rights standards recognised by international law, which foreign stakeholders are required to comply with in the course of their extraterritorial actions. According to Thomas Pogge, poverty is generated and sustained by the unjust processes and practices in which global actors engage in their operations.[323] These conditions create inequalities, which as he further explains, amount to human rights violations, necessitating the responsibility of advanced societies towards the poor within the framework of the right to development.[324] Although the world has experienced a precipitation of global action in recent years, characterised by the systematic transfer of aid to developing countries through the Millennium and Sustainable Development programmes, without clarity about the actual responsibilities of states, Pogge expresses reservation about the framing of such actions in dealing with the inequalities created by the global system.[325] In spite of Mathias Risse's scathing critique of Pogge's book as fallacious,[326]

---

320   Maastricht Guidelines on Violations of Economic, Social and Cultural Rights adopted by the International Commission of Jurists 1997.

321   Commission on Human Rights "The right to development and practical strategies for the implementation of the Millennium Development Goals, particularly Goal 8" *Note by the Secretariat E/CN4/2005/WG18/TF/CRP 1* 2 November 2005.

322   According to foundational principle 12 of the UN Guiding Principles on Business and Human Rights (pg 13), non-state actors are required to respect "internationally recognised human rights expressed in the International Bill of Human Rights" even though they are not parties to the treaties. It is further stated (pg 14) that depending on the context, "additional standards beyond the International Bill of Human Rights" may also apply, which does not exclude regional human rights treaties such as the African Charter.

323   Pogge, Thomas (ed) *Freedom from Poverty as a Human Right: Who Owes What to the Very Poor?* (Oxford: Oxford University Press, 2008) 2–11.

324   As above, 52.

325   Pogge, Thomas "The sustainable development goals: Brilliant propaganda?" (2015) *Annals of the University of Bucharest – Political Science Series ISSN 1582-2486* 1.

326   Risse, Mathias "Response to world poverty and human rights: Do we owe the global poor assistance or rectification?" (2003) *Ethics & Int'l Aff* 9–18.

the reality as Bailey and Golan rightly point out is that global arrangements usually only provide the opportunity to foreign stakeholders to impose their policy choices (with the accompanying consequences) without Africa's active involvement in the decision-making processes.[327] Owing to the recognition that non-state actors are equally accountable for human rights offences, for purposes of proper safeguard, the argument advanced here supports the need for developing an African jurisprudence "on holding non-state actors accountable for human rights violations in Africa".[328]

In adjudicating on provisions of the Charter, the African Commission is mandated to draw inspiration from international law, comprising the African instruments on human and peoples' rights, the UN Charter, the international bill of human rights, general or specialised international conventions and other instruments adopted by the United Nations.[329] To draw inspiration from the UN Charter, for example, means that the African Commission needs to interpret the purpose of international cooperation enshrined in the Charter as entailing respect for and advancement of human rights and fundamental freedoms.[330]

4.3   Relevance of the Right to Development Governance to Africa

In addition to the discussion in the early sections of this chapter with regard to the challenges in implementing the right to development in Africa, this section is intended to provide an even more vivid picture of the actual scenario, to substantiate why it is relevant to give the right to development governance particular consideration. With the setbacks to development in Africa as compared to other parts of the world,[331] Jamie Whyte is right in asking whether pursuing the right to development can in effect bring about development.[332] It is important not to lose sight of the fact that the right to development in Africa relates more to livelihood sustainability issues and thus, for Bience Gawanas, development should aim to enhance peoples' capability to overcome poverty,

---

327   Bailey, Fiona & Dolan, Anne M. "The meaning of partnership in development: Lessons for development education" (2011) 13 *Policy & Practice: A Development Education Review* 35.

328   Resolution on the Establishment of a Working Group on Extractive Industries, Environment and Human Rights Violations in Africa 2009 preamble.

329   African Charter, *supra* note 1, arts 60-61.

330   Charter of the United Nations adopted in San Francisco on 26 June 1945 art 3(1).

331   Vickers, B. "Africa and international trade: Challenges and opportunities" (d.n.a) *Thabo Mbeki Leadership Foundation – International Trade and Economic Development Division* 9.

332   Whyte, Jamie "Book review: Development as a human right edited by Bard A Andreassen and Stephen P Marks Harvard University Press London England 2006" (2007) 1:1 *The Elect J Sust Dev't* 47.

social and economic challenges and human rights violations.[333] It explains why, as Alberto Melo ascertains, issues relating to poverty eradication have constituted the primary essence of development.[334] By recognising the human person as the central subject of development, it is affirmed that through their active participation the challenges posed by poverty and human rights violations can be overcome.[335] Accordingly, theoretical guarantees suppose that the right to development should translate into practical assurances of freedom from want and fear of socio-economic deprivation.[336]

However, the African narrative proves the contrary, where according to Ivan Illich; development has rather been programmed to generate poverty.[337] Of the 55 countries that make up the AU, 38 are ranked within the bracket of "least developed" or "heavily indebted poor countries".[338] According to Melo, development in Africa as it is shaped by global politics has become just another aspect of the warfare economy that has pervaded the history of humankind and hijacked opportunities for advancement through diverse forms of domination.[339] The resultant scenario has been one of perpetual dependence through a structured world order that basically deprives the majority of African peoples of the capability to compete on a fair and equitable basis with the rest of the world. Thomas Pogge and Margot Salomon estimate that the unjust world order violates fundamental human rights through the systematic

---

333 Gawanas, Bience "The African Union: Concepts and implementation mechanisms relating to human rights" in Bosl, Anton & Diescho, Joseph (eds) *Human Rights in Africa: Legal Perspectives on their Protection and Promotion* (Windhoek: Macmillan Education Namibia, 2009) 145.

334 Melo, Alberto "Is there a right to development?" (2008) 1:2 *Rizoma Freireano – Instituto Paulo Freire de España* 4.

335 Declaration on the Right to Development, *supra* note 1, art 2.

336 UN Universal Declaration of Human Rights adopted by GA Res 217 A(III) of 10 December 1948 preamble.

337 Illich, Ivan "Development as planned poverty" in Rahnema, Majid & Bawtree, Victoria *The Post-Development Reader* (New York: Zed Books, 1997) 94–102; Melo, *supra* note 334, 3.

338 World Bank "Least developed countries: UN classification" available at: http://data.worldbank.org/region/LDC (accessed: 12 October 2016). Out of the 48 countries classified as least developed 34 are African countries and of the 39 countries classified as heavily indebted 33 are also African countries; Ondua, Henry A, Ndamsa, Dickson T. & Nkouli, Achille J.P.N. "Heavily Indebted Poor Countries Initiative (HIPC), economic stability, and economic growth in Africa" (2018) 43:1/2 *The Journal of Energy and Development* 105; Edoun, Emmanuel I. & Motsepe, Dikgang "Critical assessment of Highly Indebted Poor Countries (HIPIC) Initiative in Africa and the implication of the New Partnership for Africa's Development (NEPAD) (2001–2016): A theoretical perspective" (2016) 13:3/2 *Investment Management and Financial Innovations* 382.

339 Melo, *supra* note 334, 4.

dispossession of marginalised peoples of their proportional share in the allocation of resources, which has resulted in large-scale deficits in human well-being.[340] Of course, as Van der Have has also rightly observed, deprivation of this nature hinders the development process and thus negates people's right to participate in a manner consistent with universally acceptable human rights standards.[341]

Beyond Africa's largely corrupt leadership that accounts for the internal setbacks to development on the continent, the often-ignored problem necessitating closer attention is the dispossession of the people's productive capabilities resulting from global norms such as donor conditionalities that African countries are often obligated to comply with albeit that such conditionalities may not be relevant to the circumstances on the ground. According to the former UN High Commissioner for Human Rights Navi Pillay, dispossession stems from "denial of [the] fundamental human right to development".[342] On the contrary, Ibrahim Salama highlights the fact that the essence of the right to development is to establish an environment that enables or at least does not hinder the enjoyment of basic human rights and freedoms; an environment that is free from structural and unfair obstacles to development.[343] Salama's view is not divorced from the reasons for which Africa championed the cause for the right to development, essentially to ensure while striving to achieve substantive development that justice in development also prevails across the continent.

As a treaty provision, the right to development sets the standard that to deprive the peoples of Africa of their resources and of their capabilities to contribute to development would amount to a violation. This principle has been upheld in case law, where, alluding to the exploitative attitude of European colonisers, the African Commission noted in the *SERAC* case that:

> [T]he human and material resources of Africa were largely exploited for the benefit of outside powers, creating tragedy for Africans themselves, depriving them of their birthright and alienating them from the land. The

---

340   Pogge, Thomas "World poverty and human rights" (2005) 19:1 *Ethics & Int'l Aff* 3–5; Salomon, Margot "International economic governance and human rights accountability" (2007) *Law, Society and Economy Working Paper No 9* 1-28.

341   Van der Have, Nienke "The right to development and state responsibility: Towards idealism without a sense of realism?" (Masters Thesis, University of Amsterdam, 2012)9.

342   Sengupta, Arjun "A rights-based approach to removing poverty" in Ingram, Joseph K. & Freestone, David (eds) *Human Rights and Development* (Washington DC: World Bank Institute, 2006) 8.

343   Salama, *supra* note 7, 67 & 53.

aftermath of colonial exploitation has left Africa's precious resources and people still vulnerable to foreign misappropriation.[344]

With this observation, it is worthy to recall, as Balakrishnan Rajagopal makes clear that the right to development was conceived to achieve a "fundamental transformation of global governance"[345] and as Kiwanuka posits, to culminate the process of dissociating from colonial domination.[346] The right to development has evolved in Africa as an extension of the de-colonisation project, which unfortunately only resulted in nominal political independence.[347] The prevailing circumstances require a radical shift from development models that mostly only perpetuate paternalism to considering the right to development governance, which guarantees actual self-determination in making the policy choices that are relevant to the context in Africa.

Unlike with the prevailing political dispensation, if governance in Africa gets to be constructed on the understanding that all peoples are legitimately entitled to the right to economic, social and cultural development as the basis for the exercise of civil and political rights, policies would by law of natural selection be crafted to shape and direct governmental action towards the attainment of that ultimate goal. This is essentially what the right to development governance entails – to improve living standards for the peoples of Africa – as the argument has been advanced in this chapter. Its implementation does not demand creating new institutional mechanisms, which already exist in the form of the AU and its member states in addition to other subordinate continental and regional mechanisms. Implementation basically requires a dramatic shift in the frame of thinking that every aspect of governance in Africa must converge towards the realisation of the African peoples' entitlement to socio-economic and cultural development.

5   Concluding Remarks

Faced with the reality that Africa's development agenda is still predominantly determined by foreign stakeholders whose actions impact adversely on the well-being of the African peoples, this chapter has explored the extent to which

---

344   *SERAC* case, *supra* note 13, para 56.

345   Rajagopal, Balakrishnan "Right to development and global governance: Old and new challenges twenty-five years on" (2013) 35:4 *Hum Rts Qtly* 893.

346   Kiwanuka, *supra* note 260, 95.

347   Anghie, *supra* note 188, 66.

the right to development could be conceptualised as an alternative model to development cooperation. In doing so, it required first and foremost to look at the extent to which the right to development has been actualised both at the continental and domestic levels in relation to the obligation to adopt appropriate policies to ensure its realisation. Drawing from the conceptual nature of the right to development in Africa, which is intended to be achieved either through collective or individual state action, the AU and African states governments are identified as the mandated institutional frameworks within which the right to development is envisaged to be achieved. A cursory analysis of the AU and five randomly selected African countries is used to explain the challenges involved in the realisation of the right to development as a result of the patronising nature of development cooperation that sustains the *status quo* of dominance over the development processes in Africa.

It is accordingly stated that not until the *status quo* of foreign domination has changed, the realisation of the right to development in Africa will remain a major challenge. This claim is explained by looking at the deficiencies in development cooperation models as a justification for my argumentation in favour of a shift in paradigm from development cooperation to considering the right to development as a suitable development model for Africa. As opposed to the inordinate dependence on development cooperation, which only perpetuates foreign domination and exploitation that retards progress on the continent, it is argued that the right to development provides the opportunity for actual self-determination in making alternative development choices. Owing to the absence of a home-grown development model, the assurance that the right to development may accomplish much more for Africa than development cooperation is premised on the fact that it is by nature conceived as a tool for development policy-making.[348]

The right to development governance as it is presented in this chapter as a home-grown substitute to development cooperation is conceived from the combined conceptual formulation of the generic perception of the right to development as a policy tool and also as a development paradigm. The right to development governance model is designed to relate to the practical on-the-ground realities that the peoples of Africa are confronted with on a daily basis. In accordance, it is further explained how and what implementation of the model entails in order to drive transformation on the continent. Implementation of the right to development, particularly when it has to do with policy measures

---

348 Declaration on the Right to Development, *supra* note 1, art 2(3); African Charter, *supra* note 1, art 20(1).

for the achievement of substantive development is, as Sengupta has rightly stated, more important than legal enforcement.[349] However, the well-being of the peoples of Africa is not only compromised through denial of material entitlements but also through development injustices that contravene the right to development. Because the right to development imposes an obligation for compliance with the law as highlighted in chapter four, making the right to development governance a reality entails looking at the operational considerations with regard to the potential for violation. It is argued in this regard that when prevention fails and a violation is established, due process of the law must proceed not only because the right to development is anchored in the law but essentially because its realisation is supposed to engender the constant improvement in well-being for the peoples of Africa.

With evidence that development cooperation cannot practically ensure the realisation of the right to development as pointed out throughout this book, and in presenting the right to development governance as a suitable alternative as illustrated in this chapter, the purpose is to advance the argument for a paradigm shift in development thinking across Africa. When the peoples of Africa opted for self-determination against imperial domination under colonial rule, it took decisive collective action to break the bonds of subjugation that had been established for over seven decades. Comparatively, the manifestation of imperial domination under the present circumstances is more ideological and therefore, also needs decisive collective action but more in terms of policy making to affect a system change from the pre-existing models that continue to hold the peoples of Africa in subordination to foreign domination. To this end and in relation to the African agenda for transformation and sustainable development, the need for a home-grown functional model for development, which obtains from the range of commitments to prioritise the right to development as illustrated in this chapter, necessitates further concrete measures on the basis of which relevant policy imperatives are outlined in the concluding chapter.

---

349   Sengupta, Arjun "Right to development as a human right" (2001) 36:27 *Econ & Pol Wkly* 2533.

CHAPTER 6

Conclusion – Right to Development Imperatives for Africa

1   Concluding Highlights

This concluding chapter highlights the primary enquiry, which has been to determine why Africa should have recourse to development cooperation for the realisation of the right to development. In making this determination, the root causes to Africa's development challenges, which are established to have emanated from a compromised history of engagement with European invaders for a period of close to six centuries, are examined. It is illustrated that the right to development emerged from that background not as a solicitation for development assistance but rather as an expression of self-determination against domination and subjugation. With this background knowledge, it is pointed out that there is indeed a right to development in Africa that has evolved as a claimable entitlement but most importantly as a development paradigm that is yet to be fully explored to the benefit of the African peoples. Accordingly, the argument is advanced that the right to development, being itself a development paradigm, cannot be achieved through development cooperation, which as a mechanism for development in its own terms, only subjects Africa to the benevolence and patronage of developed countries. Africa's endemic dependence on development assistance as a means to achieve development objectives is explained to be motivated by the absence of an operational model for the continent, which has meant the inability to make alternative development choices that are relevant in addressing contemporary problems.

Drawing from the dual dimension of the right to development as a human rights concept and a development paradigm as illustrated in chapter two, it is stated that its full realisation entails exploring its dimension as a development paradigm, envisaged as a tool for policy making and also as an alternative model with the potential to yield more development benefits for Africa than can be anticipated through development cooperation. In the absence of a functional model for development in Africa, the proposition is advanced to substitute development cooperation with the right to development governance. On account of the fact that Africa remains exposed to foreign domination and exploitation in addition to internal governance malpractices and democratic deficits, as part of the operational consideration in implementing

© CAROL CHI NGANG, 2022 | DOI:10.1163/9789004467903_007

the right to development governance, it is suggested for African states governments to affirm the right and exercise the duty to formulate appropriate legislation and policies to regulate the development space, particularly taking into consideration the excessive influence that non-state actors and foreign stakeholders exert on the populations in the course of their operations. This motivates the position taken in advancing the argument for a paradigm shift from development cooperation to the right to development governance as an assurance that the right to socio-economic and cultural development guaranteed to the peoples of Africa is adequately protected.

Section 1.1 provides summary observations of the principal arguments. Section 1.2 reiterates the transformative potential of the right to development governance as an alternative perspective to development cooperation, which as it is argued is not suitable as a model for development in Africa. Section 2 further highlights the policy imperatives relating to priority measures and actions that need to be taken both at the continental level by the African Union (AU) in section 2.1 and at domestic levels by African states governments in section 2.2. Final remarks are provided in section 3.

1.1 *Summary Observations*

Pertaining to the central enquiry to determine whether the right to development in Africa is achievable through development cooperation, it is shown that conceptually, development cooperation is opposed and in fact, contradicts the African conception of the right to development. As a justification for this claim, it is illustrated in chapter two that there is indeed a right to development that has evolved in Africa not as a solicitation for development assistance but as an assertion of self-determination against the injustices perpetuated in Africa through various forms of domination. The analysis reveals that by nature, the right to development in Africa is formulated on the one hand, as a human rights concept to ensure that development processes are regulated by the principles of justice and equity and on the other hand, as a development paradigm intended to achieve improved well-being for the peoples of Africa. The African conception of the right to development therefore not only adds value to the discourse on human rights and development, but its recognition as a legal entitlement also creates a unique dispensation that allows for justice in development to prevail and for substantive development to be achieved. It is argued that the realisation of the right to development entails the fulfilment of three normative requirements: First, that African countries exercise sovereignty in formulating national development policies; second, that obstacles to development, including foreign domination and external interference are

CONCLUSION – RIGHT TO DEVELOPMENT IMPERATIVES FOR AFRICA   295

eliminated[1] and third, that an enabling environment is established to ensure that the right to development is effectively put into practice.

As to whether the right to development could be achieved through development cooperation, the mechanism of development cooperation is critically examined in chapter three in relation to the right to development in Africa. The analysis reveals that the probability to achieve the right to development through development cooperation is extremely minimal, especially considering the underlining motives behind prevailing patterns of cooperation that aim primarily at safeguarding the interests of foreign stakeholders. The patronising nature of development cooperation basically runs contrary to the entitlement to self-determination that guarantees the right to make policy alternatives. Accordingly, studies in the area of human rights and development in Africa ought to shift focus from development cooperation towards exploring the right to development as a suitable alternative, importantly because of the exigency to craft a functional development model to drive the continent's agenda for structural transformation.

Looking at the right to development dispensation in Africa, which provides for actual self-determination in making development alternatives as shown in chapter four, effective implementation remains problematic due on the one hand to internal constraints and insufficiencies and on the other hand to the dominant influence of foreign stakeholders in shaping Africa's development priorities. With regard to the latter, even though it has been argued that non-state actors, including foreign stakeholders are obligated to respect human rights extraterritorially and therefore, equally accountable for wrongful action,[2] the analysis reveals that those operating in Africa are generally insulated from accountability. The right to development dispensation not only entitles the peoples of Africa to claim entitlement to development as a matter

---

1   Declaration on the Right to Development Resolution A/RES/41/128 adopted by the UN General Assembly on 4 December 1986 art 5.

2   D'Aspremont, Jean *et al.* "Sharing responsibility between non-state actors and states in international law: Introduction" (2015) 62:1 *Neth Int'l L Rev* 50; Okafor, Obiora C. " 'Righting' the right to development: A socio-legal analysis of article 22 of the African Charter on Human and Peoples' Rights" in Marks, Stephen P. (ed) *Implementing the Right to Development: The Role of International Law* (Geneva: Friedrich-Ebert-Stiftung, 2008) 60; Chirwa, Danwood M. "Toward revitalizing economic, social and cultural rights in Africa: *Social and Economic Rights Action Centre and the Centre for Economic and Social Rights v Nigeria*" (2002) 10:1 *Hum Rts Brief* 16; Frankovits, André "Rules to live by: The human rights approach to development" (2002) 17 *PRAXIS – The Fletcher J Dev't Stud* 9; UN Universal Declaration of Human Rights adopted by General Assembly resolution 217 A(III) of 10 December 1948 preamble; Maastricht Principles on Extraterritorial Obligations of States in the area of Economic, Social and Cultural Rights adopted by the International Commission of Jurists on 28 September 2011 para 27.

of right, it also makes provision for the enforcement of that right through litigation although its full realisation cannot depend exclusively on judicial processes. With regard to legal accountability, the pre-emptive application of international law and the inadequacies in regional and domestic laws are shown to allow foreign stakeholders the opportunity to contravene the right to development in Africa with impunity.

On account of the foregoing, the discussion in chapter five explored the practical dimensions of the right to development as a development paradigm necessitating the setting of alternative priorities.[3] By conceptual formulation, in terms of which the right to development is envisaged as integral to the right to self-determination, it is demonstrated that the peoples of Africa are indeed entitled to shape the development future of the continent through contextually relevant policy choices in dealing with socio-economic realities on the ground. However, a cursory analysis of the AU and of the five countries examined shows that the right to development is yet to translate into practical reality as envisaged by the range of instruments that constitute the pillars of the right to development dispensation in Africa. Examined in relation to the deficiencies in development cooperation approaches, the argument is advanced for a paradigm shift towards greater focus on the right to development governance as an alternative development model for Africa. In terms of functional modalities, the capacity to actualise the right to development governance are examined, including through promoting socio-economic and cultural freedoms as well as the agency of the peoples of Africa to take ownership and responsibility and effectively drive their own development processes. To this end, the right to development governance is highlighted as the central focus on which the proposition for a paradigm shift is formulated. The next section proceeds to expatiate on its potential as an alternative transformative model suited to Africa.

1.2 Alternative Perspective to Development Thinking

In concurrence with Ndlovu-Gatsheni, if "genuinely African futures" would be achieved such as envisaged in Agenda 2063, the processes for development would have to be predicated on a different plane of thought and reasoning capable of rupturing established paradigms that subjugate the peoples of Africa to global patterns of coloniality.[4] The argument is reiterated in the need for Africa to consider the right to development governance as an alternative

---

3 Sengupta, Arjun "Right to development as a human right" (2001) 36:27 *Econ & Pol Wkly* 2533.
4 Ndlovu-Gatsheni, Sabelo J. "Global coloniality and the challenges of creating African futures" (2014) 36:2 *Strategic Review for Southern Africa* 196.

CONCLUSION – RIGHT TO DEVELOPMENT IMPERATIVES FOR AFRICA   297

to development cooperation, which on the most part, only promotes dependency on foreign assistance that has held back progress on the continent for several decades. Unlike development cooperation, the right to development governance provides the opportunity for independent policy making as illustrated in chapter five, to ensure the realisation of the aspirations for structural transformation and sustainable development contained in Agenda 2063.[5]

As a rights-based model, the right to development governance provides the operational framework for the realisation of the composite of human rights alongside development objectives, which otherwise may not be achieved in isolation. Where specific rights are not explicitly provided for, the right to development could be used as an interpretative guide, to establish the existence of such rights. For instance, although the right to food is not enshrined in the African Charter, the African Commission held in the *SERAC* case that it is implied in article 22 to the effect that a violation of the right to food would occasion a violation of the right to development.[6] Accordingly also, to violate the right to development would amount to a violation of the range of associated rights.

As a justiciable entitlement, the right to development imposes an obligation for legal accountability and thus guarantees protection against impunity. Litigating related violations is certain to have wide-ranging impact and therefore dramatically improve human well-being in Africa. As an interpretative guide, the right to development governance provides the basis for gauging the standards of development to be attained in Africa and as a home-grown model; it also provides a platform for development to be achieved with justice, allowing for the realisation of human rights while simultaneously pursuing economic growth objectives in an equitable manner. The right to development governance model accords priority to people-centred development programming and accordingly orients policy formulation, development planning and corresponding modalities for integrated governance. Unfortunately, prevailing theories have often stood in direct opposition to effective action.[7] This is explained by the fact that although Africa has pioneered and remains the pacesetter on the right to development, in formulating the continental policy

---

5   African Union Commission "Agenda 2063: The Africa we want" (2015) *African Union* para 66(b).

6   *Social and Economic Rights Action Centre (SERAC) & Another v Nigeria* Comm 155/96(2001) AHRLR 60 (ACHPR 2001) para 64.

7   Šlaus, Ivo & Jacobs, Garry "In search of a new paradigm for global development" (2013) 1:6 *Cadmus Journal* 2–3.

agenda for transformation, the AU Commission failed to take cognizance of the right to development as a suitable model to drive the transformation process.[8]

Similar to the haphazard manner in which independence was achieved, the vision for a new Africa outlined in Agenda 2063 includes an ambitious roadmap for development but fails to specify the applicable model for addressing concretely the issues at stake, particularly the development injustices and endemic human rights violations on the continent. Africa is burdened not only by a human development crisis but more crucially by a systems problem that requires a transformative model to ensure an overhaul of the system. While the Agenda 2063 document makes mention of an African model and approach to development and transformation,[9] it neither states concretely what the model or approach is nor does it describe how to drive the transformation process to effective realisation. The Agenda is established to be rooted in pan-Africanism and African renaissance, which, of course, are valuable political ideologies that reflect the vision for a new Africa.[10] However, these ideologies need to be harnessed and guided by the proposed right to development governance model, which as indicated in this book, is conceived in conformity with the philosophy of African solutions to African problems.

In coming to the conclusion in favour of a paradigm shift in human rights and development thinking as a prerequisite for transformation in Africa, it is further stated that the magnitude of change that is envisaged for Africa can only be achieved through decisive policies and a compelling development model in the form of the right to development governance. While this book opens up avenues for further research on the right to development governance model, on account of its pragmatic nature, requiring concrete action for its realisation, the following recommendations are intended to address the central concerns relating to the lack of a functional model to redress the set-backs to development on the continent.

---

8   The Agenda 2063 document only passively makes mention of the right to development in the last paragraph (para 76) where it is stated that "regard, we reaffirm the Rio principles of common, but differentiated responsibilities, *the right to development* and equity, mutual accountability and responsibility and policy space for nationally tailored policies and programmes on the continent".

9   AU Commission "Agenda 2063", *supra* note 5, para 74(e)&(h).

10 As above, para 1.

CONCLUSION – RIGHT TO DEVELOPMENT IMPERATIVES FOR AFRICA 299

2 Imperative for Political Action

Given that the right to development is envisaged to be achieved collectively through the concerted effort of all African countries and also through individual state action, the recommendations made in this section are intended on the one hand, to provide a reference guide to development policy-oriented research in Africa and on the other hand, to provide the baseline for priority measures and political actions that need to be taken both at the continental and domestic levels.

2.1 African Union (AU)

2.1.1 Africa's Common Policy Principle

Africa has since the year 2000, with the coming into force of the AU Constitutive Act as a guiding instrument, developed the tradition of taking common stance and policy positions on issues of collective interest and relevance to the continent at large.[11] Following this established operational principle, as custodian of the regulatory instruments on issues relating to human rights and development, the AU in its policy-making and standard-setting role is obligated to harmonise and promote a common policy position on the right to development that should become lawfully and uniformly applicable through general mainstreaming into development practice in Africa. The need for harmonisation draws from the fact that the formulation of the right to development in Africa is not standardised. For instance, the African Charter enshrines the right to development as a collective entitlement aiming at socio-economic and cultural development, while other instruments include an individual dimension and envisage its realisation to incorporate civil and political development.[12] Discrepancies of this nature render the realisation of the right to development haphazard.

Harmonisation necessitates considering the possibility of incorporating the right to development governance as a home-grown model in addressing the lack of a functional model to accelerate transformation on the African continent. A common policy position on the right to development has the advantage to ensure coordinated action that can significantly influence decision-making processes in global consultations relating to development in Africa. Thus, although Agenda 2063 calls on "the international community to respect Africa's

---

11   Constitutive Act of the African Union adopted in Lomé Togo on 11 July 2000 art 3(d); AU Commission "Agenda 2063", *supra* note 5, para 61.

12   See chapter five for details on how the various treaty and constitutional provisions that enshrine the right to development are formulated.

vision and aspirations and to align their partnerships appropriately",[13] only a rigorous policy framework in the form of the right to development governance can compel the international community to align with the African agenda for development. There certainly is a need for further research into the practical dimensions of the right to development governance, to determine how it can effectively be applied as a model for development in Africa.

As the principal development agency of the AU, the New Partnership for Africa's Development (NEPAD), including when it eventually transforms into the AU Development Agency (AUDA) owes a crucial role in advancing the right to development governance. Based on the finding that the right to development is not achievable through development cooperation, NEPAD/AUDA would need to balance its neoliberal and donor-driven approach through committed mainstreaming of right to development standards both in its programming for development and its relations with foreign stakeholders. The African Peer Review Mechanism could be used as the platform to engage African governments to become more committed to their legal obligations on the right to development, especially in terms of espousing the proposed right to development governance model for domestic implementation. The reasoning is that by using the right to development governance model as a benchmark in assessing the performance of African governments, they can be held to greater accountability for the fulfilment of the full range of human rights in their entirety as well as for the realisation of development objectives as a guarantee for the attainment of an improved standard of living for the peoples of Africa.

2.1.2   Financing for Development

The whole of Africa (represented by the AU) currently does not have any independence source of financing for development. Despite recognition that to be able to rise to the status of an influential global actor, Africa needs to demonstrate the potential to finance its own development,[14] it is not unknown that the AU is still largely funded by the European Union and China. If Africa is to achieve socio-economic and cultural self-determination, funding for development programmes will have to increasingly be sourced through the mobilisation of public and private financing from within the continent and the African diaspora. A development funding mechanism for Africa is imperative to serve as a counter measure to dependency on foreign assistance. The AU Constitutive Act indeed, makes provision for the establishment of an African Central Bank

---

13   AU Commission "Agenda 2063", *supra* note 5, para 76.
14   AU Commission "Agenda 2063", *supra* note 5, para 60.

CONCLUSION – RIGHT TO DEVELOPMENT IMPERATIVES FOR AFRICA   301

(ACB), an African Monetary Fund (AMF) and an African Investment Bank (AIB) whose roles as continental financial institutions is guaranteed to be defined in specific additional protocols.[15] While these financial institutions remain crucial in enabling Africa to achieve socio-economic and cultural self-determination, they have however, since the adoption of the Constitutive Act in July 2000 (two decades later), not been established. The protocols creating these institutions have either only been drafted or adopted. There is no indication when they would effectively become operational.[16]

Besides the continental financial institutions when they eventually become functional, to maintain a consistent flow of development financing for the purpose of collective realisation of the right to development, the AU needs to establish a *pan-African fund for development* (similar to initiatives like the Global Fund) to which, as a policy measure, every African country is obligated to make mandatory contributions. The pan-African fund should be designed to attract a steady flow of funding from the African corporate sector, philanthropic organisations, private foundations and most importantly, compulsory payment of royalties and corporate social responsibility levies by the corporate sector, including especially foreign multinational corporations operating on the continent.

The relevance of the fund is justified by the fact that the right to development engenders positive obligations requiring the mobilisation of enormous resources and also by the commitment to turn away from aid dependency towards self-sufficiency.[17] As long as Africa remains dependent on external funding, it risks remaining predisposed to the patronage of foreign donors, which as shown in chapter three, constitutes a major hindrance to effective socio-economic and cultural self-determination on the continent. As an additional remedy to financing development on the continent, the AU needs to consider reviving the initiative to create an African Monetary Fund and an African Investment Bank as alternative sources of development financing. It is only with full control over its own sources of funding that Africa can be able to gainfully manage its resources in relation to the development priorities on

---

15   AU Constitutive Act, *supra* note 11, para 19.

16   African Union "AU financial institutions" available at: https://au.int/en/ea/epr/aufi (accessed: 20 March 2010). The joint strategy on the establishment of the ACB was adopted in June 2013, the Protocol on the AIB was adopted in February 2009, pending 15 ratifications to come into force, while the Protocol on the AMF has only been drafted, date not specified.

17   AU Commission "Agenda 2063", *supra* note 5, para 72(o).

302 CHAPTER 6

the continent, particularly, with regard to the need to advance the productive capabilities of the African people.

The pan-African fund should of necessity be administered by NEPAD/AUDA, which should have as additional mandate to develop and diligently manage a donor database, particularly of foreign multinationals and the African corporate sector besides other donors and in collaboration with states governments and regional development financial institutions, device modalities for the collection of the requisite payments. The funds should be designated to the development of competitive technology, inventions of African origin, manufacturing and the conversion of the natural resources that abound in Africa into marketable commodities. Because one of the primary obstacles to development in Africa is the inability to generate requisite investment capital, the pan-African Development Fund should operate to provide such investment capital to cutting edge start-up initiatives as a means to expand opportunities for development and to advance local productive capabilities. The African Development Bank cannot necessarily do what the pan-African Development Fund could accomplish.

2.1.3 On Skills and Technology Transfer

The AU has an obligation to adopt a firm continental policy on the question of skills and technology transfer, which although has been the subject of broad consensus in international fora,[18] has never concretely been implemented. Unlike the 0.7 per cent promise of development assistance that has never been achieved, the issue of technology transfer is claimable and achievable. For instance, in keeping with the resolve to "[t]ake measures to ensure technology transfer",[19] it is in Africa's legitimate interest to ascertain that undertakings committed to by industrialised countries are fulfilled. Although natural resources constitute an essential determinant in the realisation of the right to development, Africa's resources have been the object of wanton and abusive exploitation by industrialised countries. In way of redress, Africa needs to adopt a robust policy with emphasis on the transfer of relevant technology as a precondition for resource exploitation by foreign stakeholders.

Putting such a policy in place guarantees not only gainful utilisation of the continent's resources but also ensures that the acquisition of new technology provides the opportunity to the peoples of Africa to develop their productive

---

18   Amin, Samir *Imperialism and Unequal Development* (1977) 169; See also United Nations *Compendium of International Arrangements on Transfer of Technology: Selected Instruments* (2001).

19   AU Commission "Agenda 2063", *supra* note 5, para 72(o).

CONCLUSION – RIGHT TO DEVELOPMENT IMPERATIVES FOR AFRICA 303

capabilities. The leverage to accomplish this objective might pose a challenge. However, Africa possesses the requisite resources for driving technological advancement, which could be used as a bargaining chip to secure the transfer of the necessary skills and technology to process the raw material resources at their source. Creating the necessary leverage requires, as indicated above, a common policy framework that can uniformly be applied across Africa.

2.1.4 On Attaining the Superior Purpose for Development

To accomplish prospects for development in Africa require defining in very concrete terms what development ultimately represents for the peoples of Africa and how it should be pursued. It is argued that teleological reasoning necessitates exploring decolonial narratives that perceive the imperatives for development in Africa as intended to achieve a superior purpose, defined as the bigger picture consideration of what Africa is envisaged to become and the critical self-consciousness of the strategic priorities, which should consistently trigger a rethinking of the concept of development and to redefine the processes and mechanisms thereof from a decolonial and less neo-liberalistic viewpoint.[20]

> The superior purpose could be understood to derive from the motivations that informed the struggles for decolonisation that ushered in political independence for Africa. The founding of the Organisation for African Unity (OAU) was premised on the conviction that "it is the inalienable right of all people[s] to control their own destiny, [...] to fight against neo colonialism in all its forms [...] so that the welfare and well being of their peoples can be assured". The Constitutive Act of the African Union refers to these convictions as "noble ideals" to be achieved through collective action "in all fields of human activity to raise the living standards of African peoples", akin in every sense to Article 22 of the African Charter which makes provision for the right to development (citations omitted).[21]

By setting such as a standard, every development activity would then be directed towards achieving the definitive superior purpose. For example, because the focus currently is mostly aimed at achieving economic growth and the expansion of the market economy, the need to improve livelihood is generally ignored, consequently limiting the capacity of the peoples of Africa

---

20 Ngang, Carol C. 'Right to development governance in the advent of the African Continental Free Trade Area' (2021) 65:2 *Journal of African Law* 153-178.

21 As above, 156-157.

to contribute in making their own development choices and in shaping the development future for the continent. Meanwhile, if development is defined as ultimately aiming to achieve the highest standard of living for the African peoples, the focus will shift to developing their productive capabilities and expanding their opportunities to contribute to even much higher levels of economic growth.

To achieve this purpose depends first and foremost on liberating the peoples of Africa from socio-economic and cultural deprivation and secondly, on increasingly equipping them with the relevant capabilities that are needed to accelerate transformation on the continent. Doing so is an obligation that is owed to the peoples of Africa in respect of article 22 of the African Charter and therefore, it is recommended for the AU to broaden the theoretical understanding of the right to development in order to provide greater clarity on what the populations can legitimately expect to achieve from the development process. From the perspective of the arguments advanced in this book, it entails restructuring the entire governance mechanism in Africa to be able to regulate the processes for development in a manner that every development initiative should be seen to contribute directly or indirectly to raising living standards for *all the peoples of Africa* to the highest attainable levels.

Unlike under the existing context where a huge proportion of the African populations remain dispossessed of the opportunities and the potential to contribute to development, it is evident that a shift towards expanding the production function of the African peoples would invariably augment levels of economic growth, enhance social progress, and promote cultural value systems. If Africa hopes to sustain the dream of emerging an influential global actor, it cannot afford to define development by any lesser standard. In this way, corporate ventures, extractive industry activities, foreign direct investment operations, technological advancement and mega infrastructural projects among other development programmes should then obligatorily be required to demonstrate evidence of their contribution to raising living standards and the general well-being of entire populations. As much as the peoples of Africa remain entrapped in and denied the opportunities for socio-economic and cultural self-determination, it is improbable that the kind of inclusive growth, structural transformation and sustainable development envisaged in the continental agenda for development will be achieved.

In accordance with article 66 of the African Charter that allows for the adoption of special protocols to complement provisions of the Charter, the AU may need to adopt an additional protocol on the right to development to provide normative clarity on the nature of the right to development, the role of the peoples of Africa (duty bearers) as well as the concrete obligations of

CONCLUSION – RIGHT TO DEVELOPMENT IMPERATIVES FOR AFRICA   305

member states (duty bearers) with regard to implementing the right to development. Understood as a rights-based process to development, the protocol would need to highlight the right to development as an interpretative guide to all laws and policies that regulate development practice and the associated processes in Africa. Relating to litigation, the African Commission as well as the African Court on Human and Peoples' Rights will need to improve on the nature of remedies they award so that complainants might be able to anticipate the outcomes of adjudication proportionately to what the right to development promises.

Otherwise, because adopting an additional protocol may be arduous, as an interim measure, the African Commission may need to adopt General Comments on article 22 of the Charter to enable an in-depth understanding of the African conception of the right to development in terms of substantive contents, scope of application and modalities for realisation among others. An even more realistic approach necessitates the AU to adopt a continental policy instrument in the form of a white paper to provide conceptual clarity on the right to development as a governance model for development and define the practical measures for its implementation with vividly outlined measurable outcomes.

2.2   *States Governments*

2.2.1   Socio-economic and Cultural Transformation

Besides the measures that need to be taken at the continental level as shown above, by virtue of the legal commitments undertaken under the Constitutive Act, the African Charter and other related instruments, domestic implementation remains elemental to the realisation of the right to development. In line with the forgoing recommendation, state parties to the African Charter, owe an obligation to drive socio-economic and cultural transformation to the benefit of the African peoples. It is thus, crucial to reiterate the duty they owe to lay emphasis on socio-economic and cultural development, which as stipulated in the preamble to the Charter, provides the sole guarantee for the enjoyment of civil and political rights. In this regard, as highlighted in chapter four, states governments need to demonstrate the political resolve and clarity of purpose in concretely ensuring that socio-economic and cultural transformation becomes reality.

It entails translating the commitments undertaken under treaty instruments into domestic laws and appropriate national development policies. With regard to the exploitative and abusive conduct of foreign stakeholders, it weighs on African states to improve on or adopt domestic legislation that explicitly includes provisions on regulating the activities of external actors.

The domestic legislation may not necessarily need to impose a positive duty that compels foreign stakeholders to fulfil the right to development in Africa but unavoidably must emphasise on the negative obligation to refrain from the violations that may result from their operations. National development policies should be designed to conform to the conceptual reading of the right to development as a tool for policy making that equips African states with actual self-determination in crafting concrete and realistic plans of action that must seek to better the living conditions of the African peoples.

As pointed out that development cooperation is fundamentally counterproductive to socio-economic and cultural self-determination in Africa; states governments need to demonstrate uncompromised commitment to advancing the right to development governance as a suitable alternative development model. The right to development governance provides the opportunity for Africa to either rise above prevailing forms of domination and tilt the global power dynamics in its favour or remain perpetually dependent. Given that developed countries are increasingly creating more and more geopolitical groupings to wield more influence, the nations of Africa are faced with the challenge to progressively align their domestic development policies into a standardised model for application across the continent. While it is a sovereign right bestowed on each African country to own and control its domestic development processes, it is irrational to seek to do so in isolation when greater benefits could be achieved by pulling efforts together in accordance with the African Charter requirement to ensure collectively that the right to development is achieved.

Notwithstanding the gains that may accrue to some African countries through development cooperation structures that are established outside of the pan-African framework, a decisive collective shift from development cooperation arrangements has the potential to catapult Africa into higher levels of global economic leverage and hegemony. It demands shared political conviction and unity of purpose, which as it is posited, is attainable through advancing the right to development governance as a model for development in Africa. It is by embracing this home-grown model that Africa can effectively disengage from dependency on foreign assistance and the overriding influence of developed countries. The right to development governance defines how Africa should be governed and in effect, activates thinking about the breed of leadership that is required to drive envisaged socio-economic and cultural development, which remains an unfulfilled promise to the peoples of Africa.

2.2.2 Transformative Leadership

The agenda for development in Africa and by implication, the right to development governance model proposed in this book cannot by themselves translate into reality. It requires strategic political leadership with a transformative vision to streamline what development in Africa should aim to achieve and the processes to facilitate the flourishing of collective productive capabilities. In essence, transformative leadership is envisaged in this context as a mechanism to enable the framework for development in Africa to self-regulate and patterned to transform the livelihood circumstances of the peoples of Africa. It begs for a resolute combination of the moral responsibility of the African peoples and the legal duty of states governments to create egalitarian opportunities and possibilities for the collective advancement of the African peoples.

Transformative leadership requires enlisting the full participation of the African peoples to ensure the working together of shared aspirations for the attainment of the same development objectives and the equitable redistribution of development gains. Accordingly, when the global rules for development are redefined as it frequently happens; the obligation imposed by the right to development reverts to the political leadership in Africa to set even more competitive standards for the attainment of well-being for the African peoples. According to Burns, transformative leadership is qualified by the ability to discern what the people aspire for and to seek to satisfy those higher demands.[22] In a discussion on leadership in Africa, former South African President Thabo Mbeki intimated that the outcomes expected of every process ought to determine the kind of leadership that would produce those outcomes.[23] With the expectation to achieve broad-based transformation and sustainable development within the next half a century as articulated in the 2063 agenda for development, the crucial question as Mbeki indicates is how to produce the stock of transformative leadership to accomplish that purpose.

---

22   Burns, James M. *Leadership* (New York: Harper and Row, 1978) 4; for more on transformative leadership, see Dartey-Baah, Kwasi "Effective leadership and sustainable development in Africa: Is there 'really' a link?" (2014) 5:2 *Journal of Global Responsibility* 205–208; Afegbua, Salami I. & Adejuwon, Kehinde D. "The challenges of leadership and governance in Africa" (2012)2:9 *International Journal of Academic Research in Business and Social Sciences* 147–148; Manfred, F.R. Kets de Vries; Sexton, Jennifer C. & Parker Allen III B."Destructive and transformational leadership in Africa" (2016) 2:2 *Africa Journal of Management* 12–14; Gumede, Vusi "Exploring thought leadership, thought liberation and critical consciousness for Africa's development" (2015) 40:4 *Africa Development* 91–111.

23   African Development Bank Group "High Level Event II – Leadership for the Africa we Want" Kigali, Rwanda, Wednesday 21 May 2014.

308　　　　　　　　　　　　　　　　　　　　　　　　　　　　　　　　　CHAPTER 6

It is important to admit that the thought patterns of the phasing out generation of the political leadership in Africa is still largely entangled in replicating colonial and paternalistic models for development, which is not likely to be altered in an instant. The plan to effect a change lies in beginning to put in place the systems and the policy toolkits to redirect political thinking and eventually equip emerging leaders with the working knowledge that the context and the circumstances in Africa require an alternative model to development other than those with an un-African savour. The possibility to refocus development in Africa so that it becomes substantively beneficial is dependent on genuine political commitment to meet the African peoples' aspirations for improved well-being and better living standards. Transformative leadership guarantees that the peoples of Africa can effectively exercise the right to demand accountability when right to development standards are not met and the political leadership can be able to respond favourably leaders. Because political leadership is crucial for the realisation of the agenda for transformation, a decolonised future for Africa requires a new frame of thinking on the criteria for making political choices, especially with regard to selecting the leadership that is needed to achieve that purpose.

2.2.3　　Basis for Making Political Choices

Conceptually, the right to development in Africa obligates state parties to be conscientiously responsive to the livelihood exigencies of their peoples and by implication, command the duty to take appropriate measures and to put in place functional mechanisms for the attainment of that goal. The peoples of Africa in turn have the responsibility as highlighted in article 2(2) of the Declaration on the Right to Development, to demand of the various states governments to fulfil their obligations with regard to the realisation of socio-economic and cultural development. On account of the fact that equilibrium between states' obligations and peoples' responsibilities can only be established within the framework of representative democracy, it is imperative as an inevitable prerequisite for aspirants to positions of political leadership in Africa to concretely demonstrate how their political ambitions respond to the right to socio-economic and cultural development.

In this instance, the proposed right to development governance creating a dispensation for genuine broad based accountability necessitating the crafting of resolute policies to compel African states governments to create the conditions for the attainment of socio-economic and economic self-determination. Unless prevailing development practices characterised by a combination of hostile factors, including especially the dominant influence of foreign stakeholders is reversed, prospects for socio-economic and cultural development is likely to remain constrained and therefore, also keep living standards and human well-being on the continent unacceptably low or at best, improving only very marginally. Based on the knowledge that non-state actors are imposed with an extraterritorial obligation to abide by universal human rights standards, it is important to emphasise that accountability within the context of the right to development governance does not exclude effectively regulating the operations of foreign stakeholders whose actions as illustrated in this book, often contravene with impunity the right to development guaranteed to the peoples of Africa.

The right to development governance suggests creating a political system where the well-being of the African peoples is prioritised as the focal point for development and where also, perpetrators can be compelled, at least negatively to refrain from actions that may infringe on their entitlement to socio-economic and cultural development. Accordingly, it is crucial to ensure that legislation and policies as well as development programmes at the national and continental levels provide the basis for political action and consequently guide the pursuit of socio-economic and cultural development across the continent. Such a political system can only thrive on strong institutions of accountability, including ensuring as a preliminary measure that domestic courts as jurisdictions of first instance are equipped and empowered to acknowledge that like any other human right, the right to development is justiciable and in effect, claimable through judicial processes. This is important on the most part because admissibility of cases by the African Commission and the African Court depend largely on satisfaction of the requirement to exhaust local remedies. This imposes an even greater duty on state parties that have not yet domesticated the African Charter, to proceed to do so in order to expand the jurisdiction of domestic courts to enforce the right to development at the national level.

3   Final Remarks

By positing a shift in development thinking from the pursuit of development cooperation to embracing the right to development governance as a model for development in Africa, this book has articulated in elaborate terms what early proponents like Doudou Thiam, Cardinal Etienne Duval, Sédar Senghor and Kéba M'baye intended when they, with a decolonial mindset, advocated for a proclamation of the right to development. By conceptualising the right to development governance as an alternative to the various development models that have been experimented in Africa without much success, this book has also endeavoured to expound on the African Charter preambular clause that says particular attention should be given to the right to development. To pay particular attention to the right to development virtually means and in effect, entails as a matter of governance that the framework for development is designed to equalise opportunities for all the peoples of Africa to enjoy better living standards through prioritising economic, social and cultural development and in that process also eradicate poverty and other obstacles to development on the continent.

Situated within the context of the 2063 framework for development, it is acknowledged that Africa can indeed, become an "influential global player" with the capacity to significantly shape global development politics. In reaffirming the "Rio principles of common, but differentiated responsibilities, the right to development" and a "policy space for nationally tailored policies and programmes" as the vehicle for driving the African development agenda, states governments implicitly admit that in order to achieve desired outcomes, development on the continent can be done differently.[24] The idea of common but differentiated responsibility convey the fact that because poverty and the extremely low standards of living represent the most pressing of challenges that the peoples of Africa have had to grapple with, national development policies and programmes should be tailored to respond directly to the exigencies of poverty eradication, socio-economic and cultural development as well as improved standards of living.[25] This is attainable within the scope of the right to development that makes provision for active participation in the development process and therefore, only to the extent that the peoples of Africa become the central focus of development, that is, the purpose for which development is carried out rather than objects to be used to achieve development objectives.

While the argument has been put forward that the right to development cannot be achieved through the solicitation of development assistance but rather through embracing the right to development governance as a substitute model with the potential to accelerate Africa's prospects for development, it is crucial to highlight that effective implementation cannot be accomplished without sustained evidence-based research and a consistent flow of knowledge on the subject to broaden the scope of understanding. At the instance, added to the fact that scholarship on the right to development in Africa remains scanty and more so, devoid of substance in advancing modalities for implementation, consciousness among the peoples of Africa about this important entitlement

---

24   AU Commission "Agenda 2063", *supra* note 5, para 76.
25   Ngang, Carol C. "Differentiated responsibilities under international law and the right to development paradigm for developing countries" (2017) 11:2 *HR & ILD* 270–272.

is also unacceptably low. It demands of universities and relevant research institutions within and beyond Africa to multiply efforts in generating knowledge on the right to development and essentially also in making such knowledge increasingly available and accessible to the peoples of Africa; a huge majority of whom are completely ignorant of the existence of such an entitlement to them. Regular publications and more frequent conferencing would help to advance the right to development generally and more specifically, provide the opportunity to explore the transformative potential of the right to development governanceto determine how it could accelerate and sustain prospects for development on the African continent.

Bibliography

Books

Abouharb, M. Rodwan & Cingranelli, David, 2007. *Human Rights and Structural Adjustment*. New York: Cambridge University Press.

Aguda, T. Akinola, 1989. *Human Rights and the Right to Development in Africa*. Lagos: Nigerian Institute of International Affairs.

Ake, Claude, 1996. *Democracy and Development in Africa*. Washington DC: The Brookings Institute.

Allen, Tim & Thomas, Alan (eds.), 2000. *Poverty and Development in the 21st Century*. Oxford: Oxford University Press.

Alston, Philip & Robinson, Mary, 2005. *Human Rights and Development: Towards Mutual Reinforcement*. New York: Oxford University Press.

Amïn, Samir, 1977. *Imperialism and Unequal Development*. New York/London: Monthly Review Press.

Amir, Shimeon, 1974. *Israel's Development Cooperation with Africa, Asia, and Latin America*. New York: Praeger Publishers.

Andreassen, Bård A. & Marks, Stephen (eds.), 2006. *Development as a Human Right: Legal, Political and Economic Dimensions*. Cambridge: Harvard School of Public Health.

Anghie, Anthony, 2005. *Imperialism, Sovereignty and the Making of International Law*. Cambridge: Cambridge University Press.

Arts, C.J.M.; Tamo, Atabongwung & De Feyter, K. (eds.), 2016. *UN-Declaration on the Right to Development, 1986–2016: Ways to Promote Further Progress in Practice*. The Haque: T.M.C. Asser Press.

Austen, Ralph, 2003. *African Economic History*. Oxford: James Currey.

Bartenev, Vladimir & Glazunova, Elena, 2013. *International Development Cooperation: Set of Lectures* Moscow: The World Bank.

Bass, Bernard M., 1985. *Leadership and Performance beyond Expectations*. New York: Free Press.

Bedjaoui, Mohammed (ed.), 1991. *International Law: Achievements and Prospects*. Dordrecht: Martinus Nijhoff and UNESCO.

Beegle, Khatleen, et al., 2016. *Poverty in a Rising Africa*. Washington DC: International Bank for Reconstruction and Development/The World Bank.

Bello, Emmanuel & Ajibola, Bola (eds.), 1992. *Essays in Honour of Judge Taslim Olawale Elias*. Dordrecht: Nijhoff Publishers.

Benedek, Wolfgang, et al., 2010. *The Role of Regional Human Rights Mechanisms*. Brussels: European Parliament.

Berg, Robert & Gordon, David F. (eds.), 1989. *Cooperation for International Development: The United States and the Third World in the 1990s.* Boulder: Lynne Rienner Publishers.

Bloomsbury Collections, 2014. *Connected Sociologies.* London: Bloomsbury Academic.

Bond, Patrick, 2005. *Fanon's Warning: A Civil Society Reader on the New Partnership for Africa's Development.* Asmara: Africa World Press.

Bosl, Anton & Diescho, Joseph (eds.), 2009. *Human Rights in Africa: Legal Perspectives in Their Protection and Promotion.* Windhoek: Macmillan Education Namibia.

Bourdieu, Pierre, 1998. *Practical Reason: On the Theory of Action.* Stanford: Stanford University Press.

Boyle, Alan & Chinkin, Christine, 2007. *The Making of International Law.* Oxford: Oxford University Press.

Brems, Eva; Van dee Beken, Christophe & Abay, Yimer S. (eds.), 2015. *Human Rights and Development: Legal Perspectives from and for Ethiopia.* Leiden: Brill/Nijhoff.

Burns, James M., 1978. *Leadership.* New York: Harper and Row.

Centre for Human Rights, 2016. *A Guide to the African Human Rights System: Celebrating 30 Years since the entry into force of the African Charter on Human and Peoples' Rights 1986–2016.* Pretoria: University of Pretoria Law Press.

Chazan, Naomi, et al., 1999. *Politics and Society in Contemporary Africa, 3rd Edition.* Colorado: Lynne, Rienner Publishers.

Chiambu, Sarah & Musenwa, Muchaparara (eds.), 2012. *Crisis – What Crisis?: The Multiple Dimensions of the Zimbabwean Crisis.* Cape Town: Human Science Research Council.

Chowdbury, Roy; Denters, Erik M.G. & De Waart, Paul (eds.), 1992. *The Right to Development in International Law.* Dordrecht/Boston/London: Martinus Nijhoff Publishers.

Cissé, Hassane, et al. (eds.), 2014. *The World Bank Legal Review Volume 5: Fostering Development through Opportunity, Inclusion and Equity.* Washington, DC: The World Bank.

Clapman, Andrew, 2006. *The Human Rights Obligations of Non-State Actors.* New York: Oxford University Press.

Coetzee, Jan K.; Graaff, Johann & Hendricks, Fred (eds.), 2001. *Development: Theory, Policy and Practice.* South Africa: Oxford University Press.

Cohen, Ronald; Hyden, Goran & Nagan, Winston (eds.), 1993. *Human Rights and Governance in Africa.* Gainesville: University Press of Florida.

Coleman, Andrew K., 2013. *Resolving Claims to Self-Determination: Is there a Role for the International Court of Justice?* New York: Routledge.

Cooper, J. Fenimore & Nirenberg, John, 2012. *Leadership Effectiveness* (Encyclopaedia of Leadership Edition 5). Thousand Oaks, CA: Sage Publication.

Crawford, James (ed.), 1988. *The Rights of Peoples.* Oxford: Oxford University Press.

BIBLIOGRAPHY

Currie-Alder, Bruce, et al. (eds.), 2014. *International Development: Ideas, Experience and Prospects.* Oxford/New York: Oxford University Press.

Curtin, Philip, 1973. *The Image of Africa: British Ideas and Action 1780–1850.* Madison: University of Wisconsin Press.

Dann, Philipp, 2013. *The Law of Development Cooperation: A Comparative Analysis of the World Bank, the EU and Germany.* New York: Cambridge University Press.

De Waart, Paul; Paul, Peters & Denters, Erik (eds.), 1988. *International Law and Development.* Dordrecht: Martinus Nijhoff Publishers.

Deeb, Marius K. & Deeb, Mary-Jane, 1982. *Libya since the Revolution: Aspects of Social and Political Development.* New York: Praeger Publishers.

Degnbol-Martinussen, John & Engberg-Pedersen, Poul, 2005. *Aid: Understanding International Development Cooperation.* New York: Zed Books.

Dias, Clarence J. & Gillies, David, 1993. *Human Rights, Democracy, and Development.* Montreal: The International Centre for Human Rights and Democratic Development.

Dowden, Richard, 2009. *Africa: Altered States, Ordinary Miracles.* London: Portobello Books Ltd.

Eide, Asbjørn; Krausus, Catarina & Rosas, Allan (eds.), 2001. *Economic Social and Cultural Rights* Dordrecht: Martinus Nijhoff Publishers.

El Fathaly, Omar I. & Palmer, Monte, 1980. *Political Development and Social Change in Libya.* Toronto: DC Heath and Company.

Evans, Gareth & Sahnoun, Mohamed, et al., 2001. *The Responsibility to Protect.* Ottawa: International Development Research Centre.

Evans, Malcom & Murray, Rachel (eds.), 2008. *The African Charter on Human and Peoples' Rights: The System in Practice 1986–2006.* Cambridge: Cambridge University Press.

Ewanfoh, Obehi P., 2014. *Underdevelopment in Africa: My Hands are Clean.* Morrisville, NC: Lulu Press.

Falola, Toyin (ed.), 2000. *Africa Volume 1: African History Before 1885.* Durham: Carolina Academic Press.

Fanon, Frantz (tr: Markmann, C.L.), 1986. *Black Skin, White Masks.* London: Pluto Press.

Forsythe, David P. (ed.), 2009. *Encyclopaedia of Human Rights, Vol 2.* USA: Oxford University Press.

Gauri, Varun & Brinks, Daniel (eds.), 2008. *Courting Social Justice: Judicial Enforcement of Social and Economic Rights in the Developing World.* New York: Cambridge University Press.

Giddens, Anthony, 1984. *The Constitution of Society: Outline of the Theory of Structuration.* Cambridge: Polity Press.

Ginio, Ruth, 2006. *French Colonialism Unmasked: The Vichy Years in French West Africa.* Lincoln/London: University of Nebraska Press.

Gonidec, Pierre F., 1981. *African Politics.* The Hague/Boston/London: Martinus Nijhoff.

Gros, Jean-Germain (ed.), 2003. *Cameroon: Politics and Society in Critical Perspective.* Lanham: University Press of America.

Gyimah-Boadi, Emmanuel (ed.), 2004. *Democratic Reform in Africa: The Quality of Progress.* London: Lynne Rienner Publishers.

Haas, Peter M. & Hird, John A. (eds.), 2009. *Controversies in Globalisation: Contending Approaches to International Relations.* New Delhi: SAGE Publishing.

Harvey, David, 2007. *A Brief History of Neoliberalism.* Oxford: Oxford University Press.

Hatchard, John; Perry-Kessaris, Amanda & Slinn, Peter (eds.), 2003. *Law and Development – Facing Complexities in the 21st Century: Essays in Honour of Peter Slinn.* Oregon: Cavendish Publishing Limited.

Henrard, Kristin (ed.), 2013. *The Interrelation between the Right to Identity of Minorities and their Socio-Economic Participation.* Leiden/Boston: Martinus Nijhoff Publishers.

Herderschee, Johannes; Kaiser, Kai-Alexander & Samba, Mukoko, 2012. *Resilience of an African Giant Boosting Growth and Development in the Democratic Republic of Congo.* Washington DC: The World Bank.

Hertel, Shareen & Minkler, Lanse (eds.), 2007. *Economic Rights: Conceptual, Measurement and Policy Issue.* New York: Cambridge University Press.

Heyns, Christof & Brand, Danie (eds.), 2005. *Socio-Economic Rights in South Africa.* Pretoria, Pretoria University Press.

Heyns, Christof & Killander, Magnus (eds.), 2016. *Compendium of Key Human Rights Documents of the African Union, 6th Edition.* Pretoria: Pretoria University Law Press.

Hunt, Paul; Nowak, Manfred & Osmani, Siddiq, 2004. *Human Rights and Poverty Reduction: A Conceptual Framework.* New York/Geneva: United Nations Publication.

Ingram, Joseph K. & Freestone, David (eds.), 2006. *Human Rights and Development.* Washington DC: World Bank Institute.

International Commission of Jurists (eds.), 1981. *Development, Human Rights and the Rule of Law.* Oxford: Pergamon.

Kiely, Ray & Marflect, Phil (eds.), 1998. *Globalisation and the Third World.* London/New York: Routledge.

Killander, Magnus (ed.), 2010. *International Law and Domestic Human Rights Litigation in Africa.* Pretoria: Pretoria University Law Press.

Kirchmeier, Felix; Lüke, Monika & Kalla, Britt, 2008. *Towards the Implementation of the Right to Development: Field-testing and Fine-tuning the UN Criteria on the Right to Development in the Kenyan-German Partnership.* Geneva: Friedrich-Ebert-Stiftung.

Konings, Piet & Nyamnjoh, Francis B., 2003. *Negotiating an Anglophone Identity: A Study of the Politics of Recognition and Representation in Cameroon.* Leiden/Boston: Koninklijke Brill NV.

Langendorf, Julia, et al. (eds.), 2012. *Triangular Cooperation: A Guideline for Working in Practice.* Baden-Baden: Nomos Verlag.

BIBLIOGRAPHY   317

Langford, Malcolm (ed.), 2009. *Social Rights Jurisprudence: Emerging Trend in International and Comparative Law.* Cambridge: Cambridge University Press.

Lawyers' Committee for Human Rights, 1995. *The World Bank: Governance and Human Rights, 2nd Edition.* New York: Lawyers' Committee for Human Rights.

Le Vine, Victor T., 2004. *Politics in Francophone Africa.* Boulder: Lynne Rienner.

Le Vine, Victor T., 1964. *The Cameroons: From Mandate to Independence.* Berkeley/Los Angeles: University of California Press.

Lee, Christopher J. (ed.), 2010. *Making a World after Empire: The Bandung Movement and its Political Afterlives.* Athens: Ohio University Press.

Leftwich, Adrian, 2000. *States of Development: On the Primacy of Politics in Development.* Cambridge: Polity Press.

Lloyd, Christopher; Metzer, Jacob & Sutch, Richard (eds.), 2013. *Settler Economies in World History.* Leiden: Brill.

Maathai, Wangari, 2002. *The Challenge for Africa: A New Vision.* London: William Heinemann.

Mangu, André M; Mienie, Riana & Shaik-Peremanov, Nazreen, 2009. *International Human Rights Law: Study Guide 1 for LCP409R.* Pretoria: University of South Africa.

Marks, Stephen & Andreassen, Bård A., 2006. *Development as Human Right: Legal, Political and Economic Dimensions.* Boston: Harvard School of Public Health – François-Xavier Bagnoud Centre for Health and Human Rights.

Marks, Stephen P. (ed.), 2008. *Implementing the Right to Development: The Role of International Law.* Geneva: Friedrich-Ebert-Stiftung.

Martin, Phyllis & O'Meara, Patrick O. (eds.), *Africa.* Bloomington: Indiana University Press.

Masiiwa, Medicine (ed.), 2004. *Post-Independence Land Reform in Zimbabwe: Controversies and Impact on the Economy.* Harare: Friedrich-Ebert-Stiftung and University of Zimbabwe Institute of Development Studies.

Matondi, Prosper B., 2012. *Zimbabwe's Fast Track Land Reform.* New York: Zed Books.

Mazrui, Ali A., 1986. *The Africans: A Triple Heritage.* London: BBC Publications.

Mbaku, John M. & Takougang, Joseph (eds.), 2004. *The Leadership Challenge in Africa: Cameroon under Paul Biya.* Asmara: Africa World Press Inc.

McDougal, Myres; Lasswell, Harold & Chen, Lung-Chu, 1980. *Human Rights and World Public Order: The Basic Policies of an International Law of Human Dignity.* New Haven/London: Yale University Press.

McNamara, Francis T., 1989. *France in Black Africa.* Washington DC: National Defense University Press.

Melber, Henning (ed.), 2012. *No Future without Justice: Report of the Civil Society Reflection Group on Global Development Perspectives.* Berlin: Friedrich-Ebert-Stiftung.

Mignolo, Walter, 2011. *The Darker Side of Western Modernity: Global Futures Decolonial Options.* Durham: Duke University Press.

Mlambo, Alois S., 2014. *A History of Zimbabwe.* New York: Cambridge University Press.

Monti-Belkaoui, Janice & Riahi-Belkaoui, Ahmed, 1996. *Qaddafi: The Man and His Policies.* Aldersrot: Avebury Ashgate Publishing Ltd.

Morris, Julian (ed.), 2002. *Sustainable Development: Promoting Progress or Perpetuating Poverty?* London: Profile Books.

Moyo, Sam; Helliker, Kirk & Murisa, Tendai (eds.), 2008. *Contested Terrain: Land Reform and Civil Society in Contemporary Zimbabwe.* Pietermaritzburg, South Africa: S & S Publishers.

Murray, Rachel, 2004. *Human Rights in Africa: From the OAU to the African Union.* Cambridge: Cambridge University Press.

Nelson, Jack L. & Green, Vera M. (eds.), 1980. *International Human Rights: Contemporary Issues.* New York: Human Rights Publishing Group.

Nfi, Joseph L., 2014. *The Reunification Debate in British Southern Cameroons: The Role of French Cameroon Immigrants.* Bamenda: Langaa Publishing.

Ngang, Carol C. & Kamga, Serges D. (eds.), 2020. *Insights into Policies and Practices on the Right to Development.* London/New York: Rowman & Littlefield International.

Ngang, Carol C.; Kamga, Serges D. & Gumede, Vusi (eds.), 2018. *Perspectives on the Right to Development.* Pretoria: Pretoria University Law Press.

Nkrumah, Kwame, 1963. *Africa Must Unite.* New York: Frederick A Praeger Publisher.

Nussbaum, Martha C., 2011. *Creating Capabilities: The Human Development Approach.* Cambridge/Massachusetts/London: Harvard University Press.

Olowu, Dejo, 2009. *An Integrative Rights-Based Approach to Human Development in Africa.* Pretoria: Pretoria University Law Press.

Organisation for Economic Cooperation and Development (OECD), 2014. *OECD Development Cooperation Peer Reviews: France 2013.* France: Organisation for Economic Cooperation and Development Publishing.

Ouguergouz, Fatsah, 2003. *The African Charter on Human and Peoples' Rights: A Comprehensive Agenda for Human Dignity and Sustainable Democracy in Africa.* Dordretch: Martinus Nijhoff Publishers.

Oxfam International, 2002. *Rigged Rules and Double Standards: Trade, Globalisation and the Fight against Poverty.* New York: Oxfam International.

Parker, John & Reid, Richard (eds.), 2013. *The Oxford Handbook of Modern African History.* Oxford: Oxford University Press.

Pogge, Thomas (ed.), 2008. *Freedom from Poverty as a Human Right: Who Owes What to the Very Poor?* Oxford: Oxford University Press.

Pogge, Thomas, 2002. *World Poverty and Human Rights: Cosmopolitan Responsibilities and Reforms.* Cambridge: Polity Press.

Poku, Nana & Mdee, Anna, 2011. *Politics in Africa: A New Introduction.* New York: Zed Books.

BIBLIOGRAPHY

Prada, Maritza F., 2011. *Empowering the Poor through Human Rights Litigation.* Paris: UNESCO.

Rahnema, Majid & Bawtree, Victoria, 1997. *The Post-Development Reader.* New York: Zed Books.

Ramcharan, G. Bertrand, 2010. *The Right to Development in Comparative Law: The Pressing Need for National Implementation.* Cape Town: University of Cape Town.

Robertson, Geoffrey, 2006. *Crimes against Humanity: The Struggle for Global Justice.* London: Penguin Books.

Rodney, Walter, 1973. *How Europe Underdeveloped Africa.* Dar-Es-Salaam: Tanzanian Publishing House.

Roe, Dailys; Nelson, Fred. & Sandbrook, Chris, 2009. *Communities as Resource Management Institutions: Impact, Experiences and New Directions.* London: International Institute for Environment and Development.

Salomon, Margot E., 2008. *Global Responsibility for Human Rights: World Poverty and the Development of International Law.* Oxford: Oxford University Press.

Samkange, Stanlake, 1968. *Origins of Rhodesia.* London: Heinemann, 1968.

Sen, Amartya, 1999. *Development As Freedom.* Oxford: Oxford University Press.

Sengupta, Arjun; Negi, Archna & Basu, Moushumi (eds.), 2005. *Reflections on the Right to Development.* Delhi: SAGE Publication.

Shivji, Issa G., 1989. *The Concept of Human Rights in Africa.* London: African Books Collective.

Shue, Henry, 1980. *Basic Rights.* Princeton: Princeton University Press.

Shue, Henry, 1996. *Basic Rights: Subsistence, Affluence, and U.S. Foreign Policy, 2nd Edition.* Princeton: Princeton University Press.

Sicker, Martin, 1987. *The Making of a Pariah State: The Adventurist Politics of Muammar Qaddafi.* Westport: Praeger.

Sieghart, Paul, 1983. *The International Law of Human Rights.* Oxford: Clarendon Press.

Singh, Katar, 2003. *Rural Development: Principles, Policies and Management.* New Delhi: Sage Publications.

Skinner, Gwynne; McCorquodale, Robert & De Schutter, Olivier, 2013. *The Third Pillar: Access to Judicial Remedies for Human Rights Violations by Transnational Business.* The International Corporate Accountability Roundtable, CORE and the European Coalition for Corporate Justice.

Skogly, Sigrun, 2001. *The Human Rights Obligations of the World Bank and the IMF.* London: Cavendish Publishing.

Snyder, Francis G. & Slinn, Peter (eds.), 1987. *International Law of Development: Comparative Perspectives.* Abingdon: Professional Books.

South African Human Rights Commission, 2006. *Reflections on Democracy and Human Rights: A Decade of the South African Constitution (Act 108 of 1996.)* Cape Town: South African Human Rights Commission.

320 BIBLIOGRAPHY

Ssenyonjo, Manisuli, 2009. *Economic, Social and Cultural Rights in International Law.* London: Hart Publishing.

Steiner, Henry J.; Alston, Philip & Goodman, Ryan, 2000. *International Human Rights in Context: Law, Politics, Morals, 3rd Edition.* New York: Oxford University Press.

Suhfree, Cletus S., 2016. *Africa: Where Did We Go Wrong?* Johannesburg: Muimeledi Mutangwa Publisher.

Svensson-McCarthy, Anna-Lena, 2003. *Human Rights in the Administration of Justice: A Manual on Human Rights for Judges, Prosecutors and Lawyers.* New York/ Geneva: United Nations Publication.

Sylvester, Christine, 1991. *Zimbabwe: A Terrain of Contradictory Development.* Colorado: Westview Press Inc.

Szirmai, Adam, 2005. *The Dynamics of Socio-Economic Development.* Cambridge: Cambridge University Press.

Taylor, Ian & Williams, Paul (eds.), 2004. *Africa in International Politics: External Involvement on the Continent.* London: Routledge.

Terreblanche, Sampie, 2002. *A History of Inequality in South Africa 1652–2002.* Pietermaritzburg: University of Natal Press.

The World Bank, 2000. *Can Africa Claim the 21st Century?* Washington DC: International Bank for Reconstruction and Development/The World Bank.

Thomson, Alex, 2010. *An Introduction to African Politics, 3rd Edition.* New York: Taylor & Francis.

Todaro, Michael P. & Smith, Stephen C., 2006. *Economic Development, 9th Edition.* Addison Wesley: Pearson.

Tomasevski, Katerina, 1989. *Development Aid and Human Rights: A Study for the Danish Centre of Human Rights.* London: Pinter Publishers.

Turner, Mark & Hulme, David, 1997. *Governance, Administration and Development: Making the State Work.* London: Palgrave.

United Nations, 2001. *Compendium of International Arrangements on Transfer of Technology: Selected Instruments.* Geneva: United Nations Publication.

United Nations Conference on Trade and Development, 2014. *Economic Growth in Africa Report 2014: Catalysing Investment for Transformative Growth in Africa.* New York/Geneva: United Nations Publication.

United Nations Development Programme, 2011. *Towards Human Resilience: Sustaining MDG Progress in an Age of Economic Uncertainty.* New York: United Nations Publication.

United Nations Human Rights, 2011. *Guiding Principles on Business and Human Rights: Implementing the United Nations "Protect, Respect and Remedy" Framework.* New York/Geneva: United Nations.

United Nations Human Rights, 2010. *National Human Rights Institutions: History, Principles, Roles and Responsibilities.* New York/Geneva: United Nations Publication.

United Nations Human Rights (eds.), 2013. *Realizing the Right to Development: Essays in Commemoration of 25 Years of the United Nations Declaration on the Right to Development*. Geneva: United Nations Publication.

Uvin, Peter, 2004. *Human Rights and Development*. Bloomfield: Kumarian Press.

Viljoen, Frans, 2012. *International Human Rights Law in Africa*. London: Oxford University Press.

Vincent, Raymond J. (ed.), 2009. *Foreign Policy and Human Rights: Issues and Responses*. Cambridge: Cambridge University Press.

Watson, Irene, 2015. *Aboriginal Peoples, Colonialism and International Law: Raw Law*. New York: Routledge.

Welch Jr, Claude E. & Meltzer, Roland I. (eds.), 1984. *Human Rights and Development in Africa*. New York: SUNY Press.

Wilson, Francis; Kanji, Nazneen & Bruathen, Einar, 2001. *Poverty Reduction: What Role for the State in Today's Globalised Economy?* London: Zed Books.

Wouters, Jan, et al. (eds.), 2012. *China, the European Union and Global Governance*. Cheltenham, UK: Edward Elgar Publishing.

Wright, John, 2010. *A History of Libya*. London: Hurst & Company.

Chapters in Books

Alston, Philip, 1981. "Development and the rule of law: Prevention versus cure as a human rights strategy" in International Commission of Jurists (eds.), *Development, Human Rights and the Rule of Law*. Oxford: Pergamon, 31–108.

Arbour, Louis, 2006. "Using human rights to reduce poverty" in Ingram, Jospeh K. & Freestone, David (eds) *Human Rights and Development*. Washington DC: World Bank Institute, 5–8.

Ayittey, Georges B.N., 2009. "Can foreign aid reduce poverty?: No" in Haas, Peter M. & Hird, John A. (eds.), *Controversies in Globalisation: Contending Approaches to International Relations*. New Delhi: SAGE Publishing, 88–98.

Ayittey, George B.N., 2002. "Why Africa is poor" in Morris, Julian (ed.), *Sustainable Development: Promoting Progress or Perpetuating Poverty?* London: Profile Books, 1–16.

Baricako, Gary, 2008. "Introductory preface: The African Charter and African Commission on Human and Peoples' Rights" in Evans, Malcolm & Murray, Rachel (eds.), *The African Charter on Human and Peoples' Rights: The System in Practice 1986–2006*. Cambridge: Cambridge University Press, 1–19.

Bedjaoui, Mohammed, 1987. "Some unorthodox reflections on the 'right to development'" in Snyder, Francis G. & Slinn, Peter (eds.), *International Law of Development: Comparative Perspectives*. Abingdon: Professional Books, 87–117.

Bedjaoui, Mohammed, 1991. "The right to development" in Bedjaoui, Mohammed (ed.) *International Law: Achievements and Prospects*. Dordrecht: Martinus Nijhoff & UNESCO, 1177–1204.

Beetham, David, 2006. "The right to development and its corresponding obligations" in Andreassen Bård A. & Marks, Stephen (eds.), *Development as a Human Right: Legal, Political and Economic Dimensions*. Cambridge: Harvard School of Public Health, 79–95.

Bello, Emmanuel, 1992. "Article 22 of the African Charter on Human and Peoples' Rights" in Bello, Emmanuel & A jibola, Bola (eds.), *Essays in Honour of Judge Taslim Olawale Elias*. Dordrecht: Nijhoff Publishers, 447–484.

Bhambra, Gurminder K., 2014. "Postcolonial and decolonial reconstructions" in Bloomsbury Collections *Connected Sociologies*. London: Bloomsbury Academic, 117–140.

Biholar, Ramona, 2018. "Imagining Caribbean development: The right to development and reparations nexus" in Ngang, Carol C., Kamga, Serges D. & Gumede, Vusi (eds.), *Perspectives on the Right to Development*. Pretoria: Pretoria University Law Press, 314–345.

Brand, Danie, 2005. "Introduction to socio-economic rights in the South African Constitution" in Heyns, Christophe & Brand, Danie (eds.), *Socio-Economic Rights in South Africa*. Pretoria: Pretoria University Law Press, 1–56.

Bulajic, Milan, 1988. "Principle of international development law: The right to development as an inalienable human right" in De Waart, Paul; Paul, Peters & Denters, Erik (eds.), *International Law and Development*. Dordrecht: Martinus Nijhoff Publishers, 359–370.

Chowdhury, Roy & De Waart, Paul, 1992. "Significance of the right to development in international law: An introductory view" in Chowdbury, Roy et al. (eds.), *The Right to Development in International Law*. Dordrecht: Brill/Nijhoff, 7–23.

Davis, Kevin E. & Prado, Mariana M., 2014. "Law, development and regulation" in Currie-Alder, Bruce *et al.* (eds.), *International Development: Ideas, Experience and Prospects*. Oxford: Oxford University Press, 1–47.

De Feyter, Koen, 2016. "Right to development: A treaty and its discontents" in Arts, C.J.M.; Tamo, Atabongwung & De Feyter, K. (ed.), *UN-Declaration on the Right to Development, 1986–2016: Ways to Promote Further Progress in Practice*. The Haque: T.M.C. Asser Press.

Diamond, Larry, 2004. "Promoting real reform in Africa" in Gyimah-Boadi, Emmanuel (ed.), *Democratic Reform in Africa: The Quality of Progress*. London: Lynne Rienner Publishers, 263–317.

Dicklitch, Susan & Howard-Hassmann, Rhoda, 2007. "Public policy and economic rights in Ghana and Uganda" in Hertel, Shareen & Minkler, Lanse (eds.), *Economic*

Rights: Conceptual, Measurement, and Policy Issues. New York: Cambridge University Press, 325–344.

Donnelly, Jack, 1984. "The right to development: How not to link human rights and development" in Welch Jr, Claude E. & Meltzer, Roland I. (eds.), *Human Rights and Development in Africa.* New York: SUNY Press, 261–283.

Felice, William F., 2009. "Right to development" in Forsythe, David P. (ed.), *Encyclopaedia of Human Rights, Vol 2.* USA: Oxford University Press, 21–31.

Gawanas, Bience, 2009. "The African Union: Concepts and implementation mechanisms relating to human rights" in Bosl, Anton & Diescho, Joseph (eds.), *Human Rights in Africa: Legal Perspectives on their Protection and Promotion.* Windhoek: Macmillan Namibia, 135–162.

Go, Julian, 2010. "Modeling state and sovereignty: Postcolonial constitutions in Asia and Africa" in Lee, Christopher J. (ed.), *Making a World after Empire: The Bandung Movement and its Political Afterlives.* Athens: Ohio University Press, 107–139.

Gros, Jean-Germain, 2003. "Cameroon in synopsis" in Gros, Jean-Germain (ed.), *Cameroon: Politics and Society in Critical Perspective.* Lanham: University Press of America, 1–31.

Gutto, Shadrack, 2006. "The right to development: An implied right in South Africa's constitutional order" in SAHRC *Reflections on Democracy and Human Rights: A Decade of the South African Constitution (Act 108 of 1996)* Cape Town: South African Human Rights Commission, 109–118.

Hamilton, J. Maxwell, 1989. "Development cooperation: Creating a public commitment" in Berg, Robert & Gordon, David, F. (eds.), *Cooperation for International Development: The United States and the Third World in the 1990s.* Boulder: Lynne Rienner Publishers, 211–233.

Hansungule, Michelo, 2009. "African courts and the African Commission on Human and Peoples' Rights" in Bosl, Anton & Diescho, Joseph (eds.), *Human Rights in Africa: Legal Perspectives on their Protection and Promotion.* Windhoek: Macmillan Namibia, 233–271.

Howard, Rhoda, 2009. "Is there an African concept of human rights?" in Vincent, Raymond J. (ed.), *Foreign Policy and Human Rights: Issues and Responses.* Cambridge: Cambridge University Press, 11–32.

Illich, Ivan, 1997. "Development as planned poverty" in Rahnema, Majid & Bawtree, Victoria, *The Post-Development Reader.* London/New York: Zed Books, 94–102.

Ingram, Joseph K. & Freestone, David, 2006. "Human rights and development" in Ingram, Joseph K. & Freestone, David (eds.), *Human Rights and Development.* Washington DC: World Bank Institute, 1–4.

Inikori, Joseph E., 2000. "Africa and the trans-Atlantic slave trade" in Falola, Toyin (ed) *Africa Volume 1: African History Before 1885.* Durham: Carolina Academic Press, 389–412.

Jibril, Ali A., 2015. "The right to development in Ethiopia" in Brems, Eva; Van dee Beken, Christophe & Abay, Yimer, S. (eds.), *Human Rights and Development: Legal Perspectives from and for Ethiopia, Vol III*. Leiden: Brill/Nijhoff, 68–97.

Keller, Edmond J., 1995. "Decolonisation, independence and the failure of politics" in Martin, Phyllis & O'Meara, Patrick O. (eds.), *Africa*. Bloomington: Indiana University Press, 156–171.

Kennedy, David, 2003. "The rule of law as development" in Hatchard, John; Perry-Kessaris, Amanda & Slinn, Peter (eds.), *Law and Development – Facing Complexities in the 21st Century: Essays in Honour of Peter Slinn*. New York: Cavendish Publishing Limited, 17–26.

Kiely, Ray, 1998. "The crisis of development" in Kiely, Ray & Marfleet, Phil (eds.), *Globalisation and the Third World*. London/New York: Routledge, 25–46.

Killander, Magnus & Adjolohoun, Sègnonna, 2010. "International law and domestic human rights litigation in Africa: An introduction" in Killander, Magnus (ed.), *International Law and Domestic Human Rights Litigation in Africa*. Pretoria: Pretoria University Law Press, 3–22.

Langendorf, Julia, 2012. "Triangular cooperation as a complementary strategy for development" in Langendorf, Julia, et al. (eds.), *Triangular Cooperation: A Guideline for Working in Practice*. Baden-Baden: Nomos Verlag, 21–32.

Liebenberg, Sandra, 2009. "Adjudicating social rights under a transformative constitution" in Langford, Malcolm (ed.), *Social Rights Jurisprudence: Emerging Trend in International and Comparative Law*. Cambridge: Cambridge University Press, 75–101.

Linda, Lim Y.C., 1989. "The impact of changes in the world economy on developing countries" in Berg, Robert & Gordon, David F. (eds.), *Cooperation for International Development: The United States and the Third World in the 1990s*. London: Lynne Rienner Publishers, 21–47.

Lützelschwab, Claude, 2013. "Settler colonialism in Africa" in Lloyd, Christopher; Metzer, Jacob and Sutch, Richard (eds.), *Settler Economies in World History*. Leiden: Brill, 141–167.

Madhuku, Lovemore, 2004. "Law, politics and the land reform process in Zimbabwe" in Masiiwa, Medicine (ed.), *Post-Independence Land Reform in Zimbabwe: Controversies and Impact on the Economy*. Harare: Friedrich-Ebert-Stiftung & University of Zimbabwe Institute of Development Studies, 124–147.

Marks, Stephen P., 2008. "A legal perspective on the evolving criteria of the HLTF on the right to development in commentary" in Marks, Stephen P. (ed.), *Implementing the Right to Development: The Role of International Law*. Geneva: Friedrich-Ebert -Stiftung, 72–83.

Marks, Stephen P., 2005. "The human rights framework for development: Seven approaches" in Sengupta, Arjun, Negi, Archna & Basu, Moushumi (eds.), *Reflections on the Right to Development*. Delhi: Sage Publication, 23–60.

Marks, Stephen P., 2006. "Obligations to implement the right to development: Political, legal and philosophical rationales" in Andreassen, Bård A. &Marks, Stephen P. (eds.), *Development as a Human Right: Legal, Political and Economic Dimensions.* London: Harvard University Press, 59–80.

Mojekwu, Chris C., 1980. "International human rights: The African perspective" in Nelson, Joseph L. & Green, Vera M. (eds.), *International human rights: Contemporary Issues.* New York: Human Rights Publishing Group, 85–95.

Moyo, Khulekani, 2018. "Implementing the right to development at the domestic level: A critique of the Zimbabwean Constitution of 2013" in Ngang, Carol C.; Kamga, Serges D. & Gumede, Vusi (eds.), *Perspectives on the Right to Development.* Pretoria: Pretoria University Law Press, 255–272.

Moyo, Sam & Murisa, Tendai, 2008. "Civil society: Public action towards a transformative agenda" in Moyo, Sam; Helliker, Kirk & Murisa, Tendai (eds.), *Contested Terrain: Land Reform and Civil Society in Contemporary Zimbabwe.* Pietermaritzburg: S & S Publishers, 69–107.

Ngang, Carol C., 2020. "The right to development in Africa: Implications of its ineffective implementation to prospects for development on the continent" in Kamga, Serges D. (ed.), *The Right to Development in Africa: Issues, Constraints and Prospects.* Austin, TX: Pan-African Press, 151–172.

Ngang, Carol C. & Kamga, Serges D., 2018. " 'O Cameroon, thou cradle of our fathers. ...: Land of promise' and the right to development" in Ngang, Carol C.; Kamga, Serges D. & Gumede, Vusi (eds.), *Perspectives on the Right to Development.* Pretoria: Pretoria University Law Press, 182–202.

Nwauche, Enyinna S., 2009. "Regional economic communities and human rights in West Africa and the African Arabic countries" in Bosl, Anton & Diescho, Joseph (eds.), *Human Rights in Africa: Legal Perspectives in their Protection and Promotion.* Windhoek: Macmillan Education Namibia, 319–347.

Ojo, Eric, 2020. "Making the right to development a reality in Nigeria: Policies, strategies, targets and challenges" in Ngang, Carol C. & Kamga, Serges D. (eds.), *Insights into Policies and Practices on the Right to Development.* London/New York: Rowman & Littlefield International, 103–129.

Okafor, Obiora C., 2009. " 'Righting' the right to development: A socio-legal analysis of article 22 of the African Charter on Human and Peoples' Rights" in Marks, Stephen P. (ed.), *Implementing the Right to Development: The Role of International Law.* Geneva: Friedrich-Ebert-Stiftung, 52–63.

Okafor, Obiora C., 2013. "A regional perspective: Article 22 of the African Charter on Human and Peoples' Rights" in UN Human Rights (eds.), *Realizing the Right to Development: Essays in Commemoration of 25 Years of the United Nations Declaration on the Right to Development.* Geneva: United Nations Publication, 373–384.

Okoth-Ogendo, Hastings, 1993. "Human and peoples' rights: What point is Africa trying to make?" in Cohen, Ronals; Hyden, Goran & Nagan, Winston (eds.), *Human Rights and Governance in Africa.* Gainesville: University Press of Florida, 74–86.

Osmani, Siddiq R., 2013. "The human rights-based approach to development in the era of globalization" in UN Human Rights (ed.), *Realizing the Right to Development: Essays in Commemoration of 25 Years of the United Nations Declaration on the Right to Development.* Geneva: United Nations Publication, 117–124.

Oyugi, Phoebe, 2018. "The right to development in Africa: Lessons from China" in Ngang, Carol C.; Kamga, Serges D. & Gumede, Vusi (eds.), *Perspectives on the Right to Development.* Pretoria: Pretoria University Law Press, 284–307.

Rich, Roland, 1988. "The right to development: A right of peoples?" in Crawford, James (ed.), *The Rights of Peoples.* Oxford: Oxford University Press, 39–54.

Rosas, Allan, 2001. "The right to development" in Eide, Asbjørn, Krausus, Catarina & Rosas, Allan (eds.), *Economic Social and Cultural Rights.* Dordrecht: Nijhoff Publishers, 119–132.

Sachs, Jeffrey, 2009. "Can foreign aid reduce poverty?: Yes" in Haas, Peter M. & Hird, John A. (eds.), *Controversies in Globalisation: Contending Approaches to International Relations.* New Delhi: Sage Publishing, 72–88.

Salomon, Margot E., 2008. "Legal cosmopolitanism and the normative contribution of the right to development" in Marks, Stephen P. (ed.), *Implementing the Right to Development: The Role of International Law.* Geneva: Friedrich-Ebert-Stiftung, 17–26.

Sengupta, Arjun, 2013. "Conceptualizing the right to development for the Twenty-First Century" in UN Human Rights (eds.), *Realizing the Right to Development: Essays in Commemoration of 25 Years of the United Nations Declaration on the Right to Development.* Geneva: United Nations Publication, 67–87.

Sengupta, Arjun, 2005. "On the theory and practice of the right to development"in Sengupta, Arjun (eds.), *Reflections on the Right to Development.* New Delhi: Sage Publication, 62–98.

Sharkey, Heather J., 2013. "African colonial states" in Parker, John & Reid, Richard (eds.), *The Oxford Handbook of Modern African History.* Oxford: Oxford University Press, 151–170.

Sing'Oei, Kori, 2013. "Engaging the leviathan: National development, corporate globalisation and the Endorois quest to recover their herding grounds" in Henrard, Kristin (ed.), *The Interrelation between the Right to Identity of Minorities and their Socio-Economic Participation.* Dordrecht: Martinus Nijhoff Publishers, 374–401.

Sisay, Yonas T., 2020. "Human rights and development in Ethiopia: Taking the constitutional right to development seriously" in Ngang, Carol C. & Kamga, Serges D. (eds.), *Insights into Policies and Practices on the Right to Development.* London/ New York: Rowman & Littlefield International, 15–48.

Von Schorlemer, Sabine, 2008. "Normative content of a treaty as opposed to a declaration on the right to development: A commentary" in Marks, Stephen P. (ed.), *Implementing the Right to Development: The Role of International Law.* Geneva: Friedrich-Ebert-Stiftung, 33–38.

Wang, Xigen, 2008. "On the right to sustainable development: Foundation in legal philosophy and legislative proposals" in Marks, Stephen P. (ed.), *Implementing the Right to Development: The Role of International Law.* Geneva: Friedrich-Ebert-Stiftung, 39–46.

Wenar, Leif, 2005. "The nature of human rights" in Føllesdal, Andreas & Pogge, Thomas (eds.), *Real World Justice.* Dordrecht: Springer, 285–294.

Wu, Chien-Huei, 2012. "Beyond European conditionality and Chinese non-interference: Articulating the EU-China-Africa trilateral relations" in Wouters, Jan, et al. (eds.), *China, the European Union and Global Governance.* Cheltenham, UK: Edward Elgar Publishing, 106–121.

Journal Articles

Adams, Glen & Estrada-Villalta, Sara, 2017. "Theory from the South: A decolonial approach to the psychology of global inequality", *Current Opinions in Psychology* 18, 37–42.

Afegbua, Salami I. & Adejuwon, Kehinde D., 2012. "The challenges of leadership and governance in Africa, *International Journal of Academic Research in Business and Social Sciences* 2(9), 149–151.

Ahluwalia, Montek S.; Carter, Nicholas G. & Chenery, Hollis B., 1979. "Growth and poverty in developing countries", *Journal of Development Economics* 6(3), 299–341.

Akindele, Sunday T.; Gidado, T.O. & Olaopo, O.R., 2001. "Globalisation, its implications and consequences for Africa", *Journal of Social Sciences* 5(4), 221–230.

Akyeampong, Emmanuel, 2018. "African socialism; or the search for an indigenous model of economic development?", *Economic History of Developing Regions* 33(1), 69–87.

Alemazung, J. Asongazoh, 2010. "Post-colonial colonialism: An analysis of international factors and actors marring African socio-economic and political development", *The Journal of Pan African Studies* 3(10), 62–84.

Alesina, Alberto & Dollar, David, 2000. "Who gives foreign aid to whom and why?" *Journal of Economic Growth* 5(1), 33–63.

Alston, Philip, 1982. "International trade as an instrument of positive human rights policy", *Human Rights Quarterly* 4(2), 155–183.

Alston, Philip, 1988. "Making space for new human rights: The case of the right to development", *Human Rights Yearbook* 1(3), 1–40.

Amao, Olufemi, 2008. "The African regional human rights system and multinational corporations: Strengthening the host state responsibility for control of multinational corporations", *International Journal for Human Rights* 12(5), 761–788.

American Society of International Law, 1935. "Article 27: Violation of treaty obligations", *American Journal of International Law* 29(2), 1077–1096.

Amuwo, Kunle, 1999. "France and the economic integration project in Francophone Africa", *African Journal of Political Science* 4(1), 1–20.

Anghie, Anthony, 2013. "Whose utopia?: Human rights, development and the third world", *Qui Parle: Critical Humanities and Social Sciences* 22(1), 63–80.

Anyefru, Emmanuel, 2010. "Paradoxes of internationalisation of the Anglophone problem in Cameroon", *Journal of Contemporary African Studies* 28(1), 85–101.

Appiagyei-Atua, Kwadwo, 2006. "Bumps on the road: A critique of how Africa got to NEPAD", *African Human Rights Law Journal* 6(2), 524–548.

Armiwulan, Hesti, 2009. "Development and human rights", *China Intercontinental Press*, 30–35.

Arts, Karin & Tamo, Atabongawung, 2016. "The right to development in international law: New momentum thirty years down the line?" *Netherlands International Law Review* 63(3), 221–249.

Asheim, Geir B., 2010. "Intergenerational equity", *Annual Review of Economics* 2(1), 197–222.

Asiedu, Elizabeth, 2006. "Foreign direct investment in Africa: The role of natural resources, market size, government policy, institutions and political instability", *World Economy* 29(1), 63–77.

Awasom, Nicodemus F., 2002. "Negotiating federalism: How ready were Cameroonian leaders before the February 1961 United Nations Plebiscites?", *Canadian Journal of African Studies* 36(3), 425–459.

Awung, W. J. & Atanga, Mufor, 2011. "Economic crisis and multi-party politics in Cameroon", *Cameroon Journal on Democracy and Human Rights* 5(1), 94–127.

Axelrod, Robert & Keohane, Robert O., 1985. "Achieving cooperation under anarchy: Strategies and institutions", *World Politics* 38(1), 226–254.

Aylwin, Jos, 2006. "Land and resources", *Cultural Survival Quarterly* 30(4).

Bailey, Fiona & Dolan, Anne M., 2011. "The meaning of partnership in development: Lessons for development education", *Policy & Practice: A Development Education Review* 13, 30–48.

Ball, Richard, 2001. "Individualism, collectivism and economic development", *The Annals of the American Academy of Political and Social Science* 573(1), 57–84.

Barsh, Russel L., 1991. "The right to development as a human right: Results of the global consultation", *Human Rights Quarterly* 13(3), 322–338.

Baxi, Upendra, 1983. "The new international economic order, basic needs and rights: Note towards development of the right to development", *Indian Journal of International Law* 23, 225–245.

Benedek, Wolfgang, 1993. "The African Charter and Commission on Human and Peoples' Rights: How to make it more effective", *Netherlands Quarterly of Human Rights* 11(1), 25–40.

Berthélemy, Jean-Claude, 2006. "Aid allocation: Comparing donors' behaviours", *Swedish Economic Policy Review* 13, 75–109.

Bhambra, Gurminder K., 2014. "Postcolonial and decolonial dialogues", *Postcolonial Studies* 17(2), 115–121.

Biggeri, Mario & Sanfilippo, Marco, 2009. "Understanding China's move into Africa: An empirical analysis", *Journal of Chinese Economic and Business Studies* 7(1), 31–54.

Blanton, Shannon L. & Blanton, Robert G., 2007. "What attracts foreign investors? An examination of human rights and foreign direct investment", *The Journal of Politics* 69(1), 143–155.

Boaduo, Nana A.P., 2008. "Africa's political, industrial and economic development dilemma in the contemporary era of the African Union", *Journal of Pan African Studies* 2(4), 93–110.

Bodas, João G., (d.n.a.) "The doctrine of non-retroactivity of international treaties", *Revistas,* 341–360.

Borella, François, 1971. "Le système juridique de l'Organisation de l'Unité Africaine", *Annuaire Français de Droit International* 17, 233–253.

Brand, Danie, et al., 2013. "Poverty as injustice", (2013) *Law, Democracy and Development* 17, 273–297.

Bulhan, Hussein A., 2015. "Stages of colonialism in Africa: From occupation of land to occupation of being", *Journal of Social and Political Psychology* 3(1), 239–256.

Bunn, Isabella D., 2000. "The right to development: Implications for international economic law" (2000) *American University International Law Review* 15(6), 1425–1467.

Busse, Mathia; Erdogan, Caren & Mülhen, Henning, 2016. "China's impact on Africa: The role of trade and FDI", *Kyklos – International Review for Social Sciences* 69(2), 228–262.

Canning, David, 2006. "The economics of HIV/AIDS in low income countries: The case for prevention", *Journal of Economic Perspectives* 20(3), 121–142.

Carson, Leslie R., 2009. " 'I am because we are:' Collectivism as a foundational characteristic of African American college student identity and academic achievement", *Social Psychology of Education* 12(3), 327–344.

Cassel, Douglass, 1996. "Corporate initiatives: A second human rights revolution?" *Fordham International Law Journal* 19(5), 1963–1984.

Chabeda-Barthe, Jemaiyo & Haller, Tobias, 2018. "Resilience of traditional livelihood approaches despite forest grabbing: Ogiek to the West of Mau forest, Uasin Gishu county", *Land MDPI Journal* 7(140), 1–22.

Chandra, Harish, 2012. "Right to development and world politics", *Asian Journal of Research in Social Science and Humanities* 2(4), 82–95.

Chanock, Martin, 1991. "A peculiar sharpness: An essay on property in the history of customary law in colonial Africa", *The Journal of African History* 32(1), 65–88.

Cheung, Yin-Wong, et al., 2012. "China's outward direct investment in Africa", *Review of International Economics* 20(2), 201–220.

Chingono, Heather, 2010. "Zimbabwe sanctions: An analysis of the 'lingo' guiding the perceptions of the sanctioners and the sanctionees", *African Journal of Political Science and International Relations* 4(2), 066–074.

Chirwa, Danwood M. 2008. "In search of philosophical justifications and suitable models for the horizontal application of human rights", *African Human Rights Law Journal* 8(2), 294–311.

Chirwa, Danwood M., 2004. "The doctrine of state responsibility as a potential means of making private actors accountable for human rights", *Melbourne Journal of International Law* 5(1), 1–35.

Chirwa, Danwood M., 2002. "Toward revitalizing economic, social and cultural rights in Africa: *Social and Economic Rights Action Centre and the Centre for Economic and Social Rights v. Nigeria*", *Human Rights Brief* 10(1), 14–25.

Chiviru, Theophilous, 2014. "Socio-economic rights in Zimbabwe's new Constitution", *Strategic Review for Southern Africa* 36(1), 111–119.

Clapham, Andrew, 1995. "The privatisation of human rights", *European Human Rights Law Review*, 20–31.

Claridge, Lucy, 2018. "Litigation as a tool for community empowerment: The Case of Kenya's Ogiek", *Eramus Law Review* 11(1), 57–66.

Cobbah, Josiah A.M., 1987. "African values and the human rights debate: An African perspective", *Human Rights Quarterly* 9(3), 309–331.

Cofelice, Andrea, 2018. "African Continental Free Trade Area: Opportunities and challenges", *De Gruyter – The Federalist Debate* xxxi(3),32–35.

Cornwall, Andrea & Nyamu-Musembi, Celestine, 2004. "Putting the 'rights-based approach' to development into perspective", *Third World Quarterly* 25(8), 1415–1437.

Cornwall, Andrea, 2008. "Unpacking "participation": Models, meanings and practices", *Community Development Journal* 43(3), 269–283.

Crocker, David, 2007. "Deliberative participation in local development", *Journal of Human Development* 8(3), 431–455.

Cultural Survival and the Indigenous Peoples' Caucus, 2007. "Our land, our identity, our freedom", *Cultural Survival Voices* 5(2).

D'Amato, Anthony, 1985. "Is international law really law?", *North-Western Law Review* 79,1293–1310.

D'Aspremont, Jean, et al., 2015. "Sharing responsibility between non-state actors and states in international law: Introduction", *Netherlands International Law Review* 62(1), 49–67.

BIBLIOGRAPHY

Dartey-Baah, Kwasi, 2014. "Effective leadership and sustainable development in Africa: Is there 'really' a link?", *Journal of Global Responsibility* 5(2),203–218.

Davis, Dennis M., 2003. "Constitutional burrowing: The influence of legal culture and legal history in the reconstruction of comparative influence – The South African experience", *I.CON* 1(2), 181–195.

De Feyter, Koen, 2013. "Towards a framework convention on the right to development", *Friedrich Ebert Stiftung – Global Policy and Development*, 1–20.

De Renzio, Paolo & Seifert, Jurek, 2014. "South–south cooperation and the future of development assistance: Mapping actors and options", *Third World Quarterly* 35(10), 1860–1875.

De Schutter, Olivier, et al., 2012. "Commentary to the Maastricht Principles on Extraterritorial Obligations of States in the Area of Economic, Social and Cultural Rights", *Human Rights Quarterly* 34,1084–1169.

De Siqueira, Duarte R., 2013. "Brazilian cooperation is not a free lunch: An analysis of the interests contained in the international development cooperation strategy", *Geopolítica(s)* 4(1), 137–157.

De Villiers, Bertus, 1992. "Directive principles of state policy and fundamental rights: The Indian experience", *South African Journal on Human Rights* 8(1), 29–49.

De Zwart, Pim, 2011. "South African living standards in global perspective, 1835–1910", *Economic History of Developing Regions* 26(1), 48–73.

Donnelly, Jack, 1982. "Human rights as natural rights", *Human Rights Quarterly* 4(3), 391–405.

Donnelly, Jack, 1999. "Human rights, democracy and development", *Human Rights Quarterly* 21(3), 608–632.

Donnelly, Jack, 1985. "In search of the unicorn: The jurisprudence and politics on the right to development", *California Western International Law Journal* 15(3), 473–509.

Doz Costa, Fernanda, 2008. "Poverty and human rights from rhetoric to legal obligations: A critical account of conceptual frameworks", *SUR – International Journal on Human Rights* 5(9), 81–106.

Earle, Patrick, 2001. "Human rights approach to development: Issues and challenges", *Trocaire Development Review*, 17–38.

Eckel, Jan, 2010. "Human rights and decolonization: New perspectives and open questions", *International Journal of Human Rights, Humanitarianism and Development* 1(1), 111–135.

Edoun,Emmanuel I. & Motsepe, Dikgang, 2016. "Critical assessment of Highly Indebted Poor Countries (HIPIC) Initiative in Africa and the implication of the New Partnership for Africa's Development (NEPAD) (2001–2016): A theoretical perspective", *Investment Management and Financial Innovations* 13(3), 380–386.

Egwemi, Victor, 2012. "Corruption and corrupt practices in Nigeria: An agenda for taming the monster", *Journal of Sustainable Development in Africa* 14(3), 72–85.

Eide, Asbjørn, 1989. "Realisation of social and economic rights and the minimum threshold approach", *Human Rights Law Journal* 1(2), 35–51.

Elaya, Moosa, 2016. "Lack of foreign aid effectiveness in developing countries between a hammer and an anvil", *Contemporary Arab Affairs* 9(1), 82–99.

EI-Obaid, Ahmed EI-O. & Appiagyei-Atua, Kwadwo, 1996. "Human rights in Africa: A new perspective on linking the past to the present", *McGill Law Journal* 41, 810–854.

Eltis, David, 1993. "Europeans and the rise and fall of African slavery in the Americas: An interpretation", *The American Historical Review* 98(5), 1399–1423.

Emmanuel, Nicholas G., 2013. "With a friend like this [...]: Shielding Cameroon from democratisation", *Journal of Asian and African Studies* 48(2), 145–160.

Eneh, Oonyenekenwa C., 2011. "Failed development vision, political leadership and Nigeria's underdevelopment: A critique", *Asian Journal of Rural Development* 1(1), 63–69.

Esteves, Paulo & Assunção, Manaíra, 2014. "South–south cooperation and the international development battlefield: Between the OECD and the UN", *Third World Quarterly* 35(10), 1775–1790.

Fellmeth, Aaron X., 2002. "Wiwa v. Royal Dutch Petroleum Co.: A new standard for the enforcement of international law in U.S. Courts?", *Yale Human Rights & Development Journal* 5(1), 241–254.

Feuer, Guy, 1973. "La révision des accords de coopération Franco-Africains et Franco-Malgaches", *Annuaire Français de Droit International,* 720–739.

Fikre, B. Mekuria, 2011. "The politics underpinning the non-realisation of the right to development", *Mizan Law Review* 5(2), 246–263.

Fowler, Alan, 2000. "Beyond partnership: Getting real about NGO relationships in the aid system", *Institute of Development Studies Bulletin* 31(3), 1–13.

Frankovits, André, 2002. "Rules to live by: The human rights approach to development", *PRAXIS – The Fletcher Journal of Development Studies* 17, 1–14.

Garavito, César R.; Kweitel, Joana & Waisbich, Laura T., 2012. "Development and human rights: Some ideas on how to restart the debate", *SUR – International Journal on Human Rights* 2(17), 4–13.

Gassama, Ibrahim J., 2008. "Africa and the politics of destruction: A critical re-examination of neocolonialism and its consequences", *Oregon Review of International Law* 10(2), 327–360.

Ghandhi, Sandy, 2011. "Global responsibility for human rights: World poverty and the development of international law by Margot E Salomon", *British Yearbook of International Law* 8(1), 332–334.

Golay, Christophe; Biglino, Irene & Truscan, Ivona, 2012. "The contribution of the UN special procedures to the human rights and development dialogue", *SUR–International Journal on Human Rights* 9(17), 14–37.

BIBLIOGRAPHY

Golub, Aaron; Mahoney, Maren & Harlow, John, 2013. "Sustainability and intergenerational equity: Do past injustices matter?", *Sustainable Science* 8(2),269–277.

Gonye, Jairos & Moyo, Thamsanqa, 2013. "African nationalist transformative leaders: Opportunities, possibilities and pitfalls in African fiction and politics", *Journal of African Studies and Development* 5(6), 125–134.

Gordon, Lewis R., 2004. "Fanon and development: A philosophical look", *Africa Development/Afrique Development* 29(1), 71–94.

Gore, Charles, 2013. "The new development cooperation landscape: Actors, approaches, architecture", *Journal of International Development* 25(6), 769–786.

Grabowski, Richard, 2006. "Political development, agriculture, and ethnic divisions: An African perspective", *African Development Review* 18(2), 163–182.

Gready, Paul, 2008. "Rights-based approaches to development: What is the value added?" *Development in Practice* 18(6), 734–747.

Grosfoguel, Ramón, 2011. "Decolonizing post-colonial studies and paradigms of political-economy: Transmodernity, decolonial thinking, and global coloniality", *Transmodernity: Journal of Peripheral Cultural Production of the Luso-Hispanic World* 1(1), 1–38.

Grosfoguel, Ramón, 2007. "The epistemic decolonial turn: Beyond political-economy paradigms", *Cultural Studies* 21(2–3), 211–223.

Gumede, Vusi, 2015. "Exploring thought leadership, thought liberation and critical consciousness for Africa's development", *Africa Development* 40(4), 91–111.

Gutto, Shadrack, 1984. "Responsibility and accountability of states, transnational corporations and individuals in the field of human rights to social development: A critique", *Third World Legal Studies* 3(12), 175–186.

Hamm, Brigitte I., 2001. "A human rights approach to development" *Human Rights Quarterly* 23(4), 1005–1031.

Haüsermann, Julia, 1999. "A human rights approach to development: Some practical implications for WaterAid's work", *Rights and Humanity*, 1–20.

Heidhues, Franz & Obare, Gideon, 2011. "Lessons from structural adjustment programmes and their effects in Africa", *Quarterly Journal of International Agriculture* 50(1), 55–64.

Heyns, Christof, 2001. "The African human rights system: In need of reforms?", *African Human Rights Law Journal* 1(2), 155–174.

Hoffman, Paul L., 2013. "*Kiobel v Royal Dutch Petroleum Co.*: First impressions", *Columbian Journal of Transnational Law* 52(28), 28–52.

Houanye, Paulin & Sheng, Sibao, 2012. "Foreign direct investment in Africa: securing Chinese investment for lasting development, the case of West Africa", *Review of Business & Finance Studies* 3(2), 103–117.

Ibhawoh, Bonny, 2011. "The right to development: The politics and polemics of power and resistance", *Human Rights Quarterly* 33(1), 76–104.

Inman, Derek, et al., 2018. "The (un)willingness to implement the recommendations of the African Commission on Human and Peoples' Rights: Revisiting the *Endorois* and the *Mamboleo* decisions", *African Human Rights Yearbook* 2(1), 400–426.

Inter Press Service, 2006. "DRC: Minerals flow abroad", *Africa Research Bulletin* 43(3), 16887–16922.

Iqbal, Khurshid, 2007. "The declaration on the right to development and implementation", *Political Perspectives* 1(1), 1–39.

Janus, Heiner; Klingebiel, Stephan & Paulo, Sebastian, 2015. "Beyond aid: A conceptual perspective on the transformation of development cooperation", *Journal of International Development* 27(2), 155–169.

Johnson, Glen M., 1987. "The contributions of Eleanor and Franklin Roosevelt to the development of international protection for human rights", *Human Rights Quarterly* 9(1), 19–48.

Kamga, Serges A.D. & Fombad, Charles M., 2013. "A critical review of the jurisprudence of the African Commission on the right to development", *Journal of African Law* 57(2), 1–19.

Kamga, Serges A.D. & Heleba, Siyabonga, 2012. "Can economic growth translate into access to rights?: Challenges faced by institutions in South Africa in ensuring that growth leads to better living standards", *SUR – International Journal on Human Rights* 9(17), 82–104.

Kamga, Serges A. D., 2011. "The right to development in the African human rights system: The *Endorois* case", *De Jure* 44(2), 381–391.

Kastfelt, Niels, 1976. "African Resistance to Colonialism in Adamawa", *Journal of Religion in Africa* 8(1), 1–12.

Kennedy, Paul, 1989. "The costs and benefits of British imperialism 1846–1914", *Past & Present* 125, 186–192.

King, Jeff, 2014. "Social rights, constitutionalism, and the German social state principle", *Revista Electrónica De Direito Público* 1(3), 19–40.

Kingston, Kato G., 2011. "The impacts of the World Bank and IMF structural adjustment programmes on Africa: The case study of Cote d'Ivoire, Senegal, Uganda and Zimbabwe", *Sasha Journal of Policy and Strategic Studies* 1(2), 110–130.

Kinsey, Bill H., 1983. "Emerging policy issues in Zimbabwe's land resettlement programmes", *Development Policy Review* 1(2), 163–196.

Kirchmeier, Felix, 2006. "The right to development – where do we stand?: State of the debate on the right to development", *Friedrich Ebert Stiftung–Dialogue on Globalisation* 23, 1–28.

Kiwanuka, Richard, 1988. "The meaning of 'people' in the African Charter on Human and Peoples' Rights", *American Journal of International Law* 82(1), 80–101.

Klare, Karl, 1998. "Legal culture and transformative constitutionalism", *South African Journal of Human Rights* 14(1), 146–188.

Kodjo, Edem, 1990. "The African Charter on Human and Peoples' Rights", *Human Rights Law Journal* 11(2), 271–282.

Kolstad, Ivar & Wiig, Arne, 2011. "Better the devil you know? Chinese foreign direct investment in Africa", *Journal of African Business* 12(1), 31–50.

Konings, Piet & Nyamnjoh, Francis B., 2007. "The Anglophone problem in Cameroon", *The Journal of Modern African Studies* 35(2), 207–229.

Kors, Joshua, 2010. "Blood mineral", *Current Science* 9(95), 10–12.

Kuada, John, 2010. "Culture and leadership in Africa: A conceptual model and research agenda", *African Journal of Economic and Management Studies* 1(1), 9–24.

Kwakwa, Edward, 1987. "Emerging international development law and traditional international law: Congruent or cleavage?", *Georgia Journal of International and Comparative Law* 17(3), 431–455.

Kwame, Akonor, 2008. "Foreign aid to Africa: A hollow hope?", *International Law and Politics* 40(4), 1071–1078.

Kwame, Asare L.P., 2016. "The justiciability of the right to development in Ghana: Mirage or possibility?", *Strathmore Law Review* 1(1),76–98.

Lang, Michael K., 2014. "The Presbyterian Church in Cameroon and rural missionary work: The case of the Menchum Valley in Northwest Cameroon", *Rural Theology* 12(2), 119–129.

Langa, Pius, 2006. "Transformative constitutionalism", *Prestige Lecture Stellenbosch University* 1–13.

Larschan, Bradley & Brennan, Bonnie C., 1983. "The common heritage of mankind principle in international law" *Columbia Journal of Transnational Law* 21(2), 305–337.

M'baye, Kéba, 1972. "Le droit au développement comme un droit de l'homme : Leçon inaugural de la troisième session d'enseignement de l'Institut International des Droits de l'Homme", *Revue des Droits de l'Homme* 5, 505–534.

Magnarella, Paul J., 2000. "Achieving human rights in Africa: The challenge for the new millennium", *African Studies Quarterly* 4(2), 17–27.

Mahalu, Costa R., 2009. "Human rights and development: An African perspective", *Leiden Journal of International Law* 1(1), 15–24.

Majekodunmi, Aderonke & Adejuwon, Kehinde D., 2012. "Globalization and African political economy: The Nigerian experience", *International Journal of Academic Research in Business and Social Sciences* 2(8), 189–206.

Makaye, Peter & Dube, Brian, 2014. "Zimbabwe: The challenge of democracy from below, 1980 to 2013", *International Journal of Political Science & Development* 2(10), 227–236.

Makinde, Taiwo, 2005. "Problems of policy implementation in developing nations: The Nigerian experience", *Journal of Social Science* 11(1), 63–69.

Maldonado-Torres, Nelson, 2007. "On the coloniality of being: Contributions to the development of a concept", *Cultural Studies* 21(2–3), 240–270.

Maldonado-Torres, Nelson, 2011. "Thinking through the decolonial turn: Postcontinental interventions in theory, philosophy, and critique – An introduction", *Transmodernity: Journal of Peripheral Cultural Production of the Luso-Hispanic World* 1(2), 1–15.

Maluwa, Tiyanjana, 2012. "Ratification of African Union treaties by member states: Law, policy and practice", *Melbourne Journal of International Law* 13, 1–49.

Mamdani, Mahmoud, 2002. "Amnesty or impunity? A preliminary critique of the Report of the Truth and Reconciliation Commission of South Africa (TRC)", *Diacritics* 32(3–4), 32–59.

Manby, Bronwen, 2004. "The African Union, NEPAD and human rights: The missing agenda", *Human Rights Quarterly* 26(4), 983–1027.

Manfred, F.R. Kets de Vries; Sexton, Jennifer and Parker Allen III, B., 2016. "Destructive and transformative leadership in Africa", *Africa Journal of Management* 2(2), 166–187.

Mann, Michael, 2012. "Post-colonial development in Africa" (2012) 3:1/3 *Foreign Policy Journal* 1–3.

Manzo, Kate, 2003. "Africa in the rise of rights-based development", *Geoforum* 34(4), 437–456.

Marfleet, Phil, 1998. "Globalisation and the third world", *International Socialism Journal* 2(81).

Marks, Stephen, 2004. "The human right to development: Between rhetoric and reality", *Harvard Human Rights Journal* 17(1), 137–168.

Marks, Stephen P., 2003. "The human rights framework for development: Seven approaches", *François-Xavier Bagnoud Centre for Health and Human Rights*, 1–29.

Marks, Stephen P., 2011. "The politics of the possible: The way ahead for the right to development", *Friedrich Ebert Stiftung – Dialogue on Globalisation*, 1–14.

Masaka, Dennis, 2012. "Paradoxes in the 'sanctions discourse' in Zimbabwe: A critical reflection" *African Studies Monographs* 13(1), 49–71.

Mati, Sagiru; Civcir, Irfan & Ozdeser, Hüseyin, 2019. "ECOWAS common currency: How prepared are its members?", *Investigación Económica* 78(308), 89–119.

Mattar, Mohammed, 2013. "Article 43 of the Arab Charter on Human Rights: Reconciling national, regional, and international standards", *Harvard Human Rights Journal* 26, 91–147.

Mawdsley, Emma, 2014. "Human rights and south-south development cooperation: Reflections on the "rising powers" as international development actors", *Human Rights Quarterly* 36(3), 634–635.

Mawdsley, Emma; Savage, Laura & Kim, Sung-Mi, 2014. "A 'post-aid world'?: Paradigm shift in foreign aid and development cooperation at the 2011 Busan High Level Forum", *The Geographical Journal* 180(1), 27–38.

Mazur, Robert E, 2004. "Realization or deprivation of the right to development under globalization? Debt, structural adjustment, and poverty reduction programs", *Geo Journal* 60(1), 61–71.

Mbazira, Christopher, 2006. "Enforcing the economic, social and cultural rights in the African Charter on Human and Peoples' Rights: Twenty years of redundancy, progression and significant strides", *African Human Rights Law Journal* 6(2), 333–357.

McAuslan, Patrick, 1996. "Good governance and aid in Africa", *Journal of African Law* 40(2), 168–182.

McInerney-Lankford, Siobhán, 2009. "Human rights and development: A comment on challenges and opportunities from a legal perspective", *Journal of Human Rights Practice* 1(1), 51–82.

Meilan, Laurent, 2003. "Le droit au développement et les Nations Unies: Quelques réflexions", *Droit en Quart Monde* 34,13–31.

Meir, Benjamin M. & Fox, Ashley M., 2008. "Development as health: Employing the collective right to development to achieve the goals of the individual right to health", *Human Rights Quarterly* 30(2), 259–355.

Melo, Alberto, 2008. "Is there a right to development?", *Rizoma Freireano – Instituto Paulo Freire de España* 1(2), 1–7.

Mendy, Peter K., 2003. "Portugal's civilizing mission in colonial Guinea-Bissau: Rhetoric and reality", *The International Journal of African Historical Studies* 36(1),35–58.

Mignolo, Walter, 2011. "Epistemic disobedience and the decolonial option: A manifesto", *Transmodernity,* 44–66.

Mignolo, Walter D., 2007. "Delinking: The rhetoric of modernity, the logic of coloniality and the grammar of decoloniality", *Cultural Studies* 21(2–3), 449–514.

Milani, Carlos R.S. & Muñoz, Echart E., 2013. "Does the South challenge the geopolitics of international development cooperation?", *Geopolítica(s)* 4(1), 35–41.

Minter, William & Schmidt, Elizabeth, 1988. "When sanctions worked: The case of Rhodesia re-examined", *African Affairs* 87(347), 207–237.

Mitchell, Wendy, 2006. "Notes on Thomas Pogge's 'human rights and global justice' and 'recognised and violated by international law: The human rights of the global poor' ", *International Public Policy Review* 2(2), 113–120.

Modiri, Joel, 2014. "The crisis in legal education", *Acta Academica* 46(3), 1–24.

Mohan, Gills & Holland, Jeremy, 2001. "Human rights and development in Africa: Moral intrusion or empowering opportunity?", *Review of African Political Economy* 28(88), 177–196.

Motshabi, B. Khanya, 2018. "Decolonising the university: A law perspective", *Strategic Review for Southern Africa* 40(1), 104–115.

Moyo, Sam & Skalness, Tor, 1990. "Land reform and development strategy in Zimbabwe: State autonomy, class and agrarian lobby", *Afrika Focus* 6(3–4), 201–242.

Msellemu, Sengulo A., 2013. "Common motives of Africa's anti-colonial resistance in 1890–1960", *Social Evolution & History,* 143–155.

Murray, Rachel, 1997. "Decisions by the African Commission on Human and Peoples' Rights on individual communications under the African Charter on Human and Peoples' Rights", *International and Comparative Law Quarterly* 46, 412–434.

Mutua, Makau, 2001. "Savages, victims and saviors: The metaphor of human rights", *Harvard International Law Journal* 42(1), 201–245.

Mwambazambi, Kalemba & Banza, Albert K., 2014. "Developing transformative leadership for sub-Saharan Africa: Essential missiological considerations for church workers", *Verbum et Ecclesia* 5(1), 1–19.

Nagan, Winston P., 2013. "The right to development: Importance of human and social capital as human rights issues", *Cadmus Journal* 1(6), 24–48.

Naldi, Gino & Magliveras, Konstantinos, 1998. "Reinforcing the African system of human rights: The Protocol on the establishment of a regional Court of Human and Peoples' Rights", *Netherlands Quarterly of Human Rights* 16(4), 431–456.

Nasu, Hitoshi, 2011. "The UN Security Council's responsibility and the responsibility to protect", *Max Planck Yearbook of United Nations Law* 15, 377–381.

Nathan, Laurie, 2013. "African solutions to African problems: South Africa's foreign policy", *Welt Trends Zeitschriftfürinternational Politik* 48–51.

Ndahinda, Felix M., 2016. "Peoples' rights, indigenous rights and interpretative ambiguities in decisions of the African Commission on Human and Peoples' Rights", *Human Rights Law Journal* 16(1), 29–57.

Ndlovu, Morgan, 2018. "Coloniality of knowledge and the challenge of creating African futures", *Ufahamu – A Journal of African Studies*, 40(2), 95–112.

Ndlovu-Gatsheni, Sabelo J., 2015. "Decoloniality in Africa: A continuing search for a new world order", *Australasian Review of African Studies* 32(2), 22–50.

Ndlovu-Gatsheni, Sabelo J., 2014. "Global coloniality and the challenges of creating African futures", *Strategic Review for Southern Africa* 36(2), 181–202.

Ndulo, Muna, 2003. "The democratisation process and structural adjustment in Africa", *India Journal of Global Legal Studies* 10(1), 315–368.

Ngang, Carol C., 2021. "Right to development governance in the advent of the African Continental Free Trade Area", *Journal of African Law* 65(2), 153-178.

Ngang, Carol C., 2019a. "Radical transformation and a reading of the right to development in the South African constitutional order", *South African Journal on Human Rights* 35(1), 25–49.

Ngang, Carol C., 2019b. "Systems problem and a pragmatic insight into the right to development governance for Africa", *African Human Rights Law Journal* 19(1), 365–394.

Ngang, Carol C., 2018. "Towards a right-to-development governance in Africa", *Journal of Human Rights* 17(1), 107–122.

Ngang, Carol C., 2017. "Differentiated responsibilities under international law and the right to development paradigm for developing countries", *Human Rights & International Legal Discourse* 11(2), 265–288.

Ngang, Carol C., 2015a. "Indigenous Peoples' right to sustainable development and the green economy agenda", *Africa Insight* 44(4), 31–46.

Ngang, Carol C., 2015b. "Transgression of human rights in humanitarian emergencies: The case of Somali refugees in Kenya and Zimbabwean asylum-seekers in South Africa", *Journal of Humanitarian Assistance*, 1–17.

Ngang, Carol C., 2014. "Judicial enforcement of socio-economic rights in South Africa and the separation of powers objection: The obligation to 'take other measures'", *African Human Rights Law Journal* 14(2),655–680.

Ngang, Carol C. & Kamga, Serges D., 2017. "Poverty eradication through global partnerships and the question of the right to development under international law", *African Insight* 47(3), 39–58.

Nikezic, Srdan; Purić, Sveto & Purić, Jelena, 2012. "Transactional and transformative leadership: Development through changes", *International Journal for Quality Research* 6(3), 285–296.

Niyonkuru, Fabrice, 2016. "Failure of foreign aid in developing countries: A quest for alternatives", *Business & Economics Journal* 7(3), 231–240.

Nmehielle, Vincent O., 2004. "Development of the African human rights system in the last decade", *Human Rights Brief* 11(3), 6–11.

Noyes, John, 2012. "The common heritage of mankind: Past, present and future", *Denver Journal of International Law and Policy* 40(1–3), 449–471.

Nunn, Nathan, 2006. "The long-term effects of Africa's slave trades", *Quarterly Journal of Economics* 123(1), 139–176.

Nunn, Nathan, 2005. "Slavery, institutional development and long-term growth in Africa 1400–2000", *Journal of Economic Literature*, 1–46.

Nwauche, Enyinna S. & Nwobike, Justice C., 2005. "Implementing the right to development", *SUR – International Journal on Human Rights* 2(2), 92–111.

Odinkalu, Chidi A., 2001a. "Analysis of paralysis or paralysis by analysis? Implementing economic, social, and cultural rights under the African Charter on Human and Peoples' Rights", *Human Rights Quarterly* 23(2), 327–369.

Odinkalu, Chidi A., 2001b. "The role of case and complaints procedures in the reform of the African regional human rights system", *African Human Rights Law Journal* 1(2), 225–246.

Odinkalu, Chidi A., 1998. "The individual complaints procedure of the African Commission on Human and Peoples' Rights: A preliminary assessment", *Transnational Law and Contemporary Problems* 8(2), 359–405.

Odumeru, James A. & Ifeanyi, G. Ogbonna, 2013. "Transformative vs transactional leadership theories: Evidence in literature", *International Review of Management and Business Research* 1(2), 355–361.

Oduwole, Olajumoke, 2014. "International law and the right to development: A pragmatic approach for Africa", *International Institute of Social Studies*, 1–31.

Ogbonna, Chidiebere C. 2017. "Targeted or restrictive: Impact of U.S. and EU Sanctions on education and healthcare of Zimbabweans", *African Research Review* 11(3), 31–41.

Ogbu, Osita N., 2008. "Combating corruption in Nigeria: A critical appraisal of the laws, institutions and the political will", *Annual Survey of International & Comparative Law* 14(1), 99–149.

Ogunmola, Dele, 2009. "Redesigning cooperation: The eschatology of Franco-African relations", *Journal of Social Science* 19(3), 233–242.

Okogbule, Nlerem S., 2005. "Access to justice and human rights protection in Nigeria: Problems and prospects", *SUR – International Journal on Human Rights* 2(3), 94–113.

Oloka-Onyango, Joe, 1999. "Heretical reflections on the right to self-determination: Prospects and problems for a democratic global future in the new millennium", *American University International Law Review* 15(1), 151–208.

Olusegun, Olaitan & Aiigbyoye, Oyeniyi, 2015. "Realising the right to development in Nigeria: An examination of legal barriers and challenges", *Journal of Sustainable Development Law and Policy* 6(1), 145–168.

Ondua, Henry A; Ndamsa, Dickson T. & Nkouli, Achille J.P.N., 2018. "Heavily Indebted Poor Countries Initiative (Hipc), economic stability, and economic growth in Africa", *The Journal of Energy and Development* 43(1–2), 99–124.

Ooms, Gorik & Hammonds, Rachel, 2014. "Global constitutionalism, responsibility to protect, and extra-territorial obligations to realise the right to health: Time to overcome the double standard (once again)", *International Journal for Equity in Health* 13(68), 1–6.

Organisation for Economic Cooperation and Development, 2010. "Papers on Official Development Assistance (ODA)", *OECD Journal on Development* 3(4), 9–11.

Osaghae, Eghosa E., 1991. "Colonialism and African political thought", *Ufahamu –A Journal of African Studies* 19(2–3), 20–45.

Ozoemena, Rita & Hansungule, Michelo, 2014. "Development as a right in Africa: Changing attitude for the realisation of women's substantive citizenship", *Law, Democracy and Development* 18(1), 224–239.

Paul, James C. N., 1992. "The human right to development: Its meaning and importance", *Third World Legal Studies* 11(1–2), 11–54.

Perry, Robin, 2011. "Preserving discursive spaces to promote human rights: Poverty reduction strategy, human rights and development discourse", *McGill International Journal of Sustainable Development Law and Policy* 7(1), 62–87.

Pieterse, Marius, 2005. "What do we mean when we talk about transformative constitutionalism?", *South Africa Public Law* 20(1), 155–166.

Piron, Laure-Hélène, 2005. "Rights based approaches and bilateral aid agencies: More than a metaphor?", *Institute of Development Studies Bulletin* 36(1),19–30.

Pogge, Thomas, 2005a. "Real world justice", *The Journal of Ethics* 9(1–2), 29–53.

Pogge, Thomas, 2005b. "World poverty and human rights", *Ethics and International Affairs* 19(1), 1–7.

Pollard, Elizabeth & Lee, Patrice, 2003. "Child well-being: A systematic review of the literature", *Social Indicators Research* 61(1), 9–78.

Quadir, Fahimul, 2013. "Rising donors and the new narrative of 'south–south' cooperation: What prospects for changing the landscape of development assistance programmes?", *Third World Quarterly* 34(2), 321–338.

Quane, Helen, 2012. "A further dimension to the interdependence and indivisibility of human rights?: Recent developments concerning the rights of indigenous peoples", *Harvard Human Rights Journal* 25(49), 49–83.

Radin, Margaret J., 1990. "The pragmatist and the feminist", *Southern California Law Review* 63(6), 1699-1726.

Rajagopal, Balakrishnan, 2013. "Right to development and global governance: Old and new challenges twenty-five years on", *Human Rights Quarterly* 35(4), 893–909.

Ranger, Terence, 1977. "The people in African resistance: A review", *Journal of Southern African Studies* 4(1), 125–146.

Rapatsa, Mashele, 2014. "Transformative constitutionalism in South Africa: 20 years of democracy", *Mediterranean Journal of Social Sciences* 5(27), 887–895.

Reinhold, Steven, 2013. "Good faith in international law", UCL *Journal of Law and Jurisprudence* 2, 40–63.

Rich, Roland Y., 1983. "The right to development as an emerging human right", *Virginia Journal of International Law* 23, 287–328.

Rishmawi, Mona, 2008. "Arab Charter on Human Rights 2004", *Max Planck Encyclopaedia of Public International Law*, 1–19.

Risse, Mathias, 2005. "Do we owe the global poor assistance or rectification?",*Ethics and International Affairs* 19(1), 9–18.

Ronen, Yäel, 2013. "Human rights obligations of territorial non-state actors", *Cornell International Law Journal* 46(1), 21–50.

Rono, Joseph, 2002. "The impact of the structural adjustment programmes on Kenyan society", *Journal on Social Development in Africa* 17(1), 81–98.

Rosa, Solange, 2011. "Transformative constitutionalism in a democratic developmental state", *Stellenbosch Law Review* 22(3), 452–565.

Rousselot, Juliette, 2010. "The impact of French influence on democracy and human rights in Cameroon", *Cameroon Journal on Democracy and Human Rights* 4(1), 59–71.

Roux, Theunis, 2009. "Transformative constitutionalism and the best interpretation of the South African Constitution: Distinction without difference", *Stellenbosch Law Review* 20(2), 258–285.

Rowold, Jens & Schlotz, Wolff, 2009. "Transformative and transactional leadership and followers' chronic stress", *Kravis Leadership Institute, Leadership Review* 9, 35–48.

Rutgers, Mark R., 2008. "The purpose of the state", *Administrative Theory & Praxis* 30(3), 49–354.

Salama, Ibrahim, 2005. "The right to development: Towards a new approach?", *Perceptions* 49–68.

Sanfilippo, Marco, 2010. "Chinese FDI to Africa: What is the nexus with foreign economic cooperation?", *African Development Review* 22(1), 599–614.

Sanni, Abiola, 2011. "Fundamental Rights, Enforcement Procedure, Rules, 2009 as a tool for the enforcement of the African Charter on Human and Peoples' Rights in Nigeria: The need for far-reaching reform", *African Human Rights Law Journal* 11(2), 511–531.

Sarkin, Jeremy, 2004. "The coming of age of claims for reparations for human rights abuses committed in the south", *sur – International Journal on Human Rights* 1(1), 67–125.

Sarkin, Jeremy, 1998. "The effect of constitutional borrowings on the drafting of South Africa's bill of rights and interpretation of human rights provisions", *Journal of Constitutional Law* 11(2), 176–204.

Schrijver, Nico, 2020. "A new Convention on the human right to development: Putting the cart before the horse?", *Netherlands Quarterly of Human Rights* 38(2), 84–93.

Sengupta, Arjun, 2004. "The human right to development", *Oxford Development Studies* 32(2), 179–203.

Sengupta, Arjun, 2002. "On the theory and practice of the right to development", *Human Rights Quarterly* 24(4), 837–889.

Sengupta, Arjun, 2001. "Right to development as a human right", *Economic and Political Weekly* 36(27), 2527–2536.

Sengupta, Arjun, 2000. "Realising the right to development", *Development and Change* 31(3), 553–578.

Shackelford, Scott J., 2007. "The tragedy of the common heritage of mankind", *Stanford Environmental Law Journal* 28(1), 102–157.

Shai, Isaac, 2019. "The right to development, transformative constitutionalism and radical transformation in South Africa: Postcolonial and decolonial reflections", *African Human Rights Law Journal* 19(1), 494–509.

Shepherd, George W., 1990. "The African right to development: World policy and the debt crisis", *Africa Today* 37(4), 5–14.

Sibanda, Sanele, 2011. "Not purpose-made! Transformative constitutionalism, post-independence constitutionalism and the struggle to eradicate poverty", *Stellenbosch Law Review* 22(3), 482–500.

Sinclair, Amanda, 2007. "Leadership for the disillusioned", *The Melbourne Review* 3(1), 65–71.

Singer, Joseph W., 1990. "Property and coercion in federal Indian law: The conflict between critical and complacent pragmatism", *Southern California Law Review* 63(6), 1821–1841.

Sitta, Alessandro, 2006. "The role of the right to development in the human rights framework for development", *e-Journal of Human Development and Capabilities,* 1–25.

BIBLIOGRAPHY

Siyum, Negussie, 2018. "Why Africa remains underdeveloped despite its potential?: Which theory can help Africa to develop?", *Open Access Biostatistics & Bioinformatics* 1(2), 1–5.

Skogly, Sigrun I., 2009. "Global responsibility for human rights", *Oxford Journal of Legal Studies* 29(4), 827–847.

Šlaus, Ivo & Jacobs, Garry, 2013. "In search of a new paradigm for global development", *Cadmus* 1(6),1–7.

Sohn, Louis B., 1982. "The new international law: Protection of the rights of individuals rather than states", *American University Law Review* 32(1), 1–64.

Soko, Mills & Lehmann, Jean-Pierre, 2011. "The state of development in Africa: Concepts, challenges and opportunities", *Journal of International Relations and Development* 14(1), 97–108.

Tadeg, Mesenbet A., 2010. "Reflections on the right to development: Challenges and prospects", *African Human Rights Law Journal* 10(2), 325–344.

Terry, Patrick C.R., 2015. "The Libya intervention: Neither lawful, nor successful", *Comparative and International Law Journal of Southern Africa* 48(2), 162–182.

Tinbergen, Jan, 1978. "Alternative forms of international co-operation: Comparing their efficiency", *International Social Science Journal* 30(2), 223–237.

Udombana, Nsongurua J., 2002. "A harmony or a cacophony?: The music of integration in the African treaty and the New Partnership for Africa's Development", *Indiana International and Comparative Law Review* 13(1), 185–236.

Udombana, Nsongurua J., 2000a. "The third world and the right to development: Agenda for the next millennium", *Human Rights Quarterly* 22(3), 753–787.

Udombana, Nsongurua J., 2000b. "Toward the African Court on Human and Peoples' Rights: Better late than never", *Yale Human Rights and Development Law Journal* 3(45), 45–111.

Umozurike, U. Oji, 1983. "The African Charter on Human and Peoples' Rights", *American Journal of International Law* 77(4), 902–912.

Uvin, Peter, 2002. "On high moral ground: The incorporation of human rights by the development enterprise", *Praxis – The Fletcher Journal of Development Studies* XVII, 1–11.

Van Boven, Theo, 1995. "Human rights and rights of peoples", *European Journal of International Law* 6(1), 461–476.

Van Marle, Karin, 2009. "Transformative constitutionalism as/and critique", *Stellenbosch Law Review* 20(2), 286–301.

Vandenbogaerde, Arne, 2013. "The right to development in international human rights law: A call for its dissolution", *Netherlands Quarterly of Human Rights* 31(2), 187–209.

Villaroman, Noel G., 2011. "Rescuing a troubled concept: An alternative view of the right to development", *Netherlands Quarterly of Human Rights* 29(1), 13–53.

Vitkauskaite-Meurice, Dalia, 2010. "The Arab Charter on Human Rights: The naissance of new regional human rights system or a challenge to the universality of human rights?", *Jurisprudence* 1(119),165–180.

Wanki, Justin N. & Ngang, Carol C., 2019. "Unsettling colonial paradigms: The right to development governance as framework model for African constitutionalism", *African Studies Quarterly* 18(2), 67–86.

Weinstein, Warren, 1983. "Human rights and development in Africa: Dilemmas and options", *Daedalus* 112(4), 171–196.

Welch Jr, Claude E., 1998. "The African Charter and freedom of expression in Africa", *Buffalo Human Rights Law Review* 4(7), 103–122.

Whyte, Jamie, 2007. "Book review: Development as a human right edited by Bard A Andreassen and Stephen P Marks, Harvard University Press, London England, 2006", *The Electronic Journal of Sustainable Development* 1(1), 47–49.

Williams, Carolyn, 2010. "'Am I not a man and a brother?' 'Am I not a woman and a sister?': The trans-Atlantic crusade against the slave trade and slavery", *Caribbean Quarterly* 56(1–2), 107–126.

Woldemichael, Zelalem S., (d.n.a.). "The right to development under the constitution of the federal democratic republic of Ethiopia: Some reflections", *PROLAW Student Journal of Rule of Law for Development* 4(5), 1–17.

Wolf, Anna-Lena, 2016. "Juridification of the right to development in India", *Verfassung und Recht in Übersee VRÜ* 49(2), 175–192.

Wolfrum, Rüdiger, 1983. "The principle of the common heritage of mankind", *Max-Planck – Institutfürausländischesöffentliches Recht und Völkerrecht*, 312–337.

Yeshanew, Sisay A., 2011. "Approaches to the justiciability of economic, social and cultural rights in the jurisprudence of the African Commission on Human and Peoples' Rights: Progress and perspectives", *African Journal of Human Rights* 11(2), 317–340.

Zattler, Jürgen, 1989. "The effects of structural adjustment programmes", *Verlag Weltarchiv* 24(6), 282–289.

Zhenghua, D., 2008. "Rights to development and selection in development mode", *China Human Rights,* 53–56.

Zimmermann, Felix & Smith Kimberley, 2011. "New partnerships in development co-operation", *Organisation for Economic Cooperation and Development Journal – General Papers* 2010(1), 37–45.

Zulficar, Monar, 1995. "From human rights to program reality: Vienna, Cairo and Beijing in perspective", *American University Law Review* 44(4), 1017–1036.

Conference Papers, Working Papers and Policy Papers

ActionAid, 2008. "Human rights-based approaches to poverty eradication and development", *Actionaid.*

African Development Bank Group, 2014. "High Level Event II – Leadership for the Africa we Want", Kigali, Rwanda, Wednesday, 21 May 2014.

BIBLIOGRAPHY

African Trade Policy Centre & Friedrich-Ebert-Stiftung, 2017. "Building a sustainable and inclusive continental free trade area: Nine priority recommendations from a human rights perspective", *Economic Commission for Africa – Policy Brief.*

Alonso, José A. & Glennie, Jonathan, 2015. "What is development cooperation?", *ECOSOC Development Cooperation Forum.*

Anna, Thomas, et al., 2011. "Real aid 3: Ending aid dependency", *ActionAid.*

Anyangwe, Carlson, 2010. "The African Commission's ruling in *Gumne et al. v. Cameroon*: Digest and comment", www.SouthernCameroonsIG.org.

Augenstein, Daniel & Dziedzic, Lukasz, 2011. "State responsibilities to regulate and adjudicate corporate activities under the European Convention on Human Rights", *Submission to the Special Representative of the United Nations Secretary General on the Issue of Human Rights and Transnational Corporations and Other Business Enterprises.*

Ayodele, Thomson; Nolutshungu, Temba A., & Sunwabe, Charles K., 2005. "Perspectives on aid: Foreign assistance will not pull Africa out of poverty", *African Cato Institute Economic Development Bulletin No 2 of 14 September 2005.*

Ayogu, Melvin D. & Gbadebo-Smith, Folarin, 2014. "Governance and illicit financial flows", *Political Economy Research Institute – Working Paper Series* No 366.

Bedjaoui, Mohammed, 1989. "The difficult advance of human rights towards universality in a pluralistic world", *Proceedings of the colloquium organised by the Council of Europe in co-operation with the International Institute of Human Rights Strasbourg,* 17–19 April 1989.

Benneyworth, I.J., 2011. "The ongoing relationship between France and its former African colonies", *E-International Relations* of 11 June 2011.

Besharati, Neissan A., 2013. "South African Development Partnership Agency (SADPA): Strategic aid or development packages for Africa?", *South African Institute of International Affairs – Research Report 12.*

Betteraid, 2010. "Development effectiveness in development cooperation: A rights-based perspective", *Betteraid.*

Bilal, San, 2012. "The Rise of South-South relations: Development partnerships reconsidered", *Conference Paper – European Centre for Development Policy Management.*

Birovljev, Jelena & Ćetković, Biljana, 2013. "The impact of the WTO Agreement on Agriculture on food security in developing countries", *135 EAAE Seminar – Challenges for the Global Agricultural Trade Regime after Doha.*

Brett, Evans A., 2016. "Explaining aid (in)effectiveness The political economy of aid relationships", *Department of International Development, London School of Economics – Working Paper Series No 16–176.*

Brindusa, Marian, 2007. "The dualist and monist theories: International law's comprehension of these theories", *Faculty of Economics, Law and Administrative Science, University of Târgu-Mureş Romania.*

Browning, Rebecca, 2011. "The right to development in Africa: An emerging jurisprudence?", *Kenya Law*.

Campbell, Tom, 2003. "Poverty as a violation of human rights: Inhumanity or injustice?", *Centre for Applied Philosophy and Public Ethics – Working Paper 2003/9*.

Carin, Barry, 2014. "The African Union and the post-2015 development agenda", *Centre For International Governance Innovation – Policy Brief No 45*.

Carpenter, Louisa, 2012. "Conflict minerals in the Congo: Blood minerals and Africa's under-reported first world war", *Suffolk University – Working Paper*.

Chitsike, Francis, 2003. "A critical analysis of the land reform programme in Zimbabwe", *Conference Paper – 2nd FIG Regional Conference Marrakech Morocco 2–5 December 2003*.

Clapp, Jennifer, 2006. "Developing countries and the WTO Agriculture Negotiations", *The Centre for International Governance Innovation – Working Paper No 6*.

Claridge, Lucy, 2011. "Landmark ruling provides major victory to Kenya's indigenous Endorois", *Minority Rights Group International Brief*.

Corrigan, Terence, 2009. "Socio-economic problems facing Africa: Insights from six APRM country review reports", *SAIIA Occasional Paper No 34*.

D'Hollander, David; Marx, Axel & Wouters, Jan, 2013. "Integrating human rights in development policy: Mapping donor strategies and practices", *Leuven Centre for Global Governance Studies – Working Paper No 108*.

Dąbrowska, Anna O., 2010. "Legal status of the right to development", *Haskoli Island University*.

Danailov, Silvia, 1998. "The accountability of non-state actors for human rights violations: The special case of transnational corporations", *Law and Development*.

De Feyter, Koen, 2016. "Right to development: A treaty and its discontents", *©2016 Prof Dr K De Feyter Law and Development Research Group – University of Antwerp*.

De Feyter, Koen, 2013. "The right to development in Africa", *Law and Development University of Antwerp*.

Diez, Cristina, 2014. "Policy brief and proposals: Common but differentiated responsibilities", *International Movement ATD Fourth World*.

Fagerbergm, Jan & Srholec, Martin, 2008. "The role of 'capabilities' in development: Why some countries manage to catch up while others stay poor", *DIME Working Paper 2007/8*.

Faust, Jörg & Ziaja, Sebastian, 2012. "German Aid Allocation and Partner Country Selection: Development-orientation, self-interests and path dependency", *German Development Institute – Discussion Paper 7/2012*.

Fearon, James & Laitin, David, (d.n.a.). "Cameroon", *Stanford University*.

Francioni, Francesco & Bakker, Cristine, 2013. "Responsibility to protect, humanitarian intervention and human rights: Lessons from Libya to Mali", *Transworld – Working Paper 15*.

French Ministry of Foreign Affairs, 2013. "Post-2015 Agenda on development: French position paper prepared with civil society", *Directorate-General of Global Affairs, Development and Partnerships – Working Document.*

Führer, Helmut, 1996. "The story of official development assistance: A history of the Development Assistance Committee and the Development Cooperation Directorate in dates, names and figures", *Organisation for Economic Cooperation and Development.*

Gadio, Kalidou, 2010. "The role of law in development for the African continent from a development agency perspective", *Keynote Speech Harvard African Law and Development Conference,* 17 April 2010.

Gaeta, Anthony & Vasilara, Marina, 1998. "Development and human rights: The role of the World Bank", *The International Bank for Reconstruction and Development/The World Bank.*

Gauri, Varun & Gloppen, Siri, 2012. "Human rights based approaches to development: Concepts, evidence and policy", *The World Bank Development Research Group.*

Ghai, Yash, 1989. "Whose human right to development?", *Commonwealth Secretariat – Human Rights Unit Occasional Papers.*

Girvan, Norman, 2007. "Power imbalances and development knowledge", *North-South Institute.*

Gisselquist, Rachel M., 2012. "Good governance as a concept, and why this matters for development policy", *United Nations University – World Institute for Development Economics Research.*

Grimm, Sven, 2011. "South Africa as a development partner in Africa", *EDC2020 – Policy Brief.*

Gunduz, Canan, 2004. "Human rights and development: The World Bank's need for a consistent approach", *Development Studies Institute London School of Economics and Political Science – Working Paper Series No 04-49 ISSN 1470-2320.*

Haocai, Lou, 2008. "Remarks at the opening ceremony of the Beijing forum on human rights", *China Human Rights.*

Harcourt, Wendy, 2011. "Gender equality and development effectiveness", *Open Forum for CSO Development Effective.*

Heldring, Leander & Robinson, James A. 2012. "Colonialism and economic development in Africa", *National Bureau of Economic Research – Working Paper 18566.*

Human Rights Watch, 2016. "Country summary: Zimbabwe", *Human Rights Watch.*

Hurungo, James, 2010. "An inquiry into how Rhodesia managed to survive under economic sanctions: Lessons for the Zimbabwe government", *Trane and Development Centre – Discussion Paper.*

Hynes, William & Scott, Simon, 2013. "The evolution of Official Development Assistance: Achievements, criticisms and a way forward", *Organisation for Economic Co-operation and Development.*

Ilorah, Richard, 2011. "Africa's endemic dependency on foreign aid: A dilemma for the continent", *International Conference on Information Technology Interfaces* 1-36.

International Monetary Fund, 2014. "Proposed new grouping in WEO country classifications: Low-income developing countries", *International Monetary Fund – Policy Paper*.

Ismi, Asad, 2004. "Impoverishing a Continent: The World Bank and the IMF in Africa", *Canadian Centre for Policy Alternatives*.

Jahan, Selim, 2004. "Human rights-based approach to poverty reduction: Analytical linkages, practical work and UNDP", *UNOHCHR High-Level Seminar on Global Partnership for Development on Right to Development,* 9–10 February 2004.

Janus, Heiner; Klingebiel, Stephan & Mahn, Timo, 2014. "How to shape development cooperation? The global partnership and the development cooperation forum", *German Development Institute – Briefing Paper.*

Jensen, Stephen; Corkery, Allison & Donald, Kate, 2015. "Realising rights through the Sustainable Development Goals: The role of national human rights institutions", *Danish Institute for Human Rights & Centre for Economic and Social Rights – Briefing Paper.*

Kamchedzera, Garton & Banda, Chikosa U., 2002. "The right to development, the quality of rural life and the performance of legislative duties during Malawi's first five years of multiparty politics", *Research Dissemination Seminar Number Law/2001 – 2002/001.*

Kar, Dev & Cartwright-Smith, Devon, 2010. "Illicit financial flows from Africa: Hidden resource for development", *Global Financial Integrity.*

Karpen, Ulrich, 2012. "Effectuating the constitution: Constitutional law in view of economic and social progress", *Law Faculty, University of Hamburg.*

Khadija, Sharife, 2008. "DR Congo: The heavy price of the world's high-tech" *New African,* May 2008.

Killick, Tony, 1991. "The developmental effectiveness of aid to Africa", *International Economics Department of the World Bank – Working Paper Series 646.*

Kimathi, Leah, 2012. "Contesting local marginalisation through international instruments: The Endorois community case to the African Commission on Human and Peoples' Rights", *IDEA Case Study Research.*

Kochanowicz, Kodian, 2009. "Rights-based approaches to development as a new opportunity and challenge to development cooperation", *Conference Paper on Current Challenges to Peace –Building Efforts and Development Assistance Kraków.*

Kuperman, Alan J., 2013. "Lessons from Libya: How not to intervene" *Belfer Center for Science and International Affairs, Harvard Kennedy School – Policy Brief,* September 2013.

Lagoutte, Stépanie; Kristiansen, Annli & Thonbo, Lisbeth A.N., 2006. "Review of literature on national human rights institutions", *The Danish Institute for Human Rights.*

BIBLIOGRAPHY

Levy, Brian & Fukuyama, Francis, 2010. "Development strategies: Integrating governance and growth", *The World Bank – Policy Research Working Paper 5196*.

Littmann, Julia, 2004. "A human rights approach to the New Partnership for Africa's Development (NEPAD) and the African Peer Review Mechanism (APRM)", *International Federation for Human Rights*.

Logan, Fraser, 2015. "Did structural adjustment programmes assist African development?", *E-International Relations,* 13 January 2015.

Maldonado, Nelson, 2010. "The World Bank's evolving concept of good governance and its impact on human rights", *Doctoral Workshop on Development and International Organizations Stockholm, Sweden,* 29–30 May 2010.

Manby, Bronwen, 2000. "Shell in Nigeria: Corporate social responsibility and the Ogoni crisis", *Carnegie Council on Ethics and International Affairs – Case Study No 20*.

Marshall Plan Project Group, BMZ, 2017. "Africa and Europe – A New Partnership for Development, Peace and a Better Future", *Federal Ministry for Economic Cooperation and Development (BMZ)*.

McCaston, Katherine M., 2005. "Unifying framework for poverty eradication and social justice: The evolution of CARE's development approach", *CARE International*.

McKay, Andy & Vizard, Polly, 2005. "Rights and economic growth: Inevitable conflict or "common ground"?", *Overseas Development Institute*.

Melly, Paul & Darracq, Vincent, 2013. "A new way to engage? French policy in Africa from Sarkozy to Hollande", *Chatham House*.

Merh, K. Williams, 2005. "Bringing human rights to bear on strategies to achieve the Millennium Development Goals", *Keynote address Irish Department of Foreign Affairs 7th Annual NGO Forum on Human Rights*.

Metzger, Martina, 2008. "Regional cooperation and integration in Sub-Saharan Africa", *Discussion Paper No 189 – United Nations*.

Ministry of the Economy, Planning and Regional Development, 2009. "Cameroon vision 2035: Working paper", *Republic of Cameroon*.

Morrissey, Oliver, 2002. "Aid effectiveness for growth and development", *Overseas Development Institute Opinions*.

Moyo, Sam, 2004. "The land and agrarian questions in Zimbabwe", *Conference on The Agrarian Constraint and Poverty Reduction Addis Ababa,* 17–18 December 2004.

Muscati, Samer, 2013. "Rights should be central to post-2015 development agenda", *Human Rights Watch*.

Mustafizur, Rahaman M., 2006. "Good governance: A conceptual analysis", *Osaka University Knowledge Archive:* http://hdl.handle.net/11094/6026 381–395.

Ndlovu-Gatsheni, Sabelo J., 2012. "Coloniality of power in development studies and the impact of global imperial designs on Africa", *Inaugural Lecture delivered at the University of South Africa,* 16 October 2012.

Nephew, Richard, 2018. "Libya: Sanctions removal done right – A review of the Libyan sanctions experience, 1980–2006", *Centre on Global Energy Policy*.

Ngwa, A. Kenneth, 2009. "The baobab tree lives on: Paul Biya and the logic of political survival", *African Studies Department Johns Hopkins SAIS*.

Nielsen, Lynge, 2011. "Classifications of countries based on their level of development: How it is done and how it could be done", *International Monetary Fund – Working Paper WP/11/31*.

Odutayo, Aramide, 2015. "Conditional development: Ghana crippled by structural adjustment programmes", *E-International Relations* of 1 May 2015.

Organisation for Economic Cooperation and Development (OECD), 2007. "Principles for good international engagement in fragile states and situations", *Development Assistance Committee's High Level Forum*.

Organisation for Economic Cooperation and Development-Development Assistance Committee (OECD-DAC), 2008. "Is it ODA?", *Organisation for Economic Cooperation and Development-Development Assistance Committee – Factsheet November*.

Özden, Melik, (d.n.a.). "The rights to development", *CETIM Human Rights Program*.

Özden, Melik & Golay, Christophe, 2010. "The right of peoples to self-determination and to permanent sovereignty over their natural resources seen from a human rights perspective", *CETIM*.

Panda, Manoj & Mishra, Srijit, 2005. "Poverty reduction strategy as implementation of the right to development in Maharashtra", *Indira Gandhi Institute of Development Research*.

Paulo, Sebastian, 2014. "International cooperation and development: A conceptual overview", *German Development Institute – Discussion Paper*.

Piefer, Nadine, 2014. "Triangular cooperation: Bridging south-south and north-south cooperation?", *Workshop on South-South Development Cooperation University of Heidelberg*.

Piron, Laure-Hélène, 2002. "The right to development: A review of the current state of the debate for the Department for International Development", *Department for International Development*.

Pogge, Thomas, 2015. "The Sustainable Development Goals: Brilliant propaganda?", *Annals of the University of Bucharest – Political Science Series ISSN 1582-2486*.

Pogge, Thomas W., 2003. "Severe poverty as human rights violation", *UNESCO Poverty Project*.

Prados de la Escosura, Leandro, 2011. "Human development in Africa: A long-run perspective", *University Carlos III – Working Papers in Economic History WP 11-09*.

Radelet, Stephen, 2010. "Emerging Africa: How 17 countries are leading the way" *Centre for Global Development Brief No 2 of September 2010*.

Rathgeber, Theodor, 2011. "Right to development", *Friedrich Ebert Stiftung – Summary of the Working Group/Table 1*.

BIBLIOGRAPHY

Renard, R., 2013. "Theories of development and the emergence of rights based approaches", *Lecture notes on the Right to Development – Centre for Human Rights, University of Pretoria.*

Reuter, Peters, 2017. "Illicit financial flows and governance: The importance of disintegration", *The World Bank – World Development Report Background Paper.*

Rishmawi, Mona, (d.n.a.). "The responsibility to protect and protection of civilians: The human rights story", *Office of the High Commissioner for Human Rights.*

Robinson, James A., 2013. "Why is Africa poor", *Madison Lecture – University of Groningen*, 8 April 2013.

Rutin, Yobo, 2010. "A call to re-evaluate the status of minority and indigenous rights in Kenya: Decision on the Endorois communication before the African Commission on Human and Peoples' Rights (ACHPR)", *Centre for Minority Rights Development.*

Saeed, Faisal, (d.n.a.). "The right to development as a human right: A critique with reference to GA Resolution 41/120", *Academia.edu.*

Sako, Soumana & Ogiogio, Genevesi, 2002. "Africa: Major development challenges and their capacity building dimensions", *The African Capacity Building Foundation – Occasional Paper No 1.*

Salomon, Margot, 2007. "International economic governance and human rights accountability", *Law, Society and Economy Working Paper No 9.*

Sang, Joseph K., 2001. "Case study 3 – Kenya: The Ogiek of Mau forest", *Forest People* 114–118.

Sano, Hans-Otto & Lindholt, Lone, 2000. "Human rights indicators 2000: Country data and methodology", *The Danish Institute of Human Rights.*

Sceats, Sonya, 2009. "Africa's new human rights court: Whistling in the wind?", *Chatham House – Briefing Paper.*

Schoenstein, Anna & Alemany, Cecilia, 2011. "Development cooperation beyond the aid effectiveness paradigm: A women's rights perspective", *Association for Women's Rights in Development – Discussion Paper.*

Sengupta, Arjun, 2003. "Development cooperation and the right to development", *Copyright©2003 Arjun Sengupta.*

Sengupta, Arjun, et al., 2004. "The right to development and human rights in development: A background paper", *The Norwegian Centre for Human Rights – Research Notes 07/2004.*

Siitonen, Lauri, 1990. "Political theories of development cooperation: A study of theories of international cooperation", *UN University World Institute for Development Economic Research – Working Paper 86.*

Skelton, Anne, 2010. "Public interest litigation: The South African experience", *Presentation at Public Interest Litigation Conference in Belfast.*

Skogly, Sigrun I., 2002. "Extra-national obligations towards economic and social rights", *International Council on Human Rights Policy – Background Paper.*

Skogly, Sigrun I., (d.n.a.). "Extraterritoriality: Universal human rights without universal obligations?", *Lancaster University UK*.

Stahl, Anna K., 2012. "Trilateral development cooperation between the European Union, China and Africa: What prospects for South Africa?", *University of Stellenbosch Centre for Chinese Studies – Discussion Paper No 4*.

Stewart, Francis, 2013. "Capabilities and human development: Beyond the individual – the critical role of social institutions and social competencies", *United Nations Development Programme – Occasional Paper 2013/03*.

Sun, Yun, 2014. "Africa in China's foreign policy", *John L. Thornton China Centre and Africa Growth Initiative*.

Sundaram, Jomo K. & Von Arnim, Rudiger, 2008. "Economic liberalisation and constraints to development in Sub-Saharan Africa", *UN Department of Economic and Social Affairs Working Paper No 67*.

Taiwo, Olomide, 2011. "Improving aid effectiveness for Africa's economic growth", *Foresight Africa – The Brookings Institution*.

Tamasang, Christopher F., 2017. "Illicit financial flows and the regulatory framework for mineral exploitation arrangements in Cameroon", *Trust Africa – Illicit Financial Flows Research Series*.

Thomas, J. Corbett, 2009. "Current measures and the challenges of measuring children's wellbeing", *Office for National Statistics – Working paper*.

Tortora, Piera, 2011. "Common ground between south-south and north-south cooperation principles", *Organisation for Economic Cooperation and Development – Issues Brief,* October 2011.

Touati, Sylvain, 2007. "French foreign policy in Africa: Between pré-carré and multilateralism", *Chatham House – An Africa Programme Briefing Note,* February 2007.

Unendoro, Benedict, 2007. "A sense of impunity", 1 *Zimbabwe Crises Report*.

Van der Have, Nienke S., 2013. "The right to development and state responsibility: Can states be held to account?", *Amsterdam Centre for International Law – Research Paper No 23*.

Van Wyk, Jo-Ansie, 2007. "Political leaders in Africa: Presidents, patrons or profiteers?", *Accord Occasional Paper Series*.

Vázquez, Sergio T. & Sumner, Andy, 2012. "Beyond low and middle income countries: What if there were five clusters of developing countries?", *Institute of Development Studies – Working Paper 404*.

Vickers, B., (d.n.a.). "Africa and international trade: Challenges and opportunities", *Thabo Mbeki Leadership Foundation – International Trade and Economic Development Division*.

Wachira, George M., 2008. "African Court on Human and Peoples' Rights: Ten years on and still no justice", *Minority Rights Group International*.

BIBLIOGRAPHY

Wang, Xigen, 2017. "Eradicating poverty and the role of the right to development", *Human Rights Institute of Wuhan University, China – Recommendation for the 18th Session of UN Working Group on the Right to Development.*

Ware, Anthony, 2010. "Human rights and the right to development: Insights into the Myanmar government's response to rights allegations", *Conference Paper 18th Biennial Conference of the Asian Studies Association of Australia.*

Were, Anzetse, 2008. "Debt trap? Chinese loans and Africa's development options", *South Africa Institute of International Affairs – Policy Insights 66.*

Whatley, Warren & Gillezeau, Rob, 2009. "The impact of the slave trade on African economies", *Department of Economics University of Michigan.*

Theses and Dissertations

Akum, Gawum J., 2011."The impact of foreign debt on GDP growth: Cameroon" (Msc Thesis, Ritsumeikan Asia Pacific University).

Anderssen, Maria, 2009. "Motives behind the allocation of aid: A case study regarding Swedish motives for aid allocation" (Master Essay in Political Science, Goteborg Universitet).

Assefa, A.G., 2011. "The impact of the African Charter on Human and Peoples' Rights and the Protocol on the Rights of Women on the South African judiciary" (LLM Dissertation, University of Western Cape).

Gouwenberg, Anna E., 2009. "The legal implementation of the right to development" (LLM Thesis, Leiden University).

Hrituleac, Alexandra, 2011. "The effects of colonialism on African economic development: A comparative analysis between Ethiopia, Senegal and Uganda" (Masters Dissertation, Aarhus University).

Hunter, Sarah E., 2012. "Beyond charity: The rights-based approach in theory and practice" (Honours Dissertation, Boston University).

Kamga, Serges A.D., 2011. "Human rights in Africa: Prospects for the realisation of the right to development under the New Partnership for Africa's Development" (Doctoral Thesis, University of Pretoria).

Khan, Elizabeth, 2013. "Global poverty, structural injustice and obligations to take political action" (PhD Thesis, University of York).

Khensane, Hlongwane, 2010. "Transformative leadership in Africa: Thabo Mbeki and Africa's development agenda" (Masters Dissertation, University of the Witwatersrand).

Mmari, Amanda, 2012. "The challenges surrounding the implementation of the right to development in the African Charter on Human and Peoples' Rights in light of the *Endorois* case" (LLM Dissertation, University of Pretoria).

Ngang, Carol C., 2013. "Socio-economic rights litigation: A potential strategy in the struggle for social justice in South Africa" (Masters Dissertation, University of Pretoria).

Nkonge, Christian G., 2014."The right to development under international law: Reflections from the European Union and Nigeria" (LLM Dissertation, Central European University).

Roger, Isabelle, 2003. "Le droit au développement comme droit de l'homme: Genèse et concept" (Mémoire, Instituts D'Etudes Politiques de Lyon Université Lumière Lyon 2).

Rukare, Donald, 2011. "The role of development assistance in the promotion and protection of human rights in Uganda" (LLD Thesis, University of Pretoria).

Settles, Dwayne J., 1996. "The impact of colonialism on African economic development" (Honours Dissertation, University of Tennessee).

Tadeg, Mesenbet A., 2008. "The right to development as a normative framework for the human rights obligations of international financial institutions" (LLM Dissertation, University of Pretoria).

Van der Have, Nienke, 2011. "The right to development and state responsibility: Towards idealism without a sense of realism?" (LLM Thesis, University of Amsterdam).

Cases

Abacha v Fawehinmi (2000) FWLR (Pt.4).

Abahlali baseMjondolo Movement SA & Another v Premier of the Province of KwaZulu-Natal & Others 2010 (2) BCLR 99(CC).

African Commission on Human and Peoples' Rights (Ogiek Community) v Republic of Kenya (2017) Appl No 006/2017.

Bakweri Land Claims Committee v Cameroon Comm No 260/2002 AHRLR (2004).

Centre for Minority Rights Development (Kenya) & Minority Rights Group International on Behalf of Endorois Welfare Council v Kenya Comm 276/2003 (2009) AHRLR 75 (ACHPR 2009).

Constitutional Rights Project, Civil Liberties Organisation and Media Rights Agenda v Nigeria, Comm 140/94, 141/94 and 145/95.

Democratic Republic of Congo v Burundi, Rwanda and Uganda (2009) AHRLR 9 (ACHPR 2009).

Ex Parte Chairperson of the Constitutional Assembly: In re Certification of the Constitution of the Republic of South Africa 1996(4) SA 744 (CC).

Government of the Republic of South Africa v Grootboom & Others 2000 11 BLCR 1169 (CC).

Kevin Mgwanga Gumne & Others v Cameroon Comm 266/2003 (2009) AHRLR 9 (ACHPR 2009).

BIBLIOGRAPHY

Minister of Health & Others v Treatment Action Campaign & Others (1) 2002 10 BLCR 1033 (CC).

President of the Republic of South Africa v Modderklip Boerdery (Pty) Ltd 2005 (5) SA 3 (CC).

Rev Christopher R Mtikila v Tanzania Applications 9/2011 and 11/2011 (2013).

Schubart Park & Others v City of Tshwane & Another CCT 23/12 [2012] ZACC 26.

Social and Economic Rights Action Centre (SERAC) & Another v Nigeria Comm 155/96 (2001) AHRLR 60 (ACHPR 2001).

Sudan Human Rights Organisation & Another v Sudan (2009) AHRLR 153 (ACHPR 2009).

Domestic Statutes and National Constitutions

African Charter on Human and Peoples' Rights (Ratification and Enforcement) Act No 2 of 1983 – Laws of the Federal Republic of Nigeria on the Enforcement of provisions of the African Charter on Human and Peoples' Rights.

Burkina Faso's Constitution of 1991 with Amendments through 2012 (constituteproject.org).

Cameroon's Constitution of 1972 with amendments through 2008 (constituteproject.org).

Constitution of the Democratic Republic of Benin 1990.

Constitution of the Democratic Republic of Congo 2005.

Constitution of the Federal Democratic Republic of Ethiopia 1994.

Constitution of the Federal Republic of Nigeria (Promulgation) Act 24 of 1999 Cap C23 Vol 3 (LFN 2004 Revised).

Constitution of the Republic of Malawi 1994.

Constitution of the Republic of South Africa of 1996.

Constitution of the Republic of Uganda 1995 as amended in 2005.

Constitution of Zimbabwe Amendment Act No 20 of 2013.

Libya Constitution 1969.

Libya's Constitution of 2011.

Sao Tome and Principe's Constitution of 1975 with Amendments through 1990 (constituteproject.org).

Treaties, Resolutions and Declarations

African Charter for Popular Participation in Development and Transformation, adopted in Arusha, Tanzania, 12 – 16 February 1990.

African Charter on Democracy, Elections and Governance adopted in Addis Ababa, Ethiopia on 30 January 2007.

African Charter on Human and Peoples' Rights, adopted in Nairobi, Kenya on 27 June 1981 OAU Doc CAB/LEG/67/3 Rev.5 (1981).

African Union Convention on Preventing and Combating Corruption, adopted in Maputo, Mozambique on 11 July 2003.

African Union Resolution on the Establishment of a Working group on Extractive Industries, Environmental and Human Rights Violations in Africa, 2009.

African Youth Charter, adopted in Nairobi, Kenya on 2 July 2006.

Agreement Establishing the African Continental Free Trade Area, adopted by the African Union at the 10th Extraordinary Session of the Assembly of Heads of State and Government in Kigali, Rwanda on 21 March 2018 AU Doc TI21086_E.

Arab Charter on Human Rights, adopted in Cairo, Egypt on 15 September 1994.

Association of South East Asian Nations (ASEAN) Human Rights Declaration, adopted in Phnom Penh, Cambodia on 9 November 2012.

Bangul Declaration on the 25th Anniversary of the African Charter on Human and Peoples' Rights, adopted in Banjul, The Gambia on 2 July 2006.

Charter of the United Nations and Status of the International Court of Justice, adopted in San Francisco, United States of America on 26 June 1945.

Commission on Human Rights Resolution 1998/72, adopted on 22 April 1998 appointing Arjun Sengupta, Arjun the UN Independent Expert on the Right to Development.

Constitutive Act of the African Union, adopted in Lomé, Togo on 11 July 2000.

Declaration on Principles of International Law Concerning Friendly Relations and Co-operation among States in accordance with the Charter of the United Nations, adopted by consensus by General Assembly Resolution 2625 (XXV) 24 October 1970.

Declaration on Principles of International Law concerning Friendly Relations and Co-operation among States in accordance with the Charter of the United Nations Resolution 2625 (XXV), adopted by the General Assembly on a Report from the Sixth Committee (A/8082) on 24 October 1970.

Declaration on Social Progress and Development proclaimed by the UN General Assembly, Resolution 2542 (XXIV) of 11 December 1969.

Declaration on the Granting of Independence to Colonial Countries and Peoples, adopted by the UN General Assembly, Resolution 1514 (XV) of 14 December 1960.

Declaration on the Right to Development Resolution A/RES/41/128, adopted by the UN General Assembly on 4 December 1986.

Draft International Development (Official Development Assistance Target) Bill presented to Parliament by the Secretary of State for International Development by Command of Her Majesty, January 2010.

Durban Declaration, adopted at the World Conference against Racism, Racial Discrimination, Xenophobia and Related Intolerance in Durban, South Africa on 31 August to 8 September 2001.

BIBLIOGRAPHY 357

Final Draft African Consensus and Position on Development Effectiveness, adopted by the African Union Commission in Addis Ababa, Ethiopia on 30 September 2011.

Grand Bay Declaration and Plan of Action, adopted by the First OAU Ministerial Conference on Human Rights held in Grand Bay, Mauritius, 12–16 April 1999.

International Conference on Human Rights – Proclamation of Tehran, Bagdad of 13 May 1968.

International Covenant on Civil and Political Rights, adopted by the UN General Assembly, Resolution 2200A (XXI) of 16 December 1966, 993 UNTS 3 UN Doc A/6316 (1966).

International Covenant on Economic, Social and Cultural Rights, adopted by the UN General Assembly, Resolution 2200A (XXI) of 16 December 1966, 999 UNTS 171 UN Doc A/6316 (1966).

Kigali Declaration, adopted by the AU Ministerial Conference on Human Rights in Africa held in Kigali, Rwanda in May 2003.

Kigali Declaration and Plan of Action on the 2030 Agenda for Sustainable Development and the African Agenda 2063 and the role of National Human Rights Institutions, adopted by the Network of African National Human Rights Institutions in Kigali, Rwanda on 9 November 2017.

Maastricht Guidelines on Violations of Economic, Social and Cultural Rights, adopted by the International Commission of Jurists, 26 January 1997.

Maastricht Principles on Extraterritorial Obligations of States in the area of Economic, Social and Cultural Rights, adopted by the International Commission of Jurists, 28 September 2011.

Memorandum of Understanding on the African Peer Review Mechanism, 2003.

New Partnership for Africa's Development (NEPAD) Declaration, adopted as a Programme of the African Union at the Lusaka Summit at Lusaka, Zambia in July 2001.

Optional Protocol to the International Covenant on Economic, Social and Cultural Rights, adopted by the UN General Assembly on 10 December 2008.

Paris Declaration on Aid Effectiveness and the Accra Agenda for Action (2005/2008).

Pretoria Declaration on Economic, Social and Cultural Rights in Africa, adopted by the African Commission at its 36th Session in Pretoria, South Africa, December 2004.

Principles and Guidelines on the Right to a Fair Trial and Legal Assistance in Africa 2003.

Programme of Activities for the Implementation of the International Decade for People of African Descent Resolution A/RES/69/16, adopted by the UN General Assembly on 18 November 2014.

Protocol on Amendments to the Protocol on the Statute of the African Court of Justice and Human Rights, adopted in Malabo, Equatorial Guinea on 27 June 2014.

Protocol on the Statute of the African Court of Justice and Human Rights, adopted at Sharm el-Sheikh, Egypt on 1 July 2008.

Protocol to the African Charter on Human and Peoples' Rights on the Rights of Women in Africa, adopted in Maputo, Mozambique on 11 July 2003.

Protocol to the African Charter on Human and Peoples' Rights on the Establishment of an African Court on Human and Peoples' Rights, adopted in Addis Ababa, Ethiopia on 10 June 1998.

Protocol to the Treaty Establishing the African Economic Community relating to the Pan-African Parliament, adopted in Sirte, Libya on 2 March 2001.

Report of the Meeting of Experts of the First Ministerial Conference on Human Rights in Africa Kigali 5 – 6 May 2003 EXP/CONF/HRA/RPT(II).

Report of the Panel of Experts on the Illegal Exploitation of the Natural Resources and other Forms of Wealth of the Democratic Republic of Congo 12 April 2001 UN Doc S/2001/357.

Report of the Secretary-General on the International Dimensions of the Right to Development as a Human Right UN ESCOR 35th Session paras 152-159 UN Doc E/CN.4/1334 (1979).

Resolution on the African Commission on Human and Peoples' Rights Twenty-Ninth Ordinary Session of the Assembly of Heads of States and Governments of the Organisation of African Unity Cairo, Egypt, 28–30 June 1993.

Rio Declaration on Environment and Development, adopted at the United Nations Conference on Environment and Development at Rio de Janeiro, Brazil, 3–14 June 1992.

The Limburg Principles on the Implementation of the International Covenant on Economic, Social and Cultural Rights UN Document E/CN.4/1987/17.

Transforming Our World: The 2030 Agenda for Sustainable Development Resolution A/RES/70/1, adopted by the United Nations General Assembly on 27 September 2015.

United Nations Commission on Human Rights Resolution 4 (XXXIII) of 21 February 1977.

United Nations Commission on Human Rights Resolution 5 (XXXV) of 2 March 1979.

United Nations Declaration on the Rights of Indigenous Peoples, Resolution 61/295, adopted by the UN General Assembly on 13 September 2007.

United Nations General Assembly "Final review and appraisal of the United Nations New Agenda for the Development of Africa in the 1990s and support for the New Partnership for Africa's Development" Resolution A/RES/57/7 of 4 November 2002.

United Nations General Assembly "Human rights-based approach: Statement of common understanding", adopted at the Inter-Agency Workshop on a human rights-based approach in the context of UN reform, 3–5 May 2003.

United Nations General Assembly Declaration on the New Partnership for Africa's Development Resolution A/RES/57/2 of 18 September 2002.

United Nations General Assembly Resolution A/RES/34/46 of 23 November 1979.

United Nations Millennium Declaration Resolution A/55/L.2, adopted by the United Nations General Assembly on 8 September 2000.

Universal Declaration of Human Rights, adopted by the United Nations General Assembly, Resolution 217 A(III) of 10 December 1948.

BIBLIOGRAPHY   359

Vienna Convention on the Law of Treaties, adopted by the United Nations on 22 May 1969.

Vienna Declaration and Programme of Action, adopted by the United Nations World Conference on Human Rights UN Doc. A/CONF.157/24, 25 June 1993.

World Trade Organisation Agreement on Agriculture.

Reports and Other Important Documents

African Development Bank, 2014. *Africa Development Report 2014: Regional Integration for Inclusive Growth.* African Development Bank.

African Union, 2011. "African youth decade 2009–2018 plan of action: Accelerating youth empowerment for sustainable development". *African Union.*

African Union Commission, 2015. "Agenda 2063: The Africa we want". *African Union.*

British South Africa Company, 1898. "Reports on the native disturbances in Rhodesia 1896–1897". London: British South Africa Company.

Brundtland, Gro Harlem, 1987. "Report of the World Commission on Environment and Development: Our common future". *Brundtland Commission.*

Chair Rapporteur; Zamir Akram (Pakistan) Draft Convention on the Right to Development, 2020. Human Rights Council Working Group on the Right to Development, A/HRC/WK.2/21/2 of May 2020.

Chinese White Paper on the Right to Development, 2016. "The right to development: China's philosophy, practice and contribution" adopted by China's State Council Information Office 1 December 2016.

Commission on Human Rights, 2005. "The right to development and practical strategies for the implementation of the Millennium Development Goals, particularly Goal 8", *Note by the Secretariat E/CN4/2005/WG18/TF/CRP 1* 2 November 2005.

Committee on Economic, Social and Cultural Rights, 2001. "Poverty and the International Covenant on Economic, Social and Cultural Rights", Statement adopted by the Committee on Economic, Social and Cultural Rights on 4 May 2001.

Committee on Economic, Social and Cultural Rights, 2002. "The Millennium Development Goals and economic, social and cultural rights", Joint statement by the Committee on Economic, Social and Cultural Rights and the Special Rapporteurs on economic, social and cultural rights of the Commission on Human Rights 29 November 2002.

Communication from the Commission to the European Parliament, the Council, the European Economic and Social Committee and the Committee of the Regions Brussels, 2015. "A global partnership for poverty eradication and sustainable development after 2015" 5.2.2015 COM (2015) 44 final.

Grover, Anand, 2011. "Report of the Special Rapporteur on the right of everyone to the enjoyment of the highest attainable standard of physical and mental health", *UN A/ HRC/17/25.*

International Monetary Fund, 2010. "Cameroon: Staff report for the 2010 article IV consultation and debt sustainability analysis", *IMF Country Report No 10/259 – International Monetary Fund Washington DC*.

Kunanayakam, Tamara, 2013. "Report of the Working Group on the Right to Development on its fourteenth session", *Human Rights Council A/HRC/24/37*.

New Partnership for Africa's Development (NEPAD) Planning and Coordinating Agency, 2015. "Blueprint for an integrated approach to implement Agenda 2063", *New Partnership for Africa's Development*.

Partnership Agreement between the members of the African, Caribbean and Pacific Group of States and the European Community and its Member States signed in Cotonou on 23 June 2000 (amended in 2005 and 2010).

Report of the Open-Ended Working Group of Governmental Experts on the Right to Development UN ESCOR 45th Session para 25 UN Doc E/CN.4/1989/10 (1989).

Rules of Procedure of the African Commission on Human and Peoples' Rights, 2010.

SAIFAC, 2010. "The state duty to protect, corporate obligations and extra-territorial application in the African regional human rights system", *South African Institute for Advanced Constitutional, Public, Human Rights and International Law*.

The World Bank, 2000. *Can Africa Claim the 21st Century?* Washington DC: The International Bank for Reconstruction and Development/The World Bank.

United Nations Conference on Trade and Investment, 2014. *Economic Development in Africa Report 2014: Catalysing Investment for Transformative Growth in Africa.* New York/Geneva: United Nations Publication.

United Nations Development Programme (UNDP), 2013. "Human Development Report 2013: Cameroon". *United Nations Development Programme*.

United Nations Development Programme (UNDP), 2000. *Human Development Report (2000).* New York: Oxford University Press.

United Nations Development Programme (UNDP), 1990. *Human Development Report 1990.* New York: Oxford University Press.

United Nations Economic Commission for Africa (UNECA), et al., 2013. *MDG Report 2013: Assessing Progress in Africa toward the Millennium Development Goals.* Addis Ababa: United Nations Economic Commission for Africa.

United Nations Educational, Scientific and Cultural Organisation (UNESCO), 2000. *World Education Report 2000: The Right to Education: Towards Education for all throughout Life*. Paris: UNESCO.

United Nations General Assembly, 2014. "The road to dignity by 2030: Ending poverty, transforming all lives and protecting the planet", Synbook Report of the Secretary-General on the Post-2015 Sustainable Development Agenda 4 December 2014.

United Nations High Commissioner for Human Rights (UNHCHR), 2010. "Legal capacity", *Background Conference Document – Office of the United Nations High Commissioner for Human Rights*.

BIBLIOGRAPHY   361

United Nations High Commissioner for Human Rights (UNHCHR), 2010. "The right to development – Framework for achieving the MDGs", *United Nations Office of the High Commissioner for Human Rights Infonote/MDGsR2D/15072010.*

United Nations Human Rights. "The right to development and gender", *Information Note.*

United Nations Office of the High Commission for Human Rights (UNHCHR), 2008. "Claiming the Millennium Development Goals: A human rights approach", *United Nations Office of the High Commissioner for Human Rights.*

United Nations Special Rapporteur on the situation of human rights and fundamental freedoms of indigenous peoples, 2007. Report to the Fourth Session of the UN Human Rights Council, 27 February 2007.

United Nations Task Team, 2013. "A renewed global partnership for development", *UN System Task Team on the Post-2015 UN Development Agenda.*

United Nations Women (UN Women), 2012. "The future women want: A vision of sustainable development for all", *United Nations Women.*

Media and Internet Sources and Other Web Pages

Adebayo, Bukola, "Nigeria overtakes India in extreme poverty ranking" *CNN* (Lagos, 26 June 2018) available at: https://edition.cnn.com/2018/06/26/africa/nigeria-overtakes-india-extreme-poverty-intl/index.html (accessed: 28 April 2019).

African Union, "List of countries which have signed, ratified/acceded to the African Youth Charter" available at: https://au.int/sites/default/files/treaties/7789-sl-AFRICAN%20YOUTH%20CHARTER.pdf (accessed: 29 December 2020).

African Union, "African Youth Charter, A framework defining Africa's youth agenda!" available at: http://africa-youth.org/charter (accessed: 13 October 2016).

African Union, "AU financial institutions" available at: https://au.int/en/ea/epr/aufi (accessed: 20 March 2020).

Al Jazeera, "The French African connection" (2014) *Al Jazeera* available at: http://www.aljazeera.com/programmes/specialseries/2013/08/201387113131914906.html (accessed: 24 August 2017).

Alfa, Shaban, A.R., "Ethiopia parliament passes $13bn budget after World Bank, IMF praise" *Reuters – Africa News* 8 July 2017 https://www.africanews.com/2017/07/08/ethiopia-parliament-passes-13bn-budget-after-world-bank-imf-praise// (accessed: 22 April 2019).

Aljazeera, "Inside story" Aljazeera News of 18 September 2015.

Alonso, José A.; Glennie, Jonathan & Sumner, Andy, "Recipients and contributors: Middle income countries and the future of development cooperation" (2014) available at: http://effectivecooperation.org/wordpress/wp-content/uploads/2014/04/Recipients-and-Contributors-MICs-and-the-future-of-development-cooperat.._.pdf (accessed: 09 April 2016).

American Government, "The colonial experience" available at: http://www.ushistory.org/gov/2a.asp (accessed: 16 August 2017).

Anon, "The Endorois and their struggle for the realisation of the right to development: NGLS interviews Wilson Kipsang Kipkazi of the Endorois Welfare Council and Lucy Claridge of the Minority Rights Group International" available at: http://www.un-ngls.org/spip.php?page=article_s&id_article=3607 (accessed: 17 April 2015).

Bart-Williams, Mallence, "Change your channel" *TEDTalk Berlin* 2015 available at: https://www.youtube.com/watch?v=_pvNp9gHjfk (30 October 2017).

BBC News, "Kenya's Uhuru Kenyatta urges Africa to give up aid" (12 June 2015) available at: http://www.bbc.com/news/world-africa-33108716 (accessed: 14 June 2016).

Beck's Law Dictionary, "A compendium of international law terms and phrases" available at: http://people.virginia.edu/~rjb3v/latin.html (accessed: 20 February 2015).

Boddy-Evans, Alistair, "A short history of the African slave trade" *ThoughCo* 28 December 2018available at: http://www.thoughtco.com (accessed: 20 June 2019).

Bowden, Sue & Mosley, Paul, "Politics, public expenditure and the evolution of poverty in Africa 1920–2009" (2010) available at: https://hummedia.manchester.ac.uk/institutes/gdi/publications/workingpapers/bwpi/bwpi-wp-12510.pdf (accessed: 10 February 2016).

Bradley, Penny, "The colonial pact: How France sucks the life out of Africa" (2013) *Our World Commentary* available at: https://penniwinkleb.wordpress.com/2013/01/25/the-colonial-pact-how-france-sucks-the-life-out-of-africa/ (accessed: 24 August 2017).

Branzick, Amelia, "Humanitarian aid and development assistance" (2004) *Beyond Intractability* available at: http://www.beyondintractability.org/essay/humanitarian-aid (accessed: 18 November 2017).

Chengu, Garikai, "Libya: From Africa's richest state under Gaddafi to failed state after NATOintervention"(2014)*GlobalResearch*availableat:www.globalresearch.ca/libya-from-africas-richest-state-under-gaddafi-to-failed-state-after-nato-intervention/5408740 (accessed: 29 December 2015).

Chossudovsky, Michel, "Destroying a country's standard of living: What Libya had achieved, what has been destroyed" (2013) *Global Research* available at: www.globalresearch.ca/destroying-a-country-s-standard-of-living-what-libya-had-achieved-what-has-been-destroyed/26686 (accessed: 29 December 2015).

Corruption Watch, "Mbeki: Illicit financial flows crippling the continent" (2015) *Corruption Watch* available at: http://www.corruptionwatch.org.za/mbeki-illicit-financial-flows-crippling-the-continent/ (accessed: 12 September 2017).

De Schutter, Olivier, "Millennium Development Goals need more emphasis on human rights" *The Guardian of* 21 September 2010 available at: http://www.guardian.co.uk/global-development/poverty-matters/2010/sep/21/millenniumdevelopment-goals-olivier-de-schutter (accessed: 10 March 2015).

BIBLIOGRAPHY 363

Dewast, Louise, "West Africa's eco: What difference would a single currency make?" *BBC Africa, Dakar* available at: https://www.bbc.com/news/world-africa-48882030 (accessed: 6 July 2019).

Dodson, Howard, "How slavery helped build a world economy" (2003) *National Geographic News* available at: http://news.nationalgeographic.com/news/2003/01/0131_030203_jubilee2.html (accessed: 16 August 2017).

Femi, Omojarabi W., "Adam Smith's view in *Wealth of Nations* and how it has led to the growth and consolidation of capitalism" *Academia.edu* available at: https://www.academia.edu/4057757/adam_smith_and_capitalism (accessed: 21 March 2016).

Financial Express, "China's Xi Jinping offers $60 billion Africa aid, says 'no strings attached'" 3 September 2018 https://www.financialexpress.com/world-news/chinas-xi-jinping-offers-60-billion-africa-aid-says-no-strings-attached/1301355/ (accessed: 24 October 2018).

Global Policy Centre, "Libya" available at: https://archive.globalpolicy.org/security/sanction/libya/indxirlb.htm (accessed: 30 October 2018).

Golubski, Christina M., "Africa in focus: Africa and the world poverty clock" *Brooking Institute* 18 May 2017 available at: https://www.brookings.edu/blog/africa-in-focus/2017/05/18/africa-and-the-world-poverty-clock/ (accessed: 28 April 2019).

Holman, Michael, "Sanctions have been counterproductive in Zimbabwe" *The New York Times* 21 November 2013 available at: http://www.nytimes.com/roomfordebate/2013/11/19/sanctions-successes-and-failures/sanctions-have-been-counterproductive-in-zimbabwe (accessed: 5 September 2016).

International Justice Resource Centre, "Regional systems" available at: http://www.ijrcenter.org/regional/ (accessed: 8 September 2017).

International Organisation for Migration (IOM), "International cooperation" available at: http://www.rcmvs.org/documentos/iom_emm/v1/v1s07_cm.pdf 1–21 (accessed: 16 September 2016).

Irish, John, "France says to continue military cooperation with Cameroon" *Reuters – World News* 7 February 2019 available at: https://uk.reuters.com/article/uk-france-cameroon/france-says-to-continue-military-cooperation-with-cameroon-idUKKCN1PW1RT (accessed: 30 July 2019).

Kavilu, Shadrack, "Indigenous Endorois call for implementation of African Commission ruling on their ancestral land" available at: http://www.galdu.org/web/index.php?odas=5087 (accessed: 12 June 2015).

Koutonin, Mawuna R., "14 African countries forced by France to pay colonial tax for the benefits of slavery and colonisation" (2014) *Silicon Africa* available at: http://www.siliconafrica.com/france-colonial-tax/ (accessed: 30 October 2017).

Krippahl, Cristina, "End of a 'secret' German military mission in Cameroon" *Deutsch Welle* July 2019 available at: https://www.dw.com/en/end-of-a-secret-german-military-mission-in-cameroon/a-49610889 (accessed: 30 July 2019).

Kumar, Mahendra, "Arguments for and against foreign aid" available at: http://www.economicsdiscussion.net/foreign-aid/arguments/arguments-for-and-against-foreign-aid/11838 (accessed: 6 September 2017).

Lehmann, Christof, "French Africa policy damages African and European economies" (2012) *NSNBC* available at: http://nsnbc.me/2012/10/12/french-africa-policy-damages-african-and-european-economies/ (accessed: 24 August 2017).

Libya 360° Archive, "Libya: UN HDI country profile" available at: https://libyadiary.wordpress.com/2011/03/05/libya-un-hdi-country-profile/ (accessed: 28 July 2016).

Lopes, Carlos, "Structural adjustment policies and Africa: A reply to Shantayanan Devarajan" *Think Africa Press* 15 November 2013available at: http://allafrica.com/stories/201311252050.html (accessed: 5 September 2016).

M'bokolo, Elikia, "The impact of the slave trade on Africa" *Le Monde Diplomatique* available at: http://mondediplo.com/1998/04/02africa (accessed: 12 February 2016).

Macklem, Patrick, "Global poverty and the right to development in international law" (2013) available at: http://dx.doi.org/10.2139/ssrn.2271686 (accessed: 10 March 2015) 1–63.

Mbangsi, Chi, "Cameroon/France: Does Cameroon benefit from special relationship?" (2013) *Iroko Africa* available at: http://irokoheritage.com/2013/08/22/cameroon-special-relationship-with-france-a-benefit/ (accessed: 5 September 2017).

Mbembe, Achille, "Decolonizing knowledge and the question of the archive" (2015) available at: http://wiser.wits.ac.za/system/files/Achille%20Mbembe%20%20Decolonizing%20Knowledge%20and%20the%20Question%20of%20the%20Archive.pdf (accessed: 26 April 2018).

Meena, Ruth, "Women and sustainable development" available at: http://www.un-ngls.org/orf/documents/publications.en/voices.africa/number5/vfa5.07.htm (accessed: 16 December 2017).

Mondal, Puja, "Essay on social change: Meaning, characteristics and other details" available at: http://www.yourarticlelibrary.com/sociology/essay-on-social-change-meaning-characteristics-and-other-details/8590/ (accessed: 30 June 2016).

Moody, Andrew, "China has changed discourse on Africa: Africa Programme Head at Chatham House keen to forge links with Chinese institutions" *China Daily-Africa Weekly of 10–16 July 2015*.

Moore, Olive, "From right to development to rights in development: Human rights based approaches to development" available at: http://www.nuigalway.ie/dern/documents/54_olive_moore.pdf (accessed: 10 April 2015).

Moyo, Dambisa, "Why foreign aid is hurting Africa" (2009) *The Wall Street Journal* available at: http://www.wsj.com/articles/SB123758895999200083 (accessed: 6 December 2017).

BIBLIOGRAPHY

N'Sengha, Mutombo N., "The African Charter on Human and Peoples' Rights: An African contribution to the project of global ethic" available at: http://globalethic.org/Center/mutombo1.htm (accessed: 17 April 2015).

National Archives, "Declaration of Independence: A Transcription" available at: https://www.archives.gov/founding-docs/declaration-transcript (accessed: 14 February 2016).

National Centre for Constitutional Studies, "The Declaration of Independence part of American law" available at: http://www.nccs.net/1998-06-the-declaration-of-independence-part-of-american-law.php (accessed: 20 February 2016).

New Partnership for Africa's Development (NEPAD), "Historical context: Origins and influences" available at: http://www.nepad.org/history (accessed: 4 December 2016).

New Partnership for Africa's Development (NEPAD), "NEPAD's transformation into the African Union Development Agency" available at: http://www.nepad.org/news/nepads-transformation-african-union-development-agency (accessed: 26 June 2019).

Nowosad, Orest, "A Human rights based approach to development: Strategies and challenges" available at: http://www.nhri.net/pdf/African4thNhri/Novosad%20Development.pdf (accessed: 24 April 2015).

Nunn, Nathan, "The historical origins of Africa's underdevelopment" (2007) *VOX CEPR's Policy Portal* available at: http://www.voxeu.org/article/slave-trade-and-african-underdevelopment (accessed: 13 February 2016).

Organisation for Economic Cooperation and Development (OECD), "The human rights based approach to development cooperation: Towards a common understanding among the UN agencies" available at: http://www.oecd.org/derec/finland/43966077.pdf (accessed: 22 April 2015).

Organisation for Economic Cooperation and Development (OECD), "Women in Africa" available at: http://www.oecd.org/dev/poverty/womeninafrica.htm (accessed: 3 July 2016).

Owen, Olly & Melville, Chris, "China and Africa: A new era of south-south cooperation" (2005) Open Democracy available at: https://www.opendemocracy.net/en/south_2658jsp/ (accessed: 20 April 2016).

Peta, Basildon, "Regime has turned 'breadbasket of Africa' into famished land" (2005) *The Independent – UK* available at: www.rense.com/general64/mugg.htm (accessed: 15 November 2014).

Petitjean, Olivier, "Perenco in the Democratic Republic of Congo: When oil makes the poor poorer" (2014) Multinationals Observatory available at: http://multinationales.org/Perenco-in-the-Democratic-Republic (accessed: 28 October 2016).

Rhodes, Cecil, "Confession of faith" (1877) available at: http://pages.uoregon.edu/kimball/Rhodes-Confession.htm (accessed: 20 July 2015).

Roby, Christin, "The African Union Development Agency takes shape" New Partnership for Africa's Development 4 March 2019 available at: https://www.nepad.org/african-union-development-agency-takes-shape (accessed: 26 June 2019).

Rosseel, Peter, et al., "Approaches to north-south, south-south and north-south-south collaboration: A policy document" available at: https://lirias.kuleuven.be/bitstream/123456789/229636/1/policy_paper_vlir_uwc_nss.pdf (accessed: 25 April 2016).

Schmitz, Hanz P., "Rights-based approaches to development: From rights 'talk' to joint action" (2013) Open Democracy available at: http://www.opendemocracy.net (accessed: 30 June 2015).

Searcey, Dionne; Schmitt, Eric & Gibbons-Neff, Thomas, "US reduces military aid to Cameroon over human rights abuses" *The New York Times* 7 February 2019 available at: https://www.nytimes.com/2019/02/07/world/africa/cameroon-military-abuses-united-states-aid.html (accessed: 30 July 2019).

Shah, Anup, "Foreign aid for development assistance" *Global Issues* 2004 available at: http://www.globalissues.org/article/35/foreign-aid-development-assistance (accessed: 6 September 2017).

Sklare, Aly, "Libya: Struggle for independence" available at: http://hj2009per4libya.weebly.com/struggle-for-independence.html (accessed: 10 July 2016).

South African History Online, "The fight against colonialism and imperialism in Africa" available at: https://www.sahistory.org.za/article/fight-against-colonialism-and-imperialism-africa#:~:text=To%20understand%20what%20effects%20WW2,the%20climate%20just%20before%20WW2.&text=After%201900%2C%20Europe%20began%20to,increase%20revenues%20from%20the%20colonies.&-text=Resistance%20movements%20began%20to%20rise%20in%20Africa. (accessed: 3 March 2016).

Taylor, Prue, "The common heritage of mankind: A bold doctrine kept within strict boundaries" available at: http://wealthofthecommons.org/essay/common-heritage-mankind-bold-doctrine-kept-within-strict-boundaries(accessed: 24 April 2015).

The Economist, "Development in Africa: Growth and other good things" (2013) available at: http://www.economist.com/blogs/baobab/2013/05/development-africa (accessed: 10 June 2016).

The World Bank, "Least developed countries: UN classification" available at: http://data.worldbank.org/region/LDC (accessed: 12 October 2016).

Transparency International, "Corruption on the rise in Africa poll as governments seen failing to stop it" (2016) Available at: http://www.transparency.org/news/pressrelease/corruption_on_the_rise_in_africa_poll_as_governments_seen_failing_to_stop_i (accessed: 4 May 2017).

Truman, Harry S., "Inaugural address" (1949) available at: http://www.bartleby.com/124/pres53.html (accessed: 14 October 2016) paras 1-71.

United Nations, "25th anniversary of the Declaration on the Right to Development" *Declaration on the Right to Development at 25* available at: www.un.org/en/events/righttodevelopment/ (accessed: 28 April 2019).

United Nations, "The foundation of international human rights law" available at: https://www.un.org/en/about-us/udhr/foundation-of-international-human-rights-law (accessed: 17 March 2015).

United Nations Development Programme (UNDP), "Human development reports: 2018 statistical update" *United Nations Development Programme* available at: http://hdr.undp.org/en/content/human-development-indices-indicators-2018-statistical-update (accessed: 3 April 2019).

United Nations Fund for Population Activities, "Definitions of rights based approach to development by perspective" (2003) available at: http://www.unfpa.org/derechos/docs/hrba_definitions.pdf (accessed: 30 November 2015).

United Nations Human Rights Council, "Development – right to development" available at: http://www.ohchr.org/EN/Issues/Development/Pages/Backgroundrtd.aspx (accessed: 31 January 2015).

United Nations Office of the High Commission for Human Rights (UNOHCHR), "The right to development and least developed countries" UN Human Rights, available at: https://www.ohchr.org/EN/Issues/Development/Pages/LeastDevelopedCountries.aspx (accessed: 4 November 2017).

United Nations Office of the High Commissioner for Human Rights (UNOHCHR), "TST issues brief: Human rights including the right to development" *Joint Issue Brief* available at: https://sustainabledevelopment.un.org/content/documents/2391TST%20Human%20Rights%20Issues%20Brief_FINAL.pdf (accessed: 20 October 2016).

US Department of State Office of the Historian, "Milestones: 1945–1952 – Decolonization of Asia and Africa 1945–1960" available at: https://history.state.gov/milestones/1945-1952/asia-and-africa (accessed: 14 March 2016).

Van Lennep, Tove, "The African Continental Free Trade Area III – Is Africa ready?" (2019) Helen Suzman Foundation https://hsf.org.za/publications/hsf-briefs/the-african-continental-free-trade-area-iii-2013-is-africa-ready (accessed: 26 April 2019).

Vandenhole, Wouter, "A partnership for development: International human rights law as an assessment instrument" available at: http://www2.ohchr.org/english/issues/development/docs/vandenhole.doc (accessed: 20 February 2015).

World Bulletin News Desk, "French colonial tax still enforce for Africa" *World Bulletin* available at: https://www.worldbulletin.net (accessed: 31 October 2018).

Wroughton, Lesley, "U.S. halts some Cameroon military assistance over human rights -official" *Reuters – Washington* 7 February 2019 available at: https://www.washingtonpost.com/world/africa/us-cuts-some-military-assistance-to-cameroon-citing-allegations-of-human-rights-violations/2019/02/06/aeb18052-2a4e-11e9-906e-9d55b6451eb4_story.html (accessed: 30 July 2019).

Wurong, Zu., "Respect for right to development" *China Daily* US [New York, NY] of 28 Feb 2014.

Yergin, Daniel & Stanislaw, Joseph, "Excerpt from *The Commanding Heights*" available at: http://www-tc.pbs.org/wgbh/commandingheights/shared/pdf/prof _kwamenkrumah.pdf (accessed: 14 February 2016).

Index

absence of development assistance   256
absence of political development   58
abstract rights   182
abstract theory   12
Abuja Treaty   131
abusive exploitation   162, 195, 265, 302
   direct   207
   uncontrolled   194
Accelerating youth empowerment for
     sustainable development   165, 359
access to remedy   155, 192–93
access to resources   232
accountability   9, 26, 94, 125–26, 265, 267,
     272, 295, 300, 308–9
   broad based   308
   engineered political   267
   legal   66, 126, 175, 211, 296–97
accountability of non-state actors for human
     rights violations   282, 347
acquisition of independence   46, 68
action plans   145
actions
   concerted   100, 128, 178, 226
   concrete   55, 60, 125, 153, 158, 178, 298
   consolidated   156, 279
   co-ordinate development   134
   development demands   234
   direct governmental   290
   extraterritorial   286
   gender-responsive   163
   global   50, 112, 219, 286
   liberty of   284
   pragmatic   151
   rational   98
   remedial   177
   representative   193
   sustained   85, 219, 262
   wrongful   75, 178, 189, 209, 211–12, 217, 295
actions of foreign stakeholders   84, 131, 143,
     254, 282
actions of non-state actors   175, 179, 208
actions on human livelihood   186
activism   191
   judicial   172
   political   246
   radical   234

activities of foreign stakeholders   138, 175
activities of non-state actors   177, 264
actors
   competing donor   102
   dominant   102
   external   135, 151, 189, 215, 266, 280, 284–
     85, 305
   global   180, 284, 286, 304
   international   47, 50
   key development cooperation   92
   relevant   107
actual dimensions of development
     cooperation   9
actual freedoms and capabilities   98
adequate compensation   201, 206–7
   payment of   206–7
adequate reparation   197, 205
adjudicate   88, 169, 186, 188, 345
admissibility criteria   187, 193, 275
advanced countries   117
advancement   32, 37, 41–42, 54, 56, 64, 70,
     107–8, 114, 210, 287–88
   collective   85, 307
   industrial   6
   infrastructural   76
   jurisprudential   51
   social   88
   technological   303–4
Adventurist Politics   236, 319
AfCFTA (African Continental Free Trade
     Area)   80, 147–50, 303
Africa   1–20, 22–40, 42–45, 47–65,
     67–68, 70–72, 74–87, 92–99, 101–6,
     108–16, 118–20, 122–37, 139–58, 160–70,
     173–85, 191–93, 195–96, 211–354, 356–
     59, 361–68
   colonise   118
   destabilise   87
   entangle   121
   exposed   175
   peaceful   144
   plunged   121
   positioning   37
   post-colonial   271
   unified   272
Africa and foreign stakeholders   87

INDEX

Africa and international trade 30, 287, 353
Africa arise summit 158
Africa Claim 119, 265, 320, 361
Africa command 148
Africa Growth Initiative 105, 352
African agenda 14–15, 79, 145, 147, 190, 269,
 300, 357
African aspirations for development 103
African Charter 1–2, 6–7, 14, 43–44, 49–52,
 54, 56–61, 125, 128, 147, 166–67, 194–98,
 200–202, 215, 227, 240, 243–45, 248,
 285–86, 303–5
African Charter and associated
 instruments 268
African Charter and freedom of expression in
 Africa 214, 344
African civilisation 25
African colonial states 25, 326
African colonies 29, 40, 46, 89, 122, 130, 150,
 229, 277–78, 346
African Commission 51, 157, 178, 182–85,
 187, 192–202, 206–7, 213–14, 220, 233,
 241, 273, 275, 283–84, 287, 305, 334, 338,
 345, 358
African common market 149
African common positions on issues of
 interest 128–29
African conception 12, 67, 86, 142, 151,
 294, 305
African constitutionalism 11, 344
African constructivist imagination 132
African continent 15, 22–23, 25, 32, 43, 85,
 132, 148, 151, 169, 215
African Continental Free Trade
 Agreement 80
African Continental Free Trade
 Area. *See* AfCFTA
African corporate sector 301–2
African countries 4–5, 46, 52, 80, 120–22,
 125–31, 140–42, 153, 221–22, 224–25,
 227–28, 235–37, 250, 256–57, 275–76,
 278–79, 288–89, 306
African Court 166–67, 182–83, 185–87,
 192–94, 202–7, 213, 220, 284, 305, 309,
 353, 358
 hybrid 187
African cultural patterns 29
African Cultural Renaissance 57

African decolonial theorists 11
African development agenda 52, 151,
 275, 310
African Development Bank Group 121,
 307, 345
African development landscape 122
African development space 105, 266
African diaspora 300
African economic development 22, 28, 354
African economies 23, 120–21, 128, 131, 174,
 224, 353
African forms of reasoning 29
African francophonie countries 130
African governments 120–21, 127, 143,
 145–46, 150, 157, 237, 259–60, 267–69,
 271, 300
 indebted 120
African historical tradition and values 197
African History 22, 24, 135, 315, 323, 330
African human rights architecture 146
African Human Rights Court 186,
 193, 282
African human rights jurisprudence 198
African Human Rights System 49, 51–52,
 59, 125–26, 131, 159, 167, 204, 211, 333–
 34, 339
African human rights treaties 133, 212
African identity and value systems 266
African imagination 38, 69
African jurisprudence 287
African Law 30, 36, 59, 194, 233, 303,
 334, 337–38
African leaders 15, 34–35, 38, 141, 234
African legal framework 132
African liberation leaders 33–34
African market, single 147
African model 265–66, 298
 envisaged 265
African Monetary Fund 301
African National Human Rights
 Institutions 190, 357
African nationalism 29
African nationalist 33, 262
African origins 1, 14, 18–19, 302
African patrimony 36, 69–70, 133, 265,
 273, 279
African Peer Review Mechanism
 (APRM) 141–43, 300, 349, 358

INDEX

African peoples   220, 225, 249, 256, 258, 260, 268–69, 279–80, 286, 288, 290–91, 293, 302–9

African perception   103

African political landscape   122

African political thought   25, 340

African Politics   257, 315, 320

African populations   22, 26, 32, 72, 149, 165, 223, 259, 304

African problems   259, 298, 338

African realities   54, 143

African regional human rights system   183, 340, 361

African Resistance   28, 334, 341

African resource-base   162

African ruling elites   35

Africans   24, 27, 32, 48, 290, 317
   fellow   33

African slavery   24, 332

African societies   15, 45, 63, 163–64, 224
   dysfunctional   34
   ruined   34

African solutions   298, 338

African space   59

African stakeholders   144

African state government   190

African state parties   133, 183

African states   43
   decolonised   42, 46
   five   126
   fragile independent   36
   Independent   35
   new   36

African treaty instruments   52, 56, 96, 158–59, 212

African Treaty Provisions   159

African Union   13–14, 62, 64, 103, 127–31, 141–42, 160, 165–66, 176, 178, 224–27, 299, 336, 356–59, 362

African Union Agenda   62

African Union Commission   76, 81, 144, 215, 224, 265, 297, 359

African Union Constitutive Act   166

African Union Development Agency   144, 365–66

African value systems and traditions   48

Africa's anti-colonial resistance   28, 338

Africa's constant search for assistance   262

Africa's debts   261

Africa's dependence on development assistance   227

Africa's development agenda   94, 237, 261, 291, 354

Africa's development aspirations   5, 36

Africa's development challenges   82, 84–85, 152, 260, 268, 293

Africa's development efforts   142

Africa's development history   256

Africa's development initiatives   120

Africa's development priorities   144

Africa's Development Prospects   119

Africa's Development Setbacks in Context   3–17

Africa's development trajectory   10

Africa's framework for development   269

Africa's investment destinations of choice   250

Africa's Persistent Search for New Frontiers of Assistance   260

Africa's progress and sustenance   165

Africa's support   115

Africa's underdevelopment   20–21, 23, 366

Africa's vision and aspirations   300

Africa's youth agenda, defining   165, 362

Africa to direct attack by foreign stakeholders   119

Afrique   120, 231

agencies
   foreign intelligence   122
   human   134
   moral   151

agency and leadership   164

agency and self-determination   134

agenda   14–15, 79, 81, 144–47, 248, 251, 256, 262, 265–66, 268–73, 296–302, 308, 310
   continental   304
   global   109, 147
   missing   176, 336

agenda for development   6, 14, 145, 147, 159, 224, 257, 265, 268, 307

Agenda for Sustainable Development   190, 357

aggression   137, 213

aggressive imperialistic attitude   45

Agreement Establishing   147, 356

agricultural lands   26

372 INDEX

agricultural policies, unfair 42
agriculture 42, 253, 333, 359
agriculture for economic growth 42
aid 91–92, 96, 98, 100–101, 104, 262, 269, 276,
 334, 337, 345–46, 349, 353
 military 123, 366
aid agencies 88
aid allocation 91–92, 329, 353
aid by developed countries 96
aid conditionality principle 102
aid dependency 5, 15, 102, 301, 345
aid-development-assistance 276, 367
aid donors on assistance 88
aid donors on assistance to less-developed
 countries 88
Aid Effectiveness 93–94, 104, 134, 350, 358
 foreign 109, 332
aid flow 106
aid ineffectiveness 8, 104
aid recipient countries 104
aid to developing countries 286
allegations 184, 190, 200, 202
allocation of development assistance 78
alternative model 4, 10, 13, 45, 61, 109, 256,
 291, 293, 308
alternative model to development
 cooperation 291
alternative remedies to Africa's development
 setbacks 261
alternative sabotage strategies,
 employed 121
ambiguous concept of sustainable
 development 243
amendments 171, 187, 355–56, 358
amnesty 47, 207, 336
Amnesty International 62
amounts of foreign aid to Africa 106
amplification 95
anarchy 91, 328
ancestral bond 202
ancestral lands 198–99, 223–24, 264,
 284, 364
ancestral spirituality 201
ancestral worship 199
ancestry 199
 common 200
angle, legal 166
anti-colonialism 28

anti-colonial struggles 36
apartheid 28, 47, 254
apparatus, bureaucratic 116
approaches 2, 4, 9–10, 76, 85, 95, 101–2, 229–
 30, 298, 300, 305, 333, 336
 adjudication 195
 based 134, 341, 347, 351, 365–67
 decolonial 11, 83, 327
 minimum threshold 213, 332
 misconceived 109
 pragmatic 10, 60, 196, 275, 340
 results-oriented 12
 rights-based alternative 264
 traditional livelihood 204, 330
 universal 280
appropriate development model for
 Africa 218
appropriate jurisdictions 189, 212
APRM. See African Peer Review Mechanism
APRM country review 260, 346
AQ 115, 144–45, 199, 323, 363–64, 367–68
Arab Charter 53, 336, 341, 344, 356
Arab Spring 135
arbitrariness 151
architect of independence 32
area
 good governance priority 260
 unproductive 199
 water catchment 202
argumentation 2, 13, 253, 291
arguments
 basic 97
 central 4, 153
 strong 254
armed forces 196
arms embargoes 281
article
 common 209
 transgressed 285
 violated 201
aspirants to positions of political leadership
 in Africa 308
aspirations 37, 79–81, 141, 145–46, 149, 248,
 251, 261, 264–65, 270, 272, 297, 300
 equalise 79
 frustrated 230
 legitimate 31, 38, 220
 shared 307

INDEX

aspirations for structural transformation and sustainable development 297
assassinations 130
Assembly of Heads of States and Governments 160, 358
assertion of self-determination 15, 267, 294
assessment 124, 203, 277
  country-by-country 227
  preliminary 214, 340
  theoretical 226
assimilation 29
  forced 233
assistance 3, 9, 88, 90, 92–93, 97–99, 106, 110–11, 250, 255–56, 260, 274, 276–79
  charitable 6, 253
  charity-based 208, 252
  donor 231
  global poor 286, 341
assistance for development purposes 97
assistance to Africa 9
assistance to developing countries 99, 110, 255
associated human rights instruments 161
assurance 5, 17, 33, 161, 169, 181, 186, 192, 245–46, 291, 294
  legal 146
assurances, practical 288
asymmetrical power structures 70
Atlantic Charter 21
attainment of self-determination for Africa 273
attention
  appropriate 282
  deflected 47
  requisite 103
attention by victims of violation 184
attributes responsibility 212
AU financial institutions 301, 362
austerity measures 120
  fiscal 258
  stringent 120
authoritarian regimes 191
authorities 185, 191, 214, 275
  foreign stakeholders exercise 180
  political 257
  relevant national 215
autonomy 47, 87, 101, 140, 174, 191, 217, 234, 269, 274

  cultural 41, 174, 274
  economic 118
autonomy and self-determination 217
averred political influence 192
award remedies 169

background to development cooperation 87
backwardness 85
Bakweri Lands Claim 232
balance 234, 276, 300
  equitable 99, 139, 176
  global 41, 111
balanced development 89, 140, 167, 228
bargaining strategy, collective 275
basic features of development cooperation 91
basic human rights 9, 114, 210, 236, 289
behavioural patterns 271
behaviour of foreign stakeholders and non-state actors 182
beliefs 12, 34
  spiritual 199
benchmarks 61, 300
  universal 112
beneficiaries, primary 161
benefits 25, 27, 54–55, 70–71, 73–74, 77–79, 119, 122, 147–50, 162–64, 200–201, 221, 223, 228–29, 305–6
  collective 162
  economic 230
  mutual 77, 93, 104, 107, 115, 162
  socio-economic 149
benefit to foreign stakeholders 148
benevolence 3, 6, 151, 252, 293
better living standards 17, 55, 73, 78, 99, 131, 145, 244, 248, 308, 310
betterment 5, 64
biased barometer 6
biased globalisation practices 111
bill 21, 96, 172, 240, 242, 334, 357
  comprehensive 171
  international 19, 286–87
binding character 113, 214
binding effect 3, 159, 190
binding extraterritorial obligations 220
binding force 187, 214
binding instruments 3, 180

374 INDEX

binding obligation for reliance on
development assistance 99
binding obligation on foreign stakeholders to
comply 53
binding obligations 50, 53, 59–61, 99, 110,
174, 212, 214, 275
black South Africans 47
disadvantaged 242
Blood minerals 169, 222, 335, 346
boom in international trade 23
boundaries 162, 367
strict 162, 367
Brazilian cooperation 106, 331
breadbasket of Africa 281, 366
British colonial expedition 29
British colonial rule 28, 32, 46
broad-based transformation and sustainable
development 307
broaden 135, 304, 310
broker cooperation agreements for
development 275
budgets 190, 261, 362
annual 261

Cameroon 48–49, 120–21, 123, 167–68, 225–
34, 316–17, 323, 325, 328, 335, 345, 347,
352–53, 360–61, 364
Cameroonian people 229, 252
Cameroon military assistance 123, 368
campaign, ghost city 231
campaign for independence 40
capabilities
ancillary 148
collective 64
expanding 37, 118
legal 275
people's 71
relevant 304
capabilities and choices 64
capabilities and skills-set 166
capabilities approach 13
capabilities for development 22, 266
capabilities model 13
capabilities theory 10–11, 13, 31, 174, 216, 260
capacity 64, 69, 101, 108, 134, 139, 144, 150,
196, 274, 296, 303, 310
negotiating 188
normative 69

productive 32, 81, 105, 135, 258
requisite 34, 271
resource 274, 278
technical 191
capacity of ordinary people 34
capacity to exercise 274
capital inflows, external 8
capitalism 71, 363
free market 120, 257
western-style 35
capitalist empires 24
categorisation 117–18
progressive cluster 118
categorisation ranks Africa, global 150
causal factor 91
central place in governance 280
challenges 1–3, 10–11, 14, 41–42, 83, 86, 135,
251–52, 272–73, 287–88, 330–31, 337–38,
340, 343, 353–54
bureaucratic 238
economic 288
new 290, 341
challenges of leadership and governance in
Africa 262, 307, 327
channeling of development assistance 108
changes 13, 110, 118–19, 125, 221, 230–32, 262,
298, 308, 339, 342
chaos 122, 270
engineer 210
charitable provision of development
assistance 99
charity approach 251–53
Charter for African Cultural Renaissance 57
Charter for Popular Participation
in Development and
Transformation 269, 356
Charter provisions 127, 184
child mortality 103
China 85, 119, 222, 249, 255, 262, 300
fuel 115
China-Africa South-South cooperation
framework 250
China and Africa 106, 115, 352, 366
China for development financing 250
China model 115
China's investment destinations of
choice 261
China's philosophy 106, 360

INDEX

Chinese debts 250
Chinese FDI 222, 342
Chinese loans 257, 353
choice of countries for cooperation 114
choices 37, 64, 67, 69, 200–201, 250, 253, 261, 273, 276, 283–84
cultural 74
distributive 176
choices and capabilities of local communities 201
chronic stress 262, 342
circumstances
cultural 13
prevailing 4, 130, 193, 265, 290
citizens 144, 149, 167, 213, 240, 243, 247, 283
earnable-bodied 239
individual 239
loyal 239
citizenship, substantive 183, 341
civil disobedience, massive 231
civilisation 6, 11, 25, 29–30
civilisation mission, purported 32
civilisation theory 25
civil liberties and freedoms 34
civil society 230, 318, 325, 347
robust 146
claim
indigenous 224
legal 246
legitimate 5, 111–12, 191, 194, 211
neoliberal 259
claim entitlement 295
claims approach 253–56
claim to development assistance 96, 255
clarity, normative 304
class, favoured 29
cleavages 27, 41, 116, 335
ethnic 27
coercion, economic 70, 283
coercive labour 26
collaboration 85, 87, 302
mutual 85
north-south-south 102, 366
collective action 4–5, 73, 77, 80, 125, 128, 131, 136, 147, 151, 167
decisive 292
collectivism 63–64, 97, 129, 328–29
colonial absolutism 11, 13

colonial administration 27
transferred 37
colonial allegiance to France 230
colonialism 18, 20, 22, 25, 27–37, 43, 45–46, 48, 72, 77, 254, 329, 354
experienced 237
informed 101
neo 303
coloniality 12, 29, 218, 296, 336
global 1, 11, 41, 45, 81, 83, 160, 251, 296, 333, 338
logic of 11, 83, 337
colonial legacies 35
colonial machinery 29, 35
colonial masters 34, 50, 87, 89, 102, 274
colonial matrix 11
colonial pact 130, 363
colonial possessions 234
profitable 150
colonial practices 32, 37, 39
colonial rule 5, 25–28, 30–31, 33, 35, 229, 292
reject 32
colonial tax 122, 153, 228, 278, 364
colonisation 22, 25, 27–28, 69, 118, 122, 153, 228, 364
Colonisation Continuation Pact 122, 150, 278
colonisation theory 69
colonised territories 25, 40, 87
colonization of Africa 32
combat impunity by upholding justice and equity 269
Combating Corruption 272, 356
combined theories of decoloniality 13
Commission on Human rights 47–48, 177, 286, 360
commitments 72, 76, 94, 99, 145, 150–51, 155, 157–59, 216–17, 226, 255, 301, 305
international 219
legal 52, 73, 75, 155, 212, 215, 305
moral 50, 95, 112, 253
political 76, 156, 308
shared 108
state's binding 188
sustainable 94
commodities, basic 231
commodity boycotts 281
Common Africa Positions on Post-2015 Development Agenda 129

common challenges 129
common development purpose 91
common heritage 70, 79, 147–48, 162, 203, 223, 263, 279
common heritage of mankind principle in international law 162, 335
common understanding 134, 359, 366
Communauté Financière d'Afrique 120, 231
communitarian 63
communities 23, 26, 43, 57, 63, 70, 162, 199–201, 204, 240, 243
  disadvantaged 72
  fractionalised 25
  globalised 114
  indigenous 205, 223, 284
  self-governing 22
  semi-nomadic 199
community empowerment 202, 330
comparative influence 240, 331
compensation 92, 199, 202, 205
competition 100
  foreign 148
complaint 184, 188, 192–95, 198, 202, 209, 233, 247
  admissibility of 184, 188
  handling 190
complaint procedure 184
complement Africa's efforts 114
complex dynamics 221
complexity 2, 37, 81, 262
compliance 127, 142, 174–75, 184, 204–5, 215–16, 229, 275, 281, 292
component elements 200, 244
components
  core 143, 201
  elementary 136
  important 55, 273
comprehensive development 3, 76, 219, 253
compromise state sovereignty 237
conceptions 5, 57, 59, 118, 251
  individualistic 64
  western 236
conceptual analysis 1, 14, 350
conceptual clarity 19–20, 53, 305
conceptual formulation 91, 221, 266, 296
  combined 291
conceptualising development 44, 65
concerted efforts 224, 299

concessional flows 96
Conditional development 258, 350
conditionalities 3, 98, 103, 105, 289
  donor-dictated 101
  label 104
  unattainable 108
conditional lending 257
conditions
  better 269, 280
  enabling 149
  human 60, 67, 75, 160, 283
  international 126, 138
  political 35
Conflict minerals 169, 198, 222, 346
conflicts 1, 12, 27, 99, 117, 123, 136, 154, 170, 245, 343
  armed 122–23
  endemic 136
  ethnic 46
  internal 36
  spiralling 123
  violent 169
conformity 137, 167, 245, 298
confrontational court battles 191
Congolese people 168, 197
  massacred 197
connection 21, 77, 86, 111, 130, 151, 242
  causal 87
  direct 111
  territorial 200
consciousness 22, 29, 31, 40, 310
  critical 2
  increased 36
consent 203
  free 71
conservation 202
constituencies of peoples 74
Constitution 34–35, 48, 96–97, 167–72, 197, 226, 239–43, 245–46, 267, 271, 344, 349, 355–56
  documented 35
  domestic 167, 211, 245
  transformative 242, 324
constitutional borrowings 241, 342
constitutional dispensation 240
  transformative 241–42
constitutional entitlement 127, 168–69, 243, 245
  domestic 272

INDEX 377

constitutional guarantees   167–68, 229, 238
  implicit   172
constitutionalism   267, 334
  post-independence   270, 343
constitutional order   172, 241, 323, 339
  domestic   240
Constitutive Act   14, 128–29, 131–33, 136, 160,
    166–67, 178, 268–69, 271, 299–301, 303, 305
constraints   111, 133, 165, 208, 215, 219, 227,
    238, 247–48, 270, 325
  critical   52
  internal   295
consultation   88, 118, 202, 284, 360
  effective   203
  global   299, 328
contemporary understanding of development
    cooperation   90
Contending Approaches   260, 276, 321, 326
contention   4, 99, 257
  persistent   204
context
  developmental   71
  legal   153
  prevailing   181, 261
continental agenda for development   304
continental free market   149
continental level   17, 157, 182–83, 273, 294,
    305, 309
continued external influence   227
contradictions   14, 90
  cultural   16
  recurrent development   280
Contradictions of Good Governance   256
contraventions   52, 166, 168, 190, 195, 197, 212,
    221, 230, 273, 279
contributions   12, 19, 29, 49, 106, 164–65, 170,
    253, 304, 333–34, 336
  mandatory   301
  productive   166
control   27, 37–38, 50, 75, 79, 116, 119, 130, 301,
    303, 306
  colonial   27
  economic   50
  effective   180
  excessive   280
  foreign   120
  sovereign   168
control of multinational
    corporations   207, 328

cooperation   32, 38, 40, 74–77, 85–92, 100,
    103, 112–16, 118, 125, 128–29, 131, 133
co-operation, international   89, 343
cooperation accords   228–30
  secretive   229
cooperation agreements   175–76
  broker   275
cooperation approaches   251, 256
cooperation arrangements   89, 98–99, 233
cooperation framework   67, 86–87, 89, 173
  international   4
coopération Franco-Africains   228, 332
cooperation mechanism   100
cooperation patterns   86, 102
  prevailing development   92
  rival   100
Commission's jurisprudence   193
Corporate social responsibility   210, 349
corporations   183, 198
  transnational   88, 282, 333, 345, 347
corruption   35, 79, 93, 105, 121, 130, 235, 248,
    272, 340, 367
  endemic   1, 248, 272
  political   229
countries   28, 88, 91–92, 97, 100–101, 117–19,
    121–24, 130, 166–68, 218–19, 223, 225–30,
    232–35, 238–40, 242–45, 249–50, 252–
    53, 266–67, 281–82, 288
  choice of   114, 226
  conflict-ridden   123
  decolonised   88
  emerging   105
  fragile African   149
  francophone   150, 153
  less-developed   88
  middle income   117–18, 353, 362
  recipient   92, 97–98, 104, 134
  under-developed   88
country ownership   94, 133–34
  effective   134
country's development efforts   247
country's state of human development   168
Courting Social Justice   260, 315
court of law   59
Court's ruling   204
creating domestic laws   181
creating global poverty   114
creating real self-determination for
    Africa   221

378 INDEX

crisis   123, 230, 269, 314
  economic   230, 257, 269
  global financial   255
  social   269
the crisis of development   225, 324
critique   11, 66, 83, 141, 171, 208, 248, 325, 328,
      332–33, 336
  decolonial   1
  preliminary   47, 336
cross-sectoral Youth Policies   165
crusade   216
  trans-Atlantic   24, 344
cultural arrangements in society   161
cultural challenges   52
cultural circumstances in Africa   13
cultural development   54, 56–58, 60, 69,
      78–79, 146–47, 155–56, 160–61, 173–74,
      196–97, 203–4, 245–47, 263–64, 284,
      290, 305–6, 308–10
cultural development exigencies   38, 266
cultural development realities   144
cultural homogeneity   200
Cultural Revolution   106
cultural rights   19, 56, 58–59, 73, 103, 157, 161,
      171–72, 177–78, 208, 220, 222, 258, 263,
      295, 330–31, 357–60
cultural self-determination   2, 16, 57, 83, 121,
      125, 141, 153, 300–301, 304, 306
Cultural Self-Determination   169, 169, 173
cultural sovereignty and
      self-determination   150
culture   171, 201, 239, 262, 335
  integrated   201
  legal   240, 331
  political   79
Culture and leadership in Africa   262, 335
currency   39–40, 265
  common   150, 336
  foreign   201
  single   150, 363
currency devaluation   120, 231
  undertaking   258
custodians   133, 227, 299
customary law, international   97

damages   92, 126, 130, 194, 196, 198, 201–2,
      206–7, 209, 215, 254
  irreparable   206

dangers   206, 262
dawn of independence in Africa   45
debt crisis   120, 343
debt-free economic balance sheet   238
debt relief   231, 257
debts   120, 248, 261–62, 337
  external   121
  foreign   121, 277, 353
  shady   250
debt sustainability analysis   121, 360
debt to China   261
debt trap   101, 120–21, 257, 285, 353
decisions   118, 185, 189, 201–2, 207, 214–15,
      228, 256, 273, 334, 338
  joint   94
  participation in   89, 284
  political   97
Declaration   3, 39–40, 43, 49–50, 56–59,
      73–80, 90–91, 99–100, 107, 112–14, 123,
      125–26, 135–36, 138–40, 156–58, 173, 211–
      13, 218–19, 267–69, 356–58
  NEPAD   142–43
Declaration, Paris   134, 358
Declaration of Independence   46, 367
decolonial   303
decolonial dialogues   11, 83, 329
decoloniality   11–13, 25, 83, 337–38
decoloniality and capabilities theories   13
Decoloniality of Thought in Development
      Programming   251
decolonial mindset   309
decolonial narratives   303
Decolonial Options   11, 83, 317, 337
decolonial reconstructions   11, 83, 322
decolonial reflections   12, 241, 343
decolonial revolution   12, 29
decolonial theory   10–11
decolonisation   6, 12, 30–34, 38, 40, 68, 87,
      153, 173, 224, 229
  facilitated   40
  motivated   45
decolonisation project   31, 34
decolonised states succession plans   34
decolonization   30, 159, 331, 368
deep-rooted involvement   71
deferential treatment   76
deficiencies   257, 291, 296
deficits, large-scale   289

INDEX 379

definition, new 89
definitional problem 89
degenerating 206
degree, limited 119
dehumanising practice 23
Deliberative participation 244, 330
demands of international trade 24
democracy 123, 157–58, 172, 174, 239, 241, 313, 315, 319, 323, 328–29, 331, 341–42
   constitutional 47
   representative 308
   revolutionary 245
democracy and human rights in Cameroon 123, 229, 342
democracy in South Africa 270
democratic deficits 79, 293
Democratic Development 257, 315
Democratic Reform 143, 316, 322
democratisation 230–31, 252, 260, 263, 267, 332
democratisation process 37, 231, 338
democratisation programmes 103
democratise 104
denial, calculated 80
Department of International Development 101, 346
dependence 67, 96, 118, 239, 276
   endemic 217, 293
   increasing 250
   inordinate 260, 291
   irrational 102
   perpetual 288
dependency 80, 84, 98, 100, 221–22, 252, 260–62, 269–70, 297, 300, 306
   endemic 101, 217, 252, 348
   futile 250
   hopeless 276
dependency on development assistance 67, 80, 84, 222, 260
dependency on foreign stakeholders 5
dependency theory 221
deplorable degradation 207
deposits 222
   mineral 222
   natural resource 168
deprivation 25, 31, 67, 69, 81, 161, 197–98, 229, 280, 283, 289
   chronic 67

cultural 74, 304
   socio-economic 288
design 86, 132
   political 67
destabilising 121, 136
destruction 33, 37, 137, 210, 332
destructive social consequences 258
deterioration 23, 26, 28, 168
determinants of development cooperation 158
detrimental impact 123
devaluation 120
developed countries 3, 42, 50, 73–75, 85–86, 95–96, 101–2, 110–11, 113–14, 117–18, 219–20, 255–56, 276–79, 306, 367–68
   dominant 108
   necessitating 110
   patronage of 99, 293
developed countries for assistance 276, 278
developed countries for subsistence 101
developing countries 3, 41–45, 73, 76–77, 88, 92–93, 96–110, 113, 115–19, 134, 139, 176, 209–12, 219–20, 254–55, 276, 339, 346
   aspirations of 41, 50
   efforts of 136, 219, 262
   five clusters of 118, 353
   impoverished 102
developing countries accessing opportunities 108
developing economies 117
developing nations 248, 336
development 1 65, 69, 72–87, 89–114, 118–19, 121–78, 180–201, 203–6, 208–30, 232–60, 262–80, 282–311, 313–54, 356–62, 365–68
development accords 60
development activities 65, 102, 243, 303
development actors 104
   international 100, 219, 337
development agency 141, 144, 300
development agenda 45, 164, 183, 271, 361
   economic 276
   global 147
development aid 50, 78, 88, 103, 113, 252, 320
developmental state 245
   democratic 270, 342
development and human rights 54, 328
development approach 268, 270

380 INDEX

development aspirations 265
  frustrate Africa's 122
  outlined 15
development as planned poverty 288, 323
development assistance 2–3, 8, 67, 80–81,
    83–86, 89, 93, 96–100, 102–5, 108–9,
    111–13, 139, 252, 254–56, 260, 276–
    79, 293–94
  allocating 97
  charity-based 269
  overseas 255
  soliciting 213
  story of official 87, 347
development assistance and development
    partnership 93
Development Assistance Committee 87–
    88, 347
development assistance
    programmes 100, 341
development assistance to Africa 89, 98
development benefits 293
development challenges 50, 53, 56, 95, 99–
    100, 105, 145, 152, 217, 221, 224–25
  continent's 265
  cultural 140
  defiant 144
  insurmountable 106
  redressing perennial 109
development choices 60, 67, 69, 74, 98, 111,
    133, 204, 216, 253, 304
  alternative 293
  making alternative 291
  self-reliant 83
  shaping Africa's 115
development claim 233
development contexts 54, 78, 227
development cooperation 1, 3–6, 8–10, 12–
    13, 15–18, 20, 50, 55, 75, 82–153, 164, 208,
    211–12, 218–19, 252–53, 280, 291–95, 297,
    348–49, 352
development cooperation
  causal principle 91
  dependency-based 15
  economic 80
  favoured 81
  practising 106
  south-south 100, 219, 337
development cooperation
    approaches 251, 296

development cooperation
    arrangements 306
development cooperation models 140, 291
development cooperation partner 230, 232
development cooperation prototypes 102
development discourse 248, 269, 341
  international 81
development dispensation 154–55, 159, 167,
    173–75, 213, 215–17, 219–20, 267, 269,
    271–72, 274, 295–96
development dispensation guarantees 216
Development effectiveness in development
    cooperation 101, 346
development financing 96, 250, 261–62, 301
development framework in Africa 280
development governance 5–6, 11, 17, 217–19,
    221–94, 296–300, 303, 306, 308–11,
    338–39, 344
development guarantees 113, 155
Development Imperatives 293–311
development in developing
    countries 108, 219
development injustices 11, 13, 15, 20, 22, 33–
    34, 43–44, 47–48, 67, 69, 77, 132, 135
  endemic 16
  historical 81, 127
development injustices and endemic human
    rights violations 298
development landscape 151
development law 59, 131–32
  international 41, 45, 76, 322, 335
development litigation 77, 195, 202
development model 17, 22, 34, 38, 112–13,
    151–53, 267, 270, 272, 290–91, 298
  alternative 66, 221, 271, 296, 306
  functional 33, 121, 295
  home-grown 291
  human rights-based 33
  integrated rights-based 266
development objectives 145–46, 293, 297,
    300, 307
development obligations 60, 97, 139, 191
development of human productive
    capabilities 243
development outcomes 80, 251
  optimal 140
  people-centred 166
  substantive 80
  sustainable 164

INDEX 381

development paradigm 14, 16–18, 20, 42, 45, 65, 68, 167–68, 215, 217–19, 291, 293–94, 296
   innovative 273
development partner 106, 348
Development partnerships 93–94, 101, 103, 217, 219, 346
development path 42
development policies 98, 101, 107, 109, 132, 134, 140, 237, 244, 346, 348
   appropriate 113, 259, 275
   appropriate national 73, 140, 305
   domestic 306
   global 109
   international 9, 74
   national 74, 125, 163, 175, 215, 236, 264, 271, 283, 306, 310
   people-centred 139
   radical self-reliant 236
development policy formulation 130, 140, 225
development policy framework 260
Development Policy Management 101, 217, 219, 346
development politics 45
   global 310
   international 87
development practice 20, 65, 86, 95, 131–32, 154, 171, 299, 305
development practices
   prevailing 308
   unfair 22
development priorities 5, 13, 16–17, 70, 72, 108–9, 139–40, 153, 183, 273, 283
   actual 103, 118
   shaping Africa's 295
development problems 250
   deep-seated 115
development process 55, 64, 71, 78–80, 133–35, 163–65, 200, 232–33, 242, 244, 273, 284, 286, 289, 291
development programmes 94, 134, 204, 300, 304, 309
   cultural 203
   global 224
   sustainable 286
development programming 108, 145, 167, 218, 227, 251, 268, 272
   people-centred 297
   rights-based 145

development projects 231
development setbacks 15
   understanding Africa's 16
development space 137, 294
development standards 135, 142, 189, 234, 236, 300, 308
Development Strategy 247, 338
development thinking 10, 18, 68, 251, 260–61, 266, 292, 296, 298, 309
   dependency-based 81
development trajectory 101, 236
   sustainable 261
dialectical 76
differentiation 251
dilemma 101, 217, 252, 344, 348
dimensions
   capacity building 225, 351
   developmental 274
   functional 13
   normative 51
direct attack by foreign stakeholders 119
direct investment 222, 330
   foreign 8, 221–22, 224, 329, 335
directive principles 97, 170–71, 246
Directive principles of state policy and fundamental rights 246, 331
discourse on human rights and development in Africa 83
discourse on international development 96
discretion, political 252
discriminatory treatment 233
disparities 106, 223
   economic 254
Dispensation 153–217, 308
   neo-colonial 174
   prevailing political 290
displacement, wrongful 199
dispossession 18, 22, 26, 30, 69, 133, 136, 289
   collective 63
   systematic 289
dispossession of wealth and resources 69
disruptions 11, 198
   radical 12
dissemination, appropriate 184
distribution 240
   equitable 73, 79, 189, 232, 265, 273
   fair 58
distributional patterns 119
domestic arrangements 272

382 INDEX

domesticate   52, 182, 215, 246
domestication   127, 166, 246–47
domestication Act   170
domestic challenges   37
domestic court of law   171
domestic courts   169, 171–72, 181–82, 187–89,
  192, 309
  jurisdiction of   187, 189, 309
Domestic Courts of First Instance   187
domestic development realities   140
domestic factors   20–21
domestic implementation   156, 226–27,
  300, 305
  effective   248
domestic law   9, 53, 169–70, 181, 187–89, 191–
  92, 195, 242–44, 250, 296, 305
  appropriate   283
domestic legal recognition and
  protection   250
domestic level   14, 17, 127–28, 156–57, 171, 173,
  177–78, 183–84, 188–89, 192, 211, 291, 294
domestic obligations   74
domestic policies   5, 154, 230, 237, 284
  adopted   134
  appropriate   230
  radical   244
domestic politics and governance   79
domestic remedies   181, 188, 192
  effective   188, 192
  local   192
Domestic Responsibilities   177
Domestic Statutes   170, 355
domestic warfare   24
dominance   93, 98, 113, 122, 291
  economic   42, 101
  global   128
domination   30, 33, 39–40, 45, 87, 122, 124,
  130, 133, 135–36, 283, 288, 293–94
  colonial   30, 290
  continuous external/foreign   182
  imperial   20, 29, 47, 173, 175, 236, 274, 292
donor conditionalities   289
donor countries   3, 5, 90, 92, 96, 98, 103, 112–
  13, 252, 255
  geopolitical interests of   4, 16
donor-oriented cooperation model   143
donor partners   115, 119, 134
donor-recipient   112

donors   1, 3, 55, 89, 92, 97, 100–104, 114, 117,
  143, 302
  foreign   151, 269, 301
  imperialist   107
  multilateral   96, 121
  official bilateral   121
DR Congo   223, 349
dream   304
  incomplete   12
drivers, primary   268
drive transformation   292
Durban Declaration and Programme of
  Action   254
duty
  associated   109
  collective   128
  legislative   168, 348
  overarching   186
  primary   208
duty bearers   66, 126, 135, 268, 304–5
duty bearers, primary   247
duty on African governments   146
duty to set policy standards   227

eastern provinces   196
economic blocs, regional   129, 131, 225
economic challenges and human rights
  violations   288
Economic Community   150
  coordinated African   131
economic control in Africa   50
Economic Cooperation   85, 230, 232, 270,
  278, 318, 340, 347, 349–50, 353, 366
economic development   26, 28, 57, 89, 96,
  101, 119, 252, 259, 267, 327–28
  experienced   225
  sustainable   259
economic development dilemma   120,
  260, 329
economic distress   121
economic exploitation   24, 248
  foreign   237
economic growth   53, 55, 65, 103–4, 115, 118,
  120–21, 200–201, 224–25, 258, 303–4,
  349, 352
  equitable   258
  recorded   119
economic growth in Africa   288, 340

INDEX

economic growth models 5, 265
economic growth objectives 265, 297
economic integration project in Francophone
    Africa 230, 328
economic interests 88, 122
    protecting French 231
economic policies 52, 257
economic recovery programme 257
economic sabotage 119, 122, 130
economic sanctions 122, 238, 277, 281–
    82, 348
    authorised punitive 277
    coercive 121
    survived 277
economic strength 117
Economic Uncertainty 102, 320
economic weight on Africa 105
economies
    advanced 101
    ailing 120
    capitalist 278
    debt-free 285
    emerging 85, 101, 105, 261
    flourishing 106
    global 215, 273
    industrialised 279
    market 303
    warfare 288
ECOWAS 129, 150, 336
education 27, 29, 32, 42, 57–58, 73, 121, 171,
    238–40, 260, 361
    quality 263
    universal primary 103
effective and desirable 106
effective collective measures 137
effective implementation 149, 184, 250,
    295, 310
Effective leadership and sustainable
    development in Africa 307, 331
effectiveness 93, 97, 101, 281, 346
    developmental 8, 349
effectiveness of development assistance 93
effective realisation 56, 139, 180, 264–65, 298
effective remedy 205, 207–8
effect transformation 185
egalitarian opportunities 249, 307
Elections and Good Governance 157
elements

cultural 56
defining 57
Eliminate Obstacles 135
emancipating process 201, 252, 273
emancipation 5
    cultural 34, 216
    economic 160
embezzlement 35
Emerging Africa 223, 351
emerging markets 117
Emerging Trend 242, 317, 324
empowerment 67, 141
    women's 164
enabling environment 9, 73–74, 108, 124,
    137–39, 148, 216, 240, 245, 263–64, 295
    global 89
    requisite 245
enabling environment forms 138
enabling gender-equitable framework for
    development 164
encroachment 25
    increasing 224
endemic dependence on development
    assistance 293
Endorois ancestral land 199–201
Endorois and Ogiek Community 264
Endorois community 193, 198–200
    indigenous 198
Endorois peoples 199, 284
enduring austerity 255
enforcement 155, 167, 169–70, 187, 191, 204–
    6, 208–9, 246, 332, 342, 355
    certifying 166
    judicial 13, 51
    legal 217, 292
Enforcement Act 246
enforcement measures 60
enforcement mechanisms 167, 184
    domestic 192
    regional 189, 209
    regional human rights 209
Enforcement Procedure 209, 342
engagements, contemporary 251
enjoyment 56, 58, 60, 72–73, 75, 78, 133,
    136, 138, 140, 143, 177–79, 279, 282–
    83, 285–86
enjoyment of basic human rights and
    freedoms 289

384 INDEX

enlightened self-interest   92, 106
enquiry   4, 17, 20, 84, 192, 217
   central   294
   primary   293
   robust   125
enslavement   59
enthusiasm   32
entities   41, 178–79, 187, 190
   non-state   182, 195, 285
   relevant   225
entitlement   16, 18–19, 45, 57, 59, 62, 64, 76,
   166, 173, 211–12, 245–48, 251–52, 263–
   64, 283
   absolute   263
   claimable   5, 15, 49, 110, 167, 189, 215, 228,
    255, 272, 293
   collective   15, 41, 48, 52, 64, 70–71, 200,
    221, 268, 299
   composite   244–45
   cultural   160, 263
   exclusive   199
   grants   134
   justiciable   49, 51, 163, 176, 297
   legitimate   153
   non-negotiable   173
   socio-economic   172
   substantive   56, 59–60, 182
entitlement to self-determination   16, 83,
   173, 211, 269, 283, 295
entitlement to sustainable development   163
Entrenched Provisions   167
environment   72, 126, 137, 156, 162, 194, 207,
   259, 287, 289, 359–60
   enabling domestic   121, 215
   enabling international   52
   equitable   138
   natural   137
environmental degradation   194
environmental rights   194, 240
Epistemic disobedience   11, 83, 337
equal enjoyment   54, 146, 162, 165, 203, 269
   guaranteed   73
equalising opportunities   54, 96
equality   38, 42, 58, 72–73, 77, 94, 100, 120,
   148, 232, 242
Equatorial Guinea   187, 358
equitable basis   273, 289
equitable opportunities   76

equitable social construction   69
equity   5, 65, 68, 75–77, 79, 81, 154–55, 158,
   161, 170, 173, 240, 242
   global   43
   intergenerational   243, 254, 328, 333
   social   72
era   244, 326
   contemporary   120, 260, 329
   post-independence   39
erga omnes   183
estimation   6, 128
Ethiopia   127, 129, 169, 225–27, 241–46, 250,
   261, 324, 326, 354, 356–58
   elevated   261
EU-China-Africa trilateral relations   116, 327
European colonisers   27, 289
European conditionality   116, 327
European economic interests   23
European imperialism   46
European invaders   293
European perception of civilisation   25
European plantations   23
events   21–22, 31, 33, 37, 43, 166, 170, 205–6,
   211, 231
   historical   21, 81
evidence of good governance   3
evolution of official development
   assistance   91, 348
exacerbates   102
examination   16, 135, 248, 340
   critical   86, 110
examination of human rights and foreign
   direct investment   221, 329
excessive influence   133, 179, 220, 251, 294
exchange
   disparate   23
   mutual   89
exclusion   157, 284
   social   254
exclusive entitlement by right of
   ancestry   199
exercise and enjoyment   73, 136, 138, 140, 283
exercise control   35
exercise due diligence   195
exercise influence   286
exercise of good faith   111
exercise of legality   60
exhaust   188, 190, 192, 309

INDEX 385

exigencies 11, 97, 252, 295, 310
existing rights and freedoms 285
expansion, economic 105, 119
expansive biodiversity 222
expatiate 201, 296
expectations 3, 31, 78, 80, 109, 119, 255, 262, 264, 307, 313
expenditures, public 26, 120, 257, 363
experience
    the colonial 46, 362
    shared 105
experience abuse 190
experienced sustained levels of economic growth 224
experience improvement 242
expertise 104, 107, 120
exploitation 10, 17, 21–22, 26, 30, 38–40, 42, 45, 175, 182, 198, 291, 293
    capitalist 70
    colonial 105, 235, 290
    illegal 197–98, 358
    neo-colonial 36
    resource 302
    wanton 258
exploitation by foreign stakeholders 17, 53
exploitative behaviour of foreign stakeholders 36, 74
exploitative grip 174
exploitative relationships 70
exploitative wage rates 26
exploration 21
exposure 32
    expanded 249
expropriation 232
    forceful 200
    massive 26
External actions 135
external domination 90, 216
    continuous 13, 38
external interferences 76, 283, 294
    continued 262
external pressures 181
    unwarranted 270
external state and non-state actors 8
extraction 22–23, 26, 28
    massive 25
extractive industry 198
Extra-national obligations 63, 208, 229, 352

extraterritorial activities of foreign stakeholders 180
Extraterritoriality 208–9, 352
Extraterritorial Obligations 177, 208–9, 220, 295, 309, 331, 358
extreme levels of poverty and social inequality 106
extreme poverty ranking 249, 362

facilities 253
    loan 121
    public 26
Facing Complexities 132, 176, 316, 324
Failed development vision 248, 332
failure 35, 109, 119, 121, 124, 126, 136, 250, 256–57, 259, 284
    critical 203
    government's 230
    overall economic 258
Failure of foreign aid in developing countries 109, 339
failure of politics 34, 324
Fair Trial and Legal Assistance in Africa 205, 358
faith, good 72, 111, 210, 215
Fanon's Warning 143, 314
fatigue, increasing 113
favoured destinations 8
FDI 222, 224, 329
finance development 262
financial-flows-crippling-the-continent 272, 363
financial institutions 88, 301–2
    continental 301
financial prohibitions 281
financing for development 94, 99, 255, 300
findings, clear 204
first instance, jurisdictions of 187, 309
fiscal revenues 121
flora 222, 278
focus
    central 296, 310
    dedicated 147
    institutional 166, 268
    primary 7
focus Africa's history of development injustices 20
focus on capabilities 31

focus on good governance 259
Following Sen's definition 98
food 58, 73, 171, 195, 246, 260, 263, 297
food security 42, 346
food shortages 281
force 49–50, 126, 133, 159, 185, 187, 200, 204, 237, 243, 247, 299, 301
  dynamic 144
  indomitable 47
  legal 97
  military 124
  normative 61, 155, 169–70
force and repression on Libya 237
forced labour 26
foreign aid 92, 97–98, 101, 106, 109, 252–53, 260, 276, 326–27, 335, 337, 339, 364–65
  volume of 97–98
Foreign aid to Africa 276, 335
foreign assistance 3–4, 101–2, 109, 217, 276–78, 297, 300, 306, 345
foreign conglomerates 120
foreign direct investment in Africa 116, 222, 328, 334–35
foreign direct investment operations 304
foreign domination 5, 112, 136, 159, 162, 213, 216, 218, 238, 248, 291–94
foreign domination in Libya 238
foreign economic cooperation 222, 342
foreign exploitation 236
  continuous 227
foreign extractive multinationals 169
foreign influence 239
foreign interference 213
foreign investors 221, 329
foreign multinationals 302
foreign policy 105, 135, 208, 237, 319, 321, 323, 338, 352
foreign policy agendas 115–16
foreign stakeholders 5, 8–10, 52–53, 87–88, 119, 133, 142–43, 150–51, 153–54, 175–76, 178–82, 188–89, 209, 212, 215–17, 220, 284–87, 294–96, 305–6, 308–9
foreign stakeholders and non-state actors 178–79, 182
foreign stakeholders influence 151, 248
forest 202, 204, 330
forest habitat 202
forge negotiations 275

formal recognition 20, 43
formative stages 179
formulation, convoluted 171
Fostering Development 170, 314
foundation 35, 38, 44–45, 116, 138, 167, 270, 367
  historical 20
  legal 7
foundation for post-colonial development in Africa 38
founding model, appropriate 36
founding principles 39
fragile states 37, 350
  least developed countries 117
framework
  appropriate 36
  global 41, 67, 118
  multilateral 108
  operational 145, 297
  pan-African 306
  regulatory 222, 352
  rights-based 66
framework convention 3, 9, 55, 84, 208, 331
framework mechanism 141, 149
framework model 11, 38, 110, 143, 217, 344
framework of development cooperation 5, 9, 84, 87, 111, 115, 119, 131, 135, 137–38, 140, 151, 155
framing of development cooperation 114
Françafrique 130, 229, 231, 278
Franco-African relations 228, 340
Francophone Africa 122, 130, 153, 228–30, 317, 328
freedom 31, 37–38, 45, 69–70, 72–73, 98, 133–34, 161, 174, 216, 236, 279–80, 283–86, 288–89, 318–19
  actual 98
  basic 67, 279
  collective 279
  cultural 279–81, 296
  fundamental 30, 62, 66, 78, 84, 107, 229, 287
  political 34, 36, 39, 118, 173
  real human 161
  substantive 118
freedom and identity 54, 57, 69, 133, 146, 165, 269
freedom and moral agency 151
freedom to exercise 189

INDEX 387

free trade area   148, 150
  inclusive   149
  inclusive continental   148, 345
free trade zone, largest   148
French colonial tax   278, 368
French-imposed colonial pact   130
French monetary hegemony   150
function
  core   190
  normative   114
  political   132
  regulatory   154
functional alternatives   72
functional disconnect   4
functionalist understanding   76
functional model   218, 271, 293, 298–99
  home-grown   292
Functional Requirements   271
fundamental factor   284
fundamental features   151
fundamental flaw   145
fundamental rights   246, 331, 342
funding   134, 300–301
  external   301
futile efforts   37
futures
  creating African   11, 29, 41, 83, 251,
    296, 338
  creating sustainable   12
  genuinely African   296

Gabon   234
game reserve   200
gauging development   132
GDP   99, 224, 255–56
GDP growth   121, 353
GDP quota   99, 256
gender equality   59, 103, 157, 164, 348
gender-equitable framework, enabling   164
gender perspectives   163
generations   2, 37, 70, 72, 126, 156, 161–63,
    239, 243, 254, 308
  first   161
generations of rights   161
generic concept   267
geopolitical groupings   306
geopolitical motives   151
  deep-seated   114

geopolitics of international development
    cooperation   100, 337
German social state principle   267, 334
Ghana   27–28, 32–34, 120, 196, 258, 275, 322,
    335, 350
Ghana's independence leader   46
Gidden's theory   135
global arrangement   42–43, 87, 112, 276, 287
  lop-sided   85
global development   2, 10, 77, 223, 265, 297
global development imbalances   108
Global Dynamics   83–151
global governance   4, 114, 116, 290, 321,
    327, 341
global imbalances   39, 42, 85, 118
  endemic   80
global inequalities   9, 11, 83, 164, 265, 327
  established   100
Globalisation   42, 167, 225, 260, 276, 316, 318,
    321, 324, 326–27, 335–36
  corporate   199, 253, 326
  encroaching   37
globalization   244, 248, 326, 335, 337
  uneven neoliberal   105
Global Justice   214, 319
global order   43
  more just   42
global partnership for poverty eradication
    and sustainable development   94, 360
global partnership mechanism   107
global partnership model   109
global partnerships   50, 95, 102–3, 108–10,
    112, 219
global player   79
  influential   262
global policies   41, 108, 331
global system   41–43, 99, 139, 176, 208, 286
  equitable   6, 43
goal   66, 75, 80–81, 95, 103, 108, 116, 126, 276,
    279, 286
  aspirational   170
  common   94
  fundamental   81
  ultimate   61, 145, 283, 290
Good faith in international law   210, 341
good governance   3, 103–4, 157–58, 166, 256–
    57, 259–60, 267–68, 348–50
good governance concept   257

good governance ideology 257
good governance in Africa 257
goods 147–48, 178, 210
  imported capital 119
governance 33, 35, 78–79, 147, 262–63, 266–67, 290, 307, 310, 314, 317, 320, 326–27, 349, 351
  democratic 145, 257
  effective 161
  people-centred 256
  political 143, 268
  poor 121
governance and development model 270
Governance and illicit financial flows 272, 345
governance constraints 248
governance in Africa 290
governance malpractices 1, 34, 79
  deep-rooted 268
  internal 293
governance mechanism in Africa 304
governance model 305
  good 259–60
governance model for development 305
governance paradigm 191
governance system 247
  organised 26
government actions 171, 248
government capacities 61
government policy 222, 328
governments 59–60, 146–49, 157–58, 160, 167–68, 170, 172, 191, 204, 228, 231–33, 242, 244–46, 272, 355–56
  guide 184
  home 34
grinding poverty 106
  struggle in 65
ground, high moral 229, 344
group rights 161
groups, marginalised 172
groups of people 168
growth 55, 85, 88, 104, 239, 266, 334, 349–50, 363, 367
  accelerated 65
  domestic 115
  long-term 24, 339
  self-sustaining 88
  sustainable 141, 224
Growth and poverty in developing
  countries 119, 327

growth rates 101, 225
  annual 230
  average per capita 223
  impressive economic 85, 250
growth statistics 224
guarantees 39–40, 58–59, 69–70, 72, 78, 133–34, 136, 139, 153–54, 163–64, 166, 183, 204–5, 211, 215–16, 240, 264–66
  domestic 272
  entitlements 56
  income 57
  legal 52, 95
  theoretical 288
  treaty 227
guarantees entitlement 57, 243
guarantees justice in development 132
guarantees mutuality 108
guarantees state sovereignty 264
guide, interpretative 227, 267, 272, 297, 305
guide development processes 226
guide implementation 273
Guidelines 180, 205, 207, 214, 316, 324, 358
  moral 95
guilt, collective 118

habit 276, 279
habitation 199, 284
habit of hand-stretching for assistance 279
hand
  free 174
  helping 252
hand-stretching for assistance 279
happy planet index criterion 118
hardship 269
  inflicted acute socio-economic 281
Harlow's conception 254
harm 180, 205–6, 208, 213
  avert 213
  irreparable 203, 205–6
harmonising efforts 15
haves 149, 256
HDI country profile 277, 364
health 27, 32, 95, 172, 208, 317, 336–37, 340, 355
  maternal 103
  mental 253, 360
health care 57, 73, 171, 238–39
healthcare facilities 80
health establishments 239

INDEX

389

hegemony 100, 102, 277, 306
Heretical reflections 27, 173, 340
Hidden resource 272, 349
higher levels of economic growth 304
high-handedness 193
Highly Indebted Poor Countries
  (HIPIC) 288, 332
hijacked opportunities 288
hinder development 137, 243
hinder progress 153, 272
hindrances 135, 192, 301
historical disadvantage 76, 203
historical evidence 158
history 11, 19, 30, 73, 87, 112, 190, 278, 288,
  320, 330
  complex development 19
  compromised 293
  distressful 81
  entangled 22
  focus Africa's 20
  legal 240, 331
history of humankind and hijacked
  opportunities for advancement 288
holders 126, 135, 200, 268
  potential 274
holistic concept 55
home-grown alternative model for
  development 6, 15
home-grown model for Africa 267
home-grown substitute to development
  cooperation 291
horizons, new 29
hostile factors 308
housing 58, 72–73, 171, 238
  adequate 263
human activity 303
human beings 23, 62, 134
  free 73
human capabilities 56, 69, 76, 266, 272,
  280, 284
  activating 253
human development 27–29, 34, 118, 164, 168,
  244, 252, 259, 268–69, 343, 351–52
human development index 80, 232, 240,
  244, 277
human development ranking 236
  global 223
human development targets 225
human input, requisite 24

Humanitarian aid and development
  assistance 97, 363
humanitarian emergencies 188, 281, 339
humanitarian interventions 210, 282, 347
  supposed 238
humanity 10, 18, 77, 214, 273, 319, 333
human person 2, 59, 61, 78, 213, 225, 248,
  280, 288
human rights 2–4, 7–8, 18–19, 38–41,
  47–51, 53–59, 61–62, 64–65, 71–75,
  134–39, 156–61, 180–83, 185–91, 208–11,
  257–59, 280–82, 284–89, 313–26, 328–
  54, 356–61
  collective 64
human rights abuses 25, 106, 123–24, 229,
  342, 366
  massive 33
human rights accountability 289, 351
human rights and development in Africa 7,
  16, 83, 295, 321, 323, 338, 344
human rights and foreign direct
  investment 221, 329
Human Rights and Structural
  Adjustment 258, 313
Human Rights-Based Approach to
  Development Cooperation 134
human rights concept 5, 16, 20, 53, 75, 77,
  154, 274, 293–94
human rights entitlements 145, 220
human rights framework 68
human rights impute obligations to non-state
  actors 189
human rights instruments 73, 180, 215
  international 245
human rights law 49, 132, 178–79, 182, 186–
  87, 317
human rights obligations 74, 146, 149, 186–
  87, 276, 282, 284, 319, 342, 354
Human Rights Obligations of Non-State
  Actors 282, 314
human rights offences 40, 45, 209, 287
human rights policy, positive 281, 327
human rights revolution 146, 282, 329
human rights standards 65, 123, 179–80, 282,
  286, 289
  universal 8, 59–60, 145, 180, 309
human rights theory 186
human rights treaties 209
  regional 53, 286

390   INDEX

human rights violations   178, 181, 186, 190,
    207–8, 280, 282–83, 286–88, 346–47,
    351, 356
  endemic   298
  massive   123, 206
human well-being in Africa   131, 297
hybrid African Court of Justice and human
    rights   187

idealism   125, 289, 354
ideals, noble   303
idea of capabilities   13
idea of country ownership of development
    programmes   134
idea of development   19, 39, 44, 54, 59, 142
idea of entitlement   42
idea of equality   42
idea of partnership   93
idea of poverty   67
idea of sovereignty   162
identity   54, 146, 165, 199, 203, 223, 269, 279,
    316, 326, 330
  collective   70
  common   167
  communal   57
  contested   203
  shared   105
ideological affinities   200
ideologies   30, 34–35, 101, 132, 236, 298
  conceived   35
  controversial   245
  imperial   29
  neoliberal   143
  patriarchal   70
  political   116, 237, 298
  western capitalist   87
Illicit financial flows   222, 272, 345, 349,
    352, 363
imbalances   43, 176
  structural   4, 50, 109, 114
IMF Policy Paper   117
immiserization   26
impact   22–24, 83–84, 121, 123, 162–64,
    190–91, 257, 259, 281, 317, 319, 324, 342,
    349–50, 353–54
impediment   39–40, 136, 166, 188
  greatest   35
  structural   108
  systemic   119

imperial influence of foreign
    stakeholders   271
imperialism   24, 28, 124, 238–39, 277, 302,
    313, 367
  British   27, 334
  yoke of   235
imperialistic practices   117, 175, 213, 256
  forestall   33
imperialistic tendencies   218
implementation
  actual   216
  practical   152, 176
implementation model   269
implementation of people-centred
    development policies   139
implementation of structural
    adjustment   258
implication   173, 175, 220–22, 227, 241, 243,
    248, 282, 307–8, 325, 327, 329, 332
important instrument of development
    cooperation   97
imposition   105, 122, 135, 186, 277
  external power   93
impoverished peoples of Africa   80
impoverishment   18, 269, 280
Impressive economic performance   119
improved living standards   65, 147, 169, 226,
    236, 243–45, 261, 275
improved living standards and sustainable
    development   244
improvement
  achieved   98
  constant   140, 175, 212, 244, 253, 283–84,
    286, 292
  sustained   200
Improving aid effectiveness   104, 352
impunity   47, 77, 154, 175–76, 178, 196, 209,
    265, 270, 285, 296–97
  combat   269
  condone   198, 215
  freely and with   195
  reject   178
impunity for non-state actors   196
inclusive growth   85, 224, 304, 359
inclusive growth and sustainable
    development   224
inclusive participation   71
income   58, 73
  national   98, 255

INDEX

income barometer 280
income per capita 80
  increased 27
incompatibilities, global 61
incongruous power imbalance 101
inconsistencies 14, 195, 248
increasing dependence on China for
      development financing 250
indebted poor countries 117, 288, 367
Indebted Poor Countries Initiative 288, 340
independence 25, 30–37, 39–41, 45–47,
      50, 173–74, 216, 221, 228–30, 235, 270,
      274, 367
  achieved 46
  nominal 122
  sustain 34
independence constitutions 34, 37
independence leaders 46
independence of nations 174, 216
independence project 33, 35
independence source of financing for
      development 300
independence to Africa 274
independent development policy
      making 112
in-depth analysis 128
in-depth understanding 305
indeterminate motives of development
      cooperation 86
indigenous peoples 74, 136, 157, 161, 203–4,
      223, 339, 341, 359
  fundamental freedoms of 224, 361
indigenous property rights 26
indigenous rights 185, 228, 338, 351
indigenous territories 273
industrialised countries 6, 21–22, 42, 74, 99,
      101, 117–18, 137, 153, 176, 302
  western 211, 222
ineffective implementation 221, 248–49, 325
inequalities 27, 76, 164, 271, 286
  structural 25, 79, 108, 145
Inevitable conflict 349
influence of foreign stakeholders and
      endemic corruption 248
influx, massive 281
infrastructures, public 80
injustices 44–46, 54, 59, 76, 79–80, 153, 173,
      175, 265, 270, 274
  colonial 28, 47

  endemic 158
  gross 31
  historical 18, 22, 48, 182, 254
  social 70
  systemic 25
innovation system and quality of
      governance 266
innovation system and quality of governance
      for Africa 266
inordinate dependence on development
      cooperation 291
insecurity 136, 254
instability 1, 34, 46, 122, 254
  political 27, 36, 121, 222, 328
institutional development 24, 339
institutional frameworks 87
  domestic 184
  mandated 291
institutional mechanisms 37, 210
  creating new 290
  robust 242
institutional performance 259–60
institutions 55, 91, 118, 120–21, 147, 222, 239,
      248, 328, 334, 340
  accountable 147
  indigenous 203
  strong 309
  weak judicial 25
institutions of governance 147
instruments 56, 59–60, 95–96, 142, 145, 151–
      52, 180–81, 211, 241–42, 275, 281, 296, 299
  ancillary 71, 99, 103, 142, 160, 167, 175, 212
  authoritative normative 160
  constitutive 167
  continental policy 305
  domestic development policy 241
  first hard law 49
  foundational 187
  international 2, 48, 52, 95, 349
  legal 5, 84, 153–55, 178, 216, 228
  NEPAD founding 142
  non-binding 180
  pioneer treaty 159–60
  primary 95
  regional 229
  regulatory 299
  soft law 47, 95, 156
  statutory 36
insufficiencies, democratic 1

INDEX

integration 14, 128, 131, 142, 151, 186, 217, 343, 350
  economic 131, 147
  effective 131
  socio-economic 129, 131
integration of NEPAD 142
interdependence 136, 161, 341
interdict 206–7
interests 5, 50, 88, 91, 96, 98, 106, 128–29, 184, 230, 235–36
  colonial 28
  commercial 92
  common 200
  dominant self-seeking 9
  foreign 27, 130, 237
  geopolitical 116
  ideological 115
  imperialist 162
  legitimate 302
  mutual 105, 128
  nationalistic 150
  politicised 204
  rent-seeking 151
  strategic 115
  vested 8
interests of foreign stakeholders 295
international agreements 243
international arena 144
International Arrangements 302, 320
international community 51, 59, 127, 136, 139, 141, 157, 255, 277–78, 282, 299–300
international cooperation 8–9, 15, 75, 84, 89–91, 107, 114, 208, 213, 219, 351–52
  effective 253
international customary practice 95
international decision processes 116
International Development 88, 94, 96, 100–101, 113–14, 118, 314–15, 322–24, 333–34, 346, 351, 357
international development agencies 89, 144
international development cooperation 88, 96, 100, 313, 337
international disputes 137
International economic governance 289, 351
international human rights law 19, 49, 110, 216, 237, 285, 321, 344, 367–68
international law 7, 32, 39–43, 76–77, 84, 95, 100–101, 109–14, 124, 137–38, 172–74,

180–81, 208–12, 275–76, 295–96, 313–17, 319–22, 324–33, 335–37, 339–41
international law principle 41, 90, 94, 111, 246, 264
international law requirement for development cooperation 157
international law standards 53
international level 43, 47–48, 51, 74, 125, 130–31, 138, 157, 188
international market 23
International Monetary Fund 117–18, 121, 231, 348, 350, 360
international reproach 281
international strategy 116
international trade 23–24, 30, 281, 287, 327, 353
international transactions 92
interpretative ambiguities 228, 338
intervention in Libya 123
interventions 1, 123, 142, 178, 193, 282
  military 281
interventions by foreign stakeholders 142
invasion 22, 24, 59, 234
  colonial-style 202, 273
  foreign 235
investment 85, 361
  securing Chinese 116, 334
investment capital 302
  requisite 302
investment opportunities 92
investment space 224
isolation 47, 297, 306
  diplomatic 277, 281

jeopardise enjoyment 142
judgments, contradictory 188
Judicial enforcement of socio-economic rights in South Africa 138, 263, 339
judicial processes 159, 175, 190, 200, 273, 296, 309
judicial remedies 163, 181, 211, 319
judicial review 246
judiciary 56, 192
juridification 172, 344
jurisdiction 53, 169, 181, 185–89, 209, 211, 286
  criminal 187
  domestic 179, 192
  higher 187, 189

INDEX 393

jurisdictional 209
jurisprudence 95, 194–95, 204–5, 210–11, 219, 233, 246, 331, 334, 341, 344–45
  emerging 211, 346
  established 214
  nascent 185
jurisprudential interpretation 253
jus cogens 108, 183
justice 5–6, 30–31, 75–77, 81, 132–33, 154–55, 160–61, 166–67, 187, 192–93, 204–5, 215, 239–40, 294, 339–40, 358
  dispense 182
  equitable 109
  preventive 78
  redistributive 43, 86, 192
  remedial 48
  reparative 254
  restorative 78, 254
  upholding 269
justice and freedom 6
justice demands offenders 205
justiciability 186, 195–96, 275, 335, 345
justification 5–6, 15, 19, 22, 110–11, 221, 225, 227, 250–51, 262, 266, 291, 294
  fundamental legal 94
  legitimate moral 31

Kenyan government in contravention 273
Kenyan government in violation of provisions 186
Kenyan government's decision 200
Kenyan government's failure 200
Kigali Declaration and Plan of Action 190, 357
knowledge
  generating 311
  working 308
knowledge systems 29

labour, cheap 24, 32
labour camp, massive 26
land 32, 37, 123, 199–200, 202, 223, 239, 242, 273, 325, 329–30
  famished 281, 366
land and resources 223, 328
land dispossession 206
land expropriation 26
landmark judgment 202

land ownership 199
land reform policies, controversial 281
landscape 100, 341
  new development cooperation 85, 333
largest number of people 249
largest provider of development assistance 278
law
  apartheid 26
  applicable 188
  binding 126
  enforcing 25
  fundamental statute 46
  hard 47
  national 188, 246
  positive 159
  soft 3, 51
  supreme 242
law and legal reasoning 251
law and order 27
lawful recovery 206
law guarantees 174
law obligates 177
Law on Human Rights and Development in Africa 131
law perspective 26, 338
law to remedy development injustices 87
Lawyers' Committee 259, 317
leaders 270, 308
  emerging 308
  progressive 130
  transformative 33, 262
  unprepared 37
leadership 33, 147, 164, 261–63, 306–8, 313–14, 327, 335, 345
  committed 262
  contemporary 261
  corrupt 289
  effective 134
  insensible 1
  irresponsible 35
  repressive 236, 238
  transactional 262
  transformational 307
  unfocused 262
  visionary 260
Leadership and Performance 262, 313
leadership and stakeholder structures 147

Leadership Effectiveness 262, 314
leadership for the disillusioned 262, 343
leadership in Africa 307
leadership theories 262
  transactional 262, 340
least developed 288
left Africa's precious resources and
    people 290
legacy 18, 22–23, 25, 54, 81, 261, 271
  communal 162
legal action 53, 163, 181, 192, 198, 205, 285
  joint 181
legal argument 172
legal arrangements 176
Legal Assistance 205, 358
legal barriers 135, 340
legal basis 87, 208
legal capacity to access 275
Legal culture and transformative
    constitutionalism 270, 335
legal duty, primary 175
legal duty of states governments 307
legal entitlements 4, 44, 56, 59, 146, 154,
    271, 294
  absolute 50
  claimable 18
legal experts 48
legal framework 46, 49, 75–76, 81, 90, 95, 151,
    246, 266, 271
  domestic 242
legal framework for development
    cooperation 95
legality 26, 60, 94, 242, 269, 272
legal norms 94
  international 281
legal obligations 69, 75, 88–89, 95, 99, 126–
    27, 139, 146, 182, 186, 209, 214, 220
  relevant 114
legal obligations stemming 86
legal processes 56, 159, 192, 217
legal protection 36, 181, 270
  guaranteed 51–52
legal question 158
legal reasoning 251
legal recognition 19, 43, 49, 51, 110, 223
  domestic 250
legal relationships 274
legal remedy 274
legal representatives 184

legal requirement for development
    cooperation 95
legal responsibility 47, 176–77, 179, 198, 207,
    215, 220
  direct 135, 198
  double 177
legal status 20, 53, 110, 125, 211, 347
legal strategy 76
legal theory 99, 211
legislation 184, 309
  appropriate 294
  comprehensive 245
  domestic 96, 132, 170, 175, 179,
    275, 305–6
  enacted 186
legislative framework, appropriate 263
legitimacy 18–19, 32, 60, 102, 140, 166, 239,
    242, 275
legitimacy in development cooperation 140
legitimate expectations 111, 248
level of penetration by foreign
    stakeholders 150
levels of economic growth 304
leverage, global economic 306
lex ferenda 179
lex lata 186, 212
liabilities 178–79, 189, 212, 216, 285
  corporate 187
liabilities to foreign stakeholders 216
Liability for Foreign Stakeholders and Non-
    state Actors 179
liability of foreign stakeholders on
    violations 285
liberation 30, 33, 35–36, 40, 76, 78
  political 34
  total 235
liberation leaders 32–34
liberation struggles 30
liberty 45, 52, 55, 69–70, 96, 98, 161, 165, 173–
    74, 266, 271, 273, 275
  civil 34, 36
  political 160, 280
Libya 123–24, 134–35, 226–27, 234–40,
    245, 277, 282, 285, 315, 347, 349–50,
    358, 363–64
  constrained 278
  destabilised 135
Libyan people 235–36, 238–39, 277, 282
Libyan sanctions experience 277, 350

INDEX 395

Libya's autonomy 235
life expectancy 27, 238, 285
lifestyle 238
  cultural 199
  modern 57
lifestyle characteristics 57
life-support of development assistance 103
limitations 100, 196
  structural 14
litigating 192–93, 297
litigation
  private law 189
  public interest 172, 193, 352
livelihood 33, 58, 64, 194, 202, 245, 303
  decent 136
  human 186
  improved 75, 126, 133, 140, 232
  sustainable 160
  sustained 236, 283
livelihood circumstances 225, 263, 307
livelihood exigencies 308
livelihood security 103–4, 249
livelihood sustainability challenges 248
livelihood sustainability issues 287
livelihood value 260
living conditions 78, 100, 104, 231, 258,
    264, 306
  better 281
living standards 1, 5, 26, 164, 168, 171, 225,
    228, 242, 244, 248–49, 303–4, 308
  improving 248
  raised 124
  securing better 2
living standards and sustainable
    development 244
loans 121, 259
  foreign 121
local development 244, 330
local economic initiatives 148
local productivity 148
local realities 29, 135, 273
local remedies 187–88, 190, 233, 309
  exhausted 187
logistical difficulties 193
long-term effects 22, 339
looting 26, 28, 198, 235
low income countries 117, 329
low standards 1, 310
  sustaining 213

Maastricht Guidelines on Violations 178,
    286, 357
Maastricht Principles on Extraterritorial
    Obligations of States 177, 208, 220,
    295, 331, 358
macro-economic policies 258
  well-intentioned 120
mainstreaming 145, 165–66, 299
  committed 300
Major Impediments 256
Management 121, 233, 262, 307, 319, 336, 340
  sustainable 260, 266
Mandated Entities 226
manifestation 292
  poignant 101
mankind 54, 146, 162, 165, 203, 269, 339,
    343–44, 367
mankind principle 162, 335
Mapping donor strategies 176, 346
marginalisation 254
  continuous 233
marginalisation of the poor 259
marginalised status 163
marginalising treatment, alleged 233
marketable commodities 302
market alternatives 176
market opportunities 92, 115
market size 222, 328
mass, sustained 26
masses 238
  impoverished 236
massive acquisition of independence 7
material benefits 60
material possessions 243
material resources 22, 252, 290
  raw 303
matter of governance 310
Mau forest 202–4, 206, 330, 352
Maximising benefits 221
means and facilities, appropriate 219
measurement 118, 120, 258, 267, 316, 323
measures
  adequate 113
  appropriate 60, 126, 138, 163, 204–5, 207,
    263, 308
  concrete 4, 164, 292
  counter 300
  effective 267
  legislative 128, 168, 183, 242

396 INDEX

measures *(cont.)*
   practical 158, 184, 282, 305
   precautionary 162, 184
   pre-emptive 280
   preliminary 174, 309
   redistributive 249
   regulatory 178, 265
   remedial 207
mechanism 2, 5, 9–10, 18–19, 22, 50, 86, 89,
   95–96, 112, 114, 181–82, 218–19
   active enforcement 213
   alternative remedy 190
   clear enforcement 227
   development funding 300
   domestic governance 166
   framework policy 141
   functional 109, 150, 187, 242, 308
   functional framework 147
   independent 143
   inevitable 147
   judicial remedy 192
   non-adversarial 190
   peer review 143
   protective 148
   regional 290
   regulatory 221, 225
   safeguard 211
mechanism of development assistance 96
mechanism of development cooperation 1,
   8, 16, 75, 82, 87, 100, 110, 295
member states 88, 127, 129, 133–34, 149–50,
   156–57, 159, 165, 227, 290, 305
   individual 227
merit 120
middle income 117
militarised operational commands 231
military disruptions 122
Military Disruptions Post-independence
   Africa 122
military expedition 124
military expedition in Libya 124
military operations 130, 207
military support 123
   unremitting 123
Millennium Development Goals 50, 61, 95,
   103, 108, 219, 276, 286, 350, 360–61, 363
mineral exploitation arrangements 222, 352
Minerals flow 222, 334

minimal extent 204
minimum wage 235
minority groups 185
Minority Rights Development 51, 183, 185,
   193, 198, 253, 351, 355
Minority Rights Group International 51, 183,
   193, 198, 202, 204, 253, 353, 355, 362
mobilisation 144, 276, 300–301
modalities
   device 302
   functional 253, 296
   operational 90, 92–94, 99, 104, 142
   practical 15
   recommended 86
modalities for integrated governance 297
modality of development cooperation 253
model
   applicable 2, 265, 298
   capability 253
   conceptual 262, 335
   holistic 268
   home-grown 4, 6, 266–67, 297, 299, 306
   home-growth 17
   imported 38, 260
   indigenous 28, 327
   innovative 265
   paternalistic 1, 18, 308
   post-independence 228
   pragmatic 34
   pre-existing 218, 292
   prevailing 273
   rights-based 297
   standardised 306
   unique 236
model for governance 191
Modern African 230
modernisation 76
modernity 11, 83, 337
modo-colonialism 130
modus operandi 85, 111, 143
monist theories 127, 346
monitoring and evaluation of Agenda 147
monitoring mechanism 184, 209
   universal 210
Monterrey Consensus on Financing for
   Development 99
Monterrey International Conference on
   Financing for Development 94

INDEX

moral character 50
moral conscience 136
moral obligations, positive 76
moral undertaking 156
motivation 95–96, 114, 129, 303
    primary 28, 118
motives 91–92, 105, 113, 124, 295, 353
    humanitarian 92
    mercantile 92
    primary 91, 120
movement 147
    radical opposition 231
movements, positive 224
multidimensional processes 78
multilateral forums 115
multilateralism 107, 153, 228, 353
Multilateralism and Global Partnership 107
multinational corporations 88, 186–87, 196,
    198, 207, 328
    foreign 301
mutual accountability and responsibility and
    policy space 298
Mutual Reinforcement 131, 313

narratives 170
    parochial Eurocentric 12
    reinvented universal 11
    standard theoretical 11
national constitutions 52, 127, 146, 172, 183,
    189, 191, 355
national development 169, 171, 199, 243, 245,
    253, 261, 268, 326
national development planning 163, 226, 245
national development policy
    framework 245
National Economic Empowerment and
    Development Strategy 247
national economy 239
    productive 239
national gross domestic product 99
national human rights institutions 73, 190–
    91, 320, 348–49, 357
National Implementation 139, 319
nationalisation 235
national issues 237
national levels 74, 182, 190, 309
nations 21, 44, 105, 108, 169, 174, 216, 231,
    243–44, 306, 363

civilised 210
    individual 88
native lands 26
NATO assault on Libya 282
NATO intervention 124, 135, 238, 285, 363
    humanitarian 285
natural resource endowments 102, 222
natural resources 76, 79, 167–68, 174, 195,
    197–98, 200, 202, 222–24, 228, 230, 302
natural socialism 135
natural wealth 153, 222, 278
    domestic 237
natural wealth and resources 40, 69, 79, 81,
    119, 148, 162, 171, 250
nature
    abstract 197
    asymmetrical 112
    authoritative 239
    binding 163, 189
    collective 63, 70, 132, 172
    composite 161
    conceptual 15, 20, 54, 271, 291
    cultural 84, 90, 103, 280
    dual 63
    environmental 8
    humanitarian 58, 107
    intangible 206
    legal 59, 61, 194
    mutual 93
    patronising 260
    pragmatic 20, 298
    theoretical 20
nature of development cooperation 275
nature of remedies 194, 205, 305
negative balance sheet 120
negative obligation 10, 77, 206, 213, 306
neocolonialism 33, 43, 332
neoliberal 149, 300
neo-liberal understanding 71
NEPAD and human rights 176, 336
NEPAD mechanism 149
NEPAD programme 141–42
NEPAD's transformation 144, 365
new definition of development
    cooperation 89
New Directions 162, 319
new frontiers 260
new frontiers of assistance 260

New momentum 208, 328
New Partnership for Africa's Development/
    African Union 141
New Partnership for Africa's Development
    Declaration 141
New players 87
new system of governance 35
NHRC 247
NHRI 146–47, 190–91
    projects 147
NIEO campaign 41–42
Niger Delta 194
Nigerian government in complicity 195
Nigerian government in Ogoniland 194
Nigerians, impoverished 250
Nigeria's ratification 246
Nigeria's underdevelopment 248, 332
Non-Aligned Movement 88
non-binding rulings 204
non-governmental organisations 192
    accredited 193
    based 202
non-regression 283
non-state actors 175, 177–78, 180–82, 187,
    189, 194–96, 208–10, 212, 282, 286–87,
    294–95, 309, 314
    foreign 53
    territorial 282, 342
non-state actors and foreign
    stakeholders 189, 209, 212, 294
non-state actors and states in international
    law 282, 295, 331
non-violation 212
normative framework 9, 354
normative impact 167
normativity 51
norms 41, 76, 133, 140, 154
    derivative 11
    established 41
    global 12, 251, 261, 289
    universal 53
North Atlantic Treaty Organisation 123, 238
North-South aid conditionality strategy 103
north-south cooperation principles 104, 353
North-South cooperation structure 103
North-South development cooperation 102
North-South donors 105
North-South pattern 105, 107
    dominant 104

number
    good 194
    growing 224
    largest 25, 249
    requisite 187
    total 23, 122
    unprecedented 88

OAU Charter 15, 31, 37–38, 81
objectives
    implementable 145
    intended 258
    national 170–71, 246
    primary 129, 220
obligation of African states 177
obligation on state parties 165, 175, 263
obligations 60, 72–73, 96–97, 113, 125–26,
    133–34, 137–38, 140, 145–46, 175, 177–83,
    185–86, 208–9, 211–12, 242, 263–64, 274–
    76, 280, 304–5, 307–8
    absolute 95, 112, 183
    collective 114, 129
    concrete 304
    constitutional 168, 183, 261
    core 182
    corporate 183, 361
    duty-bearer 147
    explicit 112
    extra-territorial 208, 340
    governmental 196
    international 170, 282
    justiciable 171
    mutual 75
    positive 77, 301
    primary 215
    reciprocal 94
    state's 126, 183
    universal 209, 352
obligation to take other measures 138, 263
observations 149, 209, 290, 294
ODAs 89, 96, 199, 231, 278, 340, 364
    net 232
ODA target 255
OECD 8, 85, 87–88, 90–91, 134, 163, 221, 230,
    232, 255, 366
OECD Convention 180
OECD-DAC, 96, 118, 350
OECD-DAC doctrine 107
OECD-DAC rules 104

INDEX 399

official development assistance   87–88, 91,
    96, 231, 278, 340, 347–48
Official Development Assistance
    Target   96, 357
often-uncontainable actions of foreign
    stakeholders   215
often-unresponsive   146
Ogiek Community   183, 186, 192, 202–7, 264,
    283–84, 355
    indigenous   264
Ogiek judgment   205
Ogiek peoples   202–3, 205
Ogiek Peoples' Development
    Programme   202–3
Ogoni crisis   210, 349
Ogoniland   194
    the destruction of the   195
Ogoni people   194–95, 207
OIC member countries   98
oil   198, 235, 366
    crude   194, 249
oil economy   235
oil spills, massive   194
oil wealth   236, 278
    people's   195
on-the-ground realities, practical   292
Operational Considerations   279
operational difficulties   81
operational modalities for development
    cooperation   93
operational model   2, 15, 33, 36, 227, 235,
    256, 293
    solid   46
operational principle, established   299
operational processes   205
operational strategy   141, 144
operations of foreign stakeholders   309
opportunities for economic growth   121
opposition   11
    anti-French   231
    direct   297
    political   123
    radical   231
optimistic interpretation   27
order
    judicial   214
    new global economic   43
    new international economic   8, 39, 42–
    43, 176, 329

Order for Provisional Measures   203
Organisation of African Unity Cairo
    Egypt   160
orientation   89
    developmental   36
    people-centred   149
origins
    actual   20
    historical   23, 366
    remote   21
origins of development cooperation   86–87
orthodox understanding   54, 63
outcomes
    alternative   251
    anticipated   154, 174, 216
    direct   249
    expected   99
    outlined measurable   305
    practical   99, 118
    substantive   78–80
overarching status   170
overbearing influence of foreign
    stakeholders   265
over-dependence on development
    cooperation   267
overseas territories   102
ownership   55, 69, 149, 171, 197, 202, 296
    communal   162
    domestic   108, 112
    effective   79
    private   239
    public   239
ownership rights, first   223

pace   108, 144
    slow   248
pace for development in developing
    countries   108
pacta sunt servanda   111, 210
pan-African Congresses   33
pan-African Development Fund   302
pan-Africanism   298
paradigms   10–11, 15, 83–84, 218, 221, 226, 234,
    265, 291, 333
    aid effectiveness   42, 96, 352
    colonial   11, 256, 344
    dominant   76
    established   296
    new   10, 68, 141, 265, 273, 297, 343

400 INDEX

paradigms   (*cont.*)
  a new global economic   273
  new global economic   68
  operational   45, 267
  political-economy   12, 41, 333
  standard-setting   175
  western capitalist   215
paradigm shift   18, 292, 294, 296, 298
parliamentary processes   127
participant, active   78
participation   52, 55, 89, 94, 165, 169, 232,
    236, 243–45, 249, 259, 261
  active   71, 79, 163, 288, 310
  civic   26
  youth   165
participation and freedom   42
participatory and accountable institutions of
    governance   147
participatory processes   71
particularities, regional   53
parties   9, 126, 133, 183, 189, 203, 212, 220,
    274–75, 285–86
  defaulting   281
  non-state   185, 209, 215
partners   61, 79, 91, 94
partnership   93–94, 105, 115, 135, 230, 252,
    287, 300, 328, 332, 347
  developed countries conceptualise   93
  equal horizontal   107
  equitable   88
  international   143
  supposed South-South   115
part of foreign stakeholders   143
party dictatorship, single   46
paternalism   100–101, 290
paternalistic   16, 100, 112
paternalistic colonial models   10
paternalistic nature of development
    cooperation   4, 83
patriarchal cultures   164
patriarchal forms   118
patrimonialism   29, 229
patronage   83, 100, 211, 301
patronise recipient countries   96
patronising nature of development
    cooperation   99, 280, 291, 295
patterns of development cooperation   93,
    102, 142

payment   202, 273
  compulsory   301
payments, requisite   302
peace   103, 132, 136–37, 158, 270, 349
  international   136–37
  post-war   21
peace and good governance   158
peer review processes   142
penetration   150
penetration by foreign stakeholders   150
people-centred development   104
peoples
  all   204, 223
  decolonised   274
  empowered   268
  local   210
  marginalised   289
  ordinary   34
  subjugated   234, 270
  young   149, 165
Peoples' capability   287
peoples in developing countries   62
peoples in recipient countries   104
peoples of Africa   1–2, 4–5, 29–32,
    67–70, 78–80, 111–13, 133–34, 144–49,
    153–54, 173–75, 182–85, 215–18, 253–54,
    263–65, 271, 279–80, 292, 294–96, 302–
    4, 306–11
peoples of Africa entitlement to actual
    self-determination   216
peoples of Africa in confrontational court
    battles   191
peoples of Africa in subordination to foreign
    domination   292
peoples of Africa to claim entitlement to
    development   295
peoples of Africa to global patterns of
    coloniality   296
Peoples' Rights   1, 48, 167, 184, 241, 246,
    287, 305
per capita incomes, highest   285
perception of global partnership   109
perceptions   4, 85, 95, 100, 109, 122, 124, 218–
    19, 276, 278, 281
  functionalist   76
  generic   291
  mainstream   223
  opposed   29

INDEX

401

shallow 29
subjective 210
performance 30, 154, 168, 262, 300, 313, 348
performance of African governments 300
period
   colonial 25–26, 202
   extended five-year 247
   record 148
perpetrating military assaults 123
perpetrator, actual 208
Perpetuating Poverty 278, 318, 321
persistent sabotage 86
persistent search 260
persistent search for new frontiers of
   assistance 260
personality cult 229
persons, young 165
perspective
   conceptual 100, 334
   development agency 132, 347
   divergent 4, 210
   global 26, 331
   historical 22
   regional 44, 132, 158, 233, 325
   rights-based 61, 101, 346
   theoretical 288, 332
   women's rights 42, 96, 352
   youth 165
phenomenal flow of development assistance
   to Africa 98
philanthropic organisations 301
planned liberalism 228
platform 84, 102, 108, 182, 191, 297, 300
   institutional 226
   legitimate 216
   political 40
   unified 130
platform of self-determination 40
plunging depression 120
policies 109, 111, 140, 176–77, 233–34, 236–37,
   243, 246–47, 263–64, 292–94, 305–6,
   318–19, 325–26, 339–41, 347
   appropriate 268, 291
   common 128
   continental 297, 302
   controversial 121
   decisive 298
   fiscal 153

   government's 236
   independent 297
   national 188
   progressive 228
   resolute 308
   revolutionary 236
   robust 302
   tailored 129, 298, 310
policies on development assistance 109
policy agenda 55, 273
policy alternatives 140, 285, 295, 348
policy choices 67, 248, 287, 290
   relevant 296
policy decisions 129
policy dimensions 158, 225
policy direction 191, 226
policy formulation 89, 140
   domestic 234, 240
   independent 218, 237
   orients 297
policy framework 141, 247, 256, 265,
   273, 300
   common 303
   domestic 245
   effective national development 140
   enabling people-centred pro-poor 245
   politicised 245
policy imperatives 294
   relevant 292
policy implementation 248, 336
policy instruments 271
policy measures 17, 74, 264, 273, 292, 301
   domestic 80
   regulatory 215
policy mechanism 265
policy recommendations 6
   ECA 149
policy reforms 154, 158, 168, 217, 228, 234
policy space 129, 298, 310
policy statement 231
policy structure 265
policy tool 175, 258, 265, 267, 291
political action 246, 299, 309, 354
political ambitions 308
political choices 274
   making 308
political conduct 144
political conscience 33

402 INDEX

political development 35, 50, 53, 57–58, 78, 108, 135, 149, 160–61, 327, 333
political economy 101, 346
political elites 37
political function of development policy making 132
political independence 25, 34, 41, 47, 160, 216, 303
  craved 34
  nominal 35, 47, 174, 290
political issues 58, 103
political kingdom 34, 46
Political leaders 263, 353
political leadership 76, 78, 144, 149, 248, 261–63, 281, 307–8, 332
  naive 260
  strategic 307
political leadership and governance 78
political leadership in Africa 144, 307–8
political nature and indeterminate motives of development cooperation 86
Political Perspectives 97, 334
political pluralism 239
political processes 192
political rights 39, 56, 58–59, 103, 136, 143, 155, 161, 173, 183, 191
political rights guarantees 171
political solution 205
political status 140, 174, 264
Political theories 176
Political theories of development cooperation 84, 208, 352
political turmoil 231
politicised account 76
politics 33–34, 37, 81–82, 95, 210–11, 219–21, 257, 262, 316–18, 320, 323–24, 329, 331–36
  domestic 79
  global 5, 12, 79, 288
  international 238, 320
  mainstream 205
  multiparty 168, 230, 349
  multi-party 120, 228, 328
Politics in Francophone Africa 122, 130, 153, 228, 317
politics of development assistance 81
polities 27
  functional 23

poor countries 76, 102, 115, 244, 276
  heavily indebted 288
Poor domestic political organisation 238
poorest, ranked 235
popular participation 64, 71, 266, 269–70, 356
population groupings 223
populations
  adult 28
  country's 223, 249
  indigenous 157
  large European settler 32
  largest 249
  local 26, 28
population size 202, 250
posit 189, 254
  dependency theorists 233
positions
  common 129
  common policy 299
  economic 43
  privileged 113
  recipient 117
  structured 117
  subordinate 74
positions of political leadership in Africa 308
post-2015 development agenda 129–30, 346, 350
Post-apartheid South Africa 225–27, 240, 270
Postcolonial constitutions 35, 323
post-colonial development 38, 336
post-colonial forces 42
post-colonial inequality 105
Post-continental interventions 11, 83, 336
post-independence difficulties 36, 235
post-independence model for development 228
post-independence strategy 37
poverty 25–26, 66, 76, 98, 106, 221–22, 225, 248–50, 270–71, 276, 286–88, 310, 313, 318, 321, 326–27, 345–46, 360–61
  eradicating 67, 353
  excruciating 130, 169, 250
  extreme 50, 103, 249–50
  global 50, 354, 365
  perpetual 115

INDEX

poverty and social inequality 106
poverty bracket 249
  extreme 250
poverty-clock 249
poverty eradication 9, 68, 94, 109, 249, 288,
    310, 339, 345, 349, 360
  ancillary 247
poverty in developing countries 119, 327
poverty levels 244, 263
poverty reduction 89, 105, 321, 348
poverty reduction initiatives 176
poverty reduction programs 248, 337
poverty reduction strategy 248, 269, 341, 351
poverty situation 230
power 11, 37, 41, 52, 122–23, 220, 222, 231,
    234–35, 238, 274
  colonial 148, 229
  economic 90
  foreign 237
  imperial 121
  making 223
  rising 100, 219, 337
  western 92, 235
power dynamics 232
  global 306
power imbalances 67, 101, 347
power matrix 4
power relations 94
  asymmetrical 12
practical assurances of freedom 288
practical dimensions of development
    cooperation 86
practice examples, good 226
practices 23–24, 70, 72, 106–7, 110, 112, 125,
    127, 137, 172–73, 175–76, 243–44, 313–16,
    321–22, 324–26
  administrative 190
  conservative 51
  corrupt 248, 332
  cultural 199
  customary 57
  discriminatory 136, 164, 233
  globalisation 284
  imperialist 87
  institutional 129
  legal 77
  OECD-DAC 104
  paternalistic 221

pragmatic concept 68, 111, 218
pragmatic option 282
pragmatism 12, 99, 154–55
  complacent 12, 99, 154, 343
the pragmatist and the feminist 12, 99, 154, 341
pre-condition 190, 259
  important 136
precondition for resource exploitation by
    foreign stakeholders 302
pre-eminence 112
premise 114
  central 259
prerequisites 154, 167
prerogatives 104, 204
pressure 123
  international 277
pretext 210, 282
Pretoria Declaration 59, 157, 358
prevailing patterns of development
    cooperation 5, 128
preventive measures 126
  necessitating 280
price, heavy 223, 349
prices 119, 154
  commodity 257
  increasing 231
principle of self-determination 32, 112, 134
principles 39–40, 53, 58, 72–73, 76–77, 90–
    91, 95, 100–101, 107–8, 132–33, 136–38,
    155–56, 162–64, 178–80, 187–88, 205–7,
    210, 214, 319–20, 357–58
  abstract 267, 273
  applicable 184
  characteristic 94
  defining 94
  democratic 268
  established 126
  foundational 286
  standard 220
principles of political pluralism and
    statehood 239
principles of sovereign equality and self-
    determination of states 93, 175
priorities
  alternative 109, 296
  developmental 252
  development governance model
    accords 297

404 INDEX

priorities (*cont.*)
 dominant 92
 first 224
 international 139
 low 116
 people-centred 113
 strategic 303
prioritise 6, 48, 58, 65–66, 85, 109, 130, 216,
  219, 232, 292
priority development projects 144
priority measures 294, 299
priority recommendations 148, 345
privatisation 257–58, 330
privatised public enterprises 258
privilege 27, 103, 206, 234
privileged persons 106
pro-activeness 130
problem Africa, actual 213
problems
 addressing contemporary 293
 cultural 91
 developmental 76
 global 87, 107
 historical 63
 international 58, 95
 legal 18–19, 251
 perennial 12
 recurrent 260
 resolving 108
 unsolvable 114
problem solving, global 100
Procedural Considerations 192
procedural measures, generous 192
procedure
 formal 127
 individual complaints 214, 340
processes, integrated 54, 75
processes of development cooperation 164
proclamations 33, 43–45, 47, 309, 357
production, commercial 24, 235
production function 304
productive capabilities 13, 79, 98, 148, 223,
  265, 289, 302, 304
 collective 307
 human 243
 local 302
profit maximisation 87
program development process 165
programme, appropriate 124

Programme of Activities 254, 358
programmes
 strategic 247
 youth 165–66
programmes implementation 97
progress 88, 93, 98, 109–11, 213, 215, 291, 297,
  313, 316, 322
progress in developing countries 93
project
 conservation 199
 de-colonisation 290
 economic integration 230, 328
 infrastructural 27, 304
 pragmatic 12
 unfinished 12
 virtuous 106
 wildlife 201
proliferation 122, 146
 weapons 124
Promises 199
promises of development assistance 111
Promoting Development 65
Promoting Progress 278, 318, 321
Promoting real reform in Africa 143, 322
promotion and protection of human
  rights 97, 171, 252, 354
property 12, 99, 154, 330, 343
 economic 24
property ownership 57, 235
proponents of independence 46
proposition, normative 52
proprietary rights 223
prosperity 89, 98, 236, 239
prosperity and freedom 98
protecting human rights 73, 131, 179
protection 16, 18–19, 47, 49, 62, 124, 146–47,
  160, 166–67, 181–85, 211, 216–17, 247,
  282, 323
 adequate 77, 185, 192, 195, 197
 effective 184, 186, 209
 guaranteed constitutional 241
 international 19, 170, 334
 missing 208
 requisite 182
 social 145
protection to developing countries 124
Protocol
 additional 182, 185, 301, 304–5
 special 304

INDEX

provider, largest 278
Province 172, 355
provisional measures 203, 205–6
provision for development
 assistance 86, 139
provision for development cooperation 95
provision of aid by developed countries 96
provision of assistance 93
provision of development assistance 8, 85,
 96, 103–4, 208, 212, 252, 256, 262, 277
provisions 53–54, 69–70, 74, 78, 95–97, 138–
 39, 160, 165–67, 169–71, 177–78, 181–82,
 189, 192–93, 195–96, 200–203, 211–12,
 226, 240, 244–46, 286–87
 abstract 211
 binding 38
 complement 304
 continuous 113
 contravened 198
 rights-proclaiming 170
 statutory 154
 treaty 127, 164, 289
provisions stipulate 177
psychological comfort 117
psychology of global inequality 11, 83, 327
public pronouncement, first 43
purpose
 ancillary 112
 common 90, 128
 defined 149
 developmental 96
 economic 224
 imperialistic 118
 intended 87
purposive 16, 172, 240
pursuit of development cooperation 309

Qaddafi's policies 236
Qaddafi's reign 234
quality 143, 168, 236, 247, 316, 322, 348
quality of governance 266
quasi-judicial body 206
question, important 4, 98, 129, 188, 192
quota 256

races 26, 48
 black 26
Racial Discrimination 51, 156, 254, 357
Racism 51, 156, 254, 357

racist articulations 70
raid, slave 24
ratification 127, 148, 150, 166–67, 169, 187–88,
 247, 301, 355
 achieved record 80
 historic 148
 subsequent 141
Ratification of African Union 127, 336
raw materials 92, 119, 154, 222
realisation, collective 301
realisation demands 74
Realisation of social and economic
 rights 213, 332
realism 125, 289, 354
reality
 actual 86
 global 215–16
recipient country performance 143
recipients, passive 75, 269
recipients of development assistance 89
reciprocal effect 107
reciprocity 93
recognition 8–9, 13, 18–19, 30, 32, 47–48, 55,
 57, 59–60, 62, 64, 146, 149
 additional doctrinaire 183
 collective 271
 constitutional 229, 244
 implicit 171
 mutual 21
 subsequent 146
Recognition and Representation in
 Cameroon 229, 316
recommendations 15, 184, 214, 233, 249,
 298–99, 334, 353
 making 191
recommendations to governments 184
Reconstruction, socio-cultural 34
recourse to development cooperation 4, 13,
 18, 50, 52, 219, 293
recovery strategy 120
rectification 286, 341
Redesigning cooperation 228, 340
redistribution 224
 equitable 55, 140, 149, 236, 250, 263, 267,
 279, 307
 favoured fair 237
 necessitated socialist 236
redress 39, 43, 76–77, 152–53, 155, 158, 160,
 192–93, 196, 207–8, 250, 254, 298

406   INDEX

redress   (*cont.*)
   appropriate   184, 190
   necessitating   45
redressing   14, 16, 50, 108, 188, 217, 224, 260
redressing underdevelopment   20
redress violations   206
reduction   93, 235, 257, 316
re-examination, critical   33, 332
refocus development   308
reforms   184, 213, 318, 333, 340, 359
   agricultural   258
   constitutional   185
   cultural   235
   domestic legal   185
   far-reaching   170, 342
   institutional   144
   political   146, 260
   public sector   267
refusal   25, 213, 231
regard to cases   189
regime   183, 208, 217, 281, 366
   free trade   42
   legal   9
regime change   282
regime change in Libya   282
Regional Economic Communities   150, 325
regional integration   85, 131, 149–50, 359
Regional systems   186, 364
regression   59–60, 206, 239, 283, 285
regulating development practice   131
regulatory framework for mineral
    exploitation arrangements in
    Cameroon   222, 352
rehabilitation   205
reinforcing   109, 214, 272, 338
reinforcing disarmament efforts   123
rejecting dependency on development
    assistance   279
relations   53–54, 128, 132–33, 136, 216, 219,
    226–27, 230, 234, 243, 291–92, 295–96,
    300–301
   colonial   12
   friendly   32, 58, 77, 95, 173, 357
   global economic   77
   imperial   229
   jeopardise   234
   lopsided   233
relationship   98, 115, 189, 229, 261, 346

asymmetrical   101, 261
causal   111
complex   68
dependency-based   252
horizontal   105
lopsided donor/recipient   102
post-colonial   87
special   232, 365
relevance of good governance   259
reliance   15, 99, 141, 167, 276
reliance on development assistance   99
remedies to Africa's development
    setbacks   10
remedy development injustices   87
remedy violations   178, 212
remodelling development   228
rent-seeking interests of foreign
    stakeholders   151
re-orientating   146
reparations   25, 198, 204–6, 254, 342
reparations nexus   254, 322
representation   118, 229, 274, 316
   legal   193
repression on Libya   237
reputation   127, 147
requirement
   conditionality   3
   guidelines   271
   legal   95
   normative   131, 133, 294
   resource availability   222
requirement of development
    cooperation   1, 4, 20
research   184, 260, 263, 298, 300
   policy-oriented   299
   sustained evidence-based   310
resentment   22, 238
   ignited   28
reservation   286
   expressed   50
reserves   153
   mineral   278
   national   153
resilience   45, 204, 222, 249, 316, 330
resilient imperial/colonial reason   70
resistance   11, 30, 157, 176, 220, 334
   obdurate   260
resistance movements   28

INDEX

resolute combination 307

Resolving Claims 133, 314

resonance 260, 273

resource ownership 223–24

    natural 204

Resource Potential 276

resources 26–27, 67, 69, 79–81, 148, 154, 162,
    168–69, 171, 219, 221–24, 232, 276–79,
    289, 301

    aquatic 222

    basic 58, 73

    communal 273

    continent's 256, 279, 302

    country's 24, 237, 258

    fauna 278

    human 38

    left Africa's precious 290

    oil-rich 116

    requisite 144, 276, 303

resources for development 223

respondent state 71, 233

responsibility 70, 73, 75, 112–14, 124, 180, 190,
    208–9, 220, 282, 296, 298, 308, 338, 340

    actual 112, 286

    associated legal 155, 176

    central 73

    differentiated 42, 101, 174, 176, 219, 298,
    310, 339, 347

    direct 125

    individual 125

    interpretative 56

    moral 75, 102, 307

    primary 73, 126, 139, 177

    right-bearer 147

    shared 94, 128, 147, 151

    state's 126

responsibility convey, differentiated 310

responsibility of foreign stakeholders 180

The responsibility to protect and protection
    of civilians 124, 282, 351

responsiveness 53, 272

restitution 199, 201–2, 205–6, 273

restrained action 213

    necessitating 60

restraints 10, 173, 212, 239

result of assistance 117

retarded development 218

retarded progress 15

retrenchments 257

    massive 120

revolution 134–35, 146, 236, 238–39, 315

revolutionary form 11

Rhodesia 277, 319, 337, 348, 359

right balance 122

right direction 36

right holders 18, 111, 126, 134, 138, 190

    individual 172

right judgment 269

right of participation and ownership 55

right of victims 207

rights 7–8, 18, 20–21, 42–45, 49, 51–52, 55–
    57, 59–60, 72–74, 137, 154–57, 159–63,
    171–72, 186, 194–96, 213–14, 239–43,
    297–98, 341–45, 365–67

    substantive 57

Rights and economic growth 65, 349

rights and freedoms 45, 242

rights-based approaches 5, 65–66, 137, 141,
    145–46, 286, 289, 330, 333, 349, 354

    human 134, 190, 244, 326, 348, 359

rights-based approach to development
    cooperation 286

rights-based approach to economic
    growth 200

rights-based development 44, 257, 336

rights-based process 81, 305

rights of indigenous peoples 74, 136, 161,
    203, 341, 359

rights of peoples 7, 89, 171, 314, 326, 344

Rights of Women in Africa 51, 57, 71, 96, 110,
    132, 160, 163, 241–42, 358

rights protection 160

    human 14, 167, 192, 340

rights provisions 194, 241

    human 171, 209, 241, 342

    socio-economic 172

rights to improved living standards 243, 245

rights to self-determination and
    freedom 283

right to development 3, 174, 321, 323, 351

    the human 52, 94, 201, 255, 342

    respect for 119, 368

the right to development and development
    cooperation 91

The right to development and
    gender 164, 361

Right to development and global governance 290, 341
the right to development and implementation 97, 334
The right to development and practical strategies 286, 360
The right to development and reparations nexus 254, 322
The right to development and state responsibility 70, 125, 283, 289, 353–54
right to development assistance 98, 113
the right to development for Africa 45
the right to development for women and girls 157
right to development governance for Africa 218–91, 339
right to development governance model accords priority 297
Right to Development Imperatives for Africa 295–311
right to development in Africa 1–2, 4–5, 9–10, 15–16, 52–55, 61–64, 80–87, 92–94, 96–98, 113–14, 128, 130–31, 150–52, 154–55, 174–76, 178–80, 212–13, 227, 283–84, 294–96
right to development in developing countries 3, 73, 212
the right to development in international law 3, 208, 314, 322, 328, 365
right to development paradigm for developing countries 42, 101, 174, 219, 310, 339
right to development policy framework 260
the Right to development to eliminate obstacles 113
right to economic growth 53, 55, 79
Right to Fair Trial 205, 207
right to participation 243
right to political development 78
right to self-determination 39–41, 68, 111, 136, 142, 173–74, 181, 216, 218, 233–34, 237
right to self-determination in Africa 216
right to sustainable development 74, 163–64, 243, 245, 327, 339
right to well-being and improved living standards 236
Rio Declaration 156, 359

Rising Africa 225, 313
risks 203, 257, 301
roadmap 265
    ambitious 298
    consolidated 15, 256
role
    active 191
    actual 147
    central 73
    complementary 97
    government's 247
    institutional 227, 248
    instrumental 143, 259, 279
    multifunctional 133
    primary 75, 209
    standard-setting 299
    strategic 191
    subjugated 163
    supportive 116
role of development assistance 97, 171, 252, 354
role of development cooperation 82, 112
role of NHRI 190
ruin by foreign stakeholders 240
rule of law and good governance 166, 268
the rule of law as development 132, 324
Rule of Law for Development 245, 344
rules
    global 307
    military 247
    procedural 163
rupture 74, 150, 261
Rural Development 233, 248, 319, 332
ruthless crackdown 123

sabotaged development efforts 154
sabotage theory 119
safeguard 155, 163, 177, 182, 214, 265, 270, 272, 287
safeguard measures 16, 181
sanctions 90, 121, 160, 278, 281, 337, 340, 364
sanctions on education and healthcare of Zimbabweans 121, 281, 340
sanctions removal 277, 350
SAP 120–21, 257–59, 285
scepticism 68, 77, 149
schema, systematic 81

INDEX

scholars 55, 66, 95, 97, 108, 120, 170, 212, 214, 253, 257
    proponent 7
school enrolment 27
schools 28
    missionary 32
scope 14, 128, 227, 251, 305, 310
    continental 14
    expanded 164
scrutiny, democratic 229
sector 224
    corporate 301
security 8, 67, 90, 103, 132, 136–37
    job 57
    national 91
    social 171, 240
segments, large 259
selection 137, 345
    natural 290
    partner country 115, 347
self-consciousness, critical 303
self-determination 15–16, 32–33, 39–41, 67–68, 70, 93–94, 111–12, 133–34, 153–54, 173–75, 216–18, 233–34, 256, 283, 292–96
    actual 112, 173, 216, 240, 290–91, 295, 306
    creating real 221
    economic 34, 308
self-determination of peoples 39
self-government 34, 47
    exercised 36
self-identification 200
self-identity 29
self-interests 106–7, 115, 219, 347
    national 117
self-realisation 227
self-reliance 141, 228, 256
    collective 105, 158
self-reliant efforts 15, 270
self-sufficiency 81, 301
self-sustainability 222
self-sustained development 278
Sengupta's logic 201
sentimental attachment 202
sentiments 107, 234
    anti-imperialist 235
    growing populist anti-trade 149
separation 138, 263, 339
service functionaries, public 257

services 61, 147, 178, 210, 231
    basic 120
    cloak-and-dagger secret 130
    public 80
setbacks 91, 221, 225, 256, 269, 287
    forestall 280
    internal 289
settlement 137
    amicable 203, 205
Settler colonialism in Africa 32, 324
settler colonists 46
Settler Economies 32, 317, 324
shared strategic framework 144
Sharing responsibility 282, 295, 331
shift
    decisive collective 306
    progressive 14
    radical 5, 65, 67, 141, 266, 290
    revolutionary 10
shift development thinking 15
shipment of development assistance 256
shortcomings 104, 144, 208, 215
    practical 113
shortcomings of NEPAD 144
Singer's conception 99
Singer's theorisation 155
situation 76, 93, 96, 98, 136–37, 203, 206, 221, 223, 229, 231, 251, 254
    destabilised 33
    prevailing 30
    socio-economic 120
sizeable amount of assistance 106
skills 235, 302–3
    much ignorance and few 28
    technical 105
slaveholding, motivated 24
slave raiding 24
slave routes 23
slavery 18, 22–26, 32, 34, 43, 48, 72, 77, 118, 122, 254, 339, 363–64
slaves 23–25
slave trade 23–24, 33, 344, 353, 365
    trans-Atlantic 24, 323
social and cultural rights in Africa 59, 157, 177, 295, 330, 358
Social and Economic Rights Action Centre 72, 177, 194, 220–21, 295, 297, 330, 355

Social and Political Development   135, 236, 315
social development   57, 140, 259, 264,
   333, 342
social inequality   106
socialist   89
social justice   21, 71, 120, 158, 167, 193, 243,
   349, 354
social justice in South Africa   193, 354
social life   203
Social Policy   180
social progress   40, 173, 267, 304, 349, 357
social rights   177, 191, 194, 208, 229, 242, 324,
   330, 334, 348, 352
Social Rights Jurisprudence   242, 317, 324
social state principle   267
social structures   259
societies, advanced   274, 286
society   25, 134, 151, 161, 164, 180, 239, 289,
   315–16, 323, 351
   global   43
   human   22
   unequal post-apartheid   172
socio-cultural issues   103
socio-cultural life   174
socio-economic amenities   238, 285
socio-economic demands, increased   238
socio-economic development   120–21, 136,
   142, 172, 320
socio-economic issues   103
Socio-economic problems   260, 346
socio-economic realities   296
socio-economic rights   62, 136, 138, 170–71,
   258, 263, 322, 330, 339
socio-economic rights in South Africa   62,
   138, 263, 316, 322, 339
Socio-economic rights litigation   193, 354
socio-economic rights obligations   242
socio-economic rights regime   246
socio-economic structures   136
socio-legal analysis   49, 137, 159, 295, 325
soft law nature   211
Soft Law Provisions   156
solicitation   4, 83, 125, 293–94, 310
solicitation for development assistance   83,
   125, 293–94
solicitation of development assistance   310
solidarity   49, 63, 104, 108, 110, 114, 131,
   161, 254
   compulsory   130

sound   89, 93, 120, 257
sound development practice   147
sound logic   96
source   95, 115, 169, 202, 301, 303
   agential   70
   domestic   260
   primary   24, 222
   supplementary   3
South African Constitution   62, 172, 189, 192,
   240–42, 270, 319, 322–23, 342
South African Human Rights
   Commission   172, 241, 319, 323
South Africa's transition   47
south cooperation   100, 331–32
Southern Africa   11, 26, 41, 83, 124, 170, 251,
   296, 330, 338, 343
Southern African Development
   Community   150
South-South actors   105
south-south cooperation   8, 90, 100, 104–
   7, 115
   new era of   115, 366
South-South cooperation framework   115–16
South-South cooperation patterns   104, 111
South-South partnership for
   development   107
South-South relations   101, 217, 219, 346
South-South strategy   104
sovereign equality   39, 41, 58, 90–91, 93–94,
   100, 105, 108, 111, 269, 275
sovereign equality and self-determination of
   states   93, 175
sovereign equality of African states to
   self-determination   111
sovereign obligation   74
sovereign ownership   40, 69, 79, 154, 216, 237
sovereign participants, new   43
sovereignty   70, 74, 108–9, 119, 124, 148, 153,
   162, 167, 215, 221, 228
   absolute   174
   country's   261
   cultural   150, 251
   judicial   36
   national   213
   permanent   40, 174, 350
space   100, 117, 138
special protection   203
   granted   165
   guaranteed   74

INDEX

species, rare   222
specificity   164
spheres, theoretical   237
spiritual sites   201
sporadic access   199
sprawling tropical equatorial
    rainforest   222
stability
   economic   288, 340
   political   139
stagnation   120
   economic   46
stakeholders   107–8, 204
   primary   144
stakeholder structures   147
stalled progress   22, 262
standards
   additional   286
   better   57, 67, 264
   competitive   307
   double   42, 318
   global   260
   improved   154, 222, 310
   legal   184
   minimum   36
   normative   61, 131
   rights-based   137, 280
   universal   154
standards for political conduct   144
standards for sustainable development   163
starting point for reshaping Africa's
    development   141
starvation wages   27
state action, individual   291, 299
state and domestic law   181
state and foreign stakeholders   181
state apparatus   190
state body   214
state defaults   177
state duty   183, 361
state economy   201, 273
state efforts, individual   14
statehood   36, 130, 239
   sovereign   233
statement
   political   229
   public   234
state organs   191
state-owned enterprises   120, 257

state parties   52–53, 73–74, 126, 135–37, 162–
    63, 165, 177–79, 182, 187–88, 193, 209,
    215, 263, 275, 282–83
   effect obligates   85
   enjoin   212
   monitors   184
   obligates   14, 73, 143
state policy   170–71, 246, 331
   national objectives and directive
    principles of   97, 170, 246
state power   272
state resources   263
state responsibility   75, 88, 125, 196, 283, 289,
    330, 345, 353–54
states
   autonomous   14
   decolonised   35
   donor   93, 114
   emerging   36
   external   8
   failed   124, 238, 363
   fragile developing   41
   independent   33, 36
   partner   75
   recipient   93
   respective   88, 158
   sovereign   39, 221, 232, 275
states and non-state actors   212
states governments   142, 146, 181, 227, 264,
    302, 305–8, 310
states obligations   183
state sovereignty   58
   individual   224
   limiting   210
states ruling   234
statutory recognition   228
   official   48
story, economic success   230
Strategic aid   106, 346
strategies
   good   276
   joint   301
   potential   193, 354
   short-term   92
stratification   116
strengthen   109, 144, 189
no strings attached   261, 363
structural adjustment policies   52, 143, 258,
    285, 364

412 INDEX

structural adjustment programmes 120, 141, 257–59, 333–34, 342, 349–50
  effects of 285, 345
structural adjustment strategies 120
structural transformation 17, 147, 224, 265, 295, 297, 304
  accelerated 158
structure and human agency 134
struggles for self-determination 21
stubborn loyalty 235
subjective concept 54
subject of development cooperation 4
subjects 4, 9, 14, 39, 41, 47, 63–64, 168, 175, 180, 262, 264
  central 78, 288
subjugation 30, 59, 74, 81, 133, 136, 232–34, 292–93
  alien 39–40
  colonial 31
  socio-economic 44
subjugation accord 150
subjugation laws 26
subordinates 278
  perpetual 101
subordination 153, 216, 292
Sub-Saharan Africa 98, 130, 229–30, 338, 350, 352
subservience 98
  continuous 118
subservient 122
subsistence 101, 208, 319
substance 109, 310
substantiation 82, 200
substitute 271
  home-grown 291
substitute model 310
substitute to development cooperation 271
success of international trade 24
superior purpose 303
  definitive 303
supply workforce 23
support 92, 96, 103, 105, 128, 142, 157, 219, 231–32, 359
  financial 104
  foreign 141
  indirect 116
  pledging unflinching 231
  spontaneous popular 235
supportive inclusiveness 64

support mechanism 112
supremacy, global 117
survival 11, 45, 202, 234, 249
  political 121, 231, 350
sustainability 113, 118, 254, 333
  environmental 103
sustainable development 14–15, 17, 72, 74, 128, 131, 156, 158, 163–65, 243–45, 304, 307, 318, 357, 359–61
  people-centred 268
sustainable development and participation in national development 245
Sustainable Development Goals 51, 76, 95, 103, 108, 112, 190–91, 219, 286, 348, 351
sustainable development in Africa 15, 307, 331, 248, 332
sustain impoverishment 248
sustain independence and development 34
sustain support 88
swept 146
  liberation struggles 28
systematic transfer of aid to developing countries 286
systemic attack 29
systemic barriers 79
systems 35, 41, 44, 54, 66–67, 79, 83, 130, 266, 272, 298
  alternative 32
  apartheid 271
  belief 57
  colonial 27, 30
  established functional indigenous 199
  export 27
  financial 176
  functional 144
  innovation 266
  integrated 265
  international 100, 116
  legal 132, 170, 185
  monist 188
  parliamentary 35
  political 176, 309
  regional human rights 54, 186
  unproductive global 72
systems problem 298, 339

take other measures 138, 339
taming 248, 332
target, primary 281

INDEX 413

taxes   27, 231
technical assistance   92
  specialised   8
technology transfer   302
teleological reasoning   303
tenure, customary   199
terms
  actual   100, 204
  business   237
  concrete   33, 201, 303
  legal   44–45, 65
  neo-liberal   55
territorial limitation   209
territorial possessions   229
theorisation   279
theory   3, 11–13, 83–84, 115, 117, 154, 159, 314–
  15, 326–27, 342–43, 346, 351–52, 354
  prevailing   297
The liberation struggles   30
thinking   11–12, 68, 83, 146, 290, 306,
  308, 336
  critical   75
  decolonial   4, 11, 13, 47, 83, 261, 333
  political   308
third-party effect   195
Third World   44, 88, 113, 117–18, 219, 225, 314,
  316, 323–24
Third World Aspirations   41
thought leadership   307, 333
threats   52, 133, 137, 192, 206, 211, 213, 249,
  264, 278, 284
  perceived   60
  potential   182
  real   121, 231
time immemorial   198–99, 278
tool, ineffective   211
tourism industry   199
trade   24, 42, 72, 92, 149, 222, 277, 318, 320,
  329, 361
  export   119
  informal cross-border   149
  intra-African   148
trade agreements   80, 176
trade boom   120
trade liberalisation   149, 257–58
trade negotiations   149
trade rules, free   42
Traditional forms of development
  cooperation   128

tragedy   162, 343
  creating   290
Transactional and transformative
  leadership   262, 339
trans-Atlantic routes   23
transfer   302–3, 320
  systematic   286
transformation   135, 144, 227, 265, 269–70,
  273, 292, 298–99, 304, 308, 356
  broad-based   307
  cultural   234, 305
  economic   119
  engineering   225
  facilitated   242
  fundamental   290
  radical   12, 241, 256, 268, 339, 343
  social   268
transformation agenda   256
transformation and sustainable
  development   292
transformation of development
  cooperation   100, 334
transformative constitutionalism   12, 46, 241,
  270, 335, 341–43
transformative leadership in Africa   261–62,
  336, 354
transformative model   17, 298
  alternative   296
Transgression   188, 212, 281, 339
transition   268, 270
  post-apartheid   240
transition to sustainable development   268
Transmodernity   11, 83, 333, 336–37
treaties   122, 127, 133, 148–50, 154, 175, 181,
  209, 212, 322, 327, 356, 359
  ancillary   52
  continental   147
  international   209, 329
  regional   53, 189, 191
  relevant   53, 133
treaty enforcement mechanisms   212
treaty instruments   51, 61, 132–33, 211, 220,
  227, 305
  ancillary   110, 257
  regional   51
treaty obligations   60, 142, 183, 188, 197, 233,
  240, 328
treaty ratification   127, 246
Tribal Peoples   57

tribunal 188, 214
  international 188
Trilateral development cooperation 106, 352
turnaround, radical 18

ultimate realisation 91
ultimate test 185
un-African savour 308
uncontrollable behaviour 133
uncoupling, radical 251
underdevelopment 6, 22–23, 56, 115, 130, 137, 239, 254, 315
underdevelopment
  everlasting 118
  socio-economic 47
underpinnings, theoretical 13, 16
understanding of decoloniality 12
UNDP 102, 223, 232, 236, 244, 277, 348, 361, 367
UNECA 148, 361
unforgettable historical processes 22
unified strategy 107
uniform declaration of independence 47
unique model for development 236
United Nations Development Programme 223, 236, 279, 320, 352, 361, 367
United Nations Millennium Declaration Resolution A/55/L, 276, 359
United States. *See* US
unity 131, 306
  linguistic 200
Universal Declaration 19, 21, 32, 79, 145, 180, 187, 288, 295, 359
universality 11, 59, 136, 156, 344–45
universal standards of performance and regulatory functions 154
unjustified basis 25
unorthodox reflections 174, 321
unregulated development 224
unsustainable levels 262
unsustainable relationships 67
upliftment, sustained 141
uprisings, popular 230–31
US (United States) 6, 88, 113, 118–19, 121, 123, 156, 277, 281, 323–24, 366, 368

values of solidarity and community 63
value systems, cultural 304
Very Poor 67, 286, 318

victims 181, 184, 189, 193, 198, 205, 207–8, 215, 283, 338
  violated 205
Vienna Declaration and Programme of Action 3, 95, 156, 359
viewpoint, neo-liberalistic 303
violation 60–61, 77, 177–78, 180–84, 186, 188–90, 192–98, 203–10, 212, 232–33, 246–47, 271–73, 282–86, 292, 297
  actual 182, 206, 211, 264
  alleged 193–94, 198
  flagrant 139
  gross 22
  massive 196, 202
  redressing 186, 286
  victims of 181, 190, 192
vision 233, 241, 298
  common 141
  noble 145
  pan-African 144
  transformative 145, 307
vision of sustainable development 164, 361
vulnerability 105, 203
  continent's 102
vulnerable segments 149

wanton 162, 302
war 213
  civil 124
  under-reported first world 169, 222, 346
wave of independence 46
weaknesses 34, 46, 107, 278
  political 235
wealth 69, 106, 148, 195, 197–98, 236, 239, 268, 278, 358, 363
  continent's 26
  country's 135, 168, 232, 236
  immeasurable 76
  national 154, 240
  redistribute Africa's 162
  resource 249
welfare 96, 104, 168, 201, 254, 273, 303
  equality of 72
  global 76
  social 27
wellbeing 56, 64, 207, 275, 283
  collective 31
  improved 161, 248, 264
  measuring children's 353

INDEX 415

western capitalist societies 24
withdrawal of development assistance 281
women 23, 51–52, 56–57, 59, 74, 157, 160,
163–64, 168, 171, 238, 241–42, 358, 361
Women and sustainable
development 163, 365
women in Africa 163, 366
women's rights 42, 96, 164, 285, 352
World Bank 4, 87–88, 118–21, 186, 257–61,
285, 288, 313–17, 319–20, 347–49, 351,
361–62, 367
World Bank invention 257
world economy on developing
countries 118, 324
world order 289
new 25
structured 288

world politics 91, 328
world poverty and human rights 289
World Trade Organisation 42
wrongs, historical 254

Xenophobia 51, 357

youth empowerment 165
youth organisations 165–66
youths 51, 165–66
youths of Africa 51, 165–66

Zambia 26, 33, 35, 141, 358
Zimbabwe 25–26, 121–22, 170–71, 281,
317–18, 320, 324, 334, 336, 338, 346, 348,
350, 364
Zimbabwe sanctions 122, 281, 330